TimeOut
London

Penguin Books

PENGUIN BOOKS

Published by the Penguin Group
Penguin Books Ltd, 27 Wrights Lane, London W8 5TZ, England
Penguin Books USA Inc., 375 Hudson Street, New York, New York 10014, USA
Penguin Books Australia Ltd, Ringwood, Victoria, Australia
Penguin Books Canada Ltd, 10 Alcorn Avenue, Toronto, Ontario, Canada M4V 3B2
Penguin Books (NZ) Ltd, 182-190 Wairau Road, Auckland 10, New Zealand

Penguin Books Ltd, Registered Offices: Harmondsworth, Middlesex, England

First published 1989
First Penguin edition 1990
Second edition 1992
Third edition 1994
Fourth edition 1995
Fifth edition 1997
Sixth edition 1998
Seventh edition 1999
10 9 8 7 6 5 4 3 2 1

Copyright © Time Out Group Ltd, 1989, 1990, 1992, 1994, 1995, 1997, 1998, 1999
All rights reserved

Colour reprographics by Precise Litho, 34-35 Great Sutton Street, London EC1
and Westside Digital Media, 9 Bridle Lane, London W1

Printed and bound by William Clowes Ltd, Beccles, Suffolk NR34 9QE

Edited and designed by

Time Out Guides Limited
Universal House
251 Tottenham Court Road
London W1P 0AB
Tel + 44 (0)171 813 3000
Fax+ 44 (0)171 813 6001
Email guides@timeout.com
http://www.timeout.com

Editorial

Editorial Director Peter Fiennes
Editor Jonathan Cox
Deputy Editor Lesley McCave
Listings Editor Zoë Sanders
Proofreader Tamsin Shelton
Researcher Zoë Rigden

Design

Art Director John Oakey
Art Editor Mandy Martin
Designers Benjamin de Lotz, Scott Moore, Lucy Grant
Scanner Operator Chris Quinn
Advertisement Make-up Paul Mansfield
Picture Editor Kerri Miles
Picture Researcher Olivia Duncan-Jones
Picture Admin Kit Burnet

Advertising

Group Advertisement Director Lesley Gill
Sales Director Mark Phillips
Sales Manager Alison Gray
Sales Dominic Mensah, Rhidian Thomas, Laurent Ezekiel
Display Production Manager Sally Webb
Copy Controller Sam Furniss
Advertising Assistant Ingrid Sigerson

Administration

Publisher Tony Elliott
Managing Director Mike Hardwick
Financial Director Kevin Ellis
Marketing Director Gillian Auld
General Manager Nichola Coulthard
Production Manager Mark Lamond
Accountant Catherine Bowen

Features in this guide were written and researched by:

Introduction Jonathan Cox. **London by Season** Lesley McCave, Zoë Rigden. **History** Jonathan Cox, Sarah McAlister. **London Today** Derek Hammond (*A Mayor for London* Andrew White). **The Millennium Dome** Rowan Moore. **Sightseeing** *Central London* Jonathan Cox (*Scandal!* Lesley McCave); *North London* Louise Gray, Mary Dohnal; *East & South London* Ian Cunningham; *West London* Patrick Marmion. **Museums** Jonathan Cox, Lesley McCave, Andrew White. **Art Galleries** Andrew White (*Hackney* Louise Gray). **Accommodation** Jonathan Cox, Zoë Rigden, Michael Schipper. **Restaurants** Jonathan Cox. **Pubs & Bars** Jonathan Cox. **Shopping & Services** adapted from *Time Out Shopping & Services Guide*. **Children** Jonathan Cox, Lesley McCave. **Comedy** Malcolm Hay, Andrew White. **Clubs** David Swindells. **Dance** Donald Hutera. **Film** Lesley McCave (*Movies, murder & the macabre* Kim Newman). **Gay & Lesbian** Paul Burston, Jonathan Cox, Zoë Rigden. **Music: Classical & Opera** Will Fulford-Jones. **Music: Rock, Roots & Jazz** Chris Salmon, Lily Dunn. **Sport & Fitness** Andrew White, Zoë Sanders. **Theatre** Patrick Marmion. **Trips Out of Town** Jonathan Cox (*Brighton* Mary Stevens; *Out of Town Events* Zoë Sanders). **Directory** Jonathan Cox, Lily Dunn, Zoë Sanders (*Students* Will Fulford-Jones).

The Editor would like to thank the following:

Corporation of London Press Office, Caroline Wright, the Post Office Archives, Derek Adams, Paul Burston, Selena Chalk, Bruce Dessau, Guy Dimond, Mary Dohnal, Sarah Halliwell, Sara Hannant, James Mitchell, Nana Ocran, Chloë Riess, Zoë Rigden, Nick Royle, Michael Schipper, Suzy Stammers, Mother & Father Trout, Louise Wood (London Tourist Board).

Maps by JS Graphics, 17 Beadles Lane, Old Oxted, Surrey RH8 9JG. Street maps based on material supplied by Alan Collinson and Julie Snook through Copyright Exchange.

Photography by Sara Hannant except: page 11 **Museum of London**; pages 14-15, 16, 19 and 23 **Hulton Getty**; page 27 **NMEC/Hayes Davidson/Chorley Handford**; pages 6, 50, 76, 85, 88-89, 90 and 115 **Jon Perugia**; page 87 **Mark Read**; pages 83, 165 and 182 **Dominic Dibbs**; page 167 **Roy Mehta**; page 169 **Luca Zampedri**; page 171 **Francesca Yorke**; page 185 **Frank Bauer**; page 275 (top left) **Peter Chrisp**; page 275 (top right) **JJ Waller**; pages 271, 275 (bottom left and right), 277 (top and bottom), 282, 285, 286 **Jonathan Cox**; page 219 **Ivan Kyncl**; page 254 **Rex Features**. The following pictures were supplied by the featured establishments: pages 126, 230, 268.

Contents

About the Guide

The seventh edition of the *Time Out London Guide* is our most comprehensive yet. For more than 30 years, *Time Out* magazine has been reporting on life in the capital, providing a definitive range of listings of films screened, books published, CDs released, plays staged, and cafés, bars, restaurants and clubs opened (and closed). The *London Guide* draws on this pool of knowledge and experience. At the same time it is part of an expanding series of city guides which now includes Amsterdam, Barcelona, Berlin, Brussels, Budapest, Dublin, Edinburgh & Glasgow, Florence, Las Vegas, Lisbon, Los Angeles, Madrid, Moscow & St Petersburg, New Orleans, New York, Paris, Prague, Rome, San Francisco and Sydney.

A good guide should not dictate an itinerary but, rather, open up a location to the curious visitor (and resident); it should inform, entertain and inspire by supplying contexts, insider knowledge and the wherewithal to encourage independent exploration. That has been our aim in preparing this guide.

WE'VE DONE OUR BEST

All the listings information was fully checked and correct at the time of going to press, but owners and managers can change their arrangements at any time. So it is always best to phone before you set out, to check opening times, dates of exhibitions, admission fees and other details.

The prices listed throughout should be used as guidelines. Exchange rates and inflation – even a change of government – can cause sudden changes. But if a particular set of prices or services varies greatly from those we have listed, ask why. (You can always go elsewhere; there's plenty of choice.) But do please let us know. We always aim to give the best, up-to-date advice, so we want to know if you think you've been ripped off.

TELEPHONES

All London phone numbers are prefixed by 0171 for central London and 0181 for outer London. If you are calling from an 0171 area you will have to dial 0181 to reach someone outside the centre; in an 0181 area, dial 0171 to reach someone in the heart of the city. If you dial the wrong prefix a recorded message will advise you that you have not been charged for the call. If you're calling someone in the same band, no prefix is required (unless you're using a mobile).

CREDIT CARDS

The following abbreviations have been used – **AmEx**: American Express; **DC**: Diners Club; **JCB**: Japanese Credit Bank; **MC**: MasterCard; **TC**: travellers cheques in any currency ($TC, £TC denotes currency); **V**: Visa. **Where we have listed none, they take none.**

LET US KNOW

In all cases the information we give is impartial. No organisation or enterprise has been included because its owner or manager has advertised in our publications. We hope you enjoy the *Time Out London Guide*, but if you take exception to any of our reviews, please feel free to let us know. Readers' comments are always welcome and are taken into account when preparing later editions of the guide. There's a reader's reply card at the back of the book.

There is an online version of this guide, as well as weekly events listings for several international cities, at http://www.timeout.com.

Introduction

London is a difficult city to get to know. It's a self-absorbed, unsentimental, badly mannered place that, beyond the superficial gloss of the tourist industry, makes little attempt to show visitors its true character. So, with a view to opening up the Big Smoke just a little, we've collected together a range of Londoners' opinions and prejudices in a far-from-exhaustive and entirely unscientific survey. Hopefully, though, the following will give you some understanding of what Londoners themselves like and dislike about their home town.

Most and least popular places to live

Few people want to live in the centre – the West End got only a couple of votes; most favoured the civilised, leafy northern enclaves of Hampstead, Highgate and Primrose Hill, or trendy Notting Hill.

The north/south London prejudice is strong. Those who already live north of the river tend to regard south London as untamed barbarian-ravaged wilderness; while many southerners think of north London as populated by precious middle-class snobs. There was some agreement, however, that poor old south-east London (Peckham, Deptford, New Cross) and parts of east London (Docklands, Hackney, Tower Hamlets) were beyond the pale.

Favourite and least-favourite building

Most respondents went for bold, confident structures, and not just venerable old-timers like St Paul's – Battersea Power Station, St Pancras Station, Natural History Museum, the Lloyd's Building, the Palm House at Kew were all popular choices.

Tellingly, every negative response was for a twentieth-century building. Modernism got a predictable clouting (National Theatre, Hayward Gallery), eyesore towers (NatWest Tower, Centre-point) and hideous commercial developments (the Elephant & Castle and Wandsworth Arndale shopping centres) were condemned, and recent big-money projects (Canary Wharf, Richmond Riverside, No.1 Poultry) met with much sighing and tutting.

Favourite and least-favourite street

Possibly London's best-known and most-visited street for tourists, Oxford Street, was overwhelmingly the least-popular thoroughfare for Londoners. Other hated byways were the traffic-packed, fume-filled Tottenham Court Road, and Euston and Pentonville Roads.

Favoured streets show the best of the city. Apart from relatively big names like Neal Street and Jermyn Street, nearly all were small, idiosyncratic and generally little known, such as gas-lit Goodwin's Court in Covent Garden, Launceston Place in Kensington, Sicilian Avenue, Marchmont Street and Lamb's Conduit Street in Bloomsbury, Fournier Street in Spitalfields and Northcote Road in Battersea. Small-scale shops, pubs and restaurants seem to be what Londoners want on their streets.

Favourite museum

Here, though, it was clear that the natives love the big guns as much as visitors do. Although some of the lesser-known museums (Sir John Soane's Museum, the Horniman Museum) got votes, most people went for one of the major players. The wonderful collections of the British Museum, the Science Museum, the Natural History Museum, the V&A and the National Gallery are some of the true glories of London.

Favourite view

In a city not known for its great vantage points, respondents came up with a mixed bag of opinions. Some went for the iconic (the floodlit Houses of Parliament, the Tower of London), others for the esoteric (Columbia Road Flower Market). Interestingly, though, the majority of responses were river-related – Battersea Power Station, Tower Bridge at night and, by far the most popular, the views up- and downriver from Waterloo Bridge. It inspired Ray Davies in the '60s (remember *Waterloo Sunset*?); it inspires Londoners today.

Best and worst things about living in London

No one likes to complain about London as much as Londoners. And what they complain about is the pollution, the traffic, malfunctioning public transport, the number of homeless people, the litter and the cost of living. It's all there, and it's all fairly grim. But there's plenty of pride too. Why else would we all stick it out? London is truly a world great when it comes to culture, to entertainment, to eating and drinking, to its salmagundy of races, cultures and religions. And perhaps it's that mix of the good, the bad and the ugly that gives London its individual character – a little prickly, perhaps, somewhat self-important, maybe, but, underneath its façade, a touchingly shy, loveable, non-judgmental, multi-faceted and endlessly fascinating place. Well, that's what we think. You make up your own minds.
Jonathan Cox

Simply the hottest place in town!

Situated close to the renowned **Bloomsbury** district, with easy access to London's famous **tourist** landmarks and financial square mile.

This **Traditional** yet **chic** new establishment stylishly decorated, takes you through the **gastronomic** delights of Indian cuisine.

'Spice Lunch' from £6.50.
Monday to Friday from 12 p.m. 'till 2:30 p.m.

'Spice Supper' from £7.95.
Everyday between 6 p.m. and 8 p.m.

'Spice Brunch' from £8.50.
Sunday's from 12 p.m. 'till 2:30 p.m.

Open **7** days a week.
For reservations please call 0171 833 9787.

Simply
SPICE

53 Calthorpe Street, London. WC1 tel: 0171 833 9787

In Context

London
by Season

The capital cranks up for the Millennium with a pomp- and party-packed calendar.

As the number of visitors to London has escalated over the past few years, so too has the number of festivals and events held in the capital. Although 1999 will no doubt be dominated by the build-up to New Year's Eve, the usual array of events will still take place throughout the year. We've included the pick of the best below, but there are scores more advertised in the national press and *Time Out* magazine. For some events you need to buy a ticket beforehand (sometimes several months in advance), some charge admission on the day/night, while others are free; it's always best to phone to check. All the dates given below were correct at time of going to press, but always double-check nearer the time. Although the long-term future of **Pride**, one of the capital's best-known festivals, is still in doubt, the **Pride Arts Festival** looks set to go ahead (18 June-11 July 1999), bringing together the best of gay dance, theatre, film, music and clubs in London; see *Time Out* magazine for further details nearer the time. For details of dance festivals, *see page 233*; for music festivals, *see page 246* and *page 256*. For a list of public holidays in the UK, *see page 295*.

Frequent events

Many of the big museums and galleries, such as the **National Gallery** (*see page 129*) and **British Museum** (*see page 126*), hold regular talks, films, discussions and other events. Phone the individual institutions for details.

Ceremony of the Keys
Tower of London, EC3 (0171 709 0765). Tower Hill tube. **Date** 9.53-10.05pm daily (except Christmas Day). **Maximum** in party *Apr-Oct* 8; *Nov-Mar* 15. **Map 12 R7**
This 700-year-old ceremony starts at precisely 9.53pm, when the Chief Warder leaves the Byward Tower. It's all over just after 10pm, when the last post is sounded. Apply in writing with a stamped self-addressed envelope six to eight weeks in advance.

Changing of the Guard
Buckingham Palace, Horse Guards & St James's Palace, SW1 (recorded info 0839 123411). Green Park or St James's Park tube. **Ceremonies** *Buckingham Palace* 11.30am daily or on alternate days (phone for dates).

The **Notting Hill Carnival**. *See page 9.*

St James's Palace 11.15am (dates as for Buckingham Palace). *Horse Guards* 11am Mon-Sat; 10am Sun.
The most spectacular ceremony is at **Buckingham Palace**. On guard changing days the new guard and its regimental band line up in the forecourt of Wellington Barracks, Birdcage Walk, from 10.45am. It's usually one of the five regiments of Foot Guards in their scarlet coats and bearskin hats. At 11.27am they march, accompanied by a band, to the Palace for the changing of the sentries, who stand guard in the Palace forecourt. Note that the ceremony may be cancelled in very wet weather. At **St James's Palace**, a detachment of the old guard marches off at 11.15am and back at 12.05pm. At **Horse Guards** in Whitehall it's the Household Cavalry who mount the guard (10am-4pm daily); they ride to Whitehall via The Mall from Hyde Park for an 11 o'clock changeover.

Funfairs
Alexandra Park *Muswell Hill, N22 (0181 365 2121). Wood Green tube/Alexandra Palace rail/W3 bus.* **Dates** *Easter* 1-11 Apr 1999; also *spring* 27 May-5 June

Millennium fever

Assuming we haven't all been finished off by the bug, and ignoring the fact that the millennium doesn't actually start until 1 January 2001 (there was no year '0'), the majority of London will be in a serious mood for partying on 31 December 1999. As an added bonus, Friday 31 December 1999 has been declared an extra public (bank) holiday in the UK, meaning three whole days of revelling. The following is merely a smattering of the big Millennium events that were known to be taking place at the time that this guide went to press. Phone numbers are given where possible, but most information is provisional, so phone to check before you don your glad rags and set out. Also keep an eye out in the national press and in *Time Out* magazine for further details nearer the time.

Perhaps not surprisingly, many of the major events will take place near the Millennium Dome in Greenwich: celebrations for New Year's Eve itself include the **Greenwich Party**, on Greenwich Peninsula, where some 30,000 people are expected to gather for a sound and light show. Nearby, in the grounds of the Royal Naval College, the **Greenwich & Docklands First Night** celebration will take place (phone 0181 853 4444 for details and tickets), featuring street theatre and performances from 7.30pm, with fireworks at midnight. At Flamsteed House, part of the Royal Observatory in Greenwich Park, an event called **As Time Goes By** will be staged. Expected to be one of the world's biggest Millennium celebrations, attracting around 50,000 people, this two-and-a-half-hour multimedia experience celebrating the achievements of mankind over the past 2,000 years using song, dance, narration and film will be broadcast live on BBC1 and relayed throughout the world. A decidedly family-oriented event will be the **Millennium Firework Display** at Battersea Park, SW11 (0181 871 7532), which will feature street theatre, children's entertainment and music. Those of a more sedate nature might like to join in the celebrations at **Westminster Central Hall**, SW1 (call 0171 222 8010 and ask for the church office). This evening presentation will feature a gospel concert, followed by a silent vigil at the Abbey, a midnight mass at the Cathedral and a watchnight service (which marks the passing of the old year and the beginning of the new) at Westminster Central Hall. Also on a religious theme, **Ringing in the Millennium** is a New Year peal of bells involving more than 100

churches across the country, including St Paul's Cathedral and St-Martin-in-the-Fields on Trafalgar Square.

For those who manage to crawl out of bed the next day, 1 Jan 2000 will see the grand opening of the much-derided but long-awaited **Millennium Dome** (*see page 27*). The more energetic might like to head down to central London for the **New Year's Day Parade** (0181 566 8586). This free family event will feature marching bands from around the world, clowns, cheerleaders, giant inflatables and vintage cars. The parade begins at Parliament Square at noon, and makes its way through central London, ending at Berkeley Square around 3pm. Another event of a religious note, on 2 Jan 2000, is **Fanfare for a New Generation**, billed as a 'multimedia spectacular' with a host of well-known names including Sir Cliff Richard, which will be held at either the Royal Albert Hall or the Dome at Greenwich (the venue was unconfirmed at the time of going to press).

1999; *summer* 26-31 Aug 1999; *winter fair* November 1999; phone to confirm exact dates.

Battersea Park *Albert Bridge Road, SW11 (0181 871 7530). Battersea Park or Queenstown Road rail/97, 137 bus.* **Dates** *Easter* 2-5 Apr 1999; phone for other dates.

Hampstead Heath *NW3 (0171 485 4491 for a leaflet detailing events in the park throughout the year). Belsize Park or Hampstead tube/Gospel Oak or Hampstead Heath rail/24 bus.* **Dates** *Easter* 2-5 Apr 1999; *spring bank holiday* 28-31 May 1999; *summer* 27-30 Aug 1999.

Gun Salutes
Hyde Park, W2 & the Tower of London, EC3.
Date 6 Feb (Accession Day); 21 Apr (Queen's birthday); 2 June (Coronation Day); 10 June (Duke of Edinburgh's birthday); 12 June (Trooping the Colour, *see below*); 4 Aug (Queen Mother's birthday); State Opening of Parliament (*see below*). If the date falls on a Sunday, salutes are fired on the following Monday. **Map 12 R7**
The cannons are primed on important royal occasions for gun salutes. The King's Troop of the Royal Horse Artillery makes a mounted charge through **Hyde Park**, sets up the guns and fires a 41-gun salute (noon, except for the State Opening of Parliament) opposite the Dorchester Hotel. Then, not to be outdone, at the **Tower of London**, the Honourable Artillery Company fires a 62-gun salute at 1pm.

Spring 1999

St Patrick's Day   17 Mar
London has the third largest Irish population of any city in the world, after New York and Dublin. There are no big parades, but head up to Kilburn (NW6) for a taste of boisterous Irish jubilation.

Ideal Home Exhibition   18 Mar-11 Apr
Earl's Court Exhibition Centre, Warwick Road, SW5 (box office 0171 373 8141/info 0171 244 0371). Earl's Court tube. **Map 3 A11**
The biggest consumer show in the UK draws in huge crowds from all over the country to drool over every conceivable household gadget and innovation. It's all a bit tacky, though.

Head of the River Race   27 Mar
on the Thames, from Mortlake, SW14, to Putney, SW15 (01932 220401).
Less well-known than the Oxford and Cambridge Race but just as impressive, this one goes in the opposite direction, with around 420 boat crews competing for the best time. Turn up at about 11.30am for the 12.30pm start from Mortlake. The best views of the race are to be had from Hammersmith Bridge; alternatively, watch from the finish line at Putney.

Oxford & Cambridge   3 Apr
Boat Race
on the Thames, from Putney, SW15, to Mortlake, SW14 (0171 379 3234).
Oxford and Cambridge Universities' fitter members race the four miles and 374 yards (6,819m) from Putney to Mortlake. The riverside pubs in Hammersmith and Mortlake are popular vantage points – but be prepared for huge crowds.

London Harness   5 Apr
Horse Parade
Battersea Park, Albert Bridge Road, SW11 (01733 234451). Battersea Park or Queenstown Road rail/97, 137 bus.
Working horses, traditional brewers' drays, carts and carriages tour Battersea Park, competing for rosettes.

London Marathon   18 Apr
Greenwich Park, Blackheath, to Westminster Bridge via the Isle of Dogs, Victoria Embankment & St James's Park (0171 620 4117).
The world's biggest road race, with around 35,000 starters, including celebs and record-breakers, running the 26.3 miles (16km). To run it yourself apply by the October before the race: your name will be entered into a ballot and you'll have a straight 50/50 chance of being allowed to run.

May Fayre & Puppet Festival   9 May
St Paul's Church Garden, Covent Garden, WC2 (0171 375 0441). Covent Garden tube.
Map 8 L7
A free festival of Punch and Judy and other puppetry.

FA Cup Final   22 May
Wembley Stadium, Wembley, Middx (0181 902 0902/ bookings 0181 900 1234). Wembley Park tube/Wembley Central tube/rail.
The most important day of the year for footie fans. Tickets are notoriously hard to obtain (and expensive).

Festival of Mind, Body, Spirit 22-31 May
Royal Horticultural Halls, Greycoat Street, SW1 (0171 938 3788). St James's Park tube.
Map 7 J7
A New Age festival featuring a mind-blowing array of approaches to health, spiritualism and the environment.

Rugby League Challenge   24 May
Cup Final
Wembley Stadium, Wembley, Middx (0181 902 0902/ bookings 0181 900 1234). Wembley Park tube/Wembley Central tube/rail.
Highlight of the rugby league calendar.

Chelsea Flower Show   27-28 May
grounds of Royal Hospital, Royal Hospital Road, SW3 (0171 834 4333). Sloane Square tube.
Map 4 F12
World-renowned gardening extravaganza by the river.

Victoria Embankment   30 May-25 July
Gardens Summer Events
Victoria Embankment Gardens, Villiers Street, WC2 (0171 375 0441). Embankment tube.
Map 8 L7
A series of free open-air events encompassing the **Open Air Opera** season (June, July), the **Open Dance Festival**, **Move It Mime Festival**, **Midsummer Poetry Festival** (June) and the **Summer Season of Street Theatre**. Phone for the dates and times of individual events.

Summer

Beating Retreat   2-3 June
Horse Guards Parade, Whitehall, SW1 (0171 930 4466). Westminster tube/Charing Cross tube/rail.
Map 8 K8
For those who like loud noises with their pomp, the 'Retreat' is beaten on drums by the Mounted Bands of the Household Cavalry and the Massed Bands of the Guards Division in this colourful musical ceremony.

Derby Day   4-5 June
Epsom Downs Racecourse, Epsom Downs, Surrey (enquiries/box office 01372 470047). Epsom Town Centre or Tattenham Corner rail, then shuttle bus.
The major flat race of the season is a frightfully British affair. The lower orders are herded into one enclosure, while those with fat wallets and braying voices strut about in another.

The popular **London Open House** *weekend.*

Royal Academy Summer Exhibition
7 June-22 Aug

Royal Academy, Burlington House, Piccadilly, W1 (0171 300 8000). Green Park or Piccadilly Circus tube. **Map 7 J7**

Every year around 10,000 works are submitted by artists of all styles and standards, from members of the Royal Academy to enthusiastic amateurs, and judged by a panel of eminent Academicians. The thousand or so you get to see are usually something of an artistic hotchpotch but interesting nonetheless.

Trooping the Colour
12 June

Horse Guards Parade, Whitehall, SW1 (0171 414 2479). Westminster tube/Charing Cross tube/rail. **Map 8 K8**

Even though the Queen's birthday is in April, she has an official birthday party on this day. She leaves Buckingham Palace at 10.40am and travels down The Mall to Horse Guards Parade, arriving at 11am. The route is always packed, but you may find space on the Green Park side of The Mall. Back home in the Palace by 12.30pm, the Queen takes to the balcony to watch a Royal Air Force jet zoom past at about 1pm, and there is a gun salute at the Tower of London.

Royal Ascot
15-18 June

Ascot Racecourse, Ascot, Berkshire (01344 622211). Ascot rail.

Ascot is the top toff horse racing meeting of the year. On Ladies' Day (17 June), when the Queen attends, women's outrageous hats are as much the focus of attention as the racing results.

Covent Garden Flower Festival
20-27 June

in and around Covent Garden Market (0171 379 7020). Covent Garden tube. **Map 8 L7**

The second annual flower festival promises blooms aplenty plus gardens, display areas and entertainment.

Wimbledon Lawn Tennis Championships
21 June-4 July

All England Lawn Tennis Club, PO Box 98, Church Road, SW19 (0181 944 1066/recorded info 0181 946 2244). Southfields tube/Wimbledon tube/rail.

As much about watching people as tennis. There are various ways to get tickets: apply in writing between 1 September and 31 December the previous year, sending a stamped self-addressed envelope to the above address for an application form (maximum of two tickets per household); alternatively, queue outside for tickets on the day, though be warned that people often camp out the night before. *See also p263.*

City of London Festival
22 June-15 July

venues in and around the City, EC2 (box office 0171 638 8891/info 0171 377 0540).

An international line-up of soloists, string quartets, orchestras and choirs. Also poetry and theatre in City churches.

Middlesex Show
26-27 June

Showground, Park Road, Uxbridge, Middx (0181 866 1367). Uxbridge tube.

A great family day out with morris dancing, falconry, shire-horses, veteran cars and dog agility trials.

Henley Royal Regatta
30 June-4 July

Henley Reach, Henley-on-Thames, Oxfordshire (01491 572153). Henley-on-Thames rail.

International rowing regatta; the final race is on the Sunday.

Greenwich & Docklands International Festival
9-18 July

various venues near the Thames (0181 305 1818).

In an attempt to raise the profile of the underused Thames, the festival features dance, theatre and music at locations along the river. Each year the festival's opening night and some of its events are associated with another city; in 1999 it will be Sydney. The organisers are also staging **First Night**, a New Year's Eve celebration on 31 December 1999 (*see p6* **Millennium fever**).

Website: www.festival.org

BBC Henry Wood Promenade Concerts
16 July-11 Sept

Royal Albert Hall, Kensington Gore, SW7 (0171 765 5575/box office 0171 589 8212). Gloucester Road, Knightsbridge or South Kensington tube/9, 10, 52 bus. **Map 4 D9**

Arguably the world's greatest classical music festival, presenting over 70 orchestral concerts spanning an impressive variety of composers and repertoire. *See also p245.*

Swan Upping on the Thames
20-24 July

from various points along the Thames (0171 236 1863/0171 236 7197).

This bizarre but delightfully archaic event involves a group of paddling or rowing herdsmen, who have to identify and mark swans as belonging to the Queen, the Vintners' or the Dyers' livery companies. The Dyers' swans get one mark (on the beak), the Vintners' two and, of course, the Queen's remain unblemished. You can watch the action from towpaths along the way. The route and departure time change daily; phone for details.

Royal Tournament
20 July-2 Aug

Earl's Court Exhibition Centre, Warwick Road, SW5 (box office 0171 373 8141/info 0171 244 0371). Earl's Court tube. **Map 3 A11**

The Army, Navy and RAF pit themselves against each other in displays of strength, stamina and bravery. Also, deafening military bands, plenty of pageantry and running about with gun carriages.

Great British Beer Festival
3-7 Aug

Olympia, Hammersmith Road, W14 (box office 0171 373 3113). Kensington (Olympia) tube.

This beer fest is for real ale lovers – literally: it's organised by CAMRA (Campaign for Real Ale). Introduce your tastebuds to 300 British ales and ciders and, despite the name of the festival, to a range of international beers.

Summer Rites
7 Aug

Brockwell Park, SW2 (0171 278 0995). Brixton tube/Herne Hill rail.

A burgeoning, gay-oriented festival. Things to see and do include a funfair, bars, market stalls, loads of live performances and disco tents run by top London clubs.

Solar Eclipse
11 Aug

Visible over south-west England, especially Cornwall, weather permitting; partially visible over London.

All eyes will be on the skies for this once-in-a-lifetime event, due to occur at 11.11am. Don't even think about heading down to Cornwall – facilities are expected to be stretched to – and possibly beyond – breaking point (catch in on TV if the view's not great over London).

Notting Hill Carnival   29-30 Aug
*(0181 964 0544). Ladbroke Grove, Notting Hill
or Westbourne Park tube.*
This vast and ever-popular street party features steel
bands, sound systems, colourful floats and excellent
Caribbean food. *See also p108.*

Autumn

Great River Race   5 Sept
*on the Thames, from Richmond, Surrey,
to Island Gardens, E14 (0181 398 9057).*
More than 250 'traditional' boats compete in this 22-mile
(35-km) 'marathon', aiming to scoop the UK Traditional
Boat Championship. The race sets off from Ham House,
Richmond, at 10.30am and ends at Island Gardens, opposite
Greenwich, around 1.45pm.

Thames Festival   12 & 19 Sept
*Upriver of Kew Bridge, 12 Sept, and between Waterloo
Bridge, SE1, & Blackfriars Bridge, EC4, 19 Sept
(0171 928 8998).*
An exciting, newly developed festival that aims to re-ignite
enthusiasm for London's great waterway with a series of
events celebrating the river.

Chelsea Antiques Fair   16-26 Sept
*Chelsea Old Town Hall, King's Road, SW3
(01444 482514). Sloane Square tube.*
Map 4 E12
A twice-yearly festival (also held 12-21 March), where
anyone with a budget from £20 to £50,000 should find
something of interest.

London Open House   18-19 Sept
various venues in London (recorded info 0891 600061).
On this weekend, the public have access to buildings of
architectural interest that are normally closed, free of
charge. The 400 or so participating buildings range from
hulks like the Bank of England and the amazing India &
Foreign Exchange to individual rooms in private homes –
a snooper's paradise.
Website: www.londonopenhouse.demon.co.uk

Horseman's Sunday   19 Sept
*Church of St John & St Michael, Hyde Park
Crescent, W2 (0171 262 1732). Marble Arch tube/
Paddington tube/rail.* **Map 2 E6**
Dating from 1969, when local riding stables feared closure
and held an open-air service to protest, a vicar on
horseback blesses more than 100 horses, before the animals
trot through Hyde Park.

Pearly Kings and Queens   3 Oct
Harvest Festival
*St Martin-in-the-Fields, Trafalgar Square, WC2
(0171 930 0089). Charing Cross tube/rail.* **Map 8 L7**
Dressed in their traditional flamboyant costumes, pearly
kings, queens and princesses from all over London gather
here at 3pm for a harvest thanksgiving every year.

Punch and Judy Festival   3 Oct
*Covent Garden Piazza, WC2 (0171 836 9136).
Covent Garden tube.* **Map 8 L7**
Gather round in the popular piazza to watch Punch and Judy
duff each other up.

International Festival of   7-10 Oct
Fine Wine and Food
*Olympia, Hammersmith Road, W14 (0171
453 5342). Kensington (Olympia) tube.*
This annual festival is a food-lover's paradise, with an international spread of food and wine to sample and buy.

Trafalgar Day Parade   24 Oct
*Trafalgar Square, WC2 (0171 928 8978).
Charing Cross tube/rail.* **Map 8 K7**
Nelson's victory at the Battle of Trafalgar (21 October 1805)
is commemorated with marching bands and music performances by sea cadets. It ends with the laying of a wreath
at the foot of Nelson's Column.

Cor blimey, luvvaduck – take a butcher's at the **Pearly Kings and Queens Harvest Festival**.

State Opening of Parliament late Oct/early Nov

House of Lords, Palace of Westminster, SW1
(0171 219 4272). Westminster tube. **Map 8 L9**
Members of Parliament are welcomed back from their summer hols by the Queen. It's a private (though televised) affair, but the public at least get a chance to see the Queen as she arrives and departs in her Irish or Australian State Coach, attended by the Household Cavalry. As she enters the House of Lords, a gun salute is fired. Phone nearer the time for exact details.

Christmas Lights & Tree Nov-Dec

Covent Garden, WC2 (0171 836 9136); Oxford Street, W1 (0171 629 2738); Regent Street, W1 (0171 491 4429); Bond Street, W1 (0171 821 5230); Trafalgar Square, SW1 (0171 211 2109).
Each year, in early December, London receives a fir tree from the Norwegian people in thanks for Britain's role in liberating Norway from the Nazis. The tree stands decked in lights in Trafalgar Square, and numerous main shopping streets boast impressive displays. The lights on Regent Street are switched on by a celebrity (early Nov), but other, often more charming, lights are those hanging across St Christopher's Place, W1; Bond Street, W1; and Kensington High Street, W8.

London Film Festival 4-18 Nov

National Film Theatre, South Bank, SE1 (0171 928 3535/box office 0171 928 3232). Embankment tube/Waterloo tube/rail. **Map 8 M8**
For three weeks a multitude of new international films are shown, at reduced prices, at the NFT and selected West End cinemas. Phone for the exact dates. *See also p238.*

Bonfire Night 5 Nov

all over England, Scotland and Wales (0171 971 0026).
Every year Britain commemorates the failure of the Gunpowder Plot of 1605, when Guy Fawkes attempted to blow up James I and his Parliament. In celebration, we burn the 'guy' (an effigy of Fawkes) and put our lives in danger from flying fireworks. Note that most displays are held on the weekend nearest to 5 November.

London to Brighton Veteran Car Run 7 Nov

(starting point) Serpentine Road, Hyde Park, W2 (01753 681736). Hyde Park Corner tube. **Map 2 E8**
The motors, limited to an average of 20mph (32kmph), aim to reach Brighton before 4pm. The start (7.30am) at Hyde Park has a great sense of occasion, but if you can't get there, join the crowds lining the rest of the route (via Westminster Bridge and Croydon, along the A23).

Lord Mayor's Show 13 Nov

various streets in the City (0171 606 3030).
The City gets a facelift for one day a year with a procession of 140 floats, as the new Lord Mayor travels from the Mansion House in a gilded coach. Leaving at 11am, the procession snakes through the City to the Royal Courts of Justice at 11.50am. There, the new Mayor swears solemn vows before returning to Mansion House by 2.20pm. Later, the merriment continues with fireworks launched from a barge moored between Waterloo and Blackfriars bridges.

Remembrance Sunday Ceremony 14 Nov

Cenotaph, Whitehall, SW1. Westminster tube/ Charing Cross tube/rail. **Map 8 L8**
The Queen, the Prime Minister and other dignitaries lay wreaths and observe a minute's silence (at 11am) at the Cenotaph to commemorate those who gave their lives for their country in both world wars. Afterwards, the Bishop of London takes a short service of remembrance.

Winter

International Showjumping Championships mid-Dec

Olympia, Hammersmith Road, W14 (box office 0171 373 3113). Kensington (Olympia) tube.
Plenty of horsing around, ranging from international riders' competitions to the Shetland Pony Grand National. Phone for exact dates.

New Year's Eve Celebrations 31 Dec

Trafalgar Square, W1. Charing Cross tube/rail. **Map 8 K7**
No longer the great celebration that it was: in an attempt to control the proceedings, the police have banned alcohol, resulting in near-riots as inebriated revellers pour into Trafalgar Square in a moronic stampede and try to jump in the fountain (emptied and switched off anyway). No self-respecting Londoner would be seen within a mile of the place. Better choices include the day-long celebrations in Greenwich, promising a dazzling array of light, sound and fireworks. New Year's Eve 1999 is likely to be a turbo-charged affair, though spirits may be dampened by the possibility (unconfirmed at the time this guide went to press) of a total shutdown of the underground network due to staff shortages. For specific Millennium events, *see p6* **Millennium fever**.

London International Boat Show 6-16 Jan 2000

Earl's Court Exhibition Centre, Warwick Road, SW5 (info 0990 100556). Earl's Court tube.
Map 3 A11
The latest in boats, equipment and holidays make up one of London's most popular events.

London International Mime Festival 15-30 Jan

venues throughout London (phone 0171 637 5661 for brochure, from Dec).
No, not Marcel Marceau, but mime with a difference, with artists from all over the world.

Chinese New Year Festival 5 Feb

Chinatown, around Gerrard Street, W1 (0171 439 3822). Leicester Square or Piccadilly Circus tube.
Map 8 K7
The high point of the Chinese calendar is marked with stalls selling crafts and delicacies, and dragons snaking their way through the streets, gathering gifts of money and food.

Masters Snooker Tournament 6-13 Feb

Wembley Conference Centre, Wembley, Middx (box office 0181 902 0902). Wembley Park tube/ Wembley Central tube/rail.
The world's top potters cue up for a shot at this much-desired trophy.

Clowns Service 7 Feb

Holy Trinity Church, Beechwood Road, E8 (0171 254 5062). Dalston Kingsland rail.
Commemorating the great clown and pantomimist Joey Grimaldi, 'joeys' from all over the country attend this annual church service (from 4pm). The event culminates in a clown performance.

Great Spitalfields Pancake Day Race 7 Mar

Spitalfields Market, entrance on Commercial Street or Brushfield Street, E1 (0171 375 0441). Liverpool Street tube/rail. **Map 10 R5**
On the day before Lent and its 40 days of fasting comes Pancake Day. Would-be tossers should phone a few days in advance.

History

What did the Romans ever give us? Apart from London.

Roman to Norman London

London was founded by the Trojan prince Brutus and run by a race of heroic giants descended from the Celtic King Lud. So thought the twelfth-century chronicler Geoffrey of Monmouth, and how poetic if would have been were it true. In fact, although Celtic tribes lived in scattered communities along the banks of the Thames prior to the arrival of the Romans in Britain, there's no evidence of a settlement on the site of the future metropolis before the invasion of the Emperor Claudius' legions in AD43. During the Romans' conquest of the country, they forded the Thames at its shallowest point and, later, built a timber bridge here (near the site of today's London Bridge). A settlement developed on the north side of the bridge over the next decade.

During the first two centuries AD, the Romans built roads, towns and forts; and trade flourished. The first mention of London (Londinium), by the Roman historian Tacitus, records it in AD60 as being 'filled with traders and a celebrated centre of commerce'. Progress was brought to a halt in AD61, when Boudicca, the widow of an East Anglian chieftain, rebelled against the Imperial forces who had seized her land, flogged her and raped her daughters. She led the Iceni in a savage revolt, which destroyed the Roman colony at Colchester, and marched on London. The inhabitants were massacred and the settlement burnt to the ground. Order was restored, the town rebuilt and, cAD200, a 2-mile (3-km) long, 18-foot (6-m) high defensive wall was constructed around London. Chunks of the wall survive today and the names of the original gates (Ludgate, Newgate, Bishopsgate and Aldgate) are preserved on the map of the city. The street London Wall traces part of its original course.

By the fourth century AD, racked by barbarian invasions and internal strife, the Empire was in decline. In 410, the last troops were withdrawn and London became a ghost town. The Roman way of life vanished; the only enduring legacies were roads and early Christianity.

SAXON & VIKING LONDON

During the fifth and sixth centuries, history gives way to legend. The Saxons crossed the North Sea and settled in eastern and southern England,

No, not the opening sequence of EastEnders, *but an image of Roman London, cAD120.*

apparently avoiding the ruins of London; they built farmsteads and trading posts outside the walls.

In 596, Pope Gregory sent Augustine to convert the English to Christianity. Ethelbert, Saxon King of Kent, proved a willing convert and Augustine was appointed the first Archbishop of Canterbury. Since then Canterbury has remained the centre of the English Christian Church. London's first Bishop was Mellitus, one of Augustine's missionaries, who converted the East Saxon King Sebert and, in 604, founded a wooden cathedral dedicated to St Paul inside the old city walls. On Sebert's death, his followers reverted to paganism, but later generations of Christians rebuilt St Paul's.

London continued to expand. In 731, the Venerable Bede mentions 'Lundenwic' as 'the mart of many nations resorting to it by land and sea'. This probably refers to a settlement in the area of today's Aldwych (Old English for 'old settlement').

In the ninth century, the city faced a new danger from across the North Sea. The city was sacked in 841 and, in 851, the Danish raiders returned with 350 ships, leaving London in ruins. It was not until 886 that King Alfred of Wessex (Alfred the Great) regained the city. He re-established London as a major trading centre, with a merchant navy and new wharfs at Billingsgate and Queenhithe.

Throughout the tenth century, the Saxon city prospered. Churches were built, parishes established and markets set up. Leading citizens were the Port Reeve and Shire Reeve (or Sheriff; the oldest office still existing in the City), the Bishop of London and the ealdormen (aldermen).

The eleventh century brought more Viking harassment, and the English were forced to accept a Danish king, Cnut (Canute, 1016-40). During his reign, London replaced Winchester as the capital of England. In 1042, the throne reverted to an English king, Edward the Confessor, who devoted himself to building the grandest church in England two miles (3km) west of the City at Thorn-ey ('the isle of brambles'). He replaced the timber church of St Peter's with a huge abbey, 'the West Minster' (Westminster Abbey), and moved his court to the new Palace of Westminster. The Abbey was consecrated in December 1065. A week later Edward died and was buried in his new church. Now, London grew around two hubs: Westminster as the centre for the royal court, government and law; the City of London as the commercial centre.

THE NORMAN CONQUEST

On Edward's death, there was a succession dispute. William, Duke of Normandy, claimed the Confessor (his cousin) had promised him the English crown; the English chose Edward's brother-in-law Harold. William gathered an army and invaded. On 14 October 1066, he defeated Harold at the Battle of Hastings and marched on London. City elders had little option but to offer William the throne. He was crowned in Westminster Abbey on Christmas Day 1066.

Recognising the need to win over the prosperous city merchants by negotiation rather than force, William granted the Bishop and burgesses of London a charter (still kept at Guildhall) that acknowledged their rights and independence in return for taxes. But, 'against the fickleness of the vast and fierce population', he also ordered strongholds to be built alongside the city wall, including the White Tower (the tallest building in the Tower of London) and the now-lost Baynard's Castle at Blackfriars.

The earliest surviving written account of contemporary London was written 40 years later by a monk, William Fitz Stephen, who vividly conjured up the walled city and, outside, pastures and woods for hunting, youths wrestling and fencing in Moorfields, and skating on frozen ponds.

The Middle Ages

In the growing city of London, much of the politics of the Middle Ages (late twelfth to late fifteenth centuries) revolved around a three-way struggle for power between the king and the aristocracy, the Church and the Lord Mayor and city guilds.

THE BIRTH OF PARLIAMENT

In the early Middle Ages, the king and his court frequently travelled to other parts of the kingdom and abroad, but in the fourteenth and fifteenth centuries, the Palace of Westminster became the seat of law and government. The noblemen and bishops who attended court built themselves palatial houses along the Strand, from the City to Westminster, with gardens stretching to the river.

The Model Parliament (agreeing the principles of government) was held in Westminster Hall in 1295, presided over by Edward I and attended by barons, clergy and representatives of knights and burgesses. The first step towards establishing personal rights and political liberty, and curbing the power of the king, had already been taken in 1215 with the signing of the Magna Carta by King John. In the fourteenth century, subsequent assemblies gave rise to the House of Lords (which met at the Palace of Westminster) and the House of Commons (meeting in the Chapter House at Westminster Abbey).

Relations between the monarch and the City were never less than uneasy – and often outright hostile. Londoners guarded their privileges with self-righteous intransigence and resisted all attempts by successive kings to squeeze money out of them to finance wars and building projects. Successive kings were forced to turn to Jewish and

Lombard moneylenders, but the City merchants were as intolerant of foreigners as of royal authority. Regular rioting, persecution and the occasional lynching and pogrom were less-than-laudable features of medieval London.

CITY STATUS & COMMERCIAL CLOUT

The privileges granted to the City merchants under the Norman kings, allowing independence and self-regulation, were extended by the kings who followed, in return for financial favours. In 1191, during the reign of Richard I, the City of London was formally recognised as a commune (a self-governing community) and, in 1197, won control of the Thames including lucrative fishing rights (which it retained until 1857). In 1215, King John confirmed the city's right 'to elect every year a mayor', a position of great authority with power over the Sheriff and the Bishop of London. A month later the Mayor joined the rebel barons in signing the Magna Carta.

Over the next two centuries, the power and influence of the trade and craft guilds (later the City Livery Companies) increased as trade with Europe grew. The wharfs by London Bridge were crowded with imports: fine cloth, furs, wine, spices and precious metals. Port dues and taxes were paid to customs officials, such as part-time poet Geoffrey Chaucer, whose *Canterbury Tales* became the first published work of English literature.

The city's markets, already established, drew produce from miles around: livestock at Smithfield,

Dumplings, ho!

From its earliest days, London has been a centre of commerce. And if, walking along charmless Oxford Street today, the city's great commercial tradition fails to impress, spare a thought for the loudmouthed, shifty-eyed geezers balancing trays of bootleg perfumes on rubbish bins, the *Evening Standard* men and the chestnut seller. For these are the last representatives of one of London's oldest traditions: the street vendor.

Before the rise of the shop in the second half of the nineteenth century, most of the material needs of Londoners were met by itinerant pedlars who paraded the streets advertising their wares with their distinctive cries. Most of them sold food: 'Dumplings, ho!', 'Hogs puddings', 'Spanish chestnuts', 'Ripe Turkey figs'. Others specialised in practical goods: 'Buy my matches', 'Laces, all a halfpenny a piece'. Some promoted more esoteric products: 'Ye maidens and men, come for what you lack, and buy the fair ballads I have in my pack.'

In the fifteenth century, John Lydgate commented on the great number and noise of London's street sellers. Even as late as 1851, Henry Mayhew estimated that there were 30,000 street vendors in London. The cacophony of cries was one of the first and most distinctive features of the city for many visitors. Thomas Addison wrote in *The Spectator* that, 'There is nothing which more astonishes a foreigner, than the cries of London.'

With so many traders competing to be heard, it was the tune and pitch of the cries as much as their verbal content that identified individual traders. The actual words uttered were often a mystery to listeners. JT Smith reported how a cry of 'Holloway cheese cakes' sounded exactly like 'All my teeth ache'. As Francis Grose, writing in the early nineteenth century, noted: 'An endeavour to guess at the goods they deal in through the medium of language would be a vain attempt, as few of them convey any articulate sound.' Coleridge once upbraided an old street trader whose constant, baffling call of 'Ogh clo' had been irritating him. With great dignity, the trader responded, 'Sir, I can say "old clothes" as well as you can, but if you had to say so, ten times a minute for an hour together, you would say "Ogh clo" as I do now.'

Some vendors became so well known that they achieved celebrity status. The flamboyant, dandified 'Tiddy Diddy Dol' was a fixture on Haymarket in the eighteenth century and an essential figure on public occasions. Thomas Britton, the 'musical small-coal man', founded a renowned musical club in his spare time, attracting top musicians. After hawking fuel all day, he would return to his tiny, one-room dwelling in Jerusalem Place and play his viol de gamba accompanied by Handel on the harpsichord.

The costermonger was long regarded (not least by himself) as the king of the street traders. The name is derived from 'costard', a type of large ribbed apple in which these fish, fruit and vegetable sellers once specialised. As their trade was unlicensed, the costers had to take care of themselves, evolving a form of local hereditary 'monarchy' to stand up for their rights and adjudicate in disputes. This culminated in the 1880s in the Pearly Kings and Queens whose pearl button-covered costumes reflect the flashiness of the Victorian costermongers' garb. Today's coster royalty harnesses its regal powers less to commercial than to charitable activities.

fish at Billingsgate and poultry at Leadenhall. The street markets or 'cheaps' around Westcheap (Cheapside) and Eastcheap were crammed with a variety of goods. As commerce increased, foreign traders and craftsmen settled around the port. The population within the city wall grew from about 18,000 in 1100 to over 50,000 in the 1340s.

THE BLACK DEATH &
THE PEASANTS' REVOLT

Lack of hygiene became a serious problem. Water was provided in cisterns at Cheapside and elsewhere, but the supply (more or less direct from the Thames) was limited and polluted. Houndsditch was so called because Londoners threw their dead animals into the ditch that formed the city's eastern boundary. There was no proper sewerage system, and in the streets around Smithfield (the Shambles), butchers dumped the entrails of slaughtered animals.

These conditions provided the breeding ground for the greatest catastrophe of the Middle Ages: the Black Death of 1348-9. The plague came to London from Europe, carried by rats on ships. During this period, about 30 per cent of England's population died of the disease. Though the epidemic abated, it was to recur in London on several occasions during the next three centuries.

These outbreaks left the labour market shorthanded, causing unrest among the overworked peasants. The imposition of a poll tax (a shilling a head) led to the Peasants' Revolt. In 1381, thousands marched on London, led by Jack Straw from Essex and Wat Tyler from Kent. In the rioting and looting that followed, the Savoy Palace on the Strand was destroyed, the Archbishop of Canterbury was murdered and hundreds of prisoners were set free. When the 14-year-old Richard II rode out to Smithfield to face the rioters, Wat Tyler was fatally stabbed by Lord Mayor William Walworth. The other ringleaders were subsequently rounded up and hanged. But no more poll taxes were imposed.

CHURCHES & MONASTERIES

Like every other medieval city, London had a large number of parish and monastic churches, as well as the great Gothic cathedral of St Paul's. Although allowed access to the major churches, most Londoners' lives revolved around their own

local parish places of worship, where they were baptised, married and buried. Many churches were linked with particular craft and trade guilds.

Monasteries and convents were established, all of which owned valuable acres inside and outside the city walls: the crusading Knights Templars and Knights Hospitallers were two of the earliest religious orders to settle, although the increasingly unruly Templars were disbanded in 1312 by the Pope, and their land eventually became occupied by the lawyers of Inner and Middle Temple.

The surviving church of St Bartholomew-the-Great (founded 1123) and the names of St Helen's Bishopsgate, Spitalfields and St Martin's-le-Grand are all reminders of these early monasteries and convents. The friars, who were active social workers among the poor living outside the city walls, were known by the colour of their habits: the Blackfriars (Dominicans), the Whitefriars (Carmelites) and the Greyfriars (Franciscans). Their names are still in evidence around Fleet Street and the west of the City.

Tudors & Stuarts

Under the Tudor monarchs (1485-1603), spurred by the discovery of America and the ocean routes to Africa and the Orient, London became one of Europe's largest cities. Henry VII brought to an end the Wars of the Roses by defeating Richard III at the Battle of Bosworth and marrying Elizabeth of York. The resulting Tudor rose can be seen in many of the surviving Tudor palaces. Henry VII's other great achievements were the building of a merchant navy and the Henry VII Chapel in Westminster Abbey (the resting place for himself and his queen).

HENRY VIII &
THE ENGLISH REFORMATION

He was succeeded in 1509 by arch wife-collector (and despatcher) Henry VIII. Henry's first marriage to Catherine of Aragon failed to produce an heir so the king, in 1527, determined that the union should be annulled. As the Pope refused to co-operate, Henry defied the Catholic Church, demanding that he himself be recognised as Supreme Head of the Church in England and ordering the execution of anyone who refused to go along with the plan (including his chancellor

Sir Thomas More). Thus, England became Protestant almost on a whim. The subsequent dissolution of the monasteries transformed the face of the medieval city with the confiscation and redevelopment of all property owned by the Catholic Church.

On a more positive note, Henry developed a professional navy, founding the Royal Dockyards at Woolwich in 1512 and at Deptford the following year. He also established palaces at Hampton Court and Whitehall, and built a residence at St James's Palace. Much of the land he annexed for hunting became the Royal Parks, including Hyde, Regent's, Greenwich and Richmond parks.

There was a brief Catholic revival under Queen Mary (1553-8), and her marriage to Philip II of Spain met with much opposition in London. She had 300 Protestants burned at the stake at Smithfield, earning her the nickname 'Bloody Mary'.

ELIZABETHAN LONDON

Elizabeth I's reign (1558-1603) saw a flowering of English commerce and arts. The founding of the Royal Exchange by Sir Thomas Gresham in 1566 gave London its first trading centre, allowing it to emerge as Europe's leading commercial centre.

Bring out your dead!

Ring-a-ring o' roses
A pocket full of posies
A-tishoo! A-tishoo!
We all fall down.
Dead. Epidemics were common in crowded, insanitary seventeenth-century London. There had been outbreaks of plague in 1636 and 1647, so when a number of Londoners took to their beds in late 1664 – convulsing with fever, sneezing (a-tishoo!) and covered in red swellings (rings o' roses) – few were greatly disturbed.

A bitingly cold winter, during which the Thames froze over, contained the problem, but with the arrival of spring it became clear this was not just another minor pestilence. By the end of April hundreds of people were dying agonising deaths each week. May and June were hot, causing a rapid spread of the disease and mass panic. Charles II prorogued Parliament and everyone who could leave the city did so. By the end of June the weekly death toll was 725, and it exceeded 2,000 by the first week of August.

Not since the Black Death wiped out a third of the population three centuries earlier had the city experienced anything like it – and the authorities were powerless to check the plague's progress. The Lord Mayor ordered all dogs and cats to be killed (around 40,000 dogs and 200,000 cats were slaughtered in a few days) in the belief that they were the plague carriers. Ironically this led to a surge in deaths as the real villains – rats carrying the fatal fleas – were relieved of their natural predators.

Houses where plague had been diagnosed were sealed for 40 days and had a red cross daubed on their doors. Quacks made fortunes selling useless potions and protective posies. Graveyards filled up and huge quicklime-lined pits were unable to cope with the bodies picked up in the streets by patrolling 'dead-carts'. The stench was unimaginable. Businesses collapsed through lack of custom and ships refused to dock at the Port of London, while gangs of lawless unemployed workers and abandoned servants roamed the streets.

In the third week of September at least 8,000 died. Then, suddenly, for no obvious reason, the number of deaths dropped. Weekly fatalities fell to 3,000 in the last week of September and two months later they were down to 900. The winter cold finally put paid to an epidemic that had cut the capital's population by nearly 100,000. The return of the King to St James's on 1 February 1666 signalled a return to normality. And everyone breathed a sigh of relief, unaware that only seven months later a carelessly tended fire in Pudding Lane would unleash a second catastrophe on London.

The merchant venturers and the first joint-stock companies (Russia Company and Levant Company) established new trading enterprises, and Drake, Ralegh and Hawkins sailed to the New World and beyond. In 1580, Elizabeth knighted Sir Francis Drake on his return from a three-year circumnavigation. Eight years later, Drake and Howard defeated the Spanish Armada.

As trade grew, so did London. By 1600, it was home to 200,000 people, many living in dirty, overcrowded conditions, with plague and fire constant hazards. The most complete picture of Tudor London is given in John Stow's *Survey of London* (1598), a fascinating first-hand account by a diligent Londoner whose monument stands in the City church of St Andrew Undershaft.

The glory of the Elizabethan era was the development of English drama, popular with all social classes but treated with disdain by the Corporation of London, which went so far as to ban theatres from the City in 1575. Two famous rival theatres, the Rose (1587) and the Globe (1599), were erected on the south bank of the Thames at Bankside. It was here that the plays of Marlowe and Shakespeare were performed. Deemed 'a naughty place' by royal proclamation, Bankside was the Soho of its time – home not just to the theatre, but also bear-baiting, cock-fighting, taverns and the 'Stewes' (brothels).

The Tudor dynasty ended with Elizabeth's death in 1603. Her successor, the Stuart King James I, narrowly escaped assassination on 5 November 1605, when Guy Fawkes and his gunpowder were discovered underneath the Palace of Westminster. The Gunpowder Plot was a protest at the failure to improve conditions for the persecuted Catholics, but only resulted in several messy executions and an intensification of anti-papist feelings in intolerant London. The date is commemorated as Bonfire Night. It was James I who employed Inigo Jones to design court masques and the first examples of classical Renaissance style in London, the Queen's House in Greenwich (1616) and the Banqueting House in Westminster (1619).

CIVIL WAR

Charles I succeeded his father in 1625, and gradually fell out with the City of London (from whose citizens he tried to extort taxes) and an increasingly independent-minded and antagonistic Parliament. The last straw came in 1642 when he intruded on the Houses of Parliament in an attempt to arrest five MPs. The country slid into a civil war (1642-9) between the supporters of Parliament (led by Puritan Oliver Cromwell) and those of the King.

Both sides knew that control of the country's major city and port was vital for victory. London's sympathies were firmly with the Parliamentarians and 24,000 citizens assembled at Turnham Green, west of the city, in 1642 to face Charles's army. Fatally, the king lost his nerve and withdrew. He was never to seriously threaten the capital again and, eventually, the Royalists were defeated.

Gordon Riots *in the streets (1780), but did his mum know what he was up to?*

Charles was tried for treason and, although he denied the legitimacy of the court, he was declared guilty and, on 30 January 1649, was beheaded outside the Banqueting House in Whitehall.

For the next 11 years the country was ruled as a Commonwealth by Cromwell. The closing of the theatres, banning of the supposedly Catholic superstition of Christmas and other Puritan strictures on the wickedness of any sort of fun meant that the restoration of the exiled Charles II in 1660 was greeted with considerable relief and rejoicing.

PLAGUE, FIRE &
THE 'GLORIOUS REVOLUTION'

Two major catastrophes, however, marred the first decade of Charles's reign in the capital. In 1665, the most serious outbreak of bubonic plague since the Black Death devastated London's population (*see page 15* **Bring out your dead!**).

Just as the city was breathing a sigh of relief, a second disaster struck. The fire that spread from a carelessly tended oven in a bakery in Pudding Lane in September 1666 was to rage for three days and consume four-fifths of the city, including 87 churches, 44 livery company halls and more than 13,000 houses.

Here was the chance to rebuild London as a spacious, rationally planned modern city. Many blueprints were drawn up and considered, but, in the end, Londoners were so impatient to get on with business as soon as possible that the city was reconstructed largely on its medieval street plan, albeit this time in brick and stone rather than wood. The towering figure of the period is the extraordinarily prolific Christopher Wren, who personally oversaw the work on 51 of the 54 churches that were rebuilt, including his masterwork, the new St Paul's, which was finished in 1711 and was effectively the world's first Protestant cathedral.

After the Fire, many well-to-do former City residents moved to new residential developments that were springing up in the West End. In the City, the Royal Exchange was rebuilt, but merchants increasingly used the new coffee houses to exchange news. With the expansion of the joint-stock companies and the chance to invest capital, the City was emerging as a financial, rather than manufacturing, centre.

Anti-Catholic feeling still ran high, so the accession of Catholic James II in 1685 aroused fears of a return to Catholicism, and resulted in the Dutch Protestant, William of Orange, being invited to take the throne with his wife Mary Stuart (James's daughter). James fled to France in 1688 in what became known (by its beneficiaries) as the 'Glorious Revolution'. One of the most significant developments in William III's reign was the founding of the Bank of England, in 1694, to finance the King's wars with France.

Georgian London

In accordance with the Act of Settlement (1701), after the death of Queen Anne the throne passed to George, great-grandson of James I, who had been born and brought up in Hanover, Germany. Thus a German-speaking king (who never learned English) became the first of four Georges in the Hanoverian line. During his reign (1714-27), and for several years after, the Whig party – led by Sir Robert Walpole – had the monopoly of power in Parliament. Their opponents, the Tories, supported the Stuarts and had opposed the exclusion of the Catholic James II. Walpole chaired, on the King's behalf, a group of ministers (the forerunner of today's Cabinet), becoming, in effect, Britain's first prime minister. He was also presented with 10 Downing Street as a residence; it remains the official home of all serving prime ministers.

During the eighteenth century, London grew with astonishing speed, both in terms of population and built-up area. New squares and streets of Georgian terraced houses spread over Bloomsbury, Soho, Mayfair and Marylebone as wealthy landowners and speculative developers took advantage of the demand for leasehold properties. Horse and carriage stabling, built behind the terraces, has become today's fashionable mews housing. South London became more accessible with the opening of the first new bridges, Westminster Bridge (1750) and Blackfriars Bridge (1763). Until then, London Bridge had been the only bridge across the Thames. The old city gates, most of the Roman Wall and the remaining houses on Old London Bridge were demolished, allowing easier access to the City for traffic and people.

POVERTY & CRIME

In the older districts, however, people lived in terrible squalor and poverty, far worse than that of Victorian times. Some of the most notorious slums were around Fleet Street and St Giles, only a short distance from streets of fashionable residences maintained by large numbers of servants. To make matters worse, gin ('mother's ruin') was readily available at very low prices, and many poor Londoners drank excessive amounts in an attempt to escape from the horrors of daily life.

Worse still, the well-off seemed totally complacent. They regularly amused themselves at the popular Ranelagh and Vauxhall Pleasure Gardens, and with organised trips to Bedlam (Bethlehem or Bethlem Hospital) to mock the mental patients, while public executions at Tyburn (near today's Marble Arch) were among the most popular events in the social calendar.

The outrageous imbalance in the distribution of wealth encouraged crime: robberies in the West End often took place in broad daylight. Reformers were few, though there were some notable excep-

The Yankee dollar

Americans have never liked the British climate. In fact, London's first-ever American visitor, Pocahontas, died from the effects of the unsympathetic weather within a year of her arrival in 1616. Some US citizens, however, have proved more robust, stuck it out and made lasting contributions to their adopted city. Unpalatable to patriots it may be, but several of London's best-known institutions owe their existence to the Yankee dollar and Yankee initiative.

George Peabody (1795-1869)

Thousands of Londoners had, and still have, cause to be grateful to this hardworking banker and philanthropist. Peabody arrived in London after a major US financial crisis in the 1830s and, by means of shrewd investments, gradually built up a huge fortune. He personally financed the American display at the Great Exhibition of 1851, and donated £500,000 'to ameliorate the condition of the poor and needy of this great metropolis and to promote their comfort and happiness'. The Trustees of the Peabody Donation Fund decided that a large portion of it should be used to provide 'cheap, cleanly, well-drained and healthful dwellings to the poor'. The first Peabody building was erected in Commercial Street, Spitalfields, in 1862-4. Many

more followed, including Peabody Square, SE1 (*pictured opposite*). To architectural critic Nikolaus Pevsner, the Wild Street building may have been 'familiar but nonetheless detestable' but, to many Londoners, Peabody buildings have a splendid Victorian solidity. Today the Trust maintains 12,000 properties on 72 estates in Inner London, allowing long-term residents of districts such as Chelsea to stay on in areas where property is now beyond the reach of all but the seriously wealthy. When Peabody died he was honoured with a temporary burial in Westminster Abbey (before his body was returned to his native Massachusetts) and a statue behind the Royal Exchange.

Charles Tyson Yerkes (1837-1905)

Britain led the world in the development of rail travel. And London showed the way forward in metropolitan transport when the first underground railway was opened along a four-mile (2.5-km) stretch from Baker Street to Farringdon in 1863. However, despite the success of the line, and the opening of the first electric tube line (the City and South London, now part of the Northern Line) in 1890, the British proved remarkably unwilling to invest in the system. It was left to an American, the somewhat shady

tions. Henry Fielding, the satirical writer and author of the picaresque novel *Tom Jones*, was also an enlightened magistrate at Bow Street Court. In 1751, he established, with his blind brother John, a volunteer force of 'thief-takers' to back up the often ineffective efforts of the parish constables and watchmen who were the only law-keepers in the city. This group of early cops, known as the Bow Street Runners, were the forerunners of today's Metropolitan Police (established in 1829).

Disaffection was also evident in the activities of the London mob during this period. Riots were a regular reaction to middlemen charging extortionate prices, or merchants adulterating their food. In June 1780, London was hit by the anti-Catholic Gordon Riots, named after ringleader George Gordon, which were the worst in the city's violent history, leaving 300 people dead.

Some attempt to alleviate the grosser ills of poverty was made by the establishment of five major new hospitals by private philanthropists. St Thomas's and St Bartholomew's were already long established as monastic institutions for the care of the sick, but Westminster (1720), Guy's (1725), St George's (1734), London (1740) and the Middlesex

(1745) went on to become world-famous teaching hospitals. Thomas Coram's Foundling Hospital for abandoned children was also one of the remarkable achievements of the time.

It was not only the indigenous population of London that was on the rise in the eighteenth century. Country people (who had lost their own land because of enclosures and were faced with starvation wages or unemployment) drifted into the towns in large numbers. The East End was increasingly the focus for poor immigrant labourers, especially towards the end of the eighteenth century with the buildings of the docks. By 1801, London's population had grown to almost a million, the largest in Europe. And by 1837 (the year Queen Victoria came to the throne), five more bridges and the capital's first railway line (London Bridge to Greenwich) were further signs of the expansion to follow.

The Victorian era

As well as being the administrative and financial capital of the British Empire, spanning a fifth of the globe, London was also its chief port and the

but tireless speculator and entrepreneur, Charles Tyson Yerkes, to provide the capital and vision to modernise and expand the tube network. His company, the Underground Electric Railway Company of London, bought and electrified the District Line, started the Bakerloo and Piccadilly Lines, developed the Northern Line and built the massive Lots Road power station, which still provides electricity for the tube.

Harry Gordon Selfridge (1858-1947)

Born in Wisconsin, Harry Gordon Selfridge worked for the Marshall Field department store in Chicago in 1879, rising to become a junior partner before setting up his own store in Chicago in 1904. Selfridge soon sold out and moved to Europe. In 1906, believing that the British knew how to make goods but not how to sell them, he decided to build a huge department store on Oxford Street. When Selfridges opened in 1909 it was an immediate sensation. The monumental exterior of the store, lined with Ionic columns, concealed 130 departments in a thoroughly contemporary interior, with every possible shopping need under one roof. Under the slogan 'Why not spend a day in Selfridges?', customers could eat, drink and have a haircut as well as find any conceivable consumer item. It was the model for every modern department store. *See page 202.*

world's largest manufacturing centre, with breweries, distilleries, tanneries, shipyards, engineering works and many other grimy industries lining the south bank of the Thames. On the one hand, London boasted splendid buildings, fine shops, theatres and museums; on the other, there was a city of squalor, poverty, disease and prostitution. The residential areas were becoming polarised into districts with fine terraces, maintained by squads of servants, and overcrowded, insanitary, disease-ridden slums.

The growth of the metropolis in the century before Victoria came to the throne had been spectacular enough, but during her reign (1837-1901) thousands more acres were covered with housing, roads and railway lines. Today, if you pick any street at random within five miles (8km) of central London, the chances are its houses will be mostly from the Victorian era. By the end of the nineteenth century the city's population had swelled to over six million.

Despite the social problems (most vividly depicted in the works of Charles Dickens), major steps had been taken to improve conditions for the great majority of Londoners by the turn of the century. The Metropolitan Board of Works installed an efficient sewerage system, street lighting and better roads, while the worst slums were replaced by low-cost building schemes funded by philanthropists (such as the American George Peabody; *see above*) and by the London County Council (which was created in 1888).

THE RAILWAYS

The Victorian expansion of London would not have been possible without an efficient public transport network to speed workers into and out of the city from the new suburbs. The horse-drawn bus appeared on London's streets for the first time in 1829, but it was the opening of the first passenger railway, from Greenwich to London Bridge, in 1836, that hailed the London of the future. In 1863, the first underground line – which ran between Paddington and Farringdon Road – proved an instant success, attracting more than 30,000 travellers on the first day. The world's first electric track in a deep tunnel (the 'tube') opened in 1890 between the City and Stockwell (it later became part of the present-day Northern Line). In fact, much of the vision and capital behind the modern tube was provided by an American by the name of Charles Tyson Yerkes (*see page 18* **The Yankee dollar**).

THE GREAT EXHIBITION

The Great Exhibition in 1851 captured the spirit of the age: confidence and pride, discovery and invention. Prince Albert, the Queen's Consort, was involved in the organisation of this triumphant event, for which the Crystal Palace, a giant building in iron and glass (designed not by a professional architect but by the Duke of Devonshire's talented gardener, Joseph Paxton), was erected in Hyde Park. During the five months it was open, the Exhibition drew some six million visitors from Great Britain and abroad, and the profits inspired the Prince Consort to establish a permanent centre for the study of the applied arts and sciences: the result is the South Kensington museums and Imperial College. After the Exhibition, the Palace was moved to Sydenham and used as an exhibition centre until it was destroyed by fire in 1936.

When the Victorians were not colonising the world by force, they had the foresight to combine their conquests with scientific developments. The Royal Geographical Society sent navigators to chart unknown waters, botanists to bring back new species, and geologists to study the earth. Many of the specimens that were brought back ended up in the Royal Botanic Gardens at Kew.

The twentieth century

During the brief reign of Edward VII (1901-10), London regained some of the gaiety and glamour lacking in the last dour years of Victoria's reign. A touch of Parisian chic came to London with the opening of the Ritz Hotel in Piccadilly; the Café Royal was at the height of its popularity as a meeting place for artists and writers; while 'luxury catering for the little man' was provided at the Lyons Tea Shops and new Lyons Corner Houses (the Coventry Street branch, opened in 1907, could accommodate 4,500 people). Meanwhile, the first American-style department store, Selfridges (*see page 18* **The Yankee dollar**), opened to an eager public on Oxford Street in 1909.

Entertainment for the little man (and woman) meant a night out at the music hall. Audiences cheered and jeered at the songs and jokes of Max Miller and Marie Lloyd right into the 1930s, when the variety shows lost out to cinema, radio and, eventually, television.

Road transport was revolutionised. Motor cars put-putted around the city's streets. The first motor bus was introduced in 1904, and by 1911 the use of horse-drawn buses had been abandoned. Electric trams (double-deckers) started running in 1901 (though not through the West End or the City) and continued until 1952.

WORLD WAR I (1914-18)

London suffered its first air raids in World War I. The first bomb over the city was dropped from a Zeppelin near Guildhall in September 1915, to be followed by many nightly raids. Bombing raids from planes began in July 1917. Cleopatra's Needle, on Victoria Embankment, was a minor casualty, receiving damage to the plinth and one of its sphinxes that can still be seen. In all, around 650 people lost their lives as a result of Zeppelin raids.

BETWEEN THE WARS

Political change happened quickly after World War I. Lloyd George's government averted revolution in 1918-19 by promising (but not delivering) 'homes for heroes' for the embittered returning soldiers. But the Liberal Party's days in power were numbered and, by 1924, the Labour Party had enough MPs to form its first government, led by Ramsay MacDonald.

After the trauma of World War I, a 'live for today' attitude prevailed among the young upper classes in the 'roaring twenties', who flitted from parties in Mayfair to dances at the Ritz. But this meant little to the mass of Londoners, suffering in the post-war slump. In 1921, Poplar Council in east London refused to levy the rates on its impoverished population. The entire council was sent to prison but later released, having achieved an equilisation of the rates over all London boroughs that relieved the burden on the poorest ones.

Civil disturbances, caused by rising unemployment and an increased cost of living, resulted in the nationwide General Strike of 1926, when the working classes downed tools in support of the striking miners. Prime Minister Baldwin encouraged volunteers to take over the public services and the streets teemed with army-escorted food convoys, aristocrats running soup kitchens and students driving buses. After nine days of chaos, the strike was called off by the Trades Union Congress (TUC).

The economic situation only worsened in the early 1930s following the crash of the New York Stock Exchange in 1929. By 1931, more than three million people were unemployed in Britain. During these years, the London County Council began to have a greater impact on the city's life, undertaking programmes of slum clearance and new housing, creating more parks and taking under its wing education, transport, hospitals, libraries and the fire service. London's population increased dramatically between the wars, peaking at nearly 8.7 million in 1939. To accommodate the influx, the suburbs expanded at an alarming rate, particularly to the north-west with the extension of the Metropolitan Line (an area then known as Metroland). Identical gabled, double-fronted houses sprang up in their hundreds of thousands, from Golders Green to Surbiton.

And all these new Londoners were entertained by the new media of film, radio and, later, TV. London's first radio broadcast was beamed from the roof of Marconi House in the Strand in 1922. Soon families were gathering around their enormous Bakelite wireless sets to hear the latest sounds from the British Broadcasting Company (the BBC; from 1927 called the British Broadcasting Corporation). Television broadcasts started on 26 August 1936, when the first BBC telecast went out live from Alexandra Palace studios.

WORLD WAR II (1939-45)
Neville Chamberlain's policy of appeasement towards Hitler's increasingly aggressive Germany during the 1930s finally collapsed when the Germans invaded Poland. On 3 September 1939 Britain declared war. The government implemented precautionary measures against the threat of air raids – including the digging of trench shelters in London parks, and the evacuation of 600,000 children and pregnant mothers – but the expected bombing raids did not happen during the autumn and winter of 1939-40, a period that became known as the 'Phoney War'. In July 1940, Germany began preparations for an invasion of Britain with the (ultimately unsuccessful) three months of aerial attack that came to be known as the Battle of Britain.

For Londoners, the Phoney War came to an abrupt end on 7 September 1940 when hundreds of German bombers dumped their loads of high explosives on east London and the docks. Entire streets were destroyed; the dead and injured numbered over 2,000. The Blitz had begun. The raids on London continued for 57 consecutive nights, then intermittently for a further six months. Londoners reacted with tremendous

World city

One of the first things to strike any visitor to London is the city's extraordinary ethnic diversity. You're just as likely to hear Italian, Hindi or Cantonese spoken on the streets as English, and this can't be put down solely to the huge number of tourists who visit every year; resident Londoners converse in almost 200 languages.

This multiculturalism is sometimes seen as a twentieth-century phenomenon, but London has been cosmopolitan from its beginnings. The city owes its very existence to foreigners (Romans) and much of its subsequent development has been fuelled and accelerated by injections of skills, knowledge and labour from overseas. The intentions of many of London's earliest immigrants may have been primarily hostile, but after a thousand years of invasion – initiated by the Romans, continued by the Saxons and Vikings, and culminating with the Normans – London became a magnet for foreigners, chiefly for economic reasons. This has remained the case; the Irish and Jewish merchants who came to trade in the city in the Middle Ages were motivated by the same desire to better their lot as that which drove the Italian street entertainers and ice-cream sellers of the nineteenth century and the post-war Bangladeshi restaurateurs.

Often, people from abroad have been actively encouraged to move to London in times of labour and skill shortage. In the fourteenth century, Edward III invited Flemish weavers to settle in order to develop England's laggardly cloth industry and, in more recent times, London Transport and the National Health Service ran major recruitment drives in Ireland and the West Indies to fill the labour gap following World War II.

The other major spur for immigration to London has been political and religious persecution. The first big wave of religious refugees were Protestants from Germany, France and the Low Countries in the mid-sixteenth century, followed at the end of the seventeenth century by Huguenots (French Protestants). Towards the end of the last century, Jews fleeing pogroms in Russia and eastern Europe were given refuge. The 1980s saw the arrival in London of Somalis escaping civil war in their homeland.

Some communities (such as the Huguenots) have been throughly assimilated, while others (the Punjabis of Southall, for instance) retain a strong identity. Most immigrants were poor and lived in the cheaper areas of the city, moving on as their prosperity rose. The Greek Cypriots who first settled in Soho in the 1920s and 1930s (hence the naming of Greek Street), shifted north to Camden to find cheaper accommodation in the 1940s and 1950s, and were then forced further north to Haringey in the '60s and '70s.

The East End has long been a repository for recent immigrants, and one wave frequently succeeded another, as the history of the building on the corner of Fournier Street and Brick Lane in Spitalfields illustrates. Built as a Huguenot church in 1744, it became a Wesleyan chapel at the end of the eighteenth century, a synagogue from 1898 to 1975, and is now used as a mosque by the local Bengali community.

bravery and stoicism and the period is still nostalgically referred to as 'Britain's finest hour'. After a final massive raid on 10 May 1941, the Germans focused their attention elsewhere, but by the end of the war about a third of the City and the East End was in ruins.

From 1942 the tide of the war began to turn, but Londoners still had a new terror to face – the V1 or doodlebug. In 1944, dozens of these explosive-packed pilotless planes descended on the city, causing widespread destruction. Later in the year, the more powerful V2 rocket was launched. Over the winter, 500 V2s fell on London, mostly in the East End; the last one fell on 27 March 1945 in Orpington, Kent. Victory in Europe (VE Day) was declared on 8 May 1945. Thousands of people took to the streets to celebrate.

POST-WAR LONDON

World War II left Britain almost as shattered as Germany. Soon after VE Day, a general election was held and Churchill was heavily defeated by the Labour Party under Clement Attlee. The new government established the National Health Service in 1948, and began a massive nationalisation programme that included public transport, electricity, gas, postal and telephone services. But for all the planned changes, life for most people was drab, regimented and austere.

In London, the most immediate problem was a critical shortage of housing. Prefabricated bungalows provided a temporary solution (though many were still occupied 40 years later), but huge new high-rise housing estates that the planners began to erect were often badly built and unpopular with residents.

There were bright spots, however, during this otherwise rather dour time. London hosted the Olympic Games in 1948 and three years later came the Festival of Britain (100 years after the Great Exhibition), a celebration of British technology and design. The exhibitions that took over derelict land on the south bank of the Thames for the Festival provided the incentive to build the South Bank Centre, now the largest arts centre in Europe.

THE 1950s & 1960s

As the 1950s progressed, life and prosperity gradually returned to London, leading Prime Minister Harold Macmillan in 1957 to proclaim that 'most of our people have never had it so good'. The coronation of Queen Elizabeth II in 1953 had been the biggest television broadcast in history and there was the feeling of a new age dawning.

However, many Londoners were moving out of the city. The population dropped by half a million in the late 1950s, causing a labour shortage that prompted huge recruitment drives in Britain's former colonies. London Transport and the National Health Service were particularly active in encouraging West Indians to emigrate to Britain. Unfortunately, as the Notting Hill race riots of 1958 illustrated, the welcome these new emigrants received was rarely friendly. One of the few relatively tolerant areas of the city was Soho. During the 1950s, it became famed for its seedy, bohemian pubs, clubs, and jazz joints, such as the still-jumping Ronnie Scott's.

By the mid-1960s London had started to swing. The innovative fashions of Mary Quant and others broke the stranglehold of Paris on couture; boutiques blossomed along King's Road, while Biba set the pace in Kensington. Carnaby Street became a byword for hipness, as the city basked in its new-found reputation as the music and fashion capital of the world.

The year of student unrest throughout Europe, 1968, saw the first issue of *Time Out* (a fold-up sheet for 5p) appear on the streets in August. The decade ended with the Beatles naming their final album *Abbey Road* after their recording studios in London NW8, and the Rolling Stones playing a free gig in Hyde Park (July 1969) that drew around half a million people.

THE 1970s & 1980s

The bubble had to burst: many Londoners remember the 1970s as a decade of economic strife. Inflation, the oil crisis and international debt caused chaos in the economy; and the IRA began its bombing campaign on mainland Britain. The explosion of punk in the second half of the decade, sartorially inspired by the idiosyncratic genius of Vivienne Westwood, provided some nihilistic colour.

History will regard the 1980s as the Thatcher era. When the Conservatives won the general election in 1979, Britain's first woman prime minister – the propagandist for 'market forces' and Little Englander morality – set out to expunge socialism and the influence of the 1960s and 1970s. A monetarist policy and cuts in public services savagely widened the divide between rich and poor. While the professionals and 'yuppies' (Young Urban Professionals) profited from tax cuts and easy credit, unemployment soared. In London, riots erupted in Brixton (1981) and Tottenham (1985); mass unemployment and heavy-handed policing methods were seen as contributing factors.

The Greater London Council (GLC) mounted spirited opposition to the Thatcher government, for which sin it was abolished in 1986. Since then, London has been without an elected governing body, but a referendum in May 1998 returned a resounding vote in favour of creating a mayor with authority over the whole of the city.

The spectacular rise in house prices at the end of the 1980s (peaking in August 1988) was followed by an equally alarming slump and the onset of a severe recession that only started to lift in the

Naughty but nice: saucy, seedy Soho in the '60s.

mid-1990s. The Docklands development (one of the Thatcher enterprise schemes, set up in 1981 in order to create a new business centre in the docklands to the east of the City) has faltered many times. Although it can now be counted as a qualified success in terms of attracting business to the Isle of Dogs, the bleakness of the surrounding area and lack of infrastructure make it unpopular with Docklands' office workers, and the locals in the area resent the intrusion of the yuppies.

THE 1990s

The replacement of Margaret Thatcher by John Major as leader of the Conservative Party in October 1990 signalled an upsurge of hope in London. A riot in Trafalgar Square had helped to see off both Maggie and her inequitable Poll Tax.

Yet the early years of the decade were scarred by continuing recession and an all-too-visible problem of homelessness on the streets of London. Shortly after the Conservatives were elected for yet another term in office in 1992, the IRA detonated a massive bomb in the City, killing three people and obliterating the Baltic Exchange. This was followed by a second bomb a year later, which shattered buildings around Bishopsgate. Another Docklands bomb in February 1996 broke a fragile 18-month ceasefire, but now the real possibility of finding a solution to the seemingly intractable problems of Northern Ireland has greatly reduced the danger of terrorism in the capital.

In May 1997, the British people ousted the tired Tories. Tony Blair's notably unsocialist Labour Party swept to victory on a huge wave of enthusiasm. Though the Labour Government has not yet delivered all its promises, its popularity hasn't waned (thanks in part to the lack of any credible opposition) and the general mood in London today remains one of optimism.

The funeral of Princess Diana at Westminster Abbey in September 1997 prompted extraordinary scenes and a thoroughly un-British outpouring of emotion. Far more British was the speed with which life got back to normal – the supply of flowers outside Kensington Palace dried up and the local residents started grouching about the planned 'Diana Memorial Garden' (which has now been downgraded to a far smaller garden for the disabled and a children's playground).

Nimbyism (Not In My Back Yard) is also threatening far more worthwhile projects such as Sir Norman Foster's scheme to pedestrianise part of Trafalgar Square and Westminster. But plenty of big schemes are going ahead, and if the Millennium Dome (*see page 27*) turns out to be as disastrous a waste of money as is widely feared, then there are at least a clutch of excellent projects, particularly along the South Bank (*see page 30*), that will spruce up the capital in time for 2000.

Expensive public transport, traffic-choked roads and environmental pollution remain major problems in London, but tourism to the capital has never been stronger, the city is building on the international renown for the excellence of its shops, restaurants, clubs and creative talent, and the election of a Mayor (*see page 26*) should at last give Londoners a positive voice in how their city is run in the next millennium.

London Today

Derek Hammond gets overexcited.

Roll the titles: **I LOVE LONDON** splashed over Technicolor helicopter footage of Big Ben, shot from high over the river. Roll the soundtrack: a patriotic military march, just in case Betty Windsor's at home in Buckingham Palace. Zoom along Whitehall to Nelson's Column, and children playing on the lions in Trafalgar Square. Cut to stock shots of 'bustling' Carnaby Street; to lovers lazing in 'leafy' Hyde Park – and a busy, brassy slice of psychedelia that you just know was played by 50-year-old men wearing pink ruffle shirts.

Cue plummy actor's voiceover: 'Royal London. Swinging London! Theatreland. Gangland. Dickens's London. Sherlock Holmes's London. London at war. World capital of music, media and money; fashion, food and fiction. Centre of Empire. City of dreams. Shopping. Nightlife. Fame. Fortune. The most historical, mythological, phantasmagorical... *London!*'

This is the London I love: the picture-postcard images that have been shuffled together in multilingual guidebooks and self-important film documentaries in every one of the past 40 years, spawning a never-changing fantasy of London. Nowadays, though, this classic intro sequence is just as likely to unfold into an exposé on the evils of the tourist trinket trade, its reuse exposed as clever satire; but never underestimate that kaleidoscopic jumble of cliché spliced together by dependable men in cravats. Nothing can live up to the promise of legendary London – to the *idea* of London.

Except, of course, the reality of the city itself. London exerts a magical magnetic influence all over Britain, Europe and the globe. London is The Place To Be: it takes a true Londoner to doubt that fact. Millions of visitors pour into the city every year, desperate to soak up the film-set atmosphere; maybe to put down enthusiastic Cockney roots of their own. The attraction of London grows proportionally stronger in direct relation to ambition and greed, desperation and destitution – as if the unfathomable fortune of apparently hopeless cases made good (Kate Moss, Andrew Lloyd Webber, Peter Stringfellow...) might repeat or somehow *rub off*. London has the ability to make everybody feel part of something glamorous. Exciting. Happening. London is the leader. The biggest *and* the smelliest. London means all things to all people. Freedom. Fog. Sex. Dick Van Dyke. Punk Rock. Cup Final day. Wren. The Beatles. *Cats.* Jellied eels.

'Which is all well and good,' adjudged the Time Out London Guide*'s patient editor. 'Enthusiasm. Colourful imagery. Nice. But just perhaps, for the "London Today" section, we could use a little more input on, er, London today? Traffic gridlock. Violent crime. The New Depression. Education. Healthcare. Facts. Figures. Dangerous realism...'*

As every social scientist knows, there's only one verified contemporary temperature indicator of a city statistically proven to be simultaneously red-hot and cool: a visit to a dodgy old waxworks. Around 2.5 million visitors annually troop through the portals of Madame Tussaud's on the Maryle-

bone Road, stumping up nine quid for the ultimate vicarious taste of London Today. A couple of hours in the heightened, London-rich atmosphere of Madame T's is equivalent to decades spent in real time. In Superlondon, you don't only get to notice how much taller you are than the city's movers and shakers, you get to prod them in the midriff too. My own superreal London highlights include Joanna Lumley's hands, the deliciously fleshy folds of Naomi Campbell's armpit and every square inch (by crikey, she's tiny) of our very own Kylie Minogue.

But even Mrs T's manifold faces of modern London – Mohamed al Fayed; Rosemary *Hip and Thigh Diet* Conley masquerading as Marilyn Monroe; Mr T out of the A-Team (a case of nepotism, I suspect) – are dwarfed in memory by the 'Spirit of London' ride, a two-minute, characteristic 2mph taxi ride through 400 years of history, culminating spectacularly in *the sights, the sounds, the colours, the joy...* of London Today. A friendly London bobby has just won a goldfish at the fair. There's a barrel organ playing. Twiggy frugging in a tinfoil mini-skirt. A typical light-fingered cockernee teddy-boy spiv. A roundabout packed with lions and unicorns and pearly kings and queens. A yuppie in a pleasure boat. A Chelsea Pensioner. A beefeater. Benny Hill. It's *unbelievable.* If this larger-than-life London didn't exist, someone would have to go right out and invent it.

'We were thinking along the lines of emergency response times,' admitted an increasingly beleaguered editor. *'How about the scourge of the race-hate cops? Mobies and fags and restaurants? The Princess Charlie scandal? Dog mess in Tooting?'*

London is currently setting benchmarks for state-of-the-art Art. For the first time in years, there's a real buzz about the old manor. Filmically and fashionably the city has shrugged off the millstone of Cool Britannia, and is coasting on a wave of genuine new confidence. Our own Alexander McQueen, Stella McCartney, John Galliano and Jean-Paul Gaultier lead the world at stealing ideas from London streets and selling them to continentals with too much money. London gave the world teddy-boys, mods, hippies and punks: now it offers up the ultimate cult of mix 'n' match, translated for the hard of thinking into mock-secondhand velour bumsters and couture target T-shirts.

Literary London now boasts the precocious multi-talent of football's Vinnie Jones, whose long-awaited autobiography, *You're Dead, Geezer!?!*, could almost have flowed from the pen of our giant storyteller and joined-up thriller writer, Jeffrey Archer. For so many dismal Thatcherite years there was no such thing as society, a local London authority, decent London TV or a British film industry; there weren't even any uplifting London guidebooks singing the praises of the place – just unwatched *25 Years of Pomp and Pageantry* videos, the *Sloane Rangers' Handbook* and the *Asset-Stripper's Guide to London.*

Now every gritty TV drama is set back where it belongs. At last we've relapsed into a roguish cinematic era of *slaaaags* and slappings and shooters. *Lock, Stock and Two Smoking Barrels* is the latest to tap into the rich possibilities of the Borough fruit-and-veg market and all-new suedette car-coats, benefiting greatly from the performance of a certain renaissance footballer-psychopath. Gary Oldman's *Nil By Mouth* was purest south London. Antonia Bird's *Face* was pure east, making up for its lack of Jones with a fictional soundtrack edition of Robert Elms' brilliantly gruff GLR radio show. *Elizabeth* is yet another cutting-edge London offering, set in the sixteenth century, featuring quizmaster Angus Deayton and a substitute combative footballer-poet.

'All fine and dandy,' cajoled the ever-helpful editor. *'But surely any checklist of contemporary cultural glories has to mention our metropolitan melting pot; mayoral lie-ins; millennial domesday;*

Charlton Athletic's creditable Premiership showing… Are you gonna put in some stuff we can actually use, or what?'

Truth is, it just isn't possible for anyone to draw meaningful lines around the modern-day reality of London: it's too perfectly cross-cut and superimposed with misunderstood memories of the past, with hastily rewritten myths and confidently warped nostalgia.

The only way to uncover London Today is to skive a day off work, college or tourist daytripping and simply wander about the city for eight or ten hours, with this book clutched firmly in your hand.

Last year I spent some of the most absurdly memorable days of my life more or less aimlessly treading the London streets, hoovering up the time and the place, the ghosts of the past, fact and fiction. On days I'd otherwise have spent gazing into the blank void of a computer screen, I rediscovered that old school holiday sensation of endless time, boundless possibility and zero structure. I urge you to do the same: pick a tube stop, a pub, a plaque, a park, a grave, a news story and/or a favourite myth, and go out and unpeel a tiny corner of London Tomorrow.

I could recommend ten, 20, 50 thematic, geographic, pop-historic itineraries stretching from the 27th floor of the Park Lane Hilton to Execution Dock, from Jim Bond's pad to Jayne Mansfield's spindly flyover in Chiswick (she opened it in 1962, doncha know), from the summit of St Paul's to the basement of Madame JoJo's; but I'd never be so presumptuous. Best find your own way around the maze of cracks in London's giant jigsaw picture.

Hail a hop-on hop-off trip into the very heart of London: visit Soho discos and East End strippers. Float upriver. Trail the Ripper. Learn rhyming slang. Buy a bobby's helmet. Visit Nelson, Holmes, the Krays, Minogue. Get culture, go shopping, climb landmarks, whistle *Wannabe…* and so to the jolly dodgy cockernee rub-a-dub-dub…

Derek Hammond is author of London, England – A Daytripper's Travelogue from the Coolest City in the World *(Mainstream, £7.99).*

A Mayor for London

The year 2000 will see the election of a Mayor for London. Speculation has been rife ever since the position was first mooted as to who would stand. Ken Livingstone and Lord Archer have been actively campaigning, each in his own inimitable style. Other political figures, media celebs and London luvvies have all flirted with the idea, seemingly waiting for public pressure to sweep them into the battle while they protest their modesty: Glenda Jackson MP, erstwhile Queen Bess, one-time car salesman Steve Norris, broadcasters Trevor Phillips and Darcus Howe, David 'the toe' Mellor, Tony Banks MP, Simon Hughes MP, and of course shy, retiring, Richard Branson. Even Peter Stringfellow has been mentioned, while a London cabbie has also thrown his badge into the ring.

But not Lord Levene of Portsoken KBE. Otherwise known as Lord Mayor of London, Lord Levene is elected, lives in Mansion House, and is head of the oldest municipal corporation in the world. However, the electoral system is archaic, many of his functions verge on the surreal, and his sphere of influence ceases beyond the City.

BACK TO THE PAST

The position of Lord Mayor dates back to 1192 when King John granted a royal charter to the City of London. Although supporters cried in true medieval style 'Londoners shall have no king but their Mayor,' the opposite was true: the Lord Mayor ranks before everybody *but* the sovereign.

And the post boasts a colourful past. Sir William Walworth killed Wat Tyler while wearing the chains of office in the great royal scam to defeat the Peasants' Revolt in 1381; Dick Whittington, philanthropist and cat-lover, was Mayor three times between 1397 and 1420; and John Wilkes, the populist radical, filled the post in 1774. The annual inauguration ceremony, the Lord Mayor's Show (*see page 10*), involves a golden coach, liveried aldermen, horse-drawn carriages and accompanying themed floats – an event untrammelled by the passage of time and described by Pepys as 'very silly'. As might be some of the Mayor's current activities. In one, he personally receives a fish from Billingsgate Market as annual rent. For another, he presides in full regalia while a small boy is suspended above the Thames to beat out the boundary with a birch twig.

BACK TO THE FUTURE

But the new London Mayor will have a more modern role. With five million voters, s/he will be the most personally endorsed political figure in the country. The key issue, though, and one that is still far from being decided, is how much authority the new Mayor will wield. Without tax-raising powers, and influence over key areas such as transport and education, the post will be little more than a costly, pointless political gesture, and the last thing that London needs is another toothless figurehead.

The Millennium Dome

White elephant or ugly duckling? Rowan Moore examines the evidence.

A triumph of form over content? Only you can decide.

The Millennium Dome, and the Millennium Experience it contains, are symbols of whatever you want them to be. For Tony Blair, the Dome 'embodies at once the spirit of confidence and adventure in Britain and the spirit of the future in the world'. To critics it perfectly mirrors the emptiness of the Labour Government's rhetoric, the triumph of style over substance. Even before it was built, its form – part flying saucer, part crab – had become one of Britain's best-known images, as instantly recognisable as Big Ben.

The hope is that, like the Great Exhibition of 1851, the Dome will attract the admiring, envious eyes of the rest of the world on to Britain and that,

like the Festival of Britain of 1951, it will raise the nation's spirits in a collective celebration, described by Blair as 'bold, beautiful and inspiring'. It was felt that, as the prime meridian passes through Greenwich, it would be shameful if the turn of the millennium took place without a major celebration on this site (even though the meridian line barely touches the Dome itself).

FACTS & FIGURES

Major it certainly is. The project officially weighs in at £758 million, a figure that includes all the administration and marketing costs as well as the actual building, but not the £140 million spent before construction started on decontaminating the polluted land on which the structure stands. This figure puts the Dome above the construction cost of the legendarily expensive Getty Museum in Los Angeles, and would buy the Guggenheim Museum in Bilbao ten times over.

The Dome can lay claim to endless superlatives and amazing facts. It is the biggest structure of its kind in the world and could house 13 Albert Halls, 3.8 billion pints of beer, and 18,000 double decker buses. Nelson's column could stand upright and the Eiffel Tower could lie sideways within it. Inverted under the Niagara Falls, it would take ten minutes to fill with water.

INSIDE INFORMATION
Neither its gigantism, however, nor Blair's speeches, nor the Dome's slogan of 'Time to make a difference' entirely answers the question of what it is for. At the time its structure was designed by Mike Davies of the Richard Rogers Partnership in 1996, neither this nor the other key question – what would go in it – was anywhere near being answered. By providing a huge empty space, Davies's design can, therefore, be seen as a brilliant solution to the problem of designing a building of unknown content, a monumentalisation of indecision. Its only blemish is the large hole that had to be cut to accommodate the ventilation shaft of the Blackwall Tunnel, which passes underneath and could not be moved.

Two years later at least some of the contents became clear. It was revealed that 14 'zones' would be built inside the Dome, each one dealing with a different aspect of human life at the turn of the millennium, such as the body, the mind, spirit, work, communication and national identity. These zones would be created by various designers and architects, officially billed as the best of British design. At the centre would be a spectacular theatrical and acrobatic event, with music by Peter Gabriel and designed by Mark Fisher, who is best known for his sets for the Rolling Stones.

The zone that has attracted most attention is the Body Zone, first planned as a giant human figure, whose gender, whether male, female or androgynous, was the subject of much indecision and debate. Eventually, in the hands of the architect Nigel Coates, it has managed to incorporate both sexes – a colossal, semi-abstract sculpture of a man and a woman in a 'soft embrace'. The structurally daring Mind Zone, by Zaha Hadid, is to deal with the paradoxes of human perception and thought, with the help of works by contemporary artists. Another zone, intended to make people reflect on their impact on their environment, recreates a traditional British seaside town, complete with a real beach (but hopefully without the sewage).

TO BOLDLY GO...
The idea is that the Dome should be a place where the techniques of the modern entertainment industry are put to enlightening ends. As Blair put it, the Dome 'will contain a rich texture of feelings: spiritual, emotional, fun'. It would be 'exhilarating like Disney World – yet different. Educational and interactive, like the Science Museum – yet different. Emotional and uplifting like a West End musical – yet different.'

Not everyone is convinced. If the Dome has broken records of size and cost, it is also record-breaking in the criticism it has attracted, being attacked as vacuous, bombastic and lacking in creative direction. Would the money not have been better spent on hospitals and schools? The Dome's dependence on sponsors to attract £150 million of revenue has led to accusations that its (confused) visionary ideals have been compromised. Is McDonald's really the ideal sponsor for a celebration of British achievement? Does the involvement of the arms manufacturers GEC and British Aerospace strike the right note in an event looking towards a better future?

COMEDY OF ERRORS?
Stephen Bayley, the creative director, left in a storm, saying, 'I don't do theme parks.' Designers complained that no one told them what they were meant to be doing. The original choice of roof fabric was condemned as environmentally damaging by Greenpeace and for being German-made by the tabloid press. The minister in charge of the Dome at the time, Peter Mandelson, first defended the fabric and then switched to another. The fact that this was American-made did not seem to trouble the erratic logic of tabloid xenophobia. And there have been endless problems with the extension of the Jubilee Line, which is intended to be the major means of reaching the Dome. At the time of writing it was by no means certain that the extension would be open by the start of 2000 – a potentially disastrous situation.

Religious leaders complained that there was too little mention of God in an event marking the 2,000th anniversary of Christ's birth, and the involvement of non-Christian religions from Britain's multi-ethnic society has also raised difficult issues. Sponsors fought shy of backing the Spirit Zone, which eventually was rescued by backing from a Hindu family. Even so, its budget and design were substantially cut.

To all the criticisms the Dome's backers had one answer: critics heaped scorn on the Crystal Palace and the Festival of Britain, yet both have gone down in history as triumphs. To this point Stephen Bayley riposts that, this time, 'the philistines are on the inside'. By the end of the year 2000, we should know who was right.

Rowan Moore is architecture critic of the Evening Standard.

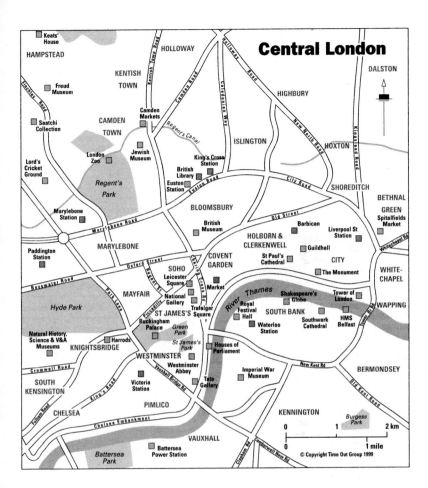

Central London

Keats' House
HAMPSTEAD
KENTISH TOWN
HOLLOWAY
Freud Museum
HIGHBURY
DALSTON
Saatchi Collection
CAMDEN TOWN
Camden Markets
ISLINGTON
HOXTON
Lord's Cricket Ground
London Zoo
Jewish Museum
King's Cross Station
SHOREDITCH
Regent's Park
British Library
Euston Station
BLOOMSBURY
BETHNAL GREEN
Spitalfields Market
Marylebone Station
British Museum
Barbican
Liverpool St Station
Paddington Station
MARYLEBONE
HOLBORN & CLERKENWELL
St Paul's Cathedral
Guildhall
CITY
WHITE-CHAPEL
COVENT GARDEN
SOHO
Leicester Square
The Monument
Hyde Park
MAYFAIR
National Gallery
Market
River Thames
Shakespeare's Globe
Tower of London
WAPPING
Natural History, Science & V&A Museums
ST JAMES'S
Trafalgar Square
Royal Festival Hall
SOUTH BANK
Southwark Cathedral
HMS Belfast
KNIGHTSBRIDGE
Buckingham Palace
Green Park
Waterloo Station
Harrods
St James's Park
Houses of Parliament
WESTMINSTER
Westminster Abbey
Imperial War Museum
BERMONDSEY
SOUTH KENSINGTON
Victoria Station
Tate Gallery
CHELSEA
PIMLICO
KENNINGTON
Burgess Park
VAUXHALL
Battersea Power Station
Battersea Park

0   1   2 km
0   1 mile

© Copyright Time Out Group 1999

Sightseeing

The South Bank

Maps 8, 11 & 12

The south bank of the Thames, from Lambeth to Tower bridges, may seem an unorthodox place to start a tour of central London, but, in terms of history, culture and the wealth of new developments leading up to the millennium, there's no more absorbing and rewarding part of the city. The south bank's greatest asset is that, while most of the north bank of the river is dominated by fume-filled expressways, the entire length of the south side can be walked without coming into contact with a single car.

Lambeth Bridge to Hungerford Bridge

Just north of Lambeth Bridge huddle the red-brick buildings of **Lambeth Palace**, official residence of the Archbishops of Canterbury since the twelfth century. Next door is the absorbing **Museum of Garden History** (*see page 127*) in the deconsecrated church of St Mary-at-Lambeth. St Thomas's Hospital, containing the **Florence Nightingale Museum** (*see page 121*), stands on one side of Westminster Bridge, but the dominant presence here is the looming bulk of the newly revamped **County Hall**. Home of the Greater London Council until its abolition in 1986, it now contains two hotels, a Chinese restaurant, a McDonald's, the **London Aquarium** (*see below*) and the two-floor arcade-game nirvana of **Namco Station**. And there's still room for more. The next addition is set to be the **FA Premier League Hall of Fame**, due to open in March 1999, which will include wax figures of famous players.

Next door, **Jubilee Gardens** will be the site of one of the most spectacular of the Millennium projects, the £19-million, 800-person capacity **BA Millennium Wheel**. When completed in early 2000, it will be the tallest Ferris wheel in the world at 450ft (137m) high. The riverside walk under Hungerford Bridge (the footbridge is soon to be rebuilt) will be familiar to fans of *Four Weddings and a Funeral* as the place where Hugh Grant made a prat of himself declaring his feelings for Andie MacDowell.

Hungerford Bridge to Blackfriars Bridge

The arts complex on the south bank represents London at its most self-consciously modern. Denys Lasdun's **Royal Festival Hall** (*see pages 232 and 245*) was built to mark the let's-all-cheer-up-after-the-war 1951 Festival of Britain. Accordingly, the new buildings were a showcase for contemporary architectural and building skills. It would be fair to say that it is not universally admired, although

appreciation is not made easier by the raised concrete walkways that stranglingly swirl about it and the proximity of the true smack-in-the-face brutalism of the **Hayward Gallery** (*see page 133*). Plans to humanise the area have been mooted since at least the 1980s, but only in December 1998 was a blueprint scheme published that is likely to be implemented (from 2001). The Royal Festival Hall will remain, but the unloved buildings housing the Hayward, the **Queen Elizabeth Hall** (RFH2) and the **Purcell Room** (RFH3) will be demolished, along with the concrete walkways, to be reborn on the other side of Hungerford Bridge in a new low-rise building. In their place, a new film complex will be constructed to house the **National Film Theatre** (*see page 238*) and the **Museum of the Moving Image** (MOMI; *see page 119*), both currently crouched under Waterloo Bridge.

Next door, and also due for some improvements, is the immense, boxy **Royal National Theatre** (*see page 265*). The glorious view over to the City from **Waterloo Bridge**, especially fine at dusk, inspired the 1967 Kinks' hit *Waterloo Sunset*. On the riverside walk under the bridge is a regular book market.

Between Waterloo and Blackfriars bridges, the most distinctive building is undoubtedly the beautifully restored **Oxo Tower Wharf**. The cleverly conceived art deco tower incorporates the word 'OXO' into its design, thereby circumventing council rules against large-scale advertising. The building now contains flats and small retail crafts units, and is topped by a glitzy restaurant and bar (*see page 156*), run by the people behind Harvey Nichols' **Fifth Floor** restaurant (*see page 155*). Anyone can enjoy the views from the top from the eighth-floor public viewing gallery. A new museum, the intriguingly titled **The Museum of...** (*see page 126*) opened in late 1998. The tower and much of the surrounding housing (plus the cutesy shops of **Gabriel's Wharf**) are maintained by the admirable, non-profit-making Coin Street Community Builders, who have done much to retain the integrity of this fast-developing area and ensure that the original inhabitants are not priced out. The annual **Coin Street Festival** is a multi-faceted celebration of local life and the arts (June-Sept; *see also page 256*). Another exciting project, a floating, Olympic-sized lido, is planned for the stretch of the Thames by the Oxo Tower.

*A symphony in concrete: the uncompromising **Royal National Theatre**.*

Around Waterloo

A pathway links the Royal Festival Hall to **Waterloo Station**, where Eurostar trains arrive and depart from under Nicholas Grimshaw's glass-roofed terminus. This short walk once involved negotiating a complicated, unpleasant route across busy roads and down stinking alleys, but, again, great strides are being taken to make the experience easier and more pleasant. The roundabout outside Waterloo Station was once home to legions of homeless people who camped out in 'cardboard city'. No longer. The massive £20-million **BFI London IMAX Cinema** (*see page 234*) has been built on the site (opening spring 1999); it will feature a ten-storey high screen, the biggest in Europe.

Behind and below the station on the other side, **Lower Marsh** has a lively market on weekdays, and leads on to the curiously named **The Cut**, home of the **Young Vic** (*see page 270*) and the **Old Vic** theatres (*see page 265*). The former contains the excellent **Konditor & Cook** café (*see page 159*), while other good eating options here include the lively tapas bar **Mesón Don Felipe** (no.53), the excellent seafood of **Livebait** (nos.41-43; *see page 165*) and the airy bar-restaurant, the **Fire Station** (150 Waterloo Road; *see page 179*).

Bankside

The original Blackfriars Bridge (1760-9) was the third to span the Thames. It was under here that Italian banker Roberto Calvi was found hanging in 1982. The area between here and London Bridge, known as **Bankside**, was, for many centuries, London's pleasure-zone. As it was outside the puritanical jurisdiction of the City, theatres, bear-baiting pits, bawdy houses, inns and other dens of iniquity could freely prosper. There's no little irony that Bankside (officially deemed 'a naughty place' by royal proclamation in 1547) fell within the sway of the Bishops of Winchester. Far from condemning the depravity, the Church made a tidy sum from its regulation, and if anyone got too unruly they could always be cast into the dank depths of the Clink Prison. The prison was destroyed in 1780, but its site, on one of the area's most appropriately dismal and Dickensian streets, is now home to the **Clink Exhibition** (*see below*). Next door are the scant remains of **Winchester Palace** – little is left beyond the rose window of the Great Hall.

Modern Bankside's commanding presence is that mighty monolithic temple of industry, **Bankside Power Station** (which only operated for 17 years before being closed in 1980). Like Battersea Power Station upriver (*see page 102*), it was designed by Giles Gilbert Scott and will make a magnificent home for the £130-million **Tate Gallery**'s modern art collection when it opens in May 2000 (and aims to pull in two million visitors annually; *see page 131*). The building will contain one of the most stunning spaces in the city, running the length, height and almost half the width of the mammoth structure – and it'll be open to all, not just those visiting the gallery. Tiny in comparison, and a reminder of the Bankside of old, is its neighbour – the reconstructed **Shakespeare's Globe** (*see below* and *page 265*).

Next to the Globe is a curious little terrace, containing the house in which Wren is said to have lived during the construction of St Paul's. One of the most worthwhile of the Millennium projects will be a new footbridge across the river here, and the clearing of the sightlines on the north bank so that the view that Wren enjoyed of his masterwork from the south side will be restored. Two minor attractions nearby are the **London Fire Brigade Museum** on Southwark Bridge Road (*see page 126*) and the **Bankside Gallery** at 48 Hopton Street, home to the Royal Watercolour Society and the Royal Society of Painter/Printmakers.

A bigger draw will be the ambitious **Vinopolis, City of Wine** project between Blackfriars and Southwark bridges, which will be 'London's first

adult visitor attraction dedicated to the world of wine and its associated pleasures' (due to open in summer 1999). Sounds promising.

Borough

If you like literature, you'll love Borough. One of the area's biggest draws is the magnificent pub **The George**, London's sole surviving galleried coaching inn. Before custom-built theatres were introduced, plays were performed in the courtyard while people watched from the galleries. The White Hart Inn, where Mr Pickwick first meets Sam Weller in *The Pickwick Papers*, stood in White Hart Yard (it was pulled down in 1889). Talbot Yard marks the site of the Tabard Inn, where Chaucer's pilgrims meet at the beginning of *The Canterbury Tales*. The church of St George-the-Martyr (corner of Borough High Street and Long Lane) is mentioned in Dickens' *Little Dorrit* – the heroine is born in Marshalsea Prison, which used to stand a few doors away. The author's father was imprisoned in Marshalsea for debt in 1824.

Borough has always been a congested place. Until 1750, London Bridge was the only crossing point into the City, and Borough High Street became a stagecoach terminus. The seventeenth-century poet Thomas Dekker described the street as 'a continued ale house with not a shop to be seen between'. The chaotic and raucous Southwark Fair was held here every September from 1462 to 1763, until it was suppressed by the spoilsport Corporation of London.

All but submerged under sweeping road and rail lines, **Southwark Cathedral** (*see below*) has recently received a £3.9-million lottery grant for the pedestrianisation and landscaping of its surrounding area. Not such good news is that Borough's unique streets, little touched this century and long popular for period film sets, may be decimated by a rail improvement scheme. The greatest tragedy would be the destruction of covered **Borough Market** – a fruit and vegetable market has been on the site since the thirteenth century. However, a new market scheme going under the umbrella name of 'London's Larder' is hoping to breathe new life into the area by attracting food retailing and wholesaling operations, restaurants, a culinary school and other food-related businesses to the area.

Not far from the cathedral, the impressive replica of Sir Francis Drake's **Golden Hinde** (*see below*) is well worth a visit. Several attractions are clustered around London Bridge Station: the **Old Operating Theatre, Museum & Herb Garret** (*see page 122*), opposite Guy's Hospital, **Winston Churchill's Britain At War Experience** (*see below*) and the gory **London Dungeon** (*see below*).

Tower Bridge & Bermondsey

The stretch of the river from London to Tower bridges is dominated by the uncompromising bulk of **HMS Belfast** (*see below*) and the massive, soaring, glass-roofed arcade of Hay's Galleria. Its centrepiece is David Kemp's splendidly silly *The Navigators* mechanical sculpture. This is the start of **Bermondsey**, an area that was long a focus for Christianity – **Tooley Street** was once home to no fewer than three abbots, a prior and the church of St Olave's. Its near-namesake, **St Olaf House**, a fabulous art deco 1930s warehouse, is worth a look.

The capital's most spectacular bridge, **Tower Bridge**, is a relatively recent addition to the London skyline, opening not much more than a century ago in 1894. If you want to find out more about it, undergo the **Tower Bridge Experience** (*see page 44*). East of here, **Butler's Wharf** is the home of a trio of Sir Terence Conran restaurants and, just a little further on, the excellent **Design Museum** (*see page 117*), which Conran, the man who did much to bring good household design to the ordinary punter, helped to establish. Around the corner is the more idiosyncratic charm of the **Bramah Tea & Coffee Museum** (*see page 125*).

Much of this area has a Dickensian feel to it – check out **St Saviour's Dock**, a muddy creek between towering warehouses, visible over a low parapet in Jamaica Road. In Dickens' day, the streets around here formed a notorious slum called Jacob's Island, where Bill Sikes gets his comeuppance in *Oliver Twist*. Bermondsey Street is home to a superb antiques market, frequented by serious collectors and dealers (*see page 193*).

Clink Exhibition

1 Clink Street, SE1 (0171 378 1558). London Bridge tube/rail. **Open** 10am-6pm daily. **Admission** £4; £3 concs; £9 family ticket. **Credit** AmEx, JCB, MC, £TC, V. **Map 11 P8**
A better job could have been made of bringing to life Bankside's ribald past than the couple of recreated cells, piped music and illustrations on display here. This was the site of the Bishops of Winchester's small jail that, until its destruction during the Gordon Riots of 1780, held misbehaving actors, prostitutes and drunks dragged from the raucous taverns, theatres and whorehouses of Bankside. The expression 'in the clink', meaning in prison, originated from this dismal place.

Golden Hinde

St Mary Overie Dock, Cathedral Street, SE1 (0171 403 0123). Monument tube or London Bridge tube/rail. **Open** 10am-6pm daily (phone to check). **Admission** £2.30; £1.50-£1.90 concs. **Credit** MC, V. **Map 11 P8**
This full-size reconstruction of Sir Francis Drake's sixteenth-century flagship looks impressively pristine considering the two decades it has spent circumnavigating the world as a seaborne museum. It's hard to believe that the dinky ship travelled over 100,000 miles, many more than the original. Years of research went into producing an authentic reproduction, and it shows: the interior has been recreated in minute detail and the diminutive proportions of the gun deck and hold feel painfully real. The atmosphere on board is fleshed out by 'crew' in Elizabethan costume, who regale visitors with tales of uncomfortable nights on the bare deck awash with saltwater, and the brutal justice imposed on any sailor who swiped more than his share of precious rations. A big hit with kids.

Ship ahoy! It's the **Golden Hinde**.

HMS Belfast

Morgan's Lane, Tooley Street, SE1 (0171 407 6434).
London Bridge tube/rail. **Open** *Mar-Oct* 10am-6pm daily;
Nov-Feb 10am-5pm daily. **Admission** £4.70; £2.40-£3.60
concs; £11.80 family ticket. **Credit** MC, £TC, V.
Map 12 R8
One of the most spectacular sights on the Thames, the
11,500-ton battlecruiser, built in 1938, was instrumental in
the sinking of the German battleship *Scharnhorst* during
World War II and remained in active service until just after
the Korean War. Exploring its seven decks, boiler and
engine rooms and massive gun turrets is great fun – especially for children. Interestingly, the front two turrets are
trained on the Scratchwood motorway services on the M1,
12.5 miles (20km) away to the north-west of London – more,
one assumes, to demonstrate the guns' great range than to
comment on the quality of motorway food.

London Aquarium

County Hall, Riverside Building, Westminster Bridge
Road, SE1 (0171 967 8000). Westminster tube or
Waterloo tube/rail. **Open** 10am-6pm daily (last admission
5pm). **Admission** £8; £6-£7 concs; £22 family ticket;
free under-2s, wheelchair-users. **Credit** AmEx, JCB, MC,
£TC, V. **Map 8 M9**
A three-level display of hundreds of varieties of fish and
sea life from around the world. The observatory, interactive
displays and friendly, touchable rays make this a hit with
children, although it's wise to come either early or late in
the day to avoid the crowds. The sharks are, understandably, popular residents. Winner of the 1998 Group Leisure
Industry Award for 'Best New Attraction'.

London Dungeon

28-34 Tooley Street, SE1 (0171 403 0606). London
Bridge tube/rail. **Open** 10am-5.30pm daily (last
admission one hour before closing). **Admission** £8.95;
£6.50-£7.95 concs; free under-5s, wheelchair users.
Credit AmEx, MC, £TC, V. **Map 12 Q8**
It's hard not to feel uneasy about the glorification of
pain, horror and death at the London Dungeon; it's equally
hard to deny that the punters – and gore-adoring older
kids in particular – love it: they pile in by the coachload.
Peer through railings amid a dank, dark, musty maze of
gloomy arches and eerie nooks, and thrill at the scenes of
medieval torture and the screams as the rack is tightened
by another notch. Groups of visitors are herded into a mock

courtroom, before being sentenced by a 'judge'. The punishment, it seems, is a scary boat ride that, frankly, isn't.
The last part of the museum centres on one of the grizzliest
episodes from British history – the ever-popular tale of jolly
old woman-mutilator Jack the Ripper: actors in costume take
you on the hunt for the madman through rooms made to
look like the East End (in pre-curry house days). Chilling
and fun or exploitative and sick? Only you can decide.

Shakespeare's Globe

New Globe Walk, Bankside, SE1 (0171 928 6406).
Mansion House tube/Cannon Street or London Bridge
tube/rail. **Open** *May-Sept* 9am-12.30pm daily; *Oct-Apr*
10am-5pm daily. **Admission** £5; £3-£4 concs; £14
family ticket. **Credit** MC, £TC, V. **Map 11 O7**
The original Globe theatre, where many of Shakespeare's
plays were first performed, burned down in 1613 during a
performance of *Henry VIII*, when a cannon spark set fire to
the roof; the only minor casualty was a man whose breech-
es caught fire. Nearly 400 years later, the Globe has been
rebuilt not far from its original site, using construction methods and materials as close to the originals as possible.
Productions (staged in summer only) are authentically
Elizabethan, relying chiefly on natural light, a simple,
unchanging set and with audience participation encouraged.
The admission price includes a fascinating guided tour (by
lively and well-informed guides who inject a real passion
into their work) and entrance to a temporary exhibition that
sets out the history of the theatre and the surrounding area
of Bankside. The exhibition is currently inside the shell of
the indoor Inigo Jones theatre (where performances will ultimately take place in winter); when the theatre is completed
in September 1999, the exhibition will expand and move to
the undercroft. There's a tranquil café and restaurant on the
site already, and plans for more shops and eateries to be
built nearby by the end of 2000.

Southwark Cathedral

Montague Close, SE1 (0171 407 3708). London Bridge
tube/rail. **Open** 8am-6pm daily (closing times vary on
religious holidays). **Services** 8am, 8.15am, 12.30pm,
12.45pm, 5.30pm, Mon-Fri; 9am, 9.15am, 4pm, Sat; 9am,
9.15am, 11am, 3pm, Sun. **Admission** free. **Map 11 P8**
Originally the monastic church of St Mary Overie, this
splendid but little-visited building became an Anglican
cathedral in 1905. The first church on the site may date
from as early as the seventh century; the oldest parts of the
present building are twelfth-century. After the Reformation,
the church fell into disrepair and was partially used as a
bakery and a pigsty. Heavy-handed Victorian restoration
added to the fascinating mix of architectural styles, including a fine Gothic choir. John Harvard, benefactor of Harvard
University, was born in Southwark in 1607 and baptised
in the church; more recently, the John Harvard Chapel was
the setting for the film *The Slipper and the Rose*. Perhaps
the greatest surprise, however, is that there's a Pizza
Express restaurant in the Chapter House.

Winston Churchill's Britain at War Experience

64-66 Tooley Street, SE1 (0171 403 3171). London
Bridge tube/rail. **Open** *Apr-Sept* 10am-5.30pm (last
admission); *Oct-Mar* 10am-4.30pm (last admission).
Admission £5.95; £2.95-£3.95 concs; £14 family ticket.
Credit AmEx, MC, £TC, V. **Map 12 Q8**
This 'real life' experience is, inevitably, nothing of the sort.
What you get is a rather shabby attempt to evoke Blitz-time
London, with rickety speakers blaring out '40s radio broadcasts and showtunes, and awkward-looking dummies
dressed up in period costumes. There is a lot of fascinating
memorabilia though, if you care to look for it among the
muddled wall displays, and children might enjoy the atmospheric reproductions of an air raid shelter, dance hall and a
huge darkened bombsite.

The City

'I have seen the West-end, the parks, the fine squares; but I love the City far better. The City seems so much more in earnest, its rush, its roar are such serious things, sights, sounds. The City is getting its living – the West-end but enjoying its pleasures. At the West-end you may be amused, but in the City you are excited.'

Charlotte Brontë, *Villette*

Maps 9-12

Not at the weekend you're not. Despite a working population of 250,000, only 6,000 live within the governance of the City's ruling body, the Corporation of London. Come on a Saturday or Sunday or after 9pm on a weekday and you'll be wandering a ghost town of deserted office buildings, shut-up shops and pubs, and empty streets. Yet visit on a weekday and you will feel something of Charlotte Brontë's excitement.

Founded as a port, commerce has always been the City's *raison d'être*: according to Tacitus, in AD60 Roman Londinium was already 'filled with traders and a celebrated centre of commerce'. And if the trading is now in virtual rather than actual commodities, it's still possible to trace a direct lineage from the chaotic, cacophonous stalls of medieval Cheapside to the chaotic, cacophonous dealing rooms of today's City. This is one of the key financial centres on the planet – there are more foreign banks in London than in any other city (around 540) and the foreign exchange market is the largest in the world. The very air seems to vibrate with millions being made and lost. Yet the City is more than blokes in suits shouting into phones.

For most of the capital's history, the City of London *was* the city of London – hence, that all-important, self-important capital letter. Apart from a brief Saxon excursion westward, it was only in the seventeenth century that there was significant, systematic building outside the boundaries of the old Roman wall.

Today's City – its 320 hectares (1¼ square miles) almost accurately known also as the Square Mile – subsumes the original site of Roman Londinium. Its boundaries are defined by Temple Bar to the west, Smithfield and Moorfields to the north, Tower Hill in the east and the Thames in the south. Flattened by the Great Fire of 1666, and again by the 1940-41 Blitz, the City has always been in such a hurry to rebuild, to get back to business, that no grand Haussmann-like scheme to rationalise the place has ever been able to get off the ground. But the City, though proud of its lack

Dr Johnson's House. *See page 42.*

of sentimentality, hasn't entirely forgotten its past. Uninspiring office blocks may line many of the streets today, but these streets still largely follow their medieval courses, their names speaking their history – Old Jewry, Ironmonger Row, Poultry, Bread Street. Several excellent museums and a magnificent crop of seventeenth-century churches (*see pages 40-41*) provide further links to the City's proud and colourful past.

Along Fleet Street

Fleet Street, once synonymous with Britain's national daily and Sunday newspapers, leads eastwards from the Strand towards Ludgate Hill and St Paul's. It still bustles, but the bitterly fought departure of the papers to Wapping and Docklands in the late 1980s has torn the heart out of Fleet Street; its individual character has gone. No more do the hot metal presses clatter into the night; no more do the booze-fuelled hacks teeter from their offices to the pub and back again. The grandiose, fieldstone grey *Daily Telegraph* building (no.135) is now occupied by finance houses; the ground-breaking black glass-and-chrome *Daily Express* building at nos.121-128 (the first glass-curtain structure in Britain when it was built in 1932) stands empty. Only the Reuters/Press Association building (no.85) remains as a reminder of the 500-year association of Fleet Street with the printed word. It all started when William Caxton's successor, Wynkyn de Worde, brought his presses here from Westminster in 1500 and set up shop at **St Bride's** (*see page 40*). It is still affectionately thought of as the printers and journalists' church, although these are not professions renowned for their piety.

Literary figures, too, were familiar with the hostelries and chophouses of Fleet Street. A plaque on Child's bank (no.1) marks the site of the Devil's Tavern, where Ben Jonson, Samuel Pepys and Samuel Johnson all supped. Johnson was also a regular at the most famous of the Fleet Street pubs, the still-standing **Ye Olde Cheshire Cheese** (on the corner with Wine Office Court). The corpulent doctor's only surviving London home in Gough Square, restored and opened to the public as **Dr Johnson's House** (*see below*), is a handy one-minute's stagger away. Nearby is Johnson's Court, where Charles Dickens delivered what was to become his first published story, 'stealthily one evening in twilight, into a dark letterbox in a dark office up a dark corner of Fleet Street'.

As you head down into the Fleet valley (the river is now underground) towards Ludgate Circus, the view of St Paul's – particularly at night, floodlit and apparently floating over the City – is magical.

Around St Paul's

Wren's masterwork may now be forced to jostle for position with graceless office blocks, but **St Paul's Cathedral** (*see below*) still stands proud as a symbol of British resilience, largely thanks to wartime photos of the flame-licked, but apparently untouched, cathedral weathering the Blitz. It actually suffered direct hits on several occasions, and in one night alone a total of 28 incendiary bombs fell in the immediate vicinity – but the Kipling-esque imagery of brave St Paul's keeping its head while all about it were losing theirs was just the tonic the nation needed.

Adjoining **Paternoster Square** fared less well: all but flattened by the Luftwaffe, it was rebuilt in the 1960s as a precinct of shops and offices that almost immediately became a byword for architectural ugliness. After a ten-year wrangle, plans were finally agreed at the end of 1997 to rebuild the square in a mixture of classical and modern styles.

The old marketplace of medieval London, **Cheapside** ('ceap' or 'chepe' is the Old English word for market), runs down from the cathedral to Bank. Shakespeare and John Donne used to drink in the raucous taverns here that once quenched the thirsts of the hoarse street sellers, while the surrounding area echoed to the work of craftsmen (no prizes for guessing what was sold and made in Milk Street and Bread Street).

Bow Lane, by the side of **St Mary-le-Bow** (*see page 41*), is now an appealing, narrow pedestrianised street, lined with shops, sandwich bars and pubs. At its southern end, **St Mary Aldermary** is one of Wren's rare experiments with the Perpendicular style, based on the pre-Fire church. Over Queen Victoria Street is Garlick Hill; its medieval name proving false the supposed antipathy between the English and the pungent bulb. At the bottom of the street is Wren's church of **St James Garlickhythe**, which has the highest roof in the City (after St Paul's). Its light-filled interior remains much as it was in the seventeenth century, and has earned the church the nickname of 'Wren's Lantern'. Between here and Cannon Street is wine and Whittington territory. The four-times Mayor of London lived on half-cobbled College Hill (a plaque on nos.19-20 marks the site of his house). He was buried in **St Michael Paternoster Royal** at the foot of the hill. Inside, 1960s stained glass by John Hayward depicts a flat-capped Dick, together with his apocryphal cat. The name of this Wren church derives from two ancient thoroughfares nearby – Paternoster Lane (where rosaries were once made) and La Reole, a wine-making region near Bordeaux, popular with London's medieval wine importers. The **Vintners' Hall** (*see page 37*) is close by, across Upper Thames Street.

South of St Paul's lies a little explored but delightful tangle of alleyways, concealing shops, pubs and the dinky Wren church of **St Andrew by the Wardrobe**. Built in 1685-95, the church's curious name dates from 1361, when the King's Wardrobe (the ceremonial clothes of the royal family) were moved to the adjoining building. Nearby, two other Wren creations, **St Benet** and **St Nicholas Cole Abbey**, are, unfortunately, usually closed. Facing the former across scruffy Queen Victoria Street is the unexpectedly neat red-brick, seventeenth-century mansion of the **College of Arms** (*see below*), which still industriously examines and records the pedigrees of those to whom such things matter. Just west of here, at traffic-swept **Blackfriars**, the Dominicans – the 'black friars' – once had a monastery (it was dissolved in 1538; all that remains is a chunk of wall in Ireland Yard), and the Normans built one of their defensive forts, **Baynard's Castle**, to keep the unruly Londoners in check.

North of Blackfriars station is **Apothecaries' Hall**, one of the most charming of the livery halls (*see page 37*), and, close by on Ludgate Hill, stands the church of **St Martin within Ludgate**, its lead spire still visible over the surrounding buildings as Wren intended (which, alas, is more than can be said for those of most of his other churches). After reflecting on the works of God, ponder upon the sins of man around the corner in the most famous court in the land, the **Old Bailey** (*see below*), built on the site of the infamous Newgate Prison.

North to Smithfield

The two major presences north of St Paul's are Smithfield Market and St Bartholomew's Hospital. Both have ancient roots. Smithfield was originally 'smooth field' – it had no blacksmithery connections, although there was an equine link. William Fitz Stephen, in 1173, wrote of 'a smoth field where every Friday there is a celebrated rendezvous of fine horses to be sold'.

As a large open space near to the City, Smithfield was much in demand for all manner of public events – jousts, sports matches, tournaments, executions and the most famous of all London's once-numerous annual fairs. Founded in 1123, **Bartholomew Fair** was renowned as a cloth fair before transmogrifying into the raucous entertainment fest that Ben Jonson captured so vividly in his seventeenth-century play of the same name. The spoilsport City authorities finally suppressed the fair in 1855, blaming it for encouraging public disorder, and built **Smithfield Market** on the site

(it opened in 1868). Livestock had been traded here for centuries, but now the slaughtering took place elsewhere and Smithfield became – and remains – a meat market (or, rather, four linked markets). Now officially known as London Central Markets, a recent £70-million refit and refurbishment has left Horace Jones's immense Victorian East and West Markets looking splendid, repainted in their original colours of deep blues, reds and green with gold stars. If you want to see the working market, an early rise will be necessary – kicking off at around 3am, all the action is over by 8am – but you can reward your dedication with a fried breakfast and a pint with the meat porters in one of the nearby pubs (which have special early licences). Traders are normally happy to sell meat to the public, but you'll have to buy in bulk.

The instigation of Bartholomew Fair was only one of the actions of Rahere, court jester to Henry I, who almost died from malarial fever on a pilgrimage to Rome, and vowed to build a hospital on his return. He kept his promise, establishing **St Bartholomew's Hospital**, as well as a priory and the wonderfully atmospheric church of **St Bartholomew-the-Great** (*see page 40*). Although under a seemingly permanent threat of closure (the accident and emergency department has already been axed), Bart's retains its position

---

Wanna be in my gang?

Since the Middle Ages, the government of the City of London has been in the hands of the **guilds** or **livery companies**, so called because of the costumes (or 'liveries') that senior members are entitled to wear. The livery companies are descendants of the ancient Saxon 'frith guilds'. These mutual aid societies provided support to members in times of need, in return for a payment ('gild' or 'geld'). In medieval times, the guilds became associated with particular trades and crafts. Members grouped together to promote their trade and to regulate standards, the training of apprentices and pricing of their goods.

Membership of a trade or craft guild, gained by seven years' apprenticeship, was the only way to be granted 'freedom of the City', still a qualification for holding civic office (today, 'freedom' can be bought). Non-freemen had no say in the government of the City; they could not keep a shop or exercise a craft or trade inside the City walls, and had to pay a fee to sell their goods at market. Apprentices had a terrible reputation, frequently running riot and

attacking 'foreigners' (from other parts of Britain) or 'aliens' (anyone from abroad).

The Weavers' Guild was the first craft guild to purchase its royal charter in 1155. The first livery company to be incorporated was the Mercers' Company (traders in fine cloth) who received their charter in 1394. By 1423, over 100 guilds and livery companies were registered and the **Guildhall** (*see page 43*) became the meeting place for the City's government.

By monopolising trade, the guilds prospered. They bought land and built imposing halls, furnished with gold and silver plate. In keeping with their charitable origins, they established schools, almshouses and other institutions for the benefit of their members and for the poor.

By the eighteenth century, the livery companies no longer dominated trade and many of the old crafts (such as the Longbowstring Makers) were defunct. Nevertheless, the Liveries continue to play a key role in the government of the City. Some companies (the Goldsmiths and Fishmongers, for example) still fulfil an active role in supervising their trades; others are more

---

as London's oldest and best-loved hospital. It was to here that Wat Tyler was brought after being stabbed at Smithfield by the Lord Mayor in 1381, although he was immediately dragged out and beheaded by the King's men (*see page 14*). A small museum of the hospital's history can be visited (*see page 122*). Nearby, on King Edward Street, the **National Postal Museum** (*see page 114*), packed with superb stamp collections, is, alas for philatelists, closed until further notice.

Around Bank

The City has no indisputable centre, but if any place can lay claim to being the heart of the Square Mile, it's the great convergence of streets at **Bank**, overlooked by the unshakeable, self-confident triumvirate of the **Bank of England**, the **Royal Exchange** and the Lord Mayor's official residence, **Mansion House** (*see below*).

Britain's national bank was founded in 1694 to provide William III with the necessary finance to fight the French. It had its ups and downs, but eventually secured its position as the government's banker, with the authority to print and issue banknotes, and the responsibility of storing the country's gold reserves, managing the national debt and safeguarding the value of the British currency. The present building dates from 1925 to 1939, although

the outer 'curtain' walls of Sir John Soane's 1788 structure have been retained. The admirably accessible exhibition of the Bank's past and present in the **Bank of England Museum** (*see page 125*) is worth a look. Behind the Bank is the modern **Stock Exchange** (closed to the public).

Overshadowing the Bank is the massive neo-classical portico of the Royal Exchange, built by William Tite and opened by Queen Victoria in 1844. Sir Thomas Gresham created the Exchange in 1566 as a meeting and trading centre for merchants – he is honoured by a statue over the entrance in Exchange Buildings and his grasshopper emblem on the bell tower. The Royal Exchange is now HQ of the futures market, but trading no longer takes place on the premises.

Around the back of the Bank of England, it's worth taking a look at the **Lothbury Gallery** (*see page 129*), inside the grand foyer of the NatWest Bank HQ at 41 Lothbury. Art from the bank's collection is displayed here, together with an exhibition on developments in banking since the seventeenth century, and a huge model of London.

Further west is the centre of the City's civic life, **Guildhall** (*see below*), base of the Corporation of London, as well as an excellent library, the **Clockmakers' Company Museum** (*see page 126*) and the church of **St Lawrence Jewry**. The

---

concerned with social and philanthropic activities; new companies are still being formed (the Information Technologists a few years ago became the 100th Company), and only officers of the livery companies can take part in the election of the Sheriffs (24 June) and the Lord Mayor (29 September), both held at the Guildhall.

Unfortunately, most of the few medieval livery halls that survived the Great Fire were destroyed in the Blitz. A handful have been restored, however, and can be visited, although some persistence and luck is required. Most halls are only open a limited number of days a year; entrance tickets for those days are also limited, and are issued via the **City Information Centre** (0171 332 1456; *see page 42*). Among the more interesting are:

Apothecaries' Hall

Blackfriars Lane, EC4 (0171 236 1180). Blackfriars tube/rail. **Map 11 O6**
Highlights of the Apothecaries' seventeenth-century hall include a fine panelled Court Room, portraits of Stuart kings James I and Charles I, a Reynolds sketch, banisters from 1671 and a splendid 1736 ormolu candelabrum. For admission contact the Hall Manager on the above number.

Fishmongers' Hall

London Bridge, off King William Street, EC4 (0171 626 3531). Monument tube. **Map 12 Q7**
This early eighteenth-century Greek revival building contains a splendid collection of seventeenth- and eighteenth-century plate, and the dagger used by Lord Mayor William Walworth (a fishmonger) to kill Wat Tyler (*see p14*).

Goldsmiths' Hall

Foster Lane, EC2 (0171 606 7010). St Paul's tube. **Map 11 P6**
The present Renaissance-style hall dates from the 1830s, although the panelling in the Court Room was rescued from the 1669 hall.

Skinners' Hall

Dowgate Hill, EC4 (0171 236 5629). Cannon Street tube/rail. **Map 11 P7**
Much altered and frequently rebuilt over the centuries, the Skinners' Hall is notable for fine panelling in its dining hall and Court Room, and an eighteenth-century Russian glass chandelier in the Outer Hall.

Vintners' Hall

Upper Thames Street, EC4 (0171 236 1863). Mansion House tube/Cannon Street tube/rail. **Map 11 P7**
The 1671 hall survives almost intact. The splendid panelling in the Court Room, a seventeenth-century staircase and a stately late nineteenth-century dining room are all worth seeing.

The inside-out **Lloyd's Building.**

Guildhall Yard East project, due to open in mid-1999, gathers together the Corporation of London's considerable art collection in one gallery for the first time in over 50 years.

Next to Mansion House stands one of the City's finest churches, **St Stephen Walbrook** (*see page 41*), Wren's trial run for St Paul's. Nearby is the heap of stones that was once the **Temple of Mithras** (*see below*). Other notable churches in the vicinity include Nicholas Hawksmoor's idiosyncratic **St Mary Woolnoth** at the junction of King William Street and Lombard Street and Wren's exquisite **St Mary Abchurch** off Abchurch Lane (for both, *see page 41*). Around the corner from St Mary Abchurch, set into the wall of the Overseas-Chinese Banking Corporation at 111 Cannon Street, is one of the City's most esoteric and, frankly, unimpressive sights: **London Stone** (*see below*).

As is the case all over the City, wandering where the fancy takes you is the best way to get to know this enigmatic part of London. Further north, a brief foray off Cornhill down St Michael's Alley takes you to the **Jamaica Wine House**, a popular pub on the site of the Jamaica Coffee House. Opened in the 1670s, sea captains and traders would meet at the Jamaica to discuss business with the West Indies and buy the best rum to be found in London.

Around the Tower of London

For more than 900 years, the **Tower of London** (*see below*) has acted as the eastern anchor of the City – there is no more potent symbol of the capital. Yet, for Londoners, the symbolism has always been complex. Built to protect the Norman con-

querors and subdue their new subjects, the Tower came later to be seen also as a stern sentinel, guarding London's freedoms from those who sought to diminish them. Sometime palace, sometime prison, sometime place of execution, the Tower's associations, stories and legends are legion. Add to this the fact that it is Britain's most perfect medieval fortress, and it comes as no surprise that the Tower is one of London's top five visitor attractions.

The entire Tower Hill area, unappealingly bisected by a busy road, is a major focus for visitors. Just outside Tower Hill tube station in Wakefield Gardens is one of the most impressive surviving chunks of London's **Roman wall**. Although medieval additions have increased the height of the wall from around 20 feet (6m) to 35 feet (10m), its scale still impresses. A 1.7-mile (2.8-km) walk, punctuated by 21 explanatory plaques, follows the course of the old wall from the Tower to the **Museum of London** (*see page 115*). The tourist-targeted **Tower Bridge Experience** (*see below*) and St Katharine's Dock are nearby, but a far greater insight into London's past – and present – can be had by stepping a little off the tourist trail.

Samuel Pepys lived and worked on Seething Lane – there's a bust of the promiscuous diarist in the tiny green oasis of Seething Lane Gardens. Also here is the church of **St Olave Hart Street** (dubbed by Dickens 'St Ghastly Grim' after the grinning skulls around the entrance to the churchyard) where Pepys and his wife worshipped and are buried. Opposite the bottom of Seething Lane stands **All Hallows by the Tower** (*see page 40*), from the tower of which Pepys surveyed the progress of the Great Fire.

Between here and London Bridge stand two reminders of London's great days as a port: the early nineteenth-century **Custom House**, with a façade by Robert Smirke, and, next door, the former **Billingsgate Market**. For many centuries, Billingsgate wharf was famed for two things: the landing of fish and the foul language of its porters. The market was moved to a larger site on the Isle of Dogs in 1982, but Horace Jones's 1870s market building has been impressively restored (look for the fish on top of the weather vanes).

The lanes behind the waterfront are a rewarding hunting ground for church-spotters. **St Magnus the Martyr** (*see page 40*), **St Mary at Hill**, **St Margaret Pattens** and **St Dunstan in the East** are all within a couple of minutes' walk of each other. The gardens of the latter are a wonderfully lush haven in which to relax after struggling to the top of the **Monument** (*see below*). In nearby Pudding Lane, in the early hours of 2 September 1666, a fire started in a bakery that was to blaze for three days, destroying four-fifths of medieval London. Although, remarkably, only nine people are thought to have died, more than

13,000 houses, 87 churches and 44 livery halls were reduced to ashes. The Lord Mayor, woken soon after the fire started, lived to regret his immediate dismissal of the danger with the words: 'Pish! A woman might piss it out.' Thankfully, though, the fire put paid to the City's brown rats, carriers of the Great Plague, which wiped out around 100,000 of the capital's population the previous year.

A little further north, around Bishopsgate, is the area with the greatest concentration of City tower blocks. Manhattan it isn't, and the lack of architectural imagination, daring and flair is depressing. The **NatWest Tower** (on Bishopsgate) is typically unexciting, although, with 52 storeys and at 660 feet (373m) high, it at least had the distinction of being the tallest office block in Europe when it was built in 1980.

The one outstanding exception is Richard Rogers' extraordinary **Lloyd's Building** (1986), on Lime Street. Its guts-on-the-outside design draws much from Paris's Pompidou Centre, also by Rogers, and is the sort of daring, uncompromising architectural vision that is so rarely seen in the conservative City. Part of the façade of the old 1928 building (on Leadenhall Street) has been left standing. Lloyd's of London, the largest insurance market in the world, is a remarkable and unique organisation; a society of underwriters ('Names') that accepts all insurance risks for personal profit or gain. It traces its roots back to Edward Lloyd's coffee shop in Tower Street in the 1680s. Traditionally, being a Name seemed to involve nothing but waiting for regular fat cheques to pop through your letterbox. That this was all too good to be true was made brutally clear in the early 1990s, when a series of disasters caused Lloyd's to suffer record losses of over a billion pounds. Many Names were personally ruined and the company came to the brink of collapse.

Next door is one of the City's most delightful surprises: **Leadenhall Market**. 'Foreigners' – meaning anyone from outside London – were allowed to sell poultry here (and, later, cheese and butter) from the fourteenth century. The current arcaded buildings, painted in green, maroon and

cream with wonderful decorative detail, are the work of Horace Jones (architect also of Smithfield Market and Tower Bridge). One of the market's greatest characters was a gander from Ostend called Old Tom. Somehow he avoided the fate of 34,000 other geese who were slaughtered in the space of two days, and became a much-loved feature of Leadenhall, waddling around the local pubs to be fed tit-bits. He died in 1835 at the venerable age of 38 and was buried in the market. Today, Leadenhall remains a great place to wander, particularly around lunchtime: don't miss the monster pan of paella cooked up at Beauchamp's (no.25). Reassuringly, the fresh produce stalls haven't been displaced – there are still fabulous cheesemongers, butchers and fishmongers.

Between Leadenhall and Liverpool Street rail station there are more churches to discover: **St Helen Bishopsgate**, off Bishopsgate (*see page 40*), **St Andrew Undershaft** on St Mary Axe, **St Botolph Aldgate** (*see page 40*) and **St Katharine Cree** on Leadenhall Street. The latter, one of the few churches to be built in England during the years preceding the Civil War, is an extraordinary hybrid of classical and Gothic styles.

Near here, on Bevis Marks, is Britain's oldest synagogue, the superbly preserved **Bevis Marks Synagogue**, in a courtyard off Bevis Marks; it was built in 1701 by Sephardic Jews who'd escaped from the Inquisition in Portugal and Spain. This area suffered considerable damage from the IRA bombs of April 1992 and April 1993, although most have now been fully restored. The tiny pre-Fire church of **St Ethelburga** (built 1390) on Bishopsgate was devastated, but, appropriately, is now being rebuilt as a £4-million 'Centre for Peace and Reconciliation'.

Around Liverpool Street Station

The broad expanse of **Finsbury Circus** offers vital breathing room for local office workers – a rare commodity in the City, where open spaces are seen less as enhancements to the quality of life than as wasted development opportunities. Tall sweeps of offices (none of the early nineteenth-century originals survives) overlook an agreeable, almost provincial, scene of manicured gardens, a bowling green, bandstand and small restaurant.

Metropolitan values unmistakably reassert themselves in the huge **Broadgate** office development along the west side of Liverpool Street Station. Design-wise, like so many City buildings, it's all very macho and conservative, yet the area around the arena, with its atria and cascading foliage, is a pleasant spot to shop, eat or drink, and the venue for concerts in the summer and an open-air ice rink in the winter (*see page 258*). Spacious, if somewhat isolated, **Exchange Square**, with its view into Liverpool Street Station, is also worth a look.

Wonderful **Leadenhall Market**.

City churches

Before the Great Fire of 1666, nearly 100 churches stood within the City walls. Of these, 87 were destroyed during the conflagration. Sir Christopher Wren was responsible for 51 of the 54 churches that were rebuilt. Thus, not only do the great majority of City churches date from a very narrow historical period (the late seventeenth century) but, uniquely, they are also almost all the work of one man. The fact that this has not resulted in a monotony of style is a testament to Wren's incomparable genius, particularly as he was forced to work only on the original cramped sites. The churches exhibit an extraordinary diversity of design and decoration although many do share certain features in common – light interiors, painted in white and gold, clear glass windows, fine wood carving, painted altarpieces and imaginative use of ironwork. The Victorian 'improvers', preferring the dim light and stained glass of the Gothic style, mangled many of Wren's churches, and bomb damage in World War II destroyed 11 more. Today, only 38 remain; St Ethelburga's in Bishopsgate – one of the few medieval churches to survive both the Great Fire and the Blitz – was almost completely destroyed by an IRA bomb in 1993. Many City churches put on free lunchtime concerts (*see page 247*).

All Hallows by the Tower

Byward Street, EC3 (0171 481 2928). Tower Hill tube. **Open** 9am-5.45pm Mon, Wed, Fri; 8am-5.45pm Tue; 9am-7pm Thur; 10am-5pm Sat, Sun. **Map 12 R7**

Samuel Pepys surveyed the progress of the Great Fire from the tower of All Hallows – the church survived the disaster, only to be all but destroyed by Luftwaffe bombs in 1940. Only the walls and seventeenth-century brick tower were left standing, but the post-war rebuilding has created a pleasingly light interior. A Saxon arch testifies to the church's ancient roots (seventh century) and other interesting relics include Saxon crosses; a Roman tessellated pavement; Tudor monuments, sword-rests and brasses; a superb carved limewood font cover (1682) by Grinling Gibbons; and a collection of model ships. William Penn was baptised and John Quincy Adams married at All Hallows.

St Bartholomew-the-Great

West Smithfield, EC1 (0171 606 5171). Farringdon tube/rail. **Open** *mid-Nov-mid-Feb* 8.30am-4pm Mon-Fri; *mid-Feb-mid-Nov* 8.30am-5pm Mon-Fri; *all year round* 10.30am-1.30pm Sat; 2-6pm Sun. **Map 9 O5**

This church is the only surviving part of the Norman priory founded by Rahere in 1123, and London's oldest and most atmospheric parish church. The nave once extended the entire length of the churchyard to the thirteenth-century gateway, now the entrance from Smithfield. The nave was torn down during Henry VIII's monastic purge, leaving only one-third of the structure standing, but even

so it's a wonderfully evocative place – most of the Norman arches are original. Look out for Rahere's early sixteenth-century tomb. Hogarth was baptised here, and in the Lady Chapel – once leased out for commerce – Benjamin Franklin served a year as a journeyman printer.

St Botolph Aldgate

Aldgate, EC3 (0171 283 1670). **Open** 10am-4pm Mon-Fri; 9.30am-1pm Sun. **Map 12 R6**

The original St Botolph, built by the City's east gate, may date back to the tenth century. The galleried interior of the current plain-brick, stone-dressed structure (built by George Dance in 1744) is notable for John Francis Bentley's weird if highly original ceiling, lined with angels. Daniel Defoe was married here in 1683. St Botolph has a distinguished history of campaigning on social issues and it maintains the tradition today; its crypt is currently used as a day centre for the homeless.

St Bride's

Fleet Street, EC4 (0171 353 1301). Blackfriars tube/rail. **Open** 8am-4.45pm Mon-Fri; 9am-4.30pm Sat; 9.30am-12.30pm, 5.30-7.30pm, Sun. **Map 11 N6**

Completed by Wren in 1703, St Bride's is one of the finest examples of the Italian style in England. The spire, at 226 feet (69m), is the architect's tallest; the four octagonal arcades of diminishing size are said to have been the inspiration for the first tiered wedding cake. The church was gutted in the Blitz, revealing Roman and Saxon remains, which are now effectively displayed and labelled in the crypt, along with information on the long-standing connections between St Bride's and the printing and newspaper publishing businesses. The press may have deserted Fleet Street, but St Bride's, where Wynkyn de Worde set up the first printing press in the City, is still known as the journalists' or printers' church.

St Helen Bishopsgate

Great St Helen's, EC3 (0171 283 2231). Bank tube/ Liverpool Street tube/rail. **Open** 9am-5pm Mon-Fri. **Map 12 R6**

Having survived the Great Fire and weathered the Blitz, St Helen's was badly damaged by the 1992 and 1993 IRA bombs in the City. Founded in the thirteenth century, the spacious building incorporates fifteenth-century Gothic arches and a fourteenth-century nuns' chapel. The unusual double nave shows that this was once two churches side by side, one belonging to a Benedictine nunnery. (In the fourteenth century the naughty nuns were chastised for kissing lay people and wearing ostentatious veils.) You can still see, on the north side, the small staircase that led to the nuns' dormitory, and the 'squint' where nuns not admitted could look through to the altar. St Helen's is known as the 'Westminster Abbey of the City' because of its splendid collection of medieval and Tudor monuments to City dignitaries. St Andrew Undershaft, nearby, and St Olave's, on Hart Street, are also pre-Fire churches.

St Magnus the Martyr

Lower Thames Street, EC3 (0171 626 4481). Monument tube. **Open** 10am-4pm Tue-Fri; 10.30am-1pm Sun. **Map 12 Q7**

The road leading to Old London Bridge (which stood downstream of the current bridge) passed by the door of the medieval church, which was rebuilt by Wren. In *The Waste Land*, TS Eliot described its interior as an 'inex-

Visions of glory: the stunning dome in **St Mary Abchurch.**

plicable splendour of Ionian white and gold'. St Magnus, incidentally, was probably a twelfth-century Norwegian Lord of the Orkneys.

St Mary Abchurch

Abchurch Yard, Abchurch Lane, EC4 (0171 626 0306). Bank tube/Cannon Street tube/rail. **Open** 10.30am-2pm Mon-Thur; 10.30am-2pm Fri. **Map 12 Q7**

The simple, Dutch-influenced red-brick exterior of this Wren church (1681-6) conceals a splendidly rich yet light interior, largely unaltered by subsequent 'improvers'. Below the shallow dome (painted by William Snow) is superb seventeenth-century woodwork. The highlight, however, has to be the limewood reredos (altar screen) – the only one in the City that can be attributed with certainty to Grinling Gibbons. The original church on the site dates from the twelfth century and may have been named 'up church' because it was upriver from its then-owner, the Priory of St Mary Overie (now Southwark Cathedral).

St Mary-le-Bow

Cheapside, EC2 (0171 248 5139). Bank or St Paul's tube. **Open** 6.30am-6pm Mon-Thur; 6.30am-4pm Fri. **Map 11 P6**

Wren's graceful white tower and spire (1670-3), topped by a huge dragon weathercock, is one of the architect's finest works. German bombers put paid to the original interior – what you see now is a post-war reconstruction. The tradition that only those born within earshot of 'Bow Bells' can claim to be a true Cockney probably dates from the fourteenth century, when the bells first rang the City's nightly curfew. The crypt of the original Norman church survives (its arches, or 'bows', give the church its name) and is now home to **The Place Below** vegetarian restaurant.

St Mary Woolnoth

Lombard Street, EC3 (0171 626 9701). Bank tube. **Open** 8am-5pm Mon-Fri. **Map 12 Q6**

Wulnoth, a Saxon noble, is believed to have founded this church on the site of a Roman temple to Concord. It was rebuilt many times, most recently by Nicholas Hawksmoor in 1716-17, and its tiny but beautifully proportioned interior, based on the Egyptian Hall of Vitruvius, is one of the architect's finest. Edward Lloyd, in whose coffee shop Lloyd's of London was founded, was buried here in 1713. When Bank tube station was built in 1897-1900 the church was undermined, the dead removed from the vaults and lift shafts sunk directly beneath the building.

St Stephen Walbrook

39 Walbrook, EC4 (0171 283 4444). Bank, Mansion House or Monument tube/Cannon Street tube/rail. **Open** 10am-4pm Mon-Thur; 10am-3pm Fri. **Map 11 P6**

Arguably Wren's finest parish church, St Stephen Walbrook was a practice run for many of the ideas that he brought to fruition in St Paul's. Its cross-in-square plan surmounted by a central dome creates a marvellous feeling of space and light and is an ingenious use of the relatively cramped site. Although badly damaged in the Blitz, the church has been superbly restored – largely thanks to the support of Lord Palumbo who commissioned the amorphous, Roman travertine central altar by Henry Moore. The rector, Prebendary Dr Chad Varah, founded the Samaritans here in 1953 'to befriend the suicidal and the despairing'. The original seventh-century Saxon church stood on the bank of the long-vanished river Walbrook.

Liverpool Street Station is one of London's busiest; daily pumping in the City's lifeblood – tens of thousands of commuters – and then returning them back to their East Anglian homes at the end of the day. An impressive redevelopment of the station in the late 1980s/early 1990s has made it fit for the next century. On its east side, Charles Barry's venerable late-Victorian Great Eastern Hotel (the only hotel in the City, though others are planned for the millennium) is currently undergoing a huge refurbishment programme, due to be completed in the second half of 1999. That the hotel is aiming high is suggested by the fact that all catering will be provided by the ubiquitous Sir Terence Conran. Within striking distance of here, to the east, are the shops and food stalls of **Spitalfields Market** (*see pages 85 & 193*) and, further east, the curry houses of **Brick Lane** (*see page 87*).

North of London Wall

Extending from the Barbican to close to Liverpool Street Station, **London Wall** follows the northerly course of the old Roman fortifications. Part of the wall, and the remains of one of the gates into the Cripplegate Roman fort, can be seen in **St Alfage Gardens**. The area just to the north of here was levelled during the Blitz. Rather than encourage lucrative office developments, the City of London and London County Council laudably purchased a 35-acre (14-ha) site in 1958 to build 'a genuine residential neighbourhood, incorporating schools, shops, open spaces and amenities'. Unfortunately, what we ended up with was the **Barbican**.

In the brave new post-war world, it must have looked great on paper. This was how we would all live in the future: 6,500 state-of-the-art flats, some in blocks of 40 storeys and more, rising higher than 400 feet (135m) – the tallest in Europe at the time – a huge arts centre with concert halls (home to the London Symphony Orchestra), a theatre (London base of the Royal Shakespeare Company), a repertory cinema, art gallery, exhibition space, cafés and restaurants. The complex also incorporates one of the city's best museums, the **Museum of London** (*see page 115*), the Guildhall School of Music and Drama and the City of London School for Girls.

Tragically – considering the immense cost of the Barbican (the arts centre alone accounted for over £150 million) – the ideas behind the development were already out of date by the time it was completed in the early 1980s. Granted, occupancy rates are high (there is little choice of residence if you want to live in the City; five-sixths of the inhabitants of the Square Mile live here) and the events programmes at the arts centre are usually first rate – it's just that, try as hard as you can to like the place, it has no soul, no warmth, no sense of community. It's a clumsy, charmless colossus, notorious for its confusing layout.

Marooned amid the towering blocks is the only pre-war building in the vicinity – the heavily restored sixteenth-century church of **St Giles**, where Oliver Cromwell was married and John Milton buried. The Nonconformist connection continues further north-east. **Bunhill Fields** was set aside as a cemetery during the Great Plague, although seemingly not used at that time. Instead, because the ground was apparently never consecrated, it became popular for Nonconformist burials, gaining the name of 'the cemetery of Puritan England'. Much of the graveyard is now cordoned off, but it's still possible to walk through and see the monuments to John Bunyan, Daniel Defoe and that most unconformist of Nonconformists, William Blake. On adjoining Bunhill Row, John Milton lived from 1662 until his death in 1674, writing some of his greatest works here, including *Paradise Lost*. Opposite Bunhill Fields on City Road is the **Museum of Methodism** and **John Wesley's House** (*see page 122*). The founder of Methodism lived his last years in the Georgian house and is buried by the unexpectedly ornate chapel. There's a museum in the crypt, while upstairs, in 1951, Denis Thatcher married Margaret Hilda Roberts. So it seems there was methodism in her madness after all.

City Information Centre

St Paul's Churchyard (south side of the Cathedral), EC4 (0171 332 1456). St Paul's tube. **Open** *Apr-Sept* 9.30am-5pm daily; *Oct-Mar* 9.30am-5pm Mon-Fri; 9.30am-12.30pm Sat. **Map 11 O6**
A source of information on sights, events, walks and talks within the Square Mile.

College of Arms

Queen Victoria Street, EC4 (0171 248 2762). Blackfriars tube/rail. **Open** 10am-4pm Mon-Fri. **Closed** public hols. **Admission** free. **Map 11 O7**
The College of Arms has been granting coats of arms and checking family pedigrees since 1484. Its seventeenth-century mini-mansion has been beautifully restored. Only the Earl Marshal's Court (the wood-panelled entrance room hung with paintings of various worthies) can be viewed without notice. Book a tour if you want to see the Record Room and the artists at work on the elaborate certificates. If you wish to trace your roots, ask to see the Officer in Waiting, though you may be charged a small fee for him to look up the information. It's also helpful if you bring any details you already have on your family background.

Dr Johnson's House

17 Gough Square, off Fleet Street, EC4 (0171 353 3745). Chancery Lane or Temple tube or Blackfriars tube/rail. **Open** *May-Sept* 11am-5.30pm Mon-Sat; *Oct-Apr* 11am-5pm Mon-Sat. **Admission** £3; £1-£2 concs; free under-10s. **Map 11 N6**
When a man is tired of London, he is probably tired of all the interminable Samuel Johnson references. This is the only surviving London residence – he had 17 – of the inimitable and inescapable doctor. Johnson lived in this late seventeenth-century house from 1748 to 1759, while working on the first comprehensive English dictionary. Visitors can wander through his home, guided by descriptions and quotes on hand-held boards, but furnishings are disappointingly few. The barest room of all is the long garret, which was 'fitted out like a counting-house' when

*Gog and Magog guard the **Guildhall**.*

Johnson and his six clerks did their lexicographing here. A video provides insights into aspects of Johnson's life and work. Curios include an alleged brick from the Great Wall of China that belonged to Johnson. Look out for the statue of the doctor's cat, Hodge, in Gough Square.

Guildhall

off Gresham Street, EC2 (0171 606 3030). Bank tube. **Open** *Guildhall* 9am-5pm daily; *clock museum* 9.30am-4.45pm Mon-Fri. **Admission** free. **Map 11 P6**
For more than 800 years Guildhall has been the centre of the City's local government (as well as the site of major trials such as those of Lady Jane Grey and Archbishop Cranmer in 1553). The fifteenth-century Great Hall was gutted during the Great Fire and again in the Blitz, but has been sensitively restored. It's decorated with the banners and shields of the 100 Livery Companies; the windows record the names of every Lord Mayor since 1189; and there are monuments to Mayor William Beckford, Wellington, Nelson, Churchill and the two Pitts. Look out for the splendid, almost oriental-looking statues of the legendary giants Gog and Magog guarding the West Gallery. They are post-war replacements for originals destroyed in the Blitz; the phoenix on Magog's shield symbolises renewal after fire. Meetings of the Court of Common Council (governing body for the Corporation of London, presided over by the Lord Mayor) are held here once a month on a Thursday at 1pm, except during August (visitors welcome; phone for dates). The hall is also used for banquets and ceremonial events. Below the Guildhall is the largest medieval crypt in London.

The buildings alongside house Corporation offices, the Guildhall Library (partly financed by Mayor Dick Whittington's estate and the first local authority-funded public library), a shop selling books on London and the **Clockmakers' Company Museum** (*see p126*). The new **Guildhall Yard East** project will provide a new home for the Corporation's art collection (*see p128*).
Free guided tours (write to: The Keeper of Guildhall, Guildhall, EC2).

London Stone

set in wall of Overseas-Chinese Banking Corporation, 111 Cannon Street, EC4. Cannon Street tube. **Map 11 P7**
One of London's oldest, least known and least spectacular sights is the rough-hewn chunk of Clipsham limestone, barely visible behind an iron grille and glass in the wall opposite Cannon Street Station. The origins of this unremarkable-looking stone, unmarked but for two grooves on the top, are murky. It probably dates from Roman times and may have been a milestone, but was already a landmark in 1198 when it was referred to as 'Lonenstane'. It was originally set in the ground on the opposite side of the road, before being swapped to the north side of the street in 1742 and embedded in the wall of St Swithin's (now demolished) church on this site in 1798. No one has ever been very sure

about the purpose of the stone, but it was considered, in some vague unspecified way, to be the symbolic cornerstone of the City. In 1450, Jack Cade, leader of the Kentish rebels, calling himself John Mortimer, is believed to have struck the stone with his sword and proclaimed, 'Now is Mortimer Lord of the City.'

Mansion House

Walbrook, EC4 (0171 626 2500). Bank tube. **Open** for group visits by written application to Ms Ann Gale, at least two months in advance (min 15, max 40 people). **Admission** free. **Map 11 P6**
Squaring up to the Bank of England and the Royal Exchange is another neo-classical portico – that of the Lord Mayor's official residence, Mansion House. Designed by George Dance, it was completed in 1753 and contains sumptuous state rooms, such as the Egyptian Hall, scene of many an official banquet. Mansion House is the only private residence in England with its own Court of Justice, complete with 11 cells – including one for women, 'the birdcage', where suffragette Emmeline Pankhurst was once imprisoned.

The Monument

Monument Street, EC3 (0171 626 2717). Monument tube. **Open** 10am-5.40pm Mon-Fri; 2-5.40pm Sat, Sun. **Admission** £1; 50p children. **Map 12 Q7**
Erected in 1671-7 by Christopher Wren and Robert Hooke, this simple Doric column, topped with a flaming urn of gilt bronze, commemorates the Great Fire of 1666 (*see p17*). At 202 feet (61m) – the distance from here to the site of the bakery on Pudding Lane where the Fire began – the Monument was the tallest isolated stone column in the world in its time. Anyone who labours up the 311 steps won't find that hard to believe (although you will at least get a certificate for your trouble on the way out). Unless you're terminally unfit, it's worth the effort for the wonderful views from the top. Although the gallery is entirely enclosed in an iron cage (it had been a notorious spot for suicides), those who suffer from vertigo may agree with James Boswell that it is 'horrid to be so monstrous a way up in the air'. Look for the gap at the bottom of the Latin inscription on the side of the Monument. After telling of how the Fire was finally extinguished, the words '(but Popish frenzy, which wrought such horrors, is not yet quenched)' were added in 1681. Not until 1830 were these bigoted (and foundationless) words erased.

Old Bailey

corner of Newgate Street & Old Bailey, EC4 (0171 248 3277). St Paul's tube. **Open** 10.30am-1pm, 2-4.30pm, Mon-Fri. **Admission** free (no under-14s admitted, 14s-16s accompanied by adults only). **Map 11 O6**
The Old Bailey – or Central Criminal Court – has dealt with some of the most publicised criminal cases in London's history (including Oscar Wilde in 1895, Dr Crippen in 1910, William 'Lord Haw-Haw' Joyce in 1945, and Peter Sutcliffe, the 'Yorkshire Ripper', in 1981). The court was built on the site of the notorious Newgate Prison (demolished in 1902) and the bronze figure of Justice on the copper-covered dome overlooks the area where convicts were once executed. Stones from the prison made up the façade with Pomeroy's sculpted group over the main entrance – representing the Recording Angel supported by Fortitude and Truth. The tradition of judges carrying a posy of flowers into court has its origin in the need to mask the foul stench and ward off germs emanating from the prison. The public are admitted to watch trials.

St Paul's Cathedral

EC4 (0171 236 4128). St Paul's tube. **Open** *cathedral* 8.30am-4pm Mon-Sat; *galleries, crypt & ambulatory* 10am-4pm Mon-Sat. **Admission** *cathedral* £4; £2-£3.50 concs; £9 family ticket; *galleries* £3.50; £1.50-£3 concs; £7.50 family ticket. **Credit** *shop* MC, £TC, V. **Map 11 O6**

Impressive enough today, the effect of Sir Christopher Wren's masterpiece in the seventeenth century can only be wondered at. A Roman temple dedicated to Diana probably stood on the site where King Ethelbert built the first wooden church in AD604. Two more Saxon cathedrals followed (all three burned down), before the Normans constructed 'Old St Paul's' at the end of the eleventh century. This colossal Gothic building, destroyed in the 1666 Great Fire, was even larger and taller than Wren's successor. Today's St Paul's is one of the few cathedrals ever to be designed by one architect, supervised by one master builder (Thomas Strong) and built within their lifetimes (construction lasted 35 years). Wren's epitaph, inscribed on the wall by his simple tomb in the crypt, could not be more appropriate: 'If you seek his monument, look around.'

With an annual maintenance cost of £4 million, it's not surprising that entrance fees are hefty (although it's possible to peek inside for nothing), but the interior is a marvellous spectacle. Rather like St Peter's in Rome, the scale of the thing means that any feeling of sanctity is sacrificed on the altar of grandeur, but there's a wonderful sense of proportion, space and harmony that even the endless stream of coach parties can't spoil. One of the biggest surprises is the dazzlingly rich, almost Byzantine-like mosaics of the Creation in the **Choir**; these, like Holman Hunt's incongruous *Light of the World* hanging in the south aisle, are late nineteenth-century additions. In the clock tower on the West Front hangs '**Great Paul**', the heaviest swinging bell in England, some five feet (3m) in diameter. It is tolled daily at 1pm.

High up in the dome, frescoed with stories from the life of St Paul by James Thornhill, people in the **Whispering Gallery** strain to hear reverberating voices above the muffled din. Higher still are the viewing galleries: the **Stone Gallery** (at the base of the dome) and the **Golden Gallery** (at the top). It's a long, hard climb, involving 530 steps, but worth it for the unrivalled views over London. The bright, whitewashed, atmosphereless **Crypt** (the largest in Europe) centres around grandiose monuments to the Duke of Wellington and Admiral Nelson; it raises a wry smile to see a modest monument to Florence Nightingale amid all the military bigwigs who did so much to keep her supplied with customers. **Painters' Corner** contains memorials to Reynolds, Lord Leighton, Alma-Tadema, Turner, Millais and Holman Hunt. The most interesting item in the **Treasury** is an extraordinary cope (a ceremonial cape), embroidered with the spires of 73 churches. There's a decent café down here too.

Temple of Mithras

On the raised courtyard in front of Sumitomo Bank/ Legal & General Building, Temple Court, 11 Queen Victoria Street, EC4. Mansion House tube. **Open** 24 hours daily. **Admission** free. **Map 11 P6**
During the third century AD, the rival cults of Mithraism and Christianity were battling for supremacy. The worship of the macho Persian god Mithras appealed particularly to Roman soldiers, and the troops on the British frontier built the small temple to their champion near this spot (cAD240-50). The reconstructed foundations (looking as they did when they were unearthed in 1954) aren't much to look at, but show the Roman influence on the later design of churches: rounded apse, central nave and side aisles. The difference is that Christian churches were built in the shape of a cross with the altar facing east. The story of the temple, and the marble sculptures found buried underneath, can be seen in the **Museum of London** (*see p115*).

Tower Bridge Experience

SE1 (0171 407 0922). Tower Hill tube or London Bridge tube/rail. **Open** *Apr-Oct* 10am-6.30pm daily; *Nov-Mar* 9.30am-6pm daily (last admission 75 mins before closing). **Admission** £6.15; £4.15 concs; £15.50 family ticket. **Credit** AmEx, MC, £TC, V. **Map 12 R8**
Despite its mock Gothic appearance, the Tower Bridge was actually a pioneering steel-framed structure. The 'Tower

Bridge Experience' might sound a bit naff, but visitors do get a fact-packed insight into the history of London's famous bridge, which opened in 1894 and was once described as 'a colossal symbol of the British genius'. The tour is helped along by lively animatronics, interactive displays and the 'ghost' of Horace Jones, the original architect of the bridge, who died shortly after foundation work began. A collection of photos of the bridge, taken during its first 100 years, are displayed along the elevated walkways. The views from here are far-reaching, if somewhat obscured by the fact that the corridors are now enclosed with glass and metal. The tour ends in the engine rooms, which house the steam pump engines used to raise the bridge until 1976 (it's all done by electrics now). To find out when the bridge will next be lifted (usually at least once a day), and the name and type of vessel passing beneath, phone 0171 378 7700.

Tower of London

Tower Hill, EC3 (0171 709 0765). Tower Hill tube/ Fenchurch Street rail. **Open** *Mar-Oct* 9am-5pm Mon-Sat; 10am-5pm Sun; *Nov-Feb* 10am-4pm Mon, Sun; 9am-4pm Tue-Sat. **Admission** £9.50; £7.15 concs; £28.40 family ticket; free under-5s. **Credit** AmEx, MC, £TC, V.
Map 12 R7
The Tower has been a castle, a palace and a prison during its long history and it remains one of the capital's most important sights. Be warned that 2.5 million people annually traipse around the Tower; arrive early if you want to avoid the worst of the crowds. A good introduction is provided by the entertaining, free, hour-long guided tours that depart every half hour, hosted by the snappable beefeaters (more soberly known as Yeoman Warders).

The oldest part of the complex is William the Conqueror's **White Tower**, begun in 1076 (its name refers to the period during Henry III's reign when it was whitewashed). It now houses a portion of the extensive **Royal Armouries** (which have recently been redisplayed, after eight years of work, in nine new galleries) and, on the second floor, the exquisite, austere **Chapel of St John**, which, dating from 1080, is the oldest church in London.

Although popularly notorious as a site of aristo beheadings, only seven people were ever executed on **Tower Green** (a plaque in the centre of the green records their names). The proprietorial ravens that squawk about the green have been protected by royal decree for more than 300 years and are a reminder of the extensive menagerie that was kept at the Tower from 1235 until it was transferred to London Zoo in 1831. The nineteenth-century Waterloo Barracks, north of the White Tower, contain the celebrated **Crown Jewels**, the centrepiece of which is the Imperial State Crown, set with a 317-carat diamond. Their popularity is such that viewing time is strictly rationed.

South of the White Tower is the gloriously named **Bloody Tower**. It was here in 1483 that the 12-year-old Edward V and his ten-year-old brother were incarcerated by their uncle, the future Richard III. Subsequent Tudor propaganda asserted that Richard had the boys murdered – and the skeletons of two children were discovered in the tower in 1674 – but the true fate of the young princes remains one of history's great mysteries. A hundred years later, Sir Walter Ralegh was imprisoned in the tower on three separate occasions, the last being for six weeks in 1618 before his execution at Westminster. On the waterfront, south of the Bloody Tower, is **Traitors' Gate**, by which prisoners used to enter the Tower, having been ferried down the Thames from the law courts at Westminster. The gate is part of **St Thomas's Tower**, which, with neighbouring **Wakefield Tower**, has been converted to resemble Edward I's medieval palace.

Despite its outward glitter, the Tower's a strangely antiseptic, soulless place, and pricey with it. It could take some lessons from **Hampton Court Palace** (*see p105*), which puts on a far more convincing, evocative and entertaining historical show.

Holborn & Clerkenwell

Maps 6 & 9

The character of **Holborn** (pronounced 'Hó-bun'), sandwiched between commercial Covent Garden, learned Bloomsbury and the money-mad City, owes something to all three districts, but is primarily formed by the straggling, anachronistic **Inns of Court** (*see page 48* **Any room at the Inn?**).

Around Aldwych

The long-vanished Holebourne river was once a tributary of the not-so-long-ago-vanished Fleet (which ran along the course of today's Farringdon Road). The western flank of modern Holborn is formed by the uncompromising car-filled conduit of Kingsway, carved out of slum-lined streets in the early 1900s in an attempt to relieve traffic congestion, and culminating in the crescent of Aldwych. The handsome **Meridien Waldorf** hotel, built here soon afterwards, and **One Aldwych** (*see page 141*), one of London's newest and most stylish five-star hotels, face a trio of unashamedly Imperial buildings: India House, Australia House and Bush House, once intended to be a huge trade centre and now home to the BBC's much-loved and much-threatened World Service. BBC mementoes and spin-offs can be bought from the shop by the entrance (*see page 205*).

Between here and the Thames lie **King's College** (its hideous 1960s buildings sitting uncomfortably with Robert Smirke's graceful 1829-31 originals) and William Chambers' grandiose late eighteenth-century **Somerset House**. This is the last of the splendid palaces that once lined the Strand; it now has the prosaic function of housing the Inland Revenue, as well as the art collection of the **Courtauld Institute** (which reopened after a refurbishment in October 1998; *see page 128*).

Two nearby curiosities are worth a glance. On Temple Place is one of a handful of still-functioning **cabmen's shelters**. These rather dainty, green-painted sheds are a legacy of the Cabmen's Shelter Fund, set up in 1874 to provide cabbies with an alternative to pubs (Victorian cab drivers were overfond of a pint) in which to hide from the elements and get a hot meal and (non-alcoholic) drink. Around the corner on Strand Lane is the **'Roman' bath**, reached via an alley off Surrey Street. David Copperfield took many a cold plunge here. It can be viewed through a window if you don't manage

to pass by during its official opening times (10am-12.30pm Mon-Fri).

Back on the Strand, literally, are the churches of **St Mary-le-Strand** (James Gibbs' first public building; built 1714-17) and **St Clement Danes** (*see below*), both isolated on traffic islands. Samuel Johnson was a regular and 'solemnly devout' member of the congregation at the latter. Just north of here loom the suitably imposing neo-Gothic **Royal Courts of Justice** (*see below*), opened in 1882 by Queen Victoria. The stress of the commission was such that the architect GE Street's crowning achievement brought him to an early grave. The fiercesome bronze griffin in the middle of the road near here marks the site of **Temple Bar** and the official boundary of the City. Just beyond is the church of **St Dunstan in the West** (*see below*) and the little-known, seventeenth-century **Prince Henry's Room** (*see below*). South of here are the labyrinthine alleyways of the **Middle** and **Inner Temples** (officially lying within the boundaries of the City; *see page 48*).

Around Lincoln's Inn Fields

The winding streets to the west of the courts bear the names of several of the now-defunct **Inns of Chancery**, such as New Inn and Clement's Inn, and are home to one-time cradle of left-wing agitation, the **LSE** (London School of Economics). Nearby, at 13 Portsmouth Street, is the **Old Curiosity Shop**, the supposed (though this is much disputed) inspiration behind the eponymous Dickens novel. It dates from about 1567.

The broad expanse of **Lincoln's Inn Fields** is London's largest square and Holborn's focal point. On the north side is the fine **Sir John Soane's Museum** (*see page 121*); to the east are the buildings of the Inn itself. Chancery Lane, running up from the Strand to High Holborn, is home of the Public Records Office and the Law Society. At its northern end are the weird, subterranean shops of the **London Silver Vaults** (*see page 186*), selling everything from silver spoons to antique clocks.

Around the corner, heading towards Holborn Circus, teeter the overhanging, half-timbered Tudor buildings of **Staple Inn**, one of the former Inns of Chancery. Across the road, by the ancient Cittie of Yorke pub, is an alley leading into the most northerly of the Inns of Court, **Gray's Inn**.

Clerkenwell

North and east of here lies the increasingly fashionable district of **Clerkenwell**. In the twelfth century, a hamlet grew up here around the religious foundations of the Priory of St John of Jerusalem and the now-vanished St Mary's Nunnery and, from the fourteenth century, the Carthusian monastery of **Charterhouse** (now an upmarket OAP home).

The original **Clerk's Well**, first mentioned in 1174, and long thought lost, was rediscovered by chance in 1924. It can now be viewed through the window of 14-16 Farringdon Lane. Over the centuries, a strong crafts tradition grew up in Clerkenwell as French Huguenots and other immigrants settled to practise their trades away from the restrictions of the City guilds. The area was thought 'an esteemed situation for gentry' until the early nineteenth century when population pressure and increasing dilapidation led to an influx of Irish, and then Italian, immigrants, looking for cheap accommodation. (Evidence of the once 10,000-strong Italian community can still be seen in **St Peter's Italian Church**, nearby on Clerkenwell Road, and **L Terroni**, the excellent deli next door.) Radicals were also attracted to Clerkenwell at this time. Clerkenwell Green was a political meeting point – Lenin edited 17 editions of the Bolshevik paper *Iskra* from a back room (which has been preserved) in the **Marx Memorial Library** (at no.37A).

Dickensian Clerkenwell

By the late nineteenth century, the district had become a 'decidedly unsavoury and unattractive locality': prime Dickens territory. Long after the demise of the saffron crocus fields, the notorious rookeries of **Saffron Hill** were depicted in all their desperate horror in *Oliver Twist*. **Bleeding Heart Yard**, off Greville Street, was where Arthur Clennam became a partner in the engineering firm of Doyce and Clennam in *Little Dorrit*, and where the ineffectual Mr Pancks tried to collect rent from his impecunious tenants. It supposedly owes its name to the brutal murder here of Elizabeth Hatton in 1646 – her heart was ripped out and said to be still pumping blood on to the cobbles when found the next morning. You can ponder the likely veracity of the legend while indulging at the **Bleeding Heart Restaurant & Wine Bar** (*see page 179*).

In nearby **Ely Place**, David Copperfield met Agnes Wakefield and renewed his friendship with Tommy Traddles. This fascinating enclave was once the site of the Bishop of Ely's London palace; all that remains is the delightful church of **St Etheldreda** (which contains a good lunchtime café; *see below*). The private, gated road, now lined by Georgian houses, is crown property and remains outside the jurisdiction of the City of London. Pub-lovers should not miss the **Olde Mitre Tavern**, on this site since 1546, secreted up a narrow alley off Ely Place. West of here, the long-established, no-nonsense **Leather Lane** street market (*see page 192*) sells clothes, food and dodgy videos, and supports a number of cheap caffs. Running parallel is **Hatton Garden** – now the centre of London's diamond trade.

Trendy Clerkenwell

The slums were eventually cleared, but little was built in their place. Consequently, the population plummeted and Clerkenwell stagnated. Since the late 1980s, however, property developers have wised up to the attractions of an area so close to the City and the West End. The tourism potential of the district is also being increasingly exploited. A heritage walk has been developed; sights that already exist include the spooky **House of Detention** (*see below*) and the sixteenth-century **St John's Gate & Museum**.

If a gauge of a district's desirability is the number of quality restaurants it maintains, then Clerkenwell has most assuredly arrived. St John Street is home to the offal-biased excellence of **St John** (no.26; *see page 161*), the relentlessly classy **Stephen Bull Smithfield** (no.71; *see pages 156-7*) and the hip bar and oriental snacks of **Cicada** (no.126; *see page 182*). Nearby Clerkenwell Green is the centre of smouldering French wonderchef Jean-Christophe Novelli's burgeoning culinary empire (**Maison Novelli** and **Novelli EC1**; *see page 167*); French chefs are also reinvigorating British cooking at the **Quality Chop House** at 94 Farringdon Road (*see page 160*). Meanwhile, at no.159, is **The Eagle** (*see page 171*), the gastropub that pioneered the idea of top-notch nosh in a boozer; and ultra-hip, modern Spanish **Moro** (*see page 176*) is leading the development of increasingly trendy Exmouth Market (nos.34-36).

The only hitch in Clerkenwell's inexorable rise is that the predominantly 'loft' accommodation drawing in most of the new blood is of a type and price to exclude all but the young, high-earning professional. Ad executives and solicitors may soon swamp the few remaining locals and artists who had previously found a haven in one of central London's quietest yet most interesting districts.

House of Detention

Clerkenwell Close, EC1 (0171 253 9494). Farringdon tube. **Open** 10am-6pm daily. **Admission** £4; £2.50-£3 concs; £10 family ticket. **Map 9 N4**
In the nineteenth century you could find yourself clapped in irons here for begging, attempting suicide or even 'stealing two grapes'. There has been a prison on this site since 1616, but it was at its busiest in 1846-78, receiving some 10,000 inmates a year. Brave the underground passageways (all that remain of the prison), and you'll get an all-too-real feeling of the dank, dark conditions that prisoners had to endure. The individual cells, at the end of the marked route, display a collection of torture weapons that go by the delightful names of 'tongue-tearer' and 'throat-catcher'. Bags of atmosphere (the BBC filmed part of *Great Expectations* here in late 1998), but not somewhere to be caught during a power cut.

Prince Henry's Room

17 Fleet Street, EC4 (0171 936 4004). Temple tube.
Open 11am-2pm Mon-Sat. **Admission** free. **Map 11 N6**
Built in 1611 and named in honour of James I's eldest son,
this is one of the few City buildings to have survived the
Great Fire, with oak panelling and plaster ceiling intact. It
now houses a collection of Samuel Pepys memorabilia.

Royal Courts of Justice

*Strand, WC2 (0171 936 6000). Temple tube (not open
Sun).* **Open** 9.30am-4.30pm Mon-Fri (no court cases
during Aug & Sept recess). **Admission** free. **Map 6 M6**
Anyone is free to take a pew at the back of any of the 88
courts. It's a fascinating and somehow reassuring experience to thus exercise one's democratic right to witness the
creaky British justice system in action. The interior of the
building is as impressive as the façade, and also houses a
coffee shop and a small exhibition of legal garb.

St Clement Danes

*Strand, WC2 (0171 242 8282). Temple tube (not open
Sun).* **Open** 8.30am-4.30pm Mon-Sat; 9am-3.30pm Sun.
Map 6 M6
The curious name of this Wren church (with a tower extension by James Gibbs) may date back to its use by Danes married to English wives who were allowed to stay behind when
Alfred the Great expelled most of their countrymen from the
kingdom. Its name is immortalised in the children's nursery
rhyme 'Oranges and lemons, Say the bells of St Clement's';
the bells still ring out the tune, and children at St Clement
Danes Primary School are given an orange and a lemon after
the annual service. Pity that the church in the rhyme almost
certainly wasn't this one, but St Clement Eastcheap, which
is near to the wharves where citrus fruit used to be unloaded.
Most of the interior was gutted during the Blitz, and has been
renovated as a suitably sedate and stately central church for
the RAF. Outside the front of the church is the controversial
1992 memorial to Marshal of the RAF, Sir Arthur 'Bomber'
Harris, the man behind the devastating saturation bombings
of German cities towards the end of World War II.

St Dunstan in the West

Fleet Street, EC4 (0171 242 6027). Chancery Lane tube.
Open 10am-2pm Tue; 2-6pm Sat; 9am-2pm Sun
(occasional concerts on Fri). **Map 11 N6**
The first mention of this church was in 1185, but the present early Gothic-revival building dates only from 1831-3,
when a widening of Fleet Street required it to shift slightly
northwards. John Donne was rector here from 1624-31; Izaak
Walton (whose *Compleat Angler* was published in the
churchyard in 1653) held the bizarrely named posts of 'scav-
enger, questman and sidesman' from 1629-44; and Samuel
Pepys popped in one day in 1667 to hear a sermon and
unsuccessfully try to fondle one of the local maidens ('…at
last I could perceive her to take pins out of her pocket to
prick me if I should touch her again').

St Etheldreda

Ely Place, EC1 (0171 405 1061). Chancery Lane tube.
Open 7.30am-7pm daily. **Map 9 N5**
Britain's oldest Catholic church (built in the 1250s) is the only
surviving building of the Bishop of Ely's once-extensive
London residence. The simple chapel, lined with the statues
of local martyrs, is London's only remaining example (except-
ing parts of Westminster Abbey) of Gothic architecture from
the reign of Edward I. The strawberries that were once grown
in the gardens were said to be the finest in the city (and
received plaudits in Shakespeare's *Richard III*); every June
the church holds a 'Strawberrie Fayre' in Ely Place.

Top: **St Mary-le-Strand** *(see page 45).*
Bottom: **Bleeding Heart Yard** *(see opposite).*

‡ See no fewer than 24 TOWERS *of* LONDON and *explore* 12 of them.

‡ *Hear* the myths and legends when you go on free Yeoman Warder 'Beefeater' tours.

‡ *Marvel* at the CROWN JEWELS and *experience* 900 years of royal history.

‡ Nearest tube - Tower Hill.

‡ Buy your entrance tickets at THE TOWER or in advance from any Underground station.

THE TOWER *of* LONDON

The Royal Fortress on the Thames

Any room at the Inn?

At one time the **Inns of Court** were thought of almost as England's third university, offering the sons of the aristrocracy and gentry a general education (which included dance classes at one time) and a few years of roistering to boot. Few completed the legal training. The Inns were so named because barristers not only trained but also ate and lodged there. Today, all barristers in England and Wales are required to work from, and eat a set number of dinners at, one of the four surviving Inns of Court (Middle Temple, Inner Temple, Lincoln's Inn and Gray's Inn) before the Inns can call them to the Bar.

The essayist Charles Lamb, who died in 1817, wrote of the joys of passing 'by unexpected ways, into its unexpected avenues, into its magnificent ample squares, its classic green recesses!' Today, the quiet alleys and open spaces of the Inns that he described remain a blessed haven from the endless traffic and choking fumes of central London.

Gray's Inn

Gray's Inn Road, WC1 (0171 458 7800). Chancery Lane or Holborn tube. **Open** 10am-4pm Mon-Fri. **Map 6 M5**
Built on the site of the manor house of Sir Reginald le Grey, Gray's was the last Inn to be founded (in 1569). Most of the present buildings are post-World War II developments and reconstructions. The Hall (open only for guided tours by appointment; phone first) contains a superb screen, said to be made from the wood of a Spanish Armada galleon. Shakespeare's *Comedy of Errors* was first performed here, in 1594. The gardens (visible from Theobald's Road) were popular for society strolling in the seventeenth century and as a venue for duels.

Lincoln's Inn

Lincoln's Inn Fields, WC2 (0171 405 1393). Chancery Lane or Holborn tube. **Open** *grounds* 9am-6pm Mon-Fri; *chapel* noon-2.30pm Mon-Fri. **Map 6 M6**
Perhaps the most majestic and attractive of the Inns (thanks in part to suffering minimal damage in the Blitz), Lincoln's is also the oldest. It was founded on its present site in 1422, and derives its name from one of two local residents: either Thomas de Lyncoln or Henry de Lacy, 3rd Earl of Lincoln. In *Bleak House*, Dickens' ferocious attack on the judicial system, he sets the impenetrable case of Jarndyce v Jarndyce in Lincoln's Inn and places vile lawyer Mr Tulkinghorn in a large house overlooking Lincoln's Inn Fields, 'let off in sets of chambers now; and in those shrunken fragments of greatness lawyers lie like maggots in nuts'. This house is thought to be the Old Hall, which, along with the Great Hall and other buildings generally closed to the public, can be visited as part of a guided tour of the fields (by written application only; phone for details). The seventeenth-century chapel is open to the public (for opening times see above).

Middle & Inner Temples

Middle Temple *Middle Temple Lane, EC4 (0171 427 4800). Temple tube (not open Sun).* **Open** 10am-11.30am, 3-4pm, Mon-Fri (the Hall is often in use in the afternoon; phone first). **Admission** free. **Map 11 N6**
Inner Temple *Inner Temple Treasury Office, EC4 (0171 797 8250). Temple tube (not open Sun).* **Open** 10am-4pm Mon-Fri. **Admission** free. **Map 11 N7**
In the second half of the twelfth century, the Knights Templars built their HQ in the area now known as Temple. On the suppression of the order in 1312, the Knights Hospitallers took over and leased part of the land to lawyers. When the Hospitallers in their turn were suppressed (in 1539), their property passed over to the crown and, in 1609, James I granted ownership of the Temple to the two Inns. Property was not formally divided between them until 1732. Incidentally, the 'Outer Temple' is the area outside Temple Bar that once belonged to the Knights Templars but was never occupied by the lawyers. Samuel Johnson often went forth on his jaunts into the City from his lodgings at 1 Inner Temple Lane, and the great jurist and judge Sir William Blackstone used to complain frequently of the riotous parties held by his 'revelling neighbour', Oliver Goldsmith.

Middle Temple Hall

Listings details as for Middle Temple above.
The most impressive feature of the Hall, completed in 1573, is its oak double hammer-beam roof. The 29-ft (9-m) Bench Table, donated by Elizabeth I, is made from a single Windsor Park oak. The smaller table in front, the 'Cupboard', was supposedly crafted from the hatch of Sir Francis Drake's *Golden Hinde*. Shakespeare's own company is said to have performed *Twelfth Night* here in 1601.

Temple Church

Inner Temple, King's Bench Walk, EC4 (0171 353 1736). Temple tube (not open Sun). **Open** 10am-4pm Wed-Sat. **Services** 8.30am, 11.15am, Sun. **Map 11 N6**
Often said to be based on the Church of Holy Sepulchre in Jerusalem, the round church of the once-powerful order of the Knights Templars was more likely based on the Dome of the Rock. Thanks to the overzealous efforts of generations of restorers, the church, despite being one of London's most ancient (built 1185), doesn't feel very old. It has been kept admirably plain, but seems somehow too light and too spick and span to cast an appropriate atmosphere over the recumbent figures of thirteenth-century knights and the grimacing gargoyles that overlook them. Traditionally, members of the Middle Temple sit in the northern stalls of the rectangular, thirteenth-century choir; Inner Temple members sit in the south stalls.

Bloomsbury

Maps 5 & 6

Between Gower Street and Great Portland Street, Euston Road and Oxford Street lies the area that during the 1930s and 1940s became known as **Fitzrovia**. Aspiring and expiring artists and writers (such as Dylan Thomas) were drawn to this seductively louche northern extension of Soho to drink away their talent in basement dens and pubs such as the **Fitzroy Tavern** on Charlotte Street. In his *Memoirs of the Forties*, Julian Maclaren-Ross recalls being warned by Tambimuttu, Sinhalese editor of *Poetry London*, to '...beware of Fitzrovia... you will stay there always day and night and get not work done ever'. The fact that few people have heard of him today suggests he failed to heed the warning.

Today, Fitzrovia's backstreets can often seem curiously devoid of life – few tourists venture north of Oxford Street, and few local workers stray from the gaggle of no-longer-very-appetising pubs in the area around **Charlotte Street** (although the restaurants here are good). The area is, however, slowly reviving as Soho overspills northwards and trendy bars such as **Jerusalem** (on Rathbone Place; *see page 223*) open up.

Beyond **Pollock's Toy Museum** (*see page 119*), **All Saint's** Margaret Street (*see below*), and the omnipresent 620-ft (385-m) **British Telecom Tower** (not open to the public), sights are few, but there's still a certain neglected charm to Fitzrovia, providing you keep clear of the scruffy, car-fume-filled canyon of Tottenham Court Road. Not much more than a century ago this was still a quiet rural road lined by cow sheds; now it's the place to head for electronic goods and computers, and classy furniture and household wares (at **Heal's**, **Habitat** and **Purves & Purves**, *see pages 202-3*).

Bookish Bloomsbury

West of Fitzrovia, and approximately bounded by Euston Road, Gray's Inn Road and Theobald's Road/Bloomsbury Way/New Oxford Street, is an area with more heavyweight literary and academic associations: **Bloomsbury**. Its main selling point is undoubtedly the magnificent **British Museum** (*see page 126*), which tops the list of London's most-visited tourist attractions. The other main influence in the area is the **University of London**, whose most striking building is the 210-ft (130-m) tower of Senate House (built in the

Not quite Little Italy, but there's a distinct continental flavour to **Sicilian Avenue**.

1930s in Portland stone), looming massively over the Malet Street campus like an Orwellian Ministry of Truth. Many of the buildings in Bloomsbury's fine Georgian squares contain offshoots of the university, including the **Percival David Foundation for Chinese Art** (*see page 117*) and the **Petrie Museum of Egyptian Archaeology** (*see page 119*). The university bookshop, **Dillons**, on the corner of Torrington Place and Gower Street, is one of London's biggest and best.

The name Bloomsbury is derived from 'Blemondisberi', meaning 'the manor of (William) Blemond', who acquired the area in the early thirteenth century. It remained largely rural until the 4th Earl of Southampton built **Southampton** (now **Bloomsbury**) **Square** around his house in the 1660s. Close by on Bloomsbury Way is the eighteenth-century church of **St George** (*see below*), identified by its unique, stepped steeple. The construction of Southampton Square marked the start of a trend and many more followed, including Bloomsbury's only surviving complete Georgian square, **Bedford Square** (1775-80), once the haunt of book publishers, and enormous **Russell Square** (laid out in 1800), dominated by the red-brick-and-terracotta fantasy of the Russell Hotel, and with a handy café in the square gardens.

Started in the 1820s, few original houses remain on **Gordon Square**, but this is nevertheless still the area most closely associated with the **Bloomsbury Group**. In various houses around here (look out for the blue plaques), Virginia and Leonard Woolf, Lytton Strachey, Roger Fry, Vanessa and Clive Bell, Duncan Grant and John Maynard Keynes flounced about practising GE Moore's belief that 'by far the most valuable things… are… the pleasures of human intercourse and the enjoyment of beautiful objects'.

Hidden corners

Further east are some of Bloomsbury's most charming corners, such as pedestrianised **Woburn Walk** (off Upper Woburn Place), with its bow-windowed shops and cafés. Equally appealing are the small-scale restaurants and shops lining **Marchmont Street**, the pleasant kids' park of **Coram's Fields** (*see page 217*), the excellent pubs on Lamb's Conduit Street (**The Lamb** is particularly recommended; *see page 180*) and **Dickens' House** on Doughty Street (*see page 120*), the author's only surviving London residence.

Traffic-packed Southampton Row, leading down to Holborn, forms Bloomsbury's lower backbone. Try the noisy, old-fashioned **Princess Louise** (on the corner of High Holborn and Newton Street) for a pint, or lunch in the blissfully quiet **October Gallery Café** (*see page 158*) on Old Gloucester Street, before browsing the second-hand books at **Skoob** (*see page 189*) in the curious, pedestrianised, colonnaded Sicilian Avenue.

It's grim up north

The north of Bloomsbury is decisively bounded by the endless traffic hurtling along Euston Road. Here stands the utilitarian **Euston Station**, simultaneously the oldest and newest of London's mainline termini. Opened in 1837, and described at the time as 'a railway station without equal', its magnificent classical portico, screen and Great Hall were, criminally, demolished in 1963 to make way for the current structure.

Equally controversial has been the endlessly criticised, hopelessly over-budget and woefully behind-schedule **British Library**, next to **St Pancras Station** (which will be the terminus of the high-speed Channel Tunnel link in 2003). Looking more like an out-of-town shopping mall than a temple of knowledge, the library should be fully functioning by mid-1999 (and the first unveiling of its interior in late 1997 actually met with considerable plaudits from users).

The station itself is a Victorian wonder. The glass-and-iron train shed, spanning 240 feet (72m) and over 100 feet (930m) high, is a remarkable feat of engineering and is fronted by Sir George Gilbert Scott's exuberant High Gothic fairytale of a building, formerly the **Midland Grand Hotel**, a structure the architect accurately if immodestly described as 'possibly too good for its purpose'. It's now known as **St Pancras Chambers** – there's a small exhibition about the hotel and the building's future in the lobby (at the west end of the building; open 11.30am-2.30pm Mon-Fri). If you want to see more, fill in a form available in the lobby for one of the occasional guided tours of the building (£5). Marriott Hotels is planning to convert part of it back to a hotel.

Next door is the more functional but unlovely **King's Cross Station**. Much of the surrounding area is seedy – unpleasantly so at night – and in desperate need of regeneration.

All Saints

Margaret Street, W1 (0171 636 1788). **Open** 7am-7pm daily. **Services** phone for details. **Map 5 J5**
This 1850s church is the major work of William Butterfield, whose diehard scarred countless London churches with his Victorian Gothic 'improvements'. The site of All Saints, however, was too small for Gothic proportions so, instead, he used an extraordinary – but surprisingly triumphant – mishmash of fourteenth-century-style details, red brick and humbug-like black stone bands à la Siena cathedral. Look for the Pre-Raphaelite Minton tile paintings on the walls.

St George Bloomsbury

Bloomsbury Way, WC1 (0171 405 3044). Holborn tube. **Open** 9.30am-5.30pm Mon-Fri; 9am-5pm Sun. **Map 6 L5**
A classical portico leads from the smoke-blackened exterior of this Hawksmoor church (1716-31) into its genteelly flaking interior (a restoration is planned). Despite its sky-blue ceiling and gilding, there's a mournful air to the place. George I, looking inappropriately heroic in a Roman toga, surmounts the remarkable tiered steeple, inspired by Pliny's description of the Mausoleum at Halicarnassus. There are free concerts in summer (1.10pm Tue; 5pm Sun).

*A rare glimpse inside the old **Midland Grand Hotel** on **London Open House** weekend. See p9.*

Marylebone

All Souls, Langham Place: Nash's mini-masterpiece.

Maps 2 & 5

Roughly defined by Oxford Street, Edgware Road, Regent's Park and Great Portland Street, the ancient manors of Lileston (Lisson) and Tyburn were thoroughly disreputable, violent places by the fourteenth century. The infamous gallows were set up at Tyburn in 1388 where they remained in use until 1783 (their site is marked by a plaque on the traffic island at the junction of Bayswater and Edgware roads). Local residents petitioned the Bishop of London for their frequently ransacked church to be moved half a mile away, to a safer site by the Tyburn stream (or bourne). The church, St Mary by the bourne, eventually gave its name to the entire district, **Marylebone**.

The small-scale shops, restaurants and pubs along today's snaking Marylebone Lane and Marylebone High Street create an agreeably laid-back, if rather upmarket, small-town ambience. Yet this coexists amid a grander, land-that-time-forgot world of sedate Georgian squares and streets.

Georgian Marylebone

In the sixteenth century, the northern half of Marylebone (now Regent's Park) became a royal hunting ground, while the southern section was bought up by the Portman family. Two centuries later, the Portmans developed many of the elegant

streets and squares that lend much of this relatively unvisited part of the city its dignified air.

One of these squares, Manchester Square, is home to the paintings, armour and other goodies of the **Wallace Collection** (*see page 131*). Nearby is Harley Street, renowned since the mid-nineteenth century for its high-charging medical specialists, while, running parallel, Wimpole Street was immortalised (not very complimentarily) by Tennyson in *In Memoriam* as a 'dark unlovely street'. It was from no.50 that Elizabeth Barrett scandalously eloped with Robert Browning in 1846; they were secretly married at **St Marylebone parish church** on Marylebone Road.

Stately **Portland Place**, leading up to Regent's Park, was the glory of eighteenth-century London and, although many of its houses have been rebuilt, its spacious proportions have been maintained. At its kink, where it links at Langham Place with Nash's Regent Street, is the BBC's HQ, **Broadcasting House**, and home to the **BBC Experience** (*see below*). Next door is Nash's delicate little Thunderbird of a church, **All Souls** (1822-4), much ridiculed in its time for the slenderness of its spire. Over the road is the expensively restored Langham Hilton, the first of London's grand hotels, opened in 1865.

Regent's Park & Baker Street

Portland Place emerges to the north at Nash's sublimely proportioned **Park Crescent** (1812-18), originally intended to be a full circus. A decade or so later, Nash's most elegant terrace, **Cumberland Terrace**, was built on the east side of **Regent's Park** (*see below*) as part of his hugely influential scheme to transform this former royal hunting ground into an urban idyll. On the west side of the park is the London Central Mosque, built in 1978 to service the spiritual needs of the city's many Muslims whose shops, cafés and restaurants are a feature of nearby **Edgware Road** and **Bayswater** (*see page 107*). The northern edge of the park is home to one of the city's major visitor attractions, **London Zoo** (*see below; and also page 218*), while the area's other main tourist draw is the permanently besieged **Madame Tussaud's** (and the **London Planetarium** next door; *see below*) on Marylebone Road. Nearby Baker Street is synonymous with the fictional junkie-detective Sherlock Holmes; devotees flock to the **Sherlock Holmes Museum** (*see below*).

All street and no Oxford

Discreet Marylebone hits snooty Mayfair at **Oxford Street**. **Marble Arch**, yet another Nash creation, marks its western extent. This almost apologetically unremarkable monument was intended to be the entrance to Buckingham Palace but, found to be too small, was moved to its current site in 1851 where it now stands, marooned on a traffic island.

London's most famous shopping street, accurately judged by Peter Ackroyd's fictional Oscar Wilde (in *The Last Testament of Oscar Wilde*) to be 'all street and no Oxford', is a scruffy, people-packed canyon of uncontrolled commerce. It's a curious mix of trash and class. Next to the tourist tat stalls and dodgy geezers flogging counterfeit perfumes on the street are huge flagship department stores (**Selfridges**, **John Lewis**, **Marks & Spencer** *et al*; *see pages 202-3*). Filling the middle ground are countless cheap clothes and shoe stores, music megastores and other high-street favourites like Gap and Next. More individual shops can be found on Marylebone High Street. The biggest name newcomer is the second London branch of Sir Terence Conran's ground-breaking **Conran Shop** (no.55; *see page 202*), showcasing the best of modern furniture and household design, and topped with **The Orrery** restaurant.

Desirable food and drink destinations – formerly not over-abundant in the area – are multiplying rapidly. Try the exemplary restaurant-cum-deli **Villandry** at 170 Great Portland Street, sausage and beer emporium **RK Stanley** (6 Little Portland Street; *see page 160*) or the recently opened branch of noodle chain **Wagamama** (101A Wigmore Street; *see page 162*).

BBC Experience

Broadcasting House, Portland Place, Regent Street, WC1 (0171 580 4468). Oxford Circus tube. **Open** 1-4.30pm Mon; 10am-4.30pm Tue-Fri; 10am-5.30pm Sat, Sun. **Admission** £6.50; £4.50-£5.50 concs; free under-5s. **Credit** MC, V. **Map 5 H5**

Within months of being occupied by the BBC in 1932, Broadcasting House was found to be too small for the burgeoning company, yet this gleaming Portland-stone construction (designed by G Val Myers, with an external sculpture of Shakespeare's Ariel by Eric Gill) has become so synonymous with 'Auntie' that it remains the heart of the nation's public service broadcasting. Daily BBC radio programmes first emanated from Savoy Hill (next to the Savoy Hotel) on 14 November 1922. In 1997, as part of celebrations marking the 75th anniversary of the Beeb, the BBC Experience was opened.

The semi-guided tour (book in advance to avoid queues) begins with an exhibition on Marconi, the single most important contributor to the invention of the wireless (look out for the transcript of the *Titanic*'s last-known wireless message – an SOS, unsurprisingly). After this, visitors get to participate in a mock radio show (the highlight of the tour), and watch montages of historic broadcasts. The tour finishes with the chance to 'direct' a short, pre-filmed scene from *EastEnders* (you don't, alas, see the finished masterpiece) and present the weather. All in all it's a rather superficial, fleeting glimpse of one of the country's greatest institutions.

London Planetarium

Marylebone Road, NW1 (0171 935 6861). Baker Street tube. **Open** *June-Aug* 10.20am-5pm daily; *Sept-May* 12.20-5pm Mon-Fri; 10.20am-5pm Sat, Sun. **Admission** £5.85; £3.85-£4.50 concs (no under-5s). **Combined ticket with Madame Tussaud's** £12; £8.05-£9.25 concs. **Credit** AmEx, MC, £$TC, V. **Map 5 G4**

Be sure to plan your visit to the Planetarium – the main attraction is a 30-minute show (there's not an awful lot more to see than this), but a 40-minute wait between performances means that if you arrive just after a show begins, you're in for a long wait. Sink back into the comfy chairs and enjoy the excellent, if inevitably, simplified history of space and the universe (as far as we know it), projected on to the dome, and livened up with computer-generated graphics.

London Zoo

Regent's Park, NW1 (0171 722 3333). Baker Street or Camden Town tube then 274, C2 bus. **Open** *Nov-Feb* 10am-4pm daily; *Mar-Oct* 10am-5.30pm daily. **Admission** £8.50; £6.50-£7.50 concs; £26 family ticket; free under-4s. **Credit** AmEx, MC, £$TC, V. **Map 5 G2**

London Zoo celebrated its 170th birthday in 1998. Whatever your view on the morality of keeping wild beasties in cages, the importance of zoos in conservation work is unquestionable. The zoo, understandably, promotes this side of its remit to the full – as well as the popular 'adopt an animal scheme' (£20 for a dung beetle; £6,000 for an elephant). One of its proudest achievements is the hand-rearing of a black rhinoceros (called Rosie), a feat rarely achieved. It's a marvellous place for kids – feeding times and special events are posted on notice boards, and close encounters of a furry kind are available at the Children's Zoo. The gardens are beautifully landscaped and it's easy to spend the best part of a day wandering between the enclosures (the newest is Bear Mountain on the Mappin Terraces). The buildings include some gems of modern architecture: look out for the Penguin Pool (1936) by Lubetkin and Tecton, Hugh Casson's Elephant House (1965) and Lord Snowdon's Aviary (1963-4).

Madame Tussaud's

Marylebone Road, NW1 (0171 935 6861). Baker Street tube. **Open** *May-Sept* 9am-5.30pm daily; *Oct-June* 10am-5.30pm Mon-Fri; 9.30am-5.30pm Sat, Sun. **Admission** £9.75; £6.60-£7.45 concs. *Combined ticket with*

Top tours: Scandal!

Marylebone is no stranger to scandal. By the early nineteenth century, it had acquired a reputation as a district inhabited by ladies who 'entertained' rich gentlemen during the day. Later, the area was the centre of some of the biggest scandals of the nineteenth and twentieth centuries. If you want to know how to get your name in the papers, follow the trail…

Start off in **Shouldham Street**, between Gloucester Place and Edgware Road. It was at **no.21** that destitute Arthur Orton, aka the **Tichborne Claimant**, died, appropriately on April Fool's Day 1898. Orton had spent his whole life convincing people that he was Sir Roger Charles Doughty Tichborne (who had actually drowned). He managed to successfully con the real man's mother into paying him the not inconsiderable annual allowance of £1,000 (no doubt the joy of seeing her long-lost son turn up alive obscured the fact that Orton was fatter than her son, barely literate and spoke with a Cockney accent). When he was eventually rumbled Orton was sentenced to 14 years in jail. The *Standard* described him as 'the most daring swindler of our times'.

Next, head a couple of streets down to **Bryanston Court**, a block of luxury flats on the corner of George Street and Seymour Place. In 1933, a certain **Mrs Wallis Simpson** began entertaining the Prince of Wales at **no.5**. Three years later, their affair brought down the monarchy and **Edward VI**, king only for ten months, was forced to abdicate.

Walk east from here along George Street to **Manchester Street**. In October 1814, the eyes of the nation were on the resident of **no.38**, one **Joanna Southcott**. The reason? The Second Coming, of

course. At the age of 64, Ms Southcott was said to be pregnant with the Messiah. She took to her bed, but nothing happened, and on 28 December she died. An autopsy revealed that there was no foetus inside her, but rather that internal flatulence and glandular enlargements of the breasts had given her the appearance of being pregnant.

Turn down Marylebone Lane towards Wimpole Street. Just off here lies quiet, secluded **Bentinck Street**. During World War II a flat at **no.5** was rented by **Guy Burgess** and **Anthony Blunt**. While he was working for MI5, Blunt would take top-secret papers back to the flat before passing them to the Russians. Burgess, meanwhile, was doing the equivalent at MI6. Burgess's exploits were discovered relatively early, in the 1950s, after he defected to Russia, but it wasn't until 1979 that Blunt was unmasked, disgraced and stripped of his knighthood.

Just round the corner, between Weymouth Street and New Cavendish Street, is **no.17 Wimpole Mews**. The flat hit the headlines in 1963 when it was discovered that its resident, osteopath **Dr Stephen Ward**, had a nice sideline introducing famous men to pretty girls – namely **Christine Keeler** and **Mandy Rice Davies** – and living off their earnings. The Cuban missile crisis was at its height, and when it was alleged that Keeler had been sleeping with both War Minister **John Profumo** and Russian diplomat Eugene Ivanov, Profumo resigned (while denying any sexual relationship with Keeler). Ward, meanwhile, was tried for immorality. The story ended in tragedy when Ward took an overdose, dying before the judge could deliver the jury's verdict of guilty.

Planetarium £12; £8.05-£9.25 concs. **Credit** AmEx, MC, £STC, V. **Map 5 G4**

If you are a child or gaspingly credulous you'll enjoy Madame Tussaud's, but it's hard to see what anyone over the age of 16 could get from the place beyond the chance to have your photo taken sticking your tongue out at Saddam Hussein. Yes, most of the models are spookily accurate (the young Norman Lamont-lookalike Elvis being a disturbing exception), but so what? There's very little information about any of the figures, no interactivity, little animatronic action. Entertainment and sporting heroes (including a lycra-clad Linford Christie plus lunchbox) mill around at the 'garden party', while close by the smouldering Pierce Brosnan/James Bond figure attracts perhaps unwanted attention (repeated female gropings caused it to be taken out of commission not long ago for retouching work, as it were).

In the main hall dummies are grouped by profession – monarchs, US presidents, dictators, etc – though the inclusion of some figures remains critically questionable (Wilde, Dickens, Shakespeare and, er, Agatha Christie?). The once-legendary Chamber of Horrors seems somewhat tame these days, particularly now that the **London Dungeon** (*see p33*) does this sort of thing more graphically and gruesomely, although this section does at least contain a few genuine exhibits (such as the guillotine blade that dispatched Marie Antoinette). Finally, punters can take a break in the café, before embarking in a 'time taxi' on a breakneck trip through 400 years of London history – a ride of such extraordinary brevity and nonsensicality that the blinking, saluting Benny Hill at journey's end seems entirely appropriate. Book tickets in advance if you want to avoid queueing.

Regent's Park

*NW1 (0171 486 7905/tennis courts 0171 486 4216). Baker Street, Camden Town, Great Portland Street or Regent's Park tube. ***Open*** park & Queen Mary's Gardens 5am-30 mins before dusk daily; tennis courts Oct-Apr 9am-dusk daily; May-Sept 8am-dusk; playgrounds 10am-30 mins before dusk daily. ***Map 5 G3**

Laid out in 1817-28 by John Nash, Regent's Park (named after Nash's faithful patron) remains central London's most well-mannered park. Originally part of the Middlesex Forest, and later a royal hunting ground, the park is particularly lively in summer, with a boating lake (herons live on the islands), three playgrounds, bandstand music, tennis courts, a café and a celebrated open-air theatre that's been running since 1932 (*see p269*). The Outer Circle, the main road running around the park, is over two miles (3.2km) long. It's bordered to the south by Marylebone Road and Park Crescent, on the west and east by Palladian mansions, and to the north by Regent's Canal. Strolling in Queen Mary's Gardens (inside the Inner Circle) on a summer evening is one of the best reasons for being in London.

Sherlock Holmes Museum

*221B Baker Street, NW1 (0171 935 8866). Baker Street tube. ***Open*** 9.30am-6pm daily. ***Admission*** £5; £3 under-16s. ***Credit*** AmEx, JCB, MC, £TC, V. ***Map 5 G4**

This re-creation of the great sleuth's fictional lodgings is well done, but you won't find any genuine historical treasures or information about Conan Doyle or the Edinburgh surgeon upon whom he based his famous detective. A fiver is rather steep for a bit of atmosphere.

Mayfair

Map 7

The late seventeenth century was a time of great dynamism in the development of London. New districts – such as Covent Garden and Soho – were laid out, and enjoyed brief vogues as fashionable addresses before the well-to-do looked further west for grander residences. The elegant Georgian streets and squares of **Mayfair** and **St James's** were part of the next wave, largely occupying their current sites by the mid-eighteenth century, but their social cachet, unlike that of their eastern neighbours, has never wavered to this day.

Piccadilly Circus

Piccadilly Circus is one of central London's pivotal points, as its constant streaming traffic indicates only too clearly. The name derives from the speciality of a tailor, Robert Baker, who made his fortune selling stiff collars known as 'picadils' and lived near here in the early seventeenth century. The commercial connection is apposite, for the posh shops of Mayfair, Piccadilly and Regent Street have long been a fixture of the district.

The Circus's great bank of neon – so untypically flashy for London – can trace its origins back to at least 1910. The other defining feature is the statue of **Eros** – a misnomer on two counts: it's actually a memorial fountain to the philanthropic Lord Shaftesbury, not a statue; and represents the Angel of Christian Charity, not the god of love. Although Eros is an enduringly popular symbol of London, the stumpy memorial, no longer marooned on a traffic island, is unimpressive. It might have been far more pleasing had the designer, Alfred Gilbert, not met with constant interference from the organising committee and council. He refused to attend the unveiling in 1893 and remained traumatised by the experience for the rest of his life.

Two big tourist attractions lie just to the east of the Circus – the bafflingly popular **Rock Circus** (*see below*) and the more obviously exciting fun palace of the **Pepsi Trocadero** (*see below*).

Leading south from here, **Haymarket**'s associations are with older forms of fun. The market, after which the street is named, traded until 1830; by then Haymarket was already famed for its theatres (the Theatre Royal opened in 1720, Her Majesty's Theatre in 1705) and notorious for its prostitutes. Today it's short on charm of any variety.

Regent Street

Curving away north-westwards from Piccadilly Circus and southwards towards Pall Mall, **Regent Street** was conceived by John Nash in the early

1800s as a dramatic boulevard to clear away unsightly slums, improve transport links and connect the Prince Regent's residence, Carlton House, with Regent's Park. His plans were continually frustrated by a variety of vested interests, but the sweep of the section just north of Piccadilly Circus – known as the Quadrant – still impresses. Nash also intended Regent Street to act as a *cordon sanitaire* between the scruffs of Soho and the toffs of Mayfair. The distinction still holds good.

Shops 'appropriated to articles of fashion and taste' were a fixture of Regent Street from the beginning. Some of the capital's most famous retailing names – the mock-Tudor department store **Liberty** (*see page 203*), the kiddie-heaven of **Hamleys** toy store (*see page 214*) – still survive amid the encroaching mainstream chains. Here too is the **Café Royal**, at no.68, ultra-fashionable bohemian hangout for artists and writers a century ago. Its plush **Grill Room** is one of Marco Pierre White's lavish affairs.

Piccadilly

Extending from Piccadilly Circus past **Green Park** (*see below*) to Hyde Park Corner, **Piccadilly** is (along with Oxford Street) one of the ancient roads heading west out of London. Despite the attractions of the street's almost equally ancient emporia such as the bookshop **Hatchards** at no.187 (founded in 1797) and **Fortnum & Mason** (*see page 202*), the constant traffic means that more pleasant window shopping can be had in the arcades leading off Piccadilly. **Burlington Arcade**, running down the side of Burlington House, now home of the **Royal Academy of Arts** (*see page 133*), is the most celebrated. The arcade was built in 1819 by the House's then-owner, Lord George Cavendish, to stop passers-by throwing rubbish over the wall into his garden. Even today, uniformed beadles ensure that shoppers don't hum, carry large packages or do anything else to upset Regency decorum.

Piccadilly is also home to several of London's luxury hotels; chief among them is **The Ritz**. Soon after the hotel opened in 1906, it became a byword for a level of glamour, glitz and extravagance unparalled in London. Even today, the word 'ritzy' conjures up high-class luxury. Booking ahead for afternoon tea is the cheapest way to gain access to the opulent Louis XVI interior (*see page 161*).

Those seeking escapism of a more low-key kind should duck in to Wren's delightful **St James's Church Piccadilly** (*see below*). The churchyard hosts a regular craft market, and the vegetarian café next door has excellent food and outdoor seating in the summer.

Retro St James's

The tiny enclave bounded by Piccadilly, Green Park, the Mall and Haymarket is a corner of London that will be forever England – that is, if your idea of England is Victorian-throwback, pin-striped old duffers puffing on cigars, reddening their faces with countless bottles of claret and lamenting the decline of empire. This is clubland – and we're not talking Ministry of Sound.

The majority of these exclusive (in every sense) establishments are lined up along **St James's Street** and **Pall Mall** (named after a croquet-like game once played here). They evolved from the seventeenth-century coffee houses as meeting places for gentlemen, although most date only from the nineteenth century. Ultra-aristocratic **White's** (Prince Charles had his stag party here), at 37 St James's Street, is the oldest (founded in 1693); the **RAC Club** (89 Pall Mall), which celebrated its centenary in 1997, is the most recent and, reputedly, the least class-conscious. The 1832 Reform Act spawned both the 'radical' **Reform Club** (104 Pall Mall) and the reactionary **Carlton Club** (69 St James's Street); the latter remains an unshakeable bastion of all-male Toryism – Margaret Thatcher had to be made an honorary man to secure entrance. **Brooks**, on the corner of St James's Street and Park Place (so exclusive it doesn't have a street number), was famed for the prodigious gambling of its members, particularly during the 1770s when Charles James Fox would drink and gamble all night before wandering down to the House of Commons to dazzle the members with the wit and cleverness of his speeches.

The material needs of the venerable gentlemen of St James's are met by the fabulously anachronistic shops and restaurants of **Jermyn** (pronounced 'jér-mun') **Street** and St James's Street. If you ignore the fact that well-to-do tourists make up most of the clientele these days, it's still a thrill to see the lovingly crafted quality of the goods and the time-warp shopfronts. For details of the best of the old St James's stores, *see page 198* **Victorian values**.

Exploring St James's

Few visitors (and equally few Londoners) venture further into St James's than Jermyn Street, yet its streets, mews and alleyways make for rewarding wandering. In particular, don't miss lively **Crown Passage** off King Street.

St James's Square was the most fashionable address in London for the 50 years after it was laid

out in the 1670s, boasting no fewer than seven dukes and seven earls as residents by the 1720s. The Prince Regent was attending a ball at no.16 in 1815 when a bloodied and dirty major arrived to announce the victory at Waterloo, much to the dismay of the hostess who was 'much annoyed with the Battle of Waterloo as it spoilt her party'. Alas, no private houses survive on the square today. In the north-west corner is the prestigious **London Library**, a private library founded by Thomas Carlyle in 1841 in disgust at the inefficiency of the British Library.

A huddle of great aristocratic houses stand in the south-west corner of St James's, the most notable being **St James's Palace**. Built by Henry VIII on the site of St James's Hospital, the palace was one of the principal royal residences for more than 300 years and is still used by Prince Charles and various minor royals. Most of what you see today is the result of a Nash remodelling in the early nineteenth century. (Nash was also responsible for **Clarence House** next door, home of the Queen Mum.) Tradition still dictates that foreign ambassadors to the UK are officially known as 'Ambassador to the Court of St James'. Although the palace is closed to the public, it is possible to explore Friary Court on Marlborough Road and attend the Sunday services at the **Chapel Royal** (October to Good Friday; 8.30am, 11.30am). It was here that Charles I took holy com-

Piccadilly Circus: *statue of Eros + bank of neon + driving rain = quintessential London.*

Piccadilly Arcade: an arcade, off Piccadilly.

munion on the morning of his execution, and Victoria and Albert (and many other royals) were married in the chapel.

Across Marlborough Road from St James's Palace, the **Queen's Chapel** was the first classical church built in England. Designed by Inigo Jones in the 1620s for Charles I's intended bride of the time, the Infanta of Castile, the chapel now stands in the grounds of **Marlborough House** and is only open to the public during Sunday services (Easter to July; 8.30am, 11.30am). The house itself was built by Christopher Wren (both father and son) for Queen Anne's bosom chum, Sarah, Duchess of Marlborough, and, as requested, is 'strong, plain and convenient'.

Further east, overlooking the Mall, is gleaming **Carlton House Terrace**, built by Nash in 1827-32 on the site of Carlton House. When the Prince Regent came to the throne as George IV he decided that his then-home was not ostentatious enough for his newly elevated station and levelled what Horace Walpole had described as 'the most perfect palace' in Europe. The terrace splits at the **Duke of York's Column**, erected in 1833. Not only did the 'Grand Old Duke' march his 10,000 men to the top of the hill and down again, but he also docked them a day's wages to pay for his own monument.

Two other notable St James's mansions overlook Green Park. At the Mall end is neo-classical **Lancaster House**, rebuilt in the 1820s by Benjamin Dean Wyatt for Frederick, Duke of York. Now used mainly for government receptions and conferences, the house much impressed Queen Victoria with its splendour (on one visit she remarked to her hostess: 'I have come from my house to your palace'). It is closed to the public. A couple of doors further north is beautiful, eighteenth-century **Spencer House** (*see below*), ancestral townhouse of Princess Diana's family and now open as a museum and art gallery.

Mayfair

To the casual observer, the huge expanse of **Mayfair**, filling the space between Oxford Street, Regent Street, Piccadilly and Park Lane, can seem little more than a homogenous mass of mansions. But there is much of interest in this vast area, named after the raucous annual fair, which moved to the site of today's Curzon Street and Shepherd Market from Haymarket in 1686 and was suppressed by the local nobs less than a century later for lowering the tone of the neighbourhood. Today, the narrow, winding streets around **Shepherd Market**, lined with restaurants, pubs and shops, make up Mayfair's quirkiest corner. The area has long held a reputation as a haunt of a better class of prostitute. Whether the oldest profession still flourishes here is a matter of debate, but the curious can always settle themselves in the congenial **Ye Grapes** pub, wave a wad of tenners around conspicuously and see what happens.

Just south of here, on **Down Street**, distinctive maroon glazed tiles betray the former entrance to one of the most interesting of London's many disused tube stations (*see opposite*). The Duke of Wellington's London home, **Apsley House** (*see below*), stands not far away at Hyde Park Corner.

Three great squares dictate the feel of the northern portion of Mayfair: Hanover Square, Berkeley Square (where no nightingales have sung in living memory) and immense **Grosvenor Square**, second in size only to Lincoln's Inn Fields. Laid out between 1725 and 1731, it has always been a prestigious address, although disappointingly few of its original houses survive. Today, the square is dominated by the looming presence of the immense US Embassy on the west side. Built in 1958-61 by Eero Saarinen, it was described by Nikolaus Pevsner as 'an impressive but decidedly embarrassing building'. A statue of Franklin D Roosevelt in the centre of the square furthers the American connection, and the **Grosvenor Chapel** on South Audley Street (where radical MP John Wilkes is buried) is still a favourite with American expats. Nearby are the peaceful **Mount Street Gardens**, next to the **Church of the Immaculate Conception** on Farm Street. One of London's few Catholic churches at which a sung Latin mass is celebrated, this splendid Gothic revival building is the British HQ of the Jesuits.

One unlikely Mayfair resident in 1968 was Jimi Hendrix, who lived with his girlfriend Kathy Etchingham in no.23 Brook Street, next door to the house where George Frideric Handel spent the last 35 years of his life. ('I haven't heard much of the guy's stuff, but I dig a bit of Bach now and again,' as Jimi said of his neighbour.) Plans to set up a Handel museum at no.25 are currently stalled.

Not far from here, on Brook Street and Carlos Place, are two of Mayfair's poshest hotels, respectively, **Claridge's** and **The Connaught**. Towards Piccadilly, on Albemarle Street, is another classic London hotel, **Brown's**, from where Alexander Graham Bell made the first successful telephone call in 1876. Another scientific pioneer, Michael Faraday,

is commemorated in the **Faraday Museum** (*see page 120*) in the basement of the Royal Institution, further up the street, at no.21.

The eastern side of Mayfair is largely devoted to commerce, albeit of a very upmarket kind. **Savile Row** has long been home to gentlemen's outfitters of a fiercely traditional stamp. At the junction of Savile Row and Vigo Street old meets new, with the venerable firm of **Gieves & Hawkes** (*see page 198*) squaring up opposite the dazzling, iconoclastic tailoring of **Ozwald Boateng** (*see page 199*).

Down Street: A lost tube station

Few people cutting up Down Street from Piccadilly towards Curzon Street give a second glance to the handsome red-tiled façade they pass on their street. Yet this is the former entrance to one of the many London tube stations that, for various reasons, are no longer used as part of the underground network. Down Street (Mayfair) station, as it was originally known, opened in 1907. Twenty-five years later, it found itself squeezed on either side when the original Green Park station was moved two streets west from Dover Street, and Hyde Park Corner station was rebuilt a similar distance further east (its original entrance now fronts Pizza on the Park at 11 Knightsbridge). Even before this, Down Street had never been heavily used – the well-heeled denizens of Mayfair tending to favour private transport – and so the station was closed in 1932.

But that wasn't the end of the line for Down Street. In 1939, with war looming, the Railway Executive Committee (responsible for co-ordinating the country's railways) decided that Down Street, close to several important ministries, was perfectly located as a bomb-proof HQ for its vital war work. Gas locks were installed and tiny offices, bedrooms, bathrooms, messes, a kitchen and a telephone exchange were constructed within the tunnels. Conditions were cramped (the passageway beside the offices was, in places, little more than two feet across – just wide enough for a tea trolley) but nevertheless considered relatively homely by those who worked down here. In the early years of the war, they included Winston Churchill and his war cabinet, who met at Down Street during the worst air raids of 1940-1 while the **Cabinet War Rooms** (*see page 116*) under Whitehall were still under construction.

After the war, Down Street was abandoned again, although it continues to fulfil an important role in the tube system, acting as a ventila-

tion shaft. Because of this function, the station remains the most complete of the disused tube stations. Although the ticket hall and most of the wartime offices have been demolished, it's still possible to see the toilets and bathrooms, complete with tubs (where Winston once splashed?), the remains of the telephone exchange and the empty shells of some of the other rooms.

Down Street is also occasionally used for parties and as a set for films and pop videos. Much of the TV series *Neverwhere* was filmed down here. One scene required a fantastical feast to be enacted on the small remaining section of the platform – London Transport staff still chortle when they recall the looks on passengers' faces on passing trains.

Although it's not widely known, London Transport conducts fascinating tours of Down Street station upon written request (you should address correspondence to: Station Manager, Green Park Station, London Underground, Piccadilly, London W1V 9HG), and, if you're lucky, the tour will finish with one of the coolest things you're ever likely to do in London – hitching a lift to Green Park station from a passing tube train.

Bond Street is equally famed for its frighteningly opulent yet clinical temples of art, couture, jewellery and antiques. In fact, there is no Bond Street as such, but, rather, **New Bond Street** and **Old Bond Street**. Here also are two of London's best-known auction houses: **Sotheby's**, at 34-35 New Bond Street (0171 493 8080), and **Phillips** (0171 629 6602), at 101 New Bond Street. The public is welcome to view items that are coming up for sale. Art fans might also like to cruise the many commercial galleries of Cork Street and Dering Street, while antique buffs shouldn't miss the **Bond Street Antiques Centre** (124 New Bond Street) and **Grays Antique Market** (58 Davies Street & 1-7 Davies Mews; *see page 186*). Nearby, pedestrianised **South Molton Street** offers more chic and bank-breakingly pricey shops.

A moment's peace from the commercial bustle can be had in the church of **St George** (1721-4) on St George Street near Hanover Square. This was the first London church to have a portico and has long been a favourite venue for society weddings.

Food options in Mayfair tend towards the unimaginative and extortionate, though there are exceptions. Marco Pierre White's exemplary (though pricey) **Mirabelle** on Curzon Street (*see page 167*) and the stunning south Indian vegetarian cooking at **Rasa W1** on Dering Street (*see page 172*) are two prime examples.

Apsley House – The Wellington Museum

149 Piccadilly, W1 (0171 499 5676). Hyde Park Corner tube. **Open** 11am-5pm Tue-Sun. **Admission** £4.50; £3 concs; free under-12s. **Credit** AmEx, DC, MC, V. **Map 7 G8**

This grand house (known at one time as 'No.1 London') was built by Robert Adam in the 1770s and was the London residence of the Duke of Wellington from 1817 until his death in 1852. His descendants still live here, but ten rooms, restored to their original state, are open to the public. The house contains the extensive collection of paintings, sculpture, ceramics, silverware and memorabilia belonging to the Iron Duke (so nicknamed not for his indomitable will but for the iron shutters he installed after rioters broke his windows in protest over his Reform Bill). Exhibits include an equestrian portrait of the great man by Goya. One of the more eccentric touches is a huge 11ft 4-in (3.4-m) statue by Canova of the diminutive Napoleon. Two new displays have recently opened in the basement: the Duke's Death and Funeral, and Medals and Memorabilia.

Green Park

SW1. Green Park tube. **Open** dawn-dusk daily. **Map 7 H7**
This literally named park was enclosed by Henry VIII and made into a Royal Park by Charles II. The park was the site of a number of early balloon ascents and firework displays. Handel composed his *Music for the Royal Fireworks* for the most famous of these pyrotechnical extravaganzas, celebrating the Peace of Aix-la-Chapelle in 1748. Today, Green Park is one of the duller of central London's open spaces, though it's an agreeable enough spot to snooze away an hour in a deckchair.

Pepsi Trocadero

1 Piccadilly Circus, W1 (0891 881100). Piccadilly Circus tube. **Open** 10am-midnight Mon-Fri; 10am-1am Sat, Sun. **Admission** varies (*see below*). **Credit** varies. **Map 8 K7**

The shy and retiring would be wise to steer clear of this entertainment mega-complex; kids, on the other hand, flock here in droves. Take the family on the **Funland Lazerbowl** (0171 287 8913), which stimulates virtually and realistically with bowling, racing cars, bumper cars and video game technology. Annoyingly, some machines dish out coupons instead of cash – you then get to 'spend' them on goods such as a Neil Sedaka video or bottom-of-the-range body spray. **Segaworld** (0171 734 2777; free) features six floors of arcade games and 'futuractive' experiences. The adventurous could try the **Emaginator** (0171 437 5723; £3.50; £3 children; £10 family ticket for 2 adults and 2 children), where you watch hyper-paced movies in seats that shudder and shake in sync. Or, if your stomach is up to it, have a go on the **Pepsi Max drop ride** (0171 434 0030; £3), where you get strapped into a seat that drops six storeys in two seconds. The **IMAX 3D cinema** (0171 494 4153; £6.75) is a less frenetic choice. Further attractions include the **Internet Exchange** and **Madison's** café (0171 437 3704) and **Old-Time Photography** (0171 734 8709), where you get kitted out in costumes of yesteryear and have your photo taken as a souvenir.

Rock Circus

Piccadilly Circus, W1 (0171 734 7203). Piccadilly Circus tube. **Open** 11am-9pm Mon, Wed, Thur, Sun; noon-9pm Tue; 11am-10pm Fri, Sat. **Admission** £7.95; £6.95 concs; £19.95 family ticket; free disabled, under-5s. **Credit** AmEx, EC, MC, £$TC, V. **Map 8 K7**

Mildly diverting but overpriced, this Madame-Tussaud's-for-pop-fans centres on wax models of the biggest stars. While a few of them are surprisingly lifelike (including Lenny Kravitz), the majority are either laughable (a camp Elvis), out of date (George Michael stuck in a late-'80s time warp) or completely unrealistic (such as a black Michael Jackson – whatever next?). Bemused punters shuffle along, wearing headphones that pipe crackled snippets of famous songs. The grand finale comes at the end of the tour in the form of a 'concert' (every 20 minutes; pray you haven't just missed one or you might be tempted to shell out more cash on drinks and popcorn). Here, rockumentary clips are interspersed with yet more dummies (including a distinctly Tracy Ullman-esque Janis Joplin) playing 'live' songs. Though the footage is watchable (if unrevealing), the lifeless, jolting models make the Thunderbirds look like the Royal Shakespeare Company. A waste of wax.

St James's Church Piccadilly

197 Piccadilly, W1 (0171 734 4511). Piccadilly Circus tube. **Open** 8am-7pm daily (phone for details of evening events). **Map 7 J7**
Offering a tranquil haven from the pounding Piccadilly traffic, this charming Wren church (1676-84) is the only one he built on an entirely new site. It was also one of the architect's favourites of his works: 'I think it may be found beautiful and convenient'. The limewood reredos, carved by Grinling Gibbons, was much admired by John Evelyn. Gibbons was also responsible for the font and organ case. James Christie, the auctioneer, and James Gillray, the caricaturist, are among the many distinguished people buried here. An excellent crafts market is held in the churchyard every Thursday to Saturday (*see p193*).

Spencer House

27 St James's Place, SW1 (0171 499 8620). Green Park tube. **Open** Feb-July, Sept-Dec 11.45am-4.45pm Sun. **Admission** £6; £5 under-16s, Friends of the RA, V&A, Tate. **Map 7 J8**
Guided tours of one of London's most splendid Palladian mansions take in a number of restored state rooms. The most notable features are the extravagant murals of the Painted Room and the beautiful painted ceiling in the Great Room. James Vardy, James Stuart and Robert Adam all worked on the house, which was completed in 1766 for Earl Spencer.

Soho

Maps 5-8

From hunting ground to boozing and cruising ground – Soho's come a long way in not much over 300 years. Sliced off from the rest of London by Oxford Street, Regent Street, Shaftesbury Avenue and Charing Cross Road, Soho is an island in the centre of the city – distinctive, proud, particular.

The integrity of this unique district has undoubtedly benefited from its lack of 'attractions', in the conventional sense. The streets are narrow, the buildings mean; there are no museums or galleries, and precious little greenery – people, not things, are the sights of Soho. While older brother Covent Garden has sobered up and scrubbed itself down, the mantle of London's pleasure-zone has passed westward. Scruffier, dirtier and noisier, Soho is where media London works and where the rest of London plays.

Most of the district was laid out in the 1670s and 1680s as part of a general expansion westward from the overcrowded City. Soho (the name derives from an old hunting call) was completed just in time to absorb an influx of Greek Christians (hence, Greek Street) fleeing Ottoman persecution, and a larger wave of French Protestants (Huguenots), forced out of France by Louis XIV's bigotry. Many were talented craftsmen and set up leather, silver and furniture workshops. Thus, from the outset, Soho has acted as a sponge and haven for outcasts and misfits; a spirit of toleration was born out of necessity, and remains one of the area's defining characteristics.

Those who didn't like what they saw got out – most of the early well-to-do residents left their Soho Square mansions for the grander, more exclusive developments of Mayfair in the early eighteenth century – and in moved the artists, writers, radicals and yet more foreign immigrants (particularly Italians). By the nineteenth century, John Galsworthy, in *The Forsyte Saga*, summed up Soho as: 'untidy, full of Greeks, Ishmaelites, cats, Italians, tomatoes, restaurants, organs, coloured stuffs, queer names…'

As the resident population dropped in the twentieth century, the area became increasingly known for its entertainments (legal and otherwise) and cheap restaurants. Jazz came to Soho in the 1950s (Ronnie Scott's on Greek Street celebrates its 40th birthday in 1999) and the sex industry expanded rapidly in the 1960s. By the mid-1970s, with operators and police in cahoots, Soho was in danger of being overrun by the sex trade. A major clampdown – which included the prosecution of several

high-ranking police officers for bribery and corruption – saw the number of premises used by the sex trade drop by five-sixths in the 1980s. At the same time, Soho was regaining its dynamism, thanks largely to its increasingly visible and energetic gay scene. Pubs like the Golden Lion on Dean Street had long been the haunt of gay servicemen, but now gay cafés, late-night bars and clubs, and fetish shops appeared along Old Compton Street, injecting a much-needed vitality and *joie de vivre* into a district in danger of becoming the sole province of dirty old men in raincoats.

That Soho is now more popular than ever is a cause for both celebration and concern. A 24-hour culture is developing, people are taking to the streets – eating, drinking, promenading; coming over all continental. Yet the chains are moving in too, bringing with them those fainthearts who previously found Soho too grimy and seedy for their tastes. No lover of cranky, louche old Soho can fail to worry at the sight of long queues at the doors of huge, characterless booze barns like the Pitcher & Piano and All Bar One on Dean Street.

The heart of Soho

The core of Soho today is **Old Compton Street** – a shopping centre since its earliest days – and its surrounding streets. Here is Soho at its most heterodox and lively – gay bars, off-licences, delis, heaving boozers, pâtisseries and cheap to chic restaurants. Perhaps the most evocative way to enter Soho, however, is via the arch of the Pillars of Hercules pub leading from Manette Street to Greek Street. The sense of passing through a portal into a different world has entranced more than one Soho neophyte in the past. Just north of here is shady **Soho Square**, initially known as King Square (a weather-beaten statue of the king in question, Charles II, stands close to the mock Tudor hut in the centre). In summer, office workers munch their lunchtime sandwiches on the grass; while, around the square's edge, London's one remaining French Protestant church and St Patrick's Catholic church provide spiritual nourishment.

The short streets leading down from here to Old Compton Street are brimful of eateries and historical associations. On **Greek Street**, Casanova and Thomas de Quincey once lodged and Josiah Wedgwood had his London showroom; famous old restaurants like **L'Escargot** (no.48; *see page 167*) and the Hungarian **Gay Hussar** (no.2) still survive; notorious Soho soak Jeffrey Bernard's favourite hangout, the undistinguished **Coach & Horses**, is at no.29.

Neighbouring **Frith Street** has been home to John Constable, Mozart and William Hazlitt (at no.6 – now one of London's most charming and discreet hotels; *see page 142*). Over the ever-vibrant **Bar Italia** (no.22; *see page 159*), with its constantly blaring TV, are, appropriately, the rooms where John Logie Baird first demonstrated the wonder of television.

Next along is **Dean Street**, site of such famed drinking haunts as the **French House** (no.49; unofficial HQ of de Gaulle and the Free French during World War II; *see page 181*) and the Colony Club (no.41), second homes to Francis Bacon and assorted literary and artistic layabouts from the 1950s, and of the **Groucho Club** (no.44), a focus for today's arts and media crowd. In two cramped rooms over **Quo Vadis** restaurant (no.28; *see page 167*), Karl Marx and family lived in 1851-6.

West of here, work begins to get an equal billing with play. **Wardour Street** has long associations with the film industry and remains home to a number of film production companies, as well as Sir Terence Conran's mega **Mezzo** restaurant (no.100), which stands on the site of the legendary Marquee Club. At the street's southern end is the churchyard of **St Anne** – only the early nineteenth-century tower of the church survived the Blitz, but it's worth a look to read the memorial slabs of William Hazlitt and the unfortunate Theodore, King of Corsica, who died penniless

Festival time in **Chinatown**.

('Fate… bestow'd a kingdom, and denied him bread'). The ashes of the author Dorothy L Sayers are buried beneath the tower.

At the eastern end of **Brewer Street** sex shops, shows and clip joints dominate (it may only be £3 to get in, but you'll be fleeced for 100 times that before you get out); the western portion contains a number of Japanese restaurants and quirky shops. Leading south to Shaftesbury Avenue is **Rupert**

Top tours: Say cheese!

Capital of cool? Do us a favour...

Are you tired of right-on guides (like, er, this one) telling you about all the hippest hang-outs and undiscovered gems of London? Do you crave the clichéd city you know from film and TV? Do you long to wallow in the unapologetic kitschy naffness that is the true glory of the capital? Then read on…

Start in the tourist mecca of **Covent Garden**. Thrill at top street entertainers, like the bloke who paints himself gold, dresses in a sheet and stands very still.

Stroll down vibrant, bustling, dirty, smelly **Oxford Street**, perhaps stopping for a pint in the street's only pub, the unappealing **Tottenham**, by Tottenham Court Road tube, before being ripped off by shifty-eyed geezers selling knocked off fake perfume from a suitcase. Maybe purchase one of those hilarious 'My dad/therapist/hamster went to London and all I got was this lousy T-shirt' T-shirts. Then some cotton and a needle to stitch up your split sides.

For lunch, what could be more tasty than a day-old slice of cardboard pizza from one of those tempting street-side stalls. Or look for a pub serving 'traditional olde English fare', like fish and chips, or curry.

Then down Regent Street to… **Carnaby Street**! The '60s! Swing your pants! The Beatles! Plastic policeman's helmets! Tower of London paperweights!

Perch on the steps of **Eros** at Piccadilly Circus with a dozen foreign students and gaze at the neon bank that puts Las Vegas in the shade – not. While you're here, don't miss out on the tourist-tacky **Trocadero** with all its 'unmissable' 'attractions'.

Be swarmed and crapped on by pestilential pigeons in the middle of central London's biggest roundabout, aka **Trafalgar Square**, before walking down the Mall and joining the crowds staring at squat, unimpressive **Buckingham Palace** in the forlorn hope that the Queen will pop out onto the balcony for a breath of fresh air.

And for dinner, it has to be an **Angus/Aberdeen Steak House**. Situated at prime spots throughout London, these culinary dinosaurs have successfully weathered food fads for decades – and a window seat is almost guaranteed.

Those with excess energy can then mill around **Leicester Square**, being subjected to further street entertainers and the attentions of genuine cock-er-ney theatre ticket touts, watching the oh, so thrilling cow herd traipse out on the hour from the Swiss Centre clock before bopping the night away with a thousand suburban teenagers at the **Hippodrome**.

A perfect day in the world's coolest city!

Street market, majoring in clothes, jewellery and CDs, while to the north is another one of Soho's portals. The tiny arch of Walkers Court leads past Paul Raymond's Revue Bar (which celebrated its 40th birthday in 1998) into **Berwick Street**, home to several excellent record and CD shops and central London's only surviving fruit and vegetable market (*see page 193*).

Branching off west is **Broadwick Street**, birthplace of William Blake (every inch the Soho misfit) and centre of a severe cholera outbreak in 1854. Local doctor John Snow became convinced that the disease was being transmitted by polluted water and had the street's water pump chained up. That Snow was proved correct led to a breakthrough in epidemiology. The doctor is commemorated by a handleless replica water pump and in the name of the street's pub (appropriately enough; the only locals who survived the outbreak were those who drank beer rather than water).

'West Soho'

Broadwick Street leads on to pedestrianised **Carnaby Street**, supposed heart of the invented district of 'West Soho'. So long has this been home to pedlars of tat and tourist trash that it's hard to believe the street could even have entered the Oxford English Dictionary in the 1960s as a byword for 'fashionable clothing for young people'. Yet, perhaps, the area is (very slowly) coming full circle. On tiny, cobbled, parallel Newburgh Street are some of the city's most genuinely cutting-edge clothing stores.

Chinatown

Curving **Shaftesbury Avenue**, extending from New Oxford Street to Piccadilly Circus, was driven through an area of slums in the 1880s, although care was taken to preserve the shape of Soho to the north. Over the next 20 years seven theatres were built along the street; six still stand, and Shaftesbury Avenue revels in being known as the heart of Theatreland. Here are also a handful of Chinese opticians, herbalists, restaurants and travel agents, providing an introduction to London's compact Chinatown.

In the 1950s, many Chinese (mainly from Hong Kong and London's original Chinatown, near the docks in Limehouse) were drawn to **Gerrard Street** and **Lisle Street** by cheap rents. Today, the ersatz oriental gates, stone lions and silly pagoda-topped phone booths suggest a Chinese theme park rather than a genuine community. Yet, despite the fact that the majority of London's Chinese live elsewhere, Chinatown remains a closely knit residential and working enclave with (beyond the many restaurants; *see pages 162-3*)

Gerrard Street: *strange fruit in the heart of Chinatown.*

few concessions made to tourism. The focus of the year here is the Chinese New Year celebrations (late Jan/early Feb; *see page 10*) which fill the streets with dancing dragons, firecrackers and revelry. Oriental foodies shouldn't miss the amazing **New Loon Fung** Supermarket on Gerrard Street, below the rooms where John Dryden once lived.

Leicester Square

Leading down from Lisle Street to Leicester Square is Leicester Place, home to one of London's cheapest yet most comfortable cinemas, the **Prince Charles** (*see page 235*) and the French Catholic church of **Notre Dame de France**. This circular symphony in concrete contains some fetching 1960 murals by Jean Cocteau.

Leicester Square itself is one of the city's great tourist meeting points. Although it started out as a chic aristo hangout in the seventeenth and eighteenth centuries (when Leicester House fronted the north side), the attractions of the theatre and the flesh had taken over by the mid-nineteenth century. Latterly, the square had become notorious as a haven for winos, junkies and general tawdriness until Westminster Council got its act together and tarted the place up in the mid-1990s.

Today, the convex-cambered square is a pleasing space, although done few favours by the undistinguished, monumental buildings that surround it. Here are London's biggest cinemas, the **Empire** and the monolithic, black-clad **Odeon** (for both, *see page 235*), venues for many a glitzy film prem.ère. Here, too, is the Society of West End Theatres' **Half-Price Ticket Booth** (*see page 265*) and, in the north-west corner, the hideous **Swiss Centre** – where the bizarre, hourly chiming cowherd clock exerts an inexplicable fascination on the milling masses.

Covent Garden

Maps 6 & 8

The designation '**Covent Garden**' nowadays refers to anywhere within the bounds of Charing Cross Road, Strand, Kingsway, High Holborn and Shaftesbury Avenue. The focus, however, remains the pedestrianised piazza where gift shops and market stalls vie for visitors' attention with street entertainers. Covent Garden's name is a corruption of the 'convent garden' of the Abbey of St Paul at Westminster that originally stood on the site. In the 1630s, the would-be property speculator 4th Earl of Bedford brought in Inigo Jones to develop the centre of Covent Garden into an area 'fitte for the habitacions of *Gentlemen* and men of ability'. Under the influence of the Italian neo-classicism of Palladio, Jones designed the bluff, no-nonsense church of **St Paul's** (*see below*) looking on to tall terraces over an arcaded, three-sided square (none of the original houses survives).

London's first planned square was an immediate hit with the well-to-do, but as the fruit and vegetable market grew to uncomfortable proportions, and newer, more exclusive developments sprung up further west, Covent Garden's reputation slumped. Coffee houses, taverns, Turkish baths and brothels thrived – John Cleland's archetypal tart-with-a-heart, Fanny Hill, picked up trade and lodged here for a while. Later, the area's grandiose Victorian gin palaces acted as 'the lighthouses which guided the thirsty soul on the road to ruin'. To the north, the squalor of the rookeries around Seven Dials and St Giles was notorious, evoking in Dickens 'wild visions of prodigies of wickedness, want and beggary'.

Theatrical Covent Garden

Yet throughout these years, Covent Garden remained a fashionable venue for theatre and opera (as celebrated at the **Theatre Museum**; *see page 123*). From the time the first **Royal Opera House** (*see pages 244-6*) opened in Bow Lane in 1732, London's beau monde has gingerly picked its way through the filth and rotting vegetables to enjoy the glittering pleasures of the stage. The **Theatre Royal** in Drury Lane was the other main attraction; it was here that Nell Gwynne performed and David Garrick revolutionised English theatre. The Royal Opera House is currently undergoing a massive £214-million redevelopment. Due to be completed by the end of 1999, the scheme will provide a permanent home for the Royal Ballet as well as the Royal Opera, and go some way towards recreating the appearance of Inigo Jones's original arcades. However, seemingly interminable controversy over mismanagement dogs the Opera House and it was announced in late 1998 that mass redundancies and a year's break from performing would be implemented in a desperate attempt to save money – and the company.

Tourist mecca

It's easy to be cynical about today's tourist-oriented Covent Garden and the influx of chain restaurants and shops – yet Covent Garden works. It's one of London's all-too-few extensive pedestrianised public spaces and, while it's true that some of the shops and market stalls dispense cheap tat, many do not. Even in the central market, there are decent goods (such as some of the jewellery on the **Apple Market** stalls in the market building) and quality entertainment (live musicians and the quirky **Cabaret Mechanical Theatre**, *see below*). The **Jubilee Market**, on the south side of the piazza, now contains mainly clothes and tatty souvenir stalls, while the old Flower Market has been converted into the **London Transport Museum** (*see page 123*).

Quality shopping

Covent Garden's concentration of hip clothes shops, many selling clubby gear, is a major draw. Floral Street, in particular, offers rich pickings for dedicated followers of fashion, while many of the more mainstream chains are represented on parallel Long Acre. Pedestrianised **Neal Street** has an agreeably offbeat ambience, with small, quirky

Cover yourself in Brussels sprouts and stand on a box – that's entertainment!

The arty crafty **Apple Market**. *See page 193.*

retailers predominating, and everything from kites to oriental tea sets on offer. **Neal's Yard** (off Shorts Gardens), a hippie haven of health food and natural remedies, is a reminder of the 'alternative' scene that did so much, through its mass squats and demonstrations, to prevent the brutal redevelopment of Covent Garden after the market moved out to Battersea in 1974.

Notable shops include the fabulous cheese-feast of **Neal's Yard Dairy** at 17 Shorts Gardens (*see page 200*) and the lush, exotic splendour of the **Wild Bunch** flower stall in nearby Earlham Street by Seven Dials (*see page 200*). The musical instrument shops of Denmark Street (close to the parish church of **St Giles-in-the-Fields**; *see below*) are as legendary in the rock world as the bookshops of Charing Cross Road are to the literate classes. In addition to the big book chains, the idiosyncratic doyen of the London book trade, **Foyles** (*see page 188*), has been trading from nos.119-125 since 1904. Look out also for the many second-hand and specialist book stores (*see page 188*).

Elsewhere in Covent Garden

East of the piazza, in **Bow Street**, stands the Magistrates' Courts that were presided over in the 1750s and 1760s by novelist and barrister Henry Fielding, and his blind half-brother John, 'the blind beak' – who was said to be able to recognise 3,000 thieves by their voices alone. It was Henry Fielding who, horrified by the lawlessness and danger of Georgian London, established the Bow Street Runners, precursors of the modern police force. Nearby on Great Queen Street stands the monolithic HQ of the United Grand Lodge of England – otherwise known as **Freemasons' Hall** (*see below*). Surprisingly, perhaps, the normally ultra-secretive Masons run guided tours of the building.

Connoisseurs of the London pub should not miss the **Lamb & Flag** (*see page 181*), at 33 Rose Street off Garrick Street. Built in 1623, it is one of central London's few surviving wooden-framed buildings. Another delightful echo of the past is the tiny alley of **Goodwin's Court**, running between St Martin's Lane and Bedfordbury, which contains a row of bow-fronted seventeenth-century houses, still lit by clockwork-operated gas street lighting.

Do the Strand

Skirting the south of Covent Garden, the Strand (or articleless 'Strand' as it's officially known) has a much more ancient pedigree. Originally a muddy bridle path, it ran directly alongside the river until the construction of Victoria Embankment in the 1860s. Built to link the City with Westminster and lined with the palatial homes of the aristocracy from the thirteenth century, it turns southward at **Charing Cross**. In front of the railway station is an 1863 monument commemorating the original cross, erected near here by the sorrowful Edward I to mark the passing of the funeral procession of his queen, Eleanor, in 1290. An appealing tradition says that Charing is a corruption of 'Chère Reine', but there was a village of Charing here long before Eleanor's body passed through.

The Strand became as notorious for pickpockets and prostitution as Covent Garden (Boswell recalls: '... last night... I met a monstrous big whore in the Strand, whom I had a great curiosity to lubricate'), but within 100 years Disraeli thought it the finest street in Europe. The building of the grand **Savoy** hotel (*see page 141*) in 1884-9 enhanced this reputation, thanks to the managerial skills of César Ritz and culinary genius of Auguste Escoffier. Around the corner in Savoy Street, the sixteenth-century **Savoy Chapel** was a fashionable venue for society weddings 100 years ago. The original chapel was part of John of Gaunt's Savoy Palace, burnt down during the Peasants' Revolt of 1381. Today's Strand, brimming with traffic and lined with offices, shops, theatres, and the odd pub and restaurant, still has grand scale, but without its former grace and distinction, it's a harsh, rather forlorn place; an impression reinforced by the many homeless people who sleep in its doorways.

The Embankment

From the Strand, pedestrianised Villiers Street leads down past Terry Farrell's monster-toy-brick **Embankment Place** development, and the claustrophobic but character-packed **Gordon's** wine bar (*see page 181*), to **Embankment Gardens** and Embankment tube station. The grand York House stood here from the thirteenth to the end of the seventeenth century. All that remains is the **York Watergate** (on Watergate Walk), which once let on to the Thames. Across

Top tours:
On the cheap

The best things in life are free

Why waste money on a travelcard when you have
been blessed with two perfectly adapted
ambulatory devices? Walking is not only free, but
it's by far the best way to get a feel of the city. A
stroll along the south bank, from the South Bank
Centre to Tower Bridge, or vice versa, offers not
only wonderful riverside views but an insight in to
many of the capital's major Millennium
developments (*see p27 & p30*).

If walking's not your thing then you can easily
pass a morning in London's major free collections
– the **British Museum** (*see p126*) or the
National Gallery (*see p129*).

Take a pew and get your energy back at one of
the free lunchtime concerts in City churches (*see
p247*) or at **St Martin-in-the-Fields** on
Trafalgar Square (all start around 1pm), followed
perhaps by a bowl of noodles in one of Chinatown's
diners, or, for more trad fare, in the ultra-budget
Stockpot restaurants (*see p158*).

Covent Garden is always bustling and there's
usually some form of street entertainment taking
place – whether it be jugglers in front of St Paul's
Church, a string trio in the market building or
hair-braiders and digeridoo players close to the
tube station.

On a sunny day you might head up to Hampstead
for a plunge in the Heath's famed bathing pools.

Late afternoon: take in one of the big museums
that allow free entrance after 4.30pm (these include
the **Museum of London** – *see p115*, **Science
Museum** – *see p116*, **Natural History Museum**
– *see p115*, and the **Victoria & Albert Museum**
– *see p116*).

Music-lovers can round off the day with a free
concert at the **Royal Festival Hall** ('commuter
jazz' 5.15-6.45pm Fri, plus most lunchtimes 12.30-
2.30pm; *see p30 & p245*), the **Barbican Centre**
(6.30pm Mon-Fri; lunchtimes Sat, Sun; *see p231
& p244*) and the foyer of the **Royal National
Theatre** (6-7.15pm Mon-Sat, plus 1-2pm Sat;
see p265).

from the gardens, sandwiched between the
river and the Embankment's constant traffic, is
Cleopatra's Needle (*see below*).

Walk along **Hungerford Bridge** (soon to be
rebuilt) towards the South Bank Centre to enjoy
one of the best views of London's riverscape, particularly at night. The huge white New Adelphi
building, with the giant clock, stands on the site of
the Adam brothers' celebrated Adelphi, built in
1768-72. This terrace of 11 houses over arches and
vaults was more of an architectural than commercial success, but it was mindless vandalism that
the whole thing was pulled down in 1936.

Cabaret Mechanical Theatre
*33-34 The Market, Covent Garden, WC2 (0171 379
7961). Covent Garden tube.* **Open** 10am-6.30pm Mon-Fri;
10am-7pm Sat; 11am-6.30pm Sun. **Admission** £1.95;
£1.20 concs; £4.95 family. **Credit** AmEx, MC, JCB, £TC,
V. **Map 8 L7**
Sue Jackson's unique venture is not a cabaret, or a theatre,
but it is mechanics in their most delightful form. More than
60 hand-built automata whirl and jump and spin at the touch
of a button. Many are a form of animated cartoon, and heart-
warmingly witty. Well worth the admission for the novelty
value alone. It's possible to try out the coin-operated
machines by the small shop without entering the exhibition.

Cleopatra's Needle
Victoria Embankment, WC2. Embankment tube. **Map 8 L7**
Nothing to do with Cleopatra, this 60-ft (37-m) high, 186-ton
granite obelisk dates from around 1475BC. Presented to
Britain in 1819, it was long thought to be too awkward to
transport to Britain. It did, however, finally make the long
journey in 1877-8. Buried beneath the needle are various
objects including, bizarrely, photographs of 12 of the best-
looking Englishwomen of the day. The sphinxes at the base
were accidentally replaced facing the wrong way after being
cleaned in the early years of this century.

Freemasons' Hall
*Great Queen Street, WC2 (0171 831 9811).
Covent Garden or Holborn tube.* **Open** Mon-Sat.
Admission free. **Map 6 L6**
You need to book a tour to enter the precincts of this monumental, strangely disturbing art deco edifice: the Grand
Lodge of the Freemasons. Though the building includes
around 20 temples, the centrepiece is undoubtedly the Grand
Temple – possibly the quietest spot in central London – with
its beautiful carved doors, superb mosaic ceiling and
stained-glass windows. Freemasons' Hall is the central
meeting place for the UK's 8,660 Masonic lodges, but, in a
bid to update the Masons' notorious reputation for secre-
tiveness, is also open for concerts and other public events
in addition to the informative guided tours (days and times
vary; phone for details).

St Giles-in-the-Fields
*St Giles High Street, WC2 (0171 240 2532). Tottenham
Court Road tube.* **Open** 9am-3.30pm Mon-Fri. **Map 6 K6**
It's hard to believe, but this church (founded in 1101) was
once surrounded by fields. The Great Plague started in the
parish of St Giles in 1665; the number of corpses buried here
was so high that subsidence caused severe structural damage to the church. The competition to design a replacement
was won by Henry Flitcroft; his church, influenced by
Gibbs's newly completed **St Martin-in-the-Fields** (*see
p70*), is little changed since the eighteenth century. The poet
Andrew Marvell was buried here in 1678, the painter Sir
Godfrey Kneller in 1723.

St Paul's
*Bedford Street, WC2 (0171 836 5221). Covent Garden
tube.* **Open** 10am-2pm Mon; 9.30am-4.30pm Tue-Fri.
Map 8 L7
When the parsimonious 4th Earl of Bedford asked Inigo
Jones to build a church on newly developed Covent Garden
piazza, he said, 'I would not have it much better than a barn,'
to which Jones replied, 'Well then, you shall have the hand-
somest barn in England.' The result (completed in 1633) was
a suitably plain Tuscan pastiche that is, indeed, little more
than a huge box inside. With Covent Garden being so inter-
twined with theatre, it's no surprise that it has long been
known as the actors' church. Lining the interior walls of the
church are memorials to stars such as Charlie Chaplin, Boris
Karloff and Vivien Leigh, interspersed with those of lesser-
known, but undoubtedly just as great in their way, entertainers such as Pantopuck the Puppetman.

Westminster

St James's Park. *See page 70.*

Maps 7 & 8

Ever since Edward the Confessor built his 'West Minster' and palace on the unpromisingly marshy Thorney Island, three miles west of the City, in the eleventh century, Westminster has been the centre of London's religious and royal life. The first Parliament met in the Abbey in the fourteenth century and politics remains the lifeblood of the district to this day. Shops and restaurants may be few, but here are London's most spectacular group of buildings and some of the easiest and most rewarding sightseeing in the capital.

Trafalgar Square

Expansive and somewhat bleak in appearance, **Trafalgar Square** only came into existence 170 years ago, when it was laid out on the site of the demolished King's Mews. Its appearance would undoubtedly be improved if it were not, in effect, a huge traffic island (although plans are currently being considered to rectify this situation), and if the verminous rats with wings that infest the place

were eradicated. Visitors, however, seem uncommonly attached to the pigeons.

The disappointingly low-key, low-rise buildings on the north side of the square, built in 1832-8, don't seem a grand enough home for the magnificent collection of the **National Gallery** (*see page 129*; the **National Portrait Gallery**, *see page 129*, can be accessed around the corner on Charing Cross Road). A more impressive structure, standing on the north-east corner of the square, is James Gibbs's perky **St Martin-in-the-Fields** (*see below*), the crypt of which contains a good café.

Trafalgar Square's centrepiece, **Nelson's Column**, surrounded by Sir Edwin Landseer's splendid lions, commemorates Britain's most famous sailor. The friezes around the base of the 171-foot (51-m) column, erected in 1843, were cast from metal from French and Spanish cannon captured at the Battle of Trafalgar in 1805.

Around St James's Park

From Trafalgar Square, the grand processional route of **The Mall** passes under Admiralty Arch and past St James's Park to the Victoria Memorial and **Buckingham Palace** (*see below*). Up close, the Palace seems rather small, squat and unimposing. More satisfying is a wander around the small portion of the royal art collection displayed in the **Queen's Gallery** (*see below*) or the carriages of the **Royal Mews** (*see below*) behind the Palace, or a stroll in **St James's Park** (*see below*) – one of London's most beautiful. On the south side of the park, the Wellington Barracks, home of the Foot Guards, contains the **Guards' Museum** (*see page 116*), only of interest to military buffs. Nearby are the wonderfully intact Georgian terraces of Queen Anne Street and Old Queen Street.

Whitehall to Parliament Square

Back in Trafalgar Square, Nelson gazes, with his one good eye, down the long, gentle curve of **Whitehall** into the heart of British governmental bureaucracy. Lined up along the street, many of the big ministries maintain at least the façade of heart-of-the-empire solidity. Halfway down the street, the Horse Guards building (try to pass by when the mounted scarlet-clad guards are changing; *see page 5*) faces the **Banqueting House** (*see below*), central London's first classical-style building and site of Charles I's execution. Near here is Edwin Lutyens's ascetically plain memorial to the dead of both world wars, the **Cenotaph**, and, on Downing Street, the disappointingly anonymous official homes of the prime minister and the chan-

Buckingham Palace: Queen's gaff and perennial tourist magnet. See page 69.

cellor of the exchequer (closed off by iron security gates since 1990).

Opposite the Cenotaph, the **Foreign and Commonwealth Office Information Centre** (0171 270 1500; 9am-5pm Mon-Fri) attempts to fulfill something of Tony Blair's commitment to more open government. An IT centre, exhibitions and a mini-cinema all trumpet what a good job the FCO is doing promoting Britain abroad. At the end of King Charles Street, the **Cabinet War Rooms** (*see page 116*) is the effectively restored operations centre used by Churchill and his cabinet during World War II air raids.

Parliament Square was laid out in 1868 on the site of what was then a notorious slum. Architecture here is on a grand scale. **Westminster Central Hall**, with its great black dome, built on the site of the old Royal Aquarium in 1905-11, is used for conferences (the first assembly of the United Nations was held here in 1946) as well as Methodist church services. Following a lengthy facelift, **Westminster Abbey** (*see below*) is now resplendent in its original pristine white (for years, many Londoners assumed it was black). Similarly shaped but much smaller, **St Margaret's** (*see below*) stands in the shadow of the Abbey, rather like a promising child next to an indulgent parent. In 1549, the church was selected to provide stone for the new Somerset House on the Strand, but when workmen arrived to demolish it they were chased off by angry parishioners armed with clubs and bows. Both Samuel Pepys and Winston Churchill were married here.

Few buildings in London dazzle – the **Houses of Parliament** (*see below*) are an exception. Built between 1834 and 1858 by Charles Barry, and fancifully decorated by Augustus Pugin, their Disneyland Gothic chutzpah simultaneously raises a smile and a gasp. Although formally still known as the Palace of Westminster, the only surviving part of the medieval royal palace is

Westminster Hall (and the **Jewel Tower**, just south of Westminster Abbey; *see below*).

London icon though it is, Parliament's clock tower, **Big Ben**, seems rather stumpy when viewed close up. The tower originally contained a small prison cell – Emmeline Pankhurst, in 1902, was its last occupant. A statue of the suffragette stands in **Victoria Tower Gardens**, by the river on the south side of Parliament. Here too is a cast of Rodin's glum-looking *Burghers of Calais* and a splendid Gothic revival drinking fountain. In the shadow of Big Ben, at the end of Westminster Bridge, stands a statue of Boudicca and her daughters gesticulating ambiguously towards Parliament – the Queen of the Iceni was no friend to Londoners, having reduced Roman Londinium to ruins and massacred its inhabitants in AD61.

Millbank

Millbank runs along the river from Parliament to Vauxhall Bridge. Just off here is **St John's Smith Square**, built as a church in 1713-28 by Thomas Archer, and now primarily a venue for classical music concerts (*see page 245*). This exuberant baroque fantasy has not been without its detractors – Dickens thought it 'a very hideous church with four towers at the corners, generally resembling some petrified monster, frightful and gigantic, on its back with its legs in the air'.

By the river, just north of Vauxhall Bridge, stood the **Millbank Penitentiary** – an attempt to build a model prison, based on the ideas of Jeremy Bentham. But it was a grim place, lasting only 70 years until 1890, before being demolished and replaced by the rather more enlightened **Tate Gallery** (*see page 131*). Overshadowing the Tate is the 387-foot (240-m) high **Millbank Tower** – a 1960s office block that is not without its fans – while, over the river, the giant toy-town-building-block bulk of **Vauxhall Cross** is the surprisingly conspicuous HQ of the internal security service, MI6.

Victoria

Victoria Street, stretching from Parliament Square to Victoria Station, links political London with backpackers' London. Victoria Coach Station is a short distance away in Buckingham Palace Road; Belgrave Road provides an almost unbroken line of cheap (and fairly grim) hotels.

The area has seldom stayed the same for long. In the eighteenth and early nineteenth centuries, it was dominated by the Grosvenor Canal, but in the 1850s much of this was buried under the new Victoria Station. A century later, many of the shops and offices along Victoria Street were pulled down and replaced by the anonymous blocks that now line it on both sides. The nearby Stag Brewery, which had stood on the site since 1641, was demolished in 1959. An aluminium statue, *The Stag*, marks the site of the old brewery in Stag Place.

Partly screened by office blocks and set well back from Victoria Street behind its own piazza, **Westminster Cathedral** (*see below*) always comes as a pleasant surprise, coming into view only when you draw level with it. Built between 1896 and 1903, the cathedral's interior has never been finished.

Further down Victoria Street, the grey concrete monstrosity that is the **Department of Trade and Industry** HQ represents 1960s architecture at its near-worst. The **Albert** pub, on the corner of Victoria Street and Buckingham Gate, standing in the shadow of two enormous office blocks, provides an oddly effective juxtaposition of old and new. The rather charming **Blewcoat School**, with its painted plaster figures on either side, is visible further down Buckingham Gate. The school was founded in 1688 for the education of poor local children.

Continuing along Victoria Street, you come to **Christchurch Gardens**, burial site of Thomas ('Colonel') Blood, the seventeenth-century rogue who very nearly got away with stealing the Crown Jewels. A memorial is dedicated to the suffragettes, who held their first meetings at **Caxton Hall**, visible on the far side of the gardens and badly in need of repair. **New Scotland Yard** – with its famous revolving sign – is in Broadway, down at the end of Caxton Street.

Strutton Ground, on the other side of Victoria Street, is home to a modest all-purpose market, flanked by sandwich shops. At the other end, the zippy **Channel Four Building**, with its outside lifts and spindly exterior design, is worth a look (corner of Chadwick Street and Horseferry Road).

Pimlico fills the triangle of land formed by Chelsea Bridge, Ebury Street, Vauxhall Bridge Road and the river. Thomas Cubitt began building elegant streets and squares here in the 1830s, as he had in Belgravia, albeit on a less grand scale. The cluster of small shops and restaurants around Warwick Way forms the heart of Pimlico, but

Belgrave Road, with its rows of solid, dazzling-white terraces, is its backbone. Close by are many dignified, beautifully maintained townhouses.

Banqueting House

Whitehall, SW1 (0171 930 4179). Westminster tube or Charing Cross tube/rail. **Open** 10am-5pm Mon-Sat (sometimes shut at short notice; phone to check). **Admission** £3.50; £2.70 concs. **Credit** EC, MC, V (on bills over £10). **Map 8 L8**

Looking perfectly in step with Whitehall buildings 200 years its junior, Inigo Jones's groundbreaking, classically inspired Banqueting House (1619-22) is the only part of the former Whitehall Palace that survived the devastating fire of 1698. There's a video and small exhibition in the undercroft, but the chief glory is the first-floor hall, designed for court ceremonials, and magnificently adorned with ceiling paintings by Rubens (1635). Charles I commissioned the Flemish artist and diplomat to glorify his less-than-prepossessing father James I and celebrate the divine right of the Stuart kings. There is no little irony that, on 30 January 1649, Charles walked beneath these very paintings on his way to stepping out of a first-floor window on to the scaffold at the front of the building to make his appointment with the executioner's axe. An excellent audio guide explaining the paintings and the hall's functions is included in the admission price.

Buckingham Palace

SW1 (0171 930 4832/recorded info 0171 799 2331/ credit card bookings 0171 321 2233/disabled info 0171 839 1377 ext 3797). St James's Park/Green Park tube or Victoria tube/rail. **Open** 6 Aug-3 Oct 9.30am-4.15pm daily. **Admission** £10; £5-£7.50 concs. **Credit** AmEx, JCB, MC, £TC, V. **Map 7 H9**

Built in 1703 for the Duke of Buckingham, the original Buckingham House was bought by George III and converted into a palace by his son George IV. In 1837, the young Queen Victoria decided to make Buckingham Palace her home, and it has been the London residence of the royal family ever since. The Royal Standard flies above the palace when the Queen is in London. You can visit the State Apartments, used for banquets and investitures, while the royals are away. The 18 rooms on view include the Throne Room, State Dining Room and Music Room, and, while some of the works of art are gems, there really is little of interest unless you're after tips on how to do up your house with upmarket nick-nackery. Tickets go on sale on the day, from 9am at the ticket office on Constitution Hill. To avoid the queue, book in advance by credit card over the phone, or by requesting an application form from the Visitor Office.

Houses of Parliament

Parliament Square, SW1 (Commons info 0171 219 4272/Lords info 0171 219 3107). Westminster tube. **Open** (always phone to check) *House of Commons Visitors' Gallery* 2.30pm onwards Mon, Tue, Thur; 9.30am-2pm, 2.30pm onwards, Wed; 9.30am-3pm Fri. *House of Lords Visitors' Gallery* 2.30pm onwards Mon-Wed; 3pm onwards Thur; phone to check. **Admission** free. **Map 8 L9**

Originally set on an island, the first Parliament was held here in 1275. Westminster became Parliament's permanent home in 1532, when Henry VIII upped sticks to Whitehall. Parliament was originally housed in the choir stalls of St Stephen's Chapel, where members sat facing each other from opposite sides; the tradition continues today. The only remaining parts of the original palace are **Westminster Hall**, with its hammer-beam roof, and the **Jewel Tower** (*see below*); the rest burned down in a great fire (1834) and was rebuilt in neo-Gothic style by Charles Barry and Augustus Pugin. There are 1,000 rooms, 100 staircases, 11 courtyards, eight bars and six restaurants (though, alas, none are open to the public).

Anyone can watch the Commons or Lords in session from the visitors' galleries; queueing outside gives you access to the central lobby, and eventually the visitors' galleries. If you arrive after 6pm (the chamber sits until at least 10pm Mon-Thur) you shouldn't have to queue. The best spectacle, however, is Prime Minister's Question Time at 2.30pm on Wednesdays (though note you will need tickets in advance for this – arrange with your MP or embassy). There's no minimum age but children must be able to sign their name in the visitors' book.

Parliament takes a break at Christmas, Easter and during the summer, but the galleries remain open to the public for pre-booked guided tours The procedure for booking is somewhat lengthy. If you are a UK resident, you should get a permit from your MP; if a tourist, you need to get a permit from the Palace of Westminster's education section. The tours are offered by staff at the Palace, and at a cost. They invariably begin at Victoria Tower, proceed through the Queen's apartments (where she dons the robes for the annual opening of Parliament), then on to the Lords' chamber and finally the Commons itself. The sense of history, grandeur and tradition is both alluring and bewildering, but the beauty and vitality of the place shines through.

Jewel Tower
Abingdon Street, SW1 (0171 222 2219). Westminster tube. **Open** *Apr-Sept* 10am-6pm daily; *Oct-Mar* 10am-4pm daily. **Admission** £1.50; 80p-£1.10 concs. **Credit** MC, £TC, V. **Map 8 L9**
Along with Westminster Hall, the moated Jewel Tower is a survivor from the medieval Palace of Westminster. It was built in 1365-6 to house Edward III's gold and jewels. From 1621 to 1864, the tower stored records of the House of Lords. Beautifully restored, it now contains an excellent exhibition and video on Parliament past and present.

Royal Mews
Buckingham Palace Road, SW1 (0171 930 4832/recorded info 0171 799 2331/disabled info 0171 839 1377). St James's Park tube or Victoria tube/rail. **Open** *Oct-July* noon-4pm Tue-Thur; *Aug-Sept* 10.30-4.30pm Mon-Thur (last admission 3.30pm). **Admission** £4; £2-£3 concs. **Credit** AmEx, MC, £TC, V. **Map 7 H9**
The Mews houses the royal carriages. The gilt palm-wood Coronation Coach, the elegant Glass Coach, the immaculately groomed horses and the finely crafted, sleek, black landaus make the Mews one of the capital's better-value collections. Closed during Royal Ascot week (June) and on state occasions.

St James's Park
The Mall, SW1 (0171 930 1793). St James's Park tube. **Open** dawn-dusk daily. **Map 8 K8**
In the seventeenth century, Charles II had the deer park of St James's Palace converted into a garden by French landscape gardener Le Nôtre, and it was landscaped further by John Nash in the early nineteenth century. The view of Buckingham Palace from the bridge over the lake is wonderful, particularly at night when the Palace is floodlit. The lake is now a sanctuary for wildfowl – pelicans (fed at 3pm daily), ducks, geese and Australian black swans. There's a playground at the Buck Palace end, and refreshments are available at the new café that replaced the unloved concrete Cake House. Many Londoners rate St James's as the loveliest and most intimate of the capital's central parks.

St Margaret's Westminster
Parliament Square, SW1 (0171 222 5152). Westminster tube. **Open** 9.30am-4.30pm daily. **Services** 11am Sun (phone to check). **Map 8 K9**
Founded in the twelfth century but rebuilt in 1486-1523 and restored many times since, it is easy to overlook this historic church, dwarfed by the adjacent Abbey. The impressive east window (1509), in richly coloured Flemish glass, commemorates the marriage of Henry VIII and Catherine of Aragon

(and not Catherine's earlier betrothal to Henry's brother Arthur as is sometimes supposed). Later windows celebrate Britain's first printer, William Caxton, buried here in 1491; the explorer Sir Walter Ralegh, executed over the road in Old Palace Yard; and the writer John Milton (1608-74) who worshipped, and married his second wife, here. John Piper's Braque-like windows on the south side date from 1966.

St Martin-in-the-Fields
Trafalgar Square, WC2 (0171 930 1862). Charing Cross tube/rail. **Open** 8am-6.30pm daily. **Map 8 L7**
A church has stood here since the thirteenth century, when it was 'in the fields' between the City and Westminster. The present church, designed by James Gibbs (1726), is embellished inside with dark woodwork and ornate Italian plasterwork; note the Royal Box to the left of the gallery – this is officially the parish church for Buckingham Palace. Free lunchtime concerts take place here every weekday around 1pm. The crypt houses the imaginatively named **Café in the Crypt** (*see p159*).

Westminster Abbey
Dean's Yard, SW1 (0171 222 5152/guided tours 0171 222 7110). St James's Park or Westminster tube.
Open *Nave* 8am-6pm Mon, Tue, Thur-Sat; 8am-7.45pm Wed; between services Sun. *Royal Chapels* 9am-4pm Mon, Tue, Thur, Fri; 9am-4pm, 6-7.45pm, Wed; 9am-1.45pm Sat. *Chapter House mid-Oct-mid-Mar* 9.30am-4pm daily; *mid-Mar-mid-Oct* 9.30am-6pm daily. *Pyx Chamber & Abbey Museum* 10.30am-4pm daily. *College Garden* Apr-Sept 10am-6pm Tue, Thur; Oct-Mar 10am-4pm Tue, Thur. **Admission** £5; £2-£3 concs; £10 family. *Chapter House, Pyx Chamber & Abbey Museum* £2.50; £1 with main entrance ticket; free with audio guide. *Audio guide* £2. **Map 8 K9**
Since Edward the Confessor built his church to St Peter (consecrated in 1065) on the site of the Saxon original, the Abbey has been bound up with British royalty. With two exceptions, every king and queen of England since William the Conqueror (1066) has been crowned here; many are buried here too – the royal chapels and tombs include Edward the Confessor's shrine and the Coronation Chair (1296).

Of the original Abbey, only the **Pyx Chamber** (the one-time royal treasury) and Norman **Undercroft** remain; the Gothic **nave** and **choir** were rebuilt by Henry III in the thirteenth century; the **Henry VII Chapel**, with its spectacular fan vaulting, was added in 1503-12; the west towers (by Hawksmoor) completed the building in 1745. The interior is cluttered with monuments to statesmen, scientists, musicians and poets. The wonderfully light, octagonal **Chapter House** (1253), with its fine thirteenth-century tiled floor, is well worth seeing (and often offers a escape from the crowds), as is the **College Garden**, especially during the free lunchtime concerts on Thursdays in July and August.

If you can avoid the dispiriting tour-group throng you'll get much more out of a visit to the Abbey. Come as early or late as possible or on midweek afternoons, when the coach parties have moved on to St Paul's. Don't bother with the astonishingly patronising audio guide (narrated by 'Brian' and 'Patience'), which seems to be aimed at particularly slow seven-year-olds. (*See also opposite* **Saints above!**).

Westminster Cathedral
Victoria Street, SW1 (0171 798 9055). Victoria tube/rail. **Open** 7am-7pm Mon-Fri, Sun; 8am-7pm Sat. **Admission** free. **Map 7 J10**
Britain's premier Catholic cathedral is a delightfully bizarre neo-Byzantine confection, with its candy-striped stone and brick bands. It was built in 1903, but the decoration still isn't complete, and the domes are bare. But the columns and mosaics (made from over 100 kinds of marble) are magnificent; the nave is the widest in Britain, Eric Gill's sculptures of the Stations of the Cross (1914-18) are especially fine and the view from the campanile is superb.

Saints above!

In a bid to show that Westminster Abbey is as much a living, developing church as a tourist magnet, ten statues of twentieth-century Christian martyrs were unveiled in July 1998. The statues stand over the west door in fifteenth-century niches that have remained vacant since the Middle Ages. Some, like Martin Luther King, are familiar figures, others are less well known, but all have in common a refusal to compromise their faith and beliefs no matter what persecution they faced.

From left to right they are…

Maximilian Kolbe

A devout Polish Catholic, Kolbe was arrested and sent to Auschwitz-Birkenau by the Nazis where he continued to celebrate mass and often gave his food to other inmates. He was murdered by lethal injection in 1941 after offering his life for that of a fellow prisoner who had been condemned to death.

Manche Masemola

Masemola's mother and father beat their young daughter to discourage her attendance at Christianity classes in Transvaal, South Africa, but she refused to be intimidated. In 1928, aged only 14, she was taken to a remote spot and murdered by her parents.

Janani Luwum

In 1974, Luwum was made Archbishop of Uganda, Rwanda, Burundi and Boga-Zaire by Idi Amin, but when he protested to Amin about the violence of the security services, Luwum was summoned to Kampala. 'They are going to kill me. I am not afraid,' he said. He disappeared without trace.

Elizabeth of Hesse-Darmstadt

In 1884, at the age of 20, Elizabeth married the fifth son of Czar Alexander II. After her husband was assassinated she gave away most of her belongings and founded the Martha and Mary Home in Moscow, which became the Sisters of Love and Charity nunnery. She was shot by the Bolsheviks in 1918.

Martin Luther King

Born in 1929, King formed the Southern Christian Leadership Conference and combined Christian zeal with an appeal to American democracy to further the cause of racial equality by non-violent means. He was shot dead in Memphis in 1964.

Oscar Romero

As archbishop of San Salvador, Romero was not afraid to speak up for the poor and the persecuted against the corrupt El Salvador government and the atrocities of the security forces. For this he was cold-shouldered by the papal hierarchy and shot dead in 1980 while celebrating mass.

Dietrich Bonhoeffer

Born in Breslau in 1906, Bonhoeffer tried to warn the German churches of the dangers of Nazism. He left Germany in the 1930s but returned as war loomed to become a significant figure in the resistance. Arrested in 1943, he was shot just days before the Soviet liberating forces arrived.

Esther John

Born Qamar Zia into an Indian Muslim family in 1929, John attended a Christian school at the age of 17. She continued to develop her faith secretly when her family moved to Pakistan after partition, but fled to teach women in the country to read. She was found murdered in her bed in 1960.

Lucian Tapiedi

The son of a sorcerer, Tapiedi was born in Papua New Guinea in 1921 but became a Christian and teacher. Fleeing the invading Japanese in 1942, he was murdered by one of the Orokaiva people. Later his killer repented, converted to Christianity and built a church in his memory.

Wang Zhiming

Wang lived in China's Yunnan province where there was a vibrant Christian community. During the 1966-76 Cultural Revolution churches were closed and Christians were forced to worship in secret, with Wang as their pastor. Arrested in 1969, he was executed in 1973 at a mass rally of more than 10,000 people.

Knightsbridge

Maps 4 & 7

The village of **Knightsbridge** was once re-nowned for its taverns and notorious for its high-waymen. The only danger of daylight robbery today comes from the inflated prices of the exclusive shops along Sloane Street and Brompton Road. Whether or not there's any truth in the suspiciously literal legend that a fight between two knights on a bridge over the now-subterranean Westbourne river (near Albert Gate in Hyde Park) gave the area its name, there's no doubt that Knightsbridge today is as posh as London gets.

The majority of visitors get no further than a devotional visit to that fabled temple of retailing, **Harrods** (*see page 202*). But, if it's Knightsbridge cachet you're after, follow the ladies-who-lunch across the street to the hipper **Harvey Nichols** (food and fashion are its strengths; *see page 202*), where the **Fifth Floor** restaurant (*see page 155*) continues to be *the* destination shop-and-scoff stop for those who consider 'work' to be deciding whether to wear the Christian Lacroix or Dolce & Gabbana number today. If your lunch budget is closer to £5 than £50, you will be relieved to discover one of London's bargain **Stockpot** restaurants on nearby Basil Street (*see page 158*), where it has been serving up ludicrously cheap, if basic, grub since 1956.

The fashion triangle of Sloane Street, Brompton Road and Beauchamp Place contains just about every big couture name on the planet. If the staggering price tags don't freeze you to the spot, the icy stares of the cooler-than-thou assistants surely will.

Belgravia

East of Sloane Street lies **Belgravia**. Until it was developed by Lord Grosvenor and Thomas Cubitt in the 1820s, the area was open fields and popular as a venue for duels. As soon as the first grand stucco houses were raised, Belgravia established a reputation as a highly exclusive, largely residential district. It retains it today, although the judgement of Benjamin Disraeli that Belgravia was 'monotonous… and so contrived as to be at the same time insipid and tawdry' might be echoed by anyone who has found themselves lost in this curiously characterless embassy-land. Characterful relief is provided in the **Grenadier** pub, in Old Barrack Yard off Wilton Row, once frequented by the Duke of Wellington and said to be haunted by the ghost of one of his officers, beaten to death for cheating at cards.

Hyde Park

Knightsbridge (the street), leading westward via Kensington Road into Kensington High Street, borders the largest of London's royal parks, **Hyde Park** (*see below*). Every morning, at 10.28am (9.28am on Sundays), soldiers of the Household Cavalry emerge from their barracks to ride through the park to Horse Guards Road for the **Changing of the Guard** (*see page 5*). Merging into Hyde Park is **Kensington Gardens** (*see below*), containing Queen Victoria's birthplace and the former home of Diana, Princess of Wales, **Kensington Palace** (*see below*). Perhaps surprisingly, vehement local opposition has caused a plan to build a £10-million Diana memorial garden here to be abandoned, although a scaled-down version might still go ahead.

South Kensington Museumland

Prince Albert's greatest legacy to the nation lies south of here in **South Kensington**. With the £186,000 profit of the 1851 Great Exhibition, and a matching government grant, he oversaw the purchase of 87 acres (35 hectares) of land for the building of institutions to 'extend the influence of Science and Art upon Productive Industry'. Although the Prince didn't live to see the completion of 'Albertopolis', the scheme was an unqualified success. Concentrated in this small area are Imperial College, the Royal Geographical Society, the Royal College of Art, the Royal College of Music (with a small museum), plus the heavyweight museum triumvirate of the **Science Museum**, the **Natural History Museum** and, arguably the best of the lot, the magnificent fine and applied art collection of the **Victoria & Albert Museum** (for all, *see page 116*). An inspired, radical design by Daniel Libeskind for an eight-storey ceramic 'spiral' extension to the V&A has been given the go-ahead, although its construction could still be thwarted by conservative killjoys.

Albert is commemorated by the recently renovated **Albert Memorial** (*see below*) on the edge of Hyde Park and, opposite, the Roman-influenced **Royal Albert Hall**, venue for the annual 'Proms' concerts (*see page 245*). Another nearby attraction renowned for its musical tradition is the extravagant, Italianate **Brompton Oratory** (*see below*). During the Cold War this church was used by the KGB as a dead letter box. Other eastern European connections in the area include the **Russian Orthodox Church** off Ennismore Gardens and the timeless Polish restaurant, **Daquise**, by South Kensington tube at 20 Thurloe Street.

So Knightsbridge, so **Harvey Nicks***! See p202.*

Well-to-do residential South Kensington stretches down to meet Chelsea somewhere around Fulham Road. Near its northern end, at no.81, stands the unique, exuberant, art nouveau **Michelin Building**, designed by Espinasse for the tyre manufacturers in 1905. It now houses book publishers, the beautiful, if pricey, **Bibendum** restaurant (*see page 155*) and Sir Terence Conran's design shrine, the **Conran Shop** (*see page 202*). Fulham Road, lined with swish antique shops, bars and restaurants (**Wok Wok** at no.140 is good for a bowl of noodles; *see page 162*), continues down to Chelsea's football ground, Stamford Bridge, and on through Fulham towards Putney Bridge.

Albert Memorial
Kensington Gardens, SW7. Knightsbridge or High Street Kensington tube then 9, 33, 49, 52, 73 bus. **Map 2 D8**
This grandiose memorial to the beloved husband of Queen Victoria was finally unveiled by the Queen in October 1998 after a decade-long restoration programme. Designed by Sir George Gilbert Scott and finished in 1872, it centres around a gilden Albert, holding a copy of the catalogue of the 1951 Great Exhibition. It is hard to believe that the modest German Prince, who explicitly said 'I would rather not be made the prominent feature of such a monument', would have approved of the pompous finished product, or the fact that its restoration cost £11 million (although this was £3 million under budget). It's quite a sight though. Guided tours of the memorial can be booked on 0171 495 0916.

Brompton Oratory
Thurloe Place, Brompton Road, SW7 (0171 589 4811). South Kensington tube. **Open** 6.30am-8pm daily.
Admission free. **Map 4 E10**
Brompton Oratory is a monument to the late nineteenth-century English Catholic revival. Built in 1880-4 to the designs of little-known (and unfortunately named) architect Herbert Gribble, after an open competition, it is a shameless attempt to imitate a florid Italian baroque church. Many of the ornate internal decorations predate the building, including Mazzuoli's late seventeenth-century statues of the apostles, which previously stood in Siena Cathedral.

Hyde Park
W2 (0171 298 2100). Hyde Park Corner, Knightsbridge, Lancaster Gate, Marble Arch or Queensway tube.
Open 5am-midnight daily. **Map 2**
Hyde Park is central London's largest park – one-and-a-half miles long and just under a mile wide – and the first to be opened to the public (in the early seventeenth century). The park later developed a reputation as a fashionable place to see and be seen, despite being plagued by highwaymen and duelling nobles. Queen Caroline, a keen landscape gardener, was behind the damming of the Westbourne river to form the park's central feature, the **Serpentine**, in the 1730s. Joseph Paxton's magnificent 'Crystal Palace' stood between the lake and the Prince of Wales Gate. This was the venue for the '**Great Exhibition** of the Works and Industry of All Nations' in 1851. Although phenomenally successful and visited by over six million people in less than six months, the palace was dismantled and rebuilt in south-east London in 1854; it burned down in 1936.

Today, Hyde Park's distractions are equally numerous – lounging in a deckchair, playing softball, boating on the lake, trotting a horse down Rotten Row (a corruption of 'route du roi', which William III laid out from the West End to Kensington Palace), listening to the Sunday soapbox orators revive the flagging British tradition of free speech at **Speaker's Corner** near Marble Arch – although its relative lack of vegetation can give it a barren appearance during the bleaker months. On royal anniversaries and other special occasions, a 41-gun salute is fired in the park, opposite the Dorchester Hotel in Park Lane.

Kensington Gardens
W8 (0171 298 2100). Bayswater, High Street Kensington, Lancaster Gate or Queensway tube.
Open dawn-dusk daily. **Map 1**
The attraction of Kensington Palace's extensive gardens (John Evelyn thought them 'very delicious') was part of the reason that William and Mary bought the house. Although the gardens now merge into Hyde Park, they were, in the early eighteenth century, laid out in a distinct formal Dutch style; they now have a considerably more natural appearance. Wander through the sunken garden, take tea at the **Orangery**, or gaze at the paintings in the recently refurbished Serpentine Gallery (*see p133*). The huge **Round Pond** in the middle is a focus for little boys (most of them over 40) sailing their model boats. Close to the Long Water is the **Peter Pan statue**. Also for children, look out for Elfin Oak, puppet shows in summer and two playgrounds (one off Broad Walk and one near Black Lion Gate).

Kensington Palace
W8 (0171 937 9561). Bayswater, High Street Kensington, Lancaster Gate or Queensway tube.
Open *from 1 May 1998* 10am-5pm daily.
Admission £7.50; £5.35-£5.90 concs; £23 family ticket.
Credit MC, £TC, V. **Map 1 B8**
Living near the river at Whitehall aggravated William III's chronic asthma, so, in 1689, he and Mary, looking for a more healthful home, bought the modest Jacobean mansion then known as Nottingham House. Wren and Hawksmoor (and, later, William Kent) were drafted in to redesign the building. Kensington Palace remained the favoured royal residence until the reign of George III, who preferred Buckingham House. The future Queen Victoria was born in the palace in 1819, and it has latterly been known as the last home of Princess Di (although she was only one of a number of royal residents). In late 1997, the Queen announced plans to turf out the remaining royals and convert the palace into a permanent memorial to the Princess and a home for the magnificent (but currently scattered) Royal Collection of art. In the shorter term, the palace is open for tours of the State Apartments, including the room where Queen Victoria was baptised, the King's Gallery with its fine seventeenth-century paintings, and the royal dress collection.

Chelsea

Map 4

The name still has cachet. Chelsea may no longer be a 'village of palaces', as it was in the sixteenth century; it may now be too pricey to support an impoverished but formidably talented artistic community, as it did in the nineteenth century; the cutting-edge King's Road fashions of the 1960s and punk may have passed into folk memory; but Chelsea still thrives. This wedge-shaped piece of land, sandwiched between Kensington and the Thames, is now the province of identikit gorgeous blonde babes (mobile phones glued to their ears, noses held high), of long-resident, venerable *grandes dames*, and of the odd well-to-do writer (the century-old Chelsea Arts Club, at 143 Old Church Street, remains as popular as ever). It is the maintenance of this arts connection, together with abundant shopping opportunities, that give Chelsea a life and spark that districts like nearby Knightsbridge – where wealth is the sole god – can only envy.

Chelsea's central axis is the ever-vibrant **King's Road**. Once the private royal route to Hampton Court, it stretches south-west from snooty Sloane Square, gradually becoming more downmarket, particularly as it rounds the bend at World's End, where the pub of the same name stands, and then proceeds (as New King's Road) all the way to Putney Bridge.

The arts and commerce stare each other in the face in **Sloane Square**, where upmarket department store **Peter Jones** (housed in one of Britain's first glass-curtain buildings, built 1935-8) faces the ground-breaking **Royal Court Theatre** (*see page 265*). Among the works premièred here were many of George Bernard Shaw's plays, John Osborne's *Look Back in Anger* and Arnold Wesker's *Roots*, and the theatre continues to pioneer challenging new works.

Shopping has long been King's Road's *raison d'être*, and fashion remains dominant. Amid the high-street chains numerous boutiques survive, providing relatively affordable garb for a mainly youthful market. Just beyond the King's Road kink is Vivienne Westwood's **World's End** clothes store (no.430; *see also page 191*), with its sloping floor and backward-spinning clock. Known as Sex in the mid-1970s, it was here that the look of punk was born. Antiques are also much in evidence – try the excellent **Antiquarius** (nos.131-141; *see page 186*). Contemporary household desirables are available from **Habitat** (no.206; *see page 202*) and **Heal's** (no.224; *see page*

203). The most welcome development of recent years on King's Road is Sir Terence Conran's **Bluebird** gastrodome (no.350; *see pages 155 & 201*), combining a restaurant, a café, a cook shop and a fabulous food hall. Surprisingly, apart from the Bluebird, this is not a fruitful area for gourmets – high prices and a lack of imagination are the norm. Budget diners can eat for remarkably little at **Chelsea Kitchen** (no.98), **Stockpot** (no.273) and **Chelsea Bun Diner** (9A Limerston Street; for all three, *see page 158*), while those with a little more to spend are probably best heading for the selection of eating spots in the peaceful Chelsea Farmers' Market on Sydney Street, near Kensington & Chelsea Town Hall.

Down by the river

Chelsea's non-commercial attractions, and historical and artistic associations, are found between King's Road and the river. Just south of the huge Lots Road Power Station (providing much of the juice for the London underground network) is the somewhat spooky **Chelsea Harbour** development. Apartments for the super-rich, a hotel, offices, unapproachably swish designer shops and a handful of restaurants cluster around the mega-yachts in the marina. But where are all the people?

More rewarding sightseeing is provided further north on **Cheyne** (pronounced 'chain-ee') **Walk**. Handsome, blue plaque-bespattered houses testify to the extraordinary concentration of artistic and literary talent that was drawn to the area in the nineteenth century. George Eliot lived the last few weeks of her life at no.4; Dante Gabriel Rossetti, Algernon Charles Swinburne and George Meredith moved into no.16 (Queen's House) in 1862, where Rossetti kept a small but noisy menagerie, much to the irritation of his neighbours; Henry James lived and died in Carlyle Mansions. Other distinguished residents of the street include Mrs Gaskell (no.93), James McNeill Whistler (no.96), Hilaire Belloc (no.104) and JMW Turner (no.119).

Nearby, Oscar Wilde lovingly decorated his house at 16 Tite Street (now no.34) in whites, yellows, reds and blues. The more sober-minded historian, Thomas Carlyle, entertained the Victorian great and good at his home at 24 Cheyne Row. **Carlyle's House** (*see page 120*) has been preserved much as it was in those days.

The first big-name resident in Chelsea was that man for all seasons, Thomas More, who fell foul of axe-happy Henry VIII in 1535 for refusing to acknowledge the King's divorce from Catherine

Three sides of Chelsea: **Albert Bridge, King's Road** *and the* **Chelsea Physic Garden**.

of Aragon. More's manor house has long since disappeared, but a gilt-faced statue of the 'scholar, saint, statesman' sits outside **Chelsea Old Church** (*see below*), where he built his own chapel, stoically gazing at the traffic pounding along Chelsea Embankment.

Past the delightful walled **Chelsea Physic Garden** (*see below*) on Royal Hospital Road is the impressive **National Army Museum** (*see page 117*). Appropriately housed in a bunker-like building, it offers an unexpectedly accessible insight into military life over the centuries. After a lifetime of service, a lucky few veterans might find themselves passing their twilight years next door in Wren's majestic **Royal Hospital Chelsea** (*see below*). Part of the hospital's grounds were once the location of **Ranelagh Gardens**, celebrated during the eighteenth century as a haunt of pleasure-seeking toffs. 'You can't set your foot without treading on a Prince, or Duke of Cumberland,' as Horace Walpole wrote. The eight-year-old Mozart gave a concert here in 1764. Canaletto's painting of the gardens can be seen in the National Gallery.

Bear in mind that most of the area is poorly served by the underground, so unless you're prepared for a fair bit of walking from Sloane Square tube, the best way to reach the sights is by bus.

Chelsea Old Church

Cheyne Walk, SW3 (0171 352 5627). Sloane Square tube/19, 39, 45, 49, 219 bus. **Open** 9.30am-1pm, 2-4.30pm, Mon, Wed-Sun. **Admission** free. **Map 4 E12**

It doesn't look very old – from the outside at least – but All Saints (as it's also known) traces its origins back to 1157. World War II bombing all but flattened the church, though there's still plenty of interest inside, including the south chapel, built in 1528 by Sir Thomas More for his own private worship; a font from 1673; monuments to eminent local families such as the Cheynes and Lawrences, and a memorial to Henry James. Look out also for the only chained books in a London church, the gift of Sir Hans Sloane, whose monument stands outside in the churchyard. Henry VIII reputedly married Jane Seymour in the church before their state wedding.

Chelsea Physic Garden

66 Royal Hospital Road (entrance in Swan Walk), SW3 (0171 352 5646). Sloane Square tube/11, 19, 22, 239 bus. **Open** 4 Apr-31 Oct noon-5pm Wed; 2-6pm Sun. **Admission** £4; £2 concs. **Credit** *shop* MC, £TC, V. **Map 4 F12**

The walled confines of London's first botanical garden provide blessed relief from the streaming traffic on Chelsea Embankment (note, though, the restricted opening hours). Established by the Apothecaries' Company in 1676, the garden was developed by Sir Hans Sloane in the early eighteenth century for 'the manifestation of the glory, power and wisdom of God, in the works of creation'. Today, it is primarily a research and educational facility, but even the uninitiated will make enlightening discoveries. Among the dye plants you'll find woad, which pre-Roman Britons fermented in stale urine to produce a violent blue face paint. In the greenhouses are the types of yams from which modern contraceptives and steroids were synthesised, as well as meadowsweet, source of the active ingredient of aspirin, discovered in 1899. The garden's other distinctions include being the site of Britain's first greenhouse and stove, and first rock garden. Cotton seed sent from Chelsea to Georgia in 1732 helped to establish the American cotton industry.

Royal Hospital Chelsea

Royal Hospital Road, SW3 (0171 730 5282). Sloane Square tube/11, 19, 22, 137 bus. **Open** *museum, chapel & Hall* 10am-noon, 2-4pm, Mon-Sat; 2-4pm Sun (closed on Sun in winter). **Admission** free. **Map 4 F12**

The grandest old age pensioners' home in the country, the Royal Hospital was inspired by Louis XIV's Hôtel des Invalides in Paris. Charles II wanted an equally splendid home for his veteran soldiers and, in 1682, commissioned the ever-industrious Christopher Wren to construct the present structure around three courtyards. 'Quiet and dignified and the work of a gentleman,' in the words of Thomas Carlyle, the hospital is still home to around 400 ex-servicemen whose uniforms of navy blue (for everyday wear) and scarlet (for ceremonial occasions) are nationally recognised. Visitors can peek at the harmonious, barrel-vaulted chapel, with its florid depiction of the *Resurrection* by Sebastiano Ricci over the altar, and the equally fine Hall opposite, still in use as the pensioners' refectory. In the central, south-facing courtyard stands a bronze statue of Charles II in Roman garb by Grinling Gibbons (1676), gazing across the grounds (site of the Chelsea Flower Show every May, *see p7*) and the river to Battersea Power Station. On Oak Apple Day (29 May), pensioners parade in the courtyard and dress the statue in oak foliage to commemorate the King's birthday and his escape from the Battle of Worcester when he hid in the Boscobel Oak.

North London

Urban buzz, urbane sophistication, green swathes, multi-ethnic mix – you name it, North London's got it.

Camden Town

You have to throw yourself in at the deep end with **Camden**; there is no shallow end. As you walk out of the tube station on to the grubby high street, waves of goths, punks, ravers and hippies try to stuff flyers, advertising small clubs or tiny shops, into your hands; the well-scrubbed denizens of the area's more respectable streets expertly sidestep incoherently cackling winos; the pungent aromas of fried onions and takeaway kebabs fill the air; cranked-up sound systems pulse out. It's all part of the Camden experience. Most people come for the cram-packed markets, some for the quieter pleasures of Sunday afternoon bookshop browsing or a cruise down the canal. More realistically, after a few hours spent here at the weekend – Camden's busiest time, when all the markets are open – your favourite place is likely to be a seat on the tube, taking you to comparative calm elsewhere.

Camden Town, an area that – in the vernacular, at least – stretches from Victorian politician Richard Cobden's statue at Mornington Crescent,

up Camden High Street to the borders of **Chalk Farm**, has undergone a sea change in the past 30 years. From 1816, when the Regent's Canal and, later, the railway were laid out, the area became built up with cheap lodging houses, which had a reputation for rough characters. After 1905, artist Walter Sickert, who lodged at Mornington Crescent and Fitzroy Street, led the so-called Camden Town Group, who rebelled against high-brow and symbolist composition.

Irish and, after 1945, Greek Cypriots migrated to Camden; traces of the latter are still visible in the scattered Greek bistros and cafés, and the Greek Orthodox church near the Royal Veterinary College (founded in 1791) on Royal College Street. Until the late 1960s, this was still a slum area; a surge in property prices, coupled with Camden's popularity with hippies as a cheap bohemian hangout (it's no coincidence that the struggling actors in the film *Withnail & I* live here) brought the place into new repute. Then the professional classes (and media celebrities such as Alan Bennett and Michael Palin) moved in, renovating

*Shady goings-on at **Camden Market**.*

Camden markets

1 Entirely avoidable tourist tat.

2 Ditto.

3 Covered section where you can pick up almost anything, including pub memorabilia and second-hand Levi's.

4 The Market Hall at Camden Lock Place contains the sort of candles, furniture and ceramics that retail in the centre of town for twice the price.

5 The place to come for (mainly silver) jewellery.

6 Army surplus.

7 New-Agey market fare including leather goods and tie-dyed shirts.

8 Among the more interesting goods in Camden Lock's second building are dried and silk flowers, games and puzzles, and furniture from Rajasthan.

9 The market's biggest concentration of food stalls – look out for the killer doughnuts.

10 Typical, unexciting market-type clothes.

11 The shops in the arches here sell great second-hand clothes and household goods.

12 Indian and African goods from the glory days of the British Empire, plus typewriters, cutlery sets and clocks.

13 Food stalls.

14 Clothes, furniture and lighting.

15 Mainly furniture and kitschy memorabilia.

16 Great second-hand clothes, many at bargain prices.

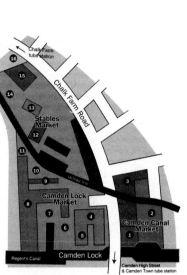

houses in some of Camden's lovely crescents. The influx of money shows itself in buildings, such as Nicholas Grimshaw's hi-tech Sainsbury's supermarket on Camden Road and the MTV building on the canal, and, most recently, in the aggressive marketing of old warehouse space as luxury loft-apartments.

Camden and its environs have plenty to offer. First, and definitely foremost, are the **markets** (*see page 192*). Since the early 1970s, these have expanded massively, becoming one of London's most popular tourist attractions.

Camden's bookshops have a breadth that reflects something of the tenor of its inhabitants – the presence of psychoanalytic specialist shop **Rathbone Books** (76 Haverstock Hill) serves one of north London's great cottage industries. The impressive **Jewish Museum** (*see page 122*) on Albert Street, just off Parkway, also deserves a visit.

After a hard few hours bargain-hunting, the hip **Mango Room** (10 Kentish Town Road) is the place to go for fine Afro-Caribbean food, or try the moules-frites minimalism of **Belgo Noord** (72 Chalk Farm Road; *see page 160*) or the top-rank beer and pub food at the **Engineer** (65 Gloucester Avenue; *see page 171*). If it's a scorcher outside, cool down with one of the great sorbets or ice-creams at **Marine Ices**, opposite Chalk Farm tube. Close by is the famous **Roundhouse** on Chalk Farm Road, originally a turning point for trams, and now a multipurpose venue for everything from exhibitions and plays to circuses, gigs and the odd illegal rave. There are currently plans to open a creative arts centre here in 2001.

Around Camden

Moving north, green relief is provided by charming **Primrose Hill** and, at the edge of Hampstead Heath, **Gospel Oak**, from which the kite-flyers of **Parliament Hill** are a short walk away. **Kentish Town**, a more downmarket and somnolent version of Camden, has, nevertheless, benefited from the social elevation of its southern neighbour. It's also the site of the **Forum** (*see page 250*), one of London's busiest rock venues.

Squeezed between Camden and King's Cross is **Somers Town**, dominated by huge '60s and '70s council housing developments, and blighted further by ongoing tensions between its young white and Asian communities. Eversholt Street

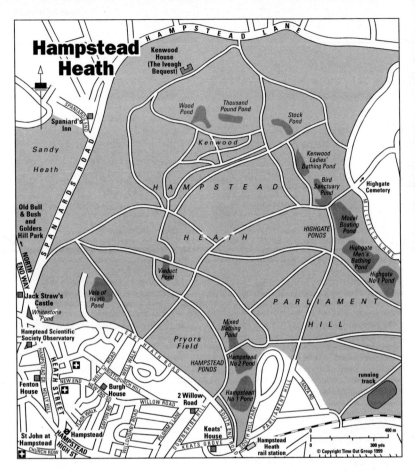

Hampstead Heath

H A M P S T E A D L A N E

Kenwood House (The Iveagh Bequest)

SPANIARDS END

Spaniard's Inn

Sandy Heath

Heath

SPANIARDS ROAD

Wood Pond

Thousand Pound Pond

Stock Pond

Kenwood

Kenwood Ladies' Bathing Pond

Bird Sanctuary Pond

Highgate Cemetery

H A M P S T E A D

Old Bull & Bush and Golders Hill Park

NORTH END WAY

MILLFIELD LANE

Model Boating Pond

HIGHGATE PONDS

H E A T H

Highgate Men's Bathing Pond

Viaduct Pond

Highgate No 1 Pond

Jack Straw's Castle

Vale of Heath Pond

Whitestone Pond

Hamptead Scientific Society Observatory

EAST HEATH ROAD

P A R L I A M E N T

Mixed Bathing Pond

H I L L

Pryors Field

HAMPSTEAD PONDS

Hampstead No 2 Pond

running track

Fenton House

HAMPSTEAD HIGH STREET

HEATH STREET

NEW END

WELL ROAD

CHRISTCHURCH HILL

WELL WALK

Burgh House

WILLOW ROAD

2 Willow Road

Hampstead No 1 Pond

FLASK WALK

WILLOUGHBY ROAD

PILGRIMS LANE

DOWNSHIRE HILL

PARLIAMENT HILL

TANZA RD

St John at Hampstead

Hampstead

CHURCH ROW

Keats' House

KEATS GROVE

SOUTH END ROAD

SOUTH HILL PARK

Hampstead Heath rail station

0   400 m
0   300 yds
© Copyright Time Out Group 1999

---

boasts the extraordinary **Transformation** (motto: 'From He to She'), the world's largest transvestite emporium. The window display is worth a picture in itself. A little further east, the **Camley Street Natural Park** offers a much-needed injection of bucolic charm amid the railway sheds and gas works. The **Regent's Canal** runs along one side of the park and enthusiasts for man-made waterways might like to check out the nearby **Canal Museum** on New Wharf Road (*see page 123*).

(*see page 123*)

Hampstead

Perched at the top of a hill and adjacent to the 800-acre (325-ha) Heath, insular, villagey **Hampstead** has long been popular with the literati and chattering classes (although not with Ezra Pound, who thought it 'a more hideous form of Boston'). Pope and Gay took the waters here during its brief time

as a spa; Wilkie Collins, Thackeray and Dickens drank at **Jack Straw's Castle** (on North End Way); and Keats strolled on the Heath with Coleridge and Wordsworth. Much of Keats's best work was composed in his house in Wentworth Place; it was in its garden that he heard his nightingale. Happily, Hampstead's hilly geography has prevented the sort of urbanisation that Camden has suffered, and it remains, together with **Highgate**, a haven for much of London's (monied) intelligentsia and literary bigwigs. It's entirely appropriate that Hampstead's current MP is ex-actress Glenda Jackson.

A tour of Hampstead

Hampstead tube station stands at the top of the steep High Street, lined with opulent but unthrilling shops and bars. Running north, and further uphill, from here is Heath Street. Don't miss the dark and inviting **Louis Pâtisserie** (no.32)

2 Willow Road – *pad of modernist architect Ernö Goldfinger. See page 83.*

for tea and fabulously sticky mittelEuropean cakes. It's a reminder of how much German, Viennese and Hungarian émigrés have contributed to NW3 since the 1930s. Just off the southern end of Heath Street is **Church Row**, one of Hampstead's most beautiful streets, with twin lines of higgeldy-piggeldy terraces leading down to **St John at Hampstead**, where painter John Constable and his wife lie at rest in the sylvan graveyard. Close by, on Holly Hill, is possibly Hampstead's nicest pub, the **Hollybush** (*see page 182*); while another minute's climb brings you to **Fenton House** (*see below*) on Hampstead Grove,

Climbing frame, **Hampstead Heath** *style.*

with its fine porcelain and paintings. The celestially inclined might like to gaze skyward at the nearby **Hampstead Scientific Society Observatory** (*see below*). On Hampstead's southern fringes, in Maresfield Gardens, is the house where Sigmund Freud lived the last year of his life, having fled Nazi persecution in Vienna in 1938 (now the **Freud Museum**; *see page 120*).

East of Heath Street is a maze of attractive streets that shelters **Burgh House** on New End Square (a Queen Anne house that now houses a small museum) and **2 Willow Road** (*see below*), a modernist terrace house built by Hungarian-born Ernö Goldfinger for himself in the 1930s. Ian Fleming hated the work of Goldfinger (who also designed Trellick Tower; *see page 108*) so much he named one of his Bond villains after him. Nearby, off Keats Grove, is the recently reopened **Keats' House** (*see page 120*). Around the corner, on South Hill Park, Ruth Ellis shot her former boyfriend outside the Magdala pub in 1955 (look for the bullet holes in the wall). She became the last woman to be hanged in the UK; her story was immortalised in the 1984 film *Dance with a Stranger*.

Nearby, on Rosslyn Hill (the southern continuation of Hampstead High Street), is one of Hampstead's few stylish all-day eating and drinking venues: **Giraffe** (no.46).

Hampstead Heath

The **Heath** (*see below*) is Hampstead's chief and enduring glory. A Sunday afternoon tramp across its varied landscapes is essential therapy for any jaded Londoner, while a dip in the swimming ponds and a picnic at one of the summer lakeside concerts at **Kenwood House** (*see below*) are equal institutions.

Top tours: Northern exposure

The best of north London's parks and gardens

Best time to do: in fine weather
Approx distance walking: 9 miles (14km)
Tube to Wood Green, then walk down Station Road to **Alexandra Park** (*see p82*) and **Alexandra Palace**, north London's (not entirely successful) rival to the long-gone **Crystal Palace** (*see p104*). Its grounds were landscaped by German prisoners of war during World War I, and the world's first TV transmitter was erected here in 1936.

Exit by Alexandra Palace Way. Cross over the road into Park Road, then right into Cranley Gardens and left into Wood Vale. You're in Highgate now. Cross **Queen's Wood** and then, over the other side of Muswell Hill Road, **Highgate Wood**. Oshobasho Café within the latter (closed Mon) is good for a spot of late breakfast or a cuppa.

Crossing over busy Archway Road, head down Southwood Lane to Highgate High Street and beautiful, hilly, mannered **Waterlow Park** (there's also a café here). Next door is **Highgate Cemetery**

(*see p82*). Although Karl Marx can be found in the East Cemetery, the West is far wilder and more romantic (but can only be visited on a guided tour).

The **Raj Tearooms** at 67 Highgate High Street are perfect as a lunchtime refuelling stop, before continuing down Swain's Lane to the south-eastern corner of mighty **Hampstead Heath** (*see p82*). Walk up **Parliament Hill** to commune with the kite-flyers and enjoy wonderful views. Then head north, via the bathing ponds or the woods, until you reach **Kenwood House** (*see p83*). There's another refreshment opportunity here, and some wonderful interiors and paintings to admire.

If you can take any more greenery, skirt along the Heath's north-western side, across Sandy Heath to the little-known **Hill Garden** (*see below*) and perhaps on to **Golders Hill Park** with its menagerie and (yet another) café. From here it's a shortish walk to Golders Green tube station or a longer one in the opposite direction back to Hampstead.

Not far from Kenwood, on the northern perimeter, is the old **Spaniard's Inn** pub (haunted, it is said, by the ghost of a highwayman). To the west lies the weather-boarded pub **Jack Straw's Castle** (named after one of the leaders of the 1381 Peasants' Revolt) and **Whitestone Pond**, where grown men play with model boats. Ignoring the gay men cruising about the **West Heath**'s leafy undergrowth, head off for **Golders Hill Park**, with its small menageries of deer, goats and birds. While you're here, drop into the **Old Bull & Bush** pub on North End Road to sing a few choruses of the music hall song, 'Come, come, come and make eyes at me/Down at the old Bull and Bush.'

Or, if you want utter tranquillity, follow the long stone walkway on the left behind the new housing development on North End Way (coming up from Jack Straw's Castle) until you stumble upon the all-but-secret **Hill Garden** with its goldfish pond and wonderful collections of plants and rare trees set in landscaped grounds. On a clear day, the views from here are superb.

St John's Wood

Follow Finchley Road towards Baker Street, passing the **Lord's Cricket Ground** on St John's Wood Road (*see page 261*), home to the **MCC Museum** (*see page 122*), and you'll come within walking distance of **Abbey Road**'s EMI Studios where, at no.3, the Beatles recorded their famous album. The zebra crossing outside is always busy with Japanese and American tourists capturing that ineffable Beatles moment on celluloid and scrawling their names on the wall. Move north up Abbey Road to 98A Boundary Road. Here, in a for-

mer paint factory, is the **Saatchi Collection** (*see page 129*). One of London's major spaces for contemporary art, Saatchi's gallery has helped turn fringe Britpack artists into the current mainstream.

Highgate

East of Hampstead Heath, and perched on a hill of its own, is graceful **Highgate**. Once a remote hilltop settlement, impassable in winter snows, the area gets its name from an old tollgate that once stood on the site of the **Gate House** pub on the High Street; dinky shops now predominate here. There are great views from the top of **Highgate Hill**. At the foot of the hill, it's said that **Dick Whittington**, on the point of leaving town, heard Bow bells peel out 'Turn again Whittington, thrice Lord Mayor of London Town'. (The bells underestimated his potential – he became mayor on four occasions in the late fourteenth/early fifteenth century.) This momentous and entirely fictitious event is commemorated on the Whittington Stone, near the eponymous hospital. He didn't have a cat either.

North of Highgate tube station, **Highgate Wood** and **Queen's Wood** offer shady walks plus refreshments in the former at **Oshobasho Café**. Highgate's best-known sight is **Highgate Cemetery** on Swain's Lane (*see below*), one of London's great metropolitan burial grounds. Adjoining the cemetery is beautiful **Waterlow Park** (*see below*). Further down Swain's Lane, you can peep through the Gothic entrance to **Holly Village**, a private village built in 1865, complete with its own village green. Hornsey Lane, on the other side of Highgate Hill, leads you to the **Archway** (or 'Suicide Bridge'), a Victorian viaduct built high over what is now the A1 and offering vertiginous views of the City and East End.

Islington

Map 9

Islington's fortunes have ebbed and flowed. Henry VIII owned several houses here and liked to hunt nearby. 'Merry Islington', then a village on a hill, was renowned for its dairy farms and local spring water. In the nineteenth century, it was known for its smart shopping streets, theatres and music halls, but its fortunes plummeted in the early twentieth century and the area became depopulated and run-down.

These days Islington is decidedly of two parts. Like so much of London, its Georgian squares and Victorian terraces have been gentrified in the past 25 years and rising property prices have succeeded in pushing out some of its poorer population. This means that the middle classes (and until a few years ago, that epitome of focaccia socialism, Richmond Crescent's Tony Blair and family) have colonised Islington. They are appropriately served by **Camden Passage**'s antique shops, **Waterstone's** bookshop (once the Collins Music Hall), bijou restaurants (including **Granita** – *see page 156* – where Blair and cohorts hatched their idea of New Labour), an independent cinema (the **Screen on the Green**; *see page 238*), music at the gorgeous Victorian **Union Chapel** (*see page 255*), and theatre at the **King's Head** (*see page 269*) and wonderful **Almeida** (*see page 268*) – a home to contemporary classical music and high-quality fringe theatre. It's easy to forget that Islington and its chic Canonbury and Highbury neighbours are close to ramshackle housing projects like Essex Road's Marquess Estate.

Islington is best taken at a stroll, starting at **Angel** tube station, continuing along **Upper Street**, past the glass façade of the **Business Design Centre** (which hides the former Royal Agricultural Hall) and triangular Green and up to Highbury, where the swimming pool is bordered by an award-winning children's playground. This way, you'll take in the shops – such as the art deco lamps at **Out of Time** on 21 Canonbury Lane, and the vinyl delights of **Reckless Records** (79 Upper Street). For sustenance, try the fish and chips at the **Upper Street Fish Shop** (no.324) or a slap-up fry-up at **Alfredo's**, opposite Islington Green on Essex Road. Indian restaurants around Penton Street and the vegetable stalls at **Chapel Market** round out the picture. The area's famous residents include Charles Lamb (64 Duncan Terrace) and Joe Orton, killed by his lover, Kenneth Halliwell, at their top-floor bedsit at 25 Noel Street in 1967.

Before striking out for **Highbury** and beyond, sample the architectural delights of Regency **Canonbury Square** and **Compton Terrace**, both well-maintained pieces of architectural history. The square, once home to George Orwell (no.27) and Evelyn Waugh (no.17A), houses the **Canonbury Tower**, which affords great views of the surrounding area (phone the Canonbury Academy on 0171 359 6888 to arrange admission). This is Islington's oldest monument, with possibly Roman foundations. In its present state, however, it is all that remains of Tudor mansion **Canonbury House**, whose former residents include Sir Francis Bacon and Oliver Goldsmith. Restored in 1907, two of the tower's rooms contain Elizabethan oak panels.

The **Little Angel Puppet Theatre** (*see page 220*) is past **St Mary's Church** (where Wesley preached) on Dagmar Passage, and, just beyond, the fine eighteenth-century houses of Cross Street line the slope towards Essex Road. **Highbury Fields**, at the north end of Upper Street, was where 200,000 Londoners fled to escape the Great Fire of 1666 (*see page 17*). Beyond this open space, on the way to Finsbury Park, lies compact **Highbury Stadium**, home to **Arsenal** Football Club: nicknamed 'the Gunners', the team's origins lie in south London's Woolwich munitions works. Of late, the club has been threatening to leave Highbury if it is not allowed to expand the stadium.

Dalston & Stoke Newington

Bishopsgate in the City passes through Shoreditch and becomes Kingsland High Street, otherwise known as the A10, the busy main road that runs out through Dalston, Stoke Newington, past the Hassidic enclave of Stamford Hill, via Tottenham and out of London altogether.

Though scruffy and, at times, intimidating, **Dalston** is also a vibrant place: there are a few kosher shops, including the 24-hour **Bagel Bakery** at 13-15 Ridley Road, and, along the same road, bustling market stalls selling Afro-Caribbean vegetables. Lots of small cafés and

Abney Park Cemetery. *See page 82.*

late-night restaurants reflect the Turkish influx into the area, as does the ubiquitous graffiti for the Kurdish PKP.

Middle-class house buyers started moving in to **Stoke Newington** in a big way after 1980. Consequently, the place sometimes seems like a poor man's Islington. Green spaces can be found at **Clissold Park** (which includes a small zoo and tearooms) and the rambling old boneyard of **Abney Park Cemetery**, which took over from Bunhill Fields as a burial ground for dissenters and Nonconformists; General Booth, founder of the Salvation Army, is buried here. Attractive, villagey Stoke Newington Church Street contains a number of good restaurants: **Rasa** (no.55; *see page 172*) is famed for its superlative vegetarian south Indian cooking, and the hippie café **Blue Legume** (no.101) has a great laid-back vibe. **Vortex** (no.139; *see page 255*) combines jazz venue, café and wine bar in one atmospheric building. At weekends, the street is enlivened by a small arts and crafts market.

Further north

Moving towards the northern perimeter of London, dull suburban streets are enlivened by the immigrant communities that have made them their home. **Golders Green**, **Hendon** (where the impressive **RAF Museum** is located; *see page 117*) and **Finchley** have large Jewish communities – although they are generally less orthodox than Hassidic **Stamford Hill**, you'll still find plenty of Jewish restaurants and shops selling kosher delicacies. Finchley is home to London's second **Jewish Museum** (*see page 122*). Golders Green is also the focus of a growing population of Japanese City workers. There has been a Jewish cemetery on Hoop Lane since 1895 – the cellist Jacqueline du Pré is buried here. Across the road, the fires of **Golders Green Crematorium** have consumed hundreds of notable bodies, including those of TS Eliot, Marc Bolan and Anna Pavlova.

Tottenham and **Haringey** retain a strong Greek Cypriot and Turkish Cypriot identity. Both areas are fun for the sweet-toothed wanting to try a few honey-soaked pastries, or the fabulous kebab shops of Green Lanes. **Cricklewood**'s Indian population has also contributed a marvellous array of shops, stocking all kinds of sugary goodies. **Muswell Hill**'s prime attraction is the giant glasshouse of **Alexandra Palace**, within **Alexandra Park** (*see below*), with its wonderful views.

Sights

Alexandra Park

Muswell Hill, N22 (park 0181 444 7696/info 0181 365 2121). Wood Green tube/Alexandra Palace rail/W3, W7, 84A, 144, 144A bus. **Open** 24 hours daily.

The views over London from **Alexandra Palace**, at the top of this steeply sloping park, are impressive on a clear day. The Palace (informally known as Ally Pally) once housed the BBC's first television studio. Now, it's an entertainment and exhibition centre with an indoor ice rink. The park's public gardens have plenty of kids' attractions and sports facilities, including a pitch-and-putt course. There are bank holiday funfairs (*see p5*) and a free fireworks display on Bonfire Night (5 Nov, but usually held on the nearest Saturday). *Boating (0181 889 9089). Jazz concerts in the Grove (summer; 0181 883 7173).*

Fenton House

Hampstead Grove, NW3 (0171 435 3471). Hampstead tube. **Open** *Mar* 2-5pm Sat, Sun; *Apr-Oct* 2-5pm Wed-Fri; 11am-5pm Sat, Sun, public hols; 11am-5pm Sat, Sun. **Admission** £4.20; £2.10 children. **Map** *see p78*.

This gem of a house, built in 1693 in William and Mary style, is one of the earliest and largest houses in Hampstead. It houses the excellent Benton Fletcher collection of early keyboard instruments, as well as a quirky range of pottery poodles in the Rockingham Room and Chinese snuffboxes and ninth-century porcelain in the Oriental Room. The four attic rooms have retained the atmosphere of a seventeenth-century property with impressive views over London. Entry to the garden (one side is beautifully landscaped; the other contains an orchard and vegetable patch) is free.

Hampstead Heath

NW3 (Parliament Hill 0171 485 4491/Golders Hill 0181 455 5183). Belsize Park or Hampstead tube/Gospel Oak or Hampstead Heath rail/24, C2, C11 bus. **Open** 24 hours daily. **Map** *see p78*.

One of London's most popular and varied green spaces, the rolling, semi-landscaped Heath has something for everyone. You can jog, stroll, sunbathe, picnic, swim in the ponds or Parliament Hill Lido, walk the dog, play football, fish, or fly a kite from the top of Parliament Hill. Alternatively, just sit and admire the views, which, on a clear day, take in the whole of central London. There are band concerts on summer Sunday afternoons on Parliament and Golders hills, as well as bowls (0171 485 4491) and guided walks (0171 482 7073). Visit **Kenwood House** (*see below*) to see the superb **Iveagh Bequest** (*see p129*) collection of paintings, and look for one of Kenwood's hidden treasures: the beautifully restored **Romany Buckland Caravan**, in a small building near the Coach House restaurant. On Saturday evenings in summer, thousands make their way to Kenwood for the lakeside concerts (*see p247*). Funfairs are held, at the upper and lower ends of the Heath, on the Easter, May and August bank holidays (*see p5*). A diary of events taking place on the Heath is available at information points.

Bathing ponds: men only, women only & mixed (summer 7am-sunset daily; admission free). Tennis courts (0171 284 3779).

Hampstead Scientific Society Observatory

Lower Terrace, NW3 (0181 346 1056/www.baesema4. demon.co.uk). Hampstead tube/46, 268 bus. **Open** (weather permitting) *Sept-Apr* 8-10pm Fri, Sat; 11am-1pm Sun. **Admission** free; donations appreciated. **Map** *see p78*.

This beautiful old observatory allows visitors in to peer through the telescopes – including a six-inch Cooke refracting telescope from 1899 – at the planets on clear nights. The observatory is also open at other times of interest, such as eclipses and the apparition of comets. The Society also welcomes new members.

Highgate Cemetery

Swain's Lane, N6 (0181 340 1834). Archway tube/C11, 271 bus. **Open** *East Cemetery Apr-Oct* 10am-5pm Mon-Fri; 11am-5pm Sat, Sun; *Nov-Mar* 10am-4pm Mon-Fri; 11am-4pm Sat, Sun. *West Cemetery tours Apr-Oct* noon,

One of **Islington**'s *less* nouveau *residents peruses* **Chapel Market**. *See page 81.*

2pm, 4pm, Mon-Fri; 11am, noon, 1pm, 2pm, 3pm, 4pm, Sat, Sun; *Nov-Mar* 11am, noon, 1pm, 2pm, 3pm, Sat, Sun. **Admission** *East Cemetery* £1; *West Cemetery* tour £3.

Opened in 1839, Highgate is London's most famous and exotic graveyard. The East Cemetery, apart from being the last resting place of Karl Marx, is rather drab, and something of a let-down, although it's worth seeking out the tombs of Yusuf Mohammed Dadoo (president of the ANC in London from 1960) and Mary Anne Evans (alias George Eliot). The West Cemetery, however, is a romantic wilderness of tombs and catacombs, but can only be visited on one of the excellent guided tours. Highlights include the mystical, family vault-lined Egyptian Avenue, the eerie catacombs and the elaborate mausoleum of seventeenth-century media tycoon Julius Beer. Eminent Victorians residing here include such contrasting figures as chemist Michael Faraday and celebrated barefist-fighter Tom Sayers (whose funeral attracted a crowd of 100,000). Note that children of eight and under are not allowed on the tours. Photography in the cemetery is only allowed with a camera permit (£2).

Kenwood House

Hampstead Lane, NW3 (0181 348 1286). Archway, Golders Green or Highgate tube/214, 210 bus.
Open *Mar & Oct* 10am-5pm, *Nov-Feb* 10am-4pm, daily. **Admission** free; donations appreciated. **Map** *see p78.*

This elegant mansion overlooking Hampstead Heath from its northern fringe was rebuilt in classical style for the Earl of Mansfield by Robert Adam in 1767-9 and bequeathed to the nation in 1927. A stroll across the Heath and around the house, with its paintings, furniture and beautiful oval-shaped library, is one of the great pleasures of living in London. The small but superb collection of Old Masters in the **Iveagh Bequest** (*see p129*) includes works

by Rembrandt, Hals, Turner, Gainsborough and Reynolds, and some wonderful Vermeers.

2 Willow Road

2 Willow Road, NW3 (0171 435 6166).
Hampstead tube. **Open** *Apr-Oct* noon-5pm Thur-Sat (last admission 4pm). **Admission** £4.10; £2 children. **Map** *see p78.*

Ernö Goldfinger's pioneering piece of domestic modernist architecture looks as striking today as it did when it was built in 1939. Its purchase by the National Trust was a brave move, but one that has paid off – the house won the London Tourist Board's 'Best Small Attraction' award in 1998. Before being taken on an informative guided tour of the house, visitors watch a short video explaining Goldfinger's philosophy of design described as 'structural rationalism'. Space is used economically throughout the building, with beds and bathrooms in closets, and a unique spiral staircase through the centre of the house. This was the Goldfinger family home and still contains much of its original contents including furniture he designed himself. There is also a collection of twentieth-century art, including works by Henry Moore and Max Ernst. Tours run from 12.15pm every 45 minutes, and last about an hour.

Waterlow Park

Highgate Hill, N6 (0171 272 2825). Archway tube/C11, 271 bus. **Open** 7.30am-dusk daily.

A small, beautiful park next to Highgate Cemetery, with steep slopes, ponds, magnificent trees and a mini-aviary. It was bequeathed to the people by former owner Sydney Waterlow as 'a garden for the gardenless'. As well as tennis courts, a putting green and a dog-free play area for under-5s, there's a garden café in sixteenth-century Lauderdale House (0181 348 8716).

East London

Lively streetlife, arty hangouts, cheap ethnic grub, poverty and new wealth – despite popular misconceptions, East London is nothing if not diverse.

Whitechapel & Spitalfields

Maps 10 & 12

Whitechapel has always been the City's poor, rather embarrassing next-door neighbour. Situated on the main route from London to Essex, it first developed as a home for bell-founders and other metalworkers who were expelled from the City for being too noisy; the **Whitechapel Bell Foundry** (established 1570) and **Gunmakers' Company Proof House** still survive in Fieldgate Street and Commercial Road respectively. By Victorian times, the area was wretchedly poor, a contemporary social historian describing it as 'a shocking place... an evil plexus of slums that hide human creeping things'. Only crime – and especially prostitution – thrived.

Poverty meant low rents – an attraction for the successive waves of immigrants who have enriched Whitechapel over the last few centuries. First, it was the French Protestant refugees, the Huguenots, in the early eighteenth century; then the Irish and Germans in the early nineteenth century; Jewish refugees from eastern Europe from 1880 to 1914; and, as the Jews prospered and moved north, Indians and Bangladeshis, who between the 1950s and 1970s took over textile businesses on Commercial Street and Commercial Road.

Exploring the East End

The best way to enter the East End is to take the 15 bus through the City and get off at Aldgate East at the stop between Goulston Street and Old Castle Street (look out for Tubby Isaacs' jellied eel stall – established 1919 – by the Aldgate Exchange pub). Commercial Street, which sweeps off to the left through Spitalfields towards Shoreditch, is for much of its length a wide swathe of Victorian warehouses.

Halfway up Commercial Street is the indoor **Spitalfields Market** (*see page 193*). The famous fruit and vegetable market, established in 1682, moved north-east to Leyton some years ago, but a small organic market continues, together with book, music and bric-a-brac stalls, on the old site surrounded by a variety of cheap eateries and small businesses.

Opposite the market is Hawksmoor's magnificent **Christ Church Spitalfields** (*see below*).

*The **East London Mosque**. See page 87.*

After dark, this stretch of Commercial Street has a distinctly Hell's Kitchen look to it, with prostitutes standing at intervals along the kerb and anonymous figures clustering around the all-night mobile caff parked outside the church railings.

Fournier Street, which runs alongside Christ Church to link Commercial Street with Brick Lane, is altogether more respectable – a reminder of the Huguenots, whose skill at silk weaving brought them prosperity in the East End. Their tall houses, with distinctive shutters and ornate, jutting porches, line the street. Similar houses can be seen in nearby Elder Street and Folgate Street, where the unique, recreated Georgian residence, **Dennis Severs' House** (*see below*), can be distinguished by its flickering gas flames over the front door.

Bargains & baltis

There are two good reasons to visit **Brick Lane** and the immediate area: **Brick Lane Market** and the plethora of cheap curry restaurants. Many of the latter are, alas, uninspiring these days – notable exceptions are (at the basic end of the scale) **Sweet & Spicy** (no.40) and (rather posher) **Le Taj** (no.134). Brick Lane's Jewish heritage survives in the **Beigel Bake** at no.159 (open 24 hours daily). Playwright Arnold Wesker was brought up in nearby Fashion Street, and *Oliver!* composer Lionel Bart lived above the shop on the corner of Brick Lane and Princelet Street, opposite the Eastern Eye restaurant. There's a dearth of good pubs around the Lane; an exception is the **Pride of Spitalfields** in Heneage Street, which attracts a friendly local crowd. The newish **Vibe Bar** (no.91) suggests that some modest trendification is being added to Brick Lane's social mix.

Most visitors to Whitechapel come for the Sunday markets at Brick Lane and nearby **Petticoat Lane** (*see page 193*), but the whole area is worth exploring. The art nouveau **Whitechapel Art Gallery** (*see page 133*) on Whitechapel High Street specialises in contemporary art. The lobby of **Whitechapel Public Library** is adorned with a painted-tile depiction of the hay market that was held in the High Street for 300 years until its abolition in 1928. A modest clothing market continues to thrive further along Whitechapel Road. Fieldgate Street (running behind the huge **East London Mosque**) is worth a detour for a look at the grim, derelict, Victorian bulk of **Tower House**, built as a hostel for the homeless. Stalin and Lenin stayed here while attending the Fifth Congress of the Russian Social Democratic Labour Party in nearby Fulbourne Street. The 'Elephant Man', Joseph Merrick, was exhibited at what is now the Bombay Saree House, before Sir Frederick Treves, a surgeon at the **Royal London Hospital** opposite, spotted him and provided a home for him in the hospital buildings. The hospital is now topped by a helipad and contains a museum with a section on Merrick plus a general run down on the history of medicine and the hospital itself (*see page 122*).

Murder in Whitechapel

The **Blind Beggar** pub (corner of Whitechapel and Cambridge Heath roads) is best known for its criminal connections. It was here, on 8 March 1966, that gangster George Cornell was shot dead by Ronnie Kray (allegedly for calling him a 'fat poof'). For ten years Ronnie and his twin brother Reggie had dominated organised crime from Woolwich to the City; Cornell was a member of the rival Richardson gang. In 1969, the Krays were each jailed for a minimum of 30 years, the judge commenting that 'society has earned a long rest from your activities'. Today, the Blind Beggar is a comfortable, rather ordinary pub, popular with traders

Canary Wharf Tower, *from Greenwich.*

and visitors to Whitechapel Road Market. **Sidney Street**, which leads off Whitechapel Road opposite Cambridge Heath Road, was the site of a famous siege on 3 January 1911. Several anarchists barricaded themselves into a house and took potshots at the police and soldiers outside before the house caught fire. Two charred bodies were recovered but the gang's leader, the enigmatically named Russian, Peter the Painter, was never found.

For decades, the alley at **Wood's Buildings** (down the side of the Bombay Saree House, across Whitechapel Road from the Royal London Hospital), led to what was arguably the most desolate spot in the whole of the East End: an almost-forgotten tract of land, dominated by a huge, ruined Victorian school. **Jack the Ripper** claimed his first victim here. The school may now have been converted into luxury flats, but the view back along the alley towards Whitechapel Road is still tinglingly Dickensian. The old East End is disappearing fast – catch it while you can.

Docklands

The history of London's **Docklands** (stretching east from Tower Bridge to the Isle of Dogs and beyond) is the history of Britain in microcosm. As the British Empire expanded in the eighteenth and nineteenth centuries, so too did the traffic along the River Thames, as ships arrived laden with booty from all corners of the globe. Different docks were built to specialise in various types of cargo: rum and hardwood at West India Docks on the Isle of Dogs; wool, sugar and rubber at St Katharine's Dock by Tower Bridge; ivory, coffee and cocoa at London Docks in Wapping. During World War II the docks suffered heavy bombing (including 57 consecutive nights of firebombing from 7 September 1940), but by the 1950s they had again reached full capacity. When it came, the end was sudden. The collapse of the Empire, a series of crippling strikes and, above all, the introduction of deep-water container ships led to the closure, one by one, of all of London's docks from Tower Bridge to Barking Creek between 1967 and 1984.

Regeneration

In 1981, the Conservative Government set up the London Docklands Development Corporation (LDDC). Its brief was to regenerate the eight-and-a-half square miles (2,200 hectares) of derelict land by building new offices and homes, and attracting new businesses. Accused from the outset of favouring wealthy outsiders over the needs of local people, the LDDC came badly unstuck in the recession of the early 1990s, when developers found themselves with brand-new empty buildings on their hands and noone to move into them. Since then, the situation has improved: the population of Docklands increased from 39,400 in 1981 to 77,000 by the time the organisation ceased operation in March 1998. Its responsibilities have been taken over by a range of other bodies.

Docklands remains one of the most intriguing areas of London to visit, and it's becoming more accessible. New, imaginatively designed pedestrian bridges across the water-filled docks have made the place more people-friendly. The Docklands Light Railway (DLR) is due to be augmented during 1999 by the long-awaited Jubilee Line extension, which will add a much-needed tube link.

St Katharine's

Just east of Tower Bridge on the north bank of the Thames, **St Katharine's** once housed over a thousand cottages, a brewery and the twelfth-century church of St Katharine – all of which were demolished (without compensation) to make way for a grandiose new docklands development scheme in 1828. St Katharine's Dock, which was built over the old settlement, remained open until 1968, re-emerging in 1973 as the first of the Docklands redevelopments. **St Katharine's Haven** is now a yacht marina; one corner of the dock houses a squadron of russet-sailed, turn-of-the-century barges. The restaurants, cafés and pubs around the dock pull in tourists by the coachload.

Wapping – crime & punishment & pubs

In 1598, London historian John Stowe described Wapping High Street as a 'filthy strait passage,

Murals in...

with alleys of small tenements or cottages... built and inhabited by sailors' victuallers'. Today, it is a quiet, rather sunless thoroughfare, though not without charm, hemmed in on either side by warehouses (those in Wapping Wall are the most spectacular) and new flats.

The river at **Wapping**, to the east of St Katharine's, brims with history. Until well into the nineteenth century, convicted pirates were taken at low tide to **Execution Dock** (near the River Police station at Wapping New Stairs), hanged, and left there in chains until three tides had washed over them. The **Captain Kidd** pub (108 Wapping High Street) commemorates one of the most famous recipients of this brand of rough justice – Kidd had been dispatched by the government to capture pirates in the Indian Ocean but decided to become one himself. Another historic pub, the **Town of Ramsgate** (62 Wapping High Street), is where the bloodthirsty Judge Jeffreys, who sent scores of pirates to Execution Dock, was himself captured as he tried to escape to Hamburg disguised as a sailor (he died in the Tower of London). 'Colonel' Blood was also caught here after attempting to steal the Crown Jewels in 1671.

While you're here, have a look at **Scandrett Street** (leading off Wapping High Street, opposite

...**Cable Street**.

interior was rebuilt after the Blitz, the exterior and monumental tower are typical of the architect.

Limehouse

Sandwiched between Wapping and the Isle of Dogs, **Limehouse** was named after the medieval lime kilns that once stood here. But, like Wapping, Limehouse's prosperity came from the sea. In 1610, a census revealed that half the working population were mariners, and Limehouse later became a centre for shipbuilding. The straw-coloured **Sail Makers' & Ship Chandlers' Building** still stands at 11 West India Dock Road.

The importance of Limehouse is reflected in the immense size of **St Anne's Limehouse** (corner of Commercial Road and Three Colt Street). Built between 1712 and 1724 in what were then open fields, this is probably Nicholas Hawksmoor's most dramatic creation. The clock tower is the second highest in Britain after Big Ben and was built by the same makers.

Britain's first wave of Chinese immigrants (mainly seamen) settled in Limehouse in the nineteenth century. Their influence survives in some of the street names (Ming Street, Canton Street) and in the few Chinese restaurants that remain around West India Dock Road. In Victorian times, Limehouse was notorious for its gambling and drug dens (Oscar Wilde's Dorian Gray comes here to buy opium) and it features in stories by Sax Rohmer (creator of oriental villain Fu Manchu) and Sir Arthur Conan Doyle. Dickens knew Limehouse well: he regularly visited his godfather in Newell Street and used the tiny, dark, and still superb, **Grapes** inn (76 Narrow Street; *see page 182*) as the model for the Six Jolly Fellowship Porters in *Our Mutual Friend* (1865). The canal path on the other side of Narrow Street takes you to Limehouse Basin, which, despite renovation and the number of pleasure-craft moored there, still looks somewhat desolate.

Isle of Dogs

For many people, Docklands *is* the **Isle of Dogs**. Redevelopment has been at its most intense here, focusing on **Canary Wharf**. Cesar Pelli's rocket-shaped 800-foot (500-m) tower is the tallest building in the UK and has dominated the London skyline since it was erected in 1991. It's only a pity that owing to fear of IRA attack (a massive bomb at South Quay in February 1996 caused a huge amount of damage and killed two people) the public aren't allowed access to enjoy the view from the top. Still, the sight of the tower through the glass-domed roof of Canary Wharf DLR station is pretty spectacular in itself. The shopping arcades here are worth a brief detour.

There's little about the Isle that isn't subject to dispute. Some insist that it isn't an island at all, but a peninsula (though the main section of West India Docks effectively splits it in two) and no one

---

Wapping Old Stairs). This was once a miniature community containing a pub, a church and a school, built in 1760 and bearing plaster figures of an eighteenth-century schoolboy and schoolgirl over the main entrance.

Dating from 1520, the **Prospect of Whitby** (57 Wapping Wall; *see page 182*) is the oldest and most famous of the Wapping riverside pubs. Pepys, Dickens, Whistler and Turner were all regulars. The **White Swan & Cuckoo** (corner of Wapping Lane and Prusom Street) lacks a riverside view but serves award-winning food, and is one of the friendliest pubs in east London.

The streets north of The Highway are solidly working-class tenements. Though not outwardly prepossessing, this area too has a colourful past. A large mural at St George's Town Hall, a few minutes' walk away in **Cable Street**, commemorates the battle between local people and marching blackshirts, led by fascist leader Sir Oswald Mosley, on 4 October 1936. The march, intended to intimidate the local Jewish population, was abandoned and the blackshirts were never seen in such numbers again in the East End. The church of **St George-in-the-East**, just off The Highway on Cannon Street Road, was built in 1714-29 to the designs of Nicholas Hawksmoor. Although the

can agree on whether 'Dogs' refers to the royal kennels that were once kept here or whether it's a corruption of the dykes that were built by Flemish engineers in the nineteenth century. Above all, argument continues to rage over whether the Isle of Dogs is a crucible of economic progress or a monstrous adventure playground for big business.

The best way to see Docklands is from the overhead Docklands Light Railway. At the undeveloped southern end of the Isle is **Mudchute City Farm** (a big hit with kids; *see page 219*). **Island Gardens**, at the very tip, offers an unparalleled view across the Thames towards **Greenwich** (a foot tunnel takes you under the river to emerge next to the Cutty Sark).

Eating and drinking options on the Isle of Dogs are not abundant. The greatest concentration of places is in the Canary Wharf complex, but most are pricey and sterile. A better bet is **Landy's at the Space** (269 Westferry Road) at Island Gardens, which offers good breakfasts and lunches upstairs from the Space arts venue.

Trinity Almshouses: *home to old sea dogs.*

Bethnal Green & Hackney

In Victorian times **Bethnal Green** was the poorest district in London. In 1889, nearly half the population lived below subsistence level, with the **Jago**, around Old Nichol Street, containing the worst ravages of poverty and squalor. The area has been completely transformed in the twentieth century, with wholesale slum clearance and the building of huge council estates, but, despite pockets of gentility, Bethnal Green remains impoverished. The **Bethnal Green Museum of Childhood** on Cambridge Heath Road (*see page 119*), originally the east London branch of the Victoria & Albert Museum, opened in 1872. Almost as ancient is the art deco inlaid Anglo-Italian caff **E Pellicci** (332 Bethnal Green Road; 0171 739 4873), which has been run by the Pellicci family since 1900.

Hackney, to the north, was originally an extended village, popular in the fifteenth and sixteenth centuries with merchants who wanted to live near, but not too near, the City. Hackney's oldest house, **Sutton House** (*see below*), dates from this period. In his diary entry for 11 June 1664, Pepys records that he went 'with my wyfe only to take ayre, it being very warm and pleasant, to Bowe and Old Ford; and thence to Hackney. There... played at shuffle board, ate cream and good cherries; and so with good refreshment home.' The rural idyll continued until the nineteenth century, when Hackney's market gardens were gradually buried under terraced houses and workshops, themselves to be replaced by housing estates after World War II.

A large, mainly poor area, Hackney is best approached selectively. **Columbia Road** and Ridley Road have excellent markets (*see page 193*); the former also has a number of pottery shops specialising in terracotta. You won't go hungry, either: the **Ridley Bagel Bakery** (13-15 Ridley Road) is open 24 hours, and fish and chip shops don't come much better than **Faulkners** (424-426 Kingsland Road). Thanks to the local Kurdish community, there are also plenty of Turkish restaurants nearby.

Mare Street features the striking **Hackney Empire** (*see page 250*), in its heyday one of London's great music halls and still a popular theatre. Look out for the striking paintwork, forming a human face, on the brick building diagonally opposite. Hackney Central Hall, built as a Methodist meeting hall in 1907, now houses the eclectic **Hackney Museum** (closed for redevelopment until the end of 1999).

Shoreditch & Hoxton

Shoreditch – or Score's Ditch as it was known in Anglo-Saxon times – was formed at the intersection of two Roman roads: Old Street, running east-west, and Kingsland Road, running north-south. Not quite the City or the East End, the place seems uncertain of its identity, and its main focal point, around Old Street tube station, is dour and rundown. But it has seen more cheerful times. James Burbage founded London's first theatre on the corner of Great Eastern Street and New Inn Yard. Called simply the Theatre, it lasted barely 20 years before decamping to Southwark and becoming the **Globe** (*see pages 33 & 265*). The same year, 1598, Ben Jonson, then Britain's foremost playwright after Shakespeare, fought a duel with an actor named Gabriel Spencer at Hoxton Fields (now Hoxton Square) and killed him. Since he was also a clergyman, Jonson escaped the gallows, but had his left thumb branded; his victim was buried in **St Leonard's Church**, in Shoreditch High Street.

Hoxton is the section of Shoreditch north of Old Street and west of Kingsland Road. From Victorian times until the outbreak of World War II, it was known chiefly for its overcrowded slums and its music halls. Both features have since disappeared under unappealing blocks of flats, but an influx of artists, musicians and other Bohemian types in recent years has given pockets of Hoxton an unexpected scruffy chic. Centred around **Hoxton Square**, home of the fine **Lux Cinema** (*see page 238*), cool bars (such as **Home** and the **Shoreditch Electricity Showrooms**; *see page 182*) are now legion in Hoxton, yet shops, restaurants and other basic facilities remain conspicuous by their absence.

Mile End, Bow & Stratford

Mostly common land until the sixteenth century, **Mile End** experienced a minor population explosion in the nineteenth century as industrialisation took hold. The area never really experienced the ravages of poverty suffered by neighbouring Whitechapel and Bethnal Green. Nevertheless, it was here that the **Trinity Almshouses** were built in 1695 (near the junction with Cambridge Heath Road) for 'twenty-eight decayed masters and commanders of ships'. Look out for the model galleons, on either side of the entrance. In the 1860s, William Booth founded the Salvation Army in Mile End.

Much of Mile End Road is filled by **Queen Mary and Westfield College**, opened by Queen Victoria in 1887 as a working men's institute. Further east, beyond Mile End tube station, lies little-known and quietly impressive **Tredegar Square** and its offshoots, Tredegar Road and Lichfield Road, each lined with beautifully restored and maintained 1830s terraced houses.

To the south-west, **Mile End Park** borders Copperfield Road, home to the **Ragged School Museum** (*see page 119*) and **Matt's Gallery** (*see page 133*). The road cuts through **Victoria Park** (*see below*), a welcome slice of green that stretches north-east towards Hackney.

Bow, to the east, has played a major role in the growth of London. In the twelfth century, the narrow Roman bridge over the River Lea at Old Ford was supplemented by a new bridge downriver. Its bow shape gave the whole area its name. Grain was transported by boat from Hertfordshire and unloaded at mills along the river. In the mid-nineteenth century, new factories sprang up, notably the Bryant and May match factory, scene of a bit-

ter but ultimately successful match-girls' strike in 1888. A quarter of a century later, Bow struck another blow for women's rights when Sylvia Pankhurst (sister of Emmeline) launched the East London Federation of Suffragettes.

Stratford ('street by the ford') formed north of the twelfth-century bridgehead. A wealthy Cisterican monastery, Stratford Langthorne Abbey, helped put Stratford on the map. The abbey was dissolved by Henry VIII in 1538, but by then Stratford's prosperity was ensured, thanks to the development of early industries such as gunpowder manufacture. In the mid-nineteenth century much of the area was covered by railway lines and marshalling yards. Stratford remains a busy transport nexus, boasting a railway, tube and DLR station, as well as a glittering new bus station resembling an upside-down umbrella.

Modern Stratford has a busy, well-defined centre, focused on Broadway, where an obelisk commemorates the nineteenth-century philanthropist Samuel Gurney. Look out too for the distinctive green dome and globe of the Transport and General Workers Union building in nearby West Ham Lane. Make your way through the big indoor shopping centre and you come to **Gerry Raffles Square**. Here the sparkling new glass-and-neon **Stratford Picture House** faces the venerable **Theatre Royal Stratford East**, currently sporting a demanding sky-blue and crimson paint scheme and resembling an over-made-up old lady. Joan Littlewood's Theatre Workshop was based here during the 1950s and 1960s, providing an early boost for the musical talents of Lionel Bart.

Walthamstow

The name comes from the Old English word 'Wilcumestowe': a place where guests are welcome. It's a description that still applies today – **Walthamstow** is a noticeably friendly place. Its borders are ancient ones: **Epping Forest** (*see page 287*) to the north, **Walthamstow Marshes** to the west. The first settlers lived here in the Bronze Age, when the whole area was still thickly forested. In medieval times much of the forest was cleared and replaced by farmland. It wasn't until the nineteenth century that Walthamstow became a wholly urban area, though most of its largely working-class population has been spared the tenements and tower blocks that litter other parts of east London.

Walthamstow has two main thoroughfares. The narrow **High Street** contains the longest and, after Brixton, most varied market in London. **Walthamstow Market** stretches for more than a mile and is lined by inexpensive shops. The second thoroughfare is undulating **Hoe Street**, consisting of a mainly uninspiring selection of kebab shops and mini-marts, although the **Dhaka Tandoori** (103 Hoe Street) is rather good.

North of Forest Road, streets such as Holmes Avenue, Diana Road and Winns Avenue are inimitably Walthamstow: ruddy brick terraced houses, with deep porches and creaking iron gates. It's the sort of dreaming suburbia immortalised in William Sansom's 1949 novel *The Body*.

Lloyd Park contains the **Waltham Forest Theatre** and a variety of imported water birds. The aviary and manicured bowling green, frequented by white-clad elderly locals, make it particularly pleasant on a summer afternoon. The eighteenth-century building with its back imperiously turned to the park is the **William Morris Gallery** (*see page 121*). From here, a short walk up Forest Road will be amply rewarded by the dramatic view of the art nouveau **Walthamstow Town Hall**. This is one of the most startling pieces of municipal architecture in London; its beautiful proportions, green-and-gold clock tower and circular reflecting pool have graced many a film and TV production (in preglasnost days it frequently stood in for Moscow or Leningrad).

The area's oldest buildings can be found in a well-concealed enclave known as **Walthamstow Village**. Vestry Road contains the **Vestry House Museum** (*see page 121*) and the **Monoux Almshouses**, built in 1795 and 'endowed for ever… for the use of six decayed tradesmen's widows of this parish and no other'. The squat, greenish exterior of nearby **St Mary's Church** conceals a modest but tranquil interior. Timbered **Ancient House**, opposite the churchyard, was once a farmhouse. Restored in 1934, it sags like an unsuccessful fruit cake. The Village continues along Orford Road, with its brace of Italian restaurants and cosy pub, imaginatively named the **Village**.

Leyton, Leytonstone & Wanstead

Badly bombed during World War II, **Leyton's** post-war development has been haphazard, and it lacks the cohesion and charm of neighbouring Walthamstow. Much of the land originally consisted of marshy, fertile farmland, and during the eighteenth century the area was best known for its market gardening. The inevitable industrialisation of the mid-nineteenth century led to much of the marshland being covered by railways and gas works, and to a downturn in the area's fortunes as the population swelled with low-paid railway workers. The proliferation of discount supermarkets and second-hand furniture and electrical shops testifies to the fact that Leyton remains one of London's poorer areas. Its best-known 'attraction' is probably its endearingly underachieving football team, **Leyton Orient**, whose home ground is in Brisbane Road.

Leytonstone, to the east of Leyton, took its name from a milestone on the Roman road from the City to Epping Forest. The Jet garage on the corner of Leytonstone High Road is on the site of a greengrocer's shop where **Alfred Hitchcock** spent his early childhood. Late in life, he recalled how, following some forgotten mischievousness, his father gave him a note and told him to take it to the nearby Harrow Green police station. There, the sergeant on duty read the note and proceeded to lock the future Master of Suspense in a cell for 20 minutes, explaining, 'This is what we do to naughty boys.'

Further east again is **Wanstead**, once the site of a Roman settlement (the remains of a villa were found in Wanstead Park in 1715). The park was formed from the grounds of Wanstead House, a favourite meeting place of Elizabethan glitterati such as Sir Philip Sidney, the Earl of Essex and the Virgin Queen herself. In the early nineteenth century, the house was demolished and sold off as building rubble, though the Temple and Grotto (scurrilously said to have been used for orgies) still stand. South of Aldersbrook Road lies **Wanstead Flats**, once the southernmost tip of Epping Forest and now a sparsely vegetated expanse of common, its perimeter marked by distant, melancholy tower blocks. At the eastern end of somnolent Overton Drive is the graceful eighteenth-century church of **St Mary the Virgin**. The rambling churchyard contains a 'Watcher's Box', once used to keep an eye out for graverobbers.

Further east

Although the London Dockland Development Corporation remit to revive the London Docks extended well to the east of the Isle of Dogs, there is little to interest visitors beyond **Blackwall**. **Canning Town**, huddled next to the River Lea, lost its main industry as early as 1912, with the closure of the Thames Ironworks and Shipbuilding Company on Bow Creek. Later, much of the area was flattened by German bombers during World War II, and large, unsympathetically designed post-war housing estates did nothing to revive the area's fortunes. Neighbouring **Newham** fared even worse: the collapse of a tower block, Ronan Point, in 1968 resulted in many deaths. **Beckton**, to the east, has done better, with better-than-average new housing. South of Beckton, **London City Airport** was opened in 1987, using the long, narrow quay between Royal Albert Dock and George V Dock as a runway for short-haul airliners (there's a good view of the airport from the DLR). Dagenham, which sprawls alongside the Thames beyond Barking, marks the outer reaches of the East End, as London gives way to Essex.

Top tours: Eastern spice

Cool bars and hot curries, hectic markets and tranquil museums

Tube to Walthamstow Central. **Walthamstow** is an unexpectedly pleasant north-east London enclave. As well as boasting Europe's longest daily (except Sun) **street market** (with 450 stalls), there are the less full-on attractions of the **Vestry House Museum** (closed Sun; *see p121*) and the **William Morris Gallery** (closed Mon, Sun; *see p121*).

Tube to Highbury & Islington, then amble down **Islington**'s Upper Street, packed with shops and restaurants, to observe liberal middle-class London in its natural habitat.

Take a tube or bus to Liverpool Street, the eastern outpost of the City, and head for the splendid indoor **Spitalfields Market** (*see p193*). There's a host of lunch options here (the steak sandwiches at the **Arkansas Café** are unbeatable; *see p157*) plus the chance to watch out-of-shape City workers puffing their way around the indoor football pitches. Once refreshed, take a peek at the neighbouring church **Christ Church Spitalfields** (*see p93*), Nicholas Hawksmoor's majestic contribution to the area.

An alternative source of sustenance can be found on nearby **Brick Lane**, a focus for the local Bangladeshi community and a well-known source of cheap curries.

South of here is **Whitechapel**, site of yet another street market, several of Jack the Ripper's murders and the go-ahead **Whitechapel Art Gallery** (*see p133*). Or you could instead head north to Kingsland

High Street to the **Geffrye Museum** (*see p117*), a wonderful collection of English domestic interiors.

Head for **Hoxton** for a late afternoon/early evening drink in one of this desolate-yet-strangely-hip area's trendy bars (*see p182*). Several also serve food, or you could try the top-notch Vietnamese food at **Viet Hoa** (70-72 Kingsland Road; *see p178*).

Christ Church Spitalfields

Commercial Street, E1 (0171 247 7202). Aldgate or Aldgate East tube/Liverpool Street tube/rail/67 bus. **Open** noon-2.30pm Mon-Fri and for concerts; otherwise apply at the rectory (2 Fournier Street, E1). **Map 10 S5**
One of Nicholas Hawksmoor's masterpieces, Christ Church is best seen at night, when its white floodlit bulk looms massively above the darkened warehouses of Commercial Street. Built in 1714 to provide a place of worship for the Huguenot silk-weavers, it later fell into disrepair and is currently undergoing restoration (mainly on the inside), though it remains open to the public.

Dennis Severs' House

18 Folgate Street, E1 (0171 247 4013). Liverpool Street tube/rail. **Open** 2-5pm first Sun of month; evening first Mon of month (phone to book); three times per week for theatrical performances, played to an audience of eight people (phone for details). **Performances** 7.30pm. **Admission** *performances* £30; *house* £7 Sun; £10 Mon. **Map 10 R5**
The current owner of this beautifully restored Georgian red-brick terraced house (built in 1724), the eccentric American-born Mr Severs, invites visitors to travel through time (for two and a half hours) and become the guests of an imaginary family who lived in the house from 1685 to 1919. As a kind of still-life radio drama, it's a highly atmospheric portrayal of lives during 250 years of east London history. You should book about three weeks in advance for the shows, though it's always worth phoning to see if there's been a cancellation. Sunday and candlelit Monday evening tours omit the theatrical element but are still worthwhile. A word

of warning: Dennis discourages children and the 'average' businessman and tourist from coming, and expects everyone to get totally immersed in the experience. It's expensive, sure, but quite unforgettable.

Sutton House

2 & 4 Homerton High Street, E9 (0181 986 2264). Bethnal Green tube then 253, 106, D6 bus/Hackney Central rail. **Open** *historic rooms* Feb-Nov 11.30am-5.30pm Wed, Sun, public hols; 2-5.30pm Sat (last admission 5pm). **Admission** £1.90; 50p under-16s; £4.50 family ticket (2 adults, 2 children). **Credit** MC, V.
The red-brick Tudor mansion, built in 1535 for Henry VIII's First Secretary of State, is the oldest house in east London. Now owned by the National Trust, it opened as a community centre in the late 1980s after a fierce debate over its future that thankfully led to the superb restoration now on view. There are Tudor, Jacobean and Georgian interiors, as well as the Edwardian chapel and medieval foundations in the cellar. It also boasts what is possibly London's oldest loo: a sixteenth-century 'garderobe'. The café and shop here are open all year round.

Victoria Park

Old Ford Road, E3 (0181 533 2057). Mile End tube/ Cambridge Heath rail/2, 8, 26, 30, 55, 253, 277, S2 bus. **Open** 6am-dusk daily.
Fringed by the Hertford Union Canal, Victoria Park is a useful detour for those weary of Hackney's plains of cement. At the main Sewardstone Road entrance, look out for the deranged-looking Dogs of Alcibiades, which have stood here since 1912. The park's large ponds and tearooms provide it with an atmosphere generally reminiscent of Regent's Park.

South London

Stretching from regal Greenwich to rarefied Richmond, there's far more south of the river than urban sprawl.

Charlton, Woolwich & Eltham

In centuries past, few travellers relished the prospect of a journey along the Old Dover Road. At **Shooters Hill** in particular the road was steep and the countryside wild; this was a favourite spot for footpads and highwaymen to lie in wait for easy prey. Robbers who were caught were themselves shown no mercy: they were hanged at a gallows at the bottom of Shooters Hill and their bodies displayed on a gibbet at the summit. In 1661, Samuel Pepys recorded that he 'rode under a man that hangs at Shooters Hill, and a filthy sight it was to see how the flesh is shrunk from his bones'.

Charlton was a nearby village, built around the Jacobean manor **Charlton House** (*see below*). Nearby **Hornfair Park** takes its name from the Charlton Horn Fair, which was held every year until 1872. According to local tradition, the fair was started after King John seduced the wife of a local miller and, in recompense, gave her wronged husband all the land visible from Charlton to Rotherhithe. The miller's neighbours named the riverside boundary of his new land Cuckold's Point and established the annual Horn Fair (horns being the symbol of cuckoldry). Hornfair Park is now tucked away at the corner of a housing estate; **Maryon Park**, used in Antonioni's film *Blow-Up* and closer to the river, is more pleasant.

One of the most spectacular sights on the river is the **Thames Barrier** (*see below*), which stretches between Silvertown on the north bank and Woolwich on the south.

Woolwich itself attracts fewer visitors than its more glamorous neighbour Greenwich, though it has plenty to offer, including an above-average shopping centre. Long, pedestrianised Powis Street also boasts two spectacular buildings at the river end: the ruddy Edwardian Central Stores building and, opposite, the creamy-tiled, art deco Co-op.

The character of Woolwich has been shaped by strong military and naval associations. Woolwich Arsenal was established in Tudor times as the country's main source of munitions. Over the centuries it spread to colossal proportions – at its peak during World War I the site stretched 3.5 miles (5.5km) along the river and employed 72,000 people. When it closed down in 1967, much of the land was used to build the new town of **Thamesmead**, and the remaining buildings – including historic

gatehouses, foundries and engraving shops – fell into disrepair. Greenwich Council has announced plans to restore the buildings to their former grandeur and open them to the public for the first time. In the meantime, you can admire **Woolwich Garrison**, historic home of the Royal Artillery, which boasts the longest Georgian façade in the country. It's best seen from Woolwich Common or from Grand Depot Road, where the remains of the **Royal Garrison Church of St George** have been left as consecrated ground after being hit by a flying bomb in 1944 (the end walls and altar still stand). For military aficionados there is the **Museum of Artillery** (*see page 116*).

Henry VIII established the Royal Dockyard at Woolwich in 1512, initially so that his new flagship, the *Great Harry*, could be built there. The dockyard closed in 1869 and moved to Chatham. Just downstream from the Woolwich Ferry terminal, the stretch of river known as Gallions Reach was the scene of the Thames' worst-ever shipping accident. In 1878, a crowded pleasure steamer, the *Princess Alice*, was struck broadside by a collier, with the loss of some 700 lives.

The Woolwich Ferry has existed since the fourteenth century; the old paddle steamers were replaced by diesels as late as 1963. (There is also a foot tunnel.) Today, the seating area outside the Waterfront Leisure Centre, next to the terminal, is a fine spot to watch a great river at work.

Despite being despoiled by numerous bleak housing estates, there are a surprising number of green spaces in this part of south-east London, connected by the excellent **Green Chain Walk** (call 0181 312 5884 for maps). This takes in wonderful ancient woodlands such as **Oxleas Wood** (accessible from Falconwood rail station), a couple of miles south of Woolwich. A mile and a half south-west of here was the site of one of the most splendid of medieval royal palaces, **Eltham Palace** (*see below*).

Greenwich & Blackheath

Greenwich was the playground of kings and queens. Henry VIII and his daughters Mary I and Elizabeth I were born here, and Greenwich Palace (then called Placentia) was Henry's favourite residence. He could hunt in Greenwich Park and visit his beloved home fleet ('the wood wall of England')

Relaxing with a lunchtime pint after a hard morning's shopping in **Greenwich Market**.

at anchor along the river. It was at Greenwich that Sir Walter Ralegh put his cloak over a puddle so Elizabeth I wouldn't get her feet wet.

After the Tudors, the palace fell on hard times. Under Oliver Cromwell, it became first a biscuit factory, then a prison. In 1660, the newly restored Charles II embarked on an ambitious scheme to return Greenwich to its former glory. Work began on a new palace, though in the event only one riverside wing was actually built. William and Mary, who succeeded Charles, preferred the royal palaces at Kensington and Hampton Court and ordered Sir Christopher Wren to design another wing for the unfinished building, to create the Royal Naval Hospital. Better known today as the **Royal Naval College** (although the Navy moved out in 1998; *see below*), this is the great façade you see from the river today, with a central gap to allow an unobscured view of **Queen's House** behind (*see below*), now part of the superb **National Maritime Museum** (*see page 115*).

The best way to arrive at Greenwich is still by river to Greenwich Pier (*see page 304*). Alternatively, you can start from Island Gardens at the tip of the Isle of Dogs and take the Greenwich Foot Tunnel under the Thames. Either way, you'll find yourself in the shadow of the **Cutty Sark** (*see below*), built in 1869 and in dry dock here since 1954, after an adventurous life as one of the fastest tea clippers in the world. Dwarfed in comparison is the yacht **Gipsy Moth IV** (occasionally open to the public; phone 0181 858 2698 for information), in which Sir Francis Chichester made the first solo round-the-world voyage in 1966-7 (on his return he was knighted with the same sword that Elizabeth I used to ennoble Francis Drake).

The town of Greenwich is a busy, traffic-ridden place. Visitors flood in every weekend to peruse the arts and crafts stalls of sprawling **Greenwich Market** (*see page 192*). Punters aren't exactly spoilt for choice when it comes to eating establishments in the area; many fill up at **Goddard's Ye Old Pie House** at 45 Greenwich Church Street, which has been serving home-baked pies since 1890.

The church of **St Alfege Greenwich** (1712-18), on Greenwich High Road, takes its name from the Archbishop of Canterbury who was martyred on the site by marauding Vikings in 1012, after courageously refusing to sanction a demand for ransom that would have secured his release.

A walkway to the right of the *Cutty Sark* takes you past the riverside front of the Royal Naval College to the **Trafalgar Tavern**, built directly on to the river and a favourite of literary chums Dickens, Thackeray and Collins, who came regularly for seafood dinners (Dickens set the wedding feast here in *Our Mutual Friend*). Tiny Crane Street, on the far side of the pub, takes you past Victorian cottages and disused Highbridge Wharf to the bizarre, white, castellated Trinity Hospital, which, since 1617, has been home to '21 retired gentlemen of Greenwich'. Despite its proximity to Greenwich town centre, this is one of the most peaceful spots anywhere on the urban Thames. The residents must have been horrified as the huge power station next door took shape in 1903, though its quiet bulk has its own grandeur. The path continues until it reaches the **Cutty Sark Tavern**, dating from 1695. Seats outside give a good view of still-active wharfs downstream, as well as the controversial **Millennium Dome** (*see page 27*) a couple of miles downriver. The **Millennium Experience Visitor Centre** (0181 305 3456; 11am-7pm Mon-Fri; 10am-6pm Sat, Sun), next to the *Cutty Sark*, provides information about

View from **Greenwich Park** *over* **Queen's House** *(p105) and the* **National Maritime Museum**.

the project. It's around a 30-minute walk from the centre to the Dome, and a further 20 minutes to the Thames Barrier.

Hilly **Greenwich Park** (*see below*) is topped by the **Royal Observatory** (*see below*), built during the reign of Charles II. Temporally speaking, this is the centre of the planet. Greenwich Mean Time, introduced in 1890, sets the world's clocks. Here too you can straddle the Greenwich Meridian Line and stand simultaneously in the eastern and western hemispheres. Every day since 1833, the red time-ball on the north-eastern turret of the Observatory has dropped at precisely 1pm as a signal to shipmasters on the river to adjust their chronometers. At the southern end of the park stands the eighteenth-century **Ranger's House** (*see below*), exhibiting paintings from Jacobean to contemporary times.

A long road, Maze Hill, runs south from Trafalgar Road, forming the eastern boundary of Greenwich Park. At the top of the hill, at the corner of Maze Hill and Westcombe Park Road, is the castle-like house built by the architect-playwright John Vanbrugh, who lived here from 1719 to 1726. From here, the view back towards the Royal Naval College and the City is superb.

Maze Hill brings you to the edge of windswept **Blackheath**. Blackheath Village, on the far side of the heath, lies just beyond the **Princess of Wales** pub, where the first ever rugby union club, Blackheath FC, was founded in 1858. The fieldstone **All Saints Church** stands nearby, its

unusually tall, sharp spire giving the building the shape of a witch's hat. With its multiplicity of restaurants and estate agents, Blackheath Village exudes middle-class values. **The Paragon**, a crescent on the edge of the heath, lined with prestigious colonnaded houses, was built in the late eighteenth century with the express purpose of attracting the right sort of people to the area when it was still struggling to lose its reputation as a no-go area, plagued by highwaymen. Allowed to fall into disrepair in the 1920s and 1930s, and badly bombed during World War II, the crescent has since been restored to its original state.

Rotherhithe

Upriver from Greenwich, the Thames curves past down-at-heel **Deptford** (where the Royal Naval Yards once built the warships with which Britain controlled the world's seas) to **Rotherhithe**. Pepys knew Rotherhithe as Redriffe, though both names may derive from the Anglo-Saxon words 'redhra' and 'hyth' – 'mariner's haven'. The old name still holds good: Rotherhithe is relatively undisturbed by visitors, with superb views across the Thames to Wapping and two of the best riverside pubs in London. The infamous Judge Jeffreys is said to have used **The Angel** (101 Bermondsey Wall East) as a vantage point to watch pirates being executed on the opposite bank. The grassy area opposite the pub, with the remains of a few walls, is all that exists of a moated manor house, built by

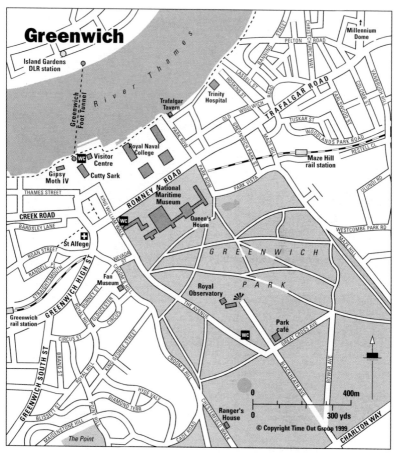

Edward III around 1355. A short walk away is **The Mayflower** (117 Rotherhithe Street), dating from 1550 and, like the Angel, built on piles so it stands directly over the river. It was given its present name when *The Mayflower* docked here in 1620 before beginning her voyage to America. Captain Christopher Jones, who commanded her, is buried in nearby **St Mary's Church**. Look out for the old school opposite the church, with its carved figures of eighteenth-century schoolchildren.

The distinctive green spire next to the approach to **Rotherhithe Tunnel** belongs to the **Norsk Kirke**, or Norwegian Church, one of a trio of Scandinavian seamen's missions in Rotherhithe (there's a Finnish one in Albion Road, and a Swedish one in Lower Road). All three of them date from the heyday of Surrey Docks, when timber-carrying ships plied the North Sea. Look out for the Norwegian street signs in St Olave Square,

immediately outside Norsk Kirke. To the south, Canada Water station forms part of the much-delayed Jubilee Line extension.

Following the line of the Thames as it flows around the Rotherhithe peninsula, **Rotherhithe Street** is one of the longest streets in London. A three-masted sailing barque, built for the French Navy in 1952 and now serving as a rather pricey restaurant, breaks the monotonous line of new, mock-Georgian residential blocks. Opposite **Surrey Docks Farm**, cut down Holyoake Close, cross Salter Road and go along Downtown Road to reach **Russia Dock Woodland and Ecological Park**, a semi-wilderness and Rotherhithe's only green space of any size. Not too far away, though, is **Southwark Park**, which contains a lido and the excellent **Café Gallery**, featuring monthly changing exhibitions of contemporary art.

Peckham, Dulwich & Camberwell

Much of south London is stigmatised as a dull, amorphous sprawl. But this (predominantly north Londoner) prejudice masks a patchwork of communities of often individual character and (sometimes hidden) charm.

Finding such charm in **Peckham** is, admittedly, a challenge. Like many districts of south London, this was a quiet rural area until the Industrial Revolution. It was a favourite stopping place for cattle drovers on their way to markets in the City; they would leave their herds grazing on the common, **Peckham Rye**, while they refreshed themselves at the inns along Peckham High Street. As a child, William Blake saw a vision of angels on the Rye, and in her novel *The Ballad of Peckham Rye* (1960), Muriel Spark refers, apparently without irony, to 'the dusky scope of the Rye's broad lyrical acres'. (Drinkers: she also maps out a useful pub crawl on page one.) The Victorian terraces that feature in the novel have now mostly gone, replaced by monolithic council estates and tower blocks.

West of here, long **Lordship Lane** is the main thoroughfare through more sedate **Dulwich**. (Its only pub of real distinction is the **East Dulwich Tavern**, on the corner of Spurling Road, but there are plenty of decent cheap restaurants.) **Dulwich Park**, with its dramatic view of the Crystal Palace TV transmitter (in **Crystal Palace Park**; *see below*), and adjoining **Dulwich Village** lie at the southern tip of Lordship Lane. Dotted with modern sculpture, the grounds of **Dulwich Picture Gallery** (*see page 128*) are a pleasant place to sit even when the gallery itself is closed (which, alas, it is until May 2000 for major refurbishment work). The rarefied atmosphere of the Village, with its distinctive dark brick, is as great a contrast to rough-and-tumble Peckham as you could imagine. Heading south out of the Village, College Road is lined with fine detached houses. At **Dulwich Common** a spectacular sight greets you: palatial, red-brick **Dulwich College**, serene in its verdant grounds. Old boys include PG Wodehouse and Raymond Chandler. Close by is the marvellously eccentric **Horniman Museum** (*see page 119*).

Between Brixton and Peckham, **Camberwell** was a country village until the mid-nineteenth century. The composer Felix Mendelssohn lived in Southampton Street; his *Spring Song*, written in 1842, was originally entitled 'Camberwell Green', after the former village green next to what is now the junction of Camberwell Road and Denmark Hill. Today, the Green is just a small, bare park. Camberwell's best feature is **Camberwell Grove**, a steep hill lined with tall Georgian houses. Its golden-lit drawing rooms, reminiscent of Henry James novels, are an enticing sight at dusk. At the eastern end of Camberwell Church Street, **St Giles**

Echoes of Egypt: **Crystal Palace Park** (*p104*).

Church, built to the designs of Sir George Gilbert Scott (1844), has grown mossy over the years and, with its 210-ft (72-m) spire, now seems embarrassingly big for its surroundings.

Stockwell, Kennington & Vauxhall

Stockwell was, at one time, a medieval manor, with the manor house on the site of present-day Stockwell Gardens, off Stockwell Road. Until the feverish house- and railway-building of the 1840s, Stockwell remained a country village. South Lambeth Common, on which cattle used to graze, has now been reduced to the scrap of green bearing the clock tower and war memorial outside Stockwell tube station.

St Mark's Church, between Prima Road and Camberwell New Road, was built in 1824 on the site of a gallows; many of the Jacobites who fought in the 1745 rebellion were hanged, drawn and quartered here. Nearby **Kennington Park** was originally Kennington Common. In the eighteenth and nineteenth centuries, preachers – among them John Wesley – addressed large audiences here. Today, Kennington is best known for its sporting connections. The **Foster's Oval** cricket ground (*see page 261*) is the home of Surrey County Cricket Club. Opened in 1845, it has hosted not only Test matches but most of the football FA Cup finals between 1870 and 1890.

The continuation of Kennington Lane beyond the junction with Kennington Road brings you to some of south London's most delightful streets – **Cardigan Street**, **Courtney Street** and **Courtney Square** are lined with clean, neat, light-brown terraced houses, all dating from 1914 and featuring matching white ironwork porches and railings. The rather unexpected glimpse of the Palace of Westminster from Cardigan Road is a reminder of how close the area is to central London.

The dull office buildings at the corner of Kennington Road and Kennington Lane stand on the site of Kennington Palace, built by the first Duke of Cornwall (the 'Black Prince') in the fourteenth century and used until the reign of Henry VII. The palace's founder is commemorated by nearby Black Prince Road (complete with Black Prince pub). Opposite the desolate, disused bingo hall by the pub is a line of forbidding four-storey Victorian houses; the young Charlie Chaplin spent part of his childhood at no.287.

Vauxhall lies between Kennington and the Thames. The wasteland bounded by Tyers Street, Goding Street and Glasshouse Walk is all that remains of the eighteenth-century pleasure park, **Vauxhall Gardens**. Henry Fielding's novel *Amelia* and Thackeray's *Vanity Fair* give a taste of the Gardens at their peak. In 1802, they were the setting for one of Britain's first balloon ascents; fittingly, the site is now used for the **London Balloon** (*see below*).

Nineties Vauxhall is not a pretty sight. Its hub, near Vauxhall station, consists of a formidable road junction, bisected by a railway viaduct. Late on Friday and Saturday nights, the area tries to put on a cheerful face, when the **Royal Vauxhall Tavern** (*see page 241*), one of south London's most popular gay venues, throbs into life. There is also a lively Portuguese community in the area (and some good restaurants, most notably **Bar Estrela**, 111-115 South Lambeth Road).

Brixton

Brixton has existed, in various guises, for around a thousand years, of which the first 985 or so were relatively uneventful. The small settlement here in the early nineteenth century underwent intense development between the 1860s and 1890s, as railways and trams linked it with the heart of London. Around the turn of the century, the social character of Brixton began to alter, as the large houses built along the trunk roads 100 years earlier were turned into flats and boarding houses. The latter were popular with theatre people working in the West End. In 1955, John Major's father, a circus and music-hall artiste, moved with his family to a two-room flat at 144 Coldharbour Lane.

Brixton's ethnic identity changed during the 1940s and 1950s, with the arrival of immigrants from the West Indies. A generation later, simmering hostility between the black community and the police, combined with economic decline, culminated in serious rioting in 1981, and again in 1985 and 1995.

Yet today the mood in Brixton is resolutely upbeat. Problems (particularly drug-related ones) certainly remain, but the recent overflow of

---

Top tours: On yer bike

A two-wheeled riverside odyssey

Hire bikes from **Bikepark** in Covent Garden (from 7.30am Mon-Fri; from 10am Sat; *see p301*) or **London Bicycle Tour Company** in Gabriel's Wharf on the South Bank (Easter-Oct from 10am daily; *see p301*).

Cycle to **Waterloo Station** and catch a train to **Richmond** (up to 12 per hour; journey time from 18 minutes).

Head for the riverside and take the waterside path heading south towards **Teddington Lock and Weir** (3 miles/5km), passing seventeenth-century **Ham House**.

At Teddington Lock cut inland through suburban Ham, asking directions to the Ham Gate of **Richmond Park**. Commune with the park's deer and enjoy fabulous views north towards the city and south over Surrey.

Leave the park by the north-westerly Richmond Gate and freewheel down Richmond Hill back in to **Richmond**.

Have a break to peruse the shops, and down a drink and a snack. Then pick up the riverside path heading north around the Old Deer Park, gazing across the river to **Syon House**, and **Kew Gardens** (3 miles/5km). Pop in for some greenhouse gazing and a stroll around the grounds.

Time for a mid-afternoon cuppa at one of the cafés in **Kew Village** (the **Hot House** is the pick) or, just over Kew Bridge on the east side, a pint or three at the trio of riverside pubs along the cutesy strip of **Strand-on-the-Green**.

Pick up the riverside path on the south bank again and continue as far as your energy and inclination take you. Trains back to Waterloo can be picked up at **Mortlake** (near Chiswick Bridge; 1.5 miles/2km from Kew), **Barnes Bridge** (1 mile/1.5km further) and **Putney** (3.5miles/5.5km further).

(Note that there may be restrictions on taking bicycles on trains during rush hour).

Top tours: Maritime London

Boats, boozers and naval gazing

Catch a riverboat to **Greenwich** from Westminster Pier, Victoria Embankment (by Westminster Bridge; approx every 30 mins; first 10.30am, or 10am June-Aug; 45 mins journey time; *see also p304*).

Check out Sir Francis Chichester's tiny circumnavigatory wonder **Gipsy Moth IV** and the celebrated tea clipper **Cutty Sark** (*see p104*).

Visit the ever-expanding and ever-more impressive **National Maritime Museum** (*see p115*).

Grab some lunch, perhaps fish and chips, at the historic riverside **Trafalgar Tavern** close to the former **Royal Naval College**.

Take the Greenwich Foot Tunnel by the Cutty Sark under the Thames to Island Gardens DLR station and jump on a train through Docklands to **Limehouse** to see what happens to once-mighty docks when they die.

Walk via Limehouse Basin west along The Highway down to redeveloped **Wapping**, a formerly vibrant if insalubrious docks-and-taverns hub, for a pint in one of the (often distressingly overtouristed) historic riverside pubs or take the East London Line tube from Wapping one stop south of the river to **Rotherhithe**, another ancient maritime village, for a jar in the **Mayflower** pub where Christopher Jones, captain of the ship of the same name, supped and then set off for the New World.

Take a bus back towards Tower Bridge or London Bridge where, if you have the stamina, there are more nautical distractions in the shape of the mighty **HMS Belfast** (*see p33*) and, on a far smaller and more personal scale, the replica of Sir Francis Drake's **Golden Hinde** (*see p32*). Both are particularly good fun for kids.

youngish, middle-class money from neighbouring Clapham (*see below*) has added a new element to the mix. A residual 'edge' remains from darker days, but, now that trendy bars, restaurants and clubs are springing up, this serves to give the place an exciting rather than dangerous vibe. A positive sign is that buzzing bar/restaurants such as the **Satay Bar** (*see page 174*) and clubs like **The Fridge** (*see page 222*), **Mass** (*see page 227*) and the **Bug Bar** (*see page 222*) attract a racially mixed crowd more concerned with cool clothes, hot music and having a good time than racial politics. The **Dogstar** (*see page 222*) is another thriving bar/club, which does a good line in comedy. Food options include the crypt-ensconced vegetarian **Bah Humbug** (*see page 178*), the modern international fare of **Helter Skelter** (*see page 167*) and the noodle bar **Fujiyama** (*see page 101* **Top tours: Deep South**). Brixton is also home to London's friendliest gay B&B, **Number Seven** (*see page 243*).

Much of the centre of Brixton does, though, for the time being at least, remain rather rundown, with few appealing shops. Emerging from the tube station to a chorus of shouts from incense-sellers, *Big Issue* vendors, drunks and the odd apocalyptic preacher can be quite a shock for the unwary. And there's plenty more noise, chaos and colour in evidence in **Brixton Market** (*see page 101*), which offers the widest selection of African and Caribbean food in Europe, as well as everything from wigs to ironing boards. Possibly the best way to experience the market is to sit at one of the tables

*Sample the colour, cacophony and Caribbean food at **Brixton Market***: *one of London's most full-on shopping experiences.*

outside tiny **Eco Brixton** (4 Market Row). The market sprawls – partly under cover – between Electric Avenue and Brixton Station Road. The former was so named in the 1880s when it became the first street in the area to be lit by electricity (and was later immortalised in song by Eddy Grant).

More serene attractions of the area include hilly **Brockwell Park**, 15 minutes' walk from the tube station, with its 1930s-built lido (*see page 259*), and the exemplary **Ritzy** cinema (*see page 238*).

Clapham

Clapham has two centres: **Clapham Junction** (technically part of Battersea) and **Clapham Common**. Until the railways arrived, Clapham Junction was a country crossroads, with **The Falcon** providing refreshment for travellers. Nowadays, the pub provides respite for shoppers: Clapham's own department store, **Arding & Hobbs**, opposite, has been serving the area since 1885. With more than 2,500 trains passing through every day, Clapham Junction is one of the busiest stations in the world.

Battersea Rise, leading towards the Common, is a somewhat arty stretch, with a good choice of restaurants, especially the decidedly non-veggie **La Pampa**, an Argentinian grill joint dishing up hefty portions of meat. **Northcote Road**, running at right angles to Battersea Rise, is a rapidly developing bar and restaurant alley that still (just) clings on to its street fruit and vegetable market. Beyond the junction with Bramfield Road is a stretch of antique shops. **The Hive**, at 53 Webb's Road (parallel to Northcote Road), is one of the most extraordinary shops in south London. Devoted entirely to bees and their products, it features a huge glass hive containing 20,000 live bees, linked to the outside world by a tunnel opening on to the street.

Battersea Rise eventually becomes Clapham Common North Side, the eastern reaches of which contain tall, stately houses with enviable views of the Common. A flat, grassy expanse within a triangle of roads, **Clapham Common** is somewhere between a park and a wild place; its bleak atmosphere has never been more vividly evoked than in Graham Greene's *The End of the Affair*. After dark, parts of the Common have gained a reputation as gay cruising grounds; it was here that ex-Welsh Secretary Ron Davies experienced his ill-defined 'moment of madness' in October 1998, leading to one of the more bizarre political scandals of recent years.

The streets around the north end of Clapham Common are transforming from down-at-heel to desirable at an extraordinary rate. A sure sign of this is the proliferation of good new bars and restaurants (try laidback French **Gastro** at 67 Venn Street; the pizzas at trendy **Eco**, 162 Clapham High Street; or cheap Thai scoff at **Pepper Tree**, 19 Clapham Common Southside).

There's more than a whiff of snobbery about genteel **Clapham Old Town**, just north-east of the Common, but it's worth a visit, if only to take in the villagey atmosphere – especially at its central point, where eighteenth-century pubs face on to an approximate square (complete with a small, countryish bus terminus). The 88 bus, rather self-consciously styled 'The Clapham Omnibus', starts its pleasantly circuitous route from here.

Famous for its lush setting on the edge of the common, **Holy Trinity Church** was well known in the nineteenth century as the headquarters of the Clapham Sect, a group of wealthy Anglicans who advocated 'muscular Christianity'; one of them was William Wilberforce, the anti-slavery campaigner. The church was rebuilt after being hit by a V2 in 1945. For breakfast, or a spot of afternoon tea, the determinedly camp **Tea-time**, at 21 The Pavement, is recommended.

Battersea

In Saxon times, **Battersea** was a small settlement known as Batrices Ege (Badric's Island), bounded by the Thames to the north and marshes to the south. Known for centuries as a centre for market gardening (part of it is still called Lavender Hill), the character of Battersea changed dramatically with the Industrial Revolution. In the nineteenth century, scores of factories sprang up, and the area was covered by a dense network of railway lines.

Battersea is still best approached by rail. The journey from Victoria Station will give you the best possible view of its best-known landmark, Sir Giles Gilbert Scott's gargantuan

Battersea Power Station (built 1929-33). Closed in 1983, it has been subject to innumerable development plans. Occasional events are held in the shell of the building, but its long-term future remains uncertain.

Battersea Park (*see below*), bordering the river, has a bloody history: in 1671 Colonel Blood hid in reeds near what is now the boating lake, waiting to shoot King Charles II as he bathed (Blood's nerve failed him); and in 1829 the Duke of Wellington fought a pistol duel here with Lord Winchilsea, who had accused him of treason for introducing the Catholic Emancipation Bill. Between the Power Station and the Park, **Adrenalin Village** (*see page 257*) offers metropolitan bungee jumping.

Battersea has long been a favourite spot for artists and writers: the old **Battersea Bridge** was the subject of Whistler's moody *Nocturnes*; Turner used to paint the river and its sunsets from **St Mary's Battersea** (and William Blake married the daughter of a local market gardener here); more recently, the Pogues celebrated **Battersea Bridge**'s next-door neighbour in 'Misty Morning, Albert Bridge'.

Putney, Mortlake & Kew

Originally a fishing and farming community, **Putney** ('Putta's landing') can claim to be London's first suburb. Thomas Cromwell was the most senior among the scores of Tudor courtiers who bought homes in the village and travelled to their jobs in the royal palaces around west London.

Away from the narrow, busy High Street, Putney is a peaceful place, especially if you head west from the bridge along the Embankment, with its ubiquitous canoe trailers hitched to Land Rovers. The annual **Boat Race** (*see page 7*) is held between here and Mortlake. Look out for the other **Putney Bridge**, this one a bar-restaurant resembling a cross between a boat and a pre-war tube station. There are a number of other good restaurants in the area (including the fine Italians **Riva** and **Del Buongustaio**; *for both see page 173*).

Striking inland across the base of the Putney peninsula eventually brings you to **Mortlake**. On the way, the main road, Queen's Ride, crosses a railway line at **Barnes Common**. On the western side of the humpbacked bridge, there's a spindly tree invariably decorated with flowers and other offerings to Marc Bolan. On 16 September 1977, the T-Rex singer's Mini collided with the tree, killing him instantly.

Like Putney, Mortlake is a former riverside village that was gradually overtaken by genteel suburbia. A little of its original character remains in Christ Church Road, with its brick workers' cottages and the cosy white-painted **Plough** (*see page 147*). Mortlake High Street takes you past the old brewery and **The Limes** (123 Mortlake High Street), a Georgian mansion built for the Countess of Strafford and now used as offices.

Kew is all but synonymous with **Kew Gardens** (more properly known as the **Royal Botanic Gardens**; *see below*), which maintains its position as the world's principal botanical research centre. In cutesy Kew Village you can find refreshment at the **Flower & Firkin** pub, whose conservatory backs on to the station platform, and the airy, arty **Hothouse** café-bar.

If you're heading for the Gardens themselves, Lichfield Road takes you to Kew Road and one of the Gardens' entrances. A few hundred metres to the north is the old-fashioned **Maids of Honour** teashop (288 Kew Road), with its fine home-made cakes and pastries, **Kew Green**, with its cricket ground surrounded by pubs, and, in a corner, long, low, elegant **St Anne's Church**, built for Queen Anne in 1714. Its interior, with fine stained glass, is superbly clear and bright.

Wimbledon

Just as most people think of Kew as its Gardens, most non-Londoners equate **Wimbledon** with its two-week tennis tournament (*see page 263*) or with the recently revived, cuddly, litter-collecting **Wombles**. For the rest of the year, the place is pretty much left to its own devices. **Wimbledon Broadway** is dominated by the massive **Centre Court** shopping centre, and, a little further east, **Wimbledon Theatre** – an entertaining example of Edwardian architecture at its most feverish. There's a scattering of decent bars and restaurants here if you don't fancy the hike up the formidably steep Wimbledon Hill Road to **Wimbledon Village**. The latter is a moneyed, country-town-ish sort of place that looks down its nose at the suburbia at the bottom of the hill. Best of the pubs here is the seventeenth-century **Rose & Crown** (near the junction of Marryat Road and Parkside).

Beyond lies **Wimbledon Common**, a huge, partially wooded expanse, criss-crossed with paths and horse tracks; it's easy to get lost here. The windmill towards the north-east corner dates from 1817. Baden-Powell (*see page 120*) wrote part of *Scouting for Boys* while living in the windmill in 1908. The museum it now houses closes during the winter, although the large tearoom is open all year round. **Putney Vale Cemetery**, in the north-east corner of the Common (accessible from Roehampton Vale), is one of the largest graveyards in London. Lillie Langtry was buried here in 1929.

On the east side of the common, the disused **Bluegate Gravel Pit** forms an idyllic lake, whose peace and quiet is barely disturbed by the murmur of traffic on Parkside. Cross the road and go down Calonne Road to discover Wimbledon's biggest surprise. Amid prime south London sub-urbia (all pre-war villas and new Rovers at rest) is a fully fledged Thai Buddhist temple, the **Buddhapadipa Temple**. Visitors are free to look around (1-6pm Sat; 8.30-10.30am, 12.30-6pm, Sun). Close by is the All England Lawn Tennis Club and the **Wimbledon Lawn Tennis Museum** (*see page 123*). Next door, **Wimbledon Park** has public tennis courts and a large boating lake.

Richmond

Richmond still resembles what it once was – a busy, cramped English country town – though the rural calm has long since been supplanted by heavy traffic and the roar of low-flying jets approaching Heathrow. Until the early sixteenth century, the whole area was called Sheen, receiving its new name when Henry VII acquired the local manor house and called it after his earldom in Yorkshire. Elizabeth I spent her last few summers at Richmond and died there in 1603, but Richmond Palace fell into neglect. All that remains is a gateway on Richmond Green, bearing the arms of Henry VII, and **Old Palace Yard** beyond. The long building on the left is **The Wardrobe**, once used to house the palace furnishings.

Richmond station stands opposite the **Bull & Bush** pub – formerly the Station Hotel and, in its heyday in the early to mid-1960s, HQ of the British blues scene. The Rolling Stones were the house band in their early days, and Elton John, Rod Stewart, the Small Faces and Long John Baldry all cut their musical teeth here.

George Street and **The Quadrant** form Richmond's nexus, lined with shops and restaurants. Alley-like Brewer's Lane, with its rows of antique shops, takes you to **Richmond Green**, bigger and less appealing than Kew Green, though it is enlivened at one end by the twin-cupola'd **Richmond Theatre**. The church of **St Mary Magdalene**, in (where else but) Paradise Road, is worth a look for its hectic combination of architectural styles, dating from 1507 to 1904.

Despite its period look, **Richmond Riverside**, near **Richmond Bridge**, was built in the 1980s, the mock Georgian-style façades concealing ordinary offices and flats. The genuinely Victorian town hall houses the public library, tourist office and **Museum of Richmond** (*see page 121*).

Good eating options are scarce in Richmond. Exceptions are the seafood and pancake-based **Chez Lindsay** (*see page 165*) and the hip **Canyon** (*see page 160*) by Richmond Bridge. For Sunday lunch try the **White Cross** on the riverside, at the bottom of Water Lane.

Ultimately, Richmond is a place for enjoying the Great Outdoors. With the exception of Epping Forest, **Richmond Park** (*see below*) is the last vestige of the great oak forests that surrounded London until medieval times. In 1727, the poet

James Thomson exclaimed of **Richmond Hill**: 'Heavens! What a goodly perspective spreads around, of hills and dales and woods and lawns and spires and glittering towns and gilded streams.' The view has changed little, except that the glittering towns have merged to form a glittering city. Close to the top of Richmond Hill, the **Terrace Gardens** descend steeply towards the river (there's a café halfway down). If the river isn't flooding, you can follow its meandering course towards **Petersham** and **Ham**. The Thames is at its most tranquil here and, in the early morning and evening, **Petersham Meadows** are almost impossibly pastoral – brown cattle grazing on water meadows beside the misty river.

Further south

Following the Thames south from Richmond (a delightful walk or bike ride) takes you close to a clutch of fine country villas. **Marble Hill House** and neighbouring **Orleans House** square up across the river to **Ham House** (for all, *see below*). Past **Twickenham** (home to the **Museum of Rugby**; *see page 123*) is Horace Walpole's idiosyncratic home, **Strawberry Hill**, before the river reaches the busy shopping centre of **Kingston** and curves around to magnificent **Hampton Court Palace** (*see below*).

Sights

Battersea Park
Albert Bridge Road, SW11 (0181 871 7530). Sloane Square tube/Battersea Park or Queenstown Road rail. **Open** 8am-dusk daily (later during events). **Map 4 F13**
Lively Battersea Park, opened in 1858 by Queen Victoria, was conceived as a means of keeping the lower orders orderly with healthful recreation. These days its patrons are more mixed, though still generally orderly. Its most famous feature, **Festival Gardens**, was one of the attractions of the 1951 Festival of Britain. There are sports facilities and playgrounds, a boating lake, a café, a children's zoo, Bank Holiday funfairs and other events throughout the year. The Peace Pagoda by the Thames was built by Japanese monks and nuns in 1985 to commemorate Hiroshima Day. The park is due to be restored to its original Victorian design as part of a massive £13-million revamp.

Charlton House
Charlton Road, SE7 (0181 856 3951). Charlton rail/53, 54, 177, 180, 380 bus. **Open** 8am-11pm Mon-Fri; 8am-5.30pm Sat (guided tours can be arranged at £25 a tour, minimum 20 people).
The finest Jacobean house in London, and possibly in the country, red-brick Charlton House was built in 1612 as a retirement gift for Adam Newton, tutor to Prince Henry, son of James I. It's not known for certain who the architect was, though John Thorpe is the most likely contender; the orangery is almost certainly the work of Inigo Jones. The building now enjoys a useful if humdrum existence as a public library and community centre.

Crystal Palace Park
SE19 (no phone). Crystal Palace rail/2B, 3, 63, 108B, 122, 137, 157, 227, 249 bus. **Open** dawn-dusk daily.

Built to house the 1851 Great Exhibition, the all-glass Crystal Palace was originally erected in Hyde Park. After the Exhibition closed, the building was moved to Sydenham, where it was used for exhibitions, plays and concerts. The extensive grounds contained an amusement park and, dotted here and there, life-sized models of dinosaurs. In 1936, the Crystal Palace caught fire and was burned to the ground; the **Crystal Palace Museum** (*see p121*) chronicles the Palace's history. The model dinosaurs, which survived the blaze and are now classified as listed buildings, are a reminder of how quirky the whole place was in its heyday. Views from the park – which contains the **National Sports Centre** (*see p263*) – are stunning.

Cutty Sark
King William Walk, SE10 (0181 858 3445). Greenwich or Maze Hill rail/Island Gardens DLR then Greenwich foot tunnel. **Open** *June-Sept* 10am-6pm Mon-Sat; noon-6pm Sun; *Oct-May* 10am-5pm Mon-Sat; noon-5pm Sun (last admission 30 mins before closing). **Admission** £3.50; £2.50 concs; £8.50 family ticket; free under-5s. **Credit** MC, V. **Map** *see p97*
The world's only surviving tea and wool clipper, this 1869 vessel smashed speed records. Visitors are free to roam the beautifully restored decks and crew's quarters, and gaze up at the rigging. Inside are collections of prints and naval relics, plus the world's largest collection of carved and painted figureheads. On summer weekends there are popular costume storytelling sessions, reliving life aboard the ship.

Eltham Palace
Eltham (off Court Road), SE9 (0181 294 2548). Eltham or Mottingham rail. **Open** *16 June-30 Sept* 10am-6pm Wed-Fri, Sun; *1-31 Oct* 10am-5pm Wed-Fri, Sun; *1 Nov-31 Mar* 10am-4pm Wed-Fri, Sun. **Admission** *house & grounds* £5.50; £2.75-£4.10 concs; *grounds only* £3.30; £1.65-£2.50 concs. **Credit** MC, V.
The only surviving parts of this once-magnificent medieval palace are the spectacular fifteenth-century Great Hall with its hammer-beam roof and the bridge over the moat. Henry VIII spent much of his childhood here, but the palace at Greenwich eventually supplanted Eltham in royal affections and was largely ruined by the seventeenth century. In the 1930s a modernist country house was built beside the old palace by the wealthy Courtauld family. It was occupied by the Ministry of Defence from World War II until 1995 when English Heritage took over the place. After renovation work, the Palace and Courtauld house (and the grounds) will be open to the public from June 1999, but ring first to check.

Greenwich Park
Charlton Way, SE10 (0181 858 2608). Blackheath, Greenwich or Maze Hill rail/Island Gardens DLR then Greenwich foot tunnel. **Open** *pedestrians* 5am-dusk daily; *traffic* 7am-dusk daily. **Map** *see p97*
The remains of 20 Saxon grave mounds and a Roman temple have been identified within its precincts, but this beautiful riverside park is more famous for its Tudor and Stuart history. Henry VIII was born at Greenwich Palace and it remained his favourite residence, surrounded by a magnificent park for hunting and hawking. In 1616, James I commissioned Inigo Jones to rebuild the Tudor palace. The result was **Queen's House** (*see below*), England's first Palladian villa. In the 1660s, the park was redesigned by André Le Nôtre, who landscaped Versailles, but Charles II's plan for a new palace was later adapted to become the **Royal Naval College** (*see below*). Crowning the hill at the top of the park are the **Royal Observatory** (*see below*) and Flamsteed House, both designed by Wren. The **Ranger's House** (*see below*), in the south of the park, is also well worth a visit. The view from the Observatory towards the river is one of the finest in London. In summer, brass bands perform in the afternoon, and there are puppet shows in the playground during August.

Top tours: Deep south

Bars and pubs, pools and clubs – and some fine museums

Take the tube to Lambeth North. Breakfast at classic Anglo-Italian caff **Perdoni's** at 18 Kennington Road (closed Sun).

Stroll across to the absorbing **Imperial War Museum** (*see p114*) for a couple of hours' pondering on the phenomenally bloody twentieth century.

If you're feeling brave, walk down St George's Road to astonishingly hideous **Elephant & Castle** for a glimpse of 1960s urban (un)planning at its worst.

Catch a bus to **Brixton**. Wander the colourful, chaotic market (closed Wed pm & Sun; *see p192*) and munch pizza at **Eco Brixton** (4 Market Row, off Electric Lane).

Walk down Effra Road and Brixton Water Lane to hilly **Brockwell Park**. On a fine day, take a plunge in **Brockwell Lido** (*see p259*) on the Dulwich Road side of the park.

Take bus P4 to the delightfully idiosyncratic **Horniman Museum** (*see p119*) in Forest Hill, then return to Brixton for evening fun.

On summer Fridays, the alfresco evening barbecues at **Brockwell Lido** are an institution (advance booking advised; *0171 274 3088*). Otherwise, check out Brixton's burgeoning restaurant scene. **Helter Skelter** (*see p167*), noodle bar **Fujiyama** (7 Vining Street; 0171 737 2369), vegetarian-in-a-crypt **Bah Humbug** (*see p178*) and the lively **Satay Bar** (*see p174*) are all winners. The **Bug Bar**, **Dogstar** and the **Fridge Bar** (*for all, see p222*) are the hippest bars – and become clubs later in the evening.

Ham House

Ham, Richmond, Surrey (0181 940 1950). Richmond tube/rail then 371 bus. **Open** *house* end Mar-Oct 1-5pm Mon-Wed, Sat, Sun; *gardens* 10.30am-6pm (or dusk) Mon-Wed, Sat, Sun. **Admission** *house & garden* £5; £2.50 children; £12.50 family ticket; *garden only* £1.50; 75p children. **Credit** AmEx, MC, £TC, V.

This handsome, red-brick, seventeenth-century riverside mansion has been restored with all its over-the-top furnishings and decorations. Surrounded by water meadows, the formal garden and 'widderness' look much as they did 300 years ago. Its recent painting in a distinctly garish shade, despite supposedly being authentic, has not met with universal approval.

Hampton Court Palace

East Molesey, Surrey (0181 781 9500). Hampton Court rail/riverboat from Westminster or Richmond to Hampton Court Pier (Apr-Oct). **Open** *Palace* Apr-Oct 10.15am-6pm Mon; 9.30am-6pm Tue-Sun; *Nov-Mar* 10.15am-4.30pm Mon; 9.30am-4.30pm Tue-Sun (last admission 45 mins before closing). *Park* dawn-dusk daily. **Admission** *Palace, courtyard, cloister & maze* £9.25; £6.10-£7 concs; £27.65 family ticket; free under-5s. *Maze only* £2.10; £1.30 concs. **Credit** AmEx, MC, £TC, V.

Yup, it's pricey – but, as you can easily spend the best part of a day wandering the corridors and gardens of Hampton Court, it's also good value for money. In 1514, the powerful Cardinal Wolsey started to build up Hampton Court as his country seat. After his fall from favour in 1529, Henry VIII took over the Palace – his additions include the fabulous vaulted ceiling of the **Chapel Royal**, which took 100 men nine months to complete. In the 1690s, William and Mary commissioned Christopher Wren to rebuild the **State Apartments** in classical Renaissance style (the **King's Apartments**, badly damaged by fire in 1986, have been splendidly restored).

Sensibly, the Palace has been split into six bite-size tours. Highlights include the **Renaissance Picture Gallery**, Henry VIII's hammer-beam-roofed **Great Hall**, and the **Tudor Kitchens**. The latter is perhaps the most fun part of the whole palace – period-dressed minions make six-teenth-century dishes, turn meat on a spit and chat to visitors. Elsewhere, costumed guides lead tours and there's foolery several times a day in **Clock Court**, overlooked by the magnificent Astronomical Clock, made for Henry VIII in 1540 by Nicholas Oursian.

The extensive gardens are an attraction in themselves. Look out for the **Great Vine**, the oldest known vine in the world. It was probably planted by Capability Brown around 1770 and still produces an annual crop of 500-700lbs (230-320kg) of black grapes, which are sold to visitors. Another must-see, or rather, must-get-lost-in, is the famous **maze**. Many a cynic has come unstuck here.

The London Balloon

Tyer Street, SE11 (0345 023842/0171 587 1111). **Open** 10am-dusk daily. **Admission** £12 adults; £7.50 under-12s. **Credit** MC, V.

Proudly advertising itself as the first tethered balloon flight in the UK, the London Balloon takes you high above the city, to heights of up to 500ft (170m), weather permitting.

Marble Hill House

Richmond Road, Twickenham, Middx (0181 892 5115). Richmond tube/rail/33, 90, 290, H22, R70 bus. **Open** *Apr-mid-Oct* 10am-6pm daily; *mid-Oct-Mar* 10am-4pm Wed-Sun. **Admission** £3; £1.50-£2.30 concs. **Credit** MC, V.

Marble Hill House, overlooking the Thames in Marble Hill Park, is a perfect Palladian villa. It was built for Henrietta Howard, the mistress of George II, and later occupied by Mrs Fitzherbert, George IV's secret wife. The interior Cube Hall has beautiful moulded decoration, and the house has been immaculately restored with original Georgian furnishings. On Sunday evenings in summer there are concerts in the park (*see p247*).

Orleans House

Riverside, Twickenham, Middx (0181 892 0221). St Margaret's rail. **Open** *Apr-Sept* 1-5.30pm Tue-Sat; 2-5.30pm Sun; *Oct-Mar* 1-4.30pm Tue-Sat; 2-4.30pm Sun. **Admission** £1; free under-16s.

Built in 1710 for James Johnston, William III's Secretary of State for Scotland, this was later home to the exiled Duke of Orléans – hence the name. The building was demolished in 1926, with the exception of the Octagon, an eight-sided turret that had formed part of the west wing. A gallery was subsequently built on the site of the main house, and both it and the Octagon are still used for exhibitions.

Queen's House

Romney Road, SE10 (0181 858 4422). Greenwich or Maze Hill rail/Island Gardens DLR then Greenwich foot

tunnel. **Open** *see note below.* **Tours** every 15 mins.
Admission *see Royal Observatory above.*
Credit AmEx, DC, JCB, MC, £TC, V. **Map** *see p97*
Furnished as it would have been in the seventeenth century, this was the first Palladian-style villa in Britain. It was designed by Inigo Jones in 1616 for James I's wife, Anne of Denmark, who died before it was finished. The tour takes visitors through the maze of rooms that makes up the first-floor apartments. Some of the original architectural features are intact, though the furniture is reproduction copies of seventeenth-century pieces.

Note that the Queen's House is closed from 4 January until 1 December 1999. Upon reopening it will house **The Story of Time** exhibition (until 31 Aug 2000; 10am-5pm daily). This will take over the entire house (all the original paintings and furniture will be removed during this period). Visitors may be charged an additional admission price (unknown at the time this guide went to press).

Ranger's House
Chesterfield Walk, SE10 (0181 853 0035). Blackheath or Maze Hill rail. **Open** *Apr-Oct* 10am-6pm daily; *Nov-Mar* 10am-4pm Wed-Sun. **Admission** £2.50; £1.30-£1.90 concs. **Map** *see p97*
A lovely red-brick eighteenth-century villa housing the Suffolk collection of Jacobean and Stuart portraits, alongside exhibitions of contemporary and local art. In the Coach House there's a study centre dedicated to seventeenth-, eighteenth- and nineteenth-century English urban architecture.

Richmond Park
Richmond, Surrey (0181 948 3209). Richmond tube/rail then 371 bus. **Open** *Mar-Sept* 7am-30 mins before dusk daily; *Oct-Feb* 7.30am-30 mins before dusk daily.
Once a royal hunting ground, Richmond Park covers a massive 2,500 acres (1,010ha), and offers superb views over London and Surrey. It's ideal for rambling, cycling and riding, and is also home to much wildlife – most famously red and fallow deer. Notable buildings here include **Pembroke Lodge** (now a café), childhood home of philosopher Bertrand Russell, and the fine Palladian villa, **White Lodge**. Don't miss the exquisite **Isabella Plantation**, a woodland haven landscaped with a stream, ponds and spectacular floral displays.

Royal Botanic Gardens (Kew Gardens)
Richmond, Surrey (0181 332 5000/recorded info 0181 940 1171). Kew Gardens tube/rail/Kew Bridge rail/ riverboat to Kew Pier. **Open** 9.30am daily, closing times vary according to time of year: 4.30pm mid-winter-7.30pm mid-summer. **Admission** £5 adults; £2.50-£3.50 concs; £13 family ticket; free under-5s. **Credit** MC, £TC, V.
Hugging the curve of the Thames, Kew Gardens was developed in the seventeenth and eighteenth centuries in the grounds of today's **Kew Palace** (closed for restoration until at least early 2000). It was landscaped by William Chambers and Capability Brown, and planted with specimens from all continents by Sir Joseph Banks. The Gardens were donated by the crown to the state in 1841. Since then, Kew has become a world-renowned centre for horticultural research (it boasts the world's largest collection of orchids).

The **Palm House** (Decimus Burton and Richard Turner, 1848) is the finest surviving glass-and-iron structure in the country, and is best seen from the galleries where you look down on a warm, damp jungle of palm and fern. The **Temperate House** is also by Burton and Turner. Don't miss the steamy **Aroid House** (John Nash, 1836), where you step into a tropical rainforest. Surrounding the glasshouses are 120ha (300 acres) filled with every imaginable variety of tree, shrub and flower. Hidden among the trees are some interesting buildings and sculptures, including the **Great Pagoda** (William Chambers, 1762) and a Japanese gateway. The **Marianne North Gallery** and the

small **Wood Museum** are also open to visitors. The former name of Jacobean **Kew Palace** was the Dutch House, because of its distinctive gables. Built in 1631, it was bought by George III in 1781 and used as a country retreat by the royal family until about 1820.

Royal Naval College
King William Walk, SE10 (0181 858 2154). Greenwich or Maze Hill rail/Island Gardens DLR then Greenwich foot tunnel. **Open** 2.30-4.45pm daily. **Admission** free. **Map** *see p97*
Founded by William III as a naval hospital, designed by Wren and built on the site of Greenwich Palace, the Royal Naval College was split in two in order to give an unimpeded view of **Queen's House** (*see above*) from the river, and vice versa. After 125 years in residence, the Navy moved out of the buildings during 1998; they are set to be replaced by several departments of the University of Greenwich among other organisations. Public access to the spectacular Painted Hall (decorated by James Thornhill in 1708-27) and chapel will remain, and it's possible that other parts of the college will be opened up to viewing in the future.

Royal Observatory
Romney Road, SE10 (0181 858 4422). Greenwich or Maze Hill rail/Island Gardens DLR then Greenwich foot tunnel. **Open** 10am-5pm daily. **Admission** *passport to all sections (National Maritime Museum, Queen's House, East Wing Exhibition & Royal Observatory, plus a free repeat visit within the next 12 months)* £5; £2.50-£4 concs; £15 family ticket; free under-5s. **Credit** AmEx, DC, JCB, MC, £TC, V. **Map** *see p97*
The Observatory was founded in 1675 by Charles II to find a solution to the problem of determining longitude at sea. It was clockmaker John Harrison, no doubt encouraged by the £20,000 prize money, who eventually found the solution in 1763. No official astronomical observation has been made here since 1954, and the cluster of buildings now houses a detailed exhibition charting the build-up to the establishment of Greenwich Mean Time and zero meridian (which divides the globe into East and West), both based here. There's a **planetarium** here too, which puts on informative shows lasting around 40 minutes at 2.30pm from Monday to Friday (£2; £1.50 children).

St Mary's Rotherhithe
St Marychurch Street, SE16 (0171 231 2465). Rotherhithe DLR. **Open** 7am-6pm Mon-Thur; 8am-6pm Sat, Sun. **Admission** free.
A gem of a church, built in 1715 by local sailors and watermen. Today, thanks to acts of burglary and vandalism, the interior can only be viewed through glass, under the watchful eye of a video camera. The communion table in the Lady Chapel and two bishop's chairs were made from timber salvaged from the warship *Fighting Temeraire*, the subject of Turner's painting now hanging in the National Gallery.

Thames Barrier Visitors' Centre
Unity Way, SE18 (0181 305 4188). Charlton rail/ riverboats to & from Greenwich Pier (0181 305 0300) & Westminster Pier (0171 930 3373)/177, 180 bus. **Open** 10am-5pm Mon-Fri; 10.30am-5.30pm Sat, Sun. **Admission** £3.40; £2 concs; £7.50 family ticket. **Credit** MC, V.
Since its completion in 1982, at a cost of over £500 million, the barrier has been raised more than 20 times to protect London from flooding. When in use, the four main gates are each the height of a five-storey building (normally they lie flat on the riverbed, allowing ships to pass over them). The Visitors' Centre has working models and an audiovisual presentation explaining how the structure was built. The barrier is raised once a month (dates and times vary; phone for details).

West London

From Bayswater hotel-land to Asian Southall, from ever-hip Notting Hill to chichi Chiswick, West London offers a microcosm of the capital's diversity.

Paddington & Bayswater

Maps 1 & 2

The name **Paddington** derives from the ancient Anglo-Saxon chieftain Padda, but most Londoners today associate this district north of Hyde Park with the railway station and its magnificent cathedral-like iron girdered roof, designed by Isambard Kingdom Brunel in 1851. It was the building of the station, along with the Grand Junction Canal (opened in 1801), that caused the population of Paddington and neighbouring **Bayswater** to boom in the mid-nineteenth century – the area was previously considered off residential limits because of the infamous Tyburn gallows nearby at present-day Marble Arch.

Despite another dip in fortune in the early twentieth century, when the district became synonymous with prostitution, poverty and neglect, Paddington and Bayswater are now relatively prosperous, largely owing to their centrality and the popularity of their classic Victorian white stuccoed townhouses. There's also an agreeably cosmopolitan ambience thanks to Middle Eastern, Greek and Jewish communities. Although hotels abound, the **Alexander Fleming Laboratory Museum** in St Mary's Hospital (*see page 121*) and the **London Toy & Model Museum** (*see page 119*) are as close as the area comes to conventional tourist attractions.

Queensway is the heart of Bayswater, but, despite some decent restaurants (particularly Chinese; *see pages 162-3*), it's something of a gaudy tourist trap. The palatial Whiteley's shopping mall labours under the ignominy of being one of Adolf Hitler's favourite buildings, but it compensates with a number of cafés, an eight-screen cinema and a good assortment of (mainly clothes) shops.

A left turn at the north end of Queensway opens up the richer pickings of **Westbourne Grove**, once known as the 'curry corridor'. The Indian restaurants here are no longer very impressive, but there are some excellent Middle Eastern and African eateries (the simple Sudanese staples of **Mandola** at no.139 are a delight, *see page 177*); or take in a few games of pool in the hip **Elbow Room** at no.103 (*see page 185*). As the road continues westward towards Portobello Road and Notting Hill, antiques take the place of fruit and

veg in shop windows. Look out for London's most stylish public toilet, complete with its own flower stall, at the junction with Colville Road.

Maida Vale, Kilburn & Queen's Park

North of the divisive Westway are the northern portion of Edgware Road, Maida Vale, Kilburn and Queen's Park. Dead-straight Edgware Road follows the course of ancient Watling Street – it's a traffic-clogged thoroughfare, redeemed only by some of London's best kebab shops (try **Patogh** or **Ranoush Juice Bar**; *see page 175*), courtesy of the thriving local Middle Eastern community.

Maida Vale (named after the Battle of Maida in southern Italy in 1806 where the British beat the French) is an affluent area characterised by Edwardian purpose-built flats, and prettified by the locks round **Little Venice**. You can walk from here along the canals to **London Zoo** (*see page 54*) – or even take a boat.

Kilburn High Road, meanwhile, is well known for its boisterous pubs, patronised primarily by the Irish expat community. **Kilburn** is also a good place for bargain shopping, and its predominantly Afro-Caribbean and Irish populations are well served by one of London's more popular and enterprising local theatres, the **Tricycle** (*see page 270*).

Queen's Park is a sanctuary away from the bedlam of Kilburn High Road and offers an excellent children's playground, a little pitch-and-putt golf course beside six well-maintained hard tennis courts and one of the best park cafés in London.

Carnival!

If Notting Hill is internationally famous for anything, it's Europe's biggest street party. Every year, the **Carnival** attracts the best part of a million revellers over its two-day duration, on the Sunday and Monday of the August bank holiday weekend (29-30 August 1999). Started as a small-scale local community event in the 1960s by the area's West Indian residents, the Carnival is now so huge and all-encompassing that many Notting Hill residents flee their homes for the period.

If you can stand the heaving crowds, however, you'll enjoy this spectacular event which centres on the massive costume parades and steel bands that inch their way around the three-mile (5-km) route via Ladbroke Grove, Westbourne Grove, Chepstow Road and the Great Western Road. Various stages feature live music (Portobello Green, Powis Square and outside Sainsbury's at the top of Ladbroke Grove), food stalls dole out great street grub, and sound systems, which get bigger and louder every year, blast out everything from lovers' rock to drum 'n' bass. Sunday is ostensibly (but not exclusively) oriented to kids, while the big day is Monday, with the streets sardine-packed almost to the point of immobility. The action gets under way around midday and winds down by 7-8pm. There are often parties afterwards but they are mostly private affairs.

Despite now attracting many more tourists and Londoners from outside Notting Hill than locals, the Carnival remains an Afro-Caribbean event at heart. Happily, it has also managed to shake off its volatile reputation after riots in the 1970s and 1980s. However, it's still wise to be wary – travel light, don't wear jewellery or carry bags or wallets. Most important of all, watch your liquid intake – toilet facilities are always hopelessly inadequate.

Map 1

Notting Hill always provokes strong reactions: Londoners long either to live here or to see it razed from the face of the earth. One reason for this extremist latter view is that this is the home of the 'trustafarian', a rich young white kid aspiring to Rastafarian, life-on-the-edge chic while living off parental trust funds. This parasitic breed is partly responsible for the lunatic local inflation of property prices, which continues unabated, meaning that no one with an income much less than £50,000 a year can afford to move into the area.

Decadent gentrification may currently dominate the image of W11, but it was not ever thus. Until a wave of white stuccoed building mapped out Notting Hill in the early 1800s, there was little but piggeries in the area. The district's fortunes declined in the twentieth century and it became solidly white and working class. During the 1950s, an influx of West Indian immigrants triggered serious race riots.

Notting Hill Gate itself is little more than a busy through road, although it boasts two cinemas: the **Gate** and the **Notting Hill Coronet** (for both, *see page 238*), the latter being one of the last cinemas in town where you can smoke. The tiny **Gate Theatre** (*see page 269*) above the Prince Albert pub on Pembridge Road is one of the best fringe theatres in town. But when people talk about Notting Hill they really mean **Portobello Road**. This narrow, snaking thoroughfare, most famous for its **market** (*see page 193*), forms the spine of this neighbourhood. Its northern end is the epicentre of the area, crowded with cafés, bars, restaurants, curiosity shops, delicatessens, vagrants and, of course, trustafarians.

Going east along Westbourne Park Road from here takes you past **All Saints Road** (currently making a remarkable transition from crack centre to ultra-hip eating alley) to the **Westbourne** pub (*see page 185*), crammed with hard-core wannabes all year round. Back on the Portobello Road, under the Westway, is a massive free-for-all jumble sale of modish second-hand clothes on Fridays and Saturdays.

At the north end of Portobello Road past another series of cafés lies **Golborne Road**, home of yet more market stalls, but where the shops and cafés assume a Portuguese and Moroccan flavour – a great place for ethnic groceries and pâtisserie. The other main feature of Golborne Road is the **Trellick Tower** – which can viewed as either a hideous carbuncle or a seminal piece of modern architecture. Built in 1973 by Ernö Goldfinger (Ian Fleming hated his work so much he named the notorious Bond villain after him), it was the tallest residential block in the country at the time, and is distinguished by a separate lift shaft adjoining the main building by concrete corridors. Contrary to popular expectation, residents are said to enjoy living there. (*See also page 82* **2 Willow Road**.)

Up at the top of Ladbroke Grove, past the gigantic Sainsbury's superstore, is **Kensal Green Cemetery** on Harrow Road. Opened in 1833, it's a huge and beautiful resting place for many a famous Londoner including Thackeray, Trollope and Isambard Kingdom Brunel, who were joined in 1997 by London's most celebrated 'lowlife' drinker, Jeffrey Bernard.

Kensington & Holland Park

Maps 1-4

No doubt to the delight of its heritage-conscious upper-class residents, **Kensington** gets a mention in the Domesday Book of 1068. In the seventeenth century the district grew up around Holland House (1606) and Campden House (1612) and was described by one contemporary historian in 1705 as a place 'inhabited by gentry and persons of note' with 'an abundance of shopkeepers and artificers'. *Plus ça change.*

Both aspects of Kensington are in evidence around the High Street. A lively mix of chainstores and individual shops stretch along the ever-busy thoroughfare while the nearby streets and squares are lined by large, pricey townhouses. The most famous of the squares, **Kensington Square**, sports an array of blue plaques denoting residents of distinction, such as the writer of *Vanity Fair*, William Makepeace Thackeray (no.16), and the philosopher John Stuart Mill (no.18).

Kensington Square is just behind the art deco splendour of **Barker's** department store (built 1905-13. Next door, on the sixth floor of Derry & Toms, is one of Europe's largest **roof gardens** (accessed from the entrance on Derry Street). Over the road from here, at the foot of Kensington Church Street, is the church of **St Mary Abbots**, distinguished by the tallest steeple in London (250ft/85m) and the pleasantly secluded gardens at its rear. **Kensington Market** is now a shadow of its former self. Opposite are two trendy stores – **Hype DF** and **Urban Outfitters** (for both, *see page 195*) – and you'll find **Amazon** (*see page 190*), with its bargain-priced designer togs, in several shops in nearby Kensington Church Street.

Down the High Street there is a classic Odeon cinema from 1926, and opposite, behind a small wood of flagpoles, lurks the ugly **Commonwealth Institute**. Behind the Institute is **Holland Park** (*see below*), the most densely activity-oriented of all London's parks. At the south end of the park is **Holland House**, originally built in 1606 (and named after an early owner, Sir Henry, Earl of Holland). The house suffered serious bomb damage during World War II and only the ground floor and arcades survived; the restored east wing con-

The old boy of High Street Ken: **Barker's.**

tains the most romantically sited youth hostel in town (*see page 150*). The open-air theatre's summer opera season (*see page 247*) is usually excellent.

Among the local historic houses worth a visit are **Leighton House** (*see below*), the nineteenth-century home of the painter Lord Leighton, and **Linley Sambourne House** (*see below*), home of Edward Linley Sambourne, cartoonist for the once-revered satirical magazine *Punch*, and now a monument to the late Victorian and Edwardian Arts and Crafts movement.

Earl's Court & Fulham

Maps 3 & 4

Earl's Court changed from hamlet to built-up urban area with the arrival of the Metropolitan Railway in 1860, and from 1914 many of its imposing houses were subdivided into flats. To this day it remains a district where many people have lived but few have settled. Previously known as Kangaroo Valley, thanks to Antipodean trekkers seeking cheap accommodation in its warren of bedsits and budget hotels, it has always had something of a seedy, though not dangerous, reputation. In the late 1970s and 1980s it became the gay centre of London, with the action centring most famously on the **Coleherne** (on the corner of Brompton and Coleherne Roads). The late Freddie Mercury of Queen also lived around here, at Garden Lodge, 1 Logan Place, and Earl's Court retains a strong gay presence today.

The area is, perhaps, more widely known as the site of the hulking **Exhibition Centre**, opposite the tube station. The 1937 structure, at its time the largest reinforced concrete building in Europe, was used as an internment camp in World War II.

The pleasantly laid-out **Brompton Cemetery** is a popular spot for sexual encounters (the proximity to graves presumably sharpening the experience), although an unmolested stroll, searching perhaps for the grave of Emmeline Pankhurst, is perfectly possible. The peace is only broken on Saturday afternoons when **Chelsea FC** are playing at home; the massive bulk of their Stamford Bridge stadium overlooks the tombs.

Neighbouring **Parsons Green** and **Fulham** are not as colourful or as promiscuous as Earl's Court, being home to déclassé Sloane Rangers (posh people said to orbit round Sloane Square). Parsons Green is centred around a small green that once, logically enough, supported a parsonage. Residents will be relieved to know that it was considered the aristocratic part of Fulham even in 1705 when Bowack pronounced it to be inhabited by 'Gentry and persons of Quality'. Appropriately, the heaving **White Horse** pub (*see page 185*) on the green serves one of the best selections of cask and bottled beers in London.

Apart from the enormously posh **Hurlingham Sports Club** and the **Queen's (Tennis & Rackets) Club**, which hosts the Stella Artois pre-Wimbledon grass court tournament, there is one place in Fulham you can enter without the requirement of a ridiculous bank balance: **Fulham Palace** (*see below*). The site was home to the Bishops of London from 704 until 1973 and boasted one of the largest moats in Britain till it was filled in 1921. Next door, small but perfectly formed **Bishop's Park** contains a paddling pool and offers beautiful leafy walks by the side of one of the prettiest stretches of the Thames.

Shepherd's Bush & Hammersmith

The approach to **Shepherd's Bush** from Holland Park Avenue is marked by Shepherd's Bush roundabout, with the **Thames Water Tower** springing out of its centre. The tower, which looks like a gigantic 'bloo-loo', is in fact a 50-foot (15-m) surge pipe for London's underground ring main. Designed by students at the Royal College of Art, it doubles as a huge barometer.

Shepherd's Bush Common itself used to be called Gagglegoose Green and formed the centre of what was, only 150 years ago, a 'pleasant village'. The name Shepherd is thought to be a personal one, but a more charming story ascribes the origin of Shepherd's Bush to the habit of shepherds watching sheep on the green while hiding in thorn bushes. Now, however, the Common is a scruffy traffic island overlooked by one of London's ugliest buildings: the Shepherd's Bush Centre.

All is not gloom in W12, however, for this is home to one of London's most prestigious new-writing theatres, **The Bush** (*see page 268*), and the neighbouring **Shepherd's Bush Empire** (*see page 250*), which has emerged in recent years as one of the most important concert venues in town. Shepherd's Bush **market** (between Shepherd's Bush and Goldhawk Road tubes) is one of west London's busier markets and, unlike Portobello Road, is very much geared to the local (Afro-Caribbean) population.

Shepherd's Bush and neighbouring **White City** are also the main base of BBC TV – **Television Centre** on Wood Lane can be readily identified by its massive satellite dishes combing the skies. Nearby is Loftus Road, the home of perennial underachievers, **Queens Park Rangers FC**. The wide open spaces of **Wormwood Scrubs** to the north are marred by one of London's most famous and forbidding Victorian jails. Less than a mile down Goldhawk Road, **Ravenscourt Park** is a much more agreeable space with an adventure playground and a number of tennis courts.

Hammersmith, south of Shepherd's Bush, is less depressing than its neighbour, but, on a similar note, is best known for its huge traffic interchange and the stone-clad corporate monstrosity of the Broadway Centre. The district is not, however, without its more notable architectural landmarks. There's the **Olympia Exhibition Centre** on Hammersmith Road, and the brown, ship-shape curiosity called the **London Ark**, the city's first ecologically friendly building, which, ironically, leans across one of the city's least ecologically friendly roadways, the A4. Then there is the **London Apollo**, previously known as the Hammersmith Odeon, where many a famous rock band has gigged. Finally, the knobbly **Hammersmith Bridge**, built in 1824 with a span of 422 feet (144m), was London's first suspension bridge (the IRA have twice attempted, and twice failed, to blow it up). **Lower Mall**, running along the river from the bridge, is a pleasant spot for a stroll or a pint at one of several riverside pubs (**The Dove** is the pick; *see page 185*).

Nor is Hammersmith without culture. On the main shopping route of King Street stands the **Lyric** theatre (*see page 269*), while the **Riverside Studios** (*see pages 133, 232, 238 & 270*) on Crisp Road is a three-theatre contemporary arts centre with a gallery and art-house repertory cinema.

Chiswick

A leafy suburb coveted by BBC senior management, actors and minor celebrities, **Chiswick** is in a world of its own. Turning your back on the tarmacked swoops of Hammersmith and walking west by the river from Hammersmith Bridge,

Chiswick Mall gives off a very different vibe. Lining this mile-long riverside stretch is an assortment of grand seventeenth- to nineteenth-century townhouses with be-flowered, wrought-iron verandahs. A stroll can be broken at one of the riverside pubs where the athletic upper classes can be observed rowing on the river – this is part of the route for the Oxford & Cambridge **Boat Race** (*see page 7*). The nearby **Fuller's Griffin Brewery** on Chiswick Lane South has stood on the same site since the seventeenth century and offers hour-and-a-half-long tours (0181 996 2063; tours at 11am, noon, 1pm and 2pm, Mon, Wed-Fri). Chiswick Mall ends at the church of **St Nicholas**. Only the ragstone tower of the original fifteenth-century building remains; the rest of the church is nineteenth-century. Gravestones commemorate local painters Hogarth and Whistler, but they are buried elsewhere. North of here, the pleasant shops and restaurants along Chiswick High Road signify the area's growing affluence. The street culminates at villagey **Turnham Green**, where cricket is still played in the summer.

Other Chiswick attractions include the Palladian magnificence of **Chiswick House** (*see below*) and **Hogarth's House** (*see below*), the country retreat of the famous eighteenth-century satirical artist. Further west are **Kew Bridge Steam Museum** (*see page 126*), housed in an impressive nineteenth-century pumping station, and the **Musical Museum** (*see page 127*), with its fine collection of self-playing instruments. South of here, overlooking Kew Gardens from the opposite side of the river, is **Syon House** (*see below*). Once a wealthy monastery, it was established by Henry V and used by Henry VIII as a prison for his wife Katherine Howard while she awaited execution.

A cutesy riverside promenade, just east of Kew Bridge on the north side of the river, runs by the mini-village of **Strand-on-the-Green**, and takes in three of the best pubs in the area.

Further west

Another notable house is a couple of miles west of Chiswick in the middle of gigantic **Osterley Park** (*see below*). Osterley House is yet another west London Robert Adam revamp.

Just north of here is the colour and curries of **Southall**. Like many of the previously sleepy parts of west London, Southall has been given a new lease of life by Indian immigrants. The predominantly Punjabi community retains a strong identity and provides a great opportunity to sample authentic north Indian cuisine in the countless cheap restaurants that line the Broadway. Try to visit on a Sunday, when the locals promenade among the market stalls, sari stores and Bollywood-packed video shops.

To the north, **Wembley** has been similarly enlivened by the mainly Gujarati community, although this deeply suburban district is better known as the home of the national sports stadium (*see page 263*), with its famous twin towers (added in 1963 to celebrate the 100th anniversary of the football league). The stadium is undergoing a massive £240-million redevelopment.

Sunday promenading along Southall Broadway.

Nearby **Neasden** is another piece of sprawling suburbia, once satirised mercilessly by the Monty Python team. Then, a Hindu sect built the multibillion-rupee **Shri Swaminarayan Mandir**, replicating the Akshardam outside Ahmedabad in Gujarat, western India. Constructed in 1995, the temple required 5,000 tons of marble and limestone and employed 1,500 sculptors for an enterprise unprecedented in this country since building the cathedrals in the Middle Ages. Visitors are welcome (dress discreetly) and there's also an informative 'Understanding Hinduism' exhibition and a good, cheap Indian café. Neasden will never be the same again.

Sights

Chiswick House

Burlington Lane, W4 (0181 995 0508). Turnham Green tube then E3 bus to Edensor Road, or Chiswick rail. **Open** *Apr-Sept* 10am-6pm daily; *first three weeks of Oct* 10am-5pm daily; *last week Oct-Mar* 10am-4pm Wed-Sun (last admission 30 mins before closing). **Closed** 24-26 Dec, 4-17 Jan and for occasional functions; phone to check. **Admission** £3; £1.50-£2.30 concs. **Credit** EC, MC, V.
Lord Burlington's 1729 design for this mansion is based on Palladio's Villa Capra (the Rotonda) in Vicenza. The interior is decked out in baroque splendour, with the lavish Blue Velvet Room winning the prize for most over-the-top décor. The formal gardens are peopled with statues, temples and obelisks as well as living picnickers. There's a good café here. Writers Jonathan Swift and Alexander Pope and the composer George Frederick Handel were all guests here.

Fulham Palace

Bishop's Avenue, off Fulham Palace Road, SW6 (0171 736 3233). Putney Bridge tube/220, 74 bus. **Open** *museum Mar-Oct* 2-5pm Wed-Sun; *Nov-Feb* 1-4pm Thur-Sun. **Admission** *museum* 50p; 25p concs (accompanied children free); *tours* £2; free under-16s.
From 704 until 1973, Fulham Palace was the official residence of the Bishops of London. The present brick house is a mishmash of periods and architectural styles; the oldest part is from 1480, while William Butterfield's neo-Gothic chapel is relatively recent, dating from 1866. The quirky museum, which traces the building's history, counts a mummified rat among its exhibits. The lovely grounds are open daily, but to get a glimpse of the (albeit rather bare) palace interior you should turn up for one of the extremely informative tours, which are held twice a month in summer and once a month in winter (on a Sunday; phone for dates).

Hogarth's House

Hogarth Lane, Great West Road, W4 (0181 994 6757). Turnham Green tube/Chiswick rail. **Open** *Apr-Oct* 1-5pm Tue-Fri; 1-6pm Sat, Sun; *Nov-Mar* 1-4pm Tue-Fri; 1-5pm Sat, Sun. **Closed** Jan. **Admission** free.
Hogarth's country retreat has been fully restored to its eighteenth-century condition and provides wall space for over 200 of the social commentator's prints, though his most famous work, *The Rake's Progress*, is a copy. (The original is in the Sir John Soane's Museum; *see page 121*.)

Holland Park

Entrances on Holland Park, Abbotsbury Road, Holland Walk & Kensington High Street, W8. High Street Kensington or Holland Park tube. **Open** 7.30am-30 mins before dusk daily. **Map 1 A8**
This is one of the most romantic parks in London, with beautiful woods and formal gardens surrounding the reconstructed Jacobean **Holland House**. The summer ballroom has been converted into a stylish, Modern British restaurant, **The Belvedere**; there's also a café. Open-air theatre and opera under an elegant canopy are staged in the park during the summer (*see p247*), and you can also make use of the squash and tennis courts, cricket and golf nets, and football pitches (phone 0171 602 2226 to book). For children, there's an adventure playground with tree-walks and rope swings, as well as tame rabbits, squirrels and peacocks. The Kyoto Japanese Garden is also worth a look.

Leighton House

12 Holland Park Road, W14 (0171 602 3316). High Street Kensington tube. **Open** 11am-5.30pm Mon-Sat. **Admission** free; donations appreciated.
Located on a quiet Kensington side street, Leighton House was designed by one-time president of the Royal Academy Lord Leighton (1864-79) in collaboration with George Aitchison. Leighton spent much of his life travelling the world, and it is from the East that the house takes most of its inspiration; its most striking feature is the exotic Arab Hall, added in 1879, and based on a Moorish palace in Palermo, Sicily. This domed structure, with its elaborate Persian tiles, mosaic floor and square fountain, has a startling cupola with stained-glass windows. Leighton, himself a distinguished artist, collected a variety of Victorian works of art by his contemporaries that are now on permanent display (*see also p129*). The house also hosts regular temporary art exhibitions. The audio tour, though slightly patronising in tone, gives an anecdote-filled insight into Leighton's life. A charge is levied for guided tours (noon Wed, Thur); phone for details.

Linley Sambourne House

18 Stafford Terrace, W8 (enquiries 0181 994 1019). High Street Kensington tube. **Open** *Mar-Oct* 10am-4pm Wed; 2-5pm Sun. **Admission** £3; £1.50-£2.50 concs. **Map 3 A9**
The former home of the noted late Victorian and Edwardian *Punch* cartoonist retains its magnificent interior, complete with pictures by Sambourne and his peers. An exceptional example of a Victorian townhouse, it's a rare chance to see how a successful artist lived and worked in Kensington.

Osterley Park

Jersey Road, Isleworth, Middx (0181 560 3918). Osterley tube. **Open** *park* dawn-dusk daily; *house Apr-Oct* 1-4.30pm Wed-Sun. **Admission** £4.10; £2.05 concs; £10.25 family ticket.
Osterley Park was built for Sir Thomas Gresham (founder of the Royal Exchange) in 1576 but transformed by Robert Adam in 1761. His revamp is dominated by the imposing colonnade of white pillars before the courtyard of the house's red-brick body. The splendour of the state rooms alone makes the house worth the visit, but the still-used Tudor stables, the vast parkland walks and the ghost said to be lurking in the basement add to Osterley's allure.

Syon House

Syon Park, Brentford, Middx (0181 560 0881). Gunnersbury tube/Kew Bridge rail/237, 267 bus. **Open** *house mid-Mar-Oct* 11am-5pm Wed, Thur, Sun, public holidays. **Admission** *house & gardens* £5.80; £4 concs; *gardens* £3; £2 concs. **Credit** MC, V.
Syon is Robert Adam's masterpiece, built in 1761 when the architect was at the height of his fame. He remodelled the existing Elizabethan house, home of the Percy family since 1594, to produce one of the most lavish and splendid eighteenth-century interiors in London. Among the many paintings on display are works by Lely, Gainsborough, Reynolds and Van Dyck. The riverside gardens, modelled by the ubiquitous 'Capability' Brown, now contain an impressive nineteenth-century conservatory, a miniature steam train, a garden centre and the **London Butterfly House** (*see p217*).

Museums & Galleries

Museums

A momentous change in museum funding means that, within a couple of years, all London's main collections will be free.

The variety and quality of London's collections are of a standard you would expect in one of the world's great cities (and their contents reflect the fact that this was once the centre of a global empire). The major museums rarely disappoint, but don't neglect the smaller places (among our favourites are **Sir John Soane's Museum**, **Carlyle's House**, the **Horniman Museum** and the **Geffrye Museum**).

Since the last edition of the guide, **Keats' House** in Hampstead has reopened following major renovation work, and the ethnographic collections of the former **Museum of Mankind** have returned to their original home at the British Museum as part of the BM's massive millennium development project (*see page 126*). Philatelists should note that the **National Postal Museum** is closed until further notice (you can phone 0171 600 8914 until July 1999 for information).

IT'S A FREE FOR ALL

To charge or not to charge. That is the question. Whether it is nobler to allow free access to the nation's great collections or suffer the slings and arrows of outraged liberal opinion and introduce admission fees. This issue has been vexing the Labour Government ever since it was elected in May 1997. Initially it appeared to be continuing its Tory predecessor's policy of pressurising the big museums and galleries into paying their own way, but in 1998 it announced a *volte face* – all entry fees were to be scrapped at the major institutions. Some, such as the **National Gallery** and the **British Museum**, had never charged admission, but others like the **Natural History Museum**, the **Science Museum**, the **Victoria & Albert Museum** and the **Imperial War Museum** will, from **April 1999**, allow children in for free. The following year pensioners will gain full access, and the year after that admission will be free for all.

Note that 'concs' in the listings indicates concessionary prices. If you are unemployed, a student, a senior citizen or fall in to any other category that may qualify for a discount (upon presentation of the relevant ID), it is always worth asking. If you're short of cash, note also that entry to a number of the big museums is free after a certain time (often 4.30pm). Credit cards are only accepted where specified.

GOSEE: LONDON WHITE CARD

If you plan to pack a lot of museums (and galleries) in to a short period of time, it may be worth buying a **GoSee: London White Card** (although we are aware of changes to museum admission prices; *see above*). This three-day or seven-day pass allows unlimited entry to 16 museums and galleries (for both permanent and temporary exhibitions) within the specified time period. Note that the **Queen's House** is closed until 1 December 1999.

Participating museums and galleries are: Apsley House – the Wellington Museum; Barbican Art Gallery; BBC Experience; Design Museum; Hayward Gallery; Imperial War Museum; London Transport Museum; Museum of London; Museum of the Moving Image; National Maritime Museum, Royal Observatory & Queen's House; Natural History Museum; Royal Academy of Arts; Science Museum; Theatre Museum; Tower Bridge Experience; Victoria & Albert Museum. **Prices are**: individual adult card £16 for three days, £26 for seven days; family card £32 for three days, £50 for seven days. The family card covers up to two adults and four children aged 16 or under. The cards can be purchased from any of the participating museums and galleries and most tourist information centres. For further details, check out the website at *www.london-gosee.com*.

Major museums

For the **British Museum**, *see page 126*.

Imperial War Museum

Lambeth Road, SE1 (0171 416 5000). Lambeth North tube/Waterloo tube/rail. **Open** 10am-6pm daily. **Admission** £5; £2.50-£4 concs; free under-5s; £13 family ticket. **Credit** MC, £TC, V. **Map 11 N10**

The early nineteenth century's most famous lunatic asylum, known as Bedlam, now houses the country's memorial to the two World Wars. A rotating clock-hand in the basement symbolises the grim cost of war in terms of human lives, a body count that it estimates will exceed 100 million by 1999.

Two of the most popular exhibits, or rather 'experiences', are **The Blitz** and **The Trench**, which do a good job at bringing history to life while avoiding vicarious thrills. In the vast atrium, you can see pristine restored and cut-away examples of a selection of hardware, including a Sopwith Camel, a V2 rocket and a Spitfire.

The lower ground floor galleries hold the excellent four-part permanent exhibition of the history of warfare in the twentieth century, while **Secret War** attempts to shed light on the clandestine world of espionage from 1909 to the present day. Exhibits range from Brezhnev's uniform to an original German 'Enigma' encrypting machine.

Signalling a deliberate move away from the solely martial, a major exhibition (designed by Sir Terence Conran) chronicling the changing face of Britain from 1945 to 1965 – **Post-War Britain: From the Bomb to the Beatles** – opened in March 1999.
Website: www.iwm.org.uk

Museum of London

150 London Wall, EC2 (0171 600 3699). Barbican or St Paul's tube/Moorgate tube/rail. **Open** 10am-5.50pm Mon-Sat, public hols; noon-5.50pm Sun. **Admission** (tickets valid for one year) £5; £3 concs; £12 family ticket; free registered disabled; **free** after 4.30pm.
Credit MC, V. **Map 9 P5**

The concrete 'drawbridge' across a 'moat' of traffic makes an appropriate, if daunting, approach to this exploration of London's history. It opened in 1976, purpose-built in the middle of a busy City roundabout, on the site of the Roman fort. Inside, you'll find one of the most imaginatively designed museums in the capital. In the **London Now** gallery, visitors can trace the growth of London from prehistoric times up to the present day with an absorbing combination of models, artefacts and reconstructions. The fast-track (45-minute) interactive computer point path round the museum, called the **Catwalk** (after Dick Whittington's persuasive, if apocryphal, moggie), provides an overview of the city's history for those pressed for time.

It's well worth lingering, however, particularly over the impressive Roman interior, with its original mosaic pavement; the Cheapside hoard (a staggering cache of fine jewels, dating from 1560 to 1640, found in a box under a shop); and the **Great Fire Experience**, an illuminated model with sound effects and commentary depicting the fire that destroyed four-fifths of London in 1666. Reconstructions of Newgate prison cells, and the Lord Mayor's ceremonial coach and shop/restaurant interiors from Victorian and Edwardian London (including Selfridges' splendid art deco elevator) all help to create an atmospheric and informative experience.

Look out also for temporary exhibitions, which, in 1999, include a look at the work of photographer **Terence Donovan** (Mar-Aug 1999).
Website: www.museumoflondon.org.uk

National Maritime Museum

Romney Road, SE10 (0181 858 4422). Greenwich or Maze Hill rail/Island Gardens DLR then Greenwich foot tunnel. **Open** 10am-5pm daily. **Tours** every 15 mins.
Admission *passport to all sections (National Maritime Museum, Queen's House, East Wing Exhibition & Old Royal Observatory, plus a free repeat visit within the next 12 months)* £5; £2.50-£4 concs; £15 family ticket; under-5s free. **Credit** AmEx, MC, £TC, V. **Map** *see p97.*

Don't be put off if you're not nautically inclined: this ever-improving museum is enjoyable for all but the terminally incurious. A series of entertaining galleries does a good job of putting Britain's maritime heritage in perspective. Particularly popular is the **Nelson Gallery** – a comprehensive monument to the naval hero, charting his achievements at sea and liaisons on land. Not surprisingly, the Battle of Trafalgar features heavily: look out for Turner's biggest ever painting (of the battle) and, on a more morbid note, the blood-soaked uniform Nelson was wearing when fatally wounded.

All Hands, popular with younger visitors, is an interactive gallery on people's livelihood and the sea; learn how to send a distress signal using Morse code, flags or radio. Other things worth seeing are the delicate scale models of ships, and the portrait gallery of explorers, navigators and their royal patrons. The major **Neptune Court** project, promising 12 new galleries, is set to open in Easter 1999, and is designed to enhance the story of the days when

Britannia ruled the waves. Note that the **Queen's House** (*see p105*) is closed until 1 December 1999, and that visitors may be charged an extra admission price to see it (not known at the time this guide went to press).
Website: www.nmm.ac.uk

Natural History Museum

Cromwell Road, SW7 (0171 938 9123/recorded info same number after hours). South Kensington tube. **Open** 10am-5.50pm Mon-Sat; 11am-5.50pm Sun.
Admission £6; £3-£3.20 concs; £16 family ticket; **free** after 4.30pm Mon-Fri; after 5pm Sat, Sun, public hols. **Credit** AmEx, MC, £TC, V. **Map 4 D10**

The Natural History Museum – built on the site of another, less popular, Great Exhibition, in 1862 – opened in 1881 to display the British Museum's burgeoning collection of natural history specimens. Split between the **Life Galleries** and the recently opened **Earth Galleries**, this is one of London's most innovative, absorbing and enjoyable museums (and deserving winner of the London Tourist Board's Large Visitor Attraction of the Year 1998). Alfred Waterhouse's stunning pink-and-gold, brick-and-terracotta building is as extraordinary as its contents, particularly in the exquisitely painted ceiling and carved fauna details in the Central Hall where the famed cast of a Diplodocus skeleton stands guard.

The Life Galleries include the ever-popular **Dinosaurs**, the interactivity-rich **Human Biology** section, the recently revamped **Creepy Crawlies** and the excellent **Mammals** and **Ecology** galleries. The **British Natural History** exhibition is due to reopen at the end of 1999. The opening of the **Earth Galleries** has transformed the old Geological Museum and achieved the seemingly impossible – making rocks interesting. Take an escalator ride through a rotating globe, feel the force of an earthquake in a mock-

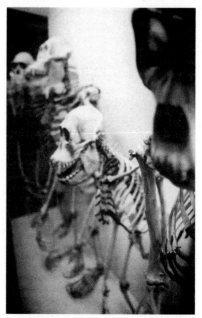

The bony **Horniman Museum**. *See page 119.*

up Kobe supermarket and walk under a volcano. A textbook example of how to make education fun. Further developments are in the pipeline.
Website: www.nhm.ac.uk

Science Museum
Exhibition Road, SW7 (0171 938 8000/8008/recorded info 0171 938 8123). South Kensington tube.
Open 10am-6pm daily. **Admission** £6.50; £3.50 concs; season tickets available; free UB40, registered disabled & carer; **free** after 4.30pm daily. **Credit** AmEx, MC, £TC, V. **Map 4 D9**
The Science Museum makes the most of Britain's pioneering industrial heritage. Many of the original machines that powered civilisation towards the millennium are lovingly preserved here. Filling five floors, the applications of technology are demonstrated, explained and celebrated. The place is crammed full of information; the synopsis (in a side gallery), which gives an overview of the exhibits, is practically a museum in itself. The big hardware includes Stephenson's Rocket, a V2 missile and the Apollo 10 command module. Take a look at inventions that were spurned in their time, such as Charles Babbage's counting machine, a precursor of the computer.

If this all sounds a bit dry, don't be fooled: this place is a huge hit with kids, particularly the **Launch Pad's** hands-on, interactive experience of how technology works and the **Flight Lab** where you can test the principles of flight for yourself by climbing into a cockpit to take the controls. Temporary exhibitions in 1999 will include **Time and Millennium** – an exhibition on atomic clocks and time measurement (from Mar) – and **Solar Eclipse** (June-Aug), exploring the history of solar eclipses, with tips for viewing the once-in-a-lifetime total eclipse on 11 August, which will be visible over southern England, especially Cornwall. The daily tours and shows, on a wide range of topics, are lively and fascinating.
Website: www.nmsi.ac.uk

Victoria & Albert Museum
Cromwell Road, SW7 (0171 938 8500). South Kensington tube. **Open** noon-5.45pm Mon; 10am-5.45pm Tue-Sun (seasonal late view on Wed 6.30-9.30pm; phone for details). **Admission** £5; £3 concs; free under-18s, students, disabled & carer, ES40s, **free** after 4.30pm; £15 season ticket. **Credit** AmEx, MC, V. **Map 4 E10**
The Victoria & Albert Museum (commonly known as the V&A) houses the world's greatest collection of decorative arts, as well as the national sculpture collection. Founded in 1852, and housed in Aston Webb's immense, sprawling, exceptionally grand building (1890), the V&A offers a staggering cross-cultural view of human achievement.

The **Art & Design** galleries are arranged thematically by place and date; the **Materials & Techniques** galleries by type of material. It is best to concentrate on certain areas of interest – it would be insane (and probably physically impossible) to try to cover all 145 galleries on one visit. Perhaps sample the world's largest collection of art from **India** outside the subcontinent, or the exceptional **Japanese Gallery** (look out for Hokusai's famous *Great Wave*), or the **Samsung Gallery of Korean Art** with ceramics dating back to around AD300. Or come more up to date in the **Frank Lloyd Wright Gallery** with some of the architect's applied art designs. The V&A's most famous exhibits are the **Raphael Cartoons** – seven vast designs for tapestries, based on episodes from the Acts of the Apostles, but almost equally popular are the superb **Dress** and **Jewellery** collections. The **British Galleries** are currently undergoing a massive £31-million refit (due to open in 2001).

The V&A held the first-ever exhibition of photography in 1858, so it's an appropriate home for the National Collection of the Art of Photography. The **Canon Photography Gallery** shows regularly changing displays – Henri Cartier-

Cabinet War Rooms: *Blitz-time memories.*

Bresson's lesser-known photographs from America and Asia are on show until 12 April 1999; Lady Hawarden's pioneering work from the mid-nineteenth century takes over from May until August 1999. Other temporary exhibitions for 1999 include **The Arts of the Sikh Kingdoms** (25 Mar-25 July) and **A Grand Design** (14 Oct-Jan 2000), a spectacular cross-section of the museum's treasures.

The museum shop is also excellent, as is the (pricey) café, and the jazz brunch/lunch on Sundays has become an institution (£9.50 including entrance to the museum).
Website: www.vam.ac.uk

Armed services

For the **Imperial War Museum**, *see page 114.*

Cabinet War Rooms
Clive Steps, King Charles Street, SW1 (0171 930 6961). St James's Park or Westminster tube. **Open** *Oct-Mar* 10am-6pm; *Apr-Sept* 9.30am-6pm daily (last admission 5.15pm). **Admission** £4.60; £2.30-£3.40 concs. **Credit** AmEx, MC, V. **Map 8 K9**
The austere underground HQ of Churchill's War Cabinet during World War II has been faithfully preserved. What you get is a guided audio tour, which takes you through the rooms rather quickly (though you can play further clips of information on subjects that take your fancy). What you don't get is a feel for the stress, smells, noises and (controlled) chaos that must have filled the rooms at the height of the war. Highlights include the key Map Room (manned night and day throughout the war to monitor the movements of Allied and Axis troops), Churchill's bedroom (complete with nightshirt and chamberpot), and the telephone hotline to the White House. The gift shop holds a small but well-chosen collection of books about the war.

Guards' Museum
Wellington Barracks, Birdcage Walk, SW1 (0171 414 3271). St James's Park tube. **Open** 10am-4pm daily. **Admission** £2; £1 concs; £4 family ticket. **Map 7 J9**
This small museum records the history of the British Army's five Guards regiments, which were founded in the seventeenth century under Charles II. The oldest medal (awarded by Oliver Cromwell to officers of his New Model Army at the Battle of Dunbar in 1651) and a bottle of Iraqi whisky captured in the Gulf War notwithstanding, this is predominantly an exhibition of uniforms and oil paintings accompanied by stirring martial music. That said, the museum is trying to emphasise its collection of curios from the everyday life of your ordinary guardsman down the ages. See the Guards in ceremonial action (every day Apr-Aug, every other day Sept-Mar, at 11.30am) when they form up to march to St James's Palace and Buckingham Palace to relieve their comrades on guard duty. The toy soldier shop claims to be the largest of its kind in London.

Museum of Artillery
The Rotunda, Repository Road, SE18 (0181 316 5402). Woolwich Dockyard rail. **Open** 1-4pm Mon-Fri. **Admission** free.

Worth visiting if only for the fine eighteenth-century architecture by John Nash. But you'll also find artillery pieces here ranging from a 1346 Bombard (a kind of stubby mortar) to a four-barrelled 14.5mm anti-aircraft gun used in the Gulf, and a section of Saddam Hussein's massive supergun, which nearly brought down a British government without firing a shot. Model weapons, guidance systems and other weaponry are dotted across the grounds.

National Army Museum

(by the Chelsea Royal Hospital) Royal Hospital Road, SW3 (0171 730 0717). Sloane Square tube/11, 19, 239 bus. **Open** 10am-5.30pm daily. **Admission** free.
Map 4 F12
An admirable attempt to make the history of the British soldier – from Agincourt to Bosnia – accessible for the non-martially inclined. The key is in focusing on individuals. The lifesize figures of soldiers from different eras do not represent anonymous ideals but real people with real stories, such as the infantryman at Waterloo who's just fallen in a ditch and got lost, and the shivering Agincourt archer fighting with his bow down as he's suffering from dysentery and doesn't want to be caught short. The imaginatively displayed permanent exhibits include **The Road to Waterloo** (featuring a huge model of the battle, complete with 75,000 mini-soldiers, and three specially commissioned films) and **The Right to Serve**, the story of women in the British army. Phone for details of other temporary exhibitions. The museum also contains a small café and a shop.

Royal Air Force Museum

Grahame Park Way, NW9 (0181 205 2266/recorded info 0181 205 9191). Colindale tube/Mill Hill Broadway rail/32, 226, 292, 303 bus. **Open** 10am-6pm daily.
Admission £6.50; £3.25-£4.90 concs; free registered disabled; £16.60 family ticket. **Credit** MC, £TC, V.
Hendon Aerodrome bills itself as the birthplace of aviation in Britain and here you can see how baby has grown. The high-tech Phantom jet dwarfs the Spitfire and Hurricane fighters that won the Battle of Britain. You can have a close look at these on a guided tour (book in advance by phone). The main hangar houses planes plucked from aviation history. Opposite you'll find the harbingers of the terrible rain from Bomber Command. There's also a Red Arrows flight simulator, a 'touch and try' Jet Provost cockpit and a walk-through Sunderland flying boat. Children especially will enjoy the 'fun 'n' flight' interactive gallery, which opened in spring 1998. Among the highlights of the museum's 1999 event programme is **Flight Activities Weekend** (5-6 June).

Art & design

For the **Victoria & Albert Museum**, *see page 116.*

Design Museum

Butlers Wharf, off Shad Thames, SE1 (0171 403 6933). London Bridge tube/rail/15, 78, 100 bus. **Open** 11.30am-6pm daily (last admission 5.30pm). **Admission** £5.25; £4 concs; free under-5s. **Credit** AmEx, MC, £TC. V.
Map 12 S9
This beautifully designed 1930s-style, sparkling white building is stark and spacious within – the perfect setting for a collection of innovative design. Incredibly user-friendly, the museum consists of just two levels with a minimum of exhibits. The first floor holds the **Review Collection** (state-of-the-art innovations from around the world) and the **Temporary Exhibition Gallery**. Temporary exhibitions for 1999 include **Modern Britain 1929-1939** (20 Jan-6 June), an exhibition of work from the modern movement encompassing, among other forms, architecture, painting, interior and product design, and sculpture.

The **Permanent Collection**, devoted to the study of design for mass production, is housed on the second floor. Arranged thematically, it focuses on different types of product. One of them is the car – look for the wooden model made up from drawings by the architect and designer Le Corbusier dating from 1928. The aim: a low-cost people's car yet with ultimate comfort; the result: something reminiscent of Fred Flintstone's runaround. There are also early televisions, washing machines, telephones, chairs (including one designed by Rennie Mackintosh that visitors can try out) and a collection of tableware. The **Blue Print Café**, which shares the building, with its balcony overlooking the Thames, is an appropriately stylish establishment (but be warned, it's a restaurant rather than a café, with prices to match).

Fan Museum

12 Crooms Hill, SE10 (0181 305 1441). Greenwich rail/riverboat to Greenwich Pier. **Open** 11am-5pm Tue-Sat; noon-5pm Sun. **Admission** £3.50; £2.50 concs; free registered disabled, OAPs 2-5pm Tue. **Credit** MC, £TC, V.
Map *see p97.*
Housed in two attractive converted Georgian townhouses, this is the world's only permanent exhibition of hand-held folding fans and other breeze-stirring contraptions. True to their coy usage, only part of the enormous collection is ever on view at one time: their elasticity necessitates periodic rest. The fans are displayed by theme, such as design, provenance or social history. Exhibitions for 1999 include a collection of advertising fans (end Mar-June).

Geffrye Museum

Kingsland Road, E2 (0171 739 9893). Old Street tube/rail then 243 bus/Liverpool Street then 149, 242 bus. **Open** 10am-5pm Tue-Sat; noon-5pm Sun, bank holiday Mon. **Admission** free (under-8s must be accompanied by an adult). **Map 10 R3**
These beautiful almshouses, built in 1715, were converted into a museum of furniture and interior design in 1914 and are now one of London's most fascinating and delightful museums. A series of rooms, reconstructed in period style, amount to an atmospheric voyage through the ages, from the Elizabethan era to the 1950s. Some are accompanied by contemporary music (listen out for the 1930s Bakelite radio, tuned into jolly, morale-boosting melodies). In the Stuart parlour, a turtle's skull, and stuffed baby crocodile and armadillo reflect the period's nascent interest in natural history. A new £5.3-million extension opened in November 1998. The space is home to twentieth-century furniture and interiors, and includes a design centre, new education facilities, a shop, restaurant and a temporary exhibition gallery. Outside, there's a walled herb garden, which makes a pleasant 'outdoor room' in fine weather. In summer, free jazz and world music concerts are given on the front lawns.

Exhibitions for 1999 include the **Ruskin Pottery Centenary Exhibition** (13 Apr-27 June), and **Mary Beale – A Woman's Perspective** (autumn 1999-Jan 2000) – an exhibition of the seventeenth-century artist's paintings. December 1999 sees the return of the Geffrye's popular annual **Christmas Past** season. The museum's atmosphere becomes magical as all the rooms are decorated with original artefacts and historically accurate replicas to reflect four centuries of Christmas traditions.

Percival David Foundation of Chinese Art

53 Gordon Square, WC1 (0171 387 3909). Euston Square, Goodge Street or Russell Square tube/Euston tube/rail. **Open** 10.30am-5pm Mon-Fri. **Admission** free; donations appreciated (under-14s must be accompanied by an adult). **Map 6 K46**
The late Percival David's collection of Chinese ceramics is the finest outside China. Temporary exhibitions are held on the ground floor. Until the end of May 1999 there will be an exhibition of rare marks on Chinese ceramics. The 1,700-

odd items of the permanent collection are found on the first and second floors. Most date from the tenth to eighteenth centuries although there are some earlier pieces, such as a rather portly hare from the Tang dynasty (eighth to tenth centuries). Aficionados will be drawn to the very rare Ru and Guan wares and the unique pair of blue-and-white Yuan dynasty temple vases (1351). Curiosity seekers look out for the late seventeenth-century Dehua ware figure of Guanyin with a swastika hanging on his chest.

Childhood & toys

Bethnal Green Museum of Childhood
Cambridge Heath Road, E2 (0181 983 5200/recorded info 0181 983 5201/0). Bethnal Green tube/rail. **Open** 10am-5.50pm Mon-Thur, Sat; 2.30-5.50pm Sun. **Admission** free (under-8s must be accompanied by an adult).
This mammoth collection of dolls, trains, cars, children's clothes, books and puppets is housed in a nineteenth-century building. The dolls' houses in cabinets, originating in seventeenth-century Holland, and the Japanese ceremonial dolls should not be missed. On the upper gallery, a selection of educational toys gives some way towards providing playthings that can be handled, but the museum is probably of more interest to nostalgic adults than kids.

London Toy & Model Museum
21-23 Craven Hill, W2 (0171 706 8000/recorded info 0171 402 5222). Bayswater, Lancaster Gate or Queensway tube/Paddington tube/rail/12, 15, 94 bus. **Open** 9am-5.30pm daily. **Admission** £5.50; £3.50-£4.50 concs; free under-4s; £15 family ticket. **Credit** JCB, MC, £TC, V. **Map 1 C6**
Marvel at the historic toys and models (both working and non-working) inside the museum's labyrinth of 20 galleries. As well as miniature planes, trains and automobiles, there's a 1920s funfair and even a mini-coalmine. Indeed, the whole place is a mine of information, detailing the long and complex history of toys, from Noah's Ark to Paddington Bear. Visitors of all ages will enjoy taking a trip in the express lift to see the imaginary Baywest City, while children especially love the walled garden with a mini-train ride and a roundabout. The museum is due to change ownership in 1999, so phone to check opening times and admission prices.

Pollock's Toy Museum
1 Scala Street, W1 (0171 636 3452). Goodge Street tube. **Open** 10am-5pm Mon-Sat. **Admission** £2.50; £1 children; free under-3s. **Credit** *shop* MC, V. **Map 5 J5**
An unlikely location – tucked away behind Goodge Street – but this museum is well worth tracking down. Most of the exhibits date from the last two centuries (but look out for the rare Egyptian clay mouse from 2000 BC), and include optical toys with such mind-boggling names as the Phenakistoscope and Heliocinegraphe. The puppet cabinets feature more familiar faces along the lines of Sooty and Sweep, Punch and Judy, and Muffin the Mule. The large collection of dolls' houses, fine examples of changing décor over the decades, display incredible attention to detail. It's also interesting to witness the evolution of teddy bears: from veteran Eric ('born' 1905) to a decidedly larger and cuddlier specimen only a few years later. Toy theatre performances can be booked for parties of children (minimum 10).

Ragged School Museum
48-50 Copperfield Road, E3 (0181 980 6405). Mile End tube. **Open** 10am-5pm Wed, Thur; 2-5pm first Sun every month. **Admission** free.
'Ragged schools' were established to educate and feed poor children. This canalside warehouse was one of the largest ragged schools in London (there were 144 in total), and was founded by Dr Barnado. Now restored to its original form, it contains a reconstructed Victorian classroom, complete with role-playing for pupils when schools visit. Free events are organised for children during school holidays and on the first Sunday of each month, and there are also good temporary exhibitions on subjects of local interest. The café is a useful refuelling stop as the museum is somewhat out of the way.

Ethnography

For the **British Museum**, *see page 112*.

Horniman Museum
London Road, SE23 (0181 699 1872, education dept ext 124/recorded info 0181 699 2339). Forest Hill rail/63, 122, 176, 185, 312, 352, P4, P13 bus. **Open** 10.30am-5.30pm Mon-Sat; 2-5.30pm Sun. **Admission** free. **Credit** MC, V.
It's a testament to this idiosyncratic museum that a journey from central London is worthwhile to discover its multifaceted charms; children enjoy the place enormously. The major ethnographic hall is undergoing extensive redevelopment and is due to reopen in spring 1999 as Britain's first permanent gallery of African art and culture. The essence of nineteenth-century tea merchant Frederick Horniman's endearingly peculiar ethnic collection is on view in the natural history hall until then. Here an immense stuffed walrus presides gruffly over an eclectic display of other specimens. The surprising Apostle's Clock enacts a famous episode from the Gospels daily at 4pm. In the Music Room you can play and listen to all kinds of instruments from around the world (there are frequent workshops for kids). Equally popular is the Living Waters Aquarium, which demonstrates the life in a river on its way to the sea. You can see inside a beehive, gaze across reedbeds and peer down microscopes in the recently added Centre for Understanding the Environment (CUE), housed in an innovative eco-friendly building. In summer, the formal and sunken gardens with fine views are an added attraction, as is the small zoo containing farmyard animals.

Petrie Museum of Egyptian Archaeology
DMS Watson Library, University College London, Malet Place (off Torrington Place), WC1 (0171 387 7050 ext 2884). Goodge Street tube. **Open** 10am-noon, 1.15-5pm, Mon-Fri; 1-5pm Sat. **Closed** Christmas, Easter and four weeks in summer. **Admission** free; donations requested. **Map 6 K4**
Father of Egyptian archaeology Sir Flinders Petrie bequeathed the result of his desert digs, a collection of the minutiae of ancient Egyptian life, to **University College London** in 1933. It's hard to find (it's best to ask a security guard once in the grounds), but even Indiana Jones would consider the effort worthwhile. On display among ranks of traditional glass cabinets full of pots, carvings and ornaments, you'll discover the oldest piece of clothing in the world (from 3000 BC) and the Qua bead-net raunchy undergarment (2400 BC). More disturbing exhibits include the exhumed pot-burial in a corner with its skeletal occupant squatting inside, and the coiffured head of a mummy with eyebrows and lashes still intact.

Film

Museum of the Moving Image
South Bank, SE1 (0171 928 3535/recorded info 0171 401 2636). Embankment tube or Waterloo tube/rail. **Open** 10am-6pm daily. **Admission** £6.25; £4.50-£5.25 concs; £17 family ticket. **Credit** MC, V. **Map 8 M8**
Squatting under Waterloo Bridge, in the multi-levelled confusion of the South Bank, MOMI offers a wealth of information for anyone interested in film or TV. The exhibition kicks off with the birth of cinema (static displays of

The **London Transport Museum**. *See p123.*

early attempts at animation, optical toys such as the Zoetrope and the first cine cameras and magic lanterns), and quickly progresses to the dawn of the silent era. This is followed by a multitude of clips covering cinema's many genres: cartoons, Russian classics (shown in an agitprop train), newsreels and Hollywood favourites.

So far, so good. It's the past decade or so that seems rather neglected. And, though the museum makes an attempt to keep up with the times by installing the inevitable 'interactive' area, it's this (albeit minor) part of the museum that lets things down, at least as far as anyone without kids in tow is concerned. Does anyone really think they're being interviewed by Zig and Zag? And just what is the point of the video screen on top of the urinal, playing clips of Alf Garnett? The Cinema 100 route, an 'interactive multimedia trail' highlighting key film facts and figures, also falls short of expectations. Yes, it's popular, and yes it's packed with info, but MOMI could do with a little reinvention here and there. The temporary exhibitions are usually good, though – **Ooh! What a Carry On** (until 19 May 1999), celebrating 40 years of nudge-nudge, wink-wink British sauciness on film, is sure to press the right buttons (ooo-er!). Bear in mind that you need at least two hours to do the museum any justice.

Literary & historical figures

Baden-Powell House
Queen's Gate, SW7 (0171 584 7030). Gloucester Road or South Kensington tube/C1, 74 bus. **Open** 7am-11pm daily. **Closed** for one week over Christmas & New Year. **Admission** free. **Map 4 D10**
This small exhibition pays tribute to Lord Robert Baden-Powell, founder of the Scout and Guide movement. Although chiefly of interest to parties of Scouts paying homage, the exhibition will move anyone susceptible to the evident sincerity of this icon of empire. A brief visit gives an insight into the attitudes and values of one individual who contributed to the culture that threw up the vast V & A over the road.

Carlyle's House
24 Cheyne Row, SW3 (0171 352 7087). Sloane Square tube. **Open** *Apr-Oct* 11am-5pm Wed-Sun. **Admission** £3.30; £1.65 under-16s.
Map 3 E12
Such was the contemporary renown of the 'Sage of Chelsea', the historian Thomas Carlyle, that within a few years of his death in 1881, the red-brick Queen Anne house where he'd lived since 1834 had been converted into a museum for public subscription. In the care of the National Trust since 1930, it is now watched over by a delightful live-in custodian who will regale visitors with stories of the many eminent visitors Carlyle and his feisty wife Jane entertained

here, including Dickens, Thackeray, George Eliot and Ruskin. The roomy yet modest house remains much as it was in the Carlyles' time; it's easy to imagine the tempestuous couple in residence. Carlyle and Tennyson would smoke by the chimney in the basement kitchen, so that Jane did not have to endure the smell.

Dickens' House
48 Doughty Street, WC1 (0171 405 2127). Chancery Lane or Russell Square tube. **Open** 9.45am-5.30pm Mon-Fri; 10am-5pm Sat. **Admission** £3.50; £1.50-£2.50 concs; £7 family ticket. **Credit** *shop* AmEx, MC, V.
Map 6 M4
This Georgian terrace house is the sole survivor of Charles Dickens's many London residences. He was able to move into this elegant (then-private) street on the strength of the phenomenal success of *The Pickwick Papers* and, although he lived here for just two and a half years (Apr 1837-Dec 1839), he managed to pen *Oliver Twist* and *Nicholas Nickleby* during that time. Only the first-floor drawing room has been restored to its original appearance, but the house is packed with Dickens memorabilia, including portraits of himself and his family, his desk, bars from the Marshalsea Prison where his father was incarcerated for debt and the room in which his sister-in-law, 16-year-old Mary Hogarth (with whom he had fallen in love), died. Every Wednesday evening from mid-March to the end of September, a one-man show, 'The Sparkler of Albion', brings the author and his characters entertainingly to life.

Faraday Museum
Royal Institution, 21 Albemarle Street, W1 (0171 409 2992). Green Park tube. **Open** 10am-6pm Mon-Fri. **Admission** £1. **Credit** *shop* MC, V.
Map 7 J7
The achievements of Michael Faraday, one-time professor at the Royal Institution and 'father of electricity', are celebrated in this small but interesting museum. Exhibits include a re-creation of the lab where Faraday discovered the laws of electromagnetics.

Freud Museum
20 Maresfield Gardens, NW3 (0171 435 2002/5167). Finchley Road tube/Finchley Road & Frognal rail. **Open** noon-5pm Wed-Sun. **Admission** £4; £2 concs; free under-12s. **Credit** AmEx, MC, V.
This pleasantly quiet Arts and Crafts-style house is where Sigmund Freud spent his last year after leaving Vienna and Nazi persecution. It was here that he finished his last master work, *Moses and Monotheism*, and received visitors such as HG Wells and Salvador Dali. On the ground floor is a faithful reproduction of Freud's Viennese study, complete with rug-bedecked couch and a few of the antique figurines he loved to collect. Upstairs are artefacts belonging to his daughter Anna, a leading child analyst who lived here until her death in 1982. Various displays and a short video illuminate the Freud clan (including a young Lucian) in action. Freud heritage stuff (cufflinks patterned with a Freud doodle, anyone?) is marketed in the small shop, alongside a small book selection. For the *echt* bookshops, scuttle down to Karnak Books opposite Finchley Road tube station or Rathbone Books on Haverstock Hill to get a better idea of the man's extraordinary significance in twentieth-century thought.

Keats' House
Wentworth Place, Keats Grove, NW3 (0171 435 2062). Hampstead tube/24, 46, 168 bus. **Open** *Apr-Oct* 10am-1pm, 2pm, Mon-Fri; 10am-1pm, 2-5pm, Sat; 2-5pm Sun; *Nov-Mar* 1-5pm Mon-Fri; 10am-1pm, 2-5pm, Sat; 2-5pm Sun. **Admission** free. **Map** *see p78.*
Keats wrote some of his best-loved poems and fell in love with Fanny Brawne while living in this cutesy Regency cottage (1818-20). A plum tree in the garden marks the site of

the original tree beneath which he is thought to have penned his *Ode to a Nightingale*. Cabinets within the house contain original manuscripts, and visitors can nose around the poet's bedroom, living room and kitchen. The house reopened in 1998 after major restoration work on the roof. There is more restoration work planned, so phone to check that the house is open before setting off.

Sir John Soane's Museum
13 Lincoln's Inn Fields, WC2 (0171 405 2107). Holborn tube. **Open** 10am-5pm Tue-Sat; 6-9pm first Tue of every month. **Admission** free; donations appreciated (entry to the exhibition £2; free concs). **Guided tours** 2.30pm Sat (£3; free concs). **Map 6 M5**
One of London's most delightful and idiosyncratic museums. Sir John Soane (1753-1837) was not only one of the leading architects of his day, but an inveterate and inspired collector. The word 'eclectic' doesn't do justice to the extraordinary accumulation of treasures stuffed (much as they were in Soane's time) into the house he reconstructed himself. Highlights include Hogarth's *Rake's Progress* and *The Election* series, and the sarcophagus of Pharaoh Seti I, but other gems include Indian drawings, Christopher Wren's watch, numerous chunks and casts of ancient sculpture, a monument to Soane's wife's dog ('Alas, poor Fanny') and Soane's own architectural plans and models. The house's atmosphere is at its most magical when lit by candles on the evening openings on the first Tuesday of the month.

William Morris Gallery
Lloyd Park, Forest Road, E17 (0181 527 3782). Walthamstow Central tube/rail then 34, 97, 215, 257 bus. **Open** 10am-1pm, 2-5pm, Tue-Sat; first Sun every month. **Admission** free. **Credit** MC, £TC, V.
Opened in 1950, this was the childhood home of William Morris, the influential late-Victorian designer, craftsman and socialist. In four rooms on the ground floor, Morris's biography is expounded through his work and political writings. Upstairs there are galleries devoted to his associates – Burne-Jones, Philip Webb and Ernest Gimson – who assisted in contributing to the considerable popularity Morris's style retains today. There are also paintings by one-time apprentice to Morris, Frank Brangwyn.

Local museums

Crystal Palace Museum
Anerley Hill, SE19 (0181 676 0700). Crystal Palace rail/ 2B, 3, 63, 108B, 122, 137, 157, 227, 249 bus. **Open** 11am-5pm Sun, bank holiday Mon. **Admission** free; donations requested.
Housed in the old engineering school, where John Logie Baird invented television, this small but informative museum tells the tale of the famed, ill-fated Crystal Palace from its arrival in Sydenham after the 1851 Great Exhibition to its destruction by fire in 1936. *See also p104* **Crystal Palace Park**.

Cuming Museum
155-157 Walworth Road, SE17 (0171 701 1342). Elephant & Castle tube/rail. **Open** 10am-5pm Tue-Sat. **Closed** closed public hols. **Admission** free.
One of London's most likeable local museums, the Cuming charts the history of Southwark from the Romans to the present day and is packed with intriguing exhibits.

Livesey Museum
682 Old Kent Road, SE15 (0171 639 5604). Elephant & Castle tube/rail then 53, 172 bus. **Open** *mid-Dec-mid-Sept* 10am-5pm Tue-Sat. **Admission** free.
Opened in 1890 as a public library (the gift of Victorian industrialist and benefactor Sir George Livesey), the small-but-perfectly-formed Livesey became a museum in 1974.

Since then, it has hosted numerous temporary exhibitions, aimed mainly at children. Not worth a journey across town, perhaps, but great if you're in the area.

Museum of Richmond
Old Town Hall, Whittaker Avenue, Richmond, Surrey (0181 332 1141). Richmond tube/rail. **Open** *May-Oct* 11am-5pm Tue-Sat; 2-5pm Sun; *Nov-Apr* 11am-5pm Tue-Sat. **Admission** £2; £1 concs; free under-16s.
The focus here is on Richmond's popularity as a royal resort, but the museum also traces the area's history from its role as a prehistoric settlement (weapons and other implements frequently turn up in the river) to life in the town during World War II. The staff are friendly and well informed.

Vestry House Museum
Vestry Road, E17 (0181 509 1917). Walthamstow Central tube/rail. **Open** 10am-1pm, 2-5.30pm, Mon-Fri; 10am-1pm, 2-5pm, Sat. **Admission** free.
This diminutive but charming museum offers a fascinating photographic history of Walthamstow, as well as focusing on two of the area's favourite sons: Alfred Hitchcock (*see p92*), born and bred in Leytonstone, and Frederick Bremer, designer of Britain's first motor car (the 1894 vehicle is on display). Strangely, there's nothing about Britain's first powered flight, by AV Roe over Walthamstow Marshes in 1909. The costume and toy sections are well worth a look.

Wandsworth Museum
The Courthouse, Garratt Lane, SW18 (0181 871 7074). East Putney tube/28, 37, 39, 44, 77A, 156, 170, 220, 270, 337 bus. **Open** 10am-5pm Tue-Sat; 2-5pm Sun. **Admission** free.
The exhibits in this welcoming local museum are dedicated to the development and social history of the borough of Wandsworth from medieval times to the present day. Many of the photos, letters and artefacts have been donated by local residents. There are interactive displays and quizzes for children.

Medicine

Alexander Fleming Laboratory Museum
St Mary's Hospital, Praed Street, W2 (0171 725 6528). Paddington tube/rail/7, 15, 27, 36 bus. **Open** 10am-1pm Mon-Thur and by appointment 2-5pm Mon-Thur, 10am-5pm Fri. **Admission** £2; £1 concs. **Map 2 D5**
On 3 September 1928, when a Petri dish of bacteria became contaminated with a mysterious mould, Alexander Fleming realised something peculiar was going on. This chance discovery of penicillin had momentous consequences and this small museum is a re-creation (in the very same room) of his laboratory, with displays and a video providing insights into his life and the role of penicillin in the fight against disease.

Florence Nightingale Museum
St Thomas's Hospital, 2 Lambeth Palace Road, SE1 (0171 620 0374). Westminster tube/Waterloo tube/ rail. **Open** 10am-5pm Tue-Sun (last admission 4pm). **Admission** £3.50; £2.50 concs; £7 family ticket. **Credit** AmEx, MC, £TC, V. **Map 8 M9**
The world's most famous nurse is celebrated in the well thought-out displays of this small museum, close to Westminster Bridge. Nightingale's chief achievement in a long career of social campaigning was to establish nursing as a disciplined profession (indeed, 'her lady and the lamp' care in the Crimea was but a small part of her life's contribution to medicine); and she set up the first nursing school at St Thomas's in 1859.

Museums of the Royal College of Surgeons

35-43 Lincoln's Inn Fields, WC2 (0171 973 2190/ recorded info 0171 312 6694/museums@rcseng.ac.uk). Holborn tube. **Open** 10am-5pm Mon-Fri. **Admission** free; donations encouraged. **Map 6 M6**

The Royal College of Surgeons runs four museums under one roof: the **Hunterian**, the **Odontological**, and the **Wellcome Museums of Pathology and Anatomy** (open by appointment only). The Hunterian Museum (perhaps the most impressive), in Lincoln's Inn Fields, consists of a collection of anatomical and pathological specimens, purchased by the British Government in 1799 from John Hunter (1728-93); it's not for the squeamish. Tall glass-fronted display cabinets hold jars of numerous (human and animal) internal organs along with foetuses at different stages of their development. A skeleton of a giant man, the Irish Giant, and a dwarf woman are also on display. Jaws, casts and skulls can be seen in the Odontological Museum, as well as the famous Waterloo teeth, extracted from the corpses on the field of battle to replace those lost by the living. The dental and surgical instruments serve to reinforce the value of anaesthetics.
Website: www.rcseng.ac.uk

Old Operating Theatre, Museum & Herb Garret

9A St Thomas's Street, SE1 (0171 955 4791). London Bridge tube/rail. **Open** 10am-4pm Tue-Sun & most Mons (phone to check). **Admission** £2.90; £1.50-£2 concs; £7.25 family ticket. **Map 12 Q8**

The only surviving example of an early nineteenth-century operating theatre is reached via a narrow flight of stairs to the belfry of an old church. Here, in an adjoining room, ancient banks of viewing stands rise in semicircles around a crude wooden bed. Close your eyes and you can almost hear the screams from an unanaesthetised, blindfolded patient as a blood-stained surgeon carefully saws through his leg. Exhibits in the garret illustrate the history of surgery, herbal medicine and nursing at Guy's and St Thomas's hospitals.

Royal London Hospital Archives & Museum

St Philip's Church, Newark Street, E1 (0171 377 7608). Whitechapel tube. **Open** 10am-4.30pm Mon-Fri. **Admission** free.

Joseph Merrick, 'the Elephant Man', was a patient, and then an exhibit, at the Royal London Hospital in the late 1880s. Part of the hospital's museum is devoted to this tragic figure. The rest charts the history of the hospital, and nursing and medicine in general. It includes a section on the heroic nurse Edith Cavell, who was executed by the Germans in 1915 for helping Allied soldiers to escape from occupied Belgium.

St Bartholomew's Hospital Museum

West Smithfield, EC1 (0171 601 8152/guided tours 0171 837 0546). Barbican, Farringdon or St Paul's tube. **Open** 10am-4pm Tue-Fri. **Admission** free. **Guided tours** 2pm Fri (£4; £3 concs). **Map 11 O5**

London's oldest and best-loved hospital, threatened with closure for many years, has thankfully been saved (for the time being at least). Inside the grounds are a small but informative museum of its history and the only survivor of its original four chapels, **St Bartholomew-the-Less**. The **Great Hall** and the staircase, its walls decorated with epic biblical murals by William Hogarth, can also be viewed from the museum, but the seasonal weekly tours offer a better view, while also taking in Smithfield and the surrounding area.

Religion

Jewish Museum, Camden

129 Albert Street, NW1 (0171 284 1997). Camden Town tube. **Open** 10am-4pm Mon-Thur, Sun. **Admission** £3; £1.50-£2 concs; free under-5s.

London's two-sited Jewish Museum has been recognised as one of Britain's pre-eminent museums. It's easy to see why. Although both sites are relatively small, they contain a wealth of information. Camden's branch is more formal: three galleries detailing Jewish British history, an exhibition area and, upstairs, a floor of effectively displayed ceremonial objects such as a series of rimmonim (the decorative silver tops of Torah scrolls), Hanukkah lamps and a magnificent Venetian synagogue ark, dating from the sixteenth century. This quiet building, smelling of fresh wood, lends itself to a thoughtful experience: there are helpful volunteers on hand always ready to furnish further information.

Jewish Museum, Finchley

80 East End Road, N3 (0181 349 1143). Finchley Central tube/13, 82, 112, 143, 260 bus. **Open** 10.30am-5pm Mon-Thur; 10.30am-4.30pm Sun. **Closed** Suns in Aug, Jewish festivals, public hols & public hol weekends, 24 Dec-4 Jan. **Admission** £2; £1 concs.

Located in the Sternberg Centre for Reform Judaism, the museum's Finchley branch may lack the gilt-edged splendour of its NW1 sibling, but it compensates admirably with its fascinating displays detailing many aspects of Jewish social history. On two levels, there is a functional sewing workshop, detailing sweatshop life at the turn of the century, plus artefacts relating to East End life and practical information for refugees from Germany ('Do not talk in a loud voice,' warns one pamphlet. 'Do not make yourself conspicuous.') Upstairs, a Holocaust exhibition follows the life of Leon Greenman, a British Jew who, alone of his family, survived Auschwitz. Overseen by friendly staff, this branch also has a 12,000-strong photographic archive, augmented by 2,000 oral history tapes.

Museum of Methodism & John Wesley's House

Wesley Chapel, 49 City Road, EC1 (0171 253 2262). Old Street tube/rail. **Open** 10am-4pm Mon-Sat; noon-2pm Sun. **Admission** *museum & house* £4; £2 concs; £10 family ticket; additional visits free within same month. **Map 10 Q4**

Appropriately enough, Bunhill Fields (*see p42*), just across the City Road, is the burial ground of many of London's dissenters. John Wesley's unorthodox assemblies resulted in the establishment of a church that now has a following of over 50 million around the world. In 1778, Wesley opened this chapel for worship, and in 1981 a museum of the man's work opened in the crypt. Highlights include the pulpit and a large oil portrait of the scene at his death bed. His house next door has been restored to its original Georgian interior design, right down to paint Wesley would have chosen. In the kitchen and study you can see his nightcap, preaching gown and personal experimental electric-shock machine.

Sport

MCC Museum

Marylebone Cricket Club, Lord's Ground, NW8 (0171 432 1033). St John's Wood tube. **Open** *guided tours* (phone for availability) *Oct-Mar* noon, 2pm daily; *Apr-Sept* 10am, noon, 2pm daily. **Admission** *guided tours* £5.80; £4.20 concs.

Cricket fans will be delighted by this anecdotal exhibition of the game's memorabilia. Among the paintings, photos and significantly battered bats, there's a reconstruction of the shot that killed a passing sparrow in 1936, complete with stuffed bird and its nemesis, the ball. The Ashes reside here: not much bigger than an egg cup, the sport's most hard-won trophy contains the charred remains of one of the bails from the 1882-3 Test series between England and Australia. The guided tour allows the empty ground to be viewed from the Mound stand, followed by a lingering wander through the pavilion, the visitors' dressing room, and the historic Long Room.

Museum of Rugby/Twickenham Stadium

Gate 8, Twickenham Rugby Stadium, Rugby Road, Twickenham, Middx (0181 892 2000). Hounslow East tube then 281 bus/Twickenham rail. **Open** 10.30am-5pm Tue-Sat; 2-5pm Sun. **Admission** *combined ticket £5;* £3 concs; £15 family ticket. **Credit** MC, V.
Rugby's increasing popularity might mean that more fans make the journey to this brand-new interactive celebration of the sport at its mecca in Twickenham. Its collection includes touch-screen information points on clubs and players, a scrum machine and a reconstruction of the old West Stand changing rooms. The tour round the spectacular stadium, from the dressing rooms to the hallowed turf itself, is excellent. Combined tours with **Wimbledon Lawn Tennis Museum** (*see below*) are also run; you should try to book two to three weeks in advance.

Wimbledon Lawn Tennis Museum

Church Road, SW19 (0181 946 6131). Southfields tube/39, 93, 200 bus. **Open** 10.30am-5pm daily. (spectators only during championships).
Admission £3; £2 concs. **Credit** MC, V.
More than 150 years of social and sporting history is encapsulated in this newly designed, well-lit museum. More interesting than the rows of cases filled with racquets and balls are a mock-up of an Edwardian tennis party and the section on tennis since 1968, with touch-screen commentaries on past and present Wimbledon stars and videos of past championships. The place is packed with unusual information: yellow balls were first used in 1986; they are stored at 20°C and can reach a speed of 140mph (224kmph). Only fanatical tennis groupies will thrill at the collection's array of personal memorabilia, such as Pat Cash's headbands and Boris Becker's autograph.

Theatre

Theatre Museum

Tavistock Street (entrance off Russell Street), WC2 (0171 836 7891/2330/First Call credit card bookings 0171 497 9977). Covent Garden tube. **Open** 11am-7pm Tue-Sun. **Admission** £4; £2.50 concs; £8 family ticket. **Credit** AmEx, MC, £TC, V. **Map 8 L6**
Appropriately sited near the oldest West End theatre, Theatre Royal Drury Lane, the basement galleries here feel like an aquarium of theatre history. Instead of water and fish, the rows of tanks contain illustrations and artefacts from Elizabethan theatre to present-day productions. The theatrical effect is enhanced by low lighting in the long corridors and flickering neon advertisements. In another gallery, **From Page to Stage** invites visitors to explore the creative development of the National Theatre's production of *The Wind in the Willows*: try on Toad's webbed gloves, play at being stage manager, or watch videos of rehearsals in progress. The **Exploding Tradition** section features ground-breaking stage designers from the nineteenth century onwards. The museum also holds the National Video Archive of Stage Performance (access by appointment). **Picturing the Players** is the Somerset Maugham collection of portraits of legendary thespians and theatres: look out for Elizabeth I's startling resemblance to Bette Davis in the first painting. Exhibitions for 1999 include a show on puppets (Apr-autumn) and **Curtain Up!**, a behind-the-scenes look at Cameron Mackintosh musicals.

The **Natural History Museum**. *See page 115.*

Transport

Canal Museum

12-13 New Wharf Road, N1 (0171 713 0836). King's Cross tube/rail. **Open** 10am-4.30pm Tue-Sun. **Admission** £2.50; £1.25 concs. **Map 6 L2**
The warehouse housing this small museum on the Regent Canal's Battlebridge Basin was built in the 1850s by an Italian immigrant, Carlo Gatti, who made his fortune importing ice from Norway. The blocks were carried from the docks on canal boats and stored here in huge ice wells. The museum tells the story of Gatti's life and the families who made their living on the canals.

London Transport Museum

39 Wellington Street, WC2 (0171 379 6344). Covent Garden tube. **Open** 10am-6pm Mon-Thur, Sat, Sun; 11am-6pm Fri. **Admission** £4.95; £2.95 concs; free under-5s; £12.85 family ticket; £19.95 family season ticket. **Credit** MC, V. **Map 8 L6**
Gathered behind the glass façade are the road and rail vehicles that have struggled to serve the city's burgeoning population since 1870. Beside the first electric trams, an audio-visual display prophesies their return to London's streets, while another extols the virtues of the timeless red double-decker. Justifiable pride is taken in the wonderful London Transport posters that have been produced over the years, and in the development of that masterpiece of design, the tube map.

The most exciting part of the exhibition is the story of the development of the much-maligned London underground. There is usually a queue to try out the tube train simulator, featuring the 'dead man's handle' emergency cutoff device. You can also practise bus-driving or watch the video wall celebrating the 1940s development of leafy

'Metroland' for Londoners made homeless by the Blitz. The excellent **KidZones** consist of a children's trail around the museum, accessible information about the environmental impact of transport and a variety of interactive activities.
Website: www.ltmuseum.co.uk

North Woolwich Old Station Museum

Pier Road, E16 (0171 474 7244). North Woolwich rail/Woolwich Dockyard or Woolwich Arsenal rail then foot tunnel/riverboat to North Woolwich Pier.
Open *Apr-Sept* 2-5pm Fri, Sun; 10am-5pm Sat; *during summer school holidays* 1-5pm Mon-Wed; 2-5pm Fri, Sun; 10am-5pm Sat. **Admission** free.
Dedicated to the London & North Eastern Railway, this museum is at its best on the first Sunday of summer months when the Coffee Pot and Pickett steam engines chug up and down outside. Inside, trains, tickets, station signs and a 1920s ticket office are on display. For railway enthusiasts it's worth a journey to this otherwise rather charmless part of London.

A design icon in its own right: the clean-lined **Design Museum.** *See page 117.*

Other specialist museums

Bank of England Museum

Bartholomew Lane, EC2 (0171 601 5545). Bank tube.
Open 10am-5pm Mon-Fri. **Admission** free.
Map 12 Q6
This unexpectedly interesting museum centres on a restoration of the bank's Stock Office, designed by Sir John Soane in 1793, complete with figures in period costume and a stuffed tabby cat. Well thought-out displays tell the bank's 300-year story, explaining its vital role in providing the stability and wherewithal for Britain to build up a global empire, and provide an enlightening, informal course in national finance for beginners. Visitors come tantalisingly close to a stack of gold bars, learn via interactive screens about the complexities of banknote production and security, and budding City high-flyers can play at foreign exchange trading.

Bramah Tea & Coffee Museum

corner of Gainsford Street & Maguire Street, SE1 (0171 378 0222). London Bridge tube/rail/P11, 15, 42, 47, 78 bus. **Open** 10am-6pm daily. **Admission** £4; £2.50 concs; £10 family ticket. **Credit** AmEx, JCB, MC, £TC, V.
Map 12 S9

British Museum

With 6.7 million visitors shuffling their way through its hallowed halls in 1997 (up from two million in 1974), the British Museum is easily London's number one tourist attraction – and it's not difficult to see why. The BM is one of only two institutions in the world – the other being the Smithsonian in Washington DC – that fulfil the Enlightenment concept of gathering all branches of human knowledge under one roof: a real-life encyclopaedia.

The museum's beginnings can be traced to royal physician Dr Hans Sloane's 'cabinet of curiosities' (bequeathed to the nation in 1753), a substantial miscellany of books, paintings, classical antiquities and stuffed animals. Over the next century the plunder of empire, including the Elgin Marbles from Greece and various massive Egyptian monuments, overwhelmed the storage space available. In 1847, Robert Smirke designed the present impressive neo-classical edifice, with its grand colonnaded façade and ample interior.

All change

The British Museum is currently in the throes of a major renovation project to mark its 250th anniversary (in 2003; although it is due to be completed by autumn 2000). The centrepiece of the new building will be the **Great Court**, a glass-covered two-acre inner courtyard designed by Sir Norman Foster and Partners. The Court will contain, among other things, an education centre, the Sainsbury African Galleries and the revamped **Reading Room**, which, for the first time, will be open to all visitors. Two new elliptical-shaped floors on the northern exterior of the Reading Room will be connected to the main building, making access considerably easier than at present. The project also marks the return of the **Ethnography collections** following a long spell at the Museum of Mankind. Note that, until building work is completed, visitors' services such as disabled access and access to toilets may be interrupted and galleries closed at short notice.

In the early 1990s, Edward Bramah, a former tea taster, set up this unusual museum to chart the history of tea and coffee drinking. The new premises allow the two infusions to be studied separately, and their important role in British society to be documented. There's also an impressive collection of coffee makers and teapots (including the world's largest) and a café where you can try out the real thing.

Clockmakers' Company Museum

The Clockroom, Guildhall Library, Aldermanbury, EC2 (0171 332 1868/1870). Bank, Mansion House or St Paul's tube/Moorgate tube/rail. **Open** 9.30am-4.45pm Mon-Fri. **Admission** free. **Map 11 P6**
This cramped but easily digestible collection of timepieces is the world's oldest. It includes the watch that Sir Edmund Hillary wore on the first successful ascent of Everest in 1953 and John Harrison's prizewinning chronometer. Anyone familiar with Dava Sobel's surprise bestseller *Longitude* will want to take a look at the latter – a remarkable invention that made it possible for ships at sea to chart their exact position, giving the edge to Britain's empire builders.

Kew Bridge Steam Museum

Green Dragon Lane, Brentford, Middx (0181 568 4757). Gunnersbury tube/Kew Bridge rail/27, 65, 237, 267, 391 bus. **Open** 11am-5pm daily. **Admission** *Mon-Fri* £2.80; £1-£1.50 concs; £7 family ticket. *Sat, Sun, public hols* £3.80; £2-£2.50 concs; £10.50 family ticket. **Credit** AmEx, EC, MC, V.

A Victorian riverside pumping station, close to the north end of Kew Bridge, is now home to this museum of water supply. The Water for Life exhibition details the history of London's use and abuse of the world's most precious commodity and includes a unique walk-through sewer experience. At 3pm on weekends one of the largest working steam engines in the world, the 90-inch (229-cm) Cornish Beam engine (built in 1845 for use in the tin mines), stirs ponderously into motion. Like the working waterwheel and five other steam engines, it has been restored by enthusiastic volunteers to its former working order.

London Fire Brigade Museum

94A Southwark Bridge Road, SE1 (0171 587 2894). Borough tube/London Bridge tube/rail. **Guided tours** 10.30am, 11.30am, 1.30pm Mon-Fri by appointment only. **Admission** £3; £2 under-14s; not recommended for under-7s. **Credit** MC, £TC, V. **Map 11 O9**
Book in advance for a two-hour guided tour of the museum, which explains the history of firefighting in London since 1666, the year of the Great Fire. Old firefighting appliances are among the exhibits, and visitors might glimpse firefighting recruits training at the adjacent centre.

The Museum of...

The Bargehouse, Oxo Tower Wharf, Bargehouse Street, SE1 (0171 928 1255). Waterloo tube/rail. **Open** 1-7.30pm Wed-Fri; noon-7.30pm Sat, Sun. **Admission** free. **Map 11 N7**

Getting to grips with the BM

The cardinal rule is: don't try to see everything. Even if it were physically possible to do so, you would end up with nothing but glazed eyes, throbbing feet and only the haziest of memories of anything you had seen. Focus your attention on specific areas of interest. If you don't know what you want to see, buy one of the excellent souvenir guides (£5) and take your pick of the highlights, or try one of the four suggested tours on the £1 leaflets. Alternatively, book yourself on to one of the 90-minute tours of the museum's top treasures at the information desk (£6) or join one of the free daily 'Eye Opener' tours that concentrate on one aspect of the museum's collections, or the specialist half-hour talks given by curators at 11.30am Monday to Saturday.

A few of the BM's many highlights are listed below. These all form part of the museum's permanent collection; note that there is also a programme of temporary exhibitions, some of which carry an admission charge.

Ancient Egypt – the monumental **statues of the pharaohs** and the **Rosetta Stone**, inscribed with a decree in three languages which enabled Egyptian hieroglyphics to be deciphered for the first time; *room 25 until June 1999, then the Rosetta Stone will form part of a major exhibition in the Special Exhibition gallery.*

Ancient Assyria – the vivid **reliefs** of battles and hunting scenes from Nineveh; *rooms 17, 19 & 21.*

Ancient Greece – the reconstructed tomb of one of the rulers of Xanthos, known as the **Nereid Monument**; *room 7 (from June 1999).* The sculptures from the Parthenon, better known as the **Elgin Marbles**; *room 8.*

The Celts – the **Lindow Man**, preserved in peat, having been ritually killed around 300 BC; *room 50.*

Roman Britain – the **Mildenhall Treasure** – 28 pieces of fourth-century silver tableware; *room 49.*

Middle Ages – the seventh-century **Sutton Hoo ship burial**, containing a fabulous cache of Anglo-Saxon treasure; *room 41.*

Islamic World – the unsurpassed collection of **Iznik pottery** from Ottoman Turkey; *John Addis Gallery.*

China – the Tang dynasty (AD618-906) **tomb figurines** buried with General Kiu Tingxun in 728; *Joseph E Hotung Gallery.*

South-east Asia – the close-to-lifesize **figure of the goddess Tara** from the eighth century; *Joseph E Hotung Gallery.*

Japan – the **Ukiyoe prints** and decorative arts, from the most comprehensive collection of Japanese applied and fine arts in Europe; *Konica & Urasenke Galleries.*

British Museum
Great Russell Street, WC1 (0171 636 1555/ recorded info 0171 580 1788). Holborn, Russell Square or Tottenham Court Road tube. **Open** 10am-5pm Mon-Sat; 2.30-6pm Sun. **Closed** 2 Apr 1999. **Admission** free; donations appreciated. **Map 6 K5**

A unique venture that aims to 'challenge the way we think about museums and… ask questions about our relationship with material culture'. What this means in practice is five separate museums running for 16 weeks each. The first, the **Museum of Collectors**, opened in mid-November 1998. This is to be followed by the **Museum of Me** (Apr-July), the **Museum of Emotions** (July-Oct) and the **Museum of the Unknown** (Nov 1999-Mar 2000).

Museum of Garden History
St Mary-at-Lambeth, Lambeth Palace Road, SE1 (0171 261 1891). Waterloo tube/rail/C10, 507 bus. **Open** *7 Mar-Dec* 10.30am-4pm Mon-Fri; 10.30am-5pm Sun. **Admission** free; donations appreciated. **Map 8 L10**
Inside St Mary-at-Lambeth church, antique horticultural tools and photographic panels on famous garden designers and plant hunters illustrate the development of the English passion for gardening. The tireless John Tradescant, gardener to James I and Charles I, is given particular prominence. A replica of a seventeenth-century knot garden has been created in the tiny church courtyard. One of the sarcophagi here contains the remains of Captain Bligh, who was abandoned by his mutinous crew in the middle of the Pacific.

Museum of the Order of St John
St John's Gate, EC1 (0171 253 6644). Barbican tube/ Farringdon tube/rail. **Open** 9am-5pm Mon-Fri; 10am-4pm Sat. **Tours** 11am, 2.30pm, Tue, Fri, Sat. **Admission** free; donations requested. **Map 9 O4**

The surviving 1504 gateway was once the entrance to the Priory of St John of Jerusalem, founded in the twelfth century, and is now the HQ of the British Order of St John. Beside the gate is a small museum tracing the history of the Order from the swashbuckling days of the crusading Knights Hospitallers, to the more mundane but more useful work of today's St John Ambulance Brigade. The Chapter Hall, Council Chamber, Old Chancery, new church and Norman crypt (the only remaining part of the original building) can only be seen on the guided tours; phone for details of times. All that remains of the priory's original circular church is its outline, traced in cobbles, in St John's Square, just north of the gate.

Musical Museum
368 High Street, Brentford, Middx (0181 560 8108). Gunnersbury tube/Brentford Central or Kew Bridge rail/ 65, 237, 267 bus. **Open** *Apr-June, Sept-Oct* 2-5pm Sat, Sun; *July-Aug* 2-4pm Wed; 2-5pm Sat, Sun. **Admission** £3.20; £2.50 concs.
Occupying a converted church, the museum concerns itself with mechanical musical devices of all types, shapes and sounds. Unusually, all the instruments are self-playing, restored to (almost) perfect pitch and working order, including not only the pianolas but also a violin. On the 90-minute tour by dedicated guides (2pm & 3.30pm), you can hear some of the most celebrated instruments, such as the Steinway Duo-Art grand piano or the Wurlitzer cinema organ. There is also a series of popular summer concerts.

Art Galleries

After the shock of the new, get back to the art of the matter.

The domination of the Young British Artists (YBAs), the endlessly hyped iconoclastic storm troops of British art, is loosening. Shockability, the essence of much YBA work, is by its nature a one-time phenomenon. The constant demands to redefine boundaries and challenge perceptions become, ultimately, rather wearying. True, the **ICA**, **Serpentine** and **White Cube** galleries continue to play host to installations and conceptual art, while performance and cyber art can still be found in many of the capital's smaller venues. Yet Damien Hirst's work is struggling to reach its reserve price, the Chapman brothers have taken to trading insults with David Bowie for exposure, Charles Saatchi (the biggest patron of the YBAs) has begun to sell, and, perhaps most tellingly, art graduates (according to tutors) are increasingly favouring decorative and ornamental work over installations and sculpture. Meanwhile Chris Ofili, one of the few new painters lauded in the past couple of years, won the 1998 Turner Prize.

There's plenty going on in the capital for fans of every sort of art. In May 2000 the magnificent **Tate Gallery of Modern Art** is due to open in the former Bankside Power Station, while the Millbank site will, by the following year, become devoted to British art since the sixteenth century. The **Courtauld Institute** reopened during 1998 after extensive renovation, and in summer 1999, the completion of the Guildhall Yard East project (off Gresham Street, EC2) will provide a new home for the **Guildhall Art Gallery**, bringing together the Corporation of London's considerable art collection for the first time in 50 years.

London's major collections are all immensely rewarding, but don't neglect the smaller commercial galleries listed towards the end of this chapter. Many of these put on shows by first-rank artists – Freud, Warhol, Picasso, Frink and Hockney have all recently graced small commercial galleries. And the beauty of them is that these exhibitions are more intimate, the selections often offer a different angle on the artist, and they are invariably less crowded than one would expect in a national collection.

Dulwich Picture Gallery: *under wraps in '99.*

Eighteenth-century Somerset House's recent restoration allows the Courtauld's 11 superb private collections (1300-1950) to be displayed in an appropriately grand setting. The best-known works are the impressionist and post-impressionist pieces. First-rank paintings by Manet, Degas, Cézanne (*The Card Players*), Monet, Pissarro, Renoir (*La Loge*), Seurat, Gauguin and Toulouse-Lautrec make up textile magnate Courtauld's private collection, while the Rubens (including a rare landscape, *Landscape by Moonlight*) are the legacy of Count Seilern. Other gems include Botticelli's *The Trinity*, Cranach's *Adam and Eve* and a delightful little Breugel. The collection also contains some masterful etchings and drawings, some of which feature in **Piranesi, Canaletto and Tiepolo: Etchings** (11 Feb-3 May 1999). Other exhibitions planned for 1999 are **The Value of Art** (27 May-30 Aug) and **Roger Fry's Vision of Art** (15 Oct-23 Jan 2000).

Collections

Courtauld Institute

Somerset House, Strand, WC2 (0171 873 2526). Covent Garden tube. **Open** 10am-6pm Mon-Sat; noon-6pm Sun. **Admission** £4; £2 concs; free 10am-2pm Mon. **Map 8 M7**

Dulwich Picture Gallery

College Road, SE21 (0181 693 5254). North Dulwich or West Dulwich rail/P4, 12, 37, 176 bus. **Closed until May 2000**.

Britain's oldest public gallery, designed by Sir John Soane in 1811, is as famous for its architecture as its paintings (mainly seventeenth- and eighteenth-century continental masters). Unfortunately, it is closed for refurbishment and building work until May 2000, although some of the collection will be on view at the Lothbury Gallery (*see below*) from September to December 1999.

Iveagh Bequest

Kenwood House, Hampstead Lane, NW3 (0181 348 1286). Golders Green tube then 210 bus. **Open** *Apr-Sept* 10am-6pm daily; *Oct-Mar* 10am-4pm daily.
Admission free, donations appreciated.
Set amid the leafy environs of the northern part of Hampstead Heath, the first Earl of Mansfield's home, Kenwood House, was remodelled in the late eighteenth century by Robert Adam. Beyond his neo-classical façade, the house contains a clutch of outstanding paintings and a number of fine pieces of furniture. Look out for one of Rembrandt's self-portraits (a guaranteed original, unlike so many others); several rare Vermeers in the dining room; and Reynolds' portrait of Nelson's mistress, Lady Hamilton, dressed up as a nun. Botticelli, Guardi and a couple of classic flirtatious Bouchers round out this wonderful collection. The sumptuous library is also worth a gawp. Exhibitions planned for 1999 include **The Art of Hilda Carline** (Stanley Spencer's wife) and **The Artist's Model II: From Etty to Spencer**.

Leighton House Museum

12 Holland Park Road, W14 (0171 602 3316). High Street Kensington tube/9, 9A, 10, 27, 33, 28, 31, 49 bus. **Open** 11am-5.30pm Mon-Sat. **Closed** public hols.
Admission free; donations appreciated.
The painter Lord Leighton fulfilled his vision of a palace of art when he had this rather severe house built in 1866. It houses his collection of Pre-Raphaelite and High Victorian work (as well as many of his own works), although the biggest attraction is the magnificent Arab Hall, a testament to his fascination with the East. Several small temporary exhibitions are held during the year, which in 1999 will include **The Holland Park Circle 1850-1900** and **The Leighton Open**, the annual exhibition for artists who live, work or study in the Royal Borough of Kensington and Chelsea (July). *See also p112.*

Lothbury Gallery

41 Lothbury, EC2 (0171 726 1642/1643). Bank tube. **Open** 10am-4pm (last admission 3.30pm) Mon-Fri.
Admission free. **Map 12 Q6**
Regularly changing displays of works from the NatWest Group's collection can be viewed in the splendid 1920s neo-classical foyer of the group's HQ. The collection stretches from the seventeenth century to the present day, but the focus is firmly on twentieth-century British artists, including Auerbach, Hodgkin, Pasmore and Caulfield. Exhibitions in 1999 include the **NatWest Art Prize**, a collection of contemporary work by under-35s (May-Aug), and, from September to December, a selection from the **Dulwich Picture Gallery**, which is closed for refurbishment until May 2000 (*see above*).

National Gallery

Trafalgar Square, WC2 (0171 839 3321). Leicester Square tube/Charing Cross tube/rail. **Open** 10am-6pm Mon, Tue, Thur-Sat; 10am-8pm Wed; noon-6pm Sun.
Admission free. **Map 8 K7**
Founded in 1824 with just 38 pictures, the National Collection of Paintings now contains more than 2,000 western European paintings from the mid-thirteenth century to 1900, including works from all the major schools. Since 1997, an exchange of more than 60 paintings with the **Tate Gallery** (*see p131*) using the year 1900 as the dividing date between the two galleries. The quality and range of pictures on display is simply stunning, with leather Chesterfield sofas, lashings of marble and creaking wooden floors adding to the hallowed atmosphere. There's a good introductory guided tour, which concentrates on the major paintings on the ground floor, or you can pick up the excellent free audioguide from either of the two main entrances. The exterior of Robert Venturi and Denise Scott Brown's **Sainsbury Wing** has its detractors, but the exhibition space provides a superb setting for the fine collection of early Renaissance works as well as playing host to numerous temporary exhibitions throughout the year. And don't miss the **Micro Gallery** (10am-5.30pm Mon-Sat; 2-5.30pm Sun), where, at the touch of a screen, you can see any painting in the collection, print out a reproduction or construct a customised tour around your own favourites, which might include Van Gogh's *Sunflowers*, Van Eyck's *The Arnolfini Portrait*, Bellini's *Portrait of the Doge Leonardo Loredan*, Constable's *The Hay Wain* or Turner's *The Fighting Temeraire*.

National Portrait Gallery

2 St Martin's Place, WC2 (0171 306 0055). Leicester Square tube/Charing Cross tube/rail. **Open** 10am-6pm Mon-Sat; noon-6pm Sun. **Admission** free. **Map 8 K7**
You can trace the history of the nation in the faces of its key players down the ages at the National Portrait Gallery. Founded in 1856 to collect pictures of royal and political figures, it now boasts as one of its most prized exhibits the only known portrait of non-royal, non-political William Shakespeare. For a chronological tour, start on the top floor and work your way downwards (although be prepared for some disruption as the gallery extends its exhibition space). The present generation of the royal family is on Level 2, including Brian Organ's portrait of the Princess of Wales. Several exhibitions are planned for 1999, including works by **John Everett Millais** until June, followed by **Icons of Pop** until September, and there's a nod to the millennium in **Faces of the Century** (22 Oct-30 Jan 2000). The winner and best-of-the-rest of the **BP Portrait Awards** are on show from 25 June to 26 September. **The Art of Cooking**, photographic portraits by Barry Marsden, runs until 1 April 1999 in the recently opened Portrait Café.

Queen's Gallery

Buckingham Palace, Buckingham Palace Road, SW1 (0171 930 4832/recorded info 0171 799 2331). St James's Park tube/Victoria tube/rail. **Open** 9.30am-4.30pm (last admission 4pm) daily. **Admission** £4; £2-£3 concs; free under-5s. **Credit** AmEx, MC, V. **Map 7 H9**
The Queen heads a committee that decides which paintings to show here from her vast collection (one of the largest private collections in the world). It's always worth looking out for the exhibitions, which in 1999 promise **Charles I: Portrait of a Martyr King** (a touch of royal bias in the titling, one suspects) and **Raphael's Drawings** (21 May-10 Oct), after which the gallery will close for remodelling until 2002.

Saatchi Collection

98A Boundary Road, NW8 (0171 624 8299/328 8299). St John's Wood or Swiss Cottage tube/139, 189 bus. **Open** noon-6pm Thur-Sun. **Admission** £4; £2 concs; free under-12s. **Credit** MC, V.
Charles Saatchi's advertising fortune enabled him to become a mover and shaker in the art world. A decade ago he visited the **Freeze** exhibition in Docklands and fell in love with contemporary British art. Whoever he buys now, everyone else will be watching. Similarly, whoever he sells is also noted. Richard Wilson's *20:50*, an installation in sump pump oil and galvanised steel, is now an immensely popular fixture at this gallery, and alone is worth a visit. Not surprisingly, the large, purpose-built space has also seen some extraordinary temporary exhibitions. Of the three shows a year, one usually concentrates on Young British Artists (in 1999 it will be an exhibition entitled **Neurotic Realism**) and on their equivalents in Europe: **Eurovision**.

Tate Gallery

Millbank, SW1 (0171 887 8000). Pimlico tube/C10, 77A, 88 bus. **Open** *10am-5.50pm daily.* **Admission** *free; special exhibitions prices vary.* **Map 8 K11**

Many people's favourite London gallery, the Tate perhaps owes its popularity to the satisfying combination of its international modern art with the national collection of British paintings (dating from the fifteenth century) housed under one splendid neo-classical roof. However, the Clore Gallery extension, designed by James Stirling to grace the marvellous collection of Turner paintings, has also been a great success and further improvements are in the offing. **ArtNow** is a newish space dedicated to young contemporary artists, staging four different shows of their work each year. Its development heralds the role that contemporary art is expected to play here and at the **Tate Gallery of Modern Art**, scheduled to open in May 2000 in the former Bankside Power Station. The conversion by Swiss architects Herzog and de Meuron will create Britain's first museum of modern art, leaving the Millbank building to become the **Tate Gallery of British Art** in 2001.

The Tate will be mounting a major retrospective of the work of **Jackson Pollock** (Mar-June 1999), organised by the Museum of Modern Art in New York. In November, **The Art of Bloomsbury** will focus on the works of Vanessa Bell, Duncan Grant and Roger Fry, while the Clore Gallery will look at **Turner's Rivers of France: The Seine** (from Oct).

Wallace Collection

Hertford House, Manchester Square, W1 (0171 935 0687). Bond Street tube. **Open** *10am-5pm Mon-Sat; 2-5pm Sun.* **Admission** *free.* **Map 5 G5**

The hallway and the state drawing room of Sir Richard Wallace's late eighteenth-century house have been meticulously restored to the splendour of his original design, down to the crimson silk hangings and damask curtains. The illegitimate heir of the Marquis of Hertford, Wallace nevertheless inherited the ardent Francophile's extraordinary collection of furniture (including a writing desk belonging to Marie-Antoinette), paintings and porcelain purchased for safekeeping in London after the Revolution. An impressive clutch of Old Masters, including Franz Hals' *The Laughing Cavalier* and Rubens' *Rainbow Landscape*, vie for space with magnificent European and Asian arms and armour and a display of Catherine the Great's crockery. The house seems like a delightfully peaceful nineteenth-century anachronism, although further galleries are being added, including a glass roof over the courtyard to house sculptures. You should also visit the splendidly tiled toilets.

Public galleries

Barbican Art Gallery

Level 3, Barbican Centre, Silk Street, EC2 (info 0171 382 7105). Barbican tube/Moorgate tube/rail. **Open** *10am-6.45pm Mon, Thur-Sat; 10am-5.45pm Tue; 10am-7.45pm Wed; noon-6.45pm Sun.* **Admission** *£6; £4 concs; £12 family.* **Credit** *AmEx, MC, £TC, V.* **Map 9 P5**

The main gallery of this formidably disorienting City arts centre regularly mounts interesting exhibitions of modern and historical works. Early in 1999, an exhibition entitled **Picasso and Photography** will explore the influence of the latter on the master's work. Later in the year **David Bailey**'s photographs will be on show, and a **Joseph Beuys** exhibition is planned for October.

Hackney's where the art is

To the untutored eye, Hackney – balanced on top of the City of London, sliding in parallel along the East End and grazing shoulders with more fashionable Islington – may appear pretty unprepossessing, but look again – this time in the right places. Damien Hirst used to live here; Rachel Whiteread, shoe designer Jimmy Choo and Matthew Flowers, who runs gallery **Flowers East** (*see page 135*), still do. For the artists and craftsmen of Europe, Hackney is simply the acme. Reputedly, there is a higher concentration of cultural businesses here than anywhere else on the Continent. Every disused warehouse in the borough now seems to house artistically inspired tenants and, according to local design and craft organisation **Hidden Art**, their numbers are growing.

While the casual visitor may have to negotiate Hackney's more unlovely aspects – dank tower blocks and unneutered skinheads with unneutered Rottweilers – to reach the heart of the art, it's all possible. Start at Hoxton Square and its environs: a host of small galleries and workshops dot the area. Drink at the nearby Bricklayer's Arms to pick up some tips and then head up Kingsland Road. Time your visit to coincide with one of Hidden Art's ever-popular open-workshop events and you can gain access to some 600 spaces. And then what? A visit to the **Geffrye Museum**'s new contemporary design wing (*see page 117*) or a peak at the new architectural college in Curtain Road. You choose.

But it isn't so surprising that Hackney is the new Boho homeland. It has strong historical associations with furniture, glass and fashion industries, while its general poverty has always meant that rents are cheap. Even Hackney Council is offering affordable work units to artists. While this has led to an atmosphere that begs comparison with New York City's Lower East Side's art boom (circa early 1980s), there's the danger that, like there, it'll end in tears and unwelcome change. Space anywhere in London is now at a premium and Hackney's proximity to the financial centre means that the Philistines are even now at the gates. It's difficult to be optimistic about anywhere once serious money gets involved, but watch this space. Hackney could yet win out.

Hidden Art

(information 0171 729 3301/www.hiddenart.co.uk)

Bellissima! It's the estimable **Estorick Collection of Modern Italian Art**.

Camden Arts Centre

Arkwright Road, corner of Finchley Road, NW3 (0171 435 2643). Finchley Road tube. **Open** 11am-7pm Tue-Thur; 11am-5.30pm Fri-Sun. **Admission** free.

The borough of Camden's community arts centre includes three gallery spaces, which host contemporary exhibitions and one historical show a year. There is a programme of talks by artists, usually responding to the current exhibition (dates and times vary; phone for details). Exhibitions for 1999 include a retrospective of British-Chinese sculptor **Kim Lim** (Aug-Oct).

Cartoon Art Trust

New House, 67-68 Hatton Garden, EC1 (0171 405 4717). Chancery Lane tube/Farringdon tube/rail. **Open** by appointment only, noon-6pm Mon-Fri. **Map 9 N5**

Britain has produced some of the world's finest cartoonists, from Hogarth and Gillray through to Gerald Scarfe and Steve Bell. The Trust organises and co-ordinates exhibitions and workshops, but not on the premises. Ring for details, or if you wish to visit its bookshop and library.

Chisenhale Gallery

64 Chisenhale Road, E3 (0181 9801 4518). Bethnal Green or Mile End tube/D6, 8, 277 bus. **Open** 1-6pm Wed-Sun. **Admission** free.

A vast late-Victorian warehouse backing on to a canal provides a forum for innovative art forms. The **New Work UK** show in July consists of three one-week exhibitions for new British talent. **Exit**, a show to end the century, focuses on film and video pieces from across the world.

Crafts Council

44A Pentonville Road, N1 (0171 278 7700). Angel tube. **Open** 11am-6pm Tue-Sat; 2-6pm Sun. **Admission** free. **Map 9 N2**

Housed in an elegantly converted Georgian house, the Council showcases the nation's craft output in a range of fields (textiles, wood, jewellery, furniture, ceramics). Exhibitions take a theme and demonstrate work in that area. **Repeat, repeat** (ceramics) will be on show from April to June 1999; and an international basket making exhibition is also planned. The finalists of the **Jerwood Prize** will be displayed in September.

Estorick Collection of Modern Italian Art

39A Canonbury Square (main entrance Canonbury Road), N1 (0171 704 9522). Highbury & Islington tube/rail/271 bus. **Open** 11am-6pm Wed-Sat; noon-5pm Sun. **Admission** £2.50; £1.50 concs; students free. **Credit** MC, V. **Map 9 O3**

Housed in a Georgian listed building, the Estorick offers Britain's first museum dedicated to modern Italian art. The collection of American academic and art dealer Eric Estorick and his wife Salome contains a truly wonderful selection of futurist work, including pieces by such leading lights as Luigi Russolo, Umberto Boccioni and Gino Severini. Many other major Italian artists are represented, including Modigliani and de Chirico. Long-term loans from other private collections and a fine café complete the picture.

Hayward Gallery

Belvedere Road, SE1 (0171 928 3144/recorded info 0171 261 0127). Embankment tube/Waterloo tube/rail. **Open** *during exhibitions* 10am-6pm Mon, Thur-Sun; 10am-8pm Tue, Wed. **Admission** varies (phone for details). **Credit** AmEx, MC, V. **Map 8 M8**

The Hayward, part of the South Bank's thriving arts scene, is one of London's finest venues for temporary exhibitions of contemporary and historical art. The relatively high admission charges are usually justified by the quality of the work. A major retrospective of **Patrick Caulfield's** work – still lifes, interiors, landscapes and figure compositions – will be on show until April 1999; and consistent with the Hayward's policy of variety, this is followed by **Cities on the Move**, an exploration of art and architecture in Asia's rapidly expanding metropolises.

ICA Gallery

The Mall, SW1 (0171 930 3647/membership enquiries 0171 930 0493/recorded info 0171 930 6393). Piccadilly Circus tube/Charing Cross tube/rail. **Open** noon-7.30pm daily. **Admission** £1.50, £1 concs Mon-Fri; £2.50, £2 concs Sat, Sun; free with membership. **Membership** *annual* £25; £15 concs. **Credit** AmEx, DC, JCB, MC, £TC, V. **Map 8 K8**

At the Institute of Contemporary Arts' opening in 1948, the art historian and anarchist Herbert Read declared that this would be different from all other galleries. Much to its credit, it has just about maintained its reputation for being a challenging place to witness all forms of artistic expression. The **Upper Gallery** hosts exhibitions of every type of avant-garde work; the **Concourse Gallery** attracts more attention because of its position by the café. Many leading artists had their first London exposure at the ICA, including Moore, Picasso, Ernst and, more recently, Helen Chadwick, Damien Hirst, Gary Hume and the Chapman brothers. Exhibitions in 1999 kick off with the first major solo exhibition of British artist **Steve McQueen** (29 Jan-21 Mar), followed by **All Kinds of Everything** (Apr-June), a collection of contemporary designs. Later in the year, the shortlisted entries for the **Cap Gemini Digital Art Prize** will be shown.

Matt's Gallery

42-44 Copperfield Road, E3 (0181 983 1771). Mile End tube. **Open** noon-6pm Wed-Sun. **Admission** free.

The latest installations can be puzzled over at Matt's Gallery. Artists are given free rein to do what they will with the space, and the results range from the epistemic to the plain incomprehensible. 1999 exhibitors include **Helen Robinson** (23 Mar-30 May), **Matthew Tickle** (23 June-31 July) and **Victor Burgin** (mid-Sept-mid-Nov).

RIBA

66 Portland Place, W1 (0171 307 3699). Oxford Circus or Regent's Park tube. **Open** 8am-6pm Mon, Wed, Fri, Sat; 8am-9pm Tue, Thur. **Admission** free. **Map 5 H5**

The Royal Institute of British Architects is housed in a monumental edifice built by Grey Wornham in 1934. The gallery celebrates the profession's great and the good, including Nicholas Grimshaw, Tadao Ando and Santiago Calatrava. The RIBA building contains a branch of the excellent **Pâtisserie Valerie** (*see p159*).

Riverside Studios

Crisp Road, W6 (0181 237 1000). Hammersmith tube. **Open** 11am-11pm Mon-Fri; noon-11pm Sat, Sun. **Closed** for special events; phone for details. **Admission** free.

Ten shows a year in the gallery and foyer space contribute to the fine art commitment of this independent west London theatre, cinema and arts centre. Expect to find sculpture, paintings, drawings and installations by young British unknowns as well as works by high-profile international artists; 1999's exhibitions will include the works of sculptor **Fiona Foster** (27 Apr-22 May).

Royal Academy of Arts

Burlington House, Piccadilly, W1 (0171 300 8000). Green Park or Piccadilly Circus tube. **Open** 10am-6pm Mon-Thur, Sat, Sun; 10am-8.30pm Fri. **Admission** varies (phone for details). **Credit** AmEx, MC, £TC, V. **Map 7 J7**

Britain's first art school (opened 1768), the Royal Academy of Arts also held the country's first annual open exhibitions of living artists. This persists as the **Summer Exhibition** (7 June-22 Aug 1999), which pulls in huge crowds to gaze at the thousands of paintings, sculptures and architectural designs on view. Following a slight departure from tradition in hosting the infamous contemporary **Sensation** exhibition in 1997, the RA is returning to the deceased in 1999. An interesting programme includes **Monet in the Twentieth Century** (until 18 Apr), **Kandinsky: Watercolours and other works on paper** (14 Apr-4 July), and an exhibition (in conjunction with the City of Antwerp) of the paintings of **Anthony van Dyck** to mark the 400th anniversary of his birth (18 Sept-15 Dec). The smaller Sackler Wing is devoted to such diverse subjects as Imperial Chinese ceramics and Sir John Soane; from 6-31 Oct 1999 it will house an exhibition of the work of British contemporary artist **John Hoyland**.

Serpentine Gallery

Kensington Gardens (near Albert Memorial), W2 (0171 402 6075). Lancaster Gate or South Kensington tube. **Open** 10am-6pm daily. **Admission** free. **Map 2 D8**

The Serpentine has pursued an independent and lively curatorial policy that has won it many regular visitors. Housed in a tranquil former tea pavilion – with french windows looking out on to Hyde Park, imbuing the exhibitions with varying qualities of natural light (depending on the weather) – it reopened in February 1998 following a big refurbishment. A major exhibition of classic works by **Bridget Riley** is planned for 1999, along with the first important UK exhibition of the works of South African artist **William Kentridge**.

Whitechapel Gallery

80-82 Whitechapel High Street, E1 (0171 522 7888/recorded info 0171 522 7878). Aldgate East tube/15, 253 bus. **Open** 11am-5pm Tue, Thur-Sun; 11am-8pm Wed. **Admission** free. **Map 12 S6**

A fine gallery space on two floors, the Whitechapel remains one of the most interesting independent galleries in London, putting on a continually challenging and interesting series of temporary shows. Exhibitions for 1999 include the calligraphic and watercolour work of **Henri Michaux**, to be displayed alongside his writings, and the large abstract paintings of the American **Terry Winters** (both until 25 April 1999). Later in the year the embroidered canvases of **Alighiero e Boetti** will be on show, but the **Whitechapel Open** (the only major show devoted to east London's heaving colony of artists) is a biennial event, and so is not due till 2000. The gallery also organises lectures and workshops. *See picture p134.*

Commercial galleries

Central: Cork Street & around

Cork Street has been at the hub of the art world since the end of World War II. A wander around the galleries in this area is likely to give you the chance to see works by many past and present masters, and will provide an insight into the shape of the market for both historical and contemporary artworks – and they're all free to enter. Many close in August, while their customary clientele are living it up in the Bahamas.

Whitechapel Gallery: *pride of E1. See p133.*

Bernard Jacobson

14A Clifford Street, W1 (0171 495 8575). Green Park or Piccadilly Circus tube. **Open** 10am-6pm Mon-Fri; 10am-1pm Sat. **Map 7 J7**
Jacobson's space, formerly an old gaming club, hosts the work of British painters such as Bomberg and Nicholson, along with contemporary works by Frank Stella, Robert Rauschenberg and William Tillyer.

Boukamel Contemporary Art (BCA)

9 Cork Street, W1 (0171 734 6444). Green Park or Piccadilly Circus tube. **Open** 10am-6pm Mon-Fri; 10am-2pm Sat. **Credit** AmEx, MC, V. **Map 7 J7**
Lively, contemporary, international figurative paintings and sculpture on a large scale are BCA's speciality. It represents an impressive range of European artists including Luciano Castelli, Daniel Spoerri, Ernesto Tatafiore and Markus Lüpertz. Ken Currie's figurative paintings are part of the British contingent.

Entwistle

6 Cork Street, W1 (0171 734 6440). Green Park or Piccadilly Circus tube. **Open** 10am-5.30pm Mon-Fri; 11am-4pm Sat. **Credit** AmEx, MC, V. **Map 7 J7**
Entwistle specialises in showing young British and American artists – indeed a group show of British painters will run from February 1999. Past exhibitions have ranged from Edward Lipski's sculptures and installations to the realist photographic paintings of Jason Brooks. Paul Finnegan and Nicky Hoberman (their works, that is) have also hung on these walls.

Helly Nahmad

2 Cork Street, W1 (0171 494 3200). Green Park or Piccadilly Circus tube. **Open** 10am-6pm Mon-Fri.
Map 7 J7
Helly Nahmad comes from a hugely influential art-dealing family, thereby giving him an inside track in the art field. The result is that this new gallery puts on shows that most public galleries would envy: Monet, Miró and Pissarro in its first show, and, more recently, a stunning collection of Picasso paintings. Plans for 1999 include a major surrealist exhibition, with important works by Dali, Miró, Magritte *et al.* Throughout the year it will also continue to show significant works, largely by twentieth-century artists.

Marlborough Fine Art

6 Albemarle Street, W1 (0171 629 5161). Green Park or Piccadilly Circus tube. **Open** 10am-5.30pm Mon-Fri; 10am-12.30pm Sat. **Closed** public holiday weekends.
Credit AmEx, MC, V. **Map 7 J7**
This gallery concentrates on exhibiting modern British masters with a figurative bias such as Moore, Kitaj, Nicholson and Pasmore. Its famed mixed summer show is an important date in the London art diary. The print room shows the Marlborough's own artists including Frank Auerbach and Paula Rego's figurative paintings.

Mayor

22A Cork Street, W1 (0171 734 3558). Green Park or Piccadilly Circus tube. **Open** 10am-5.30pm Mon-Fri; 10am-1pm Sat. **Map 7 J7**
The first gallery to open in Cork Street in 1933, the Mayor was also the first in Britain to exhibit many now-established names such as Bacon, Ernst, Klee and Miró, while also being in the forefront of pop art. Today, it shows the work of contemporary artists such as Andrew Ehrenworth, Ben Kadishman, Patrick O'Reilly and Tom Wesselmann. Mayor also claims to be the largest single exhibition space in the area, and there's the peculiar old squash court to peer into from the balcony.

Victoria Miro

21 Cork Street, W1 (0171 734 5082). Green Park or Piccadilly Circus tube. **Open** 10am-5.30pm Mon-Fri; 11am-1pm Sat. **Credit** AmEx. **Map 7 J7**
Victoria Miro's gallery – designed by Claudio Silvestrin – is well suited to the mixed clutch of contemporary artists she represents: Thomas Demand, Peter Doig, Andreas Gursky, Alex Hartley, Robin Lowe, Chris Ofili, Tracey Moffatt and Abigail Lane.

Waddington's

11, 12 & 34 Cork Street, W1 (0171 437 8611).
Green Park or Piccadilly Circus tube. **Open** 10am-5.30pm Mon-Fri; 10am-1pm Sat. **Closed** Sat mid-July-late Aug.
Map 7 J7
Leslie Waddington's galleries are one of the major forces to be reckoned with by modern and contemporary art dealers. Exhibited here are modern masters such as Picasso, Matisse and Dubuffet, as well as Peter Blake, Antoni Tàpies and Patrick Caulfield. Young contemporary artists represented include Ian Davenport and Fiona Rae. Artists who will be exhibited in 1999 include **Michael Craig Martin** (24 Mar-24 Apr), **Peter Halley** (28 Apr-22 May) and **Michael Landy** (26 May-19 June).

Central: Dering Street & around

Annely Juda Fine Art

23 Dering Street, W1 (0171 629 7578). Bond Street tube. **Open** 10am-6pm Mon-Fri; 10am-1pm Sat.
Map 5 H6
Annely Juda tends to concentrate on the early twentieth-century avant-garde as represented by Dada, Bauhaus and Russian constructivism. The fact that Christo, Leon Kossoff and David Hockney drawings are in 1999's schedule here gives some idea of the gallery's stature. Anthony Caro, Alan Green and Prunella Clough are also represented.

Anthony d'Offay

9, 21, 23 & 24 Dering Street, W1 (0171 499 4100).
Bond Street tube. **Open** 10am-5.30pm Mon-Fri; 10am-1pm Sat. **Map 5 H6**
Since opening in 1980 with Joseph Beuys and Gilbert & George, d'Offay has become renowned for exhibitions of significant modern art. Work by big names can often be seen here, including Warhol, Lichtenstein and Richter along with more contemporary figures, such as Rachel Whiteread

and Jeff Koons. D'Offay is opening another gallery around the corner in Haunch of Venison Yard in the summer of 1999.

Anthony Reynolds

5 Dering Street, W1 (0171 491 0621). Bond Street tube. **Open** 10am-6pm Tue-Sat. **Credit** AmEx. **Map 5 H6**
Since Anthony Reynolds moved to this space in 1987, he has focused mainly on contemporary British art in every type of medium. Artists recently represented include Keith Tyson, Paul Graham, Richard Billingham, Steve McQueen, Georgina Starr and Mark Wallinger.

Fine Art Society

148 New Bond Street, W1 (0171 629 5116). Bond Street tube. **Open** 9.30am-5.30pm Mon-Fri; 10am-1pm Sat. **Credit** AmEx, JCB, MC, V. **Map 5 H6**
Founded in 1876, the Fine Art Society has an olde-worlde atmosphere that complements the portfolio of artists. Once described by Walter Sickert as the 'best shop' in London, it specialises in nineteenth- and early twentieth-century work, not only paintings and sculptures, but also applied arts.

Gimpel Fils

30 Davies Street, W1 (0171 493 2488). Bond Street tube. **Open** 10am-5.30pm Mon-Fri; 10am-1pm Sat. **Closed** Sat in Aug. **Map 5 H6**
Gimpel Fils is known for its twentieth-century and contemporary European painting and sculpture. The work of British painter Gillian Ayres has been shown along with abstracts by Albert Irvin. There's also room for large works, such as Niki de Saint Phalle's sculptures.

Central: other galleries

Austin/Desmond Fine Art

Pied Bull Yard, 68-69 Great Russell Street, WC1 (0171 242 4443). Holborn tube. **Open** 10.30am-5.30pm Mon-Fri; 11am-2.30pm Sat during exhibitions only. **Map 6 L5**
John Austin specialises in modern British painting and carries a wide selection of contemporary prints by artists such as Ivan Hitchens, William Scott, Patrick Heron and David Hockney. The gallery also exhibits young British and Irish contemporary artists.

Blue Gallery

93 Walton Street, SW3 (0171 589 4690). South Kensington tube. **Open** 10am-6.30pm Mon-Sat. **Credit** MC, V. **Map 4 E10**
Giles Baker-Smith's choice of artists seems to increase in confidence and daring each year. In 1998 he promoted the work of royal portraitist Justin Mortimer, Melanie Manchot and Robert Davies. The gallery may well be moving in 1999, but where and when was not known at the time of going to press.

Frith Street

60 Frith Street, W1 (0171 494 1550). Tottenham Court Road tube. **Open** 10am-6pm Wed-Fri; 11am-4pm Sat. **Map 6 K6**
Opened in 1989, Frith Street's four interlinked rooms provide an intimate space for exhibitions of contemporary artists from home and abroad, including Juan Muñoz and newer arrivals such as Callum Innes, photographers Craigie Horsfield and John Riddy, multimedia artist Cornelia Parker and Turner-shortlisted Tacita Dean.

Rebecca Hossack

35 Windmill Street, W1 (0171 436 4899). Tottenham Court Road tube. **Open** 10am-6pm Mon-Sat. **Map 6 K5**
Rebecca Hossack combats the dominant Eurocentricity of the art world, specialising in Aboriginal art – look out for the annual **Songlines** exhibition in July and August. Other exhibitions for 1999 include paintings by **Indian artists** and **Nepalese women** (Oct-Nov).

White Cube

44 Duke Street, SW1 (0171 930 5373). Green Park tube. **Open** 10am-6pm Fri, Sat; Mon-Thur by appointment. **Map 7 J7**
Jay Jopling's one-room space, designed by Claudio Silvestrin, has witnessed some of the most promising exhibitions of recent years. Jopling has a sure eye for artists of the future and his relentless self-promotion has put White Cube at the forefront of the contemporary art scene. If evidence is needed, witness his stable of artists, which includes Damien Hirst, Tracey Emin, Gary Hume, Turner-shortlisted Sam Taylor-Wood, Antony Gormley and Mona Hatoum.

North

Lisson

52-54 Bell Street, NW1 (0171 724 2739). Edgware Road tube. **Open** 10am-6pm Mon-Fri; 10am-5pm Sat. **Credit** MC, V. **Map 2 E5**
Although slightly out of the way, this modernist gallery, with its seriously minimalist extension, is well worth a visit. The Lisson offers space to the young and the established, and represents a number of sculptors of international repute including Sol Lewitt, Tony Cragg, Anish Kapoor, Richard Deacon, Robert Mangold, Dan Graham and Julian Opie, in addition to promising newcomers Simon Patterson, Jane and Louise Wilson, Christine Borland, Mat Collishaw and Jason Martin.

East

Cabinet

20A Northburgh Street, EC1 (0171 274 4252). Farringdon tube/rail. **Open** noon-6pm Thur-Sat. **Map 9 O4**
Cabinet has moved from its original Brixton home to a light industrial space in Clerkenwell, but continues to explore interesting new developments. Youngish contemporary artists shown here include Jeremy Deller, Martin Creed and Gillian Carnegie.

E1

10 White's Row, E1 (0171 721 8687). Liverpool Street tube/rail. **Open** 10am-6pm Mon-Fri. **Credit** MC, V. **Map 12 R5**
Opened at the end of 1997, this diminutive space not far from Brick Lane represents part of the general shift eastwards of the London art world. It is run by Ivan Tennant, who is also behind the excellent London Arthouse – the art consultancy firm that counts hotel **One Aldwych** (*see p141*) among its customers – and makes a point of giving exposure to exciting young and emerging artists, with a particular emphasis on abstract colourists such as Matthew Webber, Elizabeth Hanniford and Rupert Burt.

Eagle

159 Farringdon Road, EC1 (0171 833 2674). Farringdon tube/rail. **Open** 11am-6pm Wed-Fri; 11am-4pm Sat; and by appointment. **Credit** AmEx. **Map 9 N4**
A friendly and relaxed art space, upstairs from the trendy, trail-blazing **Eagle** gastropub (*see p171*). With an aim to make art affordable and accessible, the gallery sells special cheap multiples, like monoprint books, at around £45.

Flowers East

199-205 Richmond Road, E8 (0181 985 3333). Hackney Central rail/55, 106, 253 bus. **Open** 10am-6pm Tue-Sun. **Credit** AmEx, MC, V.
With four spaces – two at Flowers East and two in London Fields – Flowers has no shortage of room to show its varied, 30-strong stable. The art is mostly British and ranges from the abstract to the figurative; among those

represented here are Nicola Hicks, Peter Howson and Patrick Hughes.
Branch: **London Fields** 282 Richmond Road, E8 (0181 533 5554).

Interim Art
21 Beck Road, E8 (0171 254 9607). Bethnal Green tube.
Open 11am-6pm Fri, Sat; and by appointment.
This important gallery in two rooms of a converted Victorian terraced house has made a broad shift in policy from innovative, international work towards Young British Artists. There are those who might consider this a risky strategy, but Interim's reputation remains secure with recent exhibitions by painters Mark Francis and Paul Noble, and Turner Prize-winner Gillian Wearing.

Laure Genillard
82-84 Clerkenwell Road, EC1 (0171 490 8853). Farringdon tube/rail. **Open** 11am-6pm Tue-Sat.
Map 5 J5
This is a small space that maintains an emphasis on installations and conceptual art. Artists represented include Douglas Allsop, Dean Hughes and Lesley Foxcroft.

Paton
282 Richmond Road, E8 (0181 986 3409). Bethnal Green tube then 106, 253 bus/London Fields rail/30, 38, bus. **Open** 11am-6pm Tue-Sat; noon-6pm Sun.
The dynamic Graham Paton moved his gallery to larger premises in London Fields in 1993. With double the space, he has expanded beyond his core artists and shown some more experimental works. One of the great successes of the ART98 show, the Paton gallery sells to New York's Metropolitan Museum and the Saatchi Collection.

West

England & Co
14 Needham Road, W11; moving during summer of 1999 to 216 Westbourne Grove, W11 (0171 221 0417). Notting Hill Gate tube. **Open** 11am-6pm Tue-Sat.
Credit AmEx, MC, V. **Map 1 A6**
Jane England is well known for her annual international Art In Boxes show, but the move to a new space sometime in summer 1999 will no doubt improve her reputation for regular successful reappraisals of contemporary and modern British and international work.

London Print Workshop
421-423 Harrow Road (opposite Bravington Road), W10 (0181 969 3247). Westbourne Park tube/18, 31, 28, 36 bus. **Open** 10am-6pm Mon; 10.30am-9pm Tue; 10.30am-6pm Wed-Fri; 1-5pm Sat.
The workshop puts on six exhibitions a year and offers open access to artists. The shows are wide-ranging in content, often affiliated to other galleries, and concentrate on contemporary work by young up-and-coming artists.

Photography

Admission to all the galleries below is free.

Association Gallery
Association of Photographers, 81 Leonard Street, EC2 (0171 739 6669). Old Street tube/rail. **Open** 9.30am-6pm Mon-Fri; noon-4pm Sat. **Credit** AmEx, MC, V.
Map 9 P4
The two-floor Association Gallery showcases work (both commissioned and non-commissioned) for advertising and editorial purposes. It puts on a show every March of Association of Photographers award-winners and stages around 20 exhibitions of good contemporary photography each year.

Camerawork
121 Roman Road, E2 (0181 980 6256). Bethnal Green tube. **Open** 1-6pm Thur-Sat; noon-6pm Sun.
Camerawork's brief is a worthy one: to show adventurous, challenging, issue-based work, by the likes of John Hansard (June 1999). In addition, it also offers extensive darkroom space and CD-Rom facilities to the public.

Hamilton's
13 Carlos Place, W1 (0171 499 9493). Bond Street or Green Park tube. **Open** 10am-6pm Tue-Sat.
Credit AmEx, MC, £$TC, V. **Map 7 H7**
Rubbing shoulders with Mayfair's fine art galleries, Hamilton's has always had an exclusive international clientele and exhibited high-profile photographers. This is photography as fine art – prices start at about £250. Choose from over 3,000 prints by names such as Bailey, Beaton, McCullin, Penn and Avedon. It's a great space, especially the gallery at the back, and has excellent exhibitions, concentrating on more fashionable contemporary names, from Peter Linbergh to the controversial Joel-Peter Witkin.

Photofusion
17A Electric Lane, SW9 (0171 738 5774). Brixton tube/rail. **Open** 10am-6pm Tue, Thur, Fri; 10am-8pm Wed; noon-4pm Sat.
Aided by council and commercial grants, this co-operative has kept to its community roots and holds an impressive library of social documentary photography, showing some unsettling images of London's communities. Spring 1999 sees an exhibition of the private collection of **David Hurn**, and later a set of photographs of burn victims by **Detlef Henrichs**.

Photographers' Gallery
5-8 Great Newport Street, WC2 (0171 831 1772). Covent Garden or Leicester Square tube. **Open** 11am-6pm Mon-Sat; noon-6pm Sun. **Membership** £25; £15 concs.
Credit AmEx, DC, MC, V. **Map 8 K6**
In 1971, the Photographers' Gallery was the first of its kind to open in England. It has been promoting contemporary photography ever since, but is now moving away from social documentary and reportage. It has also been instrumental in encouraging national galleries to hold photographic shows in addition to mounting 24 of its own each year. There's also a fine print library (for members only).

Special Photographers Company
21 Kensington Park Road, W11 (0171 221 3489). Ladbroke Grove or Notting Hill Gate tube. **Open** 10am-6pm Mon-Thur; 10am-5.30pm Fri; 11am-5pm Sat.
Credit AmEx, MC, V. **Map 1 A6**
Opened in the 1980s in trendy Notting Hill, the Special Photographers Company gallery aims to represent the work of serious snappers by exhibiting a wide range of work, from Joyce Tenneson to Clare Park and Herman Leonard's classic jazz images. Not limited by a specifically fine-art or documentary tradition, the gallery holds a large collection of prints from landscape to abstract (prices from £80). In 1999 there are a couple of exhibitions on a musical theme – **Paul Hoeffler**'s jazz photos from the 1940s-60s, and **David Redfern**'s fine portraits of musicians. The gallery is on two levels: the ground floor and a spacious basement area.

Zelda Cheatle Gallery
99 Mount Street, W1 (0171 408 4448). Bond Street or Green Park tube. **Open** 10am-6pm Tue-Fri; 11am-4.30pm Sat. **Credit** MC, V. **Map 7 G7**
Zelda Cheatle has a background in documentary work and a following of serious – particularly US – collectors. She shows some excellent British, American and European photography including Eve Arnold, Manuel Alvarez Bravo, Steve Pyke, Helen Sear and John Deakin.

Consumer London

Accommodation

These days you get more dash – if you've got the cash.

'The great advantage of a hotel is that it's a refuge from home life.' Whether you are looking for that refuge like George Bernard Shaw, or simply seeking a comfortable bed for the night, arriving in London without a hotel booking can be a daunting experience. It may be an easy option to book into a chain hotel (and we list the central numbers for the main chains below) but there are plenty of more characterful, personal and friendly options – if you know where to look.

But beware. There is no getting away from the unsavoury fact that hotel rooms in London are a) overpriced, b) small, and c) stylistically challenged. So be prepared for the implied parentheses in some of the comments below – 'rooms are a good size' (for London), 'prices are reasonable' (for London), etc. It is all too easy to end up in unsavoury accommodation with a severe dent in your bank balance. Below we have attempted to sift the class from the dross, in every price bracket.

A further problem for visitors is that London is simply too popular – there aren't enough beds to go round. The capital currently has around 95,000 hotel rooms and, although 41 new hotels have opened since 1995, it is estimated that 20,000 more beds are needed to keep up with demand.

At least hoteliers are finally becoming aware that the Empire is long gone and not every visitor to London wants to sip Darjeeling to the sound of a string quartet. Anouska Hempel's **Blakes** (*see opposite*) was a groundbreaker in this respect, bringing discreet 1980s chic to a fusty market. Her follow-up, **The Hempel** (*see page 141*), is 1990s minimalism taken to the extreme. Others are starting to muscle in on the style-hotel act. The big opening of 1997 was Christina Ong's **The Metropolitan** (*see page 141* – building on the success of her earlier **The Halkin**; 0171 333 1000), which has made an equal name for itself with its ultra-exclusive bar and its bizarre but brilliant modern Japanese restaurant, **Nobu** (*see page 173*). In 1998, the major newcomer was the lavish-yet-restrained **One Aldwych** (*see page 141*), which also has an excellent restaurant, **Axis** (*see page 155*). Indeed, there is now a proliferation of top-rank restaurants in hotels, including **Stefano Cavallini Restaurant at the Halkin** and **The Room at the Halcyon** (for both, *see page 153*).

Look out for more seriously stylish hotels opening over the next year. As this guide went to press the clean-lined, feng shui-inspired **myhotel**

bloomsbury (*see page 142*) opened its doors, and in July 1999 ultra-hip New York hotelier Ian Schrager will be unveiling his first London hotel, **The Burford** in St Martin's Lane, to be followed by **The Sanderson** in Berners Street.

Unfortunately, style only comes at a price as yet. London remains desperately short of classy budget options. The award-winning **Highfield Guest House** (*see page 149*) is a notable exception; the downside is that it's located deep in suburbia.

INFORMATION & BOOKING

If you have not booked ahead, London Tourist Board (LTB) information centres will help (*see page 296*). There is a booking fee of £5. In addition, if you book more than a few weeks in advance, a deposit for the room may also be required. *London – Where to Stay & What to Do* (£4.99), published annually by the LTB, can be found in information centres and large bookshops. Many hotels now have e-mail and/or website addresses via which reservations can be made. Below we list the central numbers for the major chains, the number of hotels run by these chains within Greater London and the price range (including VAT) for a double room.

London Tourist Board Accommodation Reservations Line *(0171 932 2020/www.londontown. com)*. **Open** 9.30am-5.30pm Mon-Fri.

Best Western *(0345 747474)*. **Open** 8am-8pm Mon-Fri; 8am-6pm Sat; 11am-4pm Sat. **Hotels** 15.

Forte Hotels Reservations Line *(0345 404040)*. **Open** 7am-10pm daily. **Hotels** 19.

Hilton *(0800 856 8000)*. **Open** 8am-8pm Mon-Fri; 10am-5pm Sat, Sun. **Hotels** 12.

Holiday Inn *(0800 897121)*. **Open** 7am-10.40pm daily. **Hotels** 13.

Marriott *(0800 221222)*. **Open** 8am-10pm daily. **Hotels** 6.

Radisson Edwardian *(0800 374411)*. **Open** 7am-7pm Mon-Fri; 8am-2pm Sat; 9am-3pm Sun. **Hotels** 10.

Stakis *(0990 909090)*. **Open** 8am-11pm Mon-Fri; 9am-6pm Sat, Sun. **Hotels** 6.

Travel Inn *(01582 414341)*. **Open** 8am-6pm Mon-Fri; 8am-4pm Sat, Sun. **Hotels** 4.

Visitors with disabilities

See also page 302 **Access all areas?**

Holiday Care Service *2nd floor, Imperial Buildings, Victoria Road, Horley, Surrey RH6 7PZ (01293 774535/ fax 01293 784647)*. **Open** 9am-5pm Mon-Fri. **Credit** AmEx, MC, V.
This advisory service can help disabled visitors find suitable accommodation.

*The wacky **Portobello Hotel**. See page 142.*

COMPLAINTS

If you have a complaint about anywhere you stay in London, you should personally inform the management at the time of the incident, and then in writing. In some circumstances, the LTB may look into complaints (regardless of whether or not you used its booking service). Please let us know if any of the hotels listed do not come up to scratch.

Hotels

You will find most of London's best-known hotels in Mayfair, while budget accommodation is often clustered around railway stations. The latter can be rather seedy but Ebury Street, SW1 (near Victoria), and Gower Street, WC1 (near Euston), have some good-quality, cheap hotels. There are also many hotels in the Earl's Court area and around Queensway, W2. For accommodation catering for a primarily gay and lesbian clientele, *see page 243*.

PRICES & CLASSIFICATION

Hotels are classified below according to the price of the cheapest **double** room for one night, **inclusive** of 17.5 per cent VAT. Many expensive hotels quote prices exclusive of VAT, so do check. **Prices were correct at time of going to press but are subject to annual increases of around five per cent.** Hotel prices tend to remain the same throughout the year; but it is always worth asking if there are any special deals available (especially weekend breaks).

All 'Deluxe' and 'Expensive' hotels will have an en suite bath and/or shower and toilet. Most 'Cheap' hotels have shared bathroom facilities. 'Including breakfast' means continental breakfast, which may consist of little more than coffee and toast. 'English breakfast' is more substantial and generally of the fry-up variety.

Deluxe (£220 and up)

Even if you are unable to afford to stay in London's most famous hotels, their restaurants and bars are open to the public, and most serve afternoon tea (*see page 161*). Unless otherwise stated, every hotel in this category offers babysitting, business services, conference facilities, currency exchange, fax, laundry, 24-hour room service, a safe and multilingual staff, and has at least one bar and restaurant; all rooms are equipped with air-conditioning, hairdryer, minibar, radio, safe, telephone and satellite TV. The services listed below each review are in addition to the above.

Blakes

33 Roland Gardens, SW7 3PF (0171 370 6701/fax 0171 373 0442/blakes@easynet.co.uk). Gloucester Road or South Kensington tube. **Rooms** 50. **Rates** *single* £153-£182; *double* £258-£364; *suite* £258-£840. **Credit** AmEx, DC, JCB, MC, TC, V. **Map 4 D11**
A unique designer hotel within the dark green shell of two Victorian mansions. Characterised throughout by Anouska Hempel's daring and dramatic design details – in black, ochre, cardinal red and white – the 50 individually decorated rooms are inspired by the themes of travel and history; one room houses the original bed of Napoleon's Empress Josephine. Blakes prides itself on protecting the privacy of its clients, a policy that hints at the type of guests it attracts. It's discreet, but fully conscious of its fashionable status. The secluded courtyard garden and restaurant are further draws. **Hotel services** *Courtyard garden. Limousine service. Restaurant. Roof terrace.* **Room services** *CD player. Room service (24-hour). VCR.*

Covent Garden Hotel

10 Monmouth Street, WC2H 9HB (0171 806 1000/ fax 0171 806 1100). Covent Garden or Leicester Square tube. **Rooms** 50. **Rates** *single* £205; *double* £235-£299; *suite* £347-£646. **Credit** AmEx, MC, V. **Map 6 L6**
In the midst of theatreland, Tim and Kit Kemp's Covent Garden Hotel is an appropriate stage for guests with a sense of the dramatic. All rooms are individual in terms of their size and impressive décor (in luxurious, bold colours). Quirky furniture and vivid upholstery plus matching tailor's mannequins (the hotel's trademark) make this a fun place to stay. All bathrooms are mahogany and granite. There is a new flower shop in the hotel, which provides the striking flowers in the lobby. **Brasserie Max** serves light meals and snacks. **Hotel services** *Café. Gym.* **Room services** *CD player. Fax/modem. Mobile phone. VCR. Voicemail. Website: www.firmdale.com*

The Halcyon

81 Holland Park, W11 3RZ (0171 727 7288/fax 0171 229 8516/halcyon_hotel@compuserve.com). Holland Park tube. **Rooms** 42. **Rates** *single* £175-£215; *double* £270; *suite* £305-£650. **Credit** AmEx, DC, MC, TC, V.*
The Halcyon prides itself on being a discreet retreat for the

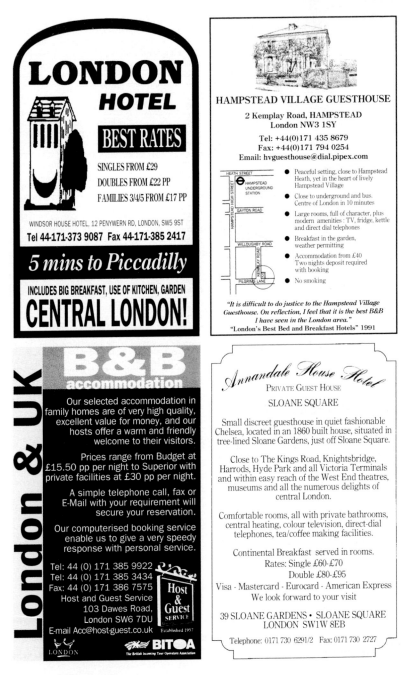

rich and famous. Wonderfully arranged flowers scent the air of the reception rooms, where antique furniture is set off against the racing green carpet and draped cream curtains. The invitingly spacious bedrooms may not be at the fore-front of modern design but their light, soothing tones, frills and flounces have a reassuringly English retro vibe. In the restaurant (*see p153*), the softly lit, unassuming interior belies a brilliantly executed menu with modern touches playing to the tastes of its younger, glitzier clientele. If you want to splash out in more ways than one, request a room with a Jacuzzi.

Hotel services *Interpreting services. Limousine service. Valet parking.* **Room services** *Fax/ISDN line. VCR (on request).*

The Hempel

31-35 Craven Hill Gardens, W2 3EA (0171 298 9000/fax 0171 402 4666/the-hempel@easynet.co.uk). Lancaster Gate or Queensway tube/Paddington tube/rail. **Rooms** 47; 6 apartments. **Rates** *double* £258-£300; *suite* £435-£911. **Credit** AmEx, DC, MC, TC, V. **Map 1 C6**
London's most minimalist hotel certainly packs a punch. Its precise, clinical design even affects the flora; on a large table almost the size of the lobby, 200 fresh white orchids stand to attention. The jaw-dropping white-on-white reception, with an atrium that extends up to the fifth floor, has no decoration or furniture except four antique Burmese oxen carts that serve as tables. The individually designed rooms are kitted out in natural fabrics; the bathrooms sport slate and sand-blasted glass. A Zen-style garden, Shadows Bar and the appropriately minimal **I-Thai** (Italian/Thai – ho, ho) restaurant complete the design package.
Hotel services *Garden. Gym. Limousine service.* **Room services** *CD player. Disabled rooms (2). Fax/modem. Website: www.hempelhotel.com*

The Lanesborough

Hyde Park Corner, SW1X 7TA (0171 259 5599/fax 0171 259 5606). Hyde Park Corner tube. **Rooms** 95. **Rates** *single* £276-£323; *double* £364-£481; *suite* £552-£4,112.* **Credit** AmEx, DC, MC, TC, V. **Map 7 G8**
Behind the relatively sober façade of the former St George's Hospital, the Lanesborough's unabashed magnificence dazzles. The luxurious Regency décor extends from the bedrooms to the Withdrawing Room and the Library Bar, which boasts one of the best collections of cognacs in London. The Conservatory restaurant, modelled on Brighton Pavilion, is the antithesis of such grandeur, reflecting a light chinoiserie theme, and serving Mediterranean/Pacific Rim cuisine (with a particularly impressive vegetarian selection) among potted palms and tinkling fountains. Only captains of industry and lottery winners with £4,000 to burn should enquire after the Royal Suite.
Hotel services *Banqueting rooms. Business centre. Car park. Gym. Limousine service. No-smoking floor.* **Room services** *Butler (24-hour). CD player. Decanter bar. Disabled room. Fax. Personalised stationery/business cards. Telephone (direct line). VCR. Website: www.lanesborough.com*

The Metropolitan

Old Park Lane, W1Y 4LB (0171 447 1000/fax 0171 447 1147/sales@metropolitan.co.uk). Green Park or Hyde Park Corner tube. **Rooms** 155. **Rates** *single* £241; *double* £270-£352; *suite* £376-£1,645. **Credit** AmEx, DC, JCB, MC, TC, V. **Map 7 G8**
Christina Ong, owner of the more business-oriented but equally stylish **Halkin** (5 Halkin Street, SW1; 0171 333 1000), has splashed out £45 million to create her most exclusive hotel yet on the site of the former Londonderry. This isn't the place for the easily intimidated: service, by the posse of model-like, DKNY-clad staff, is assertively attentive. If you want to feel like a star, though, you're on home territory: just recline on the cream leather suites in the lobby

to the sounds of piped New York hip hop, and try to foster an air of studied nonchalance. Décor in the rooms is resolutely contemporary, minimalist chic, with a well thought-out use of hardwoods, marble and natural fabrics. More wannabes try (and fail) to gain entry into the star-spangled bar than virtually any other. The Japanese restaurant, **Nobu** (*see p173*), is a cut above.
Hotel services *Beauty salon (2 treatment rooms). Car park (limited). Gym. No-smoking floor.* **Room services** *Fax/modem. ISDN line.*

One Aldwych

1 Aldwych, WC2B 4BZ (0171 300 1000/fax 0171 300 1001/sales@onealdwych.co.uk). Charing Cross, Covent Garden or Temple tube. **Rooms** 105. **Rates** *single* £270-£352; *double* £311-£376; *suite* £487-£980. **Credit** AmEx, DC, JCB, MC, TC, V. **Map 8 M7**
One Aldwych is one of a new breed of hotels arriving in London: modern, chic, sharply stylish. The imposing grey façade gives way to a clinically clean lobby, dominated by the smooth metal curves of *The Boatman* sculpture. The co-owner, Gordon Campbell Gray, has made this a multimillion-pound homage to modern art – there are over 300 pieces from his own collection here. In the rooms, bold tones strike out from placid backdrops. From the gymnasiums in the deluxe suites to the underwater Mozart symphonies in the lap pool, the clientele is bathed in luxury at every turn. Sustenance comes in the form of **Axis** (*see p155*), with its stunning spiral staircase, and **Indigo**, both offering creative, well-executed dishes.
Hotel services *Beauty salon. Car park. Gym. Limousine service. No-smoking floor.* **Room services** *CD player. Fax/modem.*

The Savoy

Strand, WC2R 0EU (0171 836 4343/fax 0171 240 6040/info@the-savoy.com). Charing Cross tube/rail. **Rooms** 207. **Rates** *single* £317; *double* £382-£400; *family room* £523; *suite* £500-£1,087. **Credit** AmEx, DC, JCB, MC, TC, V. **Map 8 L7**
Built by Richard D'Oyly Carte in 1889, The Savoy retains a reputation for effortless grandeur and trad British style (although the art deco rooms are the most thrilling). The great Escoffier first put the Savoy on the culinary map, and it's still possible to dine handsomely in the restaurant (where Ho Chi Minh was once a washer-up. Honest), take tea in the Thames Foyer and eat lunch amid assorted MPs in **The Grill Room**. In addition, The Savoy is blessed with lavish banqueting rooms, a fitness centre and a swimming pool.
Hotel services *Banqueting rooms. Beauty salon. Car park. Fitness centre & pool. Hairdressing. Limousine service. No-smoking rooms.* **Room services** *CD player. Fax/modem. ISDN line. Room/valet service (24-hour). VCR. Website: www.savoy-group.co.uk*

Expensive (£140-£220)

Unless otherwise stated, all hotels in this category have at least one bar, and offer fax and laundry services; all rooms are equipped with a hairdryer, radio, telephone and satellite TV. The services listed below each review are in addition to the above.

Dorset Square Hotel

39-40 Dorset Square, NW1 (0171 723 7874/fax 0171 724 3328/dorset@firmdale.com). Baker Street tube/Marylebone rail. **Rooms** 38 (all en suite). **Rates** *single* £115-£123; *double* £153-£253; *junior suite* £253. **Credit** AmEx, MC, £TC, V. **Map 1 F4**
Located just below Regent's Park on a grand garden square, this elegant hotel manages to retain an air of intimacy close to some of its larger peers. The rooms have a plush, Regency feel, combining boldly patterned walls with heavy floral

drapery, and in the newly fitted lounge the guests congregate on flock feather sofas around an open fire. In comparison, the feel of the Potting Shed restaurant, which serves basic English fare, is surprisingly humble.

Hotel services *Bar. Currency exchange. Lounge. Multilingual staff. Restaurant.* **Room services** *Air-conditioning. Minibar. Radio. Refrigerator. Room service (24-hour). Safe.*
Website: www.firmdale.com

The Gore

189 Queen's Gate, SW7 5EX (0171 584 6601/fax 0171 589 8127/reservations@gorehotel.co.uk). Gloucester Road tube. **Rooms** 55. **Rates** *single* £147-£176; *double* £192-£288; *suite* £264-£288. **Credit** AmEx, DC, JCB, MC, TC, V. **Map 4 D9**
The mini-palms marking the entrance add a touch of the exotic to this highly traditional Victorian hotel. Open for over a century, the Gore has retained its Victorian charm, with mahogany wall panelling and deep scarlet curtains, but its relaxed, unpretentious staff manage to keep it on the right side of stuffiness. Individual touches add to the appeal: the hotel's collection of 5,000 sketches graces the walls, the Tudor room has wonderful oak beams and a minstrel's gallery, and a carved, gilded bed once belonging to Judy Garland sits in the Venus room. The buzzing **Bistro 190** serves quality food, if not at bistro prices.

Hotel services *Babysitting. Conference facilities. Currency exchange. Multilingual staff. No-smoking rooms. Restaurants (2). Safe.* **Room services** *Minibar. Room service (7am-11.30pm). Safe. VCR (on request).*

Hazlitt's

6 Frith Street, W1V 5TZ (0171 434 1771/fax 0171 439 1524). Tottenham Court Road tube. **Rates** *single* £147; *double* £192; *suite* £227-£311. **Credit** AmEx, DC, JCB, MC, £TC, V. **Map 6 K6**
Favoured by the author Bill Bryson as 'intentionally obscure', this small, unobtrusive hotel oozes quirky charm, and enjoys a great Soho location. Essayist William Hazlitt spent his final days here and it remains a favourite haunt of literary and media types: the bookcase in the lounge contains signed copies of books by former guests, and a glance over the shelves reads like a Who's Who of '90s literati. The 23 rooms, named after previous distinguished residents and guests, are exquisitely decked out with antique four-posters, panel-backed beds and free-standing claw-footed baths. No hotel bar and no radio in rooms.

Hotel services *Lounge. Multilingual staff.*
Room services *Room service (7.30am-11.30pm).*

myhotel bloomsbury

11-13 Bayley Street, WC1B 3HD (0171 580 7766/fax 0171 580 0588/customer_service@myhotels.co.uk). Goodge Street or Tottenham Court Road tube. **Rooms** 76. **Rates** *single* £155; *double* £195-£225; *suites* £295-£395. **Credit** AmEx, DC, JCB, MC, TC, V. **Map 6 K5**
Due to open as this guide goes to press, this curiously named newcomer is the brainchild of owner Andrew Thrasyvoulou. Superlative service is the avowed intention with one 'personal assistant' looking after each customer (tipping is discouraged). Décorwise it's East meets West with interiors and furniture coming from the Conran Design Partnership and a full feng shui treatment ensuring plenty of free-flowing positive energy. It's bound to be a big hit with thirty- and fortysomething media types, but myhotel does, admirably, intend to look after the needs of kids too.
Hotel services *Alternative health treatments. Babysitting. Business services. Conference facilities. Currency exchange. Gym. Library. Limousine service. Multilingual staff. No-smoking rooms. Restaurant. Safe.* **Room services** *Air-conditioning. Fax/modem (on request). Room service (24-hour).*
Website: www.myhotels.co.uk

Number Sixteen

16 Sumner Place, SW7 3EG (0171 589 5232/fax 0171 584 8615/toll-free from US 1 800 542 5387/ reservations@numbersixteenhotel.co.uk). South Kensington tube. **Rooms** 36 (33 en suite). **Rates** (incl breakfast) *single* £85-£120; *double/twin* £155-£185; *suite* £195. **Credit** AmEx, DC, MC, £$TC, V. **Map 4 D11**
A smart yet homely (and pricey) B&B taking up four Victorian townhouses on a tree-lined street. Rooms are named by colour, and decorated with sober good taste. In winter guests can huddle around the open fire in the drawing room or browse in the library, while the conservatory and meandering garden, with fountain and statuettes, are delights in warmer weather. Terrestrial TV only.
Hotel services *Conservatory garden. Currency exchange. Fax. Multilingual staff.* **Room services** *Minibar. Radio. Room service (7am-10pm).*

Pembridge Court Hotel

34 Pembridge Gardens, W2 4DX (0171 229 9977/fax 0171 727 4982). Notting Hill Gate tube. **Rooms** 20. **Rates** (incl English breakfast) *single* £110-£145; *double* £135-£175; *triple/quad* £180-£185. **Credit** AmEx, DC, MC, £TC, V. **Map 1 A7**
Handy for Portobello Road market and Notting Hill's oh-so-trendy restaurants, the Pembridge Court is a cheery place. Many of the rooms are decorated in floral fabrics, and on the walls hang a fascinating collection of Victoriana, including fans, gloves and handbags. The restaurant, **Caps**, offers an inventive European menu. Two of the hotel's best-loved guests are the cats, Spencer and Churchill, who often prowl the picturesque patio. A place that exudes warmth, it's easy to relax and feel at home.
Hotel services *Multilingual staff. Restaurant.*
Room services *Room service (24-hour). Safe. Tea/coffee.*

Portobello Hotel

22 Stanley Gardens, W11 2NG (0171 727 2777/fax 0171 792 9641). Holland Park or Notting Hill Gate tube. **Rooms** 22. **Rates** (incl breakfast) *single* £110; *double* £150-£240. **Credit** AmEx, DC, MC, £TC, V. **Map 1 A6**
The Portobello's white Victorian façade gives no clue to the wacky curios that characterise its delightfully idiosyncratic interior. The circular bed in one of the suites is particularly exquisite. All rooms are different and, amid the clutter, you might stumble across globes, potted palms, or a wonderful Heath-Robinson bathing machine spouting taps and pipes. The restaurant, in contrast, is light and airy. No radio in the rooms. *See picture p139.*
Hotel services *Multilingual staff. Restaurant.*
Room services *Minibar. Room service (24-hour). Tea/coffee. VCR.*

Moderate (£85-£145)

All hotels in this category offer fax and laundry services, and all rooms have a TV and telephone, in addition to the services listed below.

Abbey Court

20 Pembridge Gardens, W2 4DU (0171 221 7518/fax 0171 792 0858). Notting Hill Gate tube. **Rooms** 22 (all en suite). **Rates** (incl breakfast) *single* £88-£125; *double* £130-£145; *suite* £175. **Credit** AmEx, DC, JCB, MC, £TC, V. **Map 1 A7**
An elegant, comfortable hotel close to Notting Hill Gate. Rooms are individually decorated, many with Designers Guild fabrics, antique furniture and books, and have the added bonus of a relaxing Jacuzzi bath.
Hotel services *Babysitting. Bar. Business services. Multilingual staff. No-smoking rooms. Patio.*
Room services *Hairdryer. Radio. Room service (7am-11pm). Safe.*

Teatime... the **London Elizabeth Hotel** way.

Academy Hotel

17-25 Gower Street, WC1E 6HG (0171 631 4115/fax 0171 636 3442/restaurant 0171 636 7612). Goodge Street or Russell Square tube. **Rooms** 50 (all en suite). **Rates** *single* £100-£115; *double* £125-£145; *suite* £185. **Credit** AmEx, DC, JCB, MC, TC, V. **Map 6 K4**
A £1-million development programme has left the sleek, classy Academy with gleaming pastel-painted walls and an extra 17 rooms. Two large, well laid-out patio gardens, a library, bar and restaurant are among the facilities.
Hotel services *Babysitting. Bar. Business services. Conference facilities. Currency exchange. Garden. Library. Multilingual staff. No-smoking rooms. Patio. Restaurant.* **Room services** *Air-conditioning. Radio. Room service (7am-midnight). Valet service (24-hour).*

Commodore Hotel

50 Lancaster Gate, W2 3NA (0171 402 5291/fax 0171 262 1088/reservations@commodore-hotel.u-net.com). Lancaster Gate tube. **Rooms** 90 (all en suite). **Rates** (incl breakfast) *single* £88-£96; *double* £105-£115; *triple* £140; *suite* £150. **Credit** AmEx, DC, JCB, MC, £TC, V. **Map 2 D7**
Situated a stroll away from Hyde Park, the Commodore provides good access to London's sights, in quiet surroundings. The rooms are smartly decorated in cream and light colours, with comfortably sized double rooms and bathrooms. Other features include a large collection of teddy bears and a basement tapas bar with satellite TV.
Hotel services *Bar. Business services. Meeting room. Restaurant. Safe.* **Room services** *Hairdryer. Modem. Radio. Room service (8am-8pm). Tea/coffee.*

Cranley Gardens Hotel

8 Cranley Gardens, SW7 3DB (0171 373 3232/fax 0171 373 7944). Gloucester Road tube. **Rooms** 85 (all en suite). **Rates** (incl breakfast) *single* £79-£89; *double* £109-£119; *triple* £135. **Credit** AmEx, DC, JCB, MC, £TC, V. **Map 4 D11**

Four converted Victorian townhouses make up this family-run hotel. Rooms are well appointed and all the staff are eager to please. Guests can chill out in the comfortable reception lounge and bar area, and fuel up for a day of sightseeing in the breakfast room.
Hotel services *Babysitting. Bar. Multilingual staff.* **Room services** *Hairdryer. Radio. Room service (7am-midnight).*

Five Sumner Place

5 Sumner Place, SW7 3EE (0171 584 7586/fax 0171 823 9962/no.5@dial.pipex.com/dspace.dial.pipex.com/ no.5). South Kensington tube. **Rooms** 13 (all en suite). **Rates** (incl English breakfast) *single* £88; *double* £141; *triple* £165. **Credit** AmEx, JCB, MC, £TC, V. **Map 4 D11**
Situated in a smart tree-lined street in South Kensington, this superior B&B is immaculately clean and decorated with restrained good taste. The airy blue/yellow conservatory is a lovely place to enjoy breakfast and afternoon tea.
Hotel services *Multilingual staff. No-smoking rooms. Patio. Safe.* **Room services** *Hairdryer. Minibar. Radio. Refrigerator. Room service (8am-10pm). Tea/coffee.*

Hallam

12 Hallam Street, W1N 5LF (0171 580 1166/fax 0171 323 4527). Oxford Circus tube. **Rooms** 25 (all en suite). **Rates** (incl English breakfast) *single* £81.50; *double* £97.50. **Credit** AmEx, DC, MC, £TC, V. **Map 5 H5**
Despite its central location, on a street opposite Broadcasting House and close to Oxford Street, the Hallam is a quiet spot, offering elegant, comfortable rooms and friendly service. There is a small, newly installed bar in the reception area.
Hotel services *Bar. Lounge. Multilingual staff. Safe.* **Room services** *Hairdryer. Minibar. Radio.*

London Elizabeth Hotel

4 Lancaster Terrace, W2 3PF (0171 402 6641/fax 0171 224 8900). Lancaster Gate tube. **Rooms** 49 (all en suite). **Rates** (incl continental breakfast) *single* £100; *double* £115-£150; *suite* £135-£250. **Credit** AmEx, DC, MC, £$TC, V. **Map 2 D6**
Located close to Hyde Park's Italian gardens, this hotel aims to recreate the ambience of Victorian townhouse living, with mixed success: a series of quirky features in the rooms, such as an outrageously garish stained-glass ceiling, add an air of nineteenth-century eccentricity, but the décor is outmoded and the period theme laboured. Service, however, is impeccable, and the hotel's restaurant has an exciting menu incorporating fresh herbs plucked from the hotel garden.
Hotel services *Babysitting. Bar. Business services. Car park. Conference facilities. Currency exchange. Garden. Multilingual staff. No-smoking floor. Restaurant. Safe.* **Room services** *Air-conditioning. Disabled rooms. Hairdryer. Radio. Room service (24-hour). VCR. Website: www.londonelizabethhotel.com*

Mornington Lancaster Hotel

12 Lancaster Gate, W2 3LG (0171 262 7361/fax 0171 706 1028/mornington.hotel@mornington.co.uk). Lancaster Gate tube. **Rooms** 66 (all en suite). **Rates** (incl breakfast) *single* £99; *double* £115-£140; *mini-duplexes* £140. **Credit** AmEx, DC, JCB, MC, £$TC, V. **Map D7**
Owned by a Swedish hotel group, the Mornington is a curious mix of English formality and Scandinavian pragmatism. The traditional dark greens and heavy wood veneers of the lobby and library bar are at odds with the simple pastel and pine décor of the bedrooms, but it's a combination that works surprisingly well. You'd be hard-pushed to find a similarly distinguished hotel in the environs of Hyde Park for a comparable price.
Hotel services *Bar. Car park. Conference facilities. Currency exchange. Multilingual staff. No-smoking rooms. Safe.* **Room services** *Hairdryer. Radio. Tea/coffee. VCR.*

Sandringham

3 Holford Road, NW3 1AD (0171 435 1569/fax 0171 431 5932). Hampstead tube. **Rooms** 17 (15 en suite). **Rates** *single* £70-£85; *double/twin* £115-£130; *triple* £150; *junior suite* £140. **Credit** AmEx, DC, JCB, MC, TC, V.

Close to Hampstead Heath, this elegant yet relaxing hotel is stylishly decorated and boasts an intimate home-from-home atmosphere. Breakfast and afternoon tea are served in the drawing room and there's an extensive room service menu.

Hotel services *Bar. Car park (for 5 cars). Garden. Limousine service. Lounge. Multilingual staff. No-smoking rooms.* **Room services** *Room service (24-hour). Tea/coffee.*

Topham's Hotel

28 Ebury Street, SW1W 0LU (0171 730 8147/fax 0171 823 5966). Victoria tube/rail. **Rooms** 40 (38 en suite). **Rates** (incl breakfast) *single* £110; *double/twin* £120-£140; *triple* £160. **Credit** AmEx, DC, JCB, MC, £TC, V. **Map 7 H10**

This pretty hotel in the heart of Belgravia has an unassuming, English country house feel, providing a welcome respite from its buzzing location, with the King's Road on one side and Buckingham Palace Road on the other. The rooms, decked out in cutesy pastel pinks and whites, are bright and spacious if a little lacking in warmth, and staff are welcoming.

Hotel services *Bar. Conference facilities. Restaurant. Safe.* **Room services** *Hairdryer. Tea/coffee.*

Wilbraham

1 Wilbraham Place, SW1X 9AE (0171 730 8296/fax 0171 730 6815). Sloane Square tube. **Rooms** 50 (all en suite). **Rates** *single* £79-£90; *double/twin* £100-£115; *triple* £105-£113; *suite* £130-£145. **Credit** TC. **Map 7 G10**

Just behind Sloane Square, this splendid hotel has retained many of its Victorian features, including original bathroom fittings. The rooms also have a period feel; many are decorated with a floral theme.

Hotel services *Babysitting. Bar. Currency exchange. Lounge. Multilingual staff. Safe. Restaurant.* **Room services** *Room service (7am-11pm).*

Moderate to cheap (£65-£85)

Abbey House

11 Vicarage Gate, W8 4AG (0171 727 2594). High Street Kensington or Notting Hill Gate tube. **Rooms** 16 (none en suite). **Rates** (incl English breakfast) *single* £40; *double* £65; *triple* £78; *quad* £90; *quin* £100. **Credit** £$TC. **Map 1 B8**

One of the best quality B&Bs in this price range, Abbey House is an elegant Victorian house, retaining many of its original fittings, with spacious, simply decorated rooms and comfy orthopaedic beds.

Hotel services *Multilingual staff. Payphone. Tea/coffee.* **Room services** *TV. Washbasin.*

Crescent Hotel

49-50 Cartwright Gardens, WC1H 9EL (0171 387 1515/fax 0171 383 2054). Russell Square tube/Euston tube/rail. **Rooms** 24 (18 en suite). **Rates** (incl English breakfast) *single* £40-£60; *double/twin* £75; *triple* £85. **Credit** MC, £TC, V. **Map 6 L3**

This pleasant, family-run B&B, in a Regency house in Bloomsbury dotted with antiques, overlooks crescent-shaped gardens containing tennis courts (which guests are free to use).

Hotel services *Fax. Lounge. Multilingual staff. Safe.* **Room services** *TV.*

Get switched on: **The Generator.** *See p149.*

Gate Hotel

6 Portobello Road, W11 3DG (0171 221 2403/fax 0171 221 9128). Notting Hill Gate tube. **Rooms** 6 (5 en suite). **Rates** (incl breakfast) *single* £45-£60; *double* £75-£78; *triple* £85. **Credit** MC, £TC, V. **Map 1 A6**

Notting Hill remains one of London's most fashionable districts, and the Gate, at the Notting Hill Gate end of the multicultural Portobello Road, is well located for the antique shops, market (*see p193*), and Kensington Palace and Gardens. Accommodation is fairly simple but spotlessly clean, and there's a splendid profusion of fresh flowers. Service is friendly. Note that there is a 3% surcharge on credit card payments.

Hotel services *Fax. Hairdryer (on request).* **Room services** *Radio. Refrigerator. Tea/coffee. Telephone. TV.*

Website: www.s-h-systems.co.uk/hotels/gate

Harlingford Hotel

61-63 Cartwright Gardens, WC1H 9EL (0171 387 1551/fax 0171 387 4616). Russell Square tube/Euston tube/rail. **Rooms** 43 (42 en suite). **Rates** (incl English breakfast) *single* £63; *double/twin* £78; *triple* £88; *quad* £98. **Credit** AmEx, DC, JCB, MC, £TC, V. **Map 6 L3**

Located at the end of a pretty Regency crescent, this hotel has a decidedly sophisticated feel. An impressive, softly lit front lounge overlooks public gardens and the rooms are tastefully kitted out and admirably clean. It's slightly more expensive than its neighbours: **The Crescent** (*see above*) and **Jenkins** (*see below*) hotels on the same street provide similar facilities, but the large front rooms may make it worth the extra few pounds.

Hotel services *Fax. Safe.* **Room services** *Hairdryer (on request). Tea/coffee. Telephone. TV.*

Hart House Hotel

51 Gloucester Place, W1H 3PE (0171 935 2288/ fax 0171 935 8516). Bond Street or Marble Arch tube. **Rooms** 16 (11 en suite). **Rates** (incl English breakfast) *single £53-£65; double/twin £75-£93; triple £110; quad £130.* **Credit** AmEx, JCB, £STC, V. **Map 5 G6**
A good-looking Georgian hotel located on a smart terrace with Regent's Park at one end and Oxford Street at the other. Rooms are light and subtly decorated with many of the original Georgian features.
Hotel services *Fax. Safe.* **Room services** *Hairdryer. Tea/coffee. Telephone. TV.*

Hotel 167

167 Old Brompton Road, SW5 0AN (0171 373 0672/ fax 0171 373 3360). Gloucester Road tube. **Rooms** 19 (18 en suite). **Rates** (incl breakfast) *single £66-£78; double £82-£90; triple £105.* **Credit** AmEx, MC, £TC, V. **Map 4 D11**
Featured in Jane Soloman's novel of the same name, Hotel 167 offers comfortable accommodation with real flair. Every room has been individually designed, combining funky, bright colours with antiques. The lovely reception-cum-breakfast room is decked out with marble tables and large modern paintings.
Hotel services *Fax. Multilingual staff. Safe.* **Room services** *Hairdryer. Refrigerator. Room service (8am-11pm). Satellite TV. Tea/coffee.*

Kensington Gardens Hotel

9 Kensington Gardens Square, W2 4BH (0171 221 7790/ fax 0171 792 8612/kengarhotel@compuserve.com). Bayswater or Queensway tube. **Rooms** 17 (13 en suite). **Rates** (incl breakfast) *single £50-£55; double £75; triple £95.* **Credit** AmEx, DC, MC, £TC, V.
Map 1 B6
Set on a quiet Victorian square, this comfortable B&B offers good room facilities for the price and an excellent location, near to the restaurants and multicultural buzz of Queensway.
Hotel services *Fax. Lounge. Multilingual staff.* **Room services** *Hairdryer. Minibar. Room service (2-11pm). Satellite TV. Tea/coffee. Telephone.*

Morgan Hotel

24 Bloomsbury Street & Great Russell Street, WC1B 3QJ (0171 636 3735). Tottenham Court Road tube. **Rooms** 21 (all en suite). **Rates** (incl English breakfast) *single £50-60; double/twin £75; triple £110; suite £95 for 2, £130 for 3.* **Credit** MC, £TC, V. **Map 6 K5**
The friendly owners of this Georgian terrace hotel are Londoners and proud of it: beefeaters on the walls and Toby jugs lining the breakfast room windowsill are among the giveaways. Rooms are clean and comfortable, and the location, near the British Museum, is perfect for culture vultures. The hotel is split between two houses, the second of which contains a number of suites and larger rooms, let to loyal guests or those making extended stays. There's a surcharge of 3% for credit card bookings.
Hotel services *Fax.* **Room services** *Air-conditioning (most rooms). Hairdryer. Safe. Telephone. TV.*

Parkwood

4 Stanhope Place, W2 2HB (0171 402 2241/fax 0171 402 1574). Marble Arch tube. **Rooms** 17 (13 en suite). **Rates** (incl English breakfast) *single £49.50-£69.50; double £64.50-£87.50; triple £77-£97.* **Credit** DC, MC, £TC, V. **Map 2 F6**
A quiet, centrally located B&B, on a street opposite Hyde Park and a few minutes from Oxford Street. The spruce rooms are decorated in serene colours and floral prints.
Hotel services *Fax. Lounge. Multilingual staff. No-smoking rooms. Patio.* **Room services** *Radio. Satellite TV. Tea/coffee. Telephone.*

The Plough

42 Christchurch Road, SW14 7AF (0181 876 7833/fax 0181 392 8801). Richmond tube then 33, 337 bus/ Mortlake rail. **Rooms** 7 (all en suite). **Rates** (incl English breakfast) *single £55; double £70; triple/quad £90-£100.* **Credit** AmEx, MC, TC, V.
A little gem. This picturesque sixteenth-century inn retains its beamed ceilings and thick walls, some still in wattle and daub, while providing an array of modern home comforts. Breakfast is served in the pub downstairs, where you can mingle with locals for that authentic provincial feel. Richmond Park and the river are within walking distance.
Hotel services *Car park. Fax. Garden. Laundry. Multilingual staff. Pub. Restaurant. Safe.* **Room services** *Hairdryer. Room service (noon-3pm, 7.30-9.30pm). Satellite TV. Tea/coffee. Telephone.*

Riverside Hotel

23 Petersham Road, Richmond, Surrey TW10 6UH (tel/fax 0181 940 1339). Richmond tube. **Rooms** 19 (18 en suite). **Rates** (incl English breakfast) *single £38-£55; double £70-£75; triple £85-£90; suite £110.* **Credit** AmEx, MC, TC, V.
Enjoying a superb location, overlooking the Thames at Richmond, this B&B's other plus points include clean, comfortable rooms of a good size and notably friendly owners.
Hotel services *Car park. Currency exchange. Fax. Garden. Laundry. Lounge. Multilingual staff. No-smoking rooms.* **Room services** *Hairdryer (on request). Room service (7.30am-11.30pm). Tea/coffee. Telephone. Satellite TV.*

Rushmore

11 Trebovir Road, SW5 9LS (0171 370 3839/370 6505/835 1431/fax 0171 370 0274). Earl's Court tube. **Rooms** 22 (all en suite). **Rates** (incl breakfast) *single £59-£69; double £79-£85; triple £89-£95; quad £99-£105.* **Credit** AmEx, MC, £TC, V. **Map 3 B11**
A delightful hotel, with rooms decorated in an imaginative range of styles and colours, using *trompe l'oeil* techniques and draped fabrics – each one is different. The Rushmore's Italian feel extends to the wrought-iron Tuscan furniture and glass tables in the airy conservatory.
Hotel services *Conference facilities. Fax. Laundry. Lounge. Multilingual staff. No-smoking rooms. Safe.* **Room services** *Hairdryer. Satellite TV. Tea/coffee.*

Swiss House Hotel

171 Old Brompton Road, SW5 0AN (0171 373 2769/ fax 0171 373 4983/recep@swiss-hh.demon.co.uk). Gloucester Road tube. **Rooms** 16 (15 en suite). **Rates** (incl continental breakfast) *single £42-£59; double £75-£82; triple £94; quad £106.* **Credit** AmEx, DC, JCB, MC, £TC, V. **Map 4 D11**
From the green foliage outside to dried flowers and russet carpets inside, every effort has been made to give the Swiss House the feel of an English country cottage. Rooms are decked out in pleasant lilacs and purples.
Hotel services *Fax. Laundry. Multilingual staff. No-smoking rooms. Safe.* **Room services** *Room service (noon-9pm). Satellite TV. Telephone.*
Website: www. webscape.co.uk/swisshouse

30 King Henry's Road

30 King Henry's Road, NW3 3RP (0171 483 2871/fax 0171 483 4587). Chalk Farm tube. **Rooms** 3 (all with private bathrooms). **Rates** (incl breakfast) *single £60; double £80.* **Credit** £TC.
This stylish, homely Victorian B&B in Primrose Hill, run by the welcoming Carole and Andrew Ingram, offers lovely rooms and a relaxed atmosphere. Book at least three to four weeks in advance.
Hotel services *Fax. Garden. Multilingual staff. No smoking. Telephone.* **Room services** *Hairdryer. Radio.*

Cheap (under £65)

Arosfa

83 Gower Street, WC1E 6HJ (tel/fax 0171 636 2115).
Goodge Street tube/Euston tube/rail. **Rooms** 16 (2 en
suite). **Rates** (incl English breakfast) *single* £31; *double*
£44-£58; *triple* £59-£70; *quad* £80. **Credit** TC. **Map 6 K4**
Arosfa ('place to stay' in Welsh) is run by the friendly Mr
and Mrs Dorta, who offer basic but pleasantly decorated
rooms in the former Georgian home of the artist John Everett
Millais. There's a 2% surcharge on credit cards.
Hotel services *Fax. Garden. Lounge. Multilingual staff.
Payphone.* **Room services** *TV. Washbasin.*

Ashlee House

*261-265 Gray's Inn Road, WC1X 8QT (0171 833
9400/fax 0171 833 9677).* King's Cross tube. **Rooms** 27
(150 beds). **Rates** (incl breakfast)*16-bed rooms* £10-£13;
8-bed £13-£15; *4-bed* £15-£17; *2-bed* £20-£22; *single* £32-
£34. **Credit** AmEx, MC, £TC, V. **Map 6 M3**
This brand new hostel-style accommodation caters mainly
to young backpackers. The bright yellow rooms (all with
bunk beds) take between one and 16 people; the price per
person decreases the more you share with. There's a large
dining and self-catering area downstairs and staff are
cheerful and accommodating. There's a 2% charge for
credit card payments.
Hotel services *Baggage store. Fax. Laundry. Safe.
Self-catering facilities.* **Room services** *Washbasin.*

Cartref House & James House

*129 Ebury Street, SW1W 9QU & 108 Ebury Street, SW1W
9QD (0171 730 6176 & 0171 730 7338/jamescartref@
compuserve.com).* Victoria tube/rail. **Rooms** (incl English
breakfast) *Cartref* 11 (8 en suite); *James* 10 (2 en suite).
Rates *single* £46-£56; *double* £62-£73; *triple* £75-£88;
quad £97-£107. **Credit** AmEx, DC, MC, £TC, V.
Map 7 H10
Under the same ownership, these B&Bs on a chic Georgian
street provide bright, basic rooms and a cheery welcome.
Hotel services *Fax. Multilingual staff. Payphone.*
Room services *Tea/coffee. TV.*

Coach & Horses Hotel

*8 Kew Green, Richmond, Surrey TW9 3BH (0181 940
1208/fax 0181 940 0970).* Kew Gardens tube/rail.
Rooms 6 (all en suite showers). **Rates** (incl English
breakfast) *single* £39; *double/twin* £49; *quad* £70.
Credit AmEx, MC, £TC, V.
Overlooking Kew Green, and a short stroll from Kew
Gardens, the Coach & Horses offers simply decorated rooms
above an atmospheric, friendly pub with a garden.
Hotel services *Bar. Car park. Function room. Multi-
lingual staff.* **Room services** *Tea/coffee. TV.*

Garden Court Hotel

*30-31 Kensington Gardens Square, W2 4BG (0171 229
2553/fax 0171 727 2749).* Bayswater or Queensway
tube. **Rooms** 32 (16 en suite). **Rates** (incl English
breakfast) *single* £34-£48; *double* £48-£74; *triple* £68-£82;
quad £78-£88. **Credit** MC, £TC, V. **Map 1 B6**
A popular family-run B&B overlooking a peaceful Victorian
garden square. Rooms are comfortable, warm and clean. A
hearty full English breakfast is provided each morning.
Hotel services *Fax. Garden. Lounge. Multilingual staff.
Safe.* **Room services** *Hairdryer. Telephone. TV.*

The Generator

*Compton Place (off Tavistock Place), WC1H 9SD (0171
388 7666/fax 0171 388 7644/generator@lhdr.demon.
co.uk).* Russell Square tube. **Rooms** 208 (810 beds; none
en suite). **Rates** (per person, incl breakfast) *single* £36;
twin £22.50; *3-6-bed room* £19; *7-8-bed room* £18.
Credit MC, V. **Map 6 K4**

This converted police barracks is a teenager's dream: all
coloured neon lights, *Hellraiser* posters and dark blue paint.
It's a youth hostel set-up with a huge self-catering and dining area, games machines and social areas, but each party
is accommodated separately: if there are two of you, you'll
have to get a twin room and won't be allowed to pay less to
share a dorm; the number of groups testifies to the large
number of student groups it receives. The licensed bar is
open until 2am. *See picture p145.*
Hotel services *Bar. Fax. No-smoking rooms.*
Room services *Washbasin.*
Website: *www.lhdr.demon.co.uk*

Hampstead Village Guesthouse

*2 Kemplay Road, NW3 1SY (0171 435 8679/fax 0171
794 0254/hvguesthouse@dial.pipex.com).* Hampstead
tube/Hampstead Heath rail. **Rooms** 6 (5 en suite).
Rates *single* £35-£50; *double* £55-£65; *studio* £65-£115.
Credit AmEx, DC, MC, £TC, V.
A real haven for eccentrics, this: located in a rambling Victorian Hampstead townhouse, each of its six rooms are filled
with a fabulous array of books, antiques and family clutter,
accumulated and lovingly arranged by its exuberant owner,
Anne Marie van der Meer. All the rooms are immaculately
kept, and there is a separate outhouse with a tiny corner kitch-
enette, available for use as a private suite. No smoking
throughout. Credit card payments are subject to a 5% charge.
Hotel services *Babysitting. Business services. Fax.
Garden. Laundry. Multilingual staff.* **Room services**
Hairdryer. Iron. Refrigerator. Tea/coffee. Telephone. TV.

Highfield Guest House

*12 Downhill Road, SE6 1HJ (0181 698 8038/fax 0181
698 8039).* Hither Green rail. **Rooms** 3 (1 en suite)
Rates (incl breakfast) *single* £32-£45; *double/twin* £45-
£55; *triple* £65. **Credit** JCB, MC, £TC, V.
This immaculate little guesthouse was the 1998 winner of
the London Tourist Board's best B&B award, and it's easy
to see why: the facilities are excellent, the comfortable rooms
decked out in well-chosen Ikea-style furnishings, and the
owner, Frenchman Michel Tournier, goes to great lengths
to accommodate his guests. The only disadvantage is the
location, though transport routes into central London are
numerous, and rooms like these would be at least twice the
price any further north.
Hotel services *Fax. Garden. Breakfast room/lounge.*
Room services *Hairdryer. Radio. Refrigerator.
Tea/coffee. TV.*

Jenkins Hotel

*45 Cartwright Gardens, WC1H 9EH (0171 387 2067/
fax 0171 383 3139/reservations@jenkinshotel.demon.
co.uk).* Russell Square tube/Euston tube/rail.
Rooms 14 (7 en suite). **Rates** (incl English breakfast)
single £45-£62; *double* £62-£72; *triple* £80. **Credit** MC,
£TC, V. **Map 6 L3**
Two friendly black Labradors welcome guests into this recommended B&B located on a quiet, pretty Georgian crescent. Rooms are impeccably clean and airy.
Hotel services *Fax. Garden.* **Room services** *Hairdryer. Minibar. Refrigerator. Tea/coffee. Telephone. TV.*

Oxford House Hotel

*92-94 Cambridge Street, SW1 (0171 834 6467/fax 0171
834 0225).* Victoria tube/rail. **Rooms** 17 (none en suite).
Rates (incl English breakfast) *single* £34-£36; *double*
£44-£46; *triple* £57-£60; *quad* £76-£82. **Credit** MC, £TC,
V. **Map 7 H11**
This hotel is a real find: bright, comfortable accommodation
just around the corner from Victoria Station. The shared
facilities are clean and well kept and full English breakfasts
are provided between 7.30 and 8.45 each morning.
Hotel services *Fax. Payphone.*
Room services *Radio. Washbasin.*

Ruskin Hotel

23-24 Montague Street, WC1B 5BH (0171 636 7388/ fax 0171 323 1662). Holborn, Russell Square or Tottenham Court Road tube. **Rooms** 32 (6 en suite). **Rates** (incl English breakfast) *single* £42; *double* £60-£75; *triple* £75-£85. **Credit** AmEx, DC, JCB, MC, £TC, V. **Map 6 L5**

The family-run Ruskin enjoys a great location right next to the British Museum. Rooms are very plain and a little musty, but the facilities are all there, and there's a large, plush lounge fronting on to the street. Two of the front rooms were used as offices by Sir Arthur Conan Doyle when he was writing the *Sherlock Holmes* series.
Hotel services *Fax. Multilingual staff.*
Room services *Hairdryer. Tea/coffee.*

St Margaret Hotel

26 Bedford Place, WC1B 5JL (0171 636 4277/ fax 0171 323 3066). Holborn or Russell Square tube. **Rooms** 68 (10 en suite). **Rates** (incl English breakfast) *single* £42.50-£44.50; *double* £54.50-£72. **Credit** £$TC. **Map 6 L5**

A pleasant, characterful, family-run B&B with tastefully decorated rooms and obliging staff. There are two capacious lounges and a dining room hung with chandeliers.
Hotel services *Fax. Garden. Lounge. Multilingual staff.*
Room services *Satellite TV. Telephone.*

Vicarage Hotel

10 Vicarage Gate, W8 4AG (0171 229 4030/fax 0171 792 5989/londonvicaragehotel.com). High Street Kensington or Notting Hill Gate tube. **Rooms** 18 (none en suite). **Rates** (incl English breakfast) *single* £40; *double* £63; *triple* £80; *quad* £88. **Credit** TC. **Map 1 B8**

Clean, sizeable rooms and a handy location for the shops of Kensington High Street are the chief recommendations for this homely Victorian B&B.
Hotel services *Fax. Payphone. TV lounge.*
Room services *Hairdryer (on request). Tea/coffee. Washbasin.*
Website: *www.vichotel.demon.co.uk*

Woodville House & Morgan House

107 Ebury Street, SW1W 9QU (0171 730 1048/fax 0171 730 2574) & 120 Ebury Street, SW1W 9QQ (0171 730 2384/fax 0171 730 8442). Victoria tube/rail. **Rooms** *Woodville* 12 (none en suite); *Morgan* 11 (3 en suite). **Rates** (incl English breakfast) *single* £42; *double* £58-£80; *triple* £78; *quad* £80-£100. **Credit** MC, £TC, V. **Map 7 H10**

Located close to Victoria Station, both these Georgian B&Bs are owned by exuberant couple Rachel Joplin and Ian Berry. Woodville House has traditional, flowery décor; Morgan is more contemporary. Families are very well catered for and one of the suites has an adjoining terrace that can double as a picnic area.
Hotel services *Babysitting. Fax. Kitchenette. Multilingual staff. Patio. Payphone.*
Room services *Tea/coffee. TV.*

Children's hotels

Pippa Pop-Ins

430 Fulham Road, SW6 1DU (0171 385 2457/8/fax 0171 385 5706). Fulham Broadway tube. **Rates** (incl food) £40-£50 per night; £75 per 24 hours. **Credit** MC, TC, V. **Map 3 C13**

By day, a colourful nursery school and by night, a hotel for children aged 2-12. The bright interiors spell fun from the word go. School holiday excursions, 24-hour childcare by NNEB qualified nannies, silver-service kids' dinner parties and midnight feasts are all on offer.
Hotel services *Garden. Toys.*

Women-only accommodation

Townsend House

126 Queen's Gate, SW7 5LQ (0171 589 9628/fax 0171 225 1458). Gloucester Road tube. **Open** phone enquiries 9am-5pm Mon-Fri. **Rates** *B&B: twin* £16; *hostel: single* £72; *double/twin* £65 per week; *triple* £61 per week. **Credit** £TC. **Map 4 D10**

Run by the Girls' Friendly Society, Townsend House is a clean, conveniently located women-only (aged 18-30) B&B/hostel. Most of the rooms in the house are given over to the long-stay hostel (one month minimum); the B&B (14 days maximum) consists of a few rooms on the top floor, but all guests can use the house's amenities, which include a large kitchen, two large lounges, laundry facilities and a chapel. Look for the small 'GFS' sign on the front door.

Gay & lesbian accommodation

See page 243.

Youth hostels

Most beds are in dormitories. If you are not a member of the International Youth Hostel Federation (IYHF), you'll have to pay an extra £1.70 a night to stay at hostels (after six nights you automatically become a member). Alternatively, join the IYHF for £10.20 (£5 for under-18s) at any member hostel or the YHA Adventure Shop (14 Southampton Street, WC2; 0171 836 1036/fax 0171 836 6372). Always phone hostels first to check the availability of beds. All the following hostels take MasterCard, Visa and travellers' cheques.

City of London Youth Hostel *36-38 Carter Lane, EC4 (0171 236 4965/fax 0171 236 7681). St Paul's tube.* **Beds** 199. **Reception open** 7am-11pm daily; 24-hour access. **Rates** (incl breakfast) £19-£25; £17-£21.50 under-18s. **Map 11 O6**

Earl's Court Youth Hostel *38 Bolton Gardens, SW5 (0171 373 7083/fax 0171 835 2034). Earl's Court tube.* **Beds** 155. **Reception open** 7am-11pm daily; 24-hour access. Rates (incl breakfast) £18.70; £16.45 under-18s. **Map 3 B11**

Hampstead Heath Youth Hostel *4 Wellgarth Road, NW11 (0181 458 9054/fax 0181 209 0546). Golders Green tube.* **Beds** 200. **Reception open** 6.45am-11pm daily; 24-hour access. **Rates** £15.60; £13.35 under-18s.

Holland House Youth Hostel *Holland House, Holland Walk, W8 (0171 937 0748/fax 0171 376 0667). High Street Kensington or Holland Park tube.* **Beds** 201. **Reception open** 7am-11pm daily; 24-hour access. **Rates** (incl breakfast) £18.70; £16.45 under-18s. **Map 1 A8**

Oxford Street Youth Hostel *14 Noel Street, W1 (0171 734 1618/fax 0171 734 1657). Oxford Circus tube.* **Beds** 75. **Reception open** 7am-11pm daily; 24-hour access. **Rates** £18.70; £15.25 under-18s. **Map 5 J6**

Rotherhithe Youth Hostel *Island Yard, Salter Road, SE16 (0171 232 2114/fax 0171 237 2919). Rotherhithe tube.* **Beds** 320. **Reception open** 7am-11pm; 24-hour access. **Rates** £21.30-£24.50; £17.90-£24.50 under-18s.

YMCAs & YWCAs

You may need to book months in advance. Many YMCAs specialise in long-term accommodation. A few of the larger hostels are listed below (all

Pay a £25 membership fee and enjoy some of the most fabulous and exclusive B&Bs in the country.

Host and Guest Service *103 Dawes Road, SW6 7DU (0171 385 9922/fax 0171 386 7575). Fulham Broadway tube.* **Open** 9am-5.30pm Mon-Fri. **Rates** from £16.50 per person; students from £85.90 per week. **Credit** MC, £TC, V. **Minimum stay** 2 nights.

London Bed & Breakfast Agency *71 Fellows Road, NW3 3JY (0171 586 2768/fax 0171 586 6567).* **Rates** £18-£35 per night. **Minimum stay** 2 nights.

London Homestead Services *Coombe Wood Road, Kingston-upon-Thames, Surrey KT2 7JY (0181 949 4455/fax 0181 549 5492).* **Open** *phone enquiries* 9am-7pm daily. **Rates** *single* from £16; *double* from £32. **Credit** MC, £TC, V. **Minimum stay** 3 nights.

Self-catering/service apartments

It can be very expensive to rent accommodation in London, but if you are in a group, you may be able to save money by renting a flat. The following specialise in holiday lettings. See also *Yellow Pages.*

The Apartment Service *1st floor, 5-6 Francis Grove, SW19 4DT (0181 944 1444/fax 0181 944 6744). Wimbledon tube/rail.* **Open** 9am-5.30pm Mon-Fri. **Rates** *double studio* from £90 per night. **Credit** AmEx, MC, V.

Aston's *31 Rosary Gardens, SW7 4NQ (0171 590 6000/fax 0171 590 6060). Gloucester Road tube.* **Open** 9am-6pm daily; *phone enquiries* 9am-10.30pm daily. **Rates** *single studio* from £43-£52 per night; *double studio* from £65-£74 per night. **Credit** MC, £TC, V.

Holiday Serviced Apartments *273 Old Brompton Road, SW5 9JA (0171 373 4477/fax 0171 373 4282/ reservations@holidayapartments.co.uk/www.holidayapartments.co.uk). Earl's Court tube.* **Open** 9.30am-6pm Mon-Fri. **Rates** *single/double studio* from £80 per night. **Credit** AmEx, JCB, MC, £TC, V.

The Independent Traveller *Thorverton, Exeter, Devon EX5 5NT (01392 860807/fax 01392 860552/ independenttraveller@compuserve.com).* **Rates** *apartments* £220-£2,000 per week. **Credit** MC, £TC, V. **Minimum stay** 3 nights. Properties in London and all over the UK.

London Holiday Accommodation Bureau *(tel/fax 0171 323 5120/07957 384924/sales@londonholiday.co.uk).* **Rates** from £30 per night. **Credit** Amex, MC, £TC, V.
Holiday apartments all over London, with airport/tube pickup, theatre tickets and a tour thrown in.

Palace Court Holiday Apartments *1 Palace Court, Bayswater Road, W2 4LP (0171 727 3467/fax 0171 221 7824). Notting Hill Gate or Queensway tube.* **Open** 8.30am-11pm daily. **Rates** *single studio* £55 per night; *double* £70 per night; *triple* £80 per night. **Credit** £TC.

Perfect Places *53 Margravine Gardens, W6 8RN (0181 748 6095/fax 0181 741 4213/permatch@ netcomuk.co.uk).West Kensington tube.* **Rates** from £550 per week. **Credit** AmEx, MC, TC, V.
Apartments in Kensington and Chelsea.

University residences

During university vacations much of London's student accommodation is opened up to visitors.

Arcade Halls *The Arcade, 385-401 Holloway Road, N7 0RN (0171 607 5415/fax 0171 609 0052/*

Holland House Youth Hostel*'s idyllic setting.*

are unisex), but the National Council for YMCAs (0181 520 5599) can supply a full list. Prices are around £25-£30 per night for a single room and £40-£60 for a double.

Barbican YMCA *2 Fann Street, EC2 (0171 628 0697/ fax 0171 638 2420). Barbican tube.* **Beds** 240. **Map 9 P5**

London City YMCA *8 Errol Street, EC1 (0171 628 8832/fax 0171 628 4080). Barbican tube.* **Beds** 111. **Map 9 F4**

Wimbledon YMCA *200 The Broadway, SW19 (0181 542 9055/fax 0181 542 1086). Wimbledon tube/rail.* **Beds** 110.

YWCA *Elizabeth House, 118 Warwick Way, SW1 (0171 630 0741/fax 0171 630 0740). Victoria tube/rail.* **Beds** 63. **Map 7 H11**

Staying with the locals

Staying in a Londoner's home is often more fun than being in an impersonal hotel. The following organisations can arrange accommodation (rates include breakfast).

At Home in London *70 Black Lion Lane, W6 9BE (0171 748 1943/fax 0181 748 2701/AtHomeInLondon @compuserve.com/www.athomeinlondon.co.uk).* **Open** *phone enquiries* 9.30am-5.30pm Mon-Fri. **Rates** £28-£56. **Credit** JCB, MC, £TC, V.

The Bulldog Club *14 Dewhouse Road, W14 0ET (0171 371 3202/fax 0171 371 2015/jackson@ bulldogclub.u-net.com).* **Rates** from £85 per night. **Credit** AmEx, MC, V.

summerlets@unl.ac.uk). Holloway Road tube. **Rooms** *self-contained flats (for 4-6)* £11 per night; £74 per week. **Available** 5 July-6 Sept 1999.

Butlers Wharf LSE Residence *11 Gainsford Street, SE1 2NE (0171 407 7164/fax 0171 403 0847). Tower Hill tube/London Bridge tube/rail.* **Rooms** *self-contained flats (sleeping up to 7)* 48. **Rates** from £18 per person (under-12s half-price). **Minimum stay** 4 nights. **Available** July-Sept. **Map 12 R9**

Cartwright University Halls *36 Cartwright Gardens, WC1H 9BZ (0171 388 3757/fax 0171 388 2552). Russell Square tube or Euston tube/rail.* **Rooms** *single* 153; *twin* 40. **Rates** *single* from £29; *twin* from £42.50. **Available** all year. **Map 6 L3**

Goldsmid House *36 North Row, W1R 1DH (0171 493 8911/fax 0171 491 0586). Marble Arch tube.* **Rooms** *single* 10; *double* 120. **Rates** *single* £15; *twin* £20. **Available** June-Sept. **Map 5 G6**

High Holborn Residence *178 High Holborn, WC1V 7AA (0171 379 5589/fax 0171 379 5640). Holborn tube.* **Rooms** *single* 400; *twin* 48. **Rates** *single* £25-£32; *twin* £44-£65. **Available** July-Sept. **Map 6 M5**

International Students House *229 Great Portland Street, W1N 5HD (0171 631 8300/8310/fax 0171 631 8315/accom@ish.org.uk). Great Portland Street tube.* **Rooms** *single* 158; *twin* 107. **Rates** *single* £29.50; *twin* £21 per person; *dormitory* £9.99-£17.50. **Available** all year. **Map 5 H5**

King's Campus Vacation Bureau *King's College, 127 Stamford Street, SE1 9NQ (0171 928 3777/fax 0171 928 5777). Waterloo tube/rail.* **Rates** *single* £16.50-£32.50; *twin* £28.50-£46. **Available** Easter, June-Sept. King's has eight halls offering around 2,000 beds. **Map 11 N8**

Passfield Hall *1-7 Endsleigh Place, WC1H 0PW (0171 387 7743/3584/fax 0171 387 0419). Euston tube/rail.* **Rooms** *single* 100; *twin* 34; *triple* 7. **Rates** *single* £20.50-£26.50; *twin* £42-£48; *triple* £55-£60. **Available** Easter, July-Sept. **Map 6 K4**

Walter Sickert Hall *Graham Street, N1 8LA (0171 477 8822). Angel tube.* **Rooms** *single* 220; *executive single* 6; *executive twin* 3. **Rates** *single* £30; *executive single* £38; *executive twin* £55. **Available** 1 July-18 Sept. **Map 9 P3**

Camping & caravanning

Crystal Palace Caravan Club Site *Crystal Palace Parade, SE19 1UF (0181 778 7155). Crystal Palace rail/3 bus.* **Open** *office* 8am-8pm daily. **Rates** from £3.90; plus *caravan pitch* from £5; *car & tent pitch* from £3; *motorbike & tent pitch* £2.50; *bicycle/walker & tent pitch* £1; *electricity hook-up* from £1.20. **Credit** MC, £TC, V.
Room for 100 tent and 84 caravan pitches. Good facilities plus fresh bread in the summer and restaurants nearby.

Lea Valley Campsite *Sewardstone Road, E4 7RA (0181 529 5689). Walthamstow Central tube/rail then 215 bus.* **Open** Apr-Oct 8am-10pm daily. **Rates** £5; £2.20 under-16s; *electricity hook-up* £2.25 per day. **Credit** MC, V.
Although this big site is 12 miles (19km) from central London it has good facilities and it's cheap. No single-sex groups.

Lea Valley Leisure Centre Camping & Caravan Park *Meridian Way, N9 0AS (0181 803 6900). Edmonton Green rail/W8 bus or Tottenham Hale tube/363 bus.* **Open** 8am-10pm daily. **Rates** £5.20; £2.20 5s-16s; *electricity hook-up* £2.25 per day. **Credit** MC, £TC, V.
Located behind a leisure centre, this is the ideal campsite for sport fiends. There are 160 touring caravan pitches and 100 tent pitches plus washing facilities, showers and a shop.

Tent City Acton *Old Oak Common Lane, W3 7DP (0181 743 5708). East Acton tube.* **Open** *1 June-7 Sept* 24 hours daily. **Rates** £6; £3 under-12s; free under-5s; 10% discounts for groups. **Credit** £TC.
This venerable institution provides 320 beds in a tented hostel as well as 200 tent pitches. Free showers, toilets, washing and cooking facilities. All profits go to charity.

Tent City Hackney *Millfields Road, E5 0AR (0181 985 7656). Bus 38.* **Open** *1 July-31 Aug* 24 hours daily. **Rates** £5 per person; £2.50 under-15s; free under-5s. **Credit** £TC.
This site is run by **Tent City Acton** and offers similar facilities including 90 beds in a tented hostel and 200 tent pitches.

Emergency accommodation

If you're left stranded, one of the organisations below might be able to help.

Alone in London *188 King's Cross Road, WC1 (0171 278 4224). King's Cross tube/rail.* **Drop-in centre** 9am-12.30pm Mon-Fri. **Map 6 M3**
This organisation is specifically for homeless people aged 16-25. It is best to phone beforehand for appointments, but there is also a drop-in centre on a first-come, first-served basis.

Tonbridge Club *120 Cromer Street, WC1H 8BS (0171 837 4406). King's Cross tube/rail.* **Open** 9pm-midnight daily. **Rates** £5. **Map 6 L3**
By day it's a school club, by night it's the cheapest hostel in London. If you are stranded, the Tonbridge is a godsend. You'll have to sleep on a mattress on the gym floor, but there are hot showers, TV and a games room – all for just £5. Only foreign visitors and students are allowed to stay.

Longer stay

If you are planning on staying for months rather than weeks, it may work out cheaper to rent a place (although you'll normally have to pay a month's rent in advance and a further month's rent as a deposit). Even so, accommodation is still expensive and competition fierce. The best source for places to rent is *Loot*, published daily. Buy it as early as you can and get straight on the phone. Capital Radio publishes a flatshare list, available from the foyer (30 Leicester Square, WC2H 7LA; Leicester Square tube) every Thursday around 4pm. Also try *Time Out* magazine (available from Tuesdays in central London and Wednesday further out), and *Midweek*, free from tube stations on Thursdays.

As a rough guide, you're unlikely to get a studio (no separate bedroom or, often, kitchen) or a one-bedroom flat for less than £350-£400 per month, and you'll have to settle for some of the less desirable suburbs of south and east London. If you want to stay in hip areas like Islington or Notting Hill, expect to fork out £700-£1,000; similar accommodation in Covent Garden costs £800-£1,100; and if only Knightsbridge will do, prepare to stump up around £1,400 per month. If, however, you can stomach a room in a shared flat/house, you can find accommodation for less than £250 a month in the further reaches of the East End and south London, rising to around the £500-a-month level for Fulham or Hampstead.

Restaurants

Gorge yourself on some of the greatest global grub on the planet.

London's continuing excellence in the culinary field is now so widely acknowledged that it hardly requires commenting how things weren't always this way. The range of cuisines on offer, the variety of settings and the high standards are the equal of any city on the planet. And still new places keep opening. The appetite of both Londoners and visitors for new dining experiences may seem unassuagable, but the restaurants themselves are certainly feeling the strain. Staffing is the major problem. There are simply not enough trained kitchen and waiting staff in the capital, and the result is that experienced staff flit from restaurant to restaurant, commanding ever higher wages and making consistency of service and cooking ever harder for restaurateurs to maintain.

And be warned that there is still plenty of dross out there. If you want a taste of the good old, bad old days, you'll still have no trouble finding touristy rip-off joints serving up the sort of boiled-to-death slop you wouldn't feed your pets.

PRACTICALITIES

Few places have strict dress codes these days; as a general rule, the pricier the joint, the smarter the clientele. It's only common sense that you don't turn up to Chez Nico wearing jeans and a Hawaiian shirt, yet even here you won't be forced to don a jacket and tie.

It's standard practice to pay ten per cent on top of the bill for service. Some restaurants will add this automatically (while insisting that it is 'optional'; so if service wasn't up to scratch don't hesitate to deduct the charge. In fact, it is becoming distressingly common to find 12.5 and even 15 per cent added. Be wary of places that include service in the bill but then leave the space for gratuity empty on your credit card slip.

The average prices below are for a three-course meal (or ethnic equivalent), excluding drinks and service, for one person. For more information, buy the annual *Time Out Eating & Drinking Guide* (£9).

Haute cuisine

Haute equals posh, generally. Expect formality in décor and service, high prices and classic, superlative food. Dress up and live it up.

Chez Nico at Ninety Park Lane

90 Park Lane, W1 (0171 409 1290). Hyde Park Corner or Marble Arch tube. **Lunch** noon-2pm Mon-Fri.

Dinner 7-11pm Mon-Sat. **Average** £34 lunch, £64 dinner. **Set lunch** £32 three courses. **Set dinner** £52 two courses, £64 three courses. **Credit** AmEx, MC, TC, V. **Map 7 G7**

Nico Ladenis' consummate mastery of flavours, colours and textures – whether classic French or with adroit touches of Asia and the Middle East – ensures exemplary standards of cooking in this sedate Mayfair drawing room.

Gordon Ramsay

68-69 Royal Hospital Road, SW3 (0171 352 4441/3334). Sloane Square tube. **Lunch** noon-2pm, **dinner** 6.45-11pm, Mon-Fri. **Average** £50. **Set lunch** £25 three courses. **Set meal** £50 three courses, £65 seven courses. **Credit** AmEx, DC, JCB, MC, £TC, V. **Map 4 F12**

Since his dramatic parting (together with the entire kitchen and waiting staff) from Aubergine in 1998, ex-footballer and two-star Michelin chef Ramsay has triumphantly set up on his own. The third star won't be long in coming.

Oak Room

Meridien Hotel, 21 Piccadilly, W1 (0171 437 0202). Piccadilly Circus tube. **Lunch** noon-2.30pm Mon-Fri. **Dinner** 7-11.15pm Mon-Sat. **Average** £90. **Set lunch** £29.50 three courses. **Credit** AmEx, JCB, MC, £TC, V. **Map 7 J7**

Be prepared to dig deep into your pockets to enjoy the three-star cooking of Robert Reid at Marco Pierre White's flagship London restaurant. Stick to the set lunch if you want a more affordable taste of heaven.

The Room at the Halcyon

129 Holland Park Avenue, W11 (0171 221 5411/727 7288). Holland Park tube. **Lunch** noon-2.30pm Mon-Fri, Sun. **Dinner** 7-10.30pm Mon-Thur; 7-11pm Fri, Sat; 7-10pm Sun. **Average** £37 lunch, £43 dinner. **Set lunch** £18 two courses, £23 three courses. **Set dinner** £35 two courses, £43 three courses. **Credit** AmEx, DC, MC, V.

This chic hangout attracts the glitterati of several continents. The garden terrace is as delightful a place to dine on a summer's day as you'll find in the capital, and Martin Hadden's bold, assured, inspired cooking is revelatory. *See also p139.*

Stefano Cavallini Restaurant at the Halkin

5-6 Halkin Street, SW1 (0171 333 1234/1000). Hyde Park Corner tube. **Lunch** 12.30-2.30pm Mon-Fri. **Dinner** 7.30-10.30pm Mon-Sat; 7-10pm Sun. **Average** £55. **Set lunch** £25 three courses. **Set dinner** £55 six courses. **Credit** AmEx, DC, JCB, MC, £TC, V. **Map 7 G9**

One of London's very finest. Expect profound flavours, culinary skill and a refined light touch in understated, elegant surroundings. The set lunch is one of the best deals in town.

Modern European

The restaurants in this section represent the cutting edge of modern cuisine in London. Classical European cooking usually provides the base, but ingredients and inspiration are pillaged from around the world.

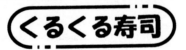

Alastair Little
*49 Frith Street, W1 (0171 734 5183). Leicester Square
or Tottenham Court Road tube.* **Lunch** 12.30-3pm Mon-
Fri. **Dinner** 6-11.30pm Mon-Sat. **Set lunch** £25 three
courses. **Set dinner** £33 three courses. **Credit** AmEx,
JCB, MC, £TC, V. **Map 6 K6**
The ground floor of this small, light-filled restaurant is a
delight (the basement is less attractive), and the daily changing menu, offering a choice of about seven Italian-inspired
dishes per course, is usually masterly prepared.
Branch: 136A Lancaster Road, W11 (0171 243 2220).

Andrew Edmunds
*46 Lexington Street, W1 (0171 437 5708). Oxford Circus
or Piccadilly Circus tube.* **Lunch** 12.30-3pm Mon-Fri; 1-3pm
Sat, Sun. **Dinner** 6-10.45pm Mon-Sat; 6-10.30pm Sun.
Average £20. **Credit** AmEx, MC, £TC, V. **Map 5 J6**
This informal bistro is tiny, and its following of thirty-
something Soho workers loyal and large, but if you love
simple, well-executed dishes, it's worth the squeeze.

Axis
*One Aldwych hotel, 1 Aldwych, WC2 (0171 300 0300).
Covent Garden tube.* **Lunch** noon-3pm Mon-Fri.
Dinner 6-11pm Mon-Sat. **Average** £50.
Credit AmEx, DC, JCB, MC, £TC, V. **Map 8 M6**
One Aldwych was *the* big hotel opening of 1998 and its stun-
ningly designed restaurant has gained almost as much press
as the hotel. Expect a measured mix of the classic and con-
temporary on the menu, cooked with conviction.

Bank
*1 Kingsway, WC2 (0171 379 9797). Covent Garden,
Holborn or Temple tube.* **Breakfast** 7.30-10.30am Mon-
Fri. **Brunch** 11.30am-3.30pm Sat, Sun. **Lunch** noon-3pm
Mon-Fri. **Dinner** 5.30-11.30pm daily. **Average** £30.
Set meal (5.30-7pm Mon-Sat) £12.90 two courses, £16.50
three courses. **Credit** AmEx, DC, MC, TC, V. **Map 6 M6**
It's huge, noisy, confusing and cost £5 million; but if you're
in the mood, dining at oh-so-fashionable Bank is exhilarating. Chef Christian Delteil's range encompasses rugged fish
soup and seared mullet with pak choi and sesame dressing.

Bibendum
*Michelin House, 81 Fulham Road, SW3 (0171 581
5817). South Kensington tube.* **Lunch** 12.30-2.30pm
Mon-Fri; 12.30-3pm Sat, Sun. **Dinner** 7-11pm Mon-Sat;
7-10.30pm Sun. **Average** £55. **Set lunch** £28 three
courses. **Credit** AmEx, DC, MC, £TC, V. **Map 4 E10**
Sir Terence Conran's design and chef Simon Hopkinson's
culinary skill made the name of this beautiful restaurant in
the 1980s, and chef Matthew Harris's kitchen continues to produce classic, unfussy cooking of the highest order.

Bluebird
*350 King's Road, SW3 (0171 559 1000). Bus 19, 22,
49.* **Brunch** 11am-4.30pm Sat, Sun. **Lunch** noon-3.30pm
Mon-Fri. **Dinner** 6-11pm Mon-Sat; 6-10.30pm Sun.
Average £33. **Set meal** (lunch, 6-7pm) £12.75 two
courses, £15.75 three courses. **Credit** AmEx, DC, JCB,
MC, TC, V. **Map 4 D12**
The most hyped opening of 1997 – this former garage is a
cleverly conceived gastro-complex consisting of a restaurant,
bar, café, fruit and veg stall, food shop and cook shop. The
arrival of chef John Torode has brought Pacific Rim influences to the menu in the big, noisy first-floor restaurant.

Circus
*1 Upper James Street, W1 (0171 534 4000). Piccadilly
Circus tube.* **Open** *winter* noon-midnight Mon-Sat; noon-
3pm Sun; *summer* noon-midnight Mon-Fri; 6pm-midnight
Sat. **Average** £26. **Set meal** (noon-3pm, 5.45-7.30pm,
10.15pm-midnight) £14.75 two courses, £16.75 three
courses. **Credit** AmEx, DC, MC, £TC, V. **Map 7 J6**

*At the centre of **Axis** lies creative cuisine.*

This newcomer is somewhat clinical in design but the menu
usually offers warming, classic combinations such as French
onion soup with Gruyère and croutons, and chicken breast
wrapped in prosciutto served on a morel and leek mash.

Clarke's
*124 Kensington Church Street, W8 (0171 221 9225).
Notting Hill Gate tube.* **Lunch** noon-2pm, **dinner** 7-
10pm, Mon-Fri. **Average** £29 lunch. **Set dinner** £42
four courses, incl coffee, service. **Credit** AmEx, MC,
£TC, V. **Map 1 B7**
Sally Clarke brought Californian-style cooking to London,
and her small, intimate, well-rounded restaurant remains a
leading light after more than a decade. The menus change
daily, but there's no choice for dinner. Great service.

Coast
*26B Albemarle Street, W1 (0171 495 5999). Green Park
tube.* **Lunch** noon-3pm Mon-Fri. **Brunch** noon-4pm
Sat, Sun. **Dinner** 6pm-midnight Mon-Sat; 6-10.30pm
Sun. **Average** £35. **Credit** AmEx, DC, MC, £TC, V.
Map 7 H7
Don your grooviest gear to visit this huge, stunningly
designed goldfish bowl. Chef Adam Gray continues where
his predecessor Stephen Terry left off, combining ingredients in unusual yet inspired ways.

The Fifth Floor
*Harvey Nichols, Knightsbridge, SW1 (0171 235 5250).
Knightsbridge tube.* **Lunch** noon-3pm Mon-Fri; noon-
3.30pm Sat, Sun. **Dinner** 6.30-11.30pm Mon-Sat.
Average £30 dinner. **Set lunch** £23.50 three courses.
Credit AmEx, DC, JCB, MC, £TC, V. **Map 4 F9**
Shop till you drop into this still-stylish, still-busy restaurant
on the same floor as the bar, café and food shop. The spa-
cious room isn't remarkable, but the menu, supplemented by
daily specials, can be relied upon to come up with the goods.

Granita

*127 Upper Street, N1 (0171 226 3222). Angel tube/
Highbury & Islington tube/rail.* **Lunch** 12.30-2.30pm
Wed-Sun. **Dinner** 6.30-10.30pm Tue-Sat; 6.30-10pm Sun.
Average £20. **Set lunch** £11.95 two courses, £13.95
three courses. **Credit** MC, £TC, V. **Map 9 O3**
Lean, sleek Granita has matured into one of Islington's best
restaurants. Dishes such as wok-fried squid with tamarind,
lime and chilli sauce are as trendy as the uniforms worn by
the charming, efficient staff.

The Ivy

*1 West Street, WC2 (0171 836 4751). Covent Garden or
Leicester Square tube.* **Lunch** noon-3pm Mon-Sat; noon-
3.30pm Sun. **Dinner** 5.30pm-midnight daily.
Average £30. **Set lunch** (Sat, Sun) £15.50 three
courses. **Credit** AmEx, DC, MC, £TC, V. **Map 6 K6**
Be prepared to book several months in advance to get a
peak-time table at this beautifully restrained thespians'
favourite. The menu is delightfully retro: nowhere will you
get a classier Welsh rarebit, hamburger or fish and chips.
The Ivy's sister restaurant, **Le Caprice** (Arlington House,
Arlington Street, SW1; 0171 629 2239), is equally exclusive,
and although both have been bought by the owners of the
mussel-and-frites **Belgo** group (*see p160*), it's unlikely that
their winning formulae will be tampered with just yet.

Lola's

*The Mall Building, 359 Upper Street, N1 (0171 359
1932). Angel tube.* **Brunch** noon-3pm Sat, Sun. **Lunch**
noon-2.30pm Mon-Fri. **Dinner** 6.30-11pm Mon-Sat.
Average £24. **Set lunch** £12 two courses, £16.50 three
courses. **Credit** AmEx, DC, JCB, MC, TC, V. **Map 9 O2**
The interior of Lola's feels rather impersonal – all the excitement comes from the plate. The eclectic menu ranges from
simple dishes like tortilla to more fancy constructions such
as sea bass with roast fennel, cherry tomatoes and basil.

Mash

*19-21 Great Portland Street, W1 (0171 637 5555). Great
Portland Street or Oxford Circus tube.* **Breakfast** 8am-
noon Mon-Fri. **Brunch** 11am-4.30pm Sat, Sun. **Lunch**
noon-3pm Mon-Fri. **Dinner** 6pm-1am daily. **Average**
£20. **Credit** AmEx, DC, JCB, MC, V. **Map 5 H5**
If you regard airport lounge décor of the 1970s as chic, Mash
is for you. Offerings at ever on-the-pulse Oliver Peyton's latest venue include breakfast, brunch, bar snacks, cocktails,
pizzas, pastas and various options from the wood-burning
oven. House beer is brewed on the premises.

Odette's

*130 Regent's Park Road, NW1 (0171 586 5486). Chalk
Farm tube/31, 168 bus.* **Wine bar Open** 12.30-2.30pm,
5.30-10.30pm, Mon-Sat; 12.30-2.30pm Sun. *Restaurant*
Lunch 12.30-2.30pm Mon-Fri. **Dinner** 7-11pm Mon-Sat.
Average £25. **Set lunch** (Mon-Fri) £10 three courses.
Credit AmEx, DC, MC, TC, V.
With its gorgeous display of gilded mirrors upstairs, and
cosy pockets of space downstairs, Odette's could revive (or
start) a relationship. And happily the quality of the food
(and a superb wine list) matches the setting.

Oxo Tower Restaurant

*Oxo Tower Wharf, Barge House Street, SE1 (0171 803
3888). Blackfriars or Waterloo tube/rail.* **Bar Open**
11am-11pm Mon-Sat; 11am-10.30pm Sun. *Brasserie*
Meals noon-3pm daily. **Average** £30. **Set meal** (5.30-
7pm Mon-Sat) £18.50 two courses, £21.50 three courses.
Restaurant **Lunch** noon-3pm Mon-Fri; noon-3.30pm Sun.
Dinner 6-11pm Mon-Sat; 6.30-10.30pm Sun. **Average**
£50. **Set lunch** £24.50 three courses. **Credit** AmEx, DC,
JCB, MC, £TC, V. **Map 11 N7**
Run by the people from Harvey Nichols' **Fifth Floor** (*see
p155*), the fabulous views over the Thames from the eighth

floor tend to overshadow the expensive, uneven food. The
brasserie is cheaper (but still pricey). Both places are better
suited for a business meal than a romantic dinner *à deux*.

The People's Palace

*Level 3, Royal Festival Hall, South Bank Centre, SE1
(0171 928 9999). Waterloo tube/rail.* **Lunch** noon-3pm,
dinner 5.30-11pm, daily. **Average** £25. **Set lunch** (Mon-
Sat) £12.50 two courses, £17 three courses. **Set meal**
(lunch Sun, 5.30-7pm daily) £15.50 two courses, £20 three
courses. **Credit** AmEx, DC, MC, TC, V. **Map 8 M8**
The mainly Med-influenced menu at this large South Bank
venue continues to maintain high standards. Service can
occasionally be slapdash, but compensation comes with the
fantastic river views and a well-chosen wine list.

Phoenix Bar & Grill

*162-164 Lower Richmond Road, SW15 (0181 780
3131). Putney Bridge tube/22, 265 bus.* **Lunch** 12.30-
2.30pm Mon-Sat; noon-3pm Sun. **Dinner** 7-11.30pm
Mon-Sat; 7-10pm Sun. **Average** £22. **Set lunch** £12
two courses. **Set Sunday lunch** £17.50 three courses.
Credit AmEx, DC, MC, £TC, V.
An excellent local restaurant, just like its sibling **Sonny's**
(94 Church Road, SW13; 0181 748 0393). Painted bright
white with a blond wood floor, the light décor is reflected in
the clean tastes of the tempting menu.

Polygon

*4 The Polygon, SW4 (0171 622 1199). Clapham
Common tube.* **Lunch** noon-3pm Fri. **Dinner** 6-11pm
Mon-Fri. **Meals** 11am-11pm Sat; 11am-10.30pm Sun.
Pre-cinema meal (6-7.30pm) £10 two courses.
Average £20. **Credit** MC, TC, V.
What could pass for a modernist bus garage in the poshest
part of Clapham is actually the hottest, most chicly designed,
eating spot in the area. The menu is jumping with salsas,
'slaws, wasabi and yakitori, plus excellent rotisserie meals.

Quaglino's

16 Bury Street, SW1 (0171 930 6767). Green Park tube.
Bar **Open** 11.30am-1am Mon-Thur; 11.30am-2am Fri,
Sat; noon-11pm Sun. **Average** £10. *Restaurant* **Lunch**
noon-3pm daily. **Dinner** 5.30pm-midnight Mon-Thur;
5.30pm-1am Fri, Sat; 5.30-11pm Sun. **Average** £30.
Set meal (noon-3pm, 5.30-6.30pm) £15.50 two courses,
£19 three courses. **Credit** AmEx, DC, JCB, MC, £TC, V.
Map 7 J7
For many years one of London's most fashionable restaurants, Quaglino's marvellous sunken dining room, polished
and gleaming, is as impressive as ever. Crustacea are always
excellent; grills, rotisserie dishes and specials can be hit and
miss. A great place for a celebration.

Ransome's Dock

*35-37 Parkgate Road, SW11 (0171 223 1611). Bus
19, 49, 319, 345.* **Meals** 11am-11pm Mon-Fri; 11am-
midnight Sat; 11.30am-3.30pm Sun. **Average** £26.
Set lunch (Mon-Fri) £11.50 two courses.
Credit AmEx, DC, MC, V.
One of those rare breeds in London: a reliable and fairly
priced neighbourhood restaurant. Martin Lam's Battersea
brasserie offers a monthly changing menu, an excellent wine
list, a relaxed atmosphere and river views.

Stephen Bull

*5-7 Blandford Street, W1 (0171 486 9696). Baker Street
or Bond Street tube.* **Lunch** 12.15-2.30pm Mon-Fri.
Dinner 6.30-10.30pm Mon-Sat. **Average** £30.
Credit AmEx, DC, MC, £TC, V. **Map 5 G5**
One of the first exponents of 'Modern British' cooking, the
self-taught Stephen Bull opened this, his original restaurant,
in 1989. The menu changes frequently, and the cooking
remains as skilful and satisfying as ever.

Internet cafés

All the places listed below serve drinks (all but **Shoot'n'Surf** are licensed to sell alcohol) and food (of varying quality). For the cheapest Net access (free, in fact) head for **Room Service @ The Vibe Bar**; for the best food and décor try **Global Café**; for the cosiest surfing space go to the **Buzz Bar**; and to see where it all started check out the pioneering **Cyberia Cyber Café**.

Buzz Bar
95 Portobello Road, W11 (0171 460 4906/ buzzbar@hotmail.com). Notting Hill Gate or Ladbroke Grove tube. **Open** 10am-7pm Mon-Sat. **Credit** DC, MC, £TC, V. **Map 1 A6**
Net access: £5 per hour. 7 terminals.
Website: www.portobellogold.com

Café Internet
22-24 Buckingham Palace Road, SW1 (0171 233 5786/ cafe@cafeinternet.co.uk). Victoria tube/rail. **Open** 7am-9pm Mon-Fri; 10am-8pm Sat, Sun. **Credit** AmEx, LV, MC, £TC, V. **Map 7 H10**
Net access: £3 per half hour. Internet training: £10 per half hour. 20 terminals.
Website: www.cafeinternet.co.uk

Cyberia Cyber Café
39 Whitfield Street, W1 (0171 681 4200/ cyberia@easynet.co.uk). Goodge Street tube. **Open** 10am-8pm Mon-Fri; 11am-7pm Sat; noon-6pm Sun. **Credit** MC, £TC, V. **Map 6 K5**
Net access: £3 per half hour. 12 terminals.
Website: www.cyberiacafe.net

Global Café
15 Golden Square, W1 (0171 287 2242/info@gold. globalcafe.co.uk). Oxford Circus or Piccadilly Circus tube. **Open** 8am-midnight Mon-Fri; 10am-midnight Sat; 1pm-midnight Sun. **Map 7 J7**

Net access: £2.75 per half hour. 11 terminals.
Website: gold.globalcafe.co.uk

Intercafé
25 Great Portland Street, W1 (0171 631 0063/ postmaster@intercafe.co.uk). Oxford Circus tube. **Open** 7.30am-7pm Mon-Fri; 9.30am-5pm Sun. **Credit** MC, £TC, V. **Map 5 J5**
Net access: £3 per half hour, £5 per hour. 9 terminals.
Website: www.intercafe.co.uk

Room Service @ The Vibe Bar
The Truman Brewery, 91 Brick Lane, E1 (0171 247 3479/claudine@vibe-bar.co.uk). Aldgate East tube. **Open** 11am-11pm Mon-Sat; noon-11pm Sun. **Credit** AmEx, MC, V. **Map 10 S5**
Net access: no charge. 4 terminals.
Website: www.vibe-bar.co.uk

Shoot'n'Surf
13 New Oxford Street, WC1 (0171 419 1183/ info@shootnsurf.co.uk). Holborn or Tottenham Court Road tube. **Open** 11am-9pm daily. **Credit** AmEx, MC, V. **Map 6 L5**
Net access: £5 per hour. 18 terminals
Website: www.shootnsurf.co.uk

Webshack
15 Dean Street, W1 (0171 439 8000/webmaster@ webshack-cafe.com). Tottenham Court Road tube. **Open** 10.30am-midnight Mon-Sat; 1-8pm Sun. **Credit** DC, MC, V. **Map 6 K6**
Net access: £3 per half hour, £5 per hour. 20 terminals.
Website: www.webshack-cafe.com

World Café
394 St John Street, EC1 (0171 713 8883/ theworldcafe@earthling.net). Angel tube. **Open** 12.30-9.30pm Mon-Sat. **Credit** AmEx, MC, V. **Map 9 O3**
Net access: £2.50 per half hour (£2.25 concs). 6 terminals.
Website: www.worldcafe.smallplanet.co.uk

Branches: Stephen Bull Smithfield 71 St John Street, EC1 (0171 490 1750); **Stephen Bull** 12 Upper St Martin's Lane, WC2 (0171 379 7811).

Sugar Club
21 Warwick Street, W1 (0171 437 7776). Oxford Circus or Piccadilly Circus tube. **Lunch** noon-3pm, **dinner** 6-11pm, daily. **Average** £28. **Credit** AmEx, DC, JCB, MC, TC, V. **Map 7 J7**
New Zealand chef Peter Gordon has moved effortlessly from Notting Hill into larger, starker premises in Soho. Dishes plunder the world's larder, but Gordon has the skill to pull together such combinations.

Teatro
93-107 Shaftesbury Avenue, W1 (0171 494 3040). Piccadilly Circus tube. **Lunch** noon-3pm Mon-Fri. **Dinner** 6-11.45pm Mon-Sat. **Average** £35 incl £1.50 cover. **Set meal** (lunch, 6-30-7.30pm) £15 two courses, £18 three courses. **Credit** AmEx, MC, £TC, V. **Map 6 K6**
Owned by footballer Lee Chapman and actress Leslie Ash, Teatro is a fine newcomer. Food is up there with the best of

them – standout dishes include roast halibut with horse-radish butter, and pig's trotter rissoles with sauce gribiche.

Afghan

Afghan Kitchen
35 Islington Green, N1 (0171 359 8019). Angel tube. **Meals** noon-midnight Tue-Sat. **Average** £8. **Map 9 O2**
Authentic, delicious, cheap Afghan food served in a pint-sized diner. The menu consists of four meat and four vege-tarian dishes, rice, bread and Afghan chutney or pickles.

American

Arkansas Café
Unit 12, Old Spitalfields Market, E1 (0171 377 6999). Liverpool Street tube/rail. **Lunch** noon-3.30pm Mon-Fri; 11.30am-4.30pm Sun. **Dinner** by arrangement. **Average** £9. **Credit** DC, MC, V. **Map 10 R5**
The best burgers and barbecued meats in town are doled

Bargain breakfasts, light lunches

Everyone agrees that London is now one of the great restaurant cities of the world; alas, everyone also agrees that it's one of the priciest. In the central London places we list below, however, it is possible to dine royally without parting with a king's ransom.

The word 'café' was once synonymous with 'caff', meaning a spit-and-sawdust fry-up joint where asking for a coffee (as opposed to a mug of tea) met with either raised eyebrows or, at best, a cup of Nescafé. Mercifully, good coffee and cakes are now rather easier to find. Fast-growing chains **Aroma**, **Caffè Nero**, **Coffee Republic**, **Pret a Manger** and **Seattle Coffee Company/Starbucks** have branches all over the centre of town.

Look also in the **Indian**, **Chinese**, **Middle Eastern** and **Vegetarian** sections of this chapter. Credit cards are not accepted unless otherwise stated.

Bloomsbury

Coffee Gallery *23 Museum Street, WC1 (0171 436 0455). Holborn or Tottenham Court Road tube.* **Open** 8am-5.30pm Mon-Fri; 10am-5.30pm Sat. **Credit** MC, £TC, V. **Map 6 L5**
Light lunches, coffee and superior cakes in this jolly, brightly coloured café near the British Museum.

Diwana Bhel Poori House *121 Drummond Street (0171 387 5556). Euston Square or Euston tube.* **Open** noon-11.30pm daily. **Credit** AmEx, DC, MC, £TC, V. **Map 5 J3**
Good south Indian veggie snacks; near Euston Station.

Museum Street Café *47 Museum Street, WC1 (0171 405 3211). Holborn or Tottenham Court Road tube.* **Open** 8am-6pm Mon-Fri; 9am-6pm Sat. **Credit** AmEx, MC, £TC, V. **Map 6 L5**
Good baking and wholesome dishes.

October Gallery Café *24 Old Gloucester Street, WC1 (0171 242 7367). Holborn tube.* **Open** 12.30-2.30pm Tue-Sat. **Map 6 L5**
Global cooking and global art in a peaceful gallery.

Pâtisserie Deux Amis *63 Judd Street, WC1 (0171 383 7029). Russell Square tube/King's Cross tube/rail.* **Open** 9am-5.30pm Mon-Sat; 9am-1.30pm Sun. **Map 6 L3**
An oasis of sophistication in a drab area, offering filled baguettes, cakes, pastries and a Mediterranean ambience.

Chelsea

Chelsea Bun Diner *9A Limerston Street (0171 352 3635). Bus 11, 19, 22, 31.* **Open** 7am-midnight Mon-Sat; 8am-midnight Sun. **Credit** MC, £TC, V. **Map 4 D12**
Fun, American-style diner with huge menu. Good breakfasts.

Chelsea Kitchen *98 King's Road (0171 589 1330). Sloane Square tube.* **Open** 8am-11.30pm daily. **Map 4 F11**
Bargain-priced, no-nonsense stomach-fillers are served in this branch of the **Stockpot** (*see below*).

The City

See also **The Place Below** (*p178*).
Lococo *9A Cullum Street, EC3 (0171 220 7722). Monument or Bank tube.* **Open** 7am-5.30pm Mon-Fri. **Map 12 R7**
Atmospheric little coffee bar with good cakes. There's a branch at 53 Charing Cross Road, WC2.

Noto Ramen House *Bow Bells House, 7 Bread St (0171 329 8056). Bank, Mansion House or St Paul's tube.* **Open** 11.30am-8.45pm Mon-Fri; 11.30am-5.45pm Sat. **Credit** £TC. **Map 11 P6**
Authentically steamy Japanese noodle bar.

Covent Garden

See also **Rock & Soul Plaice** (*p165*) and **Food For Thought** (*p178*).
India Club *2nd floor, Strand Continental Hotel, 143 Strand (0171 836 0650). Covent Garden tube.* **Open** noon-2.30pm, 6-11pm, Mon-Sat. **Credit** £TC. **Map 8 M7**
Unlicensed, quirky, utilitarian but priceless Indian diner.

Neal's Yard Beach Café *13 Neal's Yard, WC2 (0171 240 1168). Covent Garden tube.* **Open** 11am-7pm daily. **Map 6 L6**
Colourful spot for brunchy snacks and great milkshakes.

Photographers' Gallery Café *5 Great Newport Street (0171 831 1772). Leicester Square tube.* **Open** 11am-5.30pm Mon-Sat; noon-5.30pm Sun. **Map 8 K6**
Healthy lunchtime snacks amid photo exhibitions.

Holborn & Clerkenwell

Goodfellas *50 Lamb's Conduit Street, WC1 (0171 405 7088). Holborn tube/19, 38 bus.* **Open** 8am-7pm Mon-Fri; 10am-6pm Sat. **Map 6 M4**
Great sandwiches and an enormously popular lunchtime buffet (11.30am-2pm).

Lunch *60 Exmouth Market (0171 278 2420). Farringdon tube/rail.* **Open** 8.30am-6pm Mon-Fri. **Credit** £TC. **Map 9 N4** *See picture opposite.*
Tiny, modernist café/takeaway joint with good hot dishes, salads, filled bagels and wraps.

Saints' *1 Clerkenwell Road, EC1 (0171 490 4199). Barbican tube or Farringdon tube/rail.* **Open** 8am-6pm Mon-Fri (no hot food after 4pm). **Map 9 O4**
Cheap and cheery lunch spot. Service can be slow.

Knightsbridge

Gloriette Pâtisserie *128 Brompton Road, SW3 (0171 589 4750).* **Open** 7am-7pm Mon-Sat; 10am-6pm Sun. **Credit** MC, V. **Map 4 E9**
A tiny, cosy place to tuck into Austrian sweets and pastries.

Stockpot *6 Basil Street, SW3 (0171 589 8627). Knightsbridge tube.* **Open** 9.30am-11pm Mon-Sat; noon-10.30pm Sun. **Map 4 E9**
Unfeasibly cheap, if uninspiringly basic, grub. Other Stockpots can be found at 18 Old Compton St, W1; 40 Panton St, SW1; 273 King's Rd, SW3; 50 James St, W1.

Marylebone

See also **Patogh** *and* **Ranoush Juice Bar** (both *p175*).
Delizioso *90B Cleveland Street, W1 (0171 383 0497). Great Portland Street tube.* **Open** 8am-5pm Mon-Fri; 9am-3pm Sat. **Map 5 J4**
A cut above the usual sandwich bar.

& budget dinners

Love *62-64 Weymouth Street, W1 (0171 487 5683). Baker Street or Great Portland Street tube.* **Open** 8am-7pm Mon-Sat. **Credit** MC, V. **Map 5 H5**
A spare, modern café at the back of the Aveda Institute (*see p206*). Excellent organic dishes and dreamy puds.

Mad Dog Café *35 James Street, W1 (0171 486 1511). Bond Street tube.* **Open** noon-11pm Mon-Sat; noon-6pm Sun. **Credit** AmEx, DC, JCB, MC, £TC, V. **Map 5 G6**
There's a masculine feel to this concrete-clad café which offers globally influenced grub and hearty puds.

Pâtisserie Valerie at Sagne *105 Marylebone High Street, W1 (0171 935 6240). Baker Street or Bond Street tube.* **Credit** AmEx, DC, MC, £TC, V. **Map 5 G5**
Elegant café offering toothsome snacks and savouries, and fabulous cakes and tarts.

Mayfair & St James's

Richoux Coffee Co *171 Piccadilly, W1 (0171 629 4991). Green Park or Piccadilly Circus tube.* **Open** 7am-7pm Mon-Fri; 9am-7pm Sat, Sun. **Credit** AmEx, DC, MC, TC, V. **Map 7 J7**
Spacious, chic coffee house with imaginative food.

The Wren at St James's *35 Jermyn St (0171 437 9419). Piccadilly Circus tube.* **Map 7 J7**
Warming veggie fare next to Wren's St James's church. Tables outside in the churchyard in summer.

Soho

For dim sum, *see page 163. See also* **Mildred's, World Food Café** (both *p178*), **Hamine, Kulu Kulu** (both *p173*) and **Yo! Sushi** (*p174*).

Bar Italia *22 Frith Street, W1 (0171 437 4520). Leicester Square or Tottenham Court Road tube.* **Open** 7am-5am Mon-Thur; 24 hours Fri-Sun. **Map 6 K6**
Ever-green, ever-open Italian coffee bar.

Borders Café *Second floor, 203 Oxford Street, W1 (0171 292 1600). Oxford Circus tube.* **Open** 8am-10.30pm Mon-Sat; noon-5.30pm Sun. **Credit** AmEx, JCB, MC, TC, V. **Map 5 J6**
Newish US-oriented café-within-a-bookshop with views over Oxford Street and good drinks and snacks.

Café Emm *17 Frith Street, W1 (0171 437 0723). Tottenham Court Road tube.* **Open** noon-3pm Mon-Fri; 5.30-10.30pm Mon-Thur; 5.30pm-12.30am Fri; 5pm-12.30am Sat; 5-10.30pm Sun. **Credit** MC, £TC, V. **Map 6 K6**
Relaxed vibe, huge portions – a good vegetarian choice.

Hing Loon *25 Lisle St (0171 437 3602). Leicester Square tube.* **Open** noon-11.30pm daily. **Credit** AmEx, MC, £TC, V. **Map 8 K7**
One of the best of Chinatown's many diners.

Maison Bertaux *28 Greek Street, W1 (0171 437 6007). Leicester Square, Piccadilly Circus or Tottenham Court Road tube.* **Open** 9am-8pm Mon-Sat; 9am-1pm, 3-8pm, Sun. **Credit** £TC. **Map 6 K6**
Wonderfully unreconstructed French café (founded in 1871). Exquisite pastries and weak coffee.

Mildred's *58 Greek Street, W1 (0171 494 1634). Leicester Square or Tottenham Court Road tube.* **Map 6 K6**
Immensely popular and reliable vegetarian café.

Pâtisserie Valerie *44 Old Compton Street, W1 (0171 437 3466). Leicester Square or Tottenham Court Road tube.* **Open** 8am-8pm Mon-Fri; 8am-7pm Sat; 9.30am-6pm Sun. **Credit** £TC. **Map 6 K6**
Wonderful savoury flans, cakes and pastries since 1926. The only problem is its huge popularity.
Branches: 215 Brompton Road, SW3; 66 Portland Place, W1; 8 Russell Street, WC2.

Pollo *20 Old Compton Street, W1 (0171 734 5917). Leicester Square or Tottenham Court Road tube.* **Open** noon-midnight daily. **Credit** £TC. **Map 6 K6**
Probably London's best known and most popular budget diner. Bags of atmosphere and reasonable pasta. Nearby, **Presto** (4 Old Compton Street) and **Centrale** (16 Moor Street) offer similar food in a less frenetic environment.

Star Café *22 Great Chapel St (0171 437 8778). Tottenham Court Road tube.* **Open** 7am-6pm Mon-Fri. **Credit** £TC. **Map 6 K6**
Cosy oasis offering pastas, salads and five daily specials.

Tibetan Restaurant *17 Irving St (0171 839 2090). Leicester Square tube.* **Open** noon-3pm Mon, Tue, Thur-Sat; 5-10.45pm Mon-Sat. **Credit** DC, MC, £TC, V. **Map 8 K7**
An otherworldy outpost of Tibet, off Leicester Square.

The South Bank

Gourmet Pizza Company *Gabriel's Wharf, 56 Upper Ground, SE1 (0171 928 3188). Waterloo tube/rail.* **Open** noon-11pm Mon-Sat. **Credit** AmEx, DC, MC, £TC, V. **Map 11 N7**
Riverside pizzeria known for its adventurous toppings.

Konditor & Cook *Young Vic, 66 The Cut, SE1 (0171 620 2700). Waterloo tube/rail.* **Open** 8.30am-11pm Mon-Fri; 10.30am-11pm Sat. **Credit** MC, V. **Map 11 N8**
Divine cakes from their own bakery and globe-trotting grub are the attractions at the Young Vic theatre's popular café.

Westminster & Victoria

Café in the Crypt *Crypt of St Martin-in-the-Fields, Duncannon Street, WC2 (0171 839 4342). Charing Cross tube/rail.* **Open** *coffee bar* 10am-8pm Mon-Sat; noon-8pm Sun; *buffet counter* noon-3.15pm, 5-7.30pm, daily. **Map 8 K7**
Atmospheric spot for good salads and sandwiches.

Jenny Lo's Tea House *14 Eccleston Street, SW1 (0171 259 0399). Victoria tube/rail.* **Open** 11.30am-3pm, 6-10pm Mon-Fri; noon-3pm, 6-10pm Sat. **Credit** £TC. **Map 7 H10**
Simply furnished noodle bar with a Chinese theme.

out by genial, tall-hatted American Keir Helberg from his café within the Spitalfields market building.

Montana
125-129 Dawes Road, SW6 (0171 385 9500). Fulham Broadway tube. **Lunch** noon-3.30pm Fri-Sun. **Dinner** 7-11pm Mon-Thur; 7-11.30pm Fri, Sat; 7-10.30pm Sun. **Average** £21. **Credit** AmEx, MC, £TC, V.
London's first serious Southwestern restaurant continues to delight with its large picture windows, elegant blue-and-purple décor and imaginative, seasonally changing menu. Sibling restaurants **Dakota** (126 Ledbury Road, W11; 0171 792 9191) and **Canyon** (Riverside, Richmond; 0181 948 2944) continue the good work elsewhere.

Argentinian

La Pampa Grill
60 Battersea Rise, SW11 (0171 924 4774). Clapham Junction rail. **Meals** 6-11pm daily. **Average** £16. **Credit** MC, £TC, V.
For a hearty chunk of Argentina, you'd be hard-pushed to do better than La Pampa Grill. The décor is unapologetically basic, the menu unabashedly meaty and the atmosphere unreservedly fun.

Australian

Boom'rang
298 Park Road, N8 (0181 352 9372). Finsbury Park tube/rail then W7 bus. **Dinner** 6.30-11pm Tue-Sat. **Average** £21. **Set dinner** (Tue-Thur) £11.95 two courses. **Credit** MC, £TC, V.
Not exactly easily accessible, but a cracking restaurant nonetheless. The interesting, globally inspired menu contains mainly fish and vegetarian dishes plus a daily special of fish, flown in all the way from Western Australia.

Belgian

Belgo Centraal
50 Earlham Street, WC2 (0171 813 2233). Covent Garden tube. **Meals** noon-11.30pm Mon-Sat; noon-10.30pm Sun. **Average** £20. **Set lunch** £5. **Credit** AmEx, DC, JCB, MC, V. **Map 6 L6**
Celebrating the twin glories of Belgian culture – moules frites and beer – Belgo's extraordinary, noisy, *Blade Runner*-like basement restaurant is phenomenally popular. **Branch**: **Belgo Noord** 72 Chalk Farm Road, NW1 (0171 267 0718).

Brazilian

Sabor do Brasil
36 Highgate Hill, N19 (0171 263 9066). Archway tube. **Lunch** by appointment Mon-Sat; 1-3pm Sun. **Dinner** 7-11.45pm Tue-Sun. **Closed** Aug. **Average** £12. **Set dinner** (*bufe*) £9.50. **Credit** £TC.
The Anglo-Brazilian husband-and-wife team who run this friendly, relaxed restaurant do their best to provide an authentic experience of Brazil. It's bright and welcoming, and the *bufe*, a plateful of various different dishes, is superb.

British

Boisdale
15 Eccleston Street, SW1 (0171 730 6922). Victoria tube/rail. **Bar Open** noon-11pm Mon-Sat. **Average** £6.

Restaurant **Lunch** noon-2.30pm Mon-Fri. **Dinner** 7-10.30pm Mon-Sat. **Average** £30. **Set meal** £12.50, £16.90, two courses. **Credit** AmEx, DC, MC, £TC, V. **Map 7 H10**
'French classical cooking using the best Scottish ingredients and drawing from traditional British recipes' is the Boisdale's somewhat confusing-sounding but successful formula. The bar has a fantastic selection of whiskies.

Butlers Wharf Chop House
Butlers Wharf Building, 36E Shad Thames, SE1 (0171 403 3403). London Bridge tube/rail. Bar **Open** noon-3pm, 6-11pm, Mon-Sat; noon-3pm Sun. **Brunch** noon-3pm Sat, Sun. **Average** £18. **Set brunch** (Sat, Sun) £13.95 two courses, £16.25 three courses. **Set meal** (noon-3pm, 6-11pm, Mon-Fri; 6-11pm Sat) £7.75 two courses, £9.50 three courses. *Restaurant* **Lunch** noon-3pm Mon-Fri, Sun. **Dinner** 6-11pm Mon-Sat. **Average** £33. **Credit** AmEx, DC, JCB, MC, £TC, V. **Map 12 R8**
It's not cheap, but the Chop House's regularly changing, British-based menu rarely disappoints and the riverside setting near Tower Bridge is wonderful. Ask for a terrace table in summer. Brunch is especially recommended.

Greenhouse
27A Hay's Mews, W1 (0171 499 3331/3314). Green Park or Hyde Park Corner tube. **Lunch** noon-2.30pm Mon-Fri; 12.30-3pm Sun. **Dinner** 6.30-11pm Mon-Sat; 6.30-10pm Sun. **Average** £25 lunch, £35 dinner. **Set Sunday lunch** £19.50 three courses. **Credit** AmEx, DC, JCB, MC, £TC, V. **Map 7 H7**
This spacious, smart restaurant, once the demesne of Gary Rhodes, continues to produce first-rate inventive Modern British cuisine for a clientele of mainly business people and discerning tourists.

Lindsay House
21 Romilly Street, W1 (0171 439 0450). Leicester Square or Piccadilly Circus tube. **Lunch** noon-2.30pm Mon-Fri. **Dinner** 6-11pm Mon-Sat. **Average** £30 lunch. **Set dinner** £38 three courses. **Credit** AmEx, DC, MC, TC, V. **Map 6 K6**
A somewhat self-concious operation, but Richard Corrigan is a chef with a vision and his constantly evolving Modern British cooking is never less than interesting.

Quality Chop House
94 Farringdon Road, EC1 (0171 837 5093). Farringdon tube/rail/19, 38, 63 bus. **Lunch** noon-3pm Mon-Fri; noon-4pm Sun. **Dinner** 6.30-11.30pm Mon-Sat; 7-11.30pm Sun. **Average** £25. **Credit** MC, £TC, V. **Map 9 N4**
'Progressive Working Men's caterer' may be the slogan, and wooden benches and poshed-up trad grub the trademark, but the prices point to a more upmarket clientele. The recently opened fish bar has added a piscine note.

RK Stanleys
6 Little Portland Street, W1 (0171 462 0099). Oxford Circus tube. **Lunch** noon-3.30pm, **dinner** 6-11.30pm, Mon-Sat. **Average** £16. **Credit** AmEx, MC, V. **Map 5 J5**
Devoted primarily to the twin pleasures of the sausage and beer, RK Stanleys looks like a cross between an American diner and a beerhall. A quirky, fun place.

Rules
35 Maiden Lane, WC2 (0171 836 5314). Covent Garden tube/Charing Cross tube/rail. **Meals** noon-11.30pm Mon-Sat; noon-10.30pm Sun. **Average** £30. **Set meal** (3-6pm Mon-Fri) £15.95 two courses; (noon-4pm Sat, Sun) £17.95 two courses. **Credit** AmEx, DC, MC, £TC, V. **Map 8 L7**
Founded in 1798, this ancient establishment exudes history and exclusivity, yet this is no Olde England theme restau-

Time for tiffin

The big attraction of **afternoon tea** is a chance to snoop inside hotels at which you'll never afford to stay. The hotels are in on this too, so you don't have to be a millionaire or a Hollywood star to gain entry. Dress codes of jacket and tie for men are the main rules at The Ritz, The Savoy and Claridges. Other hotels have this rule but don't appear to enforce it; check when phoning to book.

As for the food: quality scones, clotted cream, jam, cakes and sandwiches for around £17 is expensive, but you are also paying for being treated like royalty in luxurious surroundings for up to two hours. During that time the world will seem an infinitely better place.

For the glitziest interior go to the **Meridien Waldorf** (*see page 45*); for the cosiest setting, try **Brown's**; for top-notch tea and sandwiches, **The Lanesborough** impresses; the tastiest pastries and the best pianist can be found at **The Dorchester**; while the service at **Claridges** and **The Lanesborough** can't be beaten. **The Ritz**, meanwhile, is the most popular: you'll need to book about three months in advance for a weekend. Unfortunately, at **The Ritz** and **The Savoy** tea-goers often feel like just another cog in a tourist-milking machine.

Brown's

33-34 Albemarle Street, W1 (The Drawing Room 0171 518 4108). Green Park tube. **Tea served** 3-6pm daily. **Set tea** £17.95. **Credit** AmEx, DC, JCB, MC, £TC, V. **Map 7 J7**

Claridges

Brook Street, W1 (0171 629 8860). Bond Street tube. **Tea served** 3-5.30pm daily. **Set tea** £18.50, £25 incl champagne. **Credit** AmEx, DC, MC, TC, V. **Map 5 H6**

The Dorchester

54 Park Lane, W1 (0171 629 8888). Hyde Park Corner or Marble Arch tube. **Afternoon tea served** 3-6pm, **high tea served** 5-8pm, daily. **Set teas** *afternoon tea* £18.50, £24.50 incl champagne; *high tea* £28. **Credit** AmEx, DC, JCB, MC, TC, V. **Map 7 G7**

The Lanesborough

Hyde Park Corner, SW1 (0171 259 5599). Hyde Park Corner tube. **Tea served** 3.30-6pm daily. **Set teas** £18.50, £23. **Credit** AmEx, DC, JCB, MC, TC, V. **Map 7 G8**

Meridien Waldorf

Aldwych, WC2 (0171 836 2400). Covent Garden or Temple tube. **Tea served** 3-5.30pm Mon-Fri. **Tea dance** 2.30-5.30pm Sat; 4-6.30pm Sun. **Set teas** £18, £21 incl champagne; £15, *chocolate tea* (Fri) £13.95; *tea dance* £25, £28 incl champagne. **Credit** AmEx, DC, TC, MC, V. **Map 8 M7**

The Ritz

Piccadilly, W1 (0171 493 8181). Green Park or Piccadilly Circus tube. **Tea served** daily; reserved sittings at 3.30pm, 5pm. **Set tea** £22.50. **Credit** AmEx, DC, JCB, MC, £TC, V. **Map 5 J7**

The Savoy

Strand, WC2 (0171 836 4343). Charing Cross tube/rail. **Tea served** 3-5.30pm daily. **Set tea** £18.50, £28 incl champagne, adults; £9.50 under-10s. **Credit** AmEx, DC, JCB, MC, TC, V. **Map 8 L7**

---

rant. Imaginatively updated versions of British classics are expertly cooked and beautifully presented. A winner.

St John

26 St John Street, EC1 (0171 251 0848/4998). Farringdon tube/rail. Bar **Open** 11am-11pm Mon-Fri; 6-11pm Sat. **Average** £7. *Restaurant* **Lunch** noon-3pm Mon-Fri. **Dinner** 6-11.30pm Mon-Sat. **Average** £25. **Credit** AmEx, DC, JCB, MC, £TC, V. **Map 9 O5**

There's a rather stark, industrial feel to this converted smokehouse – but offal fans will be in innard-heaven, enjoying dishes such as roast (veal) bone marrow and parsley salad, as well as less challenging fare. You can also eat at the bar.

Veronica's

3 Hereford Road, W2 (0171 229 5079). Bayswater or Queensway tube. **Lunch** noon-3pm Mon-Fri. **Dinner** 7-11.15pm Mon-Sat. **Average** £25. **Set meal** (lunch Mon-Fri, dinner Mon-Thur) £12.50 two courses, £16.50 three courses. **Credit** AmEx, DC, JCB, MC, £TC, V. **Map 1 B6**

Veronica Shaw's small, simply decorated restaurant serves historic British dishes, using recipes from as far back as the fourteenth century. The results are superb and the experience enjoyable, educational and unique.

Burmese

Mandalay

444 Edgware Road, W2 (0171 258 3696). Edgware Road tube. **Lunch** noon-2.30pm, **dinner** 6-10.30pm, Mon-Sat. **Average** £11. **Set lunch** £3.20 one course, £5.40 three courses. **Credit** AmEx, DC, JCB, MC, £TC, V. **Map 2 E4**

The road to Mandalay may be the traffic-choked Edgware Road, but the warmth of Dwight and Gary Ally's welcome and the quality of their cooking ensure customers leave with contented stomachs and a smile on their faces.

Caribbean

BB's

3 Chignell Place (off Uxbridge Road), W13 (0181 840 8322). Ealing Broadway tube/West Ealing rail. **Lunch** 11.30am-2.30pm Mon-Sat. **Dinner** 6.30-11.30pm Mon-Fri; 6.30pm-12.30am Sat. **Average** £15. **Set lunch** £4.50 two courses. **Credit** LV, £TC.

It may be hidden in an Ealing backwater, but Brian Benjamin's cheery Grenadian restaurant is one of the best places in London to sample such Caribbean favourites as ackee and salt fish, fried lambi and crabback.

Mango Room

10 Kentish Town Road, NW1 (0171 482 5065). Camden Town tube. **Meals** noon-midnight daily. **Average** £13. **Credit** JCB, MC, £TC, V.

The rich colours on the wall reflect the vibrancy of the Caribbean cooking at the Mango Room. Big flavours are presented with an unusual lightness and attention to detail; standout dishes include the jerk chicken.

Chinese

Golden Harvest

17 Lisle Street, WC2 (0171 287 3822). Leicester Square or Piccadilly Circus tube. **Meals** noon-2.45am daily. **Average** £14. **Minimum** £5 from 5pm. **Set meal** £7-£15 per person (minimum two). **Credit** AmEx, DC, JCB, MC, £TC, V. **Map 8 K7**

This newcomer expertly combines traditional flavours with novel ingredients. The friendly, knowledgeable proprietors

also own Chinatown's fishmonger's, so seafood – pomfret, turbot, sea bass, carp – is a speciality.

Hunan

51 Pimlico Road, SW1 (0171 730 5712). Sloane Square tube. **Lunch** noon-2.30pm, **dinner** 6-11pm, Mon-Sat. **Average** £27. **Set meal** £22-£100 per person (minimum two). **Credit** AmEx, MC, £TC, V. **Map 7 G11**

It's usually wise to avoid the set meal in Chinese restaurants, but those at Hunan can offer dishes of a revelatory standard. Be prepared to be firm, however, in insisting on real Chinese food and flavours.

Magic Wok

100 Queensway, W2 (0171 792 9767). Bayswater or Queensway tube. **Meals** noon-11pm daily. **Average** £16. **Set meal** £10.50-£22 per person (minimum two). **Credit** AmEx, DC, MC, £TC, V. **Map 1 C6**

Go for dishes from the specials list and you'll enjoy some of the best and most unusual Cantonese cooking in London, such as minced pork and aubergine.

Oodles of noodles

The Japanese have been slurping in them for eons, but it's only in the last couple of years that noodle bars have hit London in a big way. Flexibility is the key to their success. Equally appealing for groups or individuals, you can linger over several dishes or wolf down a bowl of ramen and be out in 20 minutes – and the clean, sharp flavours, fresh ingredients and low-fat dishes have a thoroughly in-tune-with-the-times healthy feel to them.

The progenitor of the trend was undoubtedly **Wagamama** (opened 1992) and it still leads the way. Of course, there were noodle bars in the capital before, but they tended to be small, steamy, relatively downmarket affairs. What Wagamama did was to take the principle of the quick-cook, quick-eat meal and give it a thoroughly 1990s twist. Big, bare spaces; young, efficient staff; and a healthy-sounding menu drawing influences from all over South-east Asia. But the real key was the quality of the food. It's high. The trickle of imitators has become a torrent of late. Below we list the best of the central London contenders.

Noho

32 Charlotte Street, W1 (0171 636 4445). Goodge Street tube. **Meals** noon-11.30pm daily. **Average** £15. **Credit** AmEx, DC, MC, £TC, V. **Map 5 J5**

Taking the rather irritating, newly invented name (standing for North Soho) for the area that was once better known as Fitzrovia (*see p51*), Noho offers a jaunt through the standard South-east Asian dishes in a cool, noisy, spartan room.

Satsuma

56 Wardour Street, W1 (0171 437 8338). Piccadilly Circus tube. **Meals** noon-11pm Mon-Thur, noon-11.30pm Fri, Sat; noon-10.30pm Sun. **Average** £9.

Set meals £8.90-£12.90. **Credit** AmEx, DC, MC, £TC, V. **Map 8 K7**

Designed by the same people as Wagamama, and looking remarkably similar, Satsuma attempts to stamp some originality on its menu by including bento lunchboxes, sushi and sashimi amid the ramen and noodle dishes. Prime location.

Wagamama

101A Wigmore Street, W1 (0171 409 0111). Bond Street or Marble Arch tube. **Meals** 11.30am-11pm Mon-Sat; 12.30-10.30pm Sun. **Average** £8. **Set meal** £8-£9.50. **Credit** AmEx, DC, MC, £TC, V. **Map 5 G6**

Wagamama's newest branch in Marylebone is very like the previous two, with a clean, stark and functional design, an open kitchen and cramped bench-like seating. The keenly priced Japanese-influenced food continues to impress. A Dublin branch opened in late 1998, and the fourth London Wagamama should appear in Piers Gough's extraordinary Glass Building on Jamestown Road, Camden in spring 1999.

Branches: 4 Streatham Street, WC1 (0171 323 9223); 10A Lexington Street, W1 (0171 292 0990).

Wok Wok

10 Frith Street, W1 (0171 437 7080). Piccadilly Circus or Tottenham Court Road tube. **Meals** noon-11pm Mon-Wed; noon-midnight Thur-Sat; 6-10.30pm Sun. **Average** £12. **Set meal** £11.50 two courses, £14.50-£19.20 three courses. **Credit** AmEx, DC, JCB, MC, £TC, V. **Map 6 K6**

Aiming to be a more upmarket (yet still very relaxed) noodle bar, Wok Wok allows diners individual tables, and provides a largely successful menu of cod South-east Asian dishes. Another good location, and the service is pleasantly breezy.

Branches: 7 Kensington High Street, W8 (0171 938 1221); 140 Fulham Road, SW10 (0171 370 5355); 67 Upper Street, N1 (0171 288 0333); 51-53 Northcote Road, SW11 (0171 978 7181).

Pan-oriental **Wagamama** *wizardry on Wigmore Street.*

Mr Kong

*21 Lisle Street, WC2 (0171 437 7341/9679). Leicester
Square tube.* **Meals** noon-3am daily. **Average** £22.
Minimum £7 after 5pm. **Set meal** £9.30 per person
(minimum two)-£22 per person (minimum four).
Credit AmEx, DC, JCB, MC, £TC, V. **Map 8 K7**
The setting may be lacking in glamour and elbow room, but
Mr Kong's menu is one of Chinatown's most enticing. A
great place to try rarely found Cantonese specials such as
fried baby squid in shrimp paste sauce.

New Four Seasons

*84 Queensway, W2 (0171 229 4320). Bayswater or
Queensway tube.* **Meals** noon-11.30pm Mon-Sat; noon-
11pm Sun. **Average** £17. **Set meal** £10.50-£16 per person
(minimum two). **Credit** AmEx, MC, £TC, V. **Map 1 C6**
Queensway now rivals Chinatown for the excellence of its
Chinese food and, despite its dingy décor, the New Four
Seasons offers a fabulous list of specials and possibly the
best Cantonese roast duck in London.

Oriental

*Dorchester Hotel, 55 Park Lane, W1 (0171 317 6328).
Green Park, Hyde Park Corner or Marble Arch tube.*
Lunch noon-2.30pm Mon-Fri. **Dinner** 7-11pm daily.
Average £35 lunch, £55 dinner. **Set lunch** £27 (dim
sum), £29.50. **Set dinner** £37-£82. **Credit** AmEx, DC,
JCB, MC, TC, V. **Map 7 G7**
It's pricey and blandly formal, but if only the highest stan-
dards of cooking will do, the Dorchester's Oriental won't let
you down. Labour-intensive dishes like stir-fried heart of
green mustard in a clear stock with dried ham are exquisite.

Dim sum

London is one of the best places in the world to try
one of the highlights of Cantonese cuisine, dim
sum. These small, delicate dumplings and snacks
are served from midday through the afternoon
(never after 6pm) at low prices: expect to pay
around £10 a head for a decent selection.

Golden Dragon

*28-29 Gerrard Street, W1 (0171 734 2763/1073).
Leicester Square or Piccadilly Circus tube.*
Meals noon-11.30pm Mon-Thur; noon-midnight Fri,
Sat; 11am-11pm Sun. **Dim sum** noon-5pm Mon-Sat;
11am-5pm Sun. **Average** £8 dim sum, £20 full menu.
Minimum £10. **Set meal** £10 per person (minimum
two)-£20 per person (minimum five). **Credit** AmEx, DC,
MC, £TC, V. **Map 8 K7**
A lively and ornate dim sum venue that offers classy ver-
sions of staples such as glutinous rice in lotus leaf and deep-
fried squid. The evening menu is less impressive, and service
can be cheerless and sloppy.
Branch: Royal Dragon 30 Gerrard Street, W1
(0171 734 0935).

Harbour City

*46 Gerrard Street, W1 (0171 439 7859/287 1526).
Leicester Square or Piccadilly Circus tube.* **Meals** noon-
11.30pm Mon-Thur; noon-midnight Fri, Sat; 11am-11pm
Sun. **Dim sum** noon-5pm Mon-Sat; 11am-5pm Sun.
Average £8 dim sum, £17 full menu. **Set meal** £12.50-
£20 per person (minimum two). **Credit** AmEx, DC, JCB,
MC, £TC, V. **Map 8 K7**
This longstanding dim sum favourite offers an 'exotic' sec-
tion including such rarely found treats as ducks' tongues in
black bean and chilli sauce, and baked mini roast pork pies.
Ask for a table on the lighter first floor.

Royal China

*13 Queensway, W2 (0171 221 2535). Bayswater or
Queensway tube.* **Meals** noon-11pm Mon-Thur; noon-
11.30pm Fri, Sat; 11am-10pm Sun. **Dim sum** noon-5pm
Mon-Sat; 11am-5pm Sun. **Average** £10 dim sum, £28
full menu. **Set meal** £23, £28, per person (minimum
two). **Credit** AmEx, DC, MC, £TC, V.
Undoubtedly the finest dim sum in London – exquisite in
flavour and presentation, and incredibly cheap. Come during the week for a quiet, leisurely meal: on Sundays the
atmosphere is pacey but queues are long.

Fish

Café Fish

*36-40 Rupert Street, W1 (0171 287 8989). Leicester
Square or Piccadilly Circus tube.* **Lunch** noon-3pm daily.
Dinner 5.30-11.30pm Mon-Sat; 5-10.30pm Sun.
Average £20. **Credit** AmEx, DC, JCB, MC, £TC, V.
Map 8 K7
Having moved from Panton Street, this good-looking,

well-lit place offers a 'canteen menu' with about ten dishes
all under a tenner, while the upstairs restaurant menu is
broader in scope and pricier.

Cave

Caviar House, 161 Piccadilly, W1 (0171 409 0445).
Green Park tube. **Lunch** noon-3pm, **dinner** 7-10.30pm,
Mon-Sat. **Average** £30. **Set lunch** £21.50 two courses.
Credit AmEx, DC, MC, £TC, V. **Map 7 J7**
An appealing postmodern grotto with a classy, nautically
themed décor. Presentation of food is strikingly modern and
is matched by the quality of execution. A great spot for a
piscine treat.

J Sheekey

28-32 St Martin's Court, WC2 (0171 240 2565).
Leicester Square tube. **Lunch** noon-3pm Mon-Sat;
noon-3.30pm Sun. **Dinner** 5.30pm-midnight daily.
Average £30. **Set meals** (lunch Sat, Sun) £15.50
three courses. **Credit** AmEx, DC, MC, V.
Map 8 K7
This moribund fish restaurant has been given a new lease
of life by Midas-touch duo Corbin and King, the men behind
Le Caprice and **The Ivy** (*see p156*). The menu maintains the
emphasis on seafood, while many other dishes are recog-
nisably Ivy (think: elevated comfort food). Book well ahead.

Livebait

21 Wellington Street, WC2 (0171 836 7161). Covent
Garden tube. **Lunch** noon-3pm, **dinner** 5.30-11.30pm,
Mon-Sat. **Average** £27. **Set meal** (noon-3pm, 5.30-7pm,
10-11.30pm) £15.50 two courses. **Credit** AmEx, DC, JCB,
MC, £TC, V. **Map 8 L7**
Although now owned by the Chez Gérard group, Livebait
remains one of the capital's most original and fun fish
restaurants. The stunning tiled interior and seafood display
of the Waterloo original have been replicated in this, the bigger Covent Garden branch.
Branch: 41-43 The Cut, SE1 (0171 928 7211).

Fish & chips

Rock & Sole Plaice

47 Endell Street, WC2 (0171 836 3785). Covent
Garden tube. **Meals** 11.30am-10pm Mon-Sat;
11.30am-9pm Sun. **Average** £10. **Credit** £TC.
Map 6 L6
Open since 1871, Rock & Sole Plaice claims to be the oldest
surviving fish and chip shop in London. Whatever the case,
it's certainly the best place in the centre of town to sample
the national dish.

Sea-Shell

49-51 Lisson Grove, NW1 (0171 723 8703). Marylebone
tube/rail. **Lunch** noon-2pm Mon-Fri; noon-2.30pm
Sun. **Dinner** 5.15-10.30pm Mon-Fri. **Meals** noon-
10.30pm Sat. **Average** £15. **Set meal** (until 7pm daily)
£9.50 three courses. **Credit** AmEx, DC, LV, MC, £TC, V.
Map 2 E4
Long a favourite of fish and chip connoisseurs (including
many cab drivers), the two-floor, dark wood and chintz-
decorated Sea-Shell maintains a consistently loyal clientele.

Upper Street Fish Shop

324 Upper Street, N1 (0171 359 1401). Angel tube/
4, 19, 30, 43 bus. **Lunch** noon-2.15pm Tue-Fri; noon-
3pm Sat. **Dinner** 6-10.15pm Mon-Thur; 5.30-10.15pm Fri,
Sat. **Average** £12. **Minimum** £7.50. **Credit** £TC.
Map 9 O1
The imaginative, frequently changing menu here offers far
more than the usual (admittedly excellent) cod and chips.
Not many chippies serve up deep-fried mussels and tem-
pura. Puddings are equally fine.

Wing your way to **Birdcage**. *See page 175.*

French

Chez Bruce

2 Bellevue Road, SW17 (0181 672 0114). Wandsworth
Common rail. **Lunch** noon-2pm Mon-Sat; 12.30-3pm Sun.
Dinner 7-10.15pm Mon-Sat. **Set lunch** £18 three
courses. **Set dinner** £25.50 three courses.
Credit AmEx, DC, JCB, MC, V.
A Wandsw zorth restaurant where standards easily exceed
many better-known West End places. The interior's plain,
the atmosphere relaxed and Bruce Poole's cooking serious
and seriously good.

Chez Lindsay

11 Hill Rise, Richmond, Surrey (0181 948 7473).
Richmond tube/rail. **Meals** 11am-11pm Mon-Sat; noon-
10pm Sun. **Average** £12.50. **Set meal** (11am-3pm, 6-11pm) £9.99
three courses. **Credit** MC, V.
Seafood and pancakes, the twin glories of Breton cooking,
are presented with great verve in this relaxed Richmond
restaurant. Try a scallop gallette, a cup of Breton cider and
a sweet crêpe to follow – a perfect meal.

Club Gascon

57 West Smithfield, EC1 (0171 796 0600). Farringdon
tube/rail. **Lunch** noon-2.15pm Mon-Fri. **Dinner**
7-10.15pm Mon-Sat. **Average** £25. **Credit** MC, V.
Map 9 O5
Specialising in the earthy goosefat-heavy cuisine of Gascony
in south-west France, Club Gascon offers a blessed relief
from self-concious, over-elaborate experimentation. Simple,
classic fare cooked with real flair and conviction.

The Criterion

224 Piccadilly, W1 (0171 930 0488). Piccadilly Circus
tube. **Lunch** noon-2.30pm Mon-Sat; noon-4pm Sun.
Dinner 6pm-midnight Mon-Sat; 6-10.30pm Sun.

Average £32. **Set meal** (noon-2.30pm, 6-6.30pm) £14.95 two courses, £17.95 three courses. **Credit** AmEx, MC, £TC, V. **Map 8 K7**
As backdrops go, they don't come much more stunning than Marco Pierre White's Criterion. The glittering mosaics, giant drapes, hanging lanterns and mirrors distract from sometimes uneven food and rushed service.

L'Escargot

48 Greek Street, W1 (0171 437 2679). Leicester Square or Tottenham Court Road tube. Ground-floor restaurant **Lunch** 12.15-2.15pm Mon-Fri. **Dinner** 6-11.30pm Mon-Sat. **Average** £26. **Set meal** (lunch, 6-7pm) £14.95 two courses, £17.95 three courses. *First-floor dining room* **Lunch** noon-2.15pm Tue-Fri. **Dinner** 6-11.30pm Tue-Sat. **Average** £35. **Set lunch** £27 three courses. **Set dinner** £42 three courses. **Credit** AmEx, DC, JCB, MC, £TC, V. **Map 6 K6**
A Soho fixture for the last 70 years, this famed eating spot still has a special aura. The modern but ungimmicky food has moved with the times and can be enjoyed in the relaxed ground-floor restaurant or the pricier first-floor Picasso Room.

Maison Novelli

29 Clerkenwell Green, EC1 (0171 251 6606). Farringdon tube/rail. **Lunch** noon-3.30pm Mon-Fri. **Dinner** 6.30-11.15pm Mon-Thur; 6.30pm-midnight Fri, Sat. **Average** £40. **Credit** AmEx, DC, JCB, MC, V. **Map 9 N4**
This is the classiest joint in smouldering wonderchef Jean-Christophe Novelli's growing empire. Expect unusual but brilliantly conceived flavour combinations. Service, alas, can leave something to be desired.
Branch: Novelli EC1 31 Clerkenwell Green, EC1 (0171 251 6606); **Novelli W8** 122 Palace Gardens Terrace, W8 (0171 229 4024); **Novelli W8, Novelli EC1** (*see below*) and **Les Saveurs** (37A Curzon Street, W1; 0171 491 8919).

Mirabelle

56 Curzon Street, W1 (0171 499 4636). Green Park tube. **Lunch** noon-3pm daily. **Dinner** 6pm-midnight Mon-Sat; 6-10.30pm Sun. **Average** £35.
Set lunch £14.95 two courses, £17.95 three courses. **Credit** AmEx, MC, V. **Map 7 H7**
This was the most acclaimed opening of 1998 – or, rather, reopening, since there's been a Mirabelle on the site for donkey's years. The new version is yet another Marco Pierre White production (*see also p165* **The Criterion** and *below* **Quo Vadis**), and one of his best yet. The set lunch is great value for superbly crafted classic dishes.

L'Odéon

65 Regent's Street, W1 (0171 287 1400). Piccadilly Circus tube. **Lunch** noon-2.45pm, **dinner** 5.30-11pm, Mon-Sat. **Average** £37. **Set meal** (lunch, 5.30-7pm) £15.50 two courses, £19.50 three courses. **Credit** AmEx, DC, JCB, MC, £TC, V. **Map 7 J7**
L'Odéon's eclectic, modern cooking with a base in French classics is most economically sampled from the fixed price menu. The long, sweeping curve of the huge dining room gives fine views out over Regent Street.

Quo Vadis

26-29 Dean Street, W1 (0171 437 9585). Leicester Square or Tottenham Court Road tube. **Lunch** noon-2.30pm Mon-Fri, Sun. **Dinner** 6-11pm Mon-Sat; 6-10.30pm Sun. **Average** £45. **Set meal** (lunch, pre-theatre 6-7.30pm, Mon-Fri) £14.95 two courses, £17.95 three courses. **Credit** AmEx, MC, £TC, V. **Map 6 K6**
The dining room at Marco Pierre White's Quo Vadis is a very pretty, serene space; the food is imaginative if a little pricey; the service, friendly and professional. Upstairs in the bar is a display of Damien Hirst's work.

Global

Helter Skelter

50 Atlantic Road, SW9 (0171 274 8600). Brixton tube/rail. **Dinner** 7-11pm Mon-Thur; 7-11.30pm Fri, Sat. **Average** £16. **Credit** AmEx, MC, £TC, V.
Sleek Helter Skelter may lie in backstreet Brixton, amid piles of market detritus, but the quality of the globe-trotting cooking and the friendly, professional service ensure a stream of returning youngish, hippish diners.

Jindivick

201 Liverpool Road, N1 (0171 607 7710). Angel tube. **Brunch** 10.30am-3.30pm Sat, Sun. **Lunch** noon-3pm Tue-Fri. **Dinner** 6-10.45pm Mon-Sat. **Average** £23. **Set meal** (noon-3pm Tue-Sat; 6-7.30pm Mon-Sat) £9.95 two courses, £11.95 three courses. **Credit** DC, MC, £TC, V. **Map 9 N1**
The award-winning brunch is one attraction at this clean, bright restaurant. The name is Australian Aboriginal, but the menu is becoming increasingly global in its influences.

The Lavender

171 Lavender Hill, SW11 (0171 978 5242). Clapham Junction rail. **Lunch** noon-3.30pm Mon-Fri; noon-4pm Sat, Sun. **Dinner** 7-10.30pm Mon-Thur, Sun; 7-11.30pm Fri, Sat. **Average** £16. **Credit** AmEx, MC, V.
Bright, loud, full of confidence – and that's just the customers. The Lavender's swinging, rainbow-painted bar/restaurant offering not just a sassy vibe and classy wine list, but unexpectedly fine modern global food.

Wiz

123A Clarendon Road, W11 (0171 229 1500). Ladbroke Grove tube. **Meals** noon-11pm Mon-Fri; 11am-4pm, 7pm-midnight, Sat; 11am-4pm, 7-10.30pm, Sun. **Average** £12. **Credit** AmEx, JCB, MC, £TC, V.

Springbok Café: *safari so goody. See p176.*

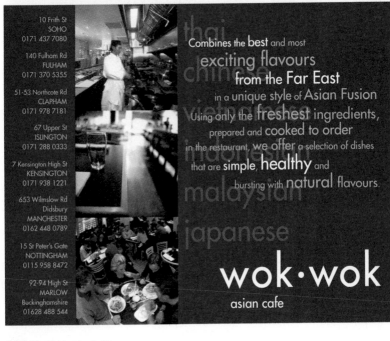

Midnight feasts

Most restaurants stop serving food between 10.30pm and 11.30pm. So if you're peckish after pub closing or a show, where do you go? Soho is the area that's most likely to offer late-night eating. The following central London places all serve food up until at least midnight on the days specified. The times given below are those for last food orders.

Bloomsbury & Fitzrovia
Birdcage (midnight daily). *See p175.*
Costa Dorada (midnight Mon-Sat) *47-55 Hanway Street, W1.* **Map 6 K5** Lively tapas and flamenco bar.

Chelsea
Chelsea Bun Diner (midnight daily). *See p158.*
Vingt Quatre (24 hours daily) *325 Fulham Road, SW10.* **Map 3 C12** Non-stop café.

Clerkenwell
Maison Novelli (midnight Fri, Sat). *See p167.*
Tinseltown (24 hours daily) *44-46 St John Street, EC1.* **Map 9 O4** American-style diner.

Covent Garden
AKA *18 West Central Avenue, WC1* (1am Mon-Sat). **Map 6 L6** Quality modern European food.
The Ivy (midnight Mon-Sat). *See p156.*
Maggiore's (midnight daily) *17-21 Tavistock Street, WC2.* **Map 8 L7** Well-priced Theatreland trattoria.
J Sheekey (midnight daily). *See p165.*

Marylebone
Iran the Restaurant (midnight daily). *See p175.*
Maroush (2am daily) *21 Edgware Road, W2.* **Map 2 F6** Dependable Middle Eastern eaterie.
Mash (1am daily). *See p156.*
Ranoush Juice Bar (3am daily). *See p175.*

Mayfair & St James's
Coast (midnight Mon-Sat). *See p155.*
Dover Street (2am daily) *8-10 Dover Street, W1.* **Map 7 J7** Jazz, soul, rhythm, blues... and food.
Down Mexico Way (1am Mon-Sat) *25 Swallow Street, W1.* **Map 7 J7** Upmarket Mexican joint; bar till 3am.
Mirabelle (midnight Mon-Sat). *See p167.*
Quaglino's (midnight Mon-Thur; 1am Fri, Sat). *See p156.*
Rasa W1 (midnight Fri, Sat). *See p172.*
Sofra Bistro (midnight daily). *See p177.*
The Sports Café (midnight Mon; 1am Tue-Sat) *80 Haymarket, SW1.* **Map 8 K7** A haven for sports fans, with decent grub to boot.

Soho
Café Emm (12.30am Fri, Sat). *See p159.*
Circus (midnight Mon-Sat). *See p155.*
The Criterion (midnight Mon-Sat). *See p165.*
Golden Harvest (2.45am daily). *See p162.*

Hamine (2.30am Mon-Fri; 1.30am Sat). *See p173.*
Hujo's (midnight Mon-Sat) *11 Berwick Street, W1.* **Map 5 J6** Backstreet brasserie.
Melati (12.30am Fri, Sat). *See p174.*
Mezzo (midnight Mon-Thur; 1am Fri, Sat) *100 Wardour Street, W1.* **Map 6 K6** Vast Conran eaterie.
Mr Kong (3am daily). *See p163.*
New Diamond (3am daily) *23 Lisle Street, WC2.* **Map 8 K7** One of Chinatown's most reliable.
Nusa Dua (midnight Fri, Sat). *See p174.*
Old Compton Café (24 hours daily) *34 Old Compton Street, W1.* **Map 6 K6.** Predominantly gay café.
Pollo (midnight daily). *See p159.*
Soho Soho (12.45am Mon-Sat) *11-13 Frith Street, W1.* **Map 6 K6** Lively rotisserie.
Soho Spice (2.30am Mon-Sat) *126 Wardour Street, W1.* **Map 6 K6** Modern Indian restaurant with a great buzz.
Wok Wok (midnight Thur-Sat). *See p162.*
Yo! Sushi (midnight daily). *See p174.*

Soho Spice *up your life.*

The ubiquitous Antony Worrall Thompson's latest creation is this top-notch 'global tapas' bar, which offers a fine range of international snacks throughout the day.

Georgian

Tbilisi
91 Holloway Road, N7 (0171 607 2536). Highbury & Islington tube/rail. **Dinner** 6.30pm-midnight daily. **Average** £14. **Credit** AmEx, MC, £TC, V.
The jumbled decoration may not be to everyone's taste, but the capital's best Georgian cooking certainly will be. Dishes such as *ajasandali*, *hachaapuri* and *kminkali* will have you reaching for your phrase book for superlatives.

Greek

Greek Valley
130 Boundary Road, NW8 (0171 624 3217). Maida Vale or Swiss Cottage tube. **Lunch** *Dec only* noon-2.30pm Mon-Sat. **Dinner** 6pm-midnight Mon-Sat. **Average** £18. **Set meal** (Mon-Thur) £8.50 three courses. **Credit** MC, V.
A kitschy atmosphere (complete with bouzouki player) doesn't detract from the flair of the kitchen. Dishes such as *spanakópitta*, *louviá* and 'valley sausage' (a house special) are executed with skill.

Lemonia
89 Regent's Park Road, NW1 (0171 586 7454). Chalk Farm tube/31, 168 bus. **Lunch** noon-3pm Mon-Fri, Sun. **Dinner** 6-11.30pm Mon-Fri; 6.30-10pm Sat. **Average** £6.75 two courses, £7.95 three courses. **Mezédes** £12.25 per person (minimum two). **Credit** MC, £TC, V.
Arguably London's best and most elegant Greek (Cypriot) restaurant. Proper attention is paid to detail in execution and presentation, although lapses are not unknown. Dishes such as *spanakópitta* and hare *stifado* are cooked with aplomb.

Indian

Central London is not well equipped with Indian restaurants; the few good ones come at a price. For the most authentic subcontinental culinary and cultural experience, visit one of the unglamorous but vibrant centres of Indian London: Wembley, Southall or Tooting.

Café Spice Namaste
16 Prescot Street, E1 (0171 488 9242). Tower Hill tube/Tower Gateway DLR. **Lunch** noon-3pm Mon-Fri. **Dinner** 6.15-10.30pm Mon-Fri; 6.30-10pm Sat. **Average** £20. **Credit** AmEx, DC, JCB, MC, £TC, V. **Map 12 S7**
No pre-made standard curry pastes and stale popadums here – Cyrus Todiwala's bright, airy restaurant shows just how exquisite and extraordinarily diverse modern Indian cooking can be. In a city brimming with retro Indian restaurants, this is the way forward. Worth a journey.
Branches: 247 Lavender Hill, SW11 (0171 738 1717).

Chor Bizarre
16 Albemarle Street, W1 (0171 629 9802). Green Park tube. **Lunch** noon-3pm, **dinner** 6-11.30pm, daily. **Average** £30. **Set lunch** (Sat, Sun) £9.95; (Mon-Fri) £12.95, £14.95. **Credit** AmEx, DC, JCB, MC, £TC, V. **Map 7 H7**
Evoking the charm and romance of old India without resorting to Raj pomp, Chor Bizarre is the perfect venue for well-heeled curry connoisseurs to enjoy classic dishes (many of them Kashmiri) cooked with considerable skill and care.

Gastropubs

Time was when the idea of eating in a pub appealed only to culinary masochists. A soggy, microwaved lard and gristle pie, a wilting spam sandwich or a reconstituted dried Vesta curry (with plenty of sultanas) used to be the most that anyone could hope to find on a pub menu. How times have changed. **The Eagle** in Farringdon blazed the trail, reopening in 1991 with a winning combination of bare-board bonhomie with seriously classy Mediterranean cooking. Within a few years everyone was jumping on the bandwagon, and today there's a stripped-down, wised-up gastropub on almost every street corner. Be warned that the prices in many of these places are the equivalent of those in good restaurants, and booking is often necessary. Most serve lunch and dinner every day (though usually only lunch on Sunday), but phone to check.

Belle Vue *1 Clapham Common Southside (0171 498 9473). Clapham Common tube.*
Bull & Last *168 Highgate Road, NW5 (0171 267 3641). Kentish Town tube/rail then C2, 214 bus.*
The Chapel *48 Chapel Street, NW1 (0171 402 9220). Edgware Road tube.* **Map 2 E5**
Duke of York *7 Roger Street, WC1 (0171 242 7230). Russell Square tube.* **Map 6 M4**
The Eagle *159 Farringdon Road, EC1 (0171 837 1353). Farringdon tube/rail/19, 38, 171A bus.* **Map 9 N4** *See picture below.*
The Engineer *65 Gloucester Avenue, NW1 (0171 722 0950). Chalk Farm tube/31, 168 bus.*
Lansdowne *90 Gloucester Avenue, NW1 (0171 483 0409). Chalk Farm tube/31, 168 bus.*
The Lord Stanley *51 Camden Park Road, NW1 (0171 428 9488). Camden Town tube or Camden Road rail then 29, 253 bus.*
Prince Bonaparte *80 Chepstow Road, W2 (0171 229 5912). Notting Hill or Westbourne Park tube/7, 20, 31 bus.* **Map 1 A5**
The Vine *86 Highgate Road, NW5 (0171 209 0038). Tufnell Park tube or Kentish Town tube/rail.*
The Westbourne *101 Westbourne Park Villas, W2 (0171 221 1332). Royal Oak or Westbourne Park tube.* **Map 1 B5**
William IV *786 Harrow Road, NW10 (0181 969 5944). Kensal Green tube.*

Gifto's Lahore Karahi
162-164 The Broadway, Southall, Middx (0181 813 8669). Southall rail/207 bus. **Meals** noon-11.30pm Mon-Fri; noon-midnight Sat, Sun. **Average** £12. **Credit** AmEx, DC, JCB, LV, MC, TC, V.
Southall's premier Pakistani restaurant is a capacious, popular place where a team of chefs performs in the open kitchen, slapping nans in the tandoor, searing kebabs over charcoal, wielding karahis over fearsome burners.

Karahi King
213 East Lane, North Wembley, Middx (0181 904 2760). North Wembley tube/245 bus. **Meals** noon-midnight daily. **Average** £12.
An out-of-the-way location means that gentrification is never likely to trouble Karahi King. Yet well-dressed Kenyan Asian families flock here, willing to overlook the cramped surroundings to enjoy some of the best karahi cooking in town.

Kastoori
188 Upper Tooting Road, SW17 (0181 767 7027). Tooting Bec or Tooting Broadway tube. **Lunch** 12.30-2.15pm Wed-Sun. **Dinner** 6-10.30pm daily. **Average** £15. **Credit** MC, V.
The best known and best regarded of the several East African Gujarati restaurants along this busy road, the simply decorated, brightly lit Kastoori is notable for its attention to detail, especially in the distinct spices of its dishes.

Masaledar
121 Upper Tooting Road, SW17 (0181 767 7676). Tooting Bec or Tooting Broadway tube. **Meals** noon-midnight daily. **Average** £10. **Credit** MC, V.
Masaledar is our pick of the meat-eating restaurants in Tooting. It's casual, yet looks quite smart; the prices are low; and the food is reliably good, at times excellent. The proprietors are Tanzanian Muslims, and there are a few East African influences in the menu; alcohol is not allowed.

Rasa W1
16 Dering Street, W1 (0171 629 1346). Oxford Circus tube. **Meals** noon-11pm Mon-Thur; noon-midnight Fri, Sat; noon-11pm Sun. **Average** £20. **Credit** AmEx, DC, JCB, MC, TC, V. **Map 5 H6**
This new branch is plusher, larger and a little pricier than the award-winning Stoke Newington original, but the unusual Keralan vegetarian dishes are just as stunning. **Branch:** 55 Stoke Newington Church Street, N16 (0171 249 0344).

Sakoni
119-121 Ealing Road, Wembley, Middx (0181 903 9601). Alperton tube/183 bus. **Meals** 11am-11pm Mon-Thur; 11am-11.30pm Fri-Sun. **Average** £8. **Credit** DC, MC, £TC, V.
Sakoni is a big, bustling snack bar, particularly popular as a meeting place for shoppers and teenagers. The kitchen never disappoints, service is unfailingly polite and the fruit juices are legendary. A wonderful slice of Wembley life.

Tamarind
20 Queen Street, W1 (0171 629 3561). Green Park tube. **Lunch** noon-3pm Mon-Fri; noon-2.30pm Sun. **Dinner** 6-11.30pm Mon-Sat; 6-10.30pm Sun. **Average** £35. **Set lunch** £8.50-£16.50. **Set dinner** (10.30-11.30pm Mon-Sat) £16.50. **Credit** AmEx, DC, JCB, MC, £TC, V. **Map 7 H7**
One of London's finest Indian restaurants is housed in one of the city's most beautifully decorated basements. Chef Atul Kochhar's assured touch with the best and freshest ingredients ensures a (pricey) treat.

Vama
438 King's Road, SW10 (0171 351 4118). Sloane Square tube then 11, 22 bus. **Lunch** 12.30-2.30pm, **dinner** 6.30-11.30pm, daily. **Average** £25. **Credit** AmEx, DC, JCB, MC, £TC, V. **Map 4 D12**
This is an Indian-run enterprise but the look is more smart Italian restaurant than flock wallpapered suburban curry house. The concise menu is also unusual, offering skilfully cooked dishes from the Pakistani borders with Afghanistan, and Baluchistan.

Veeraswamy
Mezzanine floor, Victory House, 101 Regent Street, W1 (0171 734 1401). Piccadilly Circus tube. **Lunch** noon-2.30pm Mon-Fri; 12.30-3pm Sat, Sun. **Dinner** 5.30-11.30pm Mon-Sat, 6-10.30pm Sun. **Average** £30. **Set lunch** (Mon-Sat) £12 two courses; £14.75 three courses. **Set dinner** (5.30-6.30pm, 10.30-11.30pm) £12 two courses, £14.75 three courses. **Sunday brunch** £15 three courses. **Credit** AmEx, DC, JCB, MC, V. **Map 7 J7**
A radical revamp of this ailing but affectionately remembered 70-year-old Indian stalwart has created a look that's more Scandinavian than subcontinental, but the vastly improved food remains true to classical Indian roots.

Irish

The O'Conor Bar
88 Marylebone Lane, W1 (0171 935 9311). Bond Street tube. **Lunch** noon-2.30pm Mon-Fri. **Dinner** 6-10pm Mon-Sat. **Average** £20. **Set meal** £16.50 two courses, £19 three courses. **Credit** AmEx, MC, V. **Map 5 G5**
The menu in this agreeably under-designed room (not a Guinness sign or shamrock in sight) over a pub is not really geared to summer eating but, if you crave a big bowl of steaming Irish stew and a pint of the black stuff, you won't be disappointed.

Italian

Great-value Italian eaterie chains with branches dotted throughout the centre of London include **Spaghetti House** and **Café Pasta**. See *Yellow Pages* for branches.

Arancia
52 Southwark Park Road, SE16 (0171 394 1751). Elephant & Castle tube/rail then 1, 199 bus/South Bermondsey rail. **Lunch** 12.30am-3pm Tue-Sun. **Dinner** 7-11pm Tue-Sat. **Average** £6.50 lunch, £15 dinner. **Set dinner** £7.50 three courses. **Credit** DC, JCB, MC, £TC, V.
A firm contender for best-value meal in London, this lowly caff employs the services of a former head chef at the much-loved, now-defunct Arts Theatre Café. Only a couple of dishes are available at lunch, but the splendid set dinner is a steal.

Assaggi
The Chepstow, 39 Chepstow Place, W2 (0171 792 5501). Notting Hill Gate tube. **Lunch** 12.30-2.30pm, **dinner** 7.30-11pm, Mon-Sat. **Average** £30. **Credit** AmEx, DC, MC, JCB, £TC, V. **Map 1 B6**
So widely adored is this small restaurant that diners often have to book about a month in advance. The somewhat rudimentary décor doesn't seem quite in tune with the impeccable standards of the imaginative food and size of the bill.

Bertorelli's

19 Charlotte Street, W1 (0171 636 4174). Goodge Street tube. Café. **Lunch** noon-3pm Mon-Fri. **Dinner** 6-11pm Mon-Sat. **Average** £20. *Restaurant* **Lunch** noon-3pm Mon-Fri. **Dinner** 6-11pm Mon-Sat. **Average** £32. **Credit** AmEx, DC, MC, £TC, V. **Map 5 J5**

This refurbished branch of Bertorelli's looks stunning: from its bright, fresh backdrop to tiny details like the colourful water glasses. Maddalena Bonino's admirable cooking in the upstairs restaurant is equal to the surroundings. **Branch:** 44A Floral Street, WC2 (0171 836 3969).

Del Buongustaio

283 Putney Bridge Road, SW15 (0181 780 9361). East Putney tube/Putney rail/14, 220 bus. **Lunch** noon-3pm Mon-Fri; 12.30-3.30pm Sun. **Dinner** 6.30-11.30pm Mon-Sat; 6.30-10.30pm Sun. **Average** £23. **Set lunch** £9.50 two courses. **Set dinner** £22.50 five courses. **Credit** AmEx, MC, V.

A bistro-like décor belies one of the most interesting Italian menus in London. Renaissance influences are evident in stunning dishes such as *torta rinascimenttale* (baked layers of broad bean, prosciutto, ricotta and Fontina).

Enoteca

28 Putney High Street, SW15 (0181 785 4449). East Putney tube/Putney rail/14 bus. **Lunch** 12.30-2.30pm Mon-Fri. **Dinner** 7-11pm Mon-Sat. **Average** £22. **Credit** AmEx, DC, MC, V.

Enoteca, perched on a corner site, looks inviting in a spartan kind of way, and is particularly notable for its exceptional, predominantly Italian wine list. The cooking is also handled with flair and care, and rarely disappoints.

Riva

169 Church Road (entrance in Castlenau Road), SW13 (0181 748 0434). Barnes Bridge rail. **Lunch** noon-2.30pm Mon-Fri, Sun. **Dinner** 7-11pm Mon-Thur; 7-11.30pm Fri, Sat; 7-9.30pm Sun. **Average** £22. **Credit** AmEx, MC, £TC, V.

There's a simple and understated elegance to Riva that's reflected in a fine, seasonally changing menu that might include beef carpaccio, home-cured goose and fava beans, and sweet and sour fish and seafood platter.

River Café

Thames Wharf, Rainville Road, W6 (0171 381 8824). Hammersmith tube/211, 220, 295 bus. **Lunch** 12.30-3pm daily. **Dinner** 7-9.30pm Mon-Sat. **Average** £40. **Credit** AmEx, JCB, MC, £TC, V.

It's not a café and you can't see the river, but Rose and Ruth Rogers' celebrated restaurant certainly does deliver well-executed, down-to-earth dishes using top-notch ingredients. On the down side, inflated prices and sometimes sloppy service can rankle.

Vasco & Piero's Pavilion

15 Poland Street, W1 (0171 437 8774). Oxford Circus or Tottenham Court Road tube. **Lunch** noon-3pm, **dinner** 6-11pm, Mon-Fri. **Average** £25 (lunch). **Set dinner** £14.50 two courses, £17.50 three courses. **Credit** AmEx, DC, JCB, MC, £$TC, V. **Map 5 J6**

A reliable old Soho stager that delivers carefully executed dishes in a cosy, clubby atmosphere. Service is very friendly, if slightly erratic at times.

Zafferano

15 Lowndes Street, SW1 (0171 235 5800). Knightsbridge tube. **Lunch** noon-2.30pm, **dinner** 7-11pm, Mon-Sat. **Set lunch** £17.50 two courses, £20.50 three courses. **Set dinner** £25.50 two courses, £29.50 three courses, £33.50 four courses. **Credit** AmEx, MC, £TC, V. **Map 4 F9**

One of London's best, smartest and most celebrity-packed restaurants. The food is well-nigh faultless, from imaginative pastas to more unusual dishes like sweetbreads in a Sicilian-style sweet and sour sauce with capers.

Pizzerias

Of the chains, **Pizza Express** (with branches all over the city) remains the best, although the newer **ASK** chain is growing rapidly and gaining a reputation for reliable grub. Other good bets within central London include **Condotti** (4 Mill Street, W1; 0171 499 1308), **Pizza on the Park** (11 Knightsbridge, SW1; 0171 235 5273), **Soho Pizzeria** (16-18 Beak Street, W1; 0171 434 2480), **Purple Sage** (90-92 Wigmore Street, W1; 0171 486 1912) and **La Spighetta** (43 Blandford Street, W1; 0171 486 7340). **Calzone** is a winning mini-chain, with branches in Notting Hill Gate (2A Kensington Park Road; 0171 243 2003), Hampstead (66 Heath Street, NW3; 0171 794 6775), Chelsea (335 Fulham Road, SW10; 0171 352 9797) and Islington (35 Upper Street, N1; 0171 359 9191). If you happen to find yourself in West Hampstead, **La Brocca** (273 West End Lane, NW6; 0171 433 1989) is a buzzing basement pasta/pizza joint. Another north-west London gem is **Red Pepper** (8 Formosa Street, W9; 0171 266 2708).

Japanese

Hamine

84 Brewer Street, W1 (0171 439 0785). Piccadilly Circus tube. **Meals** 11am-2.30am Mon-Fri; 11am-1.30am Sat; 11am-11.30pm Sun. **Average** £10. **Map 7 J7**

Hamine never changes. And why should it? The ramen is authentic, portions are huge, service is quick, prices are low and opening hours are a late-night lifesaver.

Kulu Kulu

76 Brewer Street, W1 (0171 734 7316). Piccadilly Circus tube. **Lunch** noon-2.30pm Mon-Sat; noon-3.45pm Sun. **Dinner** 5-10pm Mon-Sat. **Average** £12. **Credit** JCB, MC, £TC, V. **Map 7 J7**

A no-nonsense conveyor-belt sushi bar with thoroughly authentic, keenly priced, gimmick-free grub.

Matsuri

15 Bury Street, SW1 (0171 839 1101). Green Park or Piccadilly Circus tube. **Lunch** noon-2.30pm, **dinner** 6-10pm, Mon-Sat. **Average** £20 lunch, £40 dinner. **Set lunch** £5.50-£40. **Set dinner** £12-£55. **Credit** AmEx, DC, JCB, MC, £TC, V. **Map 7 J7**

Matsuri avoids the stuffiness of some top-notch Japanese places while matching all in the quality of food and service. Despite being a basement, the dining area feels light and expansive. The many-course teppan dinners are superb.

Nobu

Metropolitan Hotel, 19 Old Park Lane, W1 (0171 447 4747). Hyde Park Corner tube. **Lunch** noon-2.15pm Mon-Fri. **Dinner** 6-10.30pm Mon-Sat. **Average** £30 lunch, £57 dinner. **Set lunch** £20-£40. **Set dinner** £60. **Credit** AmEx, DC, JCB, MC, £TC, V. **Map 7 H8**

Part of the ultra-hip **Metropolitan Hotel** (*see p141*), Nobu is so cool it's chilly. And if you thought you knew Japanese food, think again. South American influences are evident in dishes such as yellowtail sashimi with jalapeño garnish and citrus sauce. Superb and unique.

t'su

118 Draycott Avenue, SW3 (0171 584 5522). South Kensington tube/49 bus. **Meals** noon-11pm Mon-Sat; noon-10pm Sun. **Average** £20. **Credit** AmEx, MC, V. **Map 4 E10**
Not the place for a purist, perhaps, but t'su's modern eclectic take on Japanese cuisine, using presentation and ingredients you won't find in traditional sushi bars, is refreshingly unhidebound – and a notable success.

Yoshino

3 Piccadilly Place, W1 (0171 287 6622). Piccadilly Circus tube. **Lunch** 11.30am-2pm, **dinner** 6-9pm, Mon-Sat. **Average** £9 lunch, £30 dinner. **Set lunch** £5.80-£20. **Set dinner** £9.80-£35. **Credit** AmEx, DC, JCB, MC, £TC, V. **Map 7 J7**
Yoshino is tucked down a narrow street off Piccadilly and marked only by a discreet (non-English) sign. Everything is written in Japanese but staff are happy to translate. The quality of the food is exemplary.

Yo! Sushi

52 Poland Street, W1 (0171 287 0443). Oxford Circus tube. **Meals** noon-midnight daily. **Average** £16. **Credit** AmEx, DC, JCB, MC, £TC, V. **Map 5 J6**
Boasting the world's longest sushi conveyor belt (176ft/60m), sushi-making machines and robotic drinks trolleys, Yo! Sushi is not backward at coming forward. The food suffers somewhat in comparison, but for fun and novelty this place is hard to beat.

Jewish

Solly's

148A Golders Green Road, NW11 (ground floor & takeaway 0181 455 2121/first floor 0181 455 0004). Golders Green tube. *Ground floor* **Lunch** 11.30am-3pm Fri. **Meals** 11am-midnight Mon-Thur, Sun. **Average** £17. **Set meal** £20 three courses. *First floor* **Dinner** 6.30-11.30pm Mon-Thur; winter one hour after sabbath-11.30pm Sat. **Meals** served 12.30pm-midnight Sun. **Average** £20. **Set dinner** £20 four courses. **Credit** AmEx, DC, MC, £TC, V.
The upstairs dining room (said to be Europe's largest kosher restaurant) is decked out in Middle Eastern style, with murals, rugs and ornamental daggers. A well-executed menu and attentive service ensure a great evening out.

Korean

Greater London's greatest concentration of Korean residents – and restaurants – is in New Malden (20 minutes from Waterloo Station).

Jin

16 Bateman Street, W1 (0171 734 0908). Leicester Square or Tottenham Court Road tube. **Lunch** noon-2.30pm Mon-Sat. **Dinner** 6-11pm daily. **Average** £16. **Set dinner** £16.90 per person (minimum two). **Credit** AmEx, DC, JCB, MC, V. **Map 6 K6**
Located in the middle of Soho, Jin is a stylish (if very dark) place offering top-class Korean cooking. Excellent quality raw ingredients and spices are handled with assurance. More of an evening venue than a lunch stop.

Kaya

42 Albemarle Street, W1 (0171 499 0622). Green Park or Piccadilly Circus tube. **Lunch** noon-3pm Mon-Sat. **Dinner** 6-11pm daily. **Average** £20 lunch, £30 dinner. **Set lunch** £13-£15. **Credit** AmEx, DC, JCB, MC, V. **Map 7 J7**

Belting out the orders at Yo! Sushi.

Kaya is London's prettiest Korean restaurant. Here, waitresses dressed in traditional costumes (*hanbok*) shuffle along to traditional Korean folk music, and serve up authentic dishes such as *pibimbap* (rice, vegetables, meat and egg).

You Me House

96 Burlington Road, New Malden, Surrey (0181 715 1079). New Malden rail. **Lunch** noon-3pm Mon, Tue, Thur-Sun. **Dinner** 6-11pm daily. **Average** £20. **Credit** MC, £TC, V.
Deservedly popular with New Malden's Korean community, the curiously named You Me House is a bastion of quality Korean home cooking. Service is polite and friendly.

Malaysian & Indonesian

Melati

21 Great Windmill Street, W1 (0171 437 2745). Leicester Square or Piccadilly Circus tube. **Meals** noon-11.30pm Mon-Thur, Sun; noon-12.30am Fri, Sat. **Average** £15. **Set meal** £17.50, £22.50, per person (minimum two). **Credit** AmEx, DC, JCB, LV, MC, TC, V. **Map 8 K7**
This long-established, cramped but ever-popular Indonesian restaurant can waver on the service front though the kitchen usually comes up with the goods. The *ikan bumbu Bali* is a particular treat.

Nusa Dua

11-12 Dean Street, W1 (0171 437 3559). Leicester Square or Tottenham Court Road tube. **Lunch** noon-2.30pm Mon-Fri. **Dinner** 6.30-11.30pm Mon-Thur; 6.30pm-midnight Fri, Sat; 6.30-10.30pm Sun. **Average** £15. **Set meal** £15, £17.50 (minimum two). **Credit** AmEx, MC, V. **Map 6 K6**
Nusa Dua is a fun-looking, cheerfully decorated two-floor restaurant that pulls in a diverse clientele. The excellent *rijsttafel* (a selection of the kitchen's best) is a bargain, especially given the location.

Satay Bar

447-450zzz Coldharbour Lane, SW9 (0171 326 5001). Brixton tube/rail. **Lunch** noon-3pm, **dinner** 6pm-midnight, Mon-Fri. **Meals** 1pm-midnight Sat, 2-10.30pm Sun. **Average** £10. **Set meal** (*rijsttafel*) £11.95 per person (minimum two). **Credit** AmEx, DC, MC, V.
This hip Brixton bar manages to be casual, welcoming and stylish in the right proportions while pulling in a boisterous multiracial crowd. And, happily, the food is as enjoyable as the vibe.

Selasih

114 Seymour Place, W1 (0171 224 8816). Edgware Road tube. **Lunch** noon-3pm, **dinner** 6-10.30pm, Mon-Sat. **Average** £12. **Set meal** £9.95 (per person). **Credit** MC, V. **Map 2 F5**

An exotic interior, sarong-clad staff and exquisite food. Try the succulent *ikan pais* (grilled fish wrapped in banana leaf) or perfectly spiced *pajri nenas* (pineapple in a sweet and spicy curry). The lunchtime 'express meals' are a good deal.

Suan Neo

31 Broadgate Circle, EC2 (0171 256 5044). Liverpool Street tube/rail. **Meals** 11.30am-9.30pm Mon-Fri. **Average** £30. **Set meal** £25 three courses. **Credit** AmEx, DC, MC, V. **Map 2 F5**

Aimed squarely at a City market, Suan Neo is furnished to match in a modern British style, with a cleverly lit low ceiling and lavishly set tables. The menu is inspiring, offering a wide choice of rarely found dishes.

Mediterranean

Oceana

Jason Court, 76 Wigmore Street, W1 (0171 224 2992). Bond Street tube. **Lunch** noon-3pm Mon-Fri. **Dinner** 6-11.15pm Mon-Sat. **Average** £25. **Set meal** (noon-3pm, 6-7.30pm) £12.50 two courses. **Credit** AmEx, DC, JCB, MC, £TC, V. **Map 5 H6**

Oceana's colourful postmodern design gives this airy basement the feel of an ocean liner. Pierre Khodja has developed a deceptively simple menu with dishes that are artfully and colourfully presented and humming with fresh flavours.

Snow's on the Green

166 Shepherd's Bush Road, W6 (0171 603 2142). Hammersmith tube. **Lunch** noon-3pm Mon-Fri. **Dinner** 6-11pm Mon-Sat. **Average** £20. **Set lunch** £12.50 two courses, £15.50 three courses. **Credit** AmEx, DC, MC, V.

Sebastian Snow's airy restaurant doesn't explode with atmosphere, but does provide a fresh, soothing environment in which to enjoy racy dishes such as sea trout lasagne and open ravioli of crab, coconut cream, chilli and fish juices.

Woz

46 Golborne Road, W10 (0181 968 2200). Ladbroke Grove or Westbourne Park tube. **Brunch** noon-4pm Sat, Sun. **Lunch** noon-4pm Tue-Fri. **Dinner** 7-11pm Mon-Sat. **Average** £15 lunch. £22.95 three courses, £24.95 four courses, £25.95 five courses. **Credit** AmEx, JCB, MC, V.

Antony Worrall Thompson played a major role in popularising Mediterranean cooking in London. Woz, his latest venture (and nickname), boldly does away with a menu, offering instead a variety of dishes to be shared – and lingered over.

Mexican

Cactus Blue

86 Fulham Road, SW3 (0171 823 7858). South Kensington tube. **Brunch** noon-4pm Sat, Sun. **Meals** 5.30-11.45pm Mon-Sat; noon-10.30pm Sun. **Average** £22. **Credit** AmEx, MC, £TC, V. **Map 4 D11**

This classy establishment is serious about its food and its design. Making full use of the palette of chillies, flavourings and regional ingredients that make up Southwestern cooking, Cactus Blue is a welcome change from fajitas and tacos.

Café Pacifico

5 Langley Street, WC2 (0171 379 7728). Covent Garden or Leicester Square tube. **Meals** noon-11.45pm Mon-Sat; noon-10.45pm Sun. **Average** £16. **Credit** AmEx, JCB, MC, £TC, V. **Map 6 L6**

Despite the odd rough edge, Café Pacifico still comes highly rated: great location, pleasant, spacious open-front room and buzzing bar, and some of the best Mexican food in town.

Middle Eastern

Iran the Restaurant

59 Edgware Road, W2 (0171 723 1344). Marble Arch tube. **Meals** noon-midnight daily. **Average** £27.50. **Credit** AmEx, JCB, MC, £TC, V. **Map 2 F6**

Iran is the closest thing we have in London to a Persian haute cuisine restaurant. The reserved staff lend a reverential air to the surroundings and splendidly refined food.

Patogh

8 Crawford Place, W1 (0171 262 4015). Edgware Road tube. **Open** noon-11.30pm daily. **Average** £8. **Credit** £TC. **Map 2 E5**

Not so much a restaurant as a chummy, New Age kebab shop, where owner and head chef Tooray Pari specialises in fresh Iranian grills using organic meat. We defy anyone to finish the superb but unfeasibly large mixed grill.

Ranoush Juice Bar

43 Edgware Road, W2 (0171 723 5929). Marble Arch tube. **Open** 9am-3am daily. **Average** £8. **Map 2 F6**

Ranoush's interior is bland (unless you have a thing for black marble), but people provide the interest during late evenings, when this is a happening place. The meze, kebabs and fruit juices are fresh and fab.

Oriental

Birdcage

110 Whitfield Street, W1 (0171 383 3346). Goodge Street or Warren Street tube. **Meals** noon-midnight Mon-Fri. **Dinner** 6pm-midnight Sat, Sun. **Average** £23. **Set lunch** £22.50 three courses. **Set dinner** £25 three courses. **Credit** AmEx, DC, JCB, MC, V. **Map 5 J4**

Thai sculptures, birdcages (of course) and serving vessels of audacious weirdness are just part of this visually incredible restaurant. The main ingredient is Michael von Hruschka's unusual and often stunning fusion cooking.

Silks & Spice

23 Foley Street, W1 (0171 636 2718). Great Portland Street tube. **Meals** noon-11pm Mon-Fri; 5.30-11pm Sat; noon-3pm, 5.30-10.30pm, Sun. **Average** £17. **Set lunch** £11 per person (minimum two), three courses. **Set meal** £16.50-£22 per person (minimum two). **Credit** AmEx, MC, £TC, V. **Map 5 J5**

Styling itself a Thai-Malaysian café-bar-restaurant, Silks & Spice is one of the most reliable oriental joints in town. The décor is warm-toned and the cooking imaginative and assured. Service can be a bit hit and miss.

Branches: 103 Boundary Road, NW8 (0171 624 1485); 28 Chalk Farm Road, NW1 (0171 267 5751); 95 Chiswick High Road, W4 (0181 995 7991).

Vong

Berkeley Hotel, Wilton Place, SW1 (0171 235 1010). Hyde Park Corner or Knightsbridge tube. **Lunch** noon-2.30pm Mon-Sat. **Dinner** 6-11.30pm Mon-Sat; 6-10pm Sun. **Average** £30. **Set lunch** £16.50 two courses, £20 three courses. **Set dinner** (6-7.30pm, 10.30-11.30pm) £17.50 two courses. **Credit** AmEx, DC, JCB, MC, £TC, V. **Map 7 G8**

Oriental and western cuisines are fused magnificently in this minimally chic branch of Jean-Georges Vongerichten's celebrated New York restaurant. Save up and treat yourself – and don't pass on the stunning desserts.

Peruvian

Fina Estampa

150 Tooley Street, SE1 (0171 403 1342). London Bridge tube/rail. **Lunch** noon-3pm, **dinner** 6.30-10.30pm, Mon-Sat. **Average** £30. **Credit** AmEx, DC, JCB, MC, £TC, V. **Map 12 Q8**

If there is one place to dispel the notion that the words 'classy' and 'Latin American' don't belong together, then Fina Estampa is it. A sleek mint-green interior, professional service and a menu of refined peasant dishes add up to a desirable package.

Pie & mash

It may surprise some people to learn that London has its own indigenous cuisine. True, it lacks finesse, but the city's last bastions of pies, eels and mash (mostly in east London) offer delicious stomach-fillers at laughably low prices. Two of the finest are **G Kelly** (414 Bethnal Green Road, E2; 0171 739 3603) and **Manze's** (87 Tower Bridge Road, SE1; 0171 407 2985).

Polish

Patio

5 Goldhawk Road, W12 (0181 743 5194). Goldhawk Road or Shepherd's Bush tube. **Lunch** noon-3pm Mon-Fri. **Dinner** 6pm-midnight daily. **Average** £10. **Set meal** £9.90 three courses. **Credit** AmEx, DC, JCB, MC, £TC, V.

A nondescript façade in an unpromising location masks a unique restaurant, where Ewa the enigmatic proprietress greets diners, and husband Michalik cooks up reassuring standards such as blinis and carp Polish-style. Short on frills, big on charm.

Wódka

12 St Alban's Grove, W8 (0171 937 6513). Gloucester Road or High Street Kensington tube. **Lunch** 12.30-2.30pm Mon-Fri. **Dinner** 7-11.15pm daily. **Average** £20. **Set lunch** £10.90 two courses, £13.50 three courses. **Credit** AmEx, DC, MC, £TC, V. **Map 3 C9**

Jan Woroniecki is on a mission to modernise Polish food. The menu covers all the classics: hearty soups, smoked fish, stuffed cabbage and the rest, but innovatively combines them with the likes of olives, sun-dried tomatoes and couscous.

Portuguese

Bar Estrela

111-115 South Lambeth Road, SW8 (0171 793 1051). Stockwell tube/Vauxhall tube/rail. **Meals** 11am-midnight daily. **Average** £12. **Credit** AmEx, DC, MC, V.

This hub of the local Portuguese enclave comes into its own when the sun shines and its french windows are flung open. Portuguese and a few others – a happy, vital mix – come to snack, drink coffee or beer, or eat a full meal.

Lisboa Patisserie

57 Golborne Road, W10 (0181 968 5242). Ladbroke Grove tube. **Open** 8am-8pm daily.

Its fame has spread way beyond London's Portuguese community, but Lisboa is still the pick of the *pastelaria*. Its *pasteis de nata* are legendary.

O Cantinho

137 Stockwell Road, SW8 (0171 924 0218). Stockwell tube/2, 322, 345 bus. **Bar Open** 11am-11pm daily. *Restaurant* **Meals** 10am-midnight daily. **Average** £13. **Credit** £TC.

Choose between the light, modern restaurant and the shiny bar area, with green mock-marble tiles, brightly lights and droning TV, where tapas for the brave might include pig's ear salad. An undilutedly Iberian experience.

Russian

Nikita's

65 Ifield Road, SW10 (0171 352 6326). Earl's Court or West Brompton tube/14, 31, 74 bus. **Dinner** 7.30-11.30pm Mon-Sat. **Average** £24. **Set meal** £18.50-£30.50 four courses. **Credit** AmEx, JCB, MC, £TC, V. **Map 3 C12**

Nikita's is delightfully over the top, from the theatrical décor to the story-book Russian classics, delineated in detail on the long menu. The owner, Mr Borsi, has overseen the fine spread of *zakuski*, chilled vodkas and caviar for 25 years.

South African

Springbok Café

42 Devonshire Road, W4 (0181 742 3149). Turnham Green tube. **Dinner** 7.30-10.30pm Mon-Sat. **Average** £17. **Credit** MC, £TC, V.

London's only exclusively South African restaurant offers such little-seen delights as peppered kudu, Plettenberg Bay linefish and morogo. The quality of the cooking, however, has much more to offer than mere novelty. *See picture p167.*

Spanish

Cambio de Tercio

163 Old Brompton Road, SW5 (0171 244 8970). Gloucester Road tube. **Lunch** 12.30-2.30pm daily. **Dinner** 7-11.30pm Mon-Sat; 7-11pm Sun. **Average** £20, £14 tapas. **Credit** AmEx, MC, V. **Map 3 C11**

This stylish restaurant has been growing in popularity, and it's easy to understand why when you sample Manolo Albuquerque's superb modern Spanish cooking.

Castilla

82 Battersea Rise, SW11 (0171 738 9597). Clapham Junction rail/35, 37, 77, 219 bus. **Meals** 6.30-1am Mon-Sat. **Average** £14, £11 tapas. **Credit** AmEx, JCB, MC, £TC, V.

A move to bigger premises – a few doors up the street from its old locale – has happily wrought no changes to the fine classic tapas, in big portions, but there are now more main courses on offer. The décor is trad; the welcome is warm.

Gaudí

63 Clerkenwell Road, EC1 (0171 608 3220). Farringdon tube/rail. **Lunch** noon-2.30pm Mon-Fri. **Dinner** 7-10.30pm Mon-Sat. **Average** £30. **Credit** AmEx, DC, JCB, MC, £TC, V. **Map 9 N4**

The flamboyance of the Gaudí-esque décor of convoluted metalwork and multicoloured tiling is matched by the cooking of Nacho Martinez – firmly based in a Spanish repertoire yet strikingly creative.

Moro

34-36 Exmouth Market, EC1 (0171 833 8336). Farringdon tube/rail. **Bar Open** noon-10.30pm Mon-Fri. **Average** £8. *Restaurant* **Lunch** noon-2.30pm Mon-Sat. **Dinner** 7-10.30pm Mon-Fri. **Average** £21. **Credit** AmEx, MC, TC, V. **Map 9 N4**

Moro has deservedly attracted much attention since it opened in 1997. It is fashionably minimal and light, and offers an innovative, frequently changing menu incorporating influences mostly from Spain but also from North Africa.

Navarro's Tapas Bar

67 Charlotte Street, W1 (0171 636 7165). Goodge Street tube. **Lunch** noon-3pm Mon-Fri. **Dinner** 6-10.30pm Mon-Sat. **Average** £12. **Credit** AmEx, DC, JCB, MC, £TC, V. **Map 5 J5**

Navarro's tapas are among the most distinctive and interesting around. Especially suited to the light and pretty décor are the deliciously refreshing salads, while gutsier offerings like lentil and chorizo stew are equally good.

Sudanese

Mandola

139-141 Westbourne Grove, W11 (0171 229 4734). Notting Hill Gate tube/23 bus. **Meals** noon-11.30pm Mon-Sat; noon-10.30pm Sun. **Average** £12. **Unlicensed.** **Corkage** £1. **Credit** £TC. **Map 1 A6**

Booking is now essential at this simply decorated yet cosy Sudanese diner. The food is equally straightforward, but tasty, freshly prepared and with plenty of options for vegetarians. Bringing your own booze keeps the bill low.

Swedish

Anna's Place

90 Mildmay Park, N1 (0171 249 9379). Canonbury rail/38, 73, 141, 171A, 236, 277 bus. **Lunch** 12.15-2.15pm Tue-Sat. **Dinner** 7.15-10.45pm Tue-Thur; 7-11pm Fri, Sat. **Average** £23. **Credit** £$TC.

Now that Anna has handed over control to new owners, a few more modern, seasonal dishes have sneaked on to the menu, but the traditional Swedish fare is still a treat. Ask to sit in the gorgeous covered garden (heated in winter).

Thai

Esarn Kheaw

314 Uxbridge Road, W12 (0181 743 8930). Shepherd's Bush tube. **Lunch** noon-3pm Mon-Fri. **Dinner** 6-11pm daily. **Average** £20. **Credit** AmEx, DC, MC, V.

Still one of the best Thai restaurants in town, Esarn Kheaw is also one of the most unusual, specialising in spicy food from north-east Thailand ('Esarn'). Despite the insalubrious setting and grotty décor, it is rarely anything but packed.

Patara

9 Beauchamp Place, SW3 (0171 581 8820). Knightsbridge tube. **Lunch** noon-2.30pm, **dinner** 6.30-10.30pm, daily. **Average** £23. **Set lunch** £8.95 two courses. **Credit** AmEx, DC, MC, £TC, V. **Map 4 F9**

OK, it's just around the corner from Harrods, so you won't find any bargains on the menu, but for top-quality food, served with charm, Patara represents good value.

Sri Siam

16 Old Compton Street, W1 (0171 434 3544). Leicester Square or Tottenham Court Road tube. **Lunch** noon-3pm Mon-Sat. **Dinner** 6-11.15pm Mon-Sat; 6-10.30pm Sun. **Average** £25. **Set meal** £12.95-£19.95 per person (minimum two). **Credit** AmEx, DC, MC, £TC, V. **Map 6 K6**

A minimalist Thai restaurant may usually be a contradiction in terms in London, but Sri Siam's wood-strip floors and brightly painted walls are a refreshing setting for reliable food, including an impressively long vegetarian menu.

Thai Bistro

99 Chiswick High Road, W4 (0181 995 5774). Turnham Green tube/27, 237, 267 bus. **Lunch** noon-3pm Mon, Wed, Fri-Sun. **Dinner** 6-11pm Mon-Sat; 6-10.30pm Sun. **Average** £15. **Credit** MC, V.

Vatcharin Bhumichitr's Thai Bistro has effortlessly established itself in Chiswick's competitive restaurantland. The minimal, canteen-like look is familiar, but the friendly staff and cheap, expertly cooked food is less common.

Thai Pot

1 Bedfordbury, WC2 (0171 379 4580). Covent Garden tube/Charing Cross tube/rail. **Lunch** noon-3pm Mon-Fri. **Dinner** 5.30-11.15pm Mon-Sat. **Average** £17. **Set lunch** £10 two courses. **Set meal** £15 three courses, £18 four courses. **Credit** AmEx, DC, MC, £TC, V. **Map 8 L7**

The unusually airy, neo-classical décor of Thai Pot makes a pleasant backdrop for a Thai menu that offers few surprises but competent, subtly spiced versions of Thai standards. The curries are particularly recommended. **Branch: Thai Pot Express** 148 Strand, WC2 (0171 497 0904).

Turkish

Many of London's best Turkish restaurants are the unprepossessing, unreconstructed kebab houses that serve north London's Turkish community. A walk along Green Lanes or Stoke Newington Road in N16 can be a culinary revelation.

Gallipoli

102 Upper Street, N1 (0171 359 0630). Angel tube/ Highbury & Islington tube/rail. **Meals** 10am-11.30pm Mon-Thur, Sun; 10am-midnight Fri, Sat. **Average** £8 (lunch), £13 (dinner). **Credit** MC, V. **Map 9 O1**

Reflecting the bucolic charm of a Turkish country hostelry, Gallipoli offers consistently high quality on its limited menu. The mezes and kebabs are especially good.

Istanbul Iskembecisi

9 Stoke Newington Road, N16 (0171 254 7291). Dalston Kingsland rail/38, 67, 149, 242, 243 bus. **Meals** noon-5am daily. **Average** £12. **Credit** AmEx, MC, V.

The signature dish here, *iskembe* (finely chopped tripe in soup), may not be to all tastes, but the wonderfully fresh ingredients in the meze and more mainstream main dishes, plus the solicitous service, will please most diners.

Iznik

19 Highbury Park, N5 (0171 354 5697). Highbury & Islington tube/rail/19 bus. **Meals** 10am-3.30pm Mon-Fri; 9am-3.30pm Sat, Sun. **Dinner** 6.30-11pm daily. **Average** £15. **Credit** MC, £TC, V.

The décor is as uncompromisingly oriental as was Selim the Grim, whose portrait scowls down at customers as they enter. Iznik's food is equally reverent of Turkish culture and includes rarely seen, labour-intensive Ottoman lamb dishes.

Sofra Bistro

18 Shepherd Market, W1 (0171 499 4099). Green Park tube. **Meals** noon-midnight daily. **Average** £17. **Credit** AmEx, MC, £TC, V. **Map 7 H8**

Perhaps the pick of the branches in this sizeable chain, the menu here is a little different from the other Sofras, including cheaper options such as an array of own-made pastas, *yahniler* (casseroles), sandwiches and even omelettes; but mixed meze still includes the wonderful *houmous kavurma*.

*Head down to **Moro** tomorrow for innovative Spanish/North African dishes. See page 176.*

Sariyer Balik Lokantasi

56 Green Lanes, N16 (0171 275 7681). Manor House tube/141, 171A bus. **Meals** 5-11.30pm daily. **Average** £10. **Unlicensed. Corkage** no charge.
Tiny and looking rather dilapidated, this wonderful fish restaurant has been a well-kept secret among its loyal customers for the last decade. The mixed meze is excellent.

Vegetarian

Other good restaurants for vegetarians include **Café Emm** and **Love** (both *page 161*), **Rasa W1** (*page 172*) and **Sri Siam** (*page 177*).

Bah Humbug

The Crypt, St Matthew's Peace Garden, Brixton Hill, SW2 (0171 738 3184). Brixton tube/rail. **Dinner** 6-11pm Mon-Thur; 6-11.30pm Fri. **Meals** 10.30am-11.30pm Sat; 10.30am-10.30pm Sun. **Average** £16. **Credit** MC, V.
Although it's in a crypt, Bah Humbug hums with life. Cool funk ricochets off the vaulted ceilings while Brixton trendies tuck into good veggie dishes (plus a few fishy choices) like spinach and mushroom timbale. There's also a hip bar.

Carnevale

135 Whitecross Street, EC1 (0171 250 3452). Barbican tube/Old Street tube/rail/55 bus. **Open** 10am-10.30pm, **lunch** noon-3pm, **dinner** 5.30-10.30pm, Mon-Sat. **Average** £16. **Set meal** (noon-3pm, 5.30-7pm) £9.50 three courses. **Credit** £TC. **Map 9 P4**
This intimate, unassuming place doubles up as a deli during the day. The tiny restaurant serves a Mediterranean-based menu that includes dishes not normally associated with the herbivore's pantheon, such as fried cassava tortilla.

Food For Thought

31 Neal Street, WC2 (0171 836 0239). Covent Garden tube. **Breakfast** 9.30-11.30am Mon-Sat. **Lunch** noon-4pm daily. **Dinner** 4-9pm Mon-Sat. **Average** £8. **Minimum** £2.50 noon-3pm, 6-7.30pm. **Unlicensed. Corkage** no charge. **Credit** £TC. **Map 6 L6**
A lengthy lunchtime queue, snaking out into Neal Street, testifies to Food For Thought's continuing popularity. On the ground floor is a chirpy takeaway; in the cramped downstairs diners sup from the daily changing menu offering quiches, salads and hot dishes.

The Gate

51 Queen Caroline Street, W6 (0181 748 6932). Hammersmith tube. **Lunch** noon-3pm Tue-Fri. **Dinner** 6-10.45pm Mon-Sat. **Average** £16. **Credit** AmEx, MC, TC, V.

Tucked away in a quiet, leafy church courtyard, the Gate's sunflower-yellow walls and stripped-wood floor are a civilised setting in which to enjoy the elaborate, imaginative but not overambitious globally inspired menu. Probably London's best vegetarian restaurant.

Mildred's

58 Greek Street, W1 (0171 494 1634). Leicester Square or Tottenham Court Road tube. **Meals** noon-11pm Mon-Sat; 12.30-6.30pm Sun. **Average** £11. **Credit** TC. **Map 6 K6**
This bustling, informal, friendly, long-established place bases its short menu around stir-fry, falafel and black-eyed bean burger with salad, all of which are around a fiver. Expect to share a table.

The Place Below

St Mary-le-Bow, Cheapside, EC2 (0171 329 0789). St Paul's tube/Bank tube/DLR. **Open** 7.30am-2.30pm, **breakfast** 7.30-10.30am, **lunch** 10.30am-2.30pm, Mon-Fri. **Average** £12. **Credit** MC, £TC, V. **Map 11 P6**
Deep within the Norman crypt of the St Mary-le-Bow church (*see also p41*), this café offers a welcome escape from City life, as well as some excellent vegetarian sustenance.

World Food Café

Neal's Yard Dining Room, 1st floor, 14 Neal's Yard, WC2 (0171 379 0298). Covent Garden tube. **Meals** noon-5pm Mon-Sat. **Average** £11. **Map 6 L6**
One of the best choices for vegetarian food in the centre of town. Cooking is inventive and globally inspired, while the atmosphere is friendly and relaxed.

Vietnamese

Huong-Viet

An Viet House, 12-14 Englefield Road, N1 (0171 249 0877). Bus 67, 149, 236, 242, 243A. **Lunch** noon-3.30pm, **dinner** 5.30-11pm, daily. **Average** £10.
This Vietnamese community centre and café offers an extensive menu of around 100 freshly prepared Vietnamese dishes, served in big portions at low prices, in a basic but convivial dining room.

Viet Hoa

70-72 Kingsland Road, E2 (0171 729 8293). Bus 26, 48, 55, 67, 149, 242. **Lunch** noon-3.30pm, **dinner** 5.30-11pm, Tue-Sun. **Average** £8. **Set lunch** £3.95 two courses. **Credit** MC, V.
This wonderfully unpretentious restaurant-cum-informal community centre is hugely popular. You won't get refinement in service or décor, just the admirably fresh, needle-sharp flavours of Vietnam in a relaxed, buzzy atmosphere.

Pubs & Bars

The classic pub is ailing in London, but trendy bar-lovers have never had it so good.

Not so long ago, going out for a drink in London was an unthrilling experience if you weren't a fan of the traditional smoky, pokey boozer. However, the wine bar started to come into its own in the 1980s, followed by the emergence of seriously stylish, thoroughly metropolitan bars and spruced-up pubs offering restaurant-quality food in the 1990s (for the best of the latter, *see page 171* **Gastropubs**). Some of London's coolest new bars also double up as clubs late in the evening as DJs take the floor and dancing takes priority over drinking. For the pick of these places, *see page 222* **Club bars**. Today's London drinker is spoilt for choice when it comes to supping spots.

Yet it's not all good news. While the city's drinking scene was undoubtedly in need of a serious kick up the backside, there is also a worrying trend towards cynical, marketing-led homogeneity, with identikit pubs and bars spreading over the capital faster than fermenting yeast on a vat of ale. The ubiquity of barn-like **Pitcher & Piano** and **All Bar One** drinking halls, of **JD Wetherspoon** and **Firkin** pubs, and of **Balls Brothers**, **Corney & Barrow** and **Davy's** wine bars may offer a brand you recognise on almost every street corner (and often good-quality drinks), but they leave no room for individuality or idiosyncrasy. Lovers of that smoky, pokey old boozer are becoming an increasingly beleaguered tribe.

Bargain-hunting boozers might like to get hold of a copy of the *London Happy Hour Timetable* (Banana Publishing; £5), which lists cheap drink times from 11am to 4am in pubs and bars.

For bars that cater for a primarily gay or lesbian clientele, *see page 241*.

see page 171

Central

South Bank

Fire Station
150 Waterloo Road, SE1 (0171 620 2226). Waterloo tube/rail. **Open** 11am-11pm Mon-Sat; noon-10.30pm Sun. **Map 11 N8**
This fiercesomely popular bar – with a good restaurant at the back – used to be, surprise, surprise, a fire station. The high ceilings partially make up for the packed floor space.

Studio Six
Gabriel's Wharf, 56 Upper Ground, SE1 (0171 928 6243). Waterloo tube/rail. **Open** noon-11pm Mon-Sat; noon-10.30pm Sun. **Map 11 N7**

Notable mainly for its wealth of outdoor, close-to-the-river seating, Studio Six also offers a good selection of drinks and reasonably priced food. The interior is very basic; go on a sunny day.

The City

Bierrex
2-3 Creed Lane, EC4 (0171 329 3188). St Paul's tube. **Open** noon-9pm Mon, Tue; noon-11pm Wed-Fri. **Map 11 O6**
Located on a small lane between Ludgate Hill and Carter Lane, Bierrex stocks a fine range of more than 50 European bottled beers – in a relaxed but rather incongruous setting akin to a Midwest American diner.

Water Poet
9 Stoney Lane, E1 (0171 626 4994). Liverpool Street tube/rail. **Open** 11am-11pm Mon-Fri. **Map 12 R6**
The drinking area of this ersatz New York bar is at one end of the long, low, white-painted room; the restaurant is at the other. Food can be excellent, service can be sloppy, and the Water Poet's popularity can make it very crowded.

Holborn & Clerkenwell

Bleeding Heart
Bleeding Heart Yard, off Greville Street, EC1 (0171 242 8238). Chancery Lane tube or Farringdon tube/rail. **Open** noon-11pm Mon-Fri. **Map 9 N5**
A popular, jolly, informal and occasionally chaotic wine bar (with a smarter dining area). A full list of over 400 bottles is available on request, but the shortened version of 50 wines under £15 also provides excellent choice and value.

Café Kick
43 Exmouth Market, EC1 (0171 837 8077). Farringdon tube/rail. **Open** 11am-11pm Mon-Sat. **Map 9 N4**
A shrine to table football, Café Kick is the scene of spirited contests on the (as the French would say) *babyfoot* tables. After joining battle, relax at the bar at the back with a drink or a coffee (which comes in 20 different guises).

Cicada
132-136 St John Street, EC1 (0171 608 1550). Farringdon tube/rail. **Open** noon-11pm Mon-Fri; 6-11pm Sat. **Map 9 O5**
Cicada's pleasingly butch, modernist interior is a fine space, with rough-hewn surfaces and big windows. Pan-oriental food is available in the bar and restaurant.

The Eagle
159 Farringdon Road, EC1 (0171 837 1353). Farringdon tube/rail. **Open** noon-11pm Mon-Sat; noon-5pm Sun. **Map 9 N4**
London's trail-blazing gastropub continues to be ridiculously popular: arrive early if you want any hope of a seat. Happily, the quality of the mainly Mediterranean dishes remains high. Many wines are available by the glass.

A dying breed: Covent Garden's thoroughly trad **Lamb & Flag**.

Fox & Anchor

115 Charterhouse Street, EC1 (0171 253 4838). Farringdon tube/rail. **Open** *7am-11pm Mon-Fri.* **Map 9 O5**
Note the opening hours of this unique pub: they are designed to meet the needs of workers at Smithfield's meat market, not to suit idlers about town. The beer is good, and food is top-of-the-range butties with the emphasis on fried flesh.

Jerusalem Tavern

55 Britton Street, EC1 (0171 490 4281). Farringdon tube/rail. **Open** *9am-11pm Mon-Fri.* **Map 9 O5**
All of Farringdon's media circus seem to squeeze into this tiny reconstructed Georgian parlour with its original fires, partitioned cubicles and distempered walls. The solicitous bar staff tend an exceptional selection of beers and wines.

LED

171 Farringdon Road, EC1 (0171 278 4400). Farringdon tube/rail. **Open** *noon-midnight Mon-Sat.* **Map 9 N4**
Yet another minimalist style bar opens in Farringdon. Warmth is provided by cheery staff and the crimson, womb-like basement lounge with its black '70s-style sofas, huge TV and Playstation consoles.

Bloomsbury & Fitzrovia

Duke of York

7 Roger Street, WC1 (0171 242 7230). Russell Square tube/19, 38, 55 bus. **Open** *noon-11pm Mon-Fri; 7-11pm Sat.* **Map 6 M4**
Making a virtue of its original dinginess, this corner boozer still looks as if it should hold a few old geezers in flat caps nursing bitter. The fashionably eclectic food menu, however, betrays the Duke's ambition to move with the times.

The Lamb

Lamb's Conduit Street, WC1 (0171 405 0713). Russell Square tube. **Open** *11am-11pm Mon-Sat; noon-4pm, 7-10.30pm, Sun.* **Map 6 M4**
Wonderfully old-fashioned pub that draws in a mixed crowd to enjoy the Young's beers and the splendid wooden bar with small, engraved, swivel-hinged glass panels dividing punter from publican.

Point 101

101 New Oxford Street, WC1 (0171 379 3112). Tottenham Court Road tube. **Open** *11am-1am Mon-Thur; 11am-2am Fri, Sat; noon-midnight Sun.* **Map 6 K6**
This retro-feel bar (from the Mean Fiddler organisation) opened beneath Centrepoint in late 1998 and is already prodigiously popular. Looking rather like a bus station from outside, it has cosy cubicles upstairs and decent food.

Truckles of Pied Bull Yard

off Bury Place, WC1 (0171 404 5338). Holborn tube. **Open** *11.30am-9pm Mon-Fri; 11.30am-3pm Sat.* **Map 6 L5**
One of the large chain of Davy's wine bars, this branch boasts a spacious two-floor interior and an attractive paved courtyard. All the classic bottles are sold, from claret to sherry to port. And there are ale and good snacks too.

Vats

51 Lamb's Conduit Street, WC1 (0171 242 8963). Holborn or Russell Square tube. **Open** *noon-11pm Mon-Fri.* **Map 6 M4**
A wine bar of the old school, blessed with a first-rate, mainly traditional wine list, a wood-panelled interior and long, dark bar, and customers who favour suits.

Marylebone

The Chapel

48 Chapel Street, NW1 (0171 402 9220). Edgware Road tube. **Open** *noon-11pm Mon-Sat; noon-3pm, 7-10.30pm, Sun.* **Map 2 E5**
This award-winning bar has a simple, bare-boarded interior, a pleasant shaded garden, plenty of wines by the glass, good cask-conditioned ales and excellent food. The only drawback is that it tends to get uncomfortably packed.

Mayfair

The Library

The Lanesborough Hotel, Hyde Park Corner, SW1 (0171 259 5599 ext 5681). Hyde Park Corner tube. **Open** *11am-11pm Mon-Sat; noon-10.30pm Sun.* **Map 7 G8**
The Lanesborough's book-lined bar has an old-fashioned air at odds with the rest of the lavishly decorated hotel. Great cocktails, great service and complimentary nibbles of a high standard. Dress: no jeans or trainers.

The Met Bar

Old Park Lane, W1 (0171 447 1000). Hyde Park Corner tube. **Open** *11am-3am Mon-Sat; 11am-10.30pm Sun.* **Map 7 H8**
The only time you're likely to get into London's hippest new bar is at midday. By night, it's so full of stellar bodies that not even the most determined lines in the book will get you through the door. Don't worry – you're not missing much.

Trader Vic's

Hilton Hotel, Park Lane, W1 (0171 493 8000 ext 420). Hyde Park Corner or Green Park tube. **Open** *5pm-12.45am Mon-Sat; 5-10.30pm Sun.* **Map 7 G8**
Spectacularly tacky and very pricey, but if you're in the mood for cocktails and kitsch, this Hawaiian-themed basement bar can be tremendous fun. On the 28th floor, **Windows** bar offers one of London's most spectacular spots to gaze out over the city while you sup.

Soho

Alphabet

61-63 Beak Street, W1 (0171 439 2190). Oxford Circus tube. **Open** *11am-11pm Mon-Sat.* **Map 7 J6**
Very hip at the time of its opening a couple of years ago, Alphabet has become something of a victim of its own success. The drinks are good, but claustrophobes steer clear.

Atlantic Bar & Grill

20 Glasshouse Street, W1 (0171 734 4888). Piccadilly Circus tube. **Open** noon-3am Mon-Sat; 6pm-midnight Sun. **Map 7 J7**

The Atlantic's bars still look mighty impressive (and remain very popular) but they've long since ceased to be *the* place in town to be seen – and the unfathomable door policy remains as irritating as ever. The drinks are good though.

Cork & Bottle

44-46 Cranbourn Street, WC2 (0171 734 7807). Leicester Square tube. **Open** 11am-11pm Mon-Sat; noon-10.30pm Sun. **Map 8 K7**

Don Hewitson's 28-year-old basement wine bar is one of London's finest. When busy (which is most of the time) it can feel cramped and airless, but brave the discomfort for the superb wine list and good food.

Dog & Duck

18 Bateman Street, W1 (0171 437 4447). Piccadilly Circus or Tottenham Court Road tube. **Open** noon-11pm Mon-Fri; 6-11pm Sat; 7-10.30pm Sun. **Map 6 K6**

A tiny, cosy, old-fashioned pub, with a lovely Edwardian interior, engraved mirrors and green-and-orange tilework. Seating is restricted to a few bar stools and benches.

The Dog House

187 Wardour Street, W1 (0171 434 2116/2118). Tottenham Court Road tube. **Open** 5-11pm Mon-Fri; 6-11pm Sat. **Map 6 K6**

An intimate space with alcove seating and a trendy but friendly crowd. There's a large selection of flavoured vodkas, from fruity versions to red-hot chilli pepper.

Ego

23-24 Bateman Street, W1 (0171 437 1977). Leicester Square or Tottenham Court Road tube. **Open** 11am-1am Mon-Sat. **Admission** £3 after 11pm. **Map 6 K6**

Ego (formerly Riki-Tik) has pulled off the seemingly impossible – attracting a fashionable crowd and keeping it. The pace inside is frenetic. House speciality: flavoured vodka.

French House

49 Dean Street, W1 (0171 437 2799). Leicester Square tube. **Open** noon-11pm Mon-Sat; noon-10.30pm Sun. **Map 6 K6**

This tiny, heaving and enormously enjoyable establishment has long been a haunt of writers and artists. Don't ask for pints here – they only serve halves, plus wines and spirits.

Covent Garden

The American Bar

Savoy Hotel, Strand, WC2 (0171 836 4343). Charing Cross tube/rail. **Open** 11am-11pm Mon-Sat; noon-3.30pm, 6.30-10.30pm, Sun. **Map 8 L7**

This art deco period piece is surprisingly relaxed (and surprisingly unimpressive) for the cocktail bar of a five-star hotel. The drinks are first class, and come with endlessly replenished crisps and olives. Dress: jacket and tie for men.

Bar des Amis

11-14 Hanover Place, WC2 (0171 379 3444). Covent Garden tube. **Open** 11.30am-11pm Mon-Sat. **Map 6 L6**

A top-notch drinks list and a first-rate cheeseboard are two good reasons to patronise this basement wine bar.

Denim

4A Upper St Martin's Lane, WC2 (0171 497 0376). Leicester Square tube. **Open** noon-1am Mon-Sat. **Map 8 L6**

With its futuristic interior and womb-like red basement, Denim can't fail to make an impression. But, design aside, it also offers friendly service and decent bar snacks.

Detroit

35 Earlham Street, WC2 (0171 240 2662). Covent Garden tube. **Open** 5pm-midnight Mon-Sat. **Map 6 K6**

Cocktails remain the speciality in this amorphous underground bar with its Flintstones-style décor. Food – such as Caesar salad and grilled chicken breast with chips – is good and affordably priced.

Freud

198 Shaftesbury Avenue, WC2 (0171 240 9933). Covent Garden or Tottenham Court Road tube. **Open** 11am-11pm Mon-Sat; noon-10.30pm Sun. **Map 6 L6**

A basement bar, enhanced by huge candlesticks, distressed walls and slate tables. The cocktails aren't bad, there's a varied selection of international bottled beers and light dishes, and the clientele is agreeably disparate.

Gordon's

47 Villiers Street, WC2 (0171 930 1408). Embankment tube or Charing Cross tube/rail. **Open** 11am-11pm Mon-Fri; 5-11pm Sat. **Map 8 L7**

Located in a dimly lit cellar, this classic wine bar scores highly for atmosphere. Prices are low, with fortified wines a strength. Fairly basic food sops up the booze admirably.

Lamb & Flag

33 Rose Street, WC2 (0171 497 9504). Covent Garden tube. **Open** 11am-11pm Mon-Thur; 11am-10.45pm Fri, Sat; noon-10.30pm Sun. **Map 8 L7**

A small, rickety pub tucked up a side alley. In the seventeenth century, Dryden was beaten up here – now it's a popular meeting place and one of the only decent pubs in Covent Garden. Upstairs is quieter – but not much.

Soho Brewing Company

41 Earlham Street, WC2 (0171 240 0606). Covent Garden tube. **Open** 11am-11pm Mon-Sat; 12.30-10.30pm Sun. **Map 6 L6**

Looking not unlike a pristine steamship engine room, this sizeable basement bar is distinguished by its home-brewed beers and above-average food in the restaurant area.

Westminster & Victoria

Boisdale

15 Eccleston Street, SW1 (0171 730 6922). Victoria tube/rail. **Open** noon-11pm Mon-Fri; 7-11pm Sat. **Map 7 H10**

The bar at the back of this Franco-Scottish restaurant has the largest collection of malt whiskies in London. And the range of champagnes and cigars is equally impressive. Suits predominate, but the atmosphere is friendly.

Chelsea & South Kensington

The Crescent

99 Fulham Road, SW3 (0171 225 2244). South Kensington tube. **Open** 11am-midnight Mon-Fri; 10am-midnight Sat; 11am-10pm Sun. **Map 4 E10**

The modern aluminium-and-glass frontage and plush banquette-lined interior is most un-wine-bar-like, but wine is the driving force here. An impressive list has over 150 names. The food is serious stuff too.

Orange Brewery

37 Pimlico Road, SW1 (0171 730 5984). Sloane Square tube/11, 211 bus. **Open** 11am-11pm Mon-Sat; noon-10.30pm Sun. **Map 7 G11**

One of a growing number of microbreweries in London. Seasonal beers and special one-offs top up the range on tap. The place itself looks a bit too done-up in a typical tied-house make-over sort of way.

Phene Arms

9 Phene Street, SW3 (0171 352 3294). Sloane Square or South Kensington tube. **Open** 11am-11pm Mon-Sat; noon-10.30pm Sun. **Map 4 E12**
This excellent local, off Oakley Street, midway between King's Road and Chelsea Embankment is full of (slightly eccentric) character, and has a fine summer terrace. Oh, and George Best has been spotted here.

Knightsbridge

Nag's Head

53 Kinnerton Street, SW1 (0171 235 1135). Hyde Park Corner or Knightsbridge tube. **Open** 11am-11pm Mon-Sat; noon-10.30pm Sun. **Map 7 G9**
A charming little chatterbox of a pub with Wilton Place, where staff are noticeably friendly and newcomers are made welcome. In summer, lack of space means that drinkers spill out into the mews.

The Albion

10 Thornhill Road, N1 (0171 607 7450). Angel tube/Highbury & Islington tube/rail. **Open** 11am-11pm Mon-Sat; 11am-10.30pm Sun. **Map 9 N1**
Ivy cascades down the broad front of this evergreen Barnsbury pub. There is a good-size garden at the back beneath another ivy canopy.

The Clifton

96 Clifton Hill, NW8 (0171 624 5233). Maida Vale or St John's Wood tube. **Open** 11am-11pm Mon-Sat; noon-10.30pm Sun.
A smart, trad establishment in a fine St John's Wood house. The tables on the leafy front terrace make this an agreeable summer hangout, while the conservatory ensures it is a pub for all seasons.

The Hollybush

22 Holly Mount, NW3 (0171 435 2892). Hampstead tube. **Open** noon-11pm Mon-Sat; noon-10.30pm Sun.
If you're looking for quiet conversation and an unspoilt bar full of nooks and crannies away from the ostentation of Hampstead village, this is the place to come.

Lansdowne

90 Gloucester Avenue, NW1 (0171 483 0409). Chalk Farm tube/31, 168 bus. **Open** 6-11pm Mon; noon-11pm Tue-Sat; noon-4pm, 7-10.30pm, Sun.
A lovely, light-filled pub where food and wine take precedence over beer. Prices are pretty high, but the eclectic modern dishes generally come up with the goods.

O'Hanlons

8 Tysoe Street, EC1 (0171 837 4112). Angel tube or Farringdon tube/rail/19, 38, 171A bus. **Open** 11am-11pm Mon-Fri; noon-11pm Sat; noon-10.30pm Sun. **Map 9 N3**
Take one pint of O'Hanlons dry stout (an unpasteurised, unfiltered gem) and one leather armchair. Add a plate of oysters and home-made soda bread plus good conversation, and you have the ingredients of a fine time.

WKD

18 Kentish Town Road, NW1 (0171 267 1869). Camden Town tube/Camden Road rail. **Open** noon-2am Mon-Thur; noon-3am Fri, Sat; noon-1am Sun.
A surprisingly successful combination of café, bar, club and exhibition space. The industrial décor is bright; music ranges from reggae, soul and world music to jamming sessions (with DJs from 9.30pm daily). The snack food is decent.

WXD

1 Ferme Park Road, N4 (0181 292 0516). Finsbury Park tube/rail. **Open** noon-midnight Mon-Fri; 10am-midnight Sat; 10am-10.30pm Sun.
Part gallery, part music venue, part café, part bar, WXD, manages to be most things to most people. The all-day brunch is excellent, and there's also a lovely garden.

Cantaloupe

35-42 Charlotte Road, EC2 (0171 613 4411). Old Street tube/rail. **Open** 11am-midnight Mon-Fri; noon-midnight Sat; noon-10.30pm Sun. **Map 10 R4**
Cantaloupe caters for Hoxton's new inhabitants (designers, artists, photographers *et al*), but thankfully it's not too posey. The place is large, with benches in the bar and a small restaurant area with a weekly changing menu at the back.

The Grapes

76 Narrow Street, E14 (0171 987 4396). West Ferry DLR. **Open** noon-3pm, 5.30-11pm, Mon-Fri; 7-11pm Sat; noon-3pm, 7-10pm, Sun.
Established in 1583, rebuilt in 1720, the quiet, characterful Grapes is mercifully off the coach-party trail and is many people's pick of the East End riverside pubs.

Great Eastern Dining Room

54-56 Great Eastern Street, EC2 (0171 613 4545). Old Street tube. **Open** noon-11pm Mon-Fri; 6-11pm Sat. **Map 10 R4**
Yet another style bar? Perhaps, but there's plenty of substance here too. A fabulous, very NOW space with a mix of retro and modern detailing, excellent food and good drinks.

Home

100-106 Leonard Street, EC2 (0171 684 8618). Old Street tube/rail. **Open** noon-midnight Mon-Fri; 6pm-midnight Sat; 3pm-midnight Sun. **Map 10 Q4**
Basically a large basement filled with knackered sofas, skipworthy tables and a relaxed, unpretentious crowd who pack in for the mix of club and retro music, and the buzz.

Hoxton Square Bar & Kitchen

2-4 Hoxton Square, N1 (0171 613 0709). Old Street tube/rail. **Open** 11am-midnight Mon-Fri; noon-midnight Sat. **Map 10 R3**
A frighteningly cool, austerely decorated (walls of sand-textured concrete) hangout, softened somewhat by comfy chairs and comforting food.

Prospect of Whitby

57 Wapping Wall, E1 (0171 481 1095). Wapping tube. **Open** 11.30am-3pm, 5.30-11pm, Mon-Fri; 11.30am-11pm Sat; noon-10.30pm Sun.
With flagstone floors, cast-iron hearths, little round windows and a famous Elizabethan pewter bar, this is an archetypal olde worlde inn. Dating back to 1520, and having once served Samuel Pepys, the pub now plays host to gawping tourists.

Shoreditch Electricity Showrooms

39A Hoxton Square, N1 (0171 739 6934). Old Street tube/rail. **Open** 11am-11pm Mon-Wed; 11am-midnight Thur-Sat; 11am-10.30pm Sun. **Map 10 R3**
There's no doubt as to the former function of this now-ultra hip bar. The décor mixes battered tables and chairs with clean-lined booths at the back and throws in a lurid alpine scene for good measure. And the beer and food are also cool.

A breath of alpine-fresh air: the snappily named **Shoreditch Electricity Showrooms**.

South

Alma Tavern
499 Old York Road, SW18 (0181 870 2537).
Wandsworth Town rail. **Open** 11am-11pm Mon-Sat;
10am-10.30pm Sun.
A beautifully renovated pub, with a big central bar and
giant painted mirrors, and – to one side – a dining room with
a huge pine table (serving international chow). The wine list
is excellent.

Belle Vue
1 Clapham Common Southside, SW4 (0171 498 9473).
Clapham Common tube. **Open** 5-11pm Mon-Fri; noon-
11pm Fri, Sat; noon-10.30pm Sun.
A mix and match spread of tables and sofas, friendly staff
and excellent food draw a young, amiable crowd. The choice
of wine is better than the beer selection.

Bread & Roses
68 Clapham Manor Street, SW4 (0171 498 1779).
Clapham Common or Clapham North tube.
Open 11am-11pm Mon-Sat; noon-10.30pm Sun.

With bare boards, classy photos on the walls, and lots of
light and space, this is a relaxed spot to drink and one of the
best places to pass a Sunday, when music from a different
African city is featured each week.

The Ship
*41 Jews Row, SW18 (0181 870 9667). Wandsworth
Town rail/28, 295 bus.* **Open** 11am-11pm Mon-Sat;
noon-10.30pm Sun.
Inside, the perennially popular Ship is a beautiful big room
with huge windows, bare boards, oak tables, a restaurant
to one side and a smaller bar at the back. But it really comes
into its own in summer when the barbecue is cranked up.

Sun & Doves
*61-63 Coldharbour Lane, SE5 (0171 733 1525). Brixton
tube/rail then 35, 45 bus or Oval tube then 36 bus.*
Open 11am-11pm Mon-Fri; noon-11pm Sat; noon-
10.30pm Sun.
A bright, clean, reconstructed boozer offering unfancy food
and a vibrant atmosphere. The nicely designed patio is perfect for alfresco drinking of cocktails, beers, fruit juices and
a balanced range of wines.

Late-night boozing

Britain's primeval licensing laws may be changing soon, but for the moment the law dictates
that most pubs and bars have to deposit their
drinkers on to the streets simultaneously at
11pm (10.30pm on a Sunday) so that they can
get a good lager-fuelled fight going. There are,
however, exceptions. Restaurants can serve
alcohol later than 11pm if you're eating, and
there are a number of drinking dens that have
managed to secure gold-dust-like late drinks
licences. The majority of these are in Soho
and Covent Garden. A selection of the best in
central London follows. The times listed are
closing times. *See also page 222* **Club bars**.
For bars that attract a largely gay clientele, *see
page 241.*

South Bank
Babushka *173 Blackfriars Road, SE1.* Midnight
Thur-Sat. **Map 11 O8**

Clerkenwell/Hoxton
Canteloupe *see p182.* Midnight Mon-Sat.
Home *see p182.* Midnight daily.
Vic Naylor *38-40 St John Street, EC1.* Midnight
Mon-Fri. **Map 9 O5**

Bloomsbury & Fitzrovia
Jerusalem *see p223.* 2am Mon-Thur; 3am Fri, Sat.
Point 101 *see p180.* 1am Mon-Thur; 2am Fri, Sat;
midnight Sun.
Sevilla Mía *22 Hanway Street, W1.* 1am Mon-Sat.
Map 6 K5

Marylebone
Mash *19-21 Great Portland Street, W1.* 1am Mon-Sat;
midnight Sun. **Map 5 H5**

Mayfair
Caspers *6 Tenterden Street, W1.* Midnight Tue-
Thur; 1am Fri, Sat. **Map 5 H6**
Corks *28 Binney Street, W1.* Midnight Mon, Tue;
2.30am Wed; 3.30am Thur-Sat. **Map 5 G6**
Dover Street *8-10 Dover Street, W1.* 3am Mon-Sat.
Map 7 J7
Havana Square *17 Hanover Square, W1.* 2am Mon-
Wed; 3am Thur-Sat; 1am Sun. **Map 5 H6**
Windows *The Hilton, Park Lane, W1.* 2am Mon-Sat.
Map 7 G8

Soho
Bar Rumba *36 Shaftesbury Avenue, W1.* 3.30am
Mon-Fri; 6am Sat; 2am Sun. **Map 8 K7**
Little Italy *21 Frith Street, W1.* 4am Mon-Sat.
Map 6 K6
Lupo *50 Dean Street, W1.* Midnight Mon; 1am Tue;
2am Wed, Thur; 3am Fri, Sat. **Map 6 K6**
O Bar *83 Wardour Street, W1.* 3am Mon-Sat.
Map 6 K6
Red *4 Greek Street, W1.* 3am Mon-Sat. **Map 6 K6**

Covent Garden
79CXR *79 Charing Cross Road, WC2.* 2am Mon-
Thur; 3am Fri, Sat. **Map 6 K6**
Fuel *21 The Market, Covent Garden, WC2.* 2am Mon-
Sat. **Map 8 L6**
Queen Mary *Victoria Embankment, WC2.* 2am Fri,
Sat. **Map 8 M7**
Roadhouse *Jubilee Hall, 35 The Piazza, WC2.* 3am
Mon-Sat; 1am Sun. **Map 8 L7**
Saint *8 Great Newport Street, WC2.* 1am Mon-Thur;
2am Fri, Sat. **Map 8 K6**
Salsa! *96 Charing Cross Road, WC2.* 2am Mon-Sat.
Map 6 K6
The Spot *29 Maiden Lane, WC2.* 1am daily.
Map 8 L6

The drugs do work at **Pharmacy**.

A pool hall like no other, with an industrial look but a relaxed feel. The long bar area widens out to the rear, where there are seven pool tables. As many people come here to drink – and nibble pub snacks – as to play.

Jac's

48 Lonsdale Road, W11 (0171 792 2838). Ladbroke Grove or Notting Hill Gate tube/7, 23, 31 bus. **Open** 6-11pm Mon-Sat; 7-10.30pm Sun. **Map 1 A6**
An agreeable bar to hang out in when it's not too crowded – which isn't often. It's dark and moody at the front and light and airy at the back. There's no name outside – blink and you'll miss it.

Julie's Bar

137 Portland Road, W11 (0171 727 7985). Holland Park tube. **Open** 11am-11pm Mon-Sat; 11am-10.30pm Sun.
A popular but surprisingly soothing haunt, decked out in a beautiful jumble of Victorian and oriental antiques and churchy wood carvings. The wine list is concise; food in the restaurant is above average.

Legless Ladder

1 Harwood Terrace, SW6 (0171 610 6131). Fulham Broadway tube. **Open** noon-11pm Mon-Sat; noon-10.30pm Sun.
This bright, spacious pub with sunny yellow walls centres on a large circular bar. Stripped to its basics, the clean, plain and simple furnishings are refreshingly free of aspirations to bohemian chic.

Paradise by Way of Kensal Green

19 Kilburn Lane, W10 (0181 969 0098). Kensal Green tube/Kensal Rise rail/18, 52, 302 bus. **Open** noon-11pm Mon-Sat; noon-10.30pm Sun.
Groovy, popular bar with an excellent restaurant at the back serving admirably unfussy international grub.

Pharmacy Restaurant & Bar

150 Notting Hill Gate, W11 (0171 221 2442). Notting Hill Gate tube. **Open** noon-3pm, 6pm-1am, Mon-Thur; noon-3pm, 6pm-2am, Fri, Sat; 11.15am-3pm, 6-10.30pm, Sun. **Map 1 A7**
Still one of London's hippest bars, Pharmacy raised a few eyebrows when it opened in 1998. On the ground floor, staff in surgical gowns serve decent cocktails and bar snacks; upstairs is the restaurant dishing up good but pricey food.

The Westbourne

101 Westbourne Park Villas, W2 (0171 221 1332). Royal Oak or Westbourne Park tube. **Open** 5-11pm Mon; noon-11pm Tue-Fri; 11am-11pm Sat; noon-10.30pm Sun. **Map 1 B5**
Phenomenally popular gastrobar where the good food is matched by the beer selection. By day it's relaxed and civilised; by night the front terrace heaves with Notting Hill's trendiest.

White Horse

1 Parsons Green, SW6 (0171 736 2115). Parsons Green tube. **Open** 11am-11pm Mon-Sat; 11am-10.30pm Sun.
Known locally as the Sloaney Pony, this invariably heaving pub provides a spectacular range of beers (57 bottled varieties, including wheat beers, smoked beer from Bavaria and a few Trappist ales) and at least five real ales on tap.

Wine Gallery

49 Hollywood Road, SW10 (0171 352 7572). Earl's Court tube. **Open** noon-4pm, 7pm-midnight, Mon-Sat; noon-4pm, 7-10.30pm, Sun. **Map 3 C12**
Almost unbelievably, this smart wine bar, with a sun-trap of a patio, sells its wines at retail prices (bottles start at £3.50 and champagne goes for around £14 upwards). You do, though, have to eat to enjoy this unique perk.

West

Albertine

1 Wood Lane, W12 (0181 743 9593). Shepherd's Bush tube. **Open** 11am-11pm Mon-Fri; 6.30-11pm Sat.
A timeless, understated wine bar: battered wood tables, dripping candles stuck into old bottles, and huge platters of wholesome grub. The long and comprehensive wine list is a treasure trove of gems at notably low prices.

Anglesea Arms

35 Wingate Road, W6 (0181 749 1291). Goldhawk Road or Ravenscourt Park tube. **Open** 11am-11pm Mon-Sat; noon-10.30pm Sun.
Locals pack the small, smoke-filled pub, waiting patiently for one of the prized tables in the back room where Dan Evans and his team dish up back-to-basic platefuls of nosh.

The Cow

89 Westbourne Park Road, W11 (0171 221 0021). Westbourne Park tube. **Open** noon-11pm Mon-Sat; noon-10.30pm Sun. **Map 1 B5**
There's more of an Irish look than feel to Tom Conran's tiny local, though the voices heard here are Trustafarian rather than County Cork. Seafood gets top billing in the bar food line-up. There's a separately run restaurant upstairs.

The Dove

19 Upper Mall, W6 (0181 748 5405). Hammersmith tube. **Open** 11am-11pm Mon-Sat; noon-10.30pm Sun.
Three small, low-ceilinged rooms huddle round the tiny central bar of this unspoilt 300-year-old tavern that proudly eschews the paraphernalia of heritage theme pubs. A small terrace at the rear looks out over the Thames.

The Elbow Room

103 Westbourne Grove, W2 (0171 221 5211). Bayswater, Notting Hill Gate or Westbourne Park tube/7, 23, 52 bus. **Open** noon-11pm Mon-Sat; noon-10.30pm Sun. **Map 1 B6**

Shopping & Services

The sharpest fashions, the choicest foodstuffs, the snazziest gifts, the coolest homewares – London has them all.

Many stores in central London are open late one night of the week (usually until 7pm or 8pm). As a rule of thumb, those in the West End (Oxford Street to Covent Garden) stay open late on Thursdays, while Wednesday is late opening in the chichi Chelsea/Knightsbridge/Kensington triangle.

YOUR RIGHTS

Statutory rights protect the consumer, and large or expensive items should come with a guarantee. You're entitled to a refund, replacement or credit note if goods are faulty (always keep the receipt). If you're returning goods for another reason, it's generally up to individual stores whether or not they refund your money. If you have a complaint about how your quibble was dealt with, report the offending trader to the **Trading Standards Department** of the relevant London borough. The **Office of Fair Trading** publishes free leaflets on all aspects of consumer purchase and runs a helpline (0345 224499; 9am-5pm Mon-Fri). The leaflets can also be obtained at **Citizens' Advice Bureaux** (*see page 292*). Staff at CABs should be able to advise you of your rights under the law.

Antiques

For **Bermondsey (New Caledonian) Market** and **Portobello Road Market**, *see page 193.*

Arcades

Admiral Vernon

141-149 Portobello Road, W11 (0171 727 5242). Notting Hill Gate tube. **Open** 5am-5pm Sat. **Credit** varies. **Map 1 A6**
One of London's smartest antiques arcades. Among the concessions you'll find old toys, Doulton pottery, clocks and twentieth-century paintings.

Alfie's Antique Market

13-25 Church Street, NW8 (0171 723 6066). Edgware Road tube/Marylebone tube/rail. **Open** 10am-6pm Tue-Sat. **Credit** varies. **Map 2 E4**
A sprawling four-storey place, aimed mainly at dealers, but with enough variety in type of goods and price that there should be something to suit every pocket.

Antiquarius

131-141 King's Road, SW3 (0171 351 5353). Sloane Square tube/19, 22, 319 bus. **Open** 10am-6pm Mon-Sat. **Credit** varies. **Map 4 F11**
A range of specialist dealers selling bronzes, rugs, ceramics, art nouveau jewellery and much, much more.

Camden Passage

Camden Passage, off Upper Street, N1 (0171 359 0150). Angel tube. **Open** *indoor shops* 10am-5pm Tue, Thur, Fri; 8am-5pm Wed; 9am-5pm Sat; *outdoor stalls* 8am-2pm Wed; 8am-4pm Sat. **Credit** varies. **Map 9 O2**
An antiques-packed enclave, with shops, arcades and, on Wednesday and Saturday, outdoor stalls.

Grays Antique Market & Grays in the Mews

58 Davies Street & 1-7 Davies Mews, W1 (0171 629 7034). Bond Street tube. **Open** 10am-6pm Mon-Fri. **Credit** varies. **Map 5 H6**
Two locations majoring in silverware, jade, jewellery and ancient Roman, Egyptian and oriental artefacts.

London Silver Vaults

Chancery House, 53-64 Chancery Lane, WC2 (0171 242 3844). Chancery Lane tube. **Open** 9am-5.30pm Mon-Fri; 9am-1pm Sat (last admission 10 mins before closing time). **Credit** AmEx, MC, V. **Map 6 M5**
These fascinating subterranean vaults have over 35 retailers offering silver, silver plate and jewellery at prices from £20 to £20,000-plus.

Architectural

LASSCo

St Michael's Church, Mark Street (off Paul Street), EC2 (0171 739 0448). Old Street tube/rail. **Open** 10am-5pm daily. **Credit** AmEx, MC, £TC, V. **Map 10 Q4**
An architectural salvage wonderland, encompassing anything from a Gothic doorway to a coffee machine from the *Queen Mary.*

Furniture & decorative

Baroque & Roll

291 Lillie Road, SW6 (0171 381 5008). Fulham Broadway or Hammersmith tube/11, 74 bus. **Open** 10.30am-5.30pm Mon-Sat.
An eclectic but well-chosen selection of outrageous decorative antiques, sumptuous fabrics and carpets, gilded furniture and delightfully camp bits and bobs.

Fine Art Society

148 New Bond Street, W1 (0171 629 5116).
Bond Street or Green Park tube. **Open** 9.30am-5.30pm
Mon-Fri; 10am-1pm Sat. **Credit** AmEx, JCB, MC, V.
Map 7 H7
Established in 1876, the Fine Art Society sells top quality
artworks, furniture, ceramics and metalwork from the
1870s onwards.

Tower Bridge Antiques

159-161 Tower Bridge Road, SE1 (0171 403 3660).
London Bridge tube/rail/47, 48 bus. **Open** 9am-5pm
Mon-Fri; 10am-6pm Sat; 11am-5pm Sun.
Map 12 R9
Multi-floored warehouse containing a bewilderingly vast
range of antique furniture.

Whiteway & Waldron

305 Munster Road, SW6 (0171 381 3195).
Fulham Broadway or Hammersmith tube/74, 211 bus.
Open 10am-6pm Mon-Fri; 11am-4pm Sat.
Whiteway & Waldron is a dusty Aladdin's Cave of ecclesi-
astica. Church and chapel paraphernalia includes pews,
stained glass, candlesticks and the like.

Glass & ceramics

Beverley

*30 Church Street, NW8 (0171 262 1576). Baker Street
or Edgware Road tube.* **Open** 10.30am-6.30pm Mon-Sat.
Map 2 E4
One of the best dealers in 1920s and 1930s ceramics in
London, featuring the likes of Clarice Cliff, Susie Cooper
and Shelley.

Jonathan Horne

*66C Kensington Church Street, W8 (0171 221 5658).
High Street Kensington or Notting Hill Gate tube.*
Open 9.30am-5.30pm Mon-Fri; by appointment Sat.
Credit AmEx, JCB, MC, £TC, V.
Jonathan Horne specialises in early English ceramics includ-
ing Staffordshire figures, delftware, Wedgwood and Surrey
borderwares.

Mark J West

*Cobb Antiques, 39B High Street, Wimbledon Village,
SW19 (0181 946 2811). Wimbledon tube/rail.*
Open 10am-5.30pm Mon-Sat. **Credit** AmEx, DC, JCB,
MC, V.
Antique glass specialist. Most pieces are eighteenth- or
nineteenth-century, but there are a few Roman examples.
Most of the business comes from selling decanters (there are
around 500 in stock) and glasses.

Metalwork

The House of Steel

*400 Caledonian Road, N1 (0171 607 5889). Caledonian
Road tube/Caledonian Road & Barnsbury rail.*
Open 11am-6pm Mon-Fri; by appointment Sat.
A shrine to antique ironwork and reproduction steel, this
company designs, makes and restores everything from
curtain poles to spiral staircases.

Mirrors & frames

Lacy Gallery

*203 Westbourne Grove, W11 (0171 229 6340). Notting
Hill Gate tube.* **Open** 10am-5pm Tue-Fri; 10am-4pm Sat.
Credit MC, V. **Map 1 B6**
Prices start at around a tenner and rise to about £3,000
at this user-friendly shop.

Textiles

Gallery of Antique Costume & Textiles

*2 Church Street, NW8 (0171 723 9981). Marylebone
tube/rail.* **Open** 10am-5.30pm Mon-Sat. **Credit** AmEx,
MC, £TC, V. **Map 2 E4**
Home to sumptuous antique brocades, appliqués, paisleys,
silks, chenilles, needlepoints, velvets and any other textile
you care to imagine. There's a delectable range of 1920s-
1940s evening wear too.

Toys

Donay Antiques

35 Camden Passage, N1 (0171 359 1880). Angel tube.
Open 8.30am-5pm Wed; 8.30am-5pm Sat; also by
appointment. **Credit** AmEx, MC, £TC, V. **Map 9 O2**
All kinds of toys and games, mainly from the 1840s to the
early twentieth century, including chess sets, inlaid skittle
boards and playing cards.

Twentieth century

John Jesse

*160 Kensington Church Street, W8 (0171 229 0312).
Notting Hill Gate tube.* **Open** 10am-6pm Mon-Fri; 11am-
4pm Sat. **Credit** AmEx, DC, MC, V. **Map 1 B8**
Art nouveau (including Lalique) and art deco pieces, plus
marvellous 1960s jewellery.

Rennies

*13 Rugby Street, WC1 (0171 405 0220). Holborn or
Russell Square tube.* **Open** 10am-6pm Tue-Sat.
Credit MC, V. **Map 6 M4**
Specialising in British artists working as designers from
1920 onwards, Paul and Karen Rennie have assembled a fine
collection of vintage posters, ceramics and Arts and Crafts
furniture plus collectable accessories.

Bookshops

Check out also the paperback-fest of the
Riverside Walk Market (10am-5pm Sat, Sun
and irregular weekdays) on the south bank under
Waterloo Bridge. The big chains have branches all
over London. These are some of their largest out-
ets: **Dillons** (82 Gower Street, WC2; 0171 636
1577), **Books etc** (120 Charing Cross Road, WC2;
0171 379 6838), **Waterstone's** (121-129 Charing
Cross Road, WC2; 0171 434 4291).

General

Blackwell's

*100 Charing Cross Road, WC2 (0171 292 5100).
Tottenham Court Road tube.* **Open** 9.30am-8.30pm
Mon-Sat; noon-6pm Sun. **Credit** AmEx, MC, V.
Map 6 K6
Although primarily an academic bookseller, Blackwell's has
a huge selection of general titles, fiction and non-fiction.

Borders

*203 Oxford Street, W1 (0171 292 1600). Oxford Circus
tube.* **Open** 8am-11pm Mon-Sat; noon-6pm Sun.
Credit AmEx, MC, V. **Map 5 J6**
An exhausting but exhaustive four-floor American-owned
book store (with a music department on the top floor, a café
on the second and a small Paperchase on the ground).
Unsurprisingly, it's particularly strong on American imports.

Compendium

234 Camden High Street, NW1 (0171 485 8944/267 1525). Camden Town or Chalk Farm tube. **Open** 10am-6pm Mon-Sat; noon-6pm Sun. **Credit** MC, £TC, V.

Alternative, beat, surrealist and generally weird stuff in addition to new fiction (home-grown and imported), an excellent selection of poetry, reference books, body art mags and anarchist newspapers. Staff know their stuff. **Branches** are too numerous to list here. Check the telephone directory for your nearest.

Foyles

113-119 Charing Cross Road, WC2 (0171 437 5660). Tottenham Court Road tube. **Open** 9am-6pm Mon-Wed, Fri, Sat; 9am-7pm Thur. **Credit** AmEx, MC, £$TC, V. **Map 6 K6**

The sheer range of titles stocked makes Foyles well worth a visit; paperbacks are irritatingly arranged by publisher.

Specialist

Books for Cooks

4 Blenheim Crescent, W11 (0171 221 1992). Ladbroke Grove tube. **Open** 9.30am-6pm Mon-Sat. **Credit** AmEx, DC, MC, £TC, V.

These small premises hold 8,000 books about food, and a tiny café. Also, cookery demonstrations. Mouth-watering.

Children's Book Centre

237 Kensington High Street, W8 (0171 937 7497). High Street Kensington tube. **Open** 9.30am-6.30pm Mon, Wed, Fri, Sat; 9.30am-6pm Tue; 9.30am-7pm Thur; noon-6pm Sun. **Credit** AmEx, MC, V. **Map 3 A9**

An attractive, well laid-out shop with plenty of room to stroll around. The ground floor stocks reading material, tapes, CD-Roms and videos. In the basement are non-fiction books, board games and toys. If you subscribe to the mailing list you get a 10% discount. The staff are helpful.

Cinema Bookshop

13-14 Great Russell Street, WC1 (0171 637 0206). Tottenham Court Road tube. **Open** 10.30am-5.30pm Mon-Sat. **Credit** JCB, MC, £TC, V. **Map 6 K5**

A huge collection of books (some rare), magazines and stills.

Daunt Books

83-84 Marylebone High Street, W1 (0171 224 2295). Baker Street or Bond Street tube. **Open** 9am-7.30pm Mon-Sat; 11am-5pm Sun. **Credit** MC, £TC, V. **Map 5 G5**

Three floors of (mainly) travel books in an attractive setting. **Branch:** 193 Haverstock Hill, NW3 (0171 794 4006).

Edward Stanford

12-14 Long Acre, WC2 (0171 836 1915). Covent Garden or Leicester Square tube. **Open** 9am-7.30pm Mon, Wed, Thur, Fri; 9.30am-7.30pm Tue; 10am-7pm Sat. **Credit** JCB, MC, £TC, V. **Map 8 L6**

Stanford's is London's best source of travel writing and guides, maps, gazetteers and globes.

Forbidden Planet

71 New Oxford Street, WC1 (0171 836 4179). Tottenham Court Road tube. **Open** 10am-6pm Mon-Wed, Sat; 10am-7pm Thur, Fri. **Credit** AmEx, MC, £TC, V. **Map 6 L5**

A range of comics, mags and books (SF, fantasy, horror).

Gay's the Word

66 Marchmont Street, WC1 (0171 278 7654). Russell Square tube. **Open** 10am-6.30pm Mon-Sat; 2-6pm Sun. **Credit** AmEx, DC, JCB, MC, £TC, V. **Map 6 L4**

London's only gay and lesbian bookshop offers a warm welcome and an impressive selection of fiction and biography.

Grant & Cutler

55-57 Great Marlborough Street, W1 (0171 734 2012). Oxford Circus tube. **Open** 9am-5.30pm Mon-Wed, Fri, Sat; 9am-7pm Thur. **Credit** JCB, MC, £TC, V. **Map 5 J6**

The leading foreign-language bookshop in town.

Murder One

71-73 Charing Cross Road, WC2 (0171 734 3485). Leicester Square tube. **Open** 10am-7pm Mon-Wed; 10am-8pm Thur-Sat. **Credit** AmEx, MC, £TC, V. **Map 8 K6**

Crime, SF, fantasy and horror, plus – rather oddly – romance.

Samuel French Theatre Bookshop

52 Fitzroy Street, W1 (0171 255 4300). Warren Street tube. **Open** 9.30am-5.30pm Mon-Fri; 11am-5pm Sat. **Credit** AmEx, DC, JCB, MC, £TC, V. **Map 5 J4**

French's aims to carry all play scripts written in the English language currently in print, plus theatre-related books.

Serpentine Gallery Bookshop

Serpentine Gallery, Kensington Gardens, W2 (0171 298 1502). Lancaster Gate or South Kensington tube. **Open** 10am-6pm daily. **Credit** AmEx, JCB, MC, TC, V. **Map 5 J4**

From Adorno to Zizek, the SG carries the most comprehensive stock of art and cultural theory books in central London. Its range of US university publications, SG's exhibition catalogues and artist monographs is breathtaking.

Silver Moon Women's Bookshop

64-68 Charing Cross Road, WC2 (0171 836 7906). Leicester Square tube. **Open** 10am-6.30pm Mon-Wed, Fri, Sat; 10am-8pm Thur; noon-6pm Sun. **Credit** AmEx, MC, £TC, V. **Map 8 K6**

A selection of fiction by women writers, plus biographies and non-fiction. The lesbian section is in the basement.

Sportspages

Caxton Walk, 94-96 Charing Cross Road, WC2 (0171 240 9604). Leicester Square tube. **Open** 9.30am-7pm Mon-Sat. **Credit** AmEx, DC, MC, £TC, V. **Map 8 K6**

Books on sport, fanzines, magazines and videos.

Talking Bookshop

11 Wigmore Street, W1 (0171 491 4117). Bond Street tube. **Open** 9.30am-5.30pm Mon-Fri; 10am-5pm Sat. **Credit** MC, V. **Map 5 G6**

The world's largest selection of spoken-word CDs and tapes.

Zwemmer Media Arts

80 Charing Cross Road, WC2 (0171 240 4157). Leicester Square tube. **Open** 10am-6.30pm Mon-Fri; 10am-6pm Sat. **Credit** AmEx, DC, MC, £TC, V. **Map 8 K6**

Photography and cinema are the specialisations at this charming link in the Zwemmer chain of specialist shops. **Branches** are too numerous to list here. Check the telephone directory for your nearest.

Second-hand/antiquarian

Bertram Rota

31 Long Acre (1st floor), WC2 (0171 836 0723). Covent Garden tube. **Open** 9.30am-5.30pm Mon-Fri (appointment recommended). **Credit** MC, £TC, V. **Map 6 L6**

Established in 1923, Bertram Rota offers a wide selection of first editions from the 1890s to the present day.

Fisher & Sperr

46 Highgate High Street, N6 (0181 340 7244). Highgate tube/214, 271 bus. **Open** 10am-5pm Mon-Sat. **Credit** MC, £TC, V.

Thousands of second-hand titles on four floors, including an excellent selection of books about London.

Maggs Brothers

50 Berkeley Square, W1 (0171 493 7160). Green Park tube. **Open** 9.30am-5pm Mon-Fri. **Credit** MC, V. **Map 7 H7**
London's most august antiquarian bookshop sells pre-twentieth-century books on travel, literature, natural history, early printing, bibliography and pre-1950 first editions.

Skoob

15 Sicilian Avenue, WC1 (0171 404 3063). Holborn tube. **Open** 10.30am-6.30pm Mon-Sat. **Credit** AmEx, JCB, MC, V. **Map 6 L5**
Impeccably well-ordered stock of non-fiction books on arts and sciences. A favourite with students.

Ulysses

40 Museum Street, WC1 (0171 831 1600/ulyssesbooks@compuserve.com). Tottenham Court Road tube. **Open** 10.30am-6pm Mon-Sat; noon-6pm Sun. **Credit** AmEx, DC, JCB, MC, £TC, V. **Map 6 L5**
This smart shop has probably the biggest collection of modern first editions in London.
Website: www.antiquarian.com/ulysses

Unsworths Bookseller

12 Bloomsbury Street, WC1 (0171 436 9836). Tottenham Court Road tube. **Open** 10am-8pm Mon-Sat; noon-8pm Sun. **Credit** AmEx, DC, JCB, MC, £TC, V. **Map 6 K5**
A roomy, modern interior holds remainders and out-of-print books as well as antiquarian stock. The second-hand section is always worth a good browse.

Woburn Book Shop

10 Woburn Walk, WC1 (0171 388 7278). Russell Square tube/Euston tube/rail. **Open** 11am-6pm Mon-Fri; 11am-5pm Sat. **Credit** JCB, MC, £TC, V. **Map 6 K3**
One of the most fascinating bookshops in London run by affable owners with a special interest in anarchist and socialist subjects.

Newsagents

A Moroni & Son

68 Old Compton Street, W1 (0171 437 2847). Piccadilly Circus tube. **Open** 7.30am-7pm Mon; 7.30am-9pm Tue-Sat; 8am-6pm Sun. **Map 6 K6**
A splendid, up-to-date array of international titles.
Branch: 308 Regent Street, W1 (0171 580 3835).

Electronics

Computers

One of the best stockists of computer games is **Virgin Megastore** (*see page 213*).

Carrera Technology

209-212 Tottenham Court Road, W1 (0171 830 0486). Goodge Street or Tottenham Court Road tube. **Open** 9am-6pm Mon-Wed, Fri; 9am-7pm Thur; 10am-5pm Sat. **Credit** AmEx, MC, £TC, V. **Map 6 K5**
An award-winning company that builds and sells its own personal computers.

Computer Exchange

219 Tottenham Court Road, W1 (0171 916 3110). Goodge Street tube. **Open** 10am-7pm Mon-Sat; 11.30am-5.30pm Sun. **Credit** AmEx, MC, £TC, V. **Map 6 K5**

The leading second-hand computer dealer in the West End for PCs. Computer exchange is also known for its range of reasonably current second-hand software. Discounts are good; staff are well informed.

Gultronics

223 & 217-218 Tottenham Court Road, W1 (0171 637 1619/mail order 0171 436 3131). Goodge Street or Tottenham Court Road tube. **Open** 9am-6pm Mon-Wed, Fri, Sat; 9am-7pm Thur. **Credit** AmEx, MC, V. **Map 6 K5**
From electric typewriters to fax machines and PCs, Gultronics stocks the lot, although laptops are a speciality. The showroom at no.223 is piled high with heavily discounted goods. Special offers change weekly.
Branch: 334 Edgware Road, W2 (0171 723 0916).

Hi-fi

The Cornflake Shop

37 Windmill Street, W1 (0171 631 0472). Goodge Street tube. **Open** 10am-6pm Tue, Wed, Fri, Sat; 10am-7pm Thur. **Credit** AmEx, MC, £TC, V. **Map 6 K5**
Mainly for buffs prepared to pay serious money for a system, but also stuff for separates fans on a budget.

Hi-Fi Experience

227 Tottenham Court Road, W1 (0171 580 3535). Tottenham Court Road tube. **Open** 10am-7pm Mon-Fri; 9am-6pm Sat. **Credit** AmEx, DC, £TC, V. **Map 6 K5**
An excellent range of quality stock, eight demo rooms and expert staff.

Richer Sounds

2 London Bridge Walk, SE1 (0171 403 1201). London Bridge tube/rail. **Open** noon-7pm Mon-Fri; 10am-5pm Sat. **Credit** MC, V. **Map 12 Q8**
Wide range of hi-fi separates at low prices, with a demo room. Some branches are open on Sunday.
Branches are too numerous to list here. Check the telephone directory for your nearest.

Photography

Jessop

63-69 New Oxford Street, WC1 (0171 240 6077). Tottenham Court Road tube. **Open** 9am-6pm Mon-Wed, Sat; 9am-8pm Thur; 9am-7pm Fri; 11am-5pm Sun. **Credit** AmEx, DC, MC, TC, V. **Map 6 L5**
This recently revamped store probably deserves its self-appointed status as 'World Photo Centre'. From 35mm hardware to digital imaging to in-house developing to second-hand gear: it's all here.
Branch: 11 Frognal Parade, NW3 (0171 794 8786).

Keith Johnson & Pelling

93-103 Drummond Street, NW1 (0171 380 1144). Euston tube/rail. **Open** 9am-5.30pm Mon-Fri. **Credit** AmEx, DC, MC, V. **Map 5 J3**
The biggest and best-known photographic business in town catering to every photographic need (pro and amateur).
Branches: 175 Wardour Street, W1 (0171 439 8811); Eagle Wharf Studios, 49 Eagle Wharf Road, N1 (0171 253 5174); 10 Heathmans Road, SW6 (0171 384 3270).

Sendean

1st floor, 105-109 Oxford Street, W1 (0171 439 8418/9419). Oxford Circus or Tottenham Court Road tube. **Open** 9.30am-5.30pm Mon-Thur; 9.30am-6pm Fri. **Credit** AmEx, MC, V. **Map 5 J6**
A friendly, family-run business that buys cameras in all conditions and offers a reliable repair service.

Snappy Snaps
23 Garrick Street, WC2 (0171 836 3040). Leicester Square tube. **Open** 8.30am-6pm Mon-Fri; noon-5pm Sat. **Map 8 L7**
Probably the best of the high-street film processing chains. **Branches** are too numerous to list here. Check the telephone directory for your nearest.

Fashion
Budget
Oxford Street is a good hunting ground for bargain seekers. Try **New Look** (nos.175 & 309; 0171 499 8497) for glitzy streetwear, **Tribe** (nos.67-71; 0171 494 1798) for natty lads' kit or **Jeffrey Rogers** (Unit G6, The Plaza, 120 Oxford Street; 0171 580 5545) for decent womenswear.

Amazon
1-22 Kensington Church Street, W8 (no phone). High Street Kensington tube. **Open** 10am Mon-Wed, Fri; 10am-7pm Thur; 9am-6pm Sat; noon-5pm Sun. **Credit** AmEx, DC, MC, V. **Map 1 B8**
Six adjoining shops offering cut-price designerwear from the likes of Nicole Farhi, Jasper Conran and Calvin Klein.

H&M
261-271 Regent Street, W1 (0171 493 4004). Oxford Circus tube. **Open** 10am-7pm Mon-Wed, Sat; 10am-8pm Thur, Fri; noon-6pm Sun. **Credit** AmEx, MC, £TC, V. **Map 7 J7**
The Swedish chain's range of well-priced womenswear seems invested with more glamour than its rivals. The kid's clothes and ranges for bigger women are worth a look too. **Branches** are too numerous to list here. Check the telephone directory for your nearest.

Miss Selfridge
40 Duke Street, W1 (0171 318 3833). Bond Street tube. **Open** 9.30am-7pm Mon-Wed, Sat; 9.30am-8pm Thur, Fri; noon-6pm Sun. **Credit** AmEx, JCB, £TC, V. **Map 5 G6**
Disposable fashion at disposable prices, primarily for teens, with a slant towards clubwear. Funky cosmetics as well. **Branches** are too numerous to list here. Check the telephone directory for your nearest.

Pink Soda
22 Eastcastle Street, W1 (0171 636 9001). Oxford Circus tube. **Open** 10am-5pm Mon-Fri. **Map 5 J6**
This tiny shop is a mecca for fashion sophisticates and extroverts on a budget. Great finger-on-the-pulse gear for gals.

Top Shop/Top Man
214 Oxford Street, W1 (0171 636 7700). Oxford Circus tube. **Open** 10am-7pm Mon-Wed, Fri, Sat; noon-6pm Sun. **Credit** AmEx, DC, MC, £TC, V. **Map 5 J6**
Following a huge revamp, a bigger, brighter and noisier Top Shop/Top Man opened in summer 1998. Rails of cheap, fashion-conscious clothes and shoes, some by top designers. **Branches** are too numerous to list here. Check the telephone directory for your nearest.

Children
See also page 214 **Cheeky Monkey** *and* **Daisy & Tom**.

Baby Gap/Gap Kids
146-148 Regent Street, W1 (0171 287 5095). Oxford Circus or Piccadilly Circus tube. **Open** 9.30am-7.30pm
Mon-Wed, Fri; 9.30am-8pm Thur; 9am-7pm Sat; noon-6pm Sun. **Credit** AmEx, MC, V. **Map 7 J7**
The clothes are spot-on, if a little pricey. Check the sale rail. **Branches** are too numerous to list here. Check the telephone directory for your nearest.

Trotters
34 King's Road, SW3 (0171 259 9620). Sloane Square tube. **Open** 9am-6.30pm Mon-Tue, Thur-Sat; 9am-7pm Wed; 10am-6pm Sun. **Credit** AmEx, MC, V.
Great, trendy clothes for young fashion victims and admirably child-friendly service. There's also a hairdresser's and a children's library on site.
Branch: 127 Kensington High Street, W8 (0171 937 9373).

Designer
Between them, Bond Street (New and Old) and Sloane Street contain just about every international designer name on the planet. If you want a wide range of labels under one roof, try **Harvey Nichols**, **Harrods** or **Liberty** (*see page 202-3*).

Agnès B
35-36 Floral Street, WC2 (0171 379 1992). Covent Garden tube. **Open** 10.30am-6.30pm Mon-Wed, Fri, Sat; 10.30am-7pm Thur; noon-5pm Sun. **Credit** MC, £TC, V. **Map 8 L6**
Agnès B has been selling the same trimmed T-shirts since she set up in business in 1973. Ranges for men, women and children just walk out of the stores.
Branches: 111 Fulham Road, SW3 (0171 225 3477); 235 Westbourne Grove, W11 (0171 792 1947); 58-62 Heath Street, NW3 (0171 431 1995).

Antoni & Alison
43 Rosebery Avenue, EC1 (0171 833 2002). Farringdon tube/rail. **Open** 10.30am-6.30pm Mon-Fri; 11am-6pm Sat. **Credit** MC, V. **Map 9 N4**
Renowned for their vacuum-packed T-shirts, A&A have just opened their first, typically idiosyncratic shop. There's distinctive underwear and groovy disco gear too. *See picture p205.*

Betty Jackson
311 Brompton Road, SW3 (0171 589 7884). South Kensington tube. **Open** 10am-6.30pm Mon-Fri; 10am-6pm Sat; noon-5pm Sun. **Credit** AmEx, MC, £TC, V. **Map 4 E10**
Unstructured, unrestrictive clothing for women. Drawstring trousers are a long-standing favourite.

Browns
23-27 South Molton Street, W1 (0171 491 7833). Bond Street tube. **Open** 10am-6.30pm Mon-Wed, Fri, Sat; 10am-7pm Thur. **Credit** AmEx, DC, JCB, MC, £$TC, V. **Map 5 H6**
Owner Joan Bernstein is an institution, as is her shop. Established designers such as Dries Van Noten sit alongside more recent finds like Arika Isogawa in the growing fashion empire that trails down South Molton Street. The Browns Focus store at no.38 sells more affordable unisex ranges. A Browns homestore was launched in 1998.

Comme des Garçons
59 Brook Street, W1 (0171 493 1258). Bond Street tube. **Open** 10am-6pm Mon-Wed, Fri, Sat; 10am-7pm Thur. **Credit** AmEx, DC, JCB, MC, £$TC, V. **Map 5 H6**
CdG designer Rei Kawakubo was one of the Japanese who changed the fashion canvas in the early 1980s by challenging our ideas about shape, fabric and tailoring. Her diffusion line is more financially accessible, her fragrance a corker.

Donna Karan

19 New Bond Street, W1 (0171 495 3100). Bond Street or Green Park tube. **Open** 10am-6pm Mon-Wed, Fri, Sat; 10am-7pm Thur. **Credit** AmEx, DC, JCB, MC, V. **Map 7 J7**

This is where you'll find just about the most glamorous understatements on the planet. Donna Karan's mainline collections are displayed over three floors and are the last word in classic, fluid formalwear (albeit at terrifying prices). The younger diffusion line is housed over the road at **DKNY** (27 Old Bond Street, W1; 0171 499 8089).

Fenwick

63 New Bond Street, W1 (0171 629 9161). Bond Street tube. **Open** 9.30am-6pm Mon-Wed, Fri, Sat; 9.30am-7.30pm Thur. **Credit** AmEx, JCB, MC, £$TC, V. **Map 5 H6**

The least intimidating of the high-fashion clothes shops in Bond Street, Fenwick has three floors of women's clothes and accessories, from Oasis to Joseph. The men's clothes in the basement are all upmarket gear.

Issey Miyake

270 Brompton Road, SW1 (0171 581 3760). South Kensington tube. **Open** 10am-6pm Mon-Sat; 1-5pm Sun. **Credit** AmEx, DC, JCB, MC, £TC, V. **Map 4 E9**

Thirty years in the biz, and fabrics remain the key to Japanese designer Miyake's creations. His trademark pleats are so popular that they've spawned their own shop. **Branch**: **Pleats Please** 20 Brook Street, W1 (0171 495 2306).

Jean-Paul Gaultier

Galerie Gaultier, 171-175 Draycott Avenue, SW3 (0171 584 4648). South Kensington tube. **Open** 10.30am-6.30pm Mon-Sat. **Credit** AmEx, DC, JCB, MC, £TC, V. **Map 4 E10**

A well-designed shop, carrying a good range of Gaultier's more wearable stuff as well as the off-the-wall (anyone for a skirt, gents?).

Jones

13 & 15 Floral Street, WC2 (0171 379 4299). Covent Garden tube. **Open** 10am-6.30pm Mon-Sat; 1-5pm Sun. **Credit** AmEx, DC, JCB, MC, £$TC, V. **Map 8 L6**

A pleasant, well-stocked shop. Alexander McQueen and W&LT are significant new additions to the womenswear. Menswear includes Thierry Mugler and Bikkembergs.

Joseph

23 Old Bond Street, W1 (0171 629 3713). Bond Street tube. **Open** 10am-6.30pm Mon-Wed, Fri, Sat; 10am-7pm Thur. **Credit** AmEx, DC, JCB, MC, £$TC, V. **Map 7 J7**

Joseph Ettedgui has one of the keenest fashion senses around and an almost magical ability to read the future. This store focuses on his own lines: knitwear, suits, jackets and jeans for men and women. The sale shop is at 53 King's Road, SW3 (0171 730 7562).

Branches are too numerous to list here. Check the telephone directory for your nearest.

Katharine Hamnett

20 Sloane Street, SW1 (0171 823 1002). Knightsbridge tube. **Open** 10am-6.30pm Mon, Tue, Thur, Fri; 10am-7pm Wed; 10am-6pm Sat. **Credit** AmEx, DC, JCB, MC, £TC, V. **Map 4 F9**

Environmental campaigner Hamnett returned to the catwalks to much acclaim. Her latest designs are full of trailer-trash chutzpah.

MaxMara

32 Sloane Street, SW1 (0171 235 7941). Knightsbridge tube. **Open** 10am-6pm Mon, Tue, Thur-Sat; 10am-7pm Wed. **Credit** AmEx, DC, JCB, MC, £TC, V. **Map 4 F9**

Upmarket continental womenswear including the perfect work suit. Designer wear, but without all the fuss.
Branch: 153 New Bond Street, W1 (0171 491 4748).

Nicole Farhi

158 New Bond Street, W1 (0171 499 8368). Bond Street tube. **Open** 10am-6pm Mon-Wed, Fri, Sat; 10am-7pm Thur. **Credit** AmEx, DC, JCB, MC, £TC, V. **Map 5 H6**

Comfortable, trend-related officewear for men (at 55-56 Long Acre, WC2; 0171 240 5240) and women.
Branches are too numerous to list here. Check the telephone directory for your nearest.

Paul Smith

40-44 Floral Street, WC2 (0171 379 7133). Covent Garden tube. **Open** 10.30am-6.30pm Mon-Wed, Fri; 10.30am-7pm Thur; 10am-6.30pm Sat. **Credit** AmEx, DC, JCB, MC, £TC, V. **Map 8 L6**

Arguably the most commercially successful of all British designers, Paul Smith is renowned for menswear (classics with a twist – the suits are particularly fine). These linked shops also stock accessories, children's clothes and womenswear. The Avery Row branch is the sale shop.
Branch: 23 Avery Row, W1 (0171 493 1287); 122 Kensington Park Road, W11 (0171 727 3553); 84-86 Sloane Avenue, SW3 (0171 589 9139).

Pellicano

63 South Molton Street, W1 (0171 629 2205). Bond Street tube. **Open** 10am-6pm Mon-Wed, Fri, Sat; 10am-7pm Thur. **Credit** AmEx, DC, JCB, MC, £$TC, V. **Map 5 H6**

A daunting, starkly designed shop, but with a great range of designers, new and old.

Vexed Generation

3 Berwick Street, W1 (0171 287 6224). Oxford Circus tube. **Open** 11.30am-6.30pm Mon-Sat. **Credit** AmEx, JCB, MC, £TC, V. **Map 5 J6**

VG's extraordinary designs for hip youngsters have made velcro fashionable again.

Vivienne Westwood

6 Davies Street, W1 (0171 629 3757). Bond Street tube. **Open** 10am-6pm Mon-Wed, Fri, Sat; 10am-7pm Thur. **Credit** AmEx, DC, JCB, MC, £$TC, V. **Map 5 H6**

Head to Davies Street for 'Gold Label' couture, or World's End for cheaper, casual items, and Conduit Street for the 'Red Label' (ready-to-wear women's clothes) and 'Man' menswear.
Branches: **World's End** 430 King's Road, SW10 (0171 352 6551); 44 Conduit Street, W1 (0171 439 1109).

Whistles

12-14 St Christopher's Place, W1 (0171 487 4484). Bond Street tube. **Open** 10am-6pm Mon-Wed, Fri, Sat; 10am-7pm Thur. **Credit** AmEx, DC, JCB, MC, £$TC, V. **Map 5 H6**

Lucille Lewin is one of the most significant fashion retailers in town. Always *à la mode*. Check out stuff by fashion's latest design *wunderkind* Jeremy Scott.
Branches are too numerous to list here. Check the telephone directory for your nearest.

Fetish

Regulation

17A St Alban's Place, N1 (0171 226 0665). Angel tube. **Open** 10.30am-6.30pm Mon-Sat; noon-5pm Sun. **Credit** AmEx, MC, JCB, £TC, V. **Map 9 O2**

The best supplier of fetish gear and industrial clothing (diving suits, fireproof suits) in London.

Market forces

There was a time when every London borough had its local street market – and was, to some degree, defined by it. Alas, many local markets are under threat from uncaring councils, and supermarket competition. Listed here are some of the biggest and best of those that remain.

General

Brick Lane Market

Brick Lane (north of railway bridge), Cygnet Street & Sclater Street, E1; Bacon Street, Cheshire Street & Chilton Street, E2. Aldgate East or Shoreditch tube or Liverpool Street tube/rail. **Open** 8am-1pm Sun.
Map 10 S5
A sprawling East End institution, which kicks off at 6am with down-at-heel traders on Bethnal Green Road offering various old tat. At 7.30am things get under way on Sclater Street, given over to pet foods, provisions, electrical goods and tools. Off Cygnet Street, new bicycles, meat, fruit and vegetables and frozen food are up for grabs. Brick Lane itself is where to find leather jackets, cheap jewellery, a fruit and veg stall and a real East End relic, a jellied eel stand. Around Cheshire Street are stalls selling cheap cassettes and household goods, lock-ups full of junk, and, further up, an indoor warehouse packed with second-hand goods, collectibles and a discount book stall.

Brixton Market

Electric Avenue, Pope's Road & Brixton Station Road, SW9. Brixton tube/rail. **Open** 8am-6pm Mon, Tue, Thur-Sat; 8am-3pm Wed.
Europe's largest collection of Afro-Caribbean foodstuffs is up for grabs at Brixton: everything from calves' heads, goat meat and pigs' tails to yams, plantain and breadfruit. Head for Electric Avenue or the slightly frayed charm of the Granville and Market Row arcades for the best of the provisions, including fabulous fish rarely seen in Britain. But there's much more than food at this fascinating market – reggae throbs out from the record stalls; herbs and potions, incense and religious tracts are on offer; and the eastern stretch of Brixton Station Road has second-hand clothes and bric-a-brac.

Camden Market

(0171 284 2084). **Camden Market open** 9am-5.30pm Thur-Sun. **Camden Lock Market open** 10am-6pm Sat, Sun (indoor stalls 10am-6pm Tue-Sun). **Stables Market open** 8am-6pm Sat, Sun. **Camden Canal Market open** 10am-6pm Sat, Sun. **Electric Market open** 9am-5.30pm Sun. **All** *Camden Town tube.*
Now London's fourth biggest tourist attraction, Camden Market has outposts in every bit of space on and off Chalk Farm Road between Camden Town tube and Hawley Street. First stop out of the tube, and just south of the junction with Dewsbury Terrace, is the Electric Ballroom, with its laundered second-hand fashions. There are more clothes, new and second-hand, around Buck Street (this is 'Camden Market' proper). The Lock – a cobbled courtyard leading to the canal – is where the market started, and it still attracts the most impenetrable crowds. Handmade crafts, hippyish clothes and vegetarian fast-food stalls are the highlights. Antiques, pine furniture, second-hand books, records and more clothes occupy the area off Chalk Farm Road. Come

early if you want to avoid the crush, but there's such an enormous variety of stuff – and people – to look at, you can easily end up spending the whole day. For a map of the market and further details of the best places to go for specific purchases, *see p77*.

Greenwich Market

Antiques market *Greenwich High Road, SE10.* **Open** 9.30am-5pm Thur. **Bosun's Yard** *59 Greenwich Church Street, SE10.* **Open** 9am-5pm Sat, Sun. **Central market** *off Stockwell Street, opposite Hotel Ibis, SE10.* **Open** *outdoor* 7am-6pm Sat; 7am-6pm Sat, Sun. *Indoor* 10am-5pm Fri, Sat; 10am-6pm Sun. **Crafts market** *College Approach, SE10.* **Open** 9.30am-5pm Fri-Sun. **Flea market** *Thames Street, SE10.* **Open** 8am-4pm Sun. **Food market** *off Stockwell Street, opposite Hotel Ibis, SE10.* **Open** 10am-4pm Sat. **All** *Greenwich rail.*
In the main covered Greenwich Market there are around 100 stalls selling handmade goods – some attractive, some ill-conceived. Typical stalls offer jumpers, pictures, coloured glass, sculpture, pottery, jewellery, toys, greeting cards, hand-painted ties and scarves. The smaller Bosun's Yard Market until recently offered a more classy range but has been disappointing of late. The tatty Village Market has mainly second-hand goods, especially jeans, leather jackets, books and furniture. In between the Village and the Greenwich Markets there is a collection of fast-food stalls offering Indian, Thai, falafel, beef burgers, crêpes and doughnuts.

Leather Lane Market

Leather Lane, EC1. Chancery Lane tube.
Open 10.30am-2pm Mon-Fri. **Map 9 N5**
This long-standing, and still thriving, street market is at

its busiest at lunchtime, when local office workers peruse the stalls while munching on grub from the Lane's caffs. Expect to find cheap clothing, household goods, bargain magazines, suspiciously cheap videos, and fruit and veg.

Petticoat Lane Market

Middlesex Street, Goulston Street, New Goulston Street, Toynbee Street, Wentworth Street, Bell Lane, Cobb Street, Leyden Street, Strype Street, Old Castle Street, Cutler Street, E1. Liverpool Street tube/rail. **Open** 9am-2pm Sun (Wentworth Street also open 10am-2.30pm Mon-Fri). **Map 12 R6**
Coachloads of tourists and bargain seekers cause pedestrian gridlock here every Sunday, making it hard to take full advantage of the best range of budget clothes and shoes in London. The top end of the market, near Aldgate East tube, has a large area devoted to leather jackets. However, prices are rarely shown, so a bit of haggling may be in order (especially if you're paying cash).

Portobello Road Market

Portobello Road, W10, W11; Golborne Road, W10. Ladbroke Grove, Notting Hill Gate or Westbourne Park tube. **Open** *Antiques* 4am-6pm Sat. *General market* 8am-6pm Mon-Wed; 9am-1pm Thur; 7am-7pm Fri, Sat. *Organic market* 11am-6pm Thur. *Clothes & bric-a-brac* 7am-4pm Fri; 8am-5pm Sat; 9am-4pm Sun. *Golborne Road market* 9am-5pm Mon-Sat. **Map 1 A6**
This is really several markets rolled into one: the top end is of most interest to antiques buffs, with more than 2,000 traders offering *objets*, jewellery, coins and medals, paintings, silverware and other collectibles. Further down the hill is a fruit and veg market (Mon-Sat). Prices are generally low. The next change comes under the Westway – food gives way to trendy clothes, jewellery, records and books. From here up to Golborne Road, it's increasingly run-down, though still worth a look for bargains.

Ridley Road Market

Ridley Road, E8. Dalston Kingsland rail/38, 149, 243 bus. **Open** 8.30am-6pm Mon-Sat.
Come for the Cockney fruit and veg sellers, Ridley Bagel Bakery, South Asian halal meat traders, the smoked salmon kiosk and wooden shacks full of Afro-Caribbean produce.

Walthamstow Market

Walthamstow High Street, E17. Walthamstow Central tube/rail. **Open** 8am-6pm Mon-Sat.
Walthamstow's answer to Petticoat Lane claims to be Europe's longest daily street market, with 450 stalls selling cheap clothing, food and household bits and bobs.

Antiques

See also above **Camden, Greenwich** *and* **Portobello Road markets.**

Bermondsey (New Caledonian) Market

Bermondsey Square, SE1. Borough tube/London Bridge tube/rail. **Open** 5am-2pm Fri (starts closing around noon). **Map 12 Q10**
The quality is high, attracting dealers from all over the South-East, but most of the good stuff has gone by 9am.

Crafts

Apple Market

North Hall, Covent Garden Market, WC2 (0171 836 9136). Covent Garden tube. **Open** 9am-7pm Mon; 10.30am-7pm Tue-Sun. **Map 7 L8**
A good range of British arts and crafts (including

special commissions) are the mainstay of the Apple Market. On Mondays the stalls are given over to antiques and quality collectables. The separately-run **Jubilee Market** in Jubilee Hall on the south side of Covent Garden Piazza is only interesting on Mondays when the usual tourist tosh is replaced by jewellery, coins, medials, ornaments and the like.

St James's Crafts Market

courtyard of St James's Church, 197 Piccadilly, W1. Green Park or Piccadilly Circus tube. **Open** *antiques* 10am-6pm Tue; *general* 10am-6pm Wed-Sat. **Map 7 J7**
Situated in a churchyard, this is the most picturesque of London markets. Unfortunately, a lot of the stuff on display is geared to tourists from nearby hotels – Fairisle sweaters, tartan shawls, Diana mugs and the like. More interesting are arty pictures of London and miniature art.

Flowers

Columbia Road Flower Market

Columbia Road (between Gosset Street & the Royal Oak pub), E2. Old Street tube/rail/26, 48, 55 bus. **Open** 8am-1pm Sun. **Map 10 S3**
Without question the prettiest street market in town. Flowers, shrubs, bedding plants and other horticultural delights spread in all directions. Shops lining the road stock garden accessories. *See picture p207.*

Fruit & veg

Berwick Street Market

Berwick Street & Rupert Street, W1. Leicester Square or Piccadilly Circus tube. **Open** 8am-6pm Mon-Sat. **Map 5 J6**
The best and cheapest selection of fruit and veg in central London, but Berwick Street Market is not what it used to be: Westminster Council has cut the number of pitches in half. However, there are also still good cheese, fish, bread, and herb and spices stalls plus some household goods and fabrics.

Leadenhall Market

Whittington Avenue, off Gracechurch Street, EC3. Monument tube/Bank tube/DLR. **Open** 7am-4pm Mon-Fri. **Map 12 Q7**
City boys and girls come to this beautiful, ancient and recently tarted-up market for its classy butchers and fishmonger's, wine bars and chocolate shops. There are few stalls as such, just shops with open store fronts. One of the best attractions is a shoe shine stall, which, for £2.50, will add a gloss to leather you never thought possible. *See also p39.*

Organic

Spitalfields Market

Commercial Street (between Lamb & Brushfield Streets), E1 (0171 247 6590). Liverpool Street tube/rail. **Open** *Organic market* 10am-5pm Fri, Sun. *General market* 11am-3pm Mon-Fri; 9.30am-5.30pm Sun. **Map 10 R5**
Crafts and antiques stalls are set up through the week, but it's on Friday and (particularly) Sunday that the market comes alive with a dozen or so organic producers selling relishes, pickles, herbs and spices, breads and cakes, and fruit and vegetables. The food court offers an excellent range of fastish foods from around the world at low prices.

Formalwear

Moss Bros
88 Regent Street, W1 (0171 494 0666). Oxford Circus or Piccadilly Circus tube. **Open** 9am-6pm Mon-Wed, Fri; 9am-7pm Thur, Sat; 11am-5pm Sun. **Credit** AmEx, DC, JCB, MC, £$TC, V. **Map 7 J7**
This shop and the Covent Garden branch have the widest selection, but all Moss Bros stores have long been famed for their hire services.
Branches are too numerous to list here. Check the telephone directory for your nearest.

Mid-range

Anvers
193-195 Brompton Road, SE3 (0171 581 9787). Knightsbridge tube. **Open** 10am-7pm Mon-Fri; 9.30am-7pm Sat; noon-5pm Sun. **Credit** AmEx, MC, £$TC, V. **Map 4 E9**
This Belgian company provide classically understated clothing for women of all ages.

Egg
36 Kinnerton Street, SW1 (0171 235 9315). Hyde Park Corner or Knightsbridge tube. **Open** 10am-6pm Tue-Sat. **Credit** AmEx, MC, £TC, V. **Map 7 G9**
Pricey, elegant clothing and beautiful accessories based largely on Chinese and Indian designs. A strange and seductive shop.

French Connection
99-103 Long Acre, WC2 (0171 379 6560). Covent Garden tube. **Open** 10am-7pm Mon-Wed, Fri, Sat; 11am-8pm Thur; noon-6pm Sun. **Credit** AmEx, DC, MC, £TC, V. **Map 8 L6**
A massive clothing store, with men's and women's ranges, toiletries and a café. Understated hip is the current look.
Branches are too numerous to list here. Check the telephone directory for your nearest.

Gap
30-31 Long Acre, WC2 (0171 379 0779). Covent Garden tube. **Open** 10am-8pm Mon-Sat; noon-6pm Sun. **Credit** AmEx, JCB, MC, £TC, V. **Map 8 L6**
Nothing to thrill, perhaps, but a reliable first stop for nicely priced casuals.
Branches are too numerous to list here. Check the telephone directory for your nearest.

Hackett
137-138 Sloane Street, SW1 (0171 730 3331). Sloane Square tube. **Open** 9.30am-6pm Mon, Tue, Thur-Sat; 9.30am-7pm Wed. **Credit** AmEx, DC, JCB, MC, £TC, V. **Map 4 F10**
This huge emporium is the place to come for classic, but not po-faced English tailoring. In the Jermyn Street branch (no.87) Sloane meets Mod.
Branches are too numerous to list here. Check the telephone directory for your nearest.

Hobbs
Unit 17, Covent Garden Piazza, WC2 (0171 836 9168). Covent Garden tube. **Open** 10.30am-7pm Mon, Wed, Fri, Sat; 11am-7pm Tue; 10.30am-7.30pm Thur; noon-5pm Sun. **Credit** AmEx, DC, JCB, MC, £TC, V. **Map 8 L7**
Unadventurous but classically sleek and reliable staples and workwear are sold at this womenswear retailer. There's a range of shoes too. Indian influences are currently in.
Branches are too numerous to list here. Check the telephone directory for your nearest.

Jane Norman
262 Oxford Street, W1 (0171 499 7454). Oxford Circus tube. **Open** 10am-7pm Mon-Wed, Fri; 10am-8pm Thur; 9.30am-7pm Sat; noon-6pm Sun. **Credit** AmEx, JCB, MC, £TC, V. **Map 5 H6**
Proving that polyster and acrylic really are here to stay, Jane Norman sells mix 'n' match separates for twentysomethings. Especially good for knock 'em dead party gear, though perhaps not the best choice for curvier women.
Branches are too numerous to list here. Check the telephone directory for your nearest.

Jigsaw
126-127 New Bond Street, W1 (0171 491 4484). Bond Street tube. **Open** 10am-6.30pm Mon-Wed, Fri, Sat; 10am-7pm Thur. **Credit** AmEx, MC, £TC, V. **Map 5 H6**
Fashion meets art at Jigsaw's flagship store, designed by architect John Pawson. Artists exhibit their work amid the slick modern tailoring and quality fabrics. It's women-only at this branch; a large outlet at 9-10 Floral Street (0171 240 5651) in Covent Garden has a groovy range of menswear.
Branches are too numerous to list here. Check the telephone directory for your nearest.

Karen Millen
22-23 James Street, WC2 (0171 836 5355). Covent Garden tube. **Open** 10am-8pm Mon-Fri; 10am-7pm Sat; 11am-6pm Sun. **Credit** AmEx, DC, JCB, MC, £TC, V. **Map 3 B9**
Smart suits and dresses with a twist, with much use made of interesting fabrics and wild colours.
Branches are too numerous to list here. Check the telephone directory for your nearest.

Monsoon
5 James Street, WC2 (0171 379 3623). Covent Garden tube. **Open** 10am-8pm Mon-Sat; 11am-6pm Sun. **Credit** AmEx, DC, JCB, MC, £$TC, V. **Map 8 L6**
Dowdiness has been dispelled and this ever-popular womenswear retailer is jazzing up its act with some warm, romantic, sexy kit.

Oasis
13 James Street, WC2 (0171 240 7445). Covent Garden tube. **Open** 10am-7pm Mon-Wed, Fri, Sat; 10am-8pm Thur; noon-7pm Sun. **Credit** AmEx, DC, JCB, MC, £$TC, V. **Map 8 L6**
Every important theme in the fashion world will eventually be interpreted reasonably well and brought to the high street in a variety of fabrics by Oasis.
Branches are too numerous to list here. Check the telephone directory for your nearest.

Ted Baker
1-2 Langley Court, WC2 (0171 497 8862). Covent Garden tube. **Open** 10am-7pm Mon-Wed, Fri; 10am-6.30pm Sat; 10am-7.30pm Thur; noon-5pm Sun. **Credit** AmEx, DC, MC, £TC, V. **Map 8 L6**
Shirts and ties are the standout items, but all sorts of (men's and women's) clothes are stocked (including the clubby Ted Baker Lite collection).
Branch: 7 Foubert's Place, W1 (0171 437 5619).

Warehouse
96 King's Road, SW3 (0171 584 0069). Sloane Square tube. **Open** 10am-6.30pm Mon, Tue, Thur-Sat; 10am-7pm Wed; noon-6pm Sun. **Credit** AmEx, JCB, MC, £TC, V. **Map 4 F11**
A reliable high-street womenswear store that always responds quickly to new trends.
Branches are too numerous to list here. Check the telephone directory for your nearest.

Second-hand

Blackout II
51 Endell Street, WC2 (0171 240 5006). Covent Garden tube. **Open** 11am-7pm Mon-Fri; 11.30am-6.30pm Sat. **Credit** AmEx, DC, JCB, MC, £TC, V. **Map 6 L6**
Clothes from the 1950s to the 1980s – evening gowns hang alongside flares and ski pants. Tack, trash and glamour in equal measure.

Cornucopia
12 Upper Tachbrook Street, SW1 (0171 828 5752). Victoria tube/rail. **Open** 11am-6pm daily. **Credit** MC, V. **Map 7 J7**
A huge stock of twentieth-century womenswear in varying states of repair, plus a good range of ornamental jewellery.

Lawrence Corner
62-64 Hampstead Road, NW1 (0171 813 1010). Warren Street tube. **Open** 9.30am-6pm Mon-Sat. **Credit** AmEx, DC, MC, V. **Map 5 J3**
This is *the* place for army surplus and militaria.

Origin, Oxfam
26 Ganton Street, W1 (0171 437 7338). Oxford Circus tube. **Open** 11am-6pm Mon-Sat. **Map 5 J6**
The charity shop's range of oldies but goodies is aimed at those 'who are fashion aware with very individual tastes'. **Branches:** 123A King's Road, SW3 (0171 351 7979); 22 Earlham Street, WC2 (0171 836 9666).

Pandora
16-22 Cheval Place, SW7 (0171 589 5289). Knightsbridge tube. **Open** 9.30am-6pm Mon-Sat. **Credit** AmEx, JCB, MC, £TC, V. **Map 4 E9**
Probably London's largest and most famous dress agency, with sections devoted to the likes of Chanel, Armani and other big-name designers.

Steinberg & Tolkien
193 King's Road, SW3 (0171 376 3660). Sloane Square tube/11, 19, 22, 49 bus. **Open** 10.30am-7pm Mon-Sat; noon-6.30pm Sun. **Credit** AmEx, DC, JCB, MC, V. **Map 4 E12**
A massive and highly rated stock of second-hand gear and accessories, with a fine vintage designer clothing section. *See picture p205.*

Street

Boxfresh
2 Shorts Gardens, WC2 (0171 240 4742). Covent Garden tube. **Open** 10.30am-6.30pm Mon-Sat; noon-4.30pm Sun. **Credit** MC, V. **Map 6 L6**
This workware store has grown up and is currently going for understated practicality from labels such as Spiewak and Enyce as well as its own range.

Burro
19A Floral Street, WC2 (0171 240 5120). Covent Garden tube. **Open** 10.30am-6.30pm Mon-Wed, Fri, Sat; 10.30am-7pm Thur; 1-5pm Sun. **Credit** AmEx, MC, £TC, V. **Map 8 L6**
Burro's warehousey shop displays 'non-branded clothing for the fashion-educated': smart shirts and well-pressed trousers for the sophisticated trendy about town.

The CM Store
121 King's Road, SW3 (0171 351 9361). Sloane Square tube/11, 19, 22 bus. **Open** 9.30am-7pm Mon-Sat; noon-6pm Sun. **Credit** AmEx, MC, £TC, V. **Map 4 F11**
A vast open-plan space with enough hip streetwear labels to satisfy the fussiest workware and clubwear devotee.

Diesel
43 Earlham Street, WC2 (0171 497 5543). Covent Garden tube. **Open** 10.30am-7pm Mon-Wed, Fri, Sat; 10.30am-8pm Thur; 11.30am-7pm Sun. **Credit** AmEx, MC, £TC, V. **Map 6 L6**
Retro jeans, T-shirts, sweatshirts and bikinis are the order of the day at London's most popular temple to kitsch excess. Such trendy gear, of course, does not come cheap. You can order your gladrags over the web if you can't make it to Covent Garden.
Website: www.diesel.com

The Dispensary
25 Pembridge Road, W11 (0171 221 9290). Notting Hill Gate tube. **Open** 10.30am-6.30pm Mon-Sat. **Credit** AmEx, JCB, MC, £TC, V. **Map 1 A7**
Once famous for sedate, impeccably cut separates, the Dispensary has decided to camp it up lately with ranges aimed at 'techno Hawaiian gigolos abroad' and 'urban, sassy London cowgirls'.
Branches: *womenswear* 9 Newburgh Street, W1 (0171 287 8145); *menswear* 15 Newburgh Street, W1 (0171 734 4095); 200 Kensington Park Road, W11 (0171 727 8797).

Duffer of St George
29 Shorts Gardens, WC2 (0171 379 4660). Covent Garden or Leicester Square tube. **Open** 10.30am-7pm Mon-Fri; 10.30am-6.30pm Sat; 1-5pm Sun. **Credit** AmEx, JCB, MC, £TC, V. **Map 6 L6**
Well-cut, natty gear hovering between designer formality and streety nonchalance.

Hype DF
48-52 Kensington High Street, W8 (0171 938 3801). High Street Kensington tube. **Open** 10am-6pm Mon-Wed, Fri; 10am-8pm Thur; noon-6pm Sun. **Credit** AmEx, DC, JCB, MC, V. **Map 3 B9**
Ultra-trendy items by Terra Firma, Dexter Wong and the like are the *raison d'acheter* at this sparkling mall.

Shop
4 Brewer Street (basement), W1 (0171 437 1259). Leicester Square tube. **Open** 10.30am-6.30pm Mon-Sat. **Credit** AmEx, JCB, MC, £TC, V. **Map 7 J7**
Humorous, tough womenswear (Fiorucci T-shirts in a tin, the Hysteric Glamour range). 'No disco shit,' says the owner.

Souled Out
Unit 25, Portobello Green Arcade, 281 Portobello Road, W10 (0181 964 1121). Ladbroke Grove or Westbourne Park tube. **Open** 10am-6pm Mon; 11am-6pm Tue-Thur; 9am-6pm Fri, Sat. **Credit** AmEx, DC, JCB, MC, £TC, V.
Funky, extrovert own-labels Soul Girl and Soul Boy make the most of global village chic.

Urban Outfitters
36-38 Kensington High Street, W8 (0171 761 1001). High Street Kensington tube. **Open** 10am-7pm Mon-Wed; 10am-8pm Thur-Sat; noon-6pm Sun. **Credit** AmEx, JCB, MC, £TC, V. **Map 3 A9**
Funky, affordable clobber, cosmetics, gadgets and home-wares all under one roof.

World
27 Litchfield Street, WC2 (0171 379 5588). Leicester Square tube. **Open** noon-7pm Mon-Sat. **Credit** MC, V. **Map 8 K6**
Gorgeously decorative global gear – African-print shirts, gold headdresses, Brazilian feather jewellery and the like.

Underwear

Marks & Spencer (*see page 203*) also sells excellent-quality yet affordable undies.

Agent Provocateur

16 Pont Street, SW1 (0171 235 0229). Knightsbridge tube. **Open** 10am-6pm Mon-Sat. **Credit** AmEx, MC, £TC, V. **Map 4 F10**

Women's lingerie with 1950s pin-up appeal, most of it from France and the States. Mail-order service available.
Branch: 6 Broadwick Street, W1 (0171 439 0229).

Janet Reger

2 Beauchamp Place, SW3 (0171 584 9360). Knightsbridge tube. **Open** 10am-6pm Mon-Sat. **Credit** AmEx, JCB, MC, V. **Map 4 F9**

For glamorous women's lingerie, at sky-rocketing prices, Janet's hard to beat.

Rigby & Peller

22A Conduit Street, W1 (0171 491 2200). Oxford Circus tube. **Open** 9.30am-6pm Mon-Wed, Fri, Sat; 9.30am-7pm Thur. **Credit** AmEx, DC, JCB, MC, V. **Map 7 J6**

R&P might be corsetière to the Queen, but there's nothing snobby about the place – and the fitters are so skilled they can tell a woman's bra size by sight alone. In addition to its own-brand underwear, you'll also find newish line Celeste, the lacy Lucetta bridal range and swimwear.
Branch: 2 Hans Road, SW3 (0171 589 9293).

Wolford

3 South Molton Street, W1 (0171 499 2549). Bond Street tube. **Open** 10am-6pm Mon-Wed, Fri, Sat; 10am-6.30pm Thur. **Credit** AmEx, DC, JCB, MC, V. **Map 5 H6**

Wolford has cornered the fashion-oriented hosiery market. Look out for the funky tights inspired by Moroccan and Indian tattoo designs. Also sold in many department stores.
Branch: 28A Kensington Church Street, W8 (0171 937 2995).

Unusual sizes

Base

55 Monmouth Street, WC2 (0171 240 8914). Leicester Square tube. **Open** 10am-6pm Mon-Sat. **Credit** AmEx, DC, MC, £TC, V. **Map 6 L6**

Sizes 16-28 are sold at Base, in both pricey and more affordable ranges.

High & Mighty

81-83 Knightsbridge, SW1 (0171 589 7454). Knightsbridge tube. **Open** 9am-6pm Mon, Tue, Thur-Sat; 9am-6.30pm Wed. **Credit** AmEx, DC, MC, £TC, V. **Map 4 F9**

Men over 6ft 3in and/or with waistlines measuring 34-60in find salvation here. There are suits, shirts and casualwear.
Branches: 145-147 Edgware Road, W2 (0171 723 8754); The Plaza, 120 Oxford Street, W1 (0171 436 4861).

Sixteen 47

69 Gloucester Avenue, NW1 (0171 483 4174). Camden Town tube. **Open** 10am-6pm Mon-Sat. **Credit** AmEx, MC, £TC, V.

Set up by comedian/actress Dawn French and designer Helen Teague – this shop aims to offer the 47% of British women who are size 16 or over something a bit different. Designs are unstructured, comfortable and fashionable.

Fashion accessories & services

General

See also page 190 **Antoni & Alison** *and page 191* **Paul Smith**.

Accessorize

Unit 22, The Market, Covent Garden, WC2 (0171 240 2107). Covent Garden tube. **Open** 10am-8pm Mon-Sat; 11am-7pm Sun. **Credit** AmEx, DC, JCB, MC, £TC, V. **Map 8 L67**

The place that proves that seasonal trends can make it to the high street at a fraction of the price. Beaded, feathery, flowery jewellery, hats, bags, cosmetics and toiletries.
Branches are too numerous to list here. Check the telephone directory for your nearest.

American Retro

35 Old Compton Street, W1 (0171 734 3477). Leicester Square tube. **Open** 10.15am-7pm Mon-Wed, Sat; 10.15am-8pm Thur, Fri. **Credit** AmEx, JCB, MC, £TC, V. **Map 6 K6**

A great range of witty accessories and cool clothing.

Emma Bernhardt

301 Portobello Road, W10 (0181 960 2929). Ladbroke Grove tube. **Open** noon-5.30pm Tue; 10.30am-5.30pm Wed, Thur; 9.30am-5.30pm Fri; 10.30am-6pm Sat. **Credit** MC, V. **Map 1 A6**

Importer of all things Mexican, EB has created Latin kitsch in W10. Technicolor, cheap and cheery.

Octopus

King's Walk Mall, 122 King's Road, SW3 (0171 589 7715). Sloane Square tube. **Open** 9.30am-6.30pm Mon-Sat; noon-6pm Sun. **Credit** AmEx, MC, V. **Map 4 F11**

Everything from the wacky to the tacky can be found at this accessories emporium; bags are a highlight.
Branches: 54 Neal Street, WC2 (0171 836 2911); 28 Carnaby Street, W1 (0171 287 3916).

Robot

37 Floral Street, WC2 (0171 836 6156). Covent Garden tube. **Open** 10am-6.30pm Mon-Wed, Fri, Sat; 10am-7pm Thur; noon-5.30pm Sun. **Credit** AmEx, DC, JCB, MC, £TC, V. **Map 8 L6**

Great accessories for men and women, including jewellery, sunglasses, bags, belts and a large range of fashion-conscious footwear.

Dry cleaning, laundries & repairs

Buckingham Dry Cleaners

83 Duke Street, W1 (0171 499 1253). Bond Street tube. **Open** 8am-6pm Mon-Fri; 9.30am-12.30pm Sat. **Credit** MC, V. **Map 5 G6**

Exemplary service is Buckingham's trademark.

Danish Express Laundry

16 Hinde Street, W1 (0171 935 6306). Bond Street tube. **Open** 8.30am-5.30pm Mon-Fri; 9.30am-12.30pm Sat. **Credit** AmEx, DC, MC, V. **Map 5 G5**

DEL will collect and return laundry.
Branch: Janet's Laundry 281A Finchley Road, NW3 (0171 435 6131).

Duds 'n' Suds

49-51 Brunswick Shopping Centre, Russell Square, WC1 (0171 837 1122). Russell Square tube. **Open** 8am-9pm Mon-Fri; 8am-8pm Sat, Sun. **Credit** AmEx, MC, V. **Map 6 L4**

Fifty-two washing machines, 25 tumble dryers, comfy chairs, pool table, pinball machines, Sky TV and snack bar.

Express Tailoring Services

3 New Burlington Place, W1 (0171 437 9345). Oxford Circus tube. **Open** 9am-6pm Mon-Fri; 9am-4pm Sat. **Map 7 J6**

An experienced and reliable company that can mend and alter almost any garment.

Michael's Shoe Care

10-12 Procter Street, WC1 (0171 405 7436). Holborn tube. **Open** 8am-6.30pm Mon-Fri. **Credit** AmEx, MC, V. **Map 6 M5**
A chain of cobblers offering most forms of shoecare, plus scarves, belts, umbrellas and briefcases.
Branches: 66 Ludgate Hill, EC4 (0171 248 4640); 9 Camomile Street, EC3 (0171 929 3887); 11A New London Street, EC3 (0171 265 1991).

Hats

See also page 198 **James Lock.**

Fred Bare

118 Columbia Road, E2 (0171 729 6962). Old Street tube/rail. **Open** 11am-5pm Sat; 9am-2pm Sun or by appointment. **Credit** MC, V. **Map 10 S3**
Opening times coincide with Columbia Road Flower Market (*see p193*). These funky hats are also sold in some department stores.

The Hat Shop

14 Lamb Street, Spitalfields, E1 (0171 247 1120). Liverpool Street tube/rail or Aldgate East tube. **Open** 10.30am-6.30pm Tue, Wed, Fri; 10.30am-7pm Thur; 11am-5pm Sat, Sun. **Credit** JCB, MC, £TC, V. **Map 6 L6**
Prices range from £10 to around £250 for the caps, hats, boaters and bonnets at this friendly, if cramped, establishment. Everything was wedding gear to street gear.

Stephen Jones

36 Great Queen Street, WC2 (0171 242 0770). Covent Garden or Holborn tube. **Open** 11am-6pm Tue-Fri; 11am-5pm Sat. **Credit** AmEx, DC, MC, £TC,V. **Map 7 J7**
Wit and wonder are Jones's specialities. Fabulously versatile unisex stuff. Prices £45-£250.

Jewellery

Angela Hale

5 The Royal Arcade, Old Bond Street, W1 (0171 495 1920). Green Park or Piccadilly Circus tube. **Open** 10am-6pm Mon-Sat. **Credit** AmEx, JCB, MC, V. **Map 7 J7**
Classic and retro-chic costume jewellery and accessories.

Argenta

82 Fulham Road, SW3 (0171 584 4480). South Kensington tube. **Open** 9.30am-5.30pm Mon-Fri; 9.30am-5pm Sat. **Credit** AmEx, JCB, MC, V. **Map 4 D11**
One of the biggest selections of silver jewellery in London with over 500 wedding and engagement rings, many by contemporary designers.

Asprey & Garrard

167 New Bond Street, W1 (0171 734 7020). Green Park tube. **Open** 9.30am-6pm Mon-Fri; 10am-5pm Sat. **Credit** AmEx, DC, JCB, MC, £TC, V. **Map 7 H7**
Asprey and Garrard, two of the most distinguished names in the business, merged in 1998. Fine English jewellery and silverware are reverentially displayed.

Beau Gems

26 Royal Exchange, Threadneedle Street, EC2 (0171 623 7634). Bank tube. **Open** 9am-5pm Mon-Fri. **Credit** AmEx, DC, MC, V. **Map 12 Q6**
Buyers, sellers, repairers of antique and modern jewellery. **Branch:** 33 Leadenhall Market, Leadenhall Place, EC3 (0171 929 6600).

Butler & Wilson

189 Fulham Road, SW3 (0171 352 8255). South Kensington tube. **Open** 10am-6pm Mon, Tue, Thur-Sat; 10am-7pm Wed. **Credit** AmEx, JCB, MC, V. **Map 4 D11**
Costume jewellery at its glittering best.
Branch: 20 South Molton Street, W1 (0171 409 2955).

ec one

28 Exmouth Market, EC1 (0171 713 6185). Angel tube/ Farringdon tube/rail. **Open** 10.30am-6pm Mon-Sat. **Credit** AmEx, JCB, MC, V. **Map 9 N4**
This newish gallery shop has made a splash with its bold, colourful contemporary designs. About 24 (predominantly local) designers are showcased.

Electrum Gallery

21 South Molton Street, W1 (0171 629 6325). Bond Street tube. **Open** 10am-6pm Mon-Fri; 10am-2pm Sat. **Credit** AmEx, DC, JCB, MC, V. **Map 5 H6**
One of the widest selections of modern craft jewellery, with work by over 100 international designers represented.

Frontiers

37 & 39 Pembridge Road, W11 (0171 727 6132). Notting Hill Gate tube. **Open** 11am-6.30pm Mon-Sat; noon-4pm Sun. **Credit** AmEx, DC, JCB, MC, £TC, V. **Map 1 A7**
Antique and tribal jewellery from around the world (but particularly Asia and North Africa) displayed in a spacious white-walled gallery.

The Great Frog

10 Ganton Street, W1 (0171 439 9357). Oxford Circus tube. **Open** 10.30am-6.30pm Mon-Sat. **Credit** AmEx, DC, JCB, MC, V. **Map 5 J6**
Silver and gold chunky rings, meaty bejewelled rings and other in-yer-face jewellery since 1971.

Into You

144 St John Street, EC1 (0171 253 5085). Angel tube/ Farringdon tube/rail. **Open** noon-7pm Tue, Wed, Fri; noon-9pm Thur; noon-6pm Sat. **Map 9 O3**
A welcoming tattoo and piercing parlour with a strong line in body jewellery, including classic designs and more ornamental pieces. Prices start around £15 for ears and noses.

Janet Fitch

37A Neal Street, W1 (0171 240 6332). Covent Garden tube. **Open** 11am-7pm Mon-Sat; 1-6pm Sun. **Credit** AmEx, MC, V. **Map 6 L6**
A small chain showing 30 or so of the best young British designers at any one time.
Branches: 25A Old Compton Street, WC2 (0171 287 3789); 188A King's Road, SW3 (0171 352 4401).

Lesley Craze Gallery/Craze 2/C2+

34-35 Clerkenwell Green, EC1 (Lesley Craze Gallery 0171 608 0393/Craze 2 0171 251 0381/C2+ 0171 251 9200). Farringdon tube/rail. **Open** 10am-5.30pm Mon-Sat. **Credit** AmEx, MC, V. **Map 9 N4**
This showcase for British contemporary designers is packed with beautiful and unusual work. No.34 specialises in pieces made of precious metals; Craze 2 is dedicated to jewellery made from non-precious materials; C2+ features a range of textiles. *See picture p206.*

Tiffany & Co

25 Old Bond Street, W1 (0171 409 2790). Green Park or Piccadilly Circus tube. **Open** 10am-5.30pm Mon-Fri; 10am-6pm Sat. **Credit** AmEx, DC, JCB, MC, £TC, V. **Map 7 J7**
The most romantic of fine jewellers. Prices are serious, but the range is spirited, not stuffy.

Victorian values

The gentleman's clubland of **St James's**, south of Piccadilly, and the southern part of **Mayfair** (*see also page 57*) contain a wonderfully anachronistic clutch of emporia where high prices are matched by superlative service and quality. Browsing in this time-warp wonderland, you can almost believe that Britain still has an empire.

Fashion

Gieves & Hawkes
1 Savile Row, W1 (0171 434 2001). Piccadilly Circus tube. **Open** 9am-6pm Mon, Tue, Fri; 10am-6pm Wed, Sat; 9am-7pm Thur. **Credit** AmEx, DC, JCB, MC, £TC, V. **Map 7 J7**
Venerable Savile Row tailors who are now focusing more on off-the-peg ranges. Three-piece bespoke suits start at around £1,800.
Branch: 18 Lime Street, EC3 (0171 283 4914).

James Lock
6 St James's Street, SW1 (0171 930 5849). Green Park tube. **Open** 9am-5.30pm Mon-Fri; 10am-5.30pm Sat. **Credit** AmEx, DC, JCB, MC £TC, V. **Map 7 J8**
This family business has been making hats to the highest standards since 1686. Past satisfied customers include Lord Byron and Harrison Ford.

John Lobb
9 St James's Street, SW1 (0171 930 3664). Green Park tube. **Open** 9am-5.30pm Mon-Fri; 9am-4.30pm Sat. **Credit** AmEx, MC, £TC, V. **Map 7 J8**
Expect to part with £1,500 and to wait eight months before you slip into a pair of John Lobb's fabulous men's shoes.

Turnbull & Asser
23 Bury Street, SW1 (0171 808 3000). Green Park or Piccadilly Circus tube. **Open** 9am-6pm Mon-Fri; 9.30am-6pm Sat. **Credit** AmEx, DC, MC, £$TC, V. **Map 7 J7**
T&A's bespoke and off-the-peg shirts have graced the backs of Winston Churchill and James Bond.
Branch: 71-72 Jermyn Street, SW1 (0171 930 0502).

Food & drink

Berry Bros & Rudd
3 St James's Street, SW1 (0171 396 9600/9666). Green Park tube. **Open** 9am-5.30pm Mon-Fri; 10am-4pm Sat. **Credit** AmEx, DC, MC, V. **Map 7 J8**
Venerable wine merchants Berry Bros is best known for German and French wines, but has a comprehensive list that takes in good New World wineries.

Charbonnel & Walker
1 The Royal Arcade, 28 Old Bond Street, W1 (0171 491 0939). Green Park or Piccadilly Circus tube. **Open** 9am-6pm Mon-Fri; 10am-5pm Sat. **Credit** AmEx, DC, JCB, MC, £TC, V. **Map 7 J7**
Traditional hand-rolled chocolates. Don't miss the fabulous champagne truffles.

JJ Fox (St James's)
19 St James's Street, SW1 (0171 493 9009). Green Park tube. **Open** 9am-5.30pm Mon-Sat. **Credit** AmEx, DC, JCB, MC, £TC, V. **Map 7 J8**
This delightful, ancient, wood-panelled shop stocks a fabulous range of cigars – Churchill and Oscar Wilde have puffed away on Fox's prime merchandise in the past.

Paxton & Whitfield
93 Jermyn Street, SW1 (0171 930 0259). Green Park or Piccadilly Circus tube. **Open** 9.30am-6pm Mon-Fri; 9am-5.30pm Sat. **Credit** AmEx, DC, MC, £TC, V. **Map 7 J7**
A pukka establishment with old-fashioned premises holding about 200 varieties of European cheeses, plus hams, pies, breads, teas, chutneys and pickles.

Health & beauty

Floris
89 Jermyn Street, SW1 (0171 930 2885). Green Park or Piccadilly Circus tube. **Open** 9.30am-5.30pm Mon-Fri; 10am-5pm Sat. **Credit** AmEx, DC, JCB, MC, £TC, V. **Map 7 J7**
Traditional toiletries have been the business of this upmarket, elegant perfumier since 1730. Expect lots of floral scents for women and no-nonsense men's colognes.

GF Trumper
9 Curzon Street, W1 (0171 499 1850). Green Park tube. **Open** 9am-5.30pm Mon-Fri; 9am-1pm Sat. **Credit** AmEx, JCB, MC, £TC, V. **Map 7 H7**
A Victorian ambience and obsequious staff perform treatments in the traditional manner at this high-class barbers. Also sells top-notch colognes.
Branches: 20 Jermyn Street, SW1 (0171 734 1370).

Penhaligon's
16-17 Burlington Arcade, W1 (0171 629 1416). Green Park or Piccadilly Circus tube. **Open** 9.30am-5.30pm Mon-Sat. **Credit** AmEx, DC, JCB, MC, £TC, V. **Map 7 J7**
Quintessentially English perfumes, toiletries and grooming products for men and women.
Branches: 20A Brook Street, W1 (0171 493 0002); 41 Wellington Street, WC2 (0171 836 2150); 8 Cornhill, EC3 (0171 283 0711); 18 Beauchamp Place, SW1 (0171 584 4008).

Leather goods

Anya Hindmarch
91 Walton Street, SW3 (0171 584 7644). South Kensington tube. **Open** 10am-5.30pm Mon-Fri; 10am-5pm Sat. **Credit** AmEx, MC, £TC, V. **Map 4 E10**
Elegant, fashionable bags at high prices. Hindmarch offers a limited bespoke service.
Branch: 15-17 Pont Street, SW1 (0171 838 9177).

Bill Amberg
10 Chepstow Road, W2 (0171 727 3560). Notting Hill Gate or Westbourne Park tube. **Open** 10am-6pm Mon, Tue, Thur-Sat; 10am-7pm Wed. **Credit** AmEx, MC, V. **Map 1 A5**
Known for his beautiful, brightly coloured soft leatherwork, Bill's bags are popular with the fashion pack. His Notting Hill shop is filled with distinctive clutch and shoulder bags, as well as cosmetic cases, watch cases and travel slippers.

Connolly
32 Grosvenor Crescent Mews, SW1 (0171 235 3883).
Hyde Park Corner tube. **Open** 10am-6pm Mon-Sat.
Credit AmEx, DC, JCB, MC, £TC, V. **Map 7 G9**
Shamelessly pricey, but fabulously classy accessories.
Connolly upholstery graces the seats of Aston Martins and
Rolls Royces.

Mulberry
11-12 Gees Court, St Christopher's Place, W1 (0171 493
2546). Bond Street tube. **Open** 10am-6pm Mon-Wed, Fri,
Sat; 10am-7pm Thur. **Credit** AmEx, DC, JCB, MC, £TC,
V. **Map 5 H6**
This flagship store carries the complete Mulberry range:
clothes, and pricey leather bags and accessories.
Branches: 41-44 New Bond Street, W1 (0171 491 3900);
185 Brompton Road, SW3 (0171 225 0313); 219 King's
Road, SW3 (0171 352 1937).

Osprey
11 St Christopher's Place, W1 (0171 935 2824). Bond
Street tube. **Open** 10.30am-6.30pm Mon-Wed, Fri; 10am-
7pm Thur; 10am-6pm Sat. **Credit** AmEx, JCB, MC, £TC,
V. **Map 5 H6**
Handmade, modern bags that look even more expensive
than they are. There are beautiful belts too.

Shoes
See also page 198 **John Lobb**.

Camper
39 Floral Street, WC2 (0171 379 8678). Covent Garden
tube. **Open** 10.30am-6.30pm Mon-Wed, Fri, Sat; 10.30am-
7pm Thur. **Credit** AmEx, DC, JCB, MC, £TC, V.
Map 8 L6
Stylish, comfy Majorcan-made shoes for both sexes.

Dr Marten Department Store
1-4 King Street, WC2 (0171 497 1460). Covent Garden
tube. **Open** 10am-7pm Mon-Wed, Fri, Sat; 10.30am-8pm
Thur; noon-6pm Sun. **Credit** AmEx, JCB, MC, £TC, V.
Map 8 L7
Five floors of footwear and clothing, plus a canteen.

Emma Hope
33 Amwell Street, EC1 (0171 833 2367). Angel tube.
Open 10am-6pm Mon-Wed, Fri, Sat; 10am-7pm Thur.
Credit MC, V. **Map 5 N3**
Elegant shoes in a range of materials by one of Britain's
best-known designers. There's a bridal collection too.
Branch: 12 Symons Street, SW3 (0171 259 9566).

Jimmy Choo
20 Motcomb Street, SW1 (0171 235 6008).
Knightsbridge tube. **Open** 10am-6pm Mon-Sat.
Credit AmEx, MC, V. **Map 7 G9**
The best place for glamorous, racy evening wear.

Manolo Blahnik
49-51 Old Church Street, SW3 (0171 352 3863). Sloane
Square tube then 11, 19, 22 bus. **Open** 10am-6pm Mon-
Fri; 10.30am-5pm Sat. **Credit** AmEx, JCB, MC, V.
Map 4 D11
Average price of shoes is £250, but they are divine creations.

Natural Shoe Store
21 Neal Street, WC2 (0171 836 5254). Covent Garden
tube. **Open** 10am-6pm Mon, Tue; 10am-7pm Wed-Fri;
10am-6.30pm Sat; noon-5.30pm Sun. **Credit** AmEx, DC,
MC, £TC, V. **Map 6 L6**
Shoes here have been produced without cruelty or environmental damage, whenever possible. Think Birkenstock.
Branch: 325 King's Road, SW3 (0171 351 3721).

Office
57 Neal Street, WC2 (0171 379 1896). Covent Garden
tube. **Open** 10am-7pm Mon-Wed, Fri, Sat; 10am-8pm
Thur; noon-6pm Sun. **Credit** AmEx, JCB, MC, £TC, V.
Map 6 L6
Funky gear with an emphasis on platforms and stilletos.
Branches are too numerous to list here. Check the
telephone directory for your nearest.

Patrick Cox
8 Symons Street, SW3 (0171 730 6504).
Sloane Square tube. **Open** 10am-6pm Mon, Tue, Thur-
Sat; 10am-7pm Wed. **Credit** AmEx, MC, £TC, V.
Map 4 F11
Inventive and unquenchably trendy, Cox's creations are so
popular that people queue to buy his wares.
Branch: Wannabe 129 Sloane Street, SW1 (0171
730 8886).

Shellys
266-270 Regent Street, W1 (0171 287 0939). Oxford
Circus tube. **Open** 10am-7pm Mon-Wed, Fri; 10am-8pm
Thur; 9.30am-7pm Sat; noon-6pm Sun. **Credit** AmEx,
DC, JCB, MC, £TC, V. **Map 5 J6**
Streetsmart boots and shoes for men and women.
Branches are too numerous to list here. Check the
telephone directory for your nearest.

Tailors
See also page 198 **Gieves & Hawkes**.

47/47A Carnaby Street
Carnaby Street, W1. Oxford Circus tube. **Map 5 J6**
Westminster Council has ensured that the traditional Soho
trade of tailoring will not completely die out by making
it impossible for anyone to use these buildings for any
other purpose. Businesses here include **Keith Watson**
(0171 437 2327), **Franco Santoro** (0171 437 8440) and
Brian Staples (0171 734 5069).

Ozwald Boateng
9 Vigo Street, W1 (0171 734 6868). Piccadilly Circus
tube. **Open** 10am-6pm Mon-Sat. **Credit** AmEx, JCB, MC,
£TC, V. **Map 7 J7**
Avant-garde tailoring for men. Bespoke starts at £1,700.

Richard James
31 Savile Row, W1 (0171 434 0605). Green Park or
Piccadilly Circus tube. **Open** 10am-6pm Mon-Fri; 11am-
5pm Sat. **Credit** AmEx, DC, MC, £$TC, V.
Map 7 J7
Unusually, a trendy, friendly tailor on Savile Row, offering
sharp suits cut in anything from cashmere to denim.

Timothy Everest
32 Elder Street, E1 (0171 377 5770). Liverpool Street
tube/rail. **Open** 9am-5.30pm Mon-Fri; 9am-4pm Sat;
also by appointment. **Credit** AmEx, MC, £TC, V.
Map 10 R5
One of the best of the new breed of tailors, who also sells
accessories, shirts and shoes.

Umbrellas & walking sticks

James Smith & Sons
53 New Oxford Street, WC1 (0171 836 4731).
Tottenham Court Road tube. **Open** 9.30am-5.25pm
Mon-Fri; 10am-5.25pm Sat. **Credit** MC, £TC, V.
Map 6 K6
There's a vast array of umbrellas and walking sticks at
this beautiful old shop, which first opened in 1857. Walking
brollies can be cut to size while you wait.

Watches

City Clocks
31 Amwell Street, EC1 (0171 278 1154). Angel tube.
Open 8.30am-5.30pm Tue-Fri; 9.30am-2.30pm Sat.
Credit AmEx, DC, MC, V. **Map 9 N3**
Any make of watch repaired, and antique pocket and wrist watches restored at this century-old business.

Simon Carter
15 Quadrant Arcade, 80-82 Regent Street, W1 (0171 287 4363). Oxford Circus or Piccadilly Circus tube.
Open 10am-6.30pm Mon-Thur; 10.30am-7.30pm Fri, Sat. **Credit** AmEx, JCB, MC, V. **Map 7 J7**
Carter makes and sells his own designs, many influenced by the decades 1920s-1960s. Prices from under £100.

The Swatch Store
313 Oxford Street, W1 (0171 493 0237). Bond Street or Oxford Circus tube. **Open** 10am-7pm Mon-Wed, Fri; 10am-8pm Thur, Sat; noon-6pm Sun. **Credit** MC, V.
Map 5 H6
Stockist of all the 160-plus Swatch watches. Prices from £25.
Branches: 104-106 Long Acre, WC2 (0171 836 7868).

Watches of Switzerland
16 New Bond Street, W1 (0171 493 5916). Green Park tube. **Open** 9.30am-5.30pm Mon, Wed-Fri; 10am-5.30pm Tue, Sat. **Credit** AmEx, DC, JCB, MC, V. **Map 7 H7**
Seriously elegant timepieces by Omega, Raymond Mercier and Ebel, at equally serious prices.
Branches are too numerous to mention here. Check the telephone directory for your nearest.

Florists

See also page 193 **Columbia Road Flower Market**.

Wild At Heart
Turquoise Island, 222 Westbourne Grove, W11 (0171 727 3095). Notting Hill Gate tube. **Open** 8am-7pm Mon-Sat. **Credit** AmEx, MC, JCB, V. **Map 1 A6**
Fabulous, if pricey, flora, sold from London's most stylish public toilet. A stunning new shop has opened recently nearby at 49A Ledbury Road, W11 (0171 727 3095).

The Wild Bunch
17 Earlham Street, WC2 (0171 497 1200). Covent Garden tube. **Open** 10am-7.30pm Mon-Sat.
Map 6 K6
A fabulous florist operating from several stalls at Seven Dials. All manner of floral styles are sold, from florid tropical blooms to a bunch of daffs, with the same easygoing charm. They also wrap your flowers splendidly.

Food & drink

For department-store food halls, *see page 202-3.*

Bakeries & pâtisseries

For other café-pâtisseries, *see also page 158-9.*

& Clarke's
122 Kensington Church Street, W8 (0171 229 2190). Notting Hill Gate tube. **Open** 8am-8pm Mon-Fri; 9am-4pm Sat. **Credit** AmEx, MC, £TC, V. **Map 1 B8**
This minute adjunct to Sally Clarke's restaurant is crammed with luxury goods (preserves, chocolate truffles, Neal's Yard cheeses). But the 30 or so breads are the draw.

Konditor & Cook
22 Cornwall Road, SE1 (0171 261 0456). Waterloo tube/rail/27 bus. **Open** 7.30am-6.30pm Mon-Fri; 8.30am-2.30pm Sat. **Credit** MC, V.
Map 11 N8.
A mouth-watering array of cakes and pastries is baked on the premises; breads are supplied by **& Clarke's** (*see above*). Many can be sampled in the café of the same name in the **Young Vic** theatre on The Cut, SE1.
Branch: 10 Stoney Street, SE1 (0171 407 5100).

Beer

The Beer Shop
14 Pitfield Street, N1 (0171 739 3701). Old Street tube/rail. **Open** 11am-7pm Mon-Fri; 10am-4pm Sat. **Credit** MC, £TC, V. **Map 10 Q4**
A wide selection of draught and bottled beers, plus the kit necessary to brew your own.

Cheese shops

See also page 198 **Paxton & Whitfield**

International Cheese Centre
21 Goodge Street, W1 (0171 631 4191). Goodge Street tube. **Open** 9.30am-6.30pm Mon-Fri; 10am-6pm Sat.
Credit AmEx, MC, £TC, V. **Map 8 K6**
This small chain of shops has done much to spread the word about quality cheese in London. The preserves and butties are good too.
Branches: 3B West Mall, Liverpool Street Station, EC2 (0171 628 6637); 41 The Parade, Platform 14-19, Victoria Station, SW1 (0171 828 2886).

Neal's Yard Dairy
17 Shorts Gardens, WC2 (0171 379 7646). Covent Garden tube. **Open** 9am-7pm Mon-Sat; 10am-5pm Sun. **Credit** JCB, MC, £TC, V. **Map 6 L6**
More than any other shop, NYD is responsible for the renaissance in British and Irish farmhouse cheeses. Most of the cheeses are matured in cellars under the shop and reach the counter in a state of rare perfection. Oils, chutneys and breads are also sold.
Branch: 6 Park Street, Borough Market, SE1 (0171 378 8195).

Coffee & tea

Algerian Coffee Stores
52 Old Compton Street, W1 (0171 437 2480). Leicester Square or Piccadilly Circus tube. **Open** 9am-7pm Mon-Sat. **Credit** AmEx, DC, JCB, MC, V.
Map 6 K6
Dispensing coffee since 1887. Coffee beans, teas, chocolates and equipment are crammed into premises steeped in charm.

The Tea House
15A Neal Street, WC2 (0171 240 7539). Covent Garden tube. **Open** 11am-7pm Mon-Wed; 10am-7pm Thur-Sat; noon-6pm Sun. **Credit** AmEx, JCB, MC, £TC, V.
Map 6 L6
A veritable temple to the goddess tea. Every imaginable type of infusion is here, plus a range of teapots.

R Twining & Co
216 Strand, WC2 (0171 353 3511). Temple tube/ Charing Cross tube/rail. **Open** 9.30am-4.30pm Mon-Fri.
Credit MC, V. **Map 6 M6**
Almost 300 years in the business, Twining & Co's long, thin shop stocks a great selection of classy tea blends, and culminates in a small museum of the firm's history.

Whittard

65-67 Regent Street, W1. Piccadilly Circus tube.
Open 9.30am-7pm Mon-Sat; noon-5pm Sun.
Credit AmEx, MC, £TC, V. **Map 7 J7**
Quirky teapots, cups and saucers, plus an impressive range of teas and coffees, from the traditional to the indulgent. **Branches** are too numerous to mention here. Check the telephone directory for your nearest.

Confectioners

See also page 198 **Charbonnel & Walker**.

Godiva

247 Regent Street, W1 (0171 495 2845).
Oxford Circus tube. **Open** 9.30am-7pm Mon-Sat; noon-6pm Sun. **Credit** AmEx, DC, MC, £TC, V.
Map 5 J6
Don't come here if you're counting the calories: you won't be able to resist the luscious handmade, hand-filled and hand-finished chocs. Seasonal goodies are a speciality.
Branches: 150 Fenchurch Street, EC3 (0171 623 2287); Selfridges, 400 Oxford Street, W1 (0171 629 1234 ext 3798); Harrods, 87 Brompton Road, SW1 (0171 730 1234 ext 4199); Brent Cross Shopping Centre, NW4 (0181 203 8886).

Rococo

321 King's Road, SW3 (0171 352 5857). Sloane Square tube. **Open** 10am-6.30pm Mon-Sat; noon-5pm Sun.
Credit AmEx, JCB, MC, £TC, V. **Map 4 D12**
Chantal Coady, of Chocolate Society fame, founded this chocoholic's paradise. Stock ranges from the serious (Valrhona rough-hewn slabs) to the frivolous (chocolate 'olives'). **The Chocolate Society** now has its own shop at 36 Elizabeth Street, SW1 (0171 259 9222).

Delicatessens

Bluebird

350 King's Road, SW3 (0171 559 1000). Sloane Square tube then 11, 19, 22, 49, 211, 319, 345 bus. **Open** 9am-8pm Mon-Wed; 9am-9pm Thur-Sat; noon-6pm Sun.
Credit AmEx, DC, JCB, MC, £TC, V. **Map 4 D12**
Welcome to foodie heaven. Sir Terence Conran's gastrodome (for the restaurant, *see p155*) is built around the ground-floor food store, which contains a bank-breaking array of fabulous provisions including oils, fruit, vegetables and breads.

Carluccio's

28A Neal Street, WC2 (0171 240 1487). Covent Garden tube. **Open** 11am-7pm Mon-Fri; 11am-6pm Sat.
Credit AmEx, MC, £TC,V. **Map 6 L6**
Beautifully packaged, pricey Italian groceries, plus exquisite fresh vegetables and prepared dishes.

Lina Stores

18 Brewer Street, W1 (0171 437 6482). Piccadilly Circus tube. **Open** 7am-5.45pm Mon-Fri; 7am-5pm Sat.
Credit AmEx, MC, V. **Map 7 J7**
A small selection of almost every Italian deli item imaginable is available at this Soho stalwart. Try the fresh tortelloni; fillings, such as pumpkin or wild mushroom, vary seasonally and are all recommended.

Villandry

170 Great Portland Street, W1 (0171 631 3131).
Great Portland Street tube. **Open** 8.30am-8pm Mon-Sat.
Credit MC, V. **Map 5 H5**
Now that Villandry (the deli and the restaurant) has settled into its capacious new premises, there's room for a vastly expanded selection of delectable cheeses, breads and choice foodstuffs from around the world.

Health & organic food

See also page 193 **Spitalfields Market**.

Planet Organic

42 Westbourne Grove, W2 (0171 221 7171). Bayswater or Queensway tube. **Open** 9am-8pm Mon-Sat; 11am-5pm Sun. **Credit** JCB, MC, V. **Map 1 B6**
A gleaming, natural food supermarket. In addition to the ten or so aisles of groceries, there's a butcher's counter (with organic sausages), a fresh fish counter, an organic juice and coffee bar, and a mini-flower stall. Organic wines sold too.

International

For the best Afro-Caribbean produce, *see page 192* **Brixton Market**.

Green Lanes

N4, N5. Manor House or Turnpike Lane tube/29, 141, 171A bus.
For the best Turkish food in town, look for the crowds on long and winding Green Lanes. Among the best to seek out are **Yasar Halim** (nos.493-495), **Ozgur** (no.397) and **Dostlar** (no.425).

Loon Fung Supermarket

42-44 Gerrard Street, W1 (0171 437 7332).
Leicester Square tube. **Open** 10am-8.30pm daily.
Credit MC, V. **Map 8 K7**
Chinatown's largest and best-stocked supermarket contains, in addition to a bewildering range of Chinese goodies, cheap woks, chopsticks and tableware, and produce from other East Asian countries.

Oriental City

399 Edgware Road, NW9 (0181 200 0009). Colindale tube. **Open** 10am-8pm Mon-Sat; noon-6pm Sun.
Credit JCB, MC, TC, V.
This Japanese shopping mall includes an excellent pan-Asian supermarket selling all kinds of products that are hard to find in the UK, plus a food court and stalls.

Reza Pâtisserie, Meats & Greengrocery

345 Kensington High Street, W8 (0171 603 0924).
High Street Kensington tube. **Open** 9am-9pm daily.
Map 3 A9
Highlights at this Iranian outlet include white salmon, unripe dates, dried morello cherries, saffron ice-cream and Middle Eastern pastries.

Southall

Southall rail/83, 105, 207 bus.
Once known for its north Indian specialities, as retailed by Sikhs, Southall has experienced a noticeable influx of Muslims from Birmingham in its Asian community. The result is a proliferation of halal butcher's shops. The tastiest street snacks are the kebabs, served Punjabi-style straight from the charcoal grill. Indian and Pakistani grocery shops remain plentiful. Try **Sira Cash & Carry**, **Gifto** or **Dokal**, all within a few hundred yards of each other on The Broadway.

Sausages

Simply Sausages

93 Berwick Street, W1 (0171 287 3482). Leicester Square or Tottenham Court Road tube. **Open** 8am-6pm Mon-Fri; 9am-6pm Sat. **Map 5 J6**
This mini-chain makes marvellous bangers, some to centuries-old British recipes, others making use of ingredients from around the world.
Branches: 341 Central Markets, EC1 (0171 329 3227).

Departments of commerce

At their worst, department stores are jacks of all trades but masters of none. Happily, London is supplied with plenty of examples of the other end of the scale, which offer high-quality service and encourage innovation. You'll find most stores in the Oxford Street/Regent Street and Knightsbridge areas, but be aware that 'department store' can be misleading. With the exceptions of Harrods, John Lewis, Liberty and Selfridges, most stores are primarily clothes shops with other departments usually little more than an afterthought.

Dickins & Jones

224-244 Regent Street, W1 (0171 734 7070). Oxford Circus tube. **Open** 10am-6.30pm Mon, Tue, Fri; 10am-7pm Wed; 10am-8pm Thur; 10am-6.30pm Sat; 11am-5pm Sun. **Credit** AmEx, DC, MC, £TC, V. **Map 5 J6**
After a refit, this House of Fraser fashion leader (devoted to clothing and beauty) has transformed itself into one of the best-looking – yet strangely soulless – stores in London. The menswear is dull, the womenswear variable, but the fashion accessories room is well worth a look.
Branches: George Street, Richmond, Surrey (0181 940 7761); **Army & Navy Stores** 101 Victoria Street, SW1 (0171 834 1234); **DH Evans** 318 Oxford Street, W1 (0171 629 8800); **Barkers of Kensington** 63 Kensington High Street, W8 (0171 937 5432).

Fortnum & Mason

181 Piccadilly, W1 (0171 734 8040). Piccadilly Circus tube. **Open** 9.30am-6pm Mon-Sat. **Credit** AmEx, DC, JCB, MC, £TC, V. **Map 7 J7**

The food halls and tearooms are the main draws at this stately old store, which comes complete with fancy-dressed assistants. Provisions are on the ground floor; upstairs you'll find classic designer clothes (Jean Muir, MaxMara, Georges Rech) and safer pieces from racier designers like Issey Miyake. An ongoing expansions programme has solved punter congestion problems.

Harrods

87 Brompton Road, SW1 (0171 730 1234).
Knightsbridge tube. **Open** 10am-6pm Mon, Tue, Sat; 10am-7pm Wed-Fri. **Credit** AmEx, DC, JCB, MC, £TC, V. **Map 4 F9**
Harrods celebrates its 150th birthday in 1999. The fabulous food halls alone fill seven elaborately decorated rooms and cover 35,000 sq ft/3,250 sq m (although not all departments are as inspiring). There are 60 fashion departments, and the toys are always worth checking out. However, there's little here that isn't done better in Harvey Nichols or Peter Jones, and many visitors find the security staff intimidating – you will probably be turned away if your clothing is deemed too skimpy (which includes shorts).

Harvey Nichols

109-125 Knightsbridge, SW1 (0171 235 5000).
Knightsbridge tube. **Open** 10am-7pm Mon, Tue, Thur-Sat; 10am-8pm Wed; noon-6pm Sun. **Credit** AmEx, DC, JCB, MC, £TC, V. **Map 4 F9**
Heaven for serial spenders and style groupies. Fashion occupies most floor space; over 200 labels are featured, although there are few surprises. Foodies are well catered for by the basement Foundation brasserie and the fifth-floor complex (food hall, café, bar and restaurant; *see p155*). Cosmetics include cult brand Ruby & Millie.

Wines & spirits

For everyday use, **Oddbins** (branches all over London – see phone book) is hard to beat. *See also page 198* **Berry Bros & Rudd**.

Bibendum

113 Regent's Park Road, NW1 (0171 722 5577). Chalk Farm tube/24, 168 bus. **Open** 10am-6.30pm Mon-Sat. **Credit** AmEx, DC, MC, V.
Not to be confused with the restaurant of the same name, this large, airy shop is one of the capital's most fashionable and dynamic wine merchants. It also has a well-annotated list for mail-order buying.

Corney & Barrow

194 Kensington Park Road, W11 (0171 221 5122). Ladbroke Grove or Notting Hill Gate tube. **Open** 10.30am-9pm Mon-Sat. **Credit** AmEx, MC, V. **Map 1 A6**
Serious wine buffs will swoon over Corney & Barrow's list, which includes Château Petrus and Domaine de la Romanee-Conti. Use it when you're after something special.

Milroy's of Soho

3 Greek Street, W1 (0171 437 9311). Tottenham Court Road tube. **Open** 10am-7pm Mon-Fri; 10am-6pm Sat. **Credit** AmEx, DC, JCB, MC, £TC, V. **Map 6 K6**
Whisky galore: Milroy's stocks over 400 lines including a huge array of single malts, plenty of bourbons and a fine selection of Irish whiskies.

Furniture

The Conran Shop

Michelin House, 81 Fulham Road, SW3 (0171 589 7401). South Kensington tube. **Open** 10am-6pm Mon, Tue, Fri; 10am-7pm Wed, Thur; 10am-6.30pm Sat; noon-6pm Sun. **Credit** AmEx, MC, £TC, V. **Map 5 G5**
The ground floor of Sir Terence Conran's design mecca holds classic modern furniture (including the recently launched Conran Collection) and soft furnishings; accessories are confined to the basement. Not to be missed.
Branch: 55 Marylebone High Street, W1 (0171 723 2223).

Furniture Union

46 Beak Street, W1 (0171 287 3424). Piccadilly Circus tube. **Open** 9am-6pm Mon-Fri. **Credit** DC, JCB, MC, V. **Map 7 J6**
Modern British furniture and quirky home accessories are showcased in this tiny shop.

Habitat

196 Tottenham Court Road, W1 (0171 631 3880). Goodge Street tube. **Open** 10am-6pm Mon-Sat; 10am-8pm Thur; 10am-6.30pm Fri; 9.30am-6.30pm Sat; noon-6pm Sun. **Credit** AmEx, MC, £TC, V. **Map 5 J4**
Sober but well-made furniture and home accessories are now the mainstay of what was the first high-street retailer to bring good, affordable, contemporary design to the masses.
Branches are too numerous to mention here. Check the telephone directory for your nearest.

John Lewis
278-306 Oxford Street, W1 (0171 629 7711).
Oxford Circus tube. **Open** 9.30am-6pm Mon-Wed, Fri;
10am-8pm Thur; 9am-6pm Sat. **Credit** £TC.
Map 5 H6
John Lewis majors on areas neglected by other stores, particularly homewares and haberdashery, and is famed for its 'never knowingly undersold' policy. Fashion tends to take a back seat, although it has been pepped up of late. **Peter Jones** on Sloane Square (0171 730 3434) is part of the same group but with added snob value.
Website: www.johnlewis.co.uk
Branches: Brent Cross Shopping Centre, NW4 (0181 202 6535); Wood Street, Kingston, Surrey (0181 547 3000).

Heal's
196 Tottenham Court Road, W1 (0171 636 1666).
Goodge Street tube. **Open** 10am-6pm Mon-Wed; 10am-8pm Thur; 10am-6.30pm Fri; 9.30am-6.30pm Sat.
Credit AmEx, DC, MC, SC, £TC, V.
Map 6 K5
One of London's oldest furniture stores, yet still one of the most fashionable. Several floors of stylish furniture, kitchenware and accessories, including pieces from the top design names.
Branch: 224 King's Road, SW3 (0171 349 8411).

Purves & Purves
80-81 & 83 Tottenham Court Road, W1 (0171 580 8223). Goodge Street or Warren Street tube.
Open 9.30am-6pm Mon-Wed, Fri, Sat; 9.30am-7.30pm Thur. **Credit** AmEx, MC, £TC, V. **Map 5 J4**
Andrew and Pauline Purves mix the best of British design with a sprinkling of top European names. There's a refreshing lack of pretension in their two stores, one of which specialises in accessories.

Tom Tom
42 New Compton Street, WC2 (0171 240 7909).
Covent Garden, Leicester Square or Tottenham Court Road tube. **Open** noon-7pm Tue-Fri; 11am-6pm Sat.
Credit AmEx, JCB, MC, £TC, V. **Map 6 K6**
A fun, eccentric shop stuffed to the gills with kitschy accessories and larger items such as 1950s fridges and Eames lounge chairs.

Liberty
214-220 Regent Street, W1 (0171 734 1234). Oxford Circus tube. **Open** 10am-6.30pm Mon-Wed, Fri, Sat; 10am-7.30pm Thur; noon-6pm Sun. **Credit** AmEx, DC, JCB, MC, TC, V. **Map 5 J6**
The Arts and Crafts heritage and faux-Tudor building give Liberty a certain quaint charm, but the store hasn't rested on its laurels. It is fast gaining a reputation for the funkiest women's fashion in London, and most departments (especially accessories, furniture, fabrics and jewellery) offer an above-average selection of goods. The best all-rounder of the upmarket department stores.

Marks & Spencer
458 Oxford Street, W1 (0171 935 7954). Bond Street or Marble Arch tube. **Open** 9am-8pm Mon-Fri; 9am-7pm Sat; noon-6pm Sun. **Credit** £$TC. **Map 5 G6**
Knickers and ready-made meals make up a hefty proportion of M&S's sales. Although it is pushing its homeware and furniture ranges, its strengths remain affordable, well-made clothes and upmarket food. This flagship store has recently undergone a huge expansion, increasing its sales space by 40%. There is another big M&S on Oxford Street (no.173), near Oxford Circus.
Website: www.marks-and-spencer.com
Branches are too numerous to list here. Check the telephone directory for your nearest.

Selfridges
400 Oxford Street, W1 (0171 629 1234).
Bond Street or Marble Arch tube. **Open** 10am-7pm Mon-Wed; 10am-8pm Thur, Fri; 9.30am-7pm Sat; noon-6pm Sun. **Credit** AmEx, DC, JCB, MC, £$TC, V.
Map 5 G6
Selfridges has the most user-friendly of London's food halls, containing a staggering range of international foodstuffs, and the biggest cosmetics hall in Europe. A major refit has spruced up the store for the next century and raised its fashion profile even further, yet the variation in quality between departments remains puzzling.

Viaduct
1-10 Summer's Street, EC1 (0171 278 8456).
Chancery Lane tube/Farringdon tube/rail.
Open 9.30am-6pm Mon-Fri; 10.30am-4pm Sat.
Credit MC, V. **Map 9 N5**
Retailers and manufacturers of modern, hip, mainly Italian and British furniture (and some accessories), from an airy warehouse-like space.

Gifts & stationery

In addition to the shops listed below, many of London's top museums have excellent gift shops, in particular the **London Transport Museum** (*see page 123*), the **British Museum** (*see page 126-7*) and the **Victoria & Albert Museum** (*see page 116*). *See also page 196* **Emma Bernhardt** and *page 195* **World**.

Anything Left-handed
57 Brewer Street, W1 (0171 437 3910). Piccadilly Circus tube. **Open** 9.30am-5pm Mon-Fri; 10am-5pm Sat.
Credit MC, £TC, V. **Map 7 J7**
A small, quirky shop for the leftie in your life. Among its bestsellers are left-handed scissors, corkscrews and books on how to improve your handwriting. It also has a mail order catalogue – handy if you can't make it to Soho.

*Baa-gains at **Antoni & Alison**. See page 190.*

BBC World Service Shop

Bush House, Strand, WC2 (0171 557 2576). Temple tube/Charing Cross tube/rail. **Open** 9.30am-6pm Mon, Tue, Thur, Fri; 10am-6pm Wed; 10am-5.30pm Sat. **Credit** AmEx, MC, £TC, V. **Map 8 M6**
Wide range of BBC spin-offs plus books on a range of arts and media subjects.

Equinox – The Astrology Shop

78 Neal Street, WC2 (0171 497 1001). Covent Garden tube. **Open** 9am-7pm Mon-Wed, Fri-Sun; 9am-8pm Thur. **Credit** AmEx, DC, MC, £TC, V. **Map 6 L6**
The name says it all… Astrological charts are a forte.

Get Stuffed

105 Essex Road, N1 (0171 226 1364). Angel tube/38, 56, 73, 171A, 277 bus. **Open** 1-5pm Mon-Fri; 1-3pm Sat. **Credit** MC, V. **Map 9 P1**
This long-established taxidermist sells creatures great and small. You won't find a more unusual or original gift anywhere in town.

Graham & Green

7 Elgin Crescent, W11 (0171 727 4594). Ladbroke Grove tube. **Open** 10am-6pm Mon-Fri; 9.30am-6pm Sat; 11am-5pm Sun. **Credit** AmEx, DC, MC, £TC, V.
The stock here – funky jewellery, pens, china, fashion accessories, picture frames and the like – is all in the best possible taste.

Steinberg & Tolkien. *See page 195.*

Branches: 4 & 10 Elgin Crescent, W11 (0171 727 4594); 164 Regent's Park Road, NW1 (0171 586 2960).

The Museum Store

37 The Market, Covent Garden Piazza, WC2 (0171 240 5760). Covent Garden tube. **Open** 10.30am-6.30pm Mon-Sat; 11am-6pm Sun. **Credit** AmEx, DC, JCB, MC, £TC, V. **Map 8 L7**
Quirky and/or stylish items from various museum shops around the world.
Branches: 4A-5A Perrin's Court, NW3 (0171 431 7156).

Mysteries

11 Monmouth Street, WC2 (0171 240 3688). Tottenham Court Road tube. **Open** 10am-6pm Mon-Sat. **Credit** MC, £TC, V. **Map 6 L6**
New Age shop packed with books and pamphlets, spacey music, posters, jewellery, charms, candles and even a phrenology head.

Neal Street East

5 Neal Street, WC2 (0171 240 0135). Covent Garden tube. **Open** 11am-7pm Mon-Wed; 10am-7pm Thur-Sat; noon-6pm Sun. **Credit** AmEx, JCB, MC, £TC, V. **Map 6 L6**
Huge range of oriental goods including Balinese animal carvings, embroidered Chinese dresses and Japanese cooking utensils.

Oggetti

133 Fulham Road, SW3 (0171 581 8088). South Kensington tube. **Open** 9.30am-6pm Mon-Sat; noon-5pm Sun. **Credit** AmEx, MC, £TC, V. **Map 4 D11**
Flash, stylish, highly desirable gizmos and gadgets for grown-ups.
Branch: 143 Fulham Road, SW3 (0171 584 9808).

Paperchase

213 Tottenham Court Road, W1 (0171 580 8496). Goodge Street tube. **Open** 9.30am-6.30pm Mon,Wed, Fri, Sat; 10am-6.30pm Tue; 9.30am-7.30pm Thur; 11am-5pm Sun. **Credit** AmEx, JCB, MC, £TC, V. **Map 6 K5**
A stationery chain with more verve than most. This flagship store has a great selection of cards, gift wrap, writing paper, pens, desk accessories and an art materials department.
Branches are too numerous to list here. Check the telephone directory for your nearest.

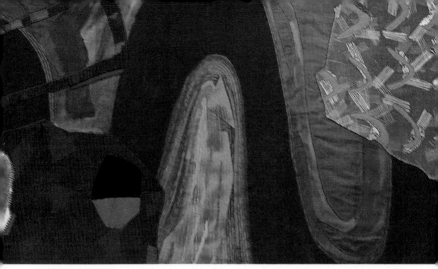

Lesley Craze Gallery: *crazy colours, terrific textiles. Great jewellery too. See page 197.*

The Pen Shop
199 Regent Street, W1 (0171 734 4088). Oxford Circus tube. **Open** 9.30am-6pm Mon, Tue, Fri, Sat; 10am-6pm Wed; 9.30am-7pm Thur. **Credit** AmEx, DC, JCB, MC, V. **Map 7 J7**
A huge range of writing implements and accessories, ranging from the mundane (£2 ballpoint) to the monumental (£85,000 Mont Blanc).
Branch: 10 West Mall, Liverpool Street Station, EC2 (0171 628 4416).

The Tintin Shop
34 Floral Street, WC2 (0171 836 1131). Covent Garden tube. **Open** 10am-6pm Mon-Sat. **Credit** AmEx, DC, JCB, MC, £TC, V. **Map 8 L6**
Devoted to the world's most famous fictional Belgian (alongside Hercule Poirot, that is), the stock at this tiny shop includes keyrings, T-shirts, towels and, of course, Hervé's comic books.
Branch: **The Big Kids Store** 394 King's Road, SW10 (0171 795 0801).

Health & beauty
Beauty services
The Green Room
21 Earl's Court Road, W8 (0171 937 6595). High Street Kensington tube. **Open** 9am-9pm Mon-Thur; 9am-6pm Fri, Sat; 10am-5pm Sun. **Credit** AmEx, DC, JCB, MC, £TC, V. **Map 3 A9**
Body Shop products are used alongside the Green Room's own aromatherapy oils at these right-on salons. Facials, manicures, massage and natural tanning are all popular treatments.
Branches are too numerous to list here. Check the telephone directory for your nearest.

Porchester Spa
225 Queensway, W2 (0171 792 3980). Bayswater, Queensway or Royal Oak tube. **Open** *Women-only* 10am-10pm Tue, Thur, Fri; 10am-4pm Sun. *Men-only* 10am-10pm Mon, Wed, Sat. *Mixed* 4-10pm Tue, Sun. **Membership** £35 a year. **Admission** £13.20 members; £17.95 non-members. **Credit** MC, V. **Map 1 B5**

As well as being equipped with two steam rooms, a Jacuzzi, swimming pool, sauna and (purely for masochists) an ice-cold plunge pool, this spa has kept its splendid original 1920s features.

The Sanctuary
11-12 Floral Street, WC2 (0171 420 5151/ gym 0171 240 0695). Covent Garden tube. **Open** *Health spa* 10am-6pm Mon, Tue, Sun; 9.30am-10pm Wed-Fri; 9.30am-8pm Sat. *Gym* 7am-9pm Mon-Fri; 10am-4.30pm Sat, Sun. **Membership** *Health spa* £1,375 per year. *Gym* full £600 per year (£60 per month) plus £175 joining fee; off-peak £445 per year (£44.50 per month) plus £150 joining fee. **Admission** *members* £49.50 day visit; £29.50 evening visit. **Credit** AmEx, MC, £$TC, V. **Map 8 L6**
A plant-filled, women-only haven equipped with a gym, two pools, Jacuzzi, steam room, sauna and sunbeds, plus more than 50 beauty treatments. You can become a member on the spot.

Cosmetics & herbalists
For London's most venerable traditional perfumiers, *see also page 198* **Penhaligon's** *and* **Floris**.

Aveda Institute
28-29 Marylebone High Street, W1 (0171 224 3157). Baker Street or Bond Street tube. **Open** 9.30am-7pm Mon-Fri; 10am-6pm Sat. **Credit** AmEx, MC, £TC, V. **Map 5 G5**
Aveda's covetable right-on lotions and potions may not be cheap, but you get what you pay for: 97% of ingredients are natural.

Crabtree & Evelyn
6 Kensington Church Street, W8 (0171 937 9335). High Street Kensington tube. **Open** 10am-6pm Mon-Wed, Fri, Sat; 10am-7pm Thur; 11am-5pm Sun. **Credit** AmEx, MC, £TC, V. **Map 1 B8**
Fanciful toiletries and gift foods, all beautifully packaged in a countrified nostalgic style. Ideal presents for the older woman in your life.
Branches are too numerous to list here. Check the telephone directory for your nearest.

Culpeper Herbalists

8 The Market, Covent Garden Piazza, WC2 (0171 379 6698). Covent Garden tube. **Open** 10am-8pm Mon-Thur; 9am-8pm Fri, Sat; 10am-6pm Sun. **Credit** AmEx, JCB, MC, £TC, V. **Map 8 L7**
Stacks of medicinal herbs and a variety of body-pampering gifts, prepared to rigorous standards and available by mail order too.
Branch: 21 Bruton Street, W1 (0171 629 4559).

Jo Malone

154 Walton Street, SW3 (0171 581 1101). Knights-bridge or South Kensington tube. **Open** 10am-6pm Mon-Sat. **Credit** MC, £TC, V. **Map 4 E10**
Gorgeous-smelling, sleekly packaged fragrances and matching body products, including the ever-popular lime, basil and mandarin. Sheer indulgence.

L'Occitane

237 Regent Street, W1 (0171 290 1426). Oxford Circus tube. **Open** 10am-7pm Mon-Wed, Fri, Sat; 10am-8pm Thur; noon-5pm Sun. **Credit** AmEx, MC, £TC, V. **Map 6 J6**
All the best French countryside whiffs and pongs, in the form of essential oils, soaps, moisturisers and the like.
Branch: 70 Kensington High Street, W8 (0171 938 4135); 67 King's Road, SW3 (0171 823 4555).

Lush

Units 7 & 11, The Piazza, Covent Garden, WC2 (0171 240 4570). Covent Garden tube. **Open** 10am-7pm Mon-Sat; noon-6pm Sun. **Credit** MC, £TC, V. **Map 8 L7**
Lush has made its name with its big tubs of freshly made enviro-friendly cosmetics, hunks of soap, wacky scents and fizzing bath bombes.
Branch: 123 King's Road, SW3 (0171 376 8348); 40 Carnaby Street, W1 (0171 287 5874).

Neal's Yard Remedies

15 Neal's Yard, WC2 (0171 379 7222). Covent Garden tube. **Open** 10am-6pm Mon; 10am-7pm Tue-Fri; 10am-5.30pm Sat; 11am-5pm Sun. **Credit** AmEx, MC, £TC, V. **Map 6 L6**
Over 200 medicinal herbs, plus skincare products and toiletries. The range of aromatherapy oils is high quality. Staff can advise customers on the right herbs to use for the right purpose.
Branches: Chelsea Farmers' Market, Sydney Street, SW3 (0171 351 6380); 9 Elgin Crescent, W11 (0171 727 3998); 68 Chalk Farm Road, NW1 (0171 284 2039).

Nelsons Homeopathic Pharmacy

73 Duke Street, W1 (0171 629 3118). Bond Street tube. **Open** 9am-5.30pm Mon-Fri; 9am-4pm Sat. **Credit** MC, £TC, V. **Map 5 G6**
More than 3,000 remedies, including Bach Flower concoctions. There are aromatherapy oils, books and nutritional supplements. Homeopathic prescriptions are fulfilled by knowledgeable staff.

Space NK Apothecary

4 Thomas Neal Centre, 37 Earlham Street, WC2 (0171 379 7030). Covent Garden tube. **Open** 10am-7pm Mon-Sat; noon-5pm Sun. **Credit** AmEx, DC, JCB, MC, V. **Map 6 L6**
Cutting-edge cosmetics, including Stila and Kiehl's, from Nicky Kinnaird's super-cool, super-successful and ever-expanding chain.
Branches: 7 Bishopsgate Arcade, 135 Bishopsgate, EC2 (0171 256 2303); 45-47 Brook Street, W1 (0171 355 1727); 307 King's Road, SW3 (0171 351 7209); 307 Brompton Road, SW3 (0171 589 8250); 73 St John's Wood High Street, NW8 (0171 536 0607).

Virgin Vie

242-244 Oxford Street, W1 (0171 629 9862). Oxford Circus tube. **Open** 10am-7pm Mon-Wed, Fri, Sat; 10am-8pm Thur; noon-6pm Sun. **Credit** AmEx, MC, TC, V. **Map 5 H6**
This tranquil shop stocks a pleasing and spot-on range of toiletries, make-up and other grooming products.

Hairdressers

See also page 198 **GF Trumper**.

Bladerunners

158 Notting Hill Gate, W11 (0171 229 2255). Notting Hill Gate tube. **Open** 8.30am-7pm Mon-Wed, Fri; 8.30am-8.30pm Thur; 10am-6pm Sat; 10am-4pm Sun.
Credit AmEx, MC, V. **Map 1 A7**
Trendy Notting Hill salon offering three methods of extensions for Euro and Afro hair, as well as all the regular stuff.

Charles Worthington

12 Charlotte Place, W1 (0171 631 1370). Goodge Street tube. **Open** 8am-8.15pm Mon-Thur; 8am-7.15pm Fri; 8am-5.15pm Sat. **Credit** AmEx, MC, V. **Map 5 J5**
Shiatsu head massage, hot towels, tea, wine, Buck's Fizz… It's easy to forget you came in for a haircut.
Branches: 34 Great Queen Street, WC2 (0171 831 5303); 1 Exchange Place, The Broadgate Club, EC2 (0171 638 0802); Dorchester Hotel, Park Lane, W1 (0171 317 6321); The Broadgate Club West, Triton Square, Regents Place, W1 (0171 383 4840).

Columbia Road Flower Market. *See p193.*

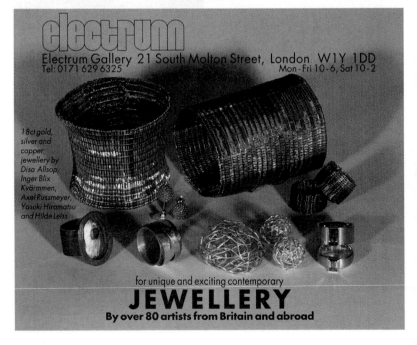

Fish

30 D'Arblay Street, W1 (0171 494 2398).
Tottenham Court Road tube. **Open** 10am-7pm Mon-Wed,
Fri; 10am-8pm Thur; 10am-5pm Sat. **Credit** MC, V.
Map 6 K6
A style-conscious, youngish crowd are expertly coiffed in
the friendly atmosphere of a former fishmonger's. Look out
for the original tiles.

Stuart Phillips

25 Monmouth Street, WC2 (0171 379 5304). Covent
Garden tube. **Open** 10am-6.30pm Mon-Fri; 10am-5.15pm
Sat. **Credit** MC, V. **Map 6 L6**
A supremely relaxing, classy, up-and-coming salon. A cut
and blow-dry is around £30 for women/£26 for men.

Vasos

5 Grape Street, WC2 (0171 813 6570). Covent Garden,
Holborn or Tottenham Court Road tube. **Open** 8.30am-
6pm Mon-Fri; 9am-1pm Sat. **6 L6**
Cheery basement barber that can deliver a decent basic cut
for around a tenner.

Vidal Sassoon

60 South Molton Street, W1 (0171 491 8848).
Bond Street tube. **Open** 10.30am-6pm Mon, Tue, Wed,
Fri; 10.30am-6.45pm Thur; 9am-5.15pm Sat.
Credit AmEx, MC, £TC, V. **Map 5 H6**
The emphasis is on precision cutting at this world-famous,
long-established chain. Call the VS School in 56 Davies
Mews, W1 (0171 629 4635); appointments 10am-3pm Mon-
Fri) for a bargain-priced cut from a (supervised) trainee.
Branches are too numerous to list here. Check the
telephone directory for your nearest.

Opticians

Arthur Morrice

13 Beauchamp Place, SW3 (0171 584 4661).
Knightsbridge tube. **Open** 9.30am-6pm Mon, Tue, Thur-
Sat; 9.30am-7pm Wed. **Credit** AmEx, DC, JCB, MC, V.
Map 4 F9
Attentive service is offered to buyers of both specs and con-
tact lenses at this beautifully decorated shop.

Boots Opticians

127A Kensington High Street, W8 (0171 938 1620).
High Street Kensington tube. **Open** 8.30am-7pm Mon-Fri;
9am-7pm Sat; 11am-5pm Sun. **Credit** AmEx, MC, V.
Map 3 B9
Not the greatest range of frames, but frequent sales, and
Boots' ubiquitousness, make this a useful step stop.
Branches are too numerous to list here. Check the
telephone directory for your nearest.

Vision Express

291 Oxford Street, W1 (0171 409 7880). Oxford
Circus tube. **Open** 9.30am-7.30pm Mon-Wed, Fri;
9.30am-8pm Thur; 9am-7pm Sat; noon-6pm Sun.
Map 5 H6
Offering 20-minute eye tests, Vision Express claims to be
able to make 95% of its customers new glasses within the
hour. Check the phone book for other branches.

Hobbies

Atlantis

146 Brick Lane, E1 (0171 377 8855). Aldgate East tube.
Open 9am-6pm Mon-Sat; 10am-5pm Sun. **Credit** AmEx,
MC, £TC, V. **Map 10 S5**
Britain's largest art materials store has it all – the place to
buy in bulk.

Chilling outside the **Bluebird.** *See page 201.*

The Bead Shop

21A Tower Street, WC2 (0171 240 0931). Leicester
Square tube. **Open** 1-6pm Mon; 10.30am-6pm Tue-Fri;
11.30am-5pm Sat. **Credit** AmEx, JCB, MC, £TC, V.
Map 6 K6
A kaleidoscopic selection of beads, plus thread, thongs, find-
ings and clasps.

Beatties

202 High Holborn, WC1 (0171 405 6285/8592).
Holborn tube. **Open** 10am-6pm Mon; 9am-6pm Tue-
Fri; 9am-5.30pm Sat. **Credit** AmEx, DC, MC, £TC, V.
Map 6 L5
Kits for all sorts of models, and everything a model railway
enthusiast could require.
Branches are too numerous to list here. Check the
telephone directory for your nearest.

The Cloth Shop

290 Portobello Road, W10 (0181 968 6001). Ladbroke
Grove or Notting Hill Gate tube. **Open** 10.30am-6pm
Mon-Thur; 10am-6pm Fri, Sat. **Credit** MC, £TC, V.
Map 1 A6
The Cloth Shop has over 400 types of cloth, many of which
are available in short lengths.

Creative Quilting

3 Bridge Road, Hampton Court, East Molesey, Surrey
(0181 941 7075). Hampton Court rail. **Open** 9.30am-
5.30pm Mon-Sat; noon-4pm Sun. **Credit** MC, V.
London's only quilting and patchwork shop.

Creativity

45 New Oxford Street, WC1 (0171 240 2945). Holborn
or Tottenham Court Road tube. **Open** 9.30am-6pm Mon-
Wed, Fri, Sat; 9.30am-7pm Thur. **Credit** MC, £TC, V.
Map 6 L5
Needlecraft essentials for knitting, tapestry, needlepoint and
embroidery. Staff are knowledgeable and friendly.

Falkiner Fine Papers

76 Southampton Row, WC1 (0171 831 1151). Holborn
tube. **Open** 9.30am-5.30pm Mon-Fri; 9.30am-1pm,
2-5.30pm, Sat. **Credit** (over £10) AmEx, MC, £TC, V.
Map 6 L5
Beautiful rare papers from around the world, including
hand-marbled, parchment and sheets containing pressed
flowers.

London Dolls House Company

29 Covent Garden Market, WC2 (0171 240 8681).
Covent Garden tube. **Open** 10.30am-7pm Mon-Sat;
noon-5pm Sun. **Credit** AmEx, MC, £TC, V.
Map 8 L7
Reproduction Victorian designs plus more modern dolls'
houses and a large stock of accessories.

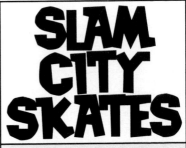

London Graphic Centre

16-18 Shelton Street, WC2 (0171 240 0095). Covent Garden tube. **Open** 9.30am-6pm Mon-Fri; 10.30am-6pm Sat. **Credit** AmEx, JCB, MC, £TC, V. **Map 6 L6**
Home to a great range of fine art, graphic and reprographic materials, and computer products.
Branches: 13 Tottenham Street, W1 (0171 637 2199); 254 Upper Richmond Road, SW15 (0181 785 9797).

MacCulloch & Wallis

25-26 Dering Street, W1 (0171 409 0725). Bond Street tube. **Open** 9am-6pm Mon-Wed, Fri; 9am-7pm Thur; 10.30am-5pm Sat. **Credit** AmEx, JCB, MC, £TC, V. **Map 5 H6**
The ultimate haberdasher, with a fabulous range of fabrics.

Spink & Son

5 King Street, SW1 (0171 930 7888). Green Park tube. **Open** 9am-5.30pm Mon-Fri. **Credit** AmEx, MC, £TC, V. **Map 7 J8**
Britain's leading authority on numismatic matters is also a fascinating and beautiful shop.

Stanley Gibbons International

399 Strand, WC2 (0171 836 8444). Covent Garden tube/ Charing Cross tube/rail. **Open** 8.30am-6pm Mon-Fri; 9am-5.30pm Sat. **Credit** AmEx, DC, MC, V. **Map 8 L7**
Founded in 1856, the most famous name in philately has more than three million stamps for sale.

Home accessories

See also **The Conran Shop, Purves & Purves** and **Heal's** *(pages 202-3).*

After Noah

121 Upper Street, N1 (0171 359 4281). Angel tube. **Open** 10am-6pm Mon-Sat; noon-5pm Sun. **Credit** AmEx, MC, V. **Map 9 O1**
A desirable mix of second-hand and new household accessories and furniture with a neat sideline in jewellery.
Branch: 261 King's Road, SW3 (0171 351 2610).

Barclay & Bodie

7 Blenheim Terrace, NW8 (0171 372 5705). St John's Wood tube. **Open** 9.30am-5.30pm Mon-Sat. **Credit** AmEx, MC, £TC, V.
Inspiring, eclectic, exclusive stock (from funky shower curtains to stylish napkin rings) featuring many unusual items.

The Candle Shop

30 The Market, Covent Garden, WC2 (0171 836 9815). Covent Garden tube. **Open** 10am-8pm Mon-Sat; 10.30am-7.30pm Sun. **Credit** AmEx, MC, £TC, V. **Map 8 L 6/7**
The more adventurous candle shopper should nose around here for candles in all shapes, shades and forms.

Cath Kidston

8 Clarendon Cross, W11 (0171 221 4000). Holland Park tube. **Open** 10.30am-6pm Mon-Fri; 11am-6pm Sat. **Credit** JCB, MC, £TC, V.
New and second-hand items from or inspired by the 1950s: painted furniture, fabrics, utensils and crockery. Expect lots of floral prints and gingham.

Designers Guild

267-271 & 275-277 King's Road, SW3 (0171 351 5775). Sloane Square tube. **Open** 9.30am-5.30pm Mon, Tue; 10am-6pm Wed-Sat; noon-5pm Sun. **Credit** AmEx, MC, V. **Map 4 E12**
Bright, energising colours are the hallmark of Tricia Guild's linen, crockery, glassware, soft furnishings and furniture.

David & Charles Wainwright

28 Rosslyn Hill, NW3 (0171 431 5900). Hampstead tube. **Open** 10am-7pm Mon-Sat; 11am-6.30pm Sun. **Credit** AmEx, MC, V.
Desirable goods from Rajasthan, Indonesia, Java and the Malaccan Straits.
Branches: 251 Portobello Road, W11 (0171 792 1988); 63 Portobello Road, W11 (0171 727 0707).

Divertimenti

45-47 Wigmore Street, W1 (0171 935 0689). Bond Street tube. **Open** 9.30am-6pm Mon-Fri; 10am-6pm Sat. **Credit** AmEx, DC, MC, £TC, V. **Map 5 G6**
Seriously cool cookware shop selling items large and small.
Branch: 139-141 Fulham Road, SW3 (0171 581 8065).

Elizabeth David Cookshop

3A North Row, The Market, Covent Garden, WC2 (0171 836 9167). Covent Garden tube. **Open** 10.30am-6.30pm Mon-Fri; 10am-7pm Sat; noon-5pm Sun. **Credit** AmEx, MC, £TC, V. **Map 8 L7**
Excellent range of pots, pans, cutlery and kitchen gadgets.

Haus

23-25 Mortimer Street, W1 (0171 255 2557). Goodge Street or Tottenham Court Road tube. **Open** 10am-6pm Mon-Fri; 11.30am-6pm Sat. **Credit** JCB, MC, £TC, V. **Map 5 J5**
Fierce furniture, arty accessories and up-to-the-minute design *savoir-faire* is what you get at Haus.

The Holding Company

241-245 King's Road, SW3 (0171 352 1600). Sloane Square tube then 11, 19, 22 bus. **Open** 10am-7pm Mon-Sat; noon-6pm Sun. **Credit** AmEx, MC, £TC, V. **Map 4 D12**
A wonderful, inventive range of storage ideas.

Inventory

26-40 Kensington High Street, W8 (0171 937 2626). High Street Kensington tube. **Open** 10am-7pm Mon-Sat; noon-6pm Sun. **Credit** AmEx, JCB, MC, £TC, V. **Map 3 B9**
Modern home accessories galore, at very reasonable prices.

Jerry's Home Store

163-167 Fulham Road, SW3 (0171 581 0909). South Kensington tube. **Open** 10am-6pm Mon-Fri; 10am-6.30pm Sat; 11.30am-5.30pm Sun. **Credit** AmEx, MC, £TC, V. **Map 4 D11**
This American homewares store sells a comprehensive

Late chemists

Bliss

5-6 Marble Arch, W1 (0171 723 6116). Marble Arch tube/N3, N56, N99 night bus. **Open** 9am-midnight daily. **Credit** AmEx, DC, MC, £TC, V. **Map 2 F6**
The two branches of Bliss listed below open till 7pm and 9pm respectively.
Branches: 33 Sloane Square, SW1 (0171 730 1023); 149 Edgware Road, W2 (0171 723 2336).

Boots

75 Queensway, W2 (0171 229 9266). Bayswater or Queensway tube. **Open** 9am-10pm Mon-Sat; 5-10pm Sun. **Credit** AmEx, MC, V. **Map 1 C6**

range of kitchenware (including electrical gadgets) and party goods, plus a few accessories for the rest of the house. **Branches:** 57-61 Heath Street, NW3 (0171 794 8622); Bentalls Centre, Kingston, Surrey (0181 549 5393).

Muji
187 Oxford Street, W1 (0171 437 7503). Oxford Circus tube. **Open** 10.30am-7pm Mon-Wed; 10.30am-8pm Thur; 10.30am-7.30pm Fri; 10am-7pm Sat; noon-6pm Sun. **Credit** AmEx, DC, JCB, MC, £TC, V. **Map 6 K6**
Pared-down designs in stationery, storage, kitchen and bathroom accessories, and clothing from this Japanese chain. **Branches** are too numerous to list here. Check the telephone directory for your nearest.

Titri
82D Portobello Road, W11 (0171 229 2023). Notting Hill Gate tube. **Open** 10.30am-5.30pm Tue-Sat. **Credit** MC, V. **Map 1 A6**
Brigitte Singh's northern Indian textiles include tablecloths, quilts and clothes, all printed by hand-blocking.

Walter Castellazzo
84 Highgate High Street, N6 (0181 340 3001). Archway or Highgate tube. **Open** 11am-6pm Tue-Sun. **Credit** MC, V.
When you're sick of chainstore homogeneity, check out this treasure trove of unusual objects and furniture.

Crafts

See also page 197 **Lesley Craze Gallery/ Craze 2/C2+.**

Ceramica Blue
10 Blenheim Crescent, W11 (0171 727 0288). Ladbroke Grove tube. **Open** 11am-5pm Mon; 10am-6.30pm Tue-Sat; noon-4pm first Sun of month. **Credit** AmEx, MC, £TC, V.
Bright and distinctive tiles and tableware from around the world at reasonable prices.

Contemporary Applied Arts
2 Percy Street, W1 (0171 436 2344). Tottenham Court Road tube. **Open** 10.30am-5.30pm Mon-Sat. **Credit** AmEx, MC, £TC, V. **Map 6 K5**
One of the largest, most varied and dynamic ranges of new craft/design work in London.

Contemporary Ceramics
William Blake House, 7 Marshall Street, W1 (0171 437 7605). Oxford Circus tube. **Open** 10am-5.30pm Mon-Wed, Fri, Sat; 10am-7pm Thur. **Credit** AmEx, MC, £TC, V. **Map 5 J6**
The retail outlet of the Craft Potters' Association sells an inventive and affordable selection of its members' work. There are regular exhibitions here too.

Crafts Council Shop
44A Pentonville Road, N1 (0171 806 2559). Angel tube. **Open** 11am-6pm Tue-Sat; 2-6pm Sun. **Credit** AmEx, JCB, MC, £TC, V. **Map 9 N2**
The Crafts Council's headquarters house a small, attractive shop with a frequently changing stock of high-quality work in a variety of media.
Branch: Victoria & Albert Museum, Cromwell Road, SW7 (0171 589 5070).

Fitch's Ark
6 Clifton Road, W9 (0181 201 1199). Warwick Avenue tube. **Open** 11am-7pm Mon-Sat; 11am-4pm Sun. **Credit** MC, V. **Map 1 C4**
Fitch's Ark specialises in creative work based on animal imagery, from animal-head doorknobs to sculpture, via glassware and kids' games.

Gabriel's Wharf & Oxo Tower
Upper Ground, SE1 (recorded info 0171 401 2255). Waterloo tube/rail. **Open** 11am-6pm Tue-Sun. **Credit** varies. **Map 11 N7**
Gabriel's Wharf has two rows of design and craft shops/ workshops including silversmiths, workers in papier mâché and ceramicists. A few hundred yards away, the **Oxo Tower** boasts a fine selection of outlets for individual artists' and designers' products, including Karen Gledhill's organic-looking gold and silver rings, Devi Khakhria's music-inspired tableware, Little & Collins hand-tufted rugs and wallhangings and Salt's inventive, original textiles.

The Glasshouse
21 St Alban's Place, N1 (0171 359 8162). Angel tube. **Open** 10am-5.30pm Tue-Fri; 10am-5pm Sat. **Credit** AmEx, JCB, MC, V. **Map 9 O2**
All the beautiful, innovative glassware on sale here is made on the premises; clients are welcome to witness the glassblowing process (Tue-Fri only).

Musical instruments

Andy's Guitar Centre & Workshop
27 Denmark Street, WC2 (0171 916 5080). Tottenham Court Road tube. **Open** 10am-7pm Mon-Sat; 12.30-6.30pm Sun. **Credit** AmEx, DC, MC, £TC, V. **Map 6 K6**
Long-established retail and repair centre. Acoustic guitars upstairs; electric downstairs. Great vintage models.

Bill Lewington
144 Shaftesbury Avenue, WC2 (0171 240 0584). Leicester Square or Tottenham Court Road tube. **Open** 9.30am-5.30pm Mon-Sat. **Credit** AmEx, DC, MC, £TC, V. **Map 6 K6**
Huge selection of brass instruments. Well-informed staff.

Boosey & Hawkes
295 Regent Street, W1 (0800 731 4778/0171 580 2060). Oxford Circus tube. **Open** 9am-6pm Mon-Fri; 10am-4pm Sat. **Credit** AmEx, DC, MC, £TC, V. **Map 5 J6**
Specialists in classical sheet music.

Hobgoblin Music
24 Rathbone Place, W1 (0171 323 9040). Tottenham Court Road tube. **Open** 10am-5.30pm Mon-Sat. **Credit** AmEx, MC, V. **Map 6 K5**
The spectrum of folk – from traditional Irish to Asian – by means of instruments, sheet music, CDs and so on.

Music & Video Exchange
56 Notting Hill Gate, W11 (0171 229 4805). Notting Hill Gate tube. **Open** 10am-8pm daily. **Credit** AmEx, DC, JCB, MC, £TC, V. **Map 1 A7**
There are plenty of bargains to be had at this well-stocked second-hand store, including pop and classical instruments.

Rayman
29 Monmouth Street, WC2 (0171 240 1776). Covent Garden tube. **Open** 10.30am-6pm Mon-Sat. **Credit** AmEx, MC, £TC, V. **Map 6 L6**
A pan-world collection of instruments including pan pipes, *pinquillos* and rainsticks.

Soundhouse/Turnkey
114 Charing Cross Road, WC2 (0171 379 5148). Tottenham Court Road tube. **Open** 10am-6pm Mon-Wed, Fri, Sat; 10am-7pm Thur. **Credit** AmEx, DC, MC, £TC, V. **Map 6 K6**
Guitars, keyboards and one of the best ranges of studio and computer equipment in town.

World of Music

8, 20 & 21-24 Denmark Street, WC2 (0171 240 7696).
Tottenham Court Road tube. **Open** 10am-6pm Mon-Sat.
Credit AmEx, DC, MC, £TC, V. **Map 6 K6**
The king of Denmark Street. Most of the music shops in this
tiny thoroughfare are part of the WoM group and encom-
pass sheet music, pianos, recording gear, drums, basses,
classical/electric guitars and amps.

Music shops

Megastores

HMV

150 Oxford Street, W1 (0171 631 3423). Oxford Circus
tube. **Open** 9.30am-8pm Mon-Fri; 9am-7.30pm Sat; noon-
6pm Sun. **Credit** AmEx, DC, MC, £TC, V.
Map 5 J6
The ground floor holds rock, pop and soul sections; in the
basement are jazz, soundtrack, classical, spoken word and
world music sections. Less tiring than other megastores.
Branches: 363 Oxford Street, W1 (0171 629 1240);
4 Trocadero, Coventry Street, W1 (0171 439 0447).

Tower Records

1 Piccadilly Circus, W1 (0171 439 2500). Piccadilly Circus
tube. **Open** 9am-midnight Mon-Sat; noon-6pm Sun.
Credit AmEx, MC, £TC, V. **Map 7 J7**
In terms of sheer quantity, Tower is hard to beat. The choice
of import CDs, particularly from Japan, is one of its most
impressive features.
Branches: 62-64 Kensington High Street, W8 (0171 938
3511); 151B Queensway, W2 (0171 229 4550); 162 Camden
High Street, NW1 (0171 424 2800).

Virgin Megastore

14-16 Oxford Street, W1 (0171 631 1234). Tottenham
Court Road tube. **Open** 9am-9pm Mon-Sat; noon-6pm
Sun. **Credit** AmEx, MC, £TC, V. **Map 6 K6**
Music still rules at this four-floor giant, but only just, as
more and more space is taken over by computer games, plus
videos and books (and even a travel agency). There's a
decent classical selection on the top floor.
Branch: 527-531 Oxford Street, W1 (0171 491 8582).

Specialist music shops

Cut a corner (Tottenham Court Road and Oxford
Street – one of London's unloveliest corners) and
dive into Hanway Street for second-hand sounds:
at no.22 there's **On the Beat**, at no.36 **Division
One**. Soho is also a music mecca – **Selectadisc**
(no.34) and **Sister Ray** (no.94) are particularly
strong on indie, **Reckless Records** (no.30) is
good for quality mainstream, there's Jamaican
music at **Daddy Kool** (no.12) and general cut-
price CDs at **Mr CD** (no.80).

Black Market

25 D'Arblay Street, W1 (0171 437 0478). Oxford
Circus tube. **Open** noon-7pm Mon; 11am-7pm Tue-Sat.
Credit AmEx, MC, £TC, V. **Map 6 K6**
The latest clubland imports are stocked at this hip outlet.

Cheapo Cheapo Records

53 Rupert Street, W1 (0171 437 8272). Piccadilly
Circus tube. **Open** 11am-10pm Mon-Sat. **Credit** £TC.
Map 8 K7
The stuff of legends. They sell records! And they're cheap!
'Nuff said.

Farringdon's Records

64-72 Leadenhall Market, EC3 (0171 623 9605).
Monument tube. **Open** 10am-6pm Mon-Fri.
Credit AmEx, DC, MC, £TC, V. **Map 12 Q6/7**
Consistently impressive, elegant classical music store. Well-
informed staff.

Honest Jon's

276 & 278 Portobello Road, W10 (0181 969 9822).
Ladbroke Grove tube. **Open** 10am-6pm Mon-Sat; 11am-
5pm Sun. **Credit** AmEx, DC, JCB, MC, £TC, V.
Map 1 A6
A favourite for black music, with jazz, soul, Latin, reggae
and dance all well represented.

Intoxica!

231 Portobello Road, W11 (0171 229 8010). Ladbroke
Grove tube. **Open** 10.30am-6pm Mon-Fri; 10am-6pm Sat;
noon-4pm Sun. **Credit** AmEx, MC, £TC, V.
Map 1 A6
Second-hand jazz, soundtracks, exotica, soul and 1960s,
plus new US independents and dance in the basement.

MDC Classic Music

437 Strand, WC2 (0171 240 2157). Charing Cross
tube/rail. **Open** 9.30am-7.30pm Mon-Fri; 9.30am-7pm
Sat; 11am-5.30pm Sun. **Credit** AmEx, MC, V.
Map 8 L7
Unashamedly populist, MDC covers most branches of the
classical world. Good for special offers.
Branches are too numerous to list here. Check the
telephone directory for your nearest.

Mole Jazz

311 Gray's Inn Road, WC1 (0171 278 0703).
King's Cross tube/rail. **Open** 10am-6pm Mon-Thur, Sat;
10am-8pm Fri. **Credit** AmEx, DC, MC, £TC, V.
Map 6 M3
Jazz from the early days to the hottest current artists: the
ground floor has CDs and books; upstairs are second-hand
LPs, with a great many collector's items.

Rare Discs Ltd

18 Bloomsbury Street, WC1 (0171 580 3516).
Holborn or Tottenham Court Road tube. **Open** 10am-
6.30pm Mon-Sat. **Credit** AmEx, DC, MC, £TC, V.
Map 6 K5
An unsurpassed collection of film soundtracks, plus shows
and musicals, mainly on vinyl.

Rhythm Records

281 Camden High Street, NW1 (0171 267 0123).
Camden Town tube. **Open** 10.30am-6.30pm daily.
Credit MC, V.
One of London's best selections of specialist independent
music: hardcore punk, 1960s psychedelia, electronic, folk
and country – on CD and vinyl.

Rough Trade

130 Talbot Road, W11 (0171 229 8541). Notting Hill
Gate tube. **Open** 10am-6.30pm Mon-Sat. **Credit** AmEx,
JCB, £TC, MC, V. **Map 1 A5**
A great selection of independent releases, from punk and
hardcore to trip hop and world music. There's also a fabu-
lous stock of fanzines.
Branch: 16 Neal's Yard, WC2 (0171 240 0105).

Stern's African Record Centre

293 Euston Road, NW1 (0171 387 5550). Warren Street
tube. **Open** 10.30am-6.30pm Mon-Sat. **Credit** AmEx,
MC, £TC, V. **Map 5 J4**
African music from every country in the continent, on all
formats. Sounds from other parts of the globe are increasingly represented.

Sport

Body Active
Charing Cross Underground Concourse, Adelaide Street,
WC2 (0171 240 1363). Charing Cross tube/rail.
Open 9am-5.30pm Mon-Fri; 10am-5.30pm Sat.
Credit MC, V. **Map 8 L7**
Claiming to be Europe's largest fitness centre, Body Active
caters for bodybuilders as much as aerobics junkies.

Cycle Surgery
9 Steward Street, E1 (0171 375 3088). Liverpool Street
tube/rail. **Open** 8.30am-6pm Mon-Fri; 10am-5pm Sat;
10am-4pm Sun. **Credit** AmEx, MC, £TC, V. **Map 10 R5**
Bikes and components sold; machines repaired and serviced.
And there's cycle parking in the basement (30p a day).

The Kite Store
48 Neal Street, WC2 (0171 836 1666). Covent Garden
tube. **Open** 10am-6pm Mon-Wed, Fri; 10am-7pm Thur;
10.30am-6pm Sat. **Credit** AmEx, MC, £TC, V.
Map 6 L6
Over 100 different kites always in stock, from basic models
to fantastic stunt designs. Staff are happy to advise novice
flyers on the most suitable models.

Lillywhite's
24-36 Lower Regent Street, SW1 (0171 930 3181).
Piccadilly Circus tube. **Open** 10am-8pm Mon-Wed, Fri;
10am-9pm Thur; 9am-7pm Sat; 11am-5pm Sun.
Credit AmEx, JCB, MC, V. **Map 8 K7**
An all-rounder, with six floors containing everything from
US brand-name leisurewear to specialist diving gear.

Skate Attack
95 Highgate Road, NW5 (0171 485 0007). Kentish
Town tube. **Open** 9.30am-6pm Mon-Fri; 9am-6pm Sat;
10am-2pm Sun. **Credit** AmEx, MC, £TC, V.
Everything skate-like can be found at Skate Attack, the
largest shop of its kind in Europe. Also does repairs.

World of Football
119-121 Oxford Street, W1 (0171 287 5088). Oxford
Circus or Tottenham Court Road tube. **Open** 10am-7pm
Mon-Wed, Fri, Sat; 10am-8pm Thur; noon-6pm Sun.
Credit AmEx, JCB, MC, £TC, V. **Map 5 J6**
Two-floor football megastore.

YHA Adventure Shop
14 Southampton Street, WC2 (0171 836 8541). Covent
Garden tube. **Open** 10am-6pm Mon, Tue; 10.30am-6pm
Wed; 10am-7pm Thur, Fri; 9am-6.30pm Sat; 11am-5pm
Sun. **Credit** AmEx, DC, JCB, MC, £TC, V. **Map 8 L7**
Good range of walking and camping gear.

Toys, games & magic

See also the toy and game departments of
Debenhams (334-348 Oxford Street, W1;
0171 580 3000), **Harrods**, **John Lewis**, **Marks
& Spencer** and **Selfridges** (for all, *see pages
202-3*). For antique toys, *see page 187* **Donay
Antiques**; for computer games, *see page 189*
Electronics: Computers.

Benjamin Pollock's Toy Shop
44 The Market, Covent Garden, WC2 (0171 379 7866).
Covent Garden tube. **Open** 10.30am-6pm Mon-Sat; noon-
5pm Sun. **Credit** AmEx, JCB, MC, £TC, V. **Map 8 L7**
Quaint and cluttered, this delightful shop specialises in
old-style toys.

Cheeky Monkey
202 Kensington Park Road, W11 (0171 792 9022).
Notting Hill Gate tube. **Open** 9.30am-5.30pm Mon-Fri;
10am-5.30pm Sat. **Credit** AmEx, MC, £TC, V. **Map 1 A6**
A fine selection of new toys and nursery accessories, including handmade quilt and cot sets, nursery friezes and wood-
en toys. Good new and second-hand clothes too.
Branch: 24 Abbeville Road, SW4 (0181 673 5215);
1 Bennett Court, Bellevue Road, SW17 (0181 672 2025).

Daisy & Tom
181 King's Road, SW3 (0171 352 5000). Sloane Square
tube then 11, 19, 22 bus/49 bus. **Open** 10am-6pm Mon,
Tue, Thur, Fri; 10am-7pm Wed; 9am-6.30pm Sat; noon-
6pm Sun. **Credit** AmEx, MC, £TC, V. **Map 4 E12**
Top toys, hip clothes, an in-store merry-go-round, a soda
bar and a general hands-on play feel – what more could any
kid or parent ask for?

Davenport's Magic Shop
7 Charing Cross Underground Shopping Concourse,
Strand, WC2 (0171 836 0408). Charing Cross tube/rail.
Open 9.30am-5.30pm Mon-Fri; 10.15am-4pm Sat.
Map 8 L7
In 1998 this family business celebrated its 100th year of
magic. The shop provides for both professionals and new-
comers, and staff are keen to encourage novices.

Disney Store
140-144 Regent Street, W1 (0171 287 6558). Oxford
Circus tube. **Open** 10am-8pm Mon-Sat; noon-6pm Sun.
Credit AmEx, JCB, MC, £TC, V. **Map 7 J7**
Get your Snow White dress, Hercules action figure or
singalong videos here.
Branches are too numerous to list here. Check the
telephone directory for your nearest.

Early Learning Centre
Unit 7, King's Mall, Hammersmith, W6 (0181 741
2469). Hammersmith tube. **Open** 9am-5.30pm Mon-Sat.
Credit AmEx, MC, £TC, V.
A flourishing chain of shops with large stocks of brightly
coloured, chunky toys. As well as their own well-priced toys,
stores carry the full Duplo and Brio ranges.
Branches are too numerous to list here. Check the
telephone directory for your nearest.

Hamleys
188-196 Regent Street, W1 (0171 734 3161). Oxford
Circus tube. **Open** 10am-8pm Mon-Fri; 9.30am-8pm Sat;
noon-6pm Sun. **Credit** AmEx, DC, JCB, MC, £TC, V.
Map 7 J7
As much tourist attraction as shop, Hamleys is five floors
of noise, colour, beaming staff, crazed children and harassed
parents. Plus points is London's biggest selection of board
games, and a video arcade in the basement. Prices are high.
Branch: 3 The Plaza, Covent Garden, WC2 (0171 240 4646).

Tridias
25 Bute Street, SW7 (0171 584 2330). South
Kensington tube. **Open** 9.30am-6pm Mon-Fri; 10am-6pm
Sat. **Credit** MC, £TC, V. **Map 4 D10**
One of the UK's top traditional toy shops. Original, reasonably priced equipment: a good place to look for rainy-day
activity toys, scientific toys and dressing-up gear.

Warner Brothers Studio Store
178-182 Regent Street, W1 (0171 434 3334). Oxford
Circus tube. **Open** 10am-7pm Mon-Wed, Fri; 10am-8pm
Thur, Sat; noon-6pm Sun. **Credit** AmEx, DC, JCB, MC,
£TC, V. **Map 7 J7**
Bugs Bunny, Daffy Duck and chums are emblazoned on
T-shirts, mugs and toothbrushes, or moulded into chunks
of loud plastic.

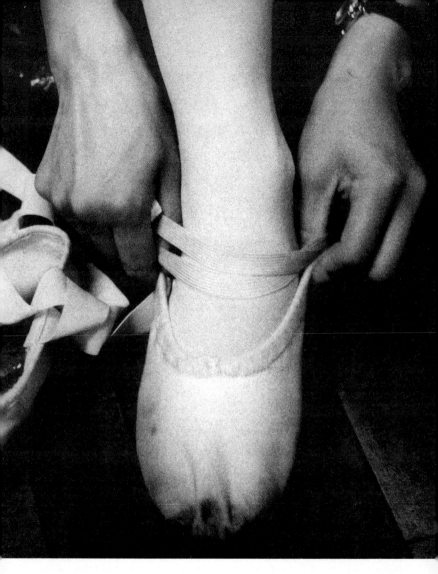

Arts & Entertainment

Children

London's a capital place for cavorting with kids.

The British famously love their pets more than they do their children, so it may come as a surprise to find so much child-centred entertainment on offer in the capital. Romping in the park, zapping aliens in a mega video arcade, stroking an iguana, laughing at a puppet show – there's more than enough to keep your offspring entertained in town. For details of current events and activities, see London's monthly magazine for parents, *Kids Out*.

Grand days out

With the capital so chock-full of child-friendly sights, it's easy to plan whole days around one area. Most of the sights in **bold** have fuller entries elsewhere in the guide; *see pages 315-21* **Index**.

South Bank

Start at County Hall, next to Westminster Bridge, which houses the **London Aquarium**, with fish and sea life from around the world, and the (expensive) video game palace of **Namco Station**. Downstream from here is the **Royal Festival Hall**, where there are cafés, free foyer exhibitions and special events on summer weekends. (Behind here, in the middle of a huge roundabout outside Waterloo Station, is the new **BFI London IMAX cinema**, due to open spring 1999.) Then stroll along the south bank to **Gabriel's Wharf**, with its shops, tearoom, restaurants, and open-air events in the summer. Nearby are the **National Film Theatre**, the **Museum of the Moving Image** and the **National Theatre**. Keep walking and you come to…

Bankside

HMS Belfast is a great place for children, with seven huge decks to explore. Nearby are **Tower Bridge** and the ghoulish pleasures of **London Dungeon** (not suitable for those of a sensitive disposition). Upstream from here, between London and Southwark bridges, is the wonderful reconstruction of Sir Francis Drake's **Golden Hinde**.

Covent Garden

One of London's only pedestrianised areas. The old fruit and vegetable market is now full of shops, stalls and street entertainers, including several toy shops. The **Cabaret Mechanical Theatre**, on the lower level of the market, contains more than 60 visitor-operated quirky contraptions to keep even the most hyperactive child busy. Nearby are the **London Transport Museum**, **Theatre Museum** and **St Paul's Church** garden (secluded and pretty, it's a good spot for a picnic, although it gets crowded when sunny).

Piccadilly Circus

The big attractions here include the **Rock Circus**, **Planet Hollywood** and the **Trocadero**, which houses an **IMAX cinema**. There's enough to keep kids happy all day, but the cost will have you reeling. Evenings are the best time to visit (all these places stay open late). Nearby are Chinatown and the Leicester Square cinemas.

Trafalgar Square

A cheap option. Marvel at how long the kids enjoy feeding the pigeons, climbing on the lions (not real, of course), playing around the fountains and watching the world go by. Then cross the road to the **National Gallery**, which has excellent (free) trails for kids to follow, via various paintings. Nearby are the **National Portrait Gallery**, The Mall (leading to **Buckingham Palace**) and Downing Street. A two-in-one treat can be had at **St Martin-in-the-Fields**: go first to the **Café in the Crypt**, then burn off all that energy at the **Brass Rubbing Centre**.

St Paul's Cathedral

Climb to the dome for breathtaking City views (you need a head for heights and lots of stamina). Nearby are **Postman's Park**, the **Museum of London** and the **Barbican Centre**.

Royal London

The first stop should be **Buckingham Palace**, although don't expect to see Liz through the windows doing a little light dusting. The best place to see the **Changing of the Guard** is near the barracks in Birdcage Walk; in the nearby **Royal Mews** you'll find groomed horses and burnished coaches. If Queenie's not at home, she'll probably be at **Windsor Castle**, which makes for a lovely day out of London, as does **Hampton Court Palace**. Whining children should be taken to the **Tower of London** and introduced to the story of the Princes in the Tower.

Greenwich

Choose a fine day and take the riverboat to explore Greenwich and **Greenwich Park** (a 15-minute walk from the pier), then walk under the Thames (through the pedestrian tunnel from Greenwich

by contrast, the lovely dolls' houses and back copies of the *Beano* at the **Bethnal Green Museum of Childhood** are better suited to older children and adults. For other museums of childhood, *see page 119*. One of the city's quirkiest museums is the **Horniman Museum** in south London (exhibits include a great collection of musical instruments and a stuffed walrus).

For something a bit different, take the kids to one of the superb talks on armour at the **Wallace Collection** (book well in advance). Also, look out for **Art Trolleys**, hands-on arts and craft areas for kids to get stuck into, at various museums.

Parks & playgrounds

London's parks are great fun for all ages. Below are a few not listed elsewhere in the guide, but there are scores more. **Regent's Park** has two boating lakes (one for children), three playgrounds and **London Zoo**; **Kensington Gardens** contains two playgrounds and the huge Round Pond for sailing model boats. Sprawling **Hampstead Heath** in the north and **Richmond Park** (lovely for cycle rides) in the south are where Londoners go to pretend they're in deepest Devon. You can also fly kites on **Parliament Hill**, or unleash your kids on the ramshackle adventure playground in **Battersea Park**. **Alexandra Park** and **Clissold Park**, both in north London, and **Victoria Park**, the pride of east London, also have attractions specifically for children. The parks mentioned below are all free.

Coram's Fields
93 Guilford Street, WC1 (0171 837 6138). Russell Square tube. **Open** *Easter-end Oct* 9am-8pm daily; *Nov-Mar* 9am-dusk daily. **Map 6 L4**
Under-5s play area, paddling pool, pet animal corner and café. No dogs, and no adults admitted without a child.

Crystal Palace Park
Thicket Road, SE20 (0181 778 9496). Crystal Palace rail. **Open** 7.30am-dusk daily.
Farmyard, horse cart rides, a maze, a funfair, two cafés, a boating lake with bizarre Victorian dinosaurs on the islands, and a 'land train' (that's a dressed-up tractor to most of us).

Highgate Wood
Muswell Hill Road, N6 (0181 444 6129). Highgate tube. **Open** 9am-one hour before dusk Tue-Fri; 8.30am-one hour before dusk Sat, Sun.
Trails, a playground (one of the best in town), a nature hut and the Oshobasho café in a restful corner of north London.

Syon Park & London Butterfly House
Syon Park, Brentford, Middx (0181 560 0378/ recorded info 0181 560 7272). Gunnersbury tube then 237, 267 bus. **Open** *May-Sept* 10am-5.30pm daily; *Oct-Apr* 10am-3.30pm daily. **Admission** *London Butterfly House* £3.20; £1.90-£2 concs; £7.50 family ticket; free under-3s. **Credit** MC, V.
Miniature steam train, playground, conservatory and garden centre, in the grounds of a huge tropical greenhouse with foliage and gorgeous butterflies from around the world. *See also p112.*

Bramley's Big Adventure. *See page 218.*

Pier to the Isle of Dogs) to return on the DLR from Island Gardens to Tower Gateway or Bank. In the park itself are the **National Maritime Museum**, **Queen's House** and the **Royal Observatory**, and within striking distance are the **Cutty Sark**, **Gipsy Moth IV** and **Greenwich Market**.

Boat trips
Cruise London's waterways. Trips run along the Regent's Canal in north London between Little Venice and **London Zoo**: phone the London Waterbus Company (0171 482 2550) or Jason's Trip (0171 286 3428), and along the Thames between **Hampton Court** in the west and the **Thames Barrier** in the east, calling at all points and piers on the way (various companies run this route; phone 0171 345 5122 for details). *See also page 304.*

Museums & collections
Of the Exhibition Road trio, the **Science Museum** is probably most popular with kids. One of its major attractions is the Launch Pad, with hands-on experiments for tots to teenagers; it also organises Science Nights, when children can explore the museum after dark (book ahead), and sleepovers. Not to be missed is the hands-on gallery, Garden and Things (phone first to check it's open). The **Natural History Museum** is also a favourite with children, especially the Dinosaur section and the earthquake simulation in the Earth Galleries. The **Victoria & Albert Museum**, too, is not without its younger fans.

The **Museum of London** holds regular workshops and shows films for both children and adults, including a diorama about the Great Fire of London. The **National Maritime Museum** in Greenwich has exciting exhibitions, plus the All Hands interactive gallery for younger children. The mammoth scale of much of the ancient plunder in the **British Museum** impresses all ages; there's an excellent children's guide to the collections.

The **London Toy & Model Museum** is splendidly hands-on and practically indestructible;

Supervised play areas

HAPA

HAPA (Hurtwood Adventure Playground Association) has a handful of parks across London where disabled and able-bodied children can play safely, supervised by fully trained staff. For a list of parks phone 0171 731 1435.

One o'clock clubs

One o'clock clubs are areas within parks where pre-school children can play in safety. Most have sandpits, playhouses, paints, crayons, toys, slides and climbing frames. Children playing in these enclosed, dog-free places must be accompanied by an adult. Supervised opening hours are from 1pm. Most Greater London boroughs run a One o'clock club: look in the telephone book and contact any borough for a list.

Indoor adventure playgrounds

Bramley's Big Adventure

136 Bramley Road, W10 (0181 960 1515). Ladbroke Grove or Latimer Road tube. **Open** 10am-6.30pm daily. **Admission** *weekends & school holidays* £3.95 over-5s; £2.95 under-5s; *weekdays & termtime* £3.50 over-5s; £2.50 under-5s; free babies & toddlers free with paying sibling. **Credit** MC, V.

A smart, cool playground with a separate area for tinies and some excellent climbing equipment (with sound effects) for older children. There's decent coffee, food and reading matter for accompanying adults.

Discovery Zone

1st floor, The Junction Shopping Centre, Clapham Junction, SW11 (0171 223 1717). Clapham Junction rail. **Open** 10am-6pm Mon-Fri; 10am-7pm Sat, Sun, school holidays. **Admission** £3.99 (£4.99 Sat, Sun) 2s-12s; £2.99 (£3.99 Sat, Sun) under-2s. **Credit** MC, V.

An enormously popular playground within Clapham Junction Station Shopping Centre, which has room for 500, although staff usually stop at 300. An exciting maze of ball pools, tunnels, slides, swings and pulleys keeps children up to 12 active and happy.

The Playhouse

The Old Gymnasium, Highbury Grove School, corner of Highbury Grove & Highbury New Park, N5 (0171 704 9424). Highbury & Islington tube. **Open** 10am-7pm daily. **Admission** £2.95 per session, £2.20 third & subsequent children; £2.20 under-2s.

This medium-sized playroom has space for up to 70 children aged from six months to 12 years. Facilities include a three-level playframe, a 40-ft (14-m) slide, ball ponds, crawl tunnels and rope bridges, plus an under-5s soft play area.

Rascals Adventure Centre

Waterfront Leisure Centre, High Street Woolwich, SE18 (0181 317 5000). Woolwich Arsenal rail/177, 180 bus. **Open** 9.30am-6pm Mon-Fri; 9.30am-2pm Sat, Sun. **Admission** *(members)* £2.10 first child; £1 any subsequent child; *(non-members)* £3; £1 per two-hour session.

There's room for up to 70 children in the play area, which is divided into a spacious soft play area for tinies and a large maze of runways, slides and other activities for five-to-eight-year-olds. Children who have had their fill of the play equipment can relax in the video corner. The management provides a 'drop and shop' session on Saturday mornings, when the play zone operates as a crèche (phone for details). Note that a maximum of three children are admitted per adult.

Swimming

There are swimming pools and leisure centres all over London. Below we list some of the best for children. For more, *see page 259.*

Finchley Lido

Great North Leisure Park, High Road, Finchley, N12 (0181 343 9830). Finchley Central tube. **Open** 6.45-8.30am, 9am-6.30pm, Mon; 6.45-8.30am, 9am-9.30pm, Tue, Thur, Fri; 6.45-8.30am, 9am-8pm, Wed; 8am-4pm Sat, Sun. **Admission** £2.50; £1.25 concs; free under-5s.

As well as the 25-m main pool, there's a leisure pool with a wave machine, hot tubs, rapids, water jets, a shallow area for babies and slides for small children. There is a fun session with inflatables on Tuesdays 4.30-6pm. The small outdoor pool is open May-Sept. Busy in the evenings.

Latchmere Leisure Centre

Burns Road, SW11 (0171 207 8004). Clapham Common tube then 345 bus/Clapham Junction rail then 49, 319, 344 bus. **Open** 7am-9.30pm Mon-Thur; 7am-6pm Fri; 7am-7.30pm Sat; 7am-9.30pm Sun. **Admission** *off-peak* 9am-5pm £2.20; *peak* £2.45; £1.65 concs; free under-5s & disabled.

A leisure pool with a beach, slides, wave machine and deliciously warm learners' pool, plus a gym and café.

Waterfront Leisure Centre

High Street Woolwich, SE18 (0181 317 5000). Woolwich Arsenal rail/177, 180 bus. **Open** 7.15am-11pm Mon-Fri; 9am-10pm Sat; 9am-9.30pm Sun. **Admission** £1.20; 70p children (additional charge for activities).

The Wild and Wet Adventure Park (open 3-8pm Mon-Fri; 9am-5pm Sat, Sun) has a 25-m fitness pool and four themed pools. Safari Oasis has interactive water toys for toddlers and a five-lane slide for all ages. Anaconda is a 103-ft (65-m) serpent-shaped slide; the ride is fast and in pitch-darkness (a height restriction of 3ft 2in – 1m – applies). The main leisure pool has a wave machine, rapids, jets, a volcano, a waterfall, a hot tub and entertainers in costumes to organise games.

Animal encounters

There are plenty of places in the city where your kids can see some cuddly (and not-so-cuddly) creatures. There are around 20 city farms in and around London. For a full list contact: National Federation of City Farms, The Green House, Hereford Street, Bedminster, Bristol BS3 4NA (0117 923 1800/fax 0117 923 1900).

Battersea Park Children's Zoo

Battersea Park, SW11 (0181 871 7540). Sloane Square tube then 19, 137 bus/Battersea Park rail. **Open** *Apr-Sept* 10am-5pm daily (last admission 4.30pm); *Oct-Mar* 11am-3pm Sat, Sun. **Admission** £1.45; 70p-95p concs. **Map 4 F13**

A small zoo near the river. There are pony rides, a hillside infested with meerkats, monkey cages and lots of small animals, including pygmy goats, rabbits and a pot-bellied pig.

London Zoo

Regent's Park, NW1 (0171 722 3333). Camden Town tube then 274 bus. **Open** *Nov-Feb* 10am-4pm, *Mar-Oct* 10am-5.30pm, daily. **Admission** £8.50; £6-£7.50 concs; £26 family ticket; free under-4s. **Credit** AmEx, MC, £STC, V. **Map 5 G2**

One of the world's best collections of animals, London Zoo also has a strong educational slant, even if most children

Hansel and Gretel *get some stick at the* **Unicorn Theatre for Children.** *See page 220.*

are here to shriek at the gorillas, rhinos, elephants and wolves. Bear Mountain, on Mappin Terraces, is a sure-fire hit. While you're here, you can adopt a little beast (animal, that is). If possible, time your visit to coincide with one of the feeding times or animal shows (phone for details). *See also p54.*

Mudchute City Farm
Pier Street, Isle of Dogs, E14 (0171 515 5901/riding reservations 0171 515 0749). Crossharbour DLR.
Open 9.30am-4.30pm (pony rides 2-3pm) daily.
Admission free (prices vary for pony rides). **Map 5 G2**
Five acres of land stocked with cows, goats, free-range chickens and horses.

Theme parks

There are a number of major theme parks just outside London including **Chessington World of Adventures**, **Thorpe Park** and **Legoland Windsor**. For these, and other family attractions outside the capital, *see pages 282-3.*

Eating with kids

Lacking the same relaxed attitude to family dining that comes naturally in most southern European countries, the majority of London restaurants are not particularly welcoming to children. No decent local Italian or Spanish restaurant would bat an eyelid if you arrive with kids, but it is the American-owned or influenced places that really make children feel welcome. Below are some of the best.

Babe Ruth's
172-176 The Highway, E1 (0171 481 8181). Shadwell DLR/D1, 100 bus. **Meals** noon-11pm Mon-Thur; noon-midnight Fri, Sat; noon-10.30pm Sun. **Credit** AmEx, MC, V.
Not exactly central, but this huge sports restaurant is great fun for families. Kids can slam-dunk in the mini-basketball court and play on games machines while they stock up on huge portions of decent US and global staples.

The Big Easy
332-334 King's Road, SW3 (0171 352 4071). Sloane Square tube then 11, 19, 22 bus. **Meals** noon-midnight Mon-Thur; noon-12.30pm Fri, Sat; noon-11.30pm Sun.
Credit AmEx, MC, £TC, V. **Map 4 D12**
With crayons, high chairs and a kids' menu, this all-American restaurant has the added attraction for families of allowing one child under ten to eat for free when accompanied by an adult who is eating a main meal (subsequent children each for £3.95).

Pizza Express
30 Coptic Street, WC1 (0171 636 3232). Holborn or Tottenham Court Raod tube. **Meals** 11.30am-midnight daily. **Credit** AmEx, DC, MC, £TC, V. **Map 6 L5**
Wot no Americans? Britain's premier pizza chain (with more than 50 branches in London alone) may not provide anything specific for kids, but they'll love the pizzas and will always be made welcome.

Rainforest Café
20 Shaftesbury Avenue, W1 (0171 434 3111). Piccadilly Circus tube. **Meals** noon-11pm Mon-Thur, Sun; noon-midnight Fri, Sat. **Credit** AmEx, MC, V. **Map 8 K7**
Dine amid a cacophony of wildlife noises and rainforest mists. Certainly an experience, but apallingly commercialised and overpriced.

Smollensky's on the Strand
105 Strand, WC2 (0171 497 2101). Charing Cross tube/rail. **Meals** noon-midnight Mon-Wed; noon-12.30am Thur-Sat; noon-5.30pm, 6.30-10.30pm, Sun.
Credit AmEx, DC, MC, £TC, V. **Map 8 L7**
A classy theme joint with live music in the evening for grown-ups and kids' entertainment from noon to 4pm on Saturdays and Sundays (plus toys, crayons and high chairs). The food is a cut above the usual burger fare.

Sticky Fingers
1A Phillimore Gardens, W8 (0171 938 5338). High Street Kensington tube. **Meals** noon-11.30pm Mon-Sat; noon-11pm Sun. **Credit** AmEx, DC, MC, V.
Map 3 A9
Less frenetic than **Planet Hollywood** (Trocadero, 13 Coventry Street, W1; 0171 287 100) or the **Hard Rock Café** (150 Old Park Lane, W1; 0171 629 0382), Bill Wyman's Sticky Fingers is a more relaxed theme restaurant experience – and there's all that Stones memorabilia. The food's better in the other two, though.

TGI Friday's
6 Bedford Street, WC2 (0171 379 0585). Covent Garden tube/Charing Cross tube/rail. **Meals** 10am-11.30pm Mon-Sat; 10am-11pm Sun. **Credit** AmEx, MC, £TC, V.
Map 8 L7
The décor's loud, the staff are loud, the music's loud – and, hey, they just lurve kids here. Burgers and fries are good; having fun is compulsory. Load of branches.

Entertainment

Little Angel Theatre
14 Dagmar Passage, off Cross Street, N1 (0171 226 1787). Angel tube/Highbury & Islington tube/rail.
Performances 11am, 3pm, Sat, Sun; half-terms and some holidays. **Closed** Aug. **Admission** £4.50-£6.50.
Credit AmEx, MC, V.
London's only permanent puppet theatre, founded in 1961, has seating for 110. It's a delightful place, with regular weekend shows by the resident company and visiting puppeteers. There is a minimum age of three, but some performances are suitable for older children only; phone to check.

London Symphony Orchestra Family Concerts
Barbican Centre, Silk Street, EC2 (0171 638 8891). Barbican tube. **Performances** once a term (usually Sun).
Admission £6; £3 under-16s. **Credit** AmEx, MC, V.
Map 9 P5
These concerts provide children with the opportunity to listen to and learn about classical music in a fun and stimulating environment. During the interval, LSO players meet children and demonstrate their instruments in the foyer. Children are also invited to bring along an instrument and join in the audience participation piece.

National Film Theatre
South Bank, SE1 (0171 928 3535). Embankment tube/ Waterloo tube/rail. **Admission** £6.25; £1 under-16s accompanied by adults. **Credit** AmEx, £TC, V. **Map 8 M7**
Matinées for children are held on irregular Saturdays and Sundays at 4pm. Phone for details.

Polka Theatre for Children
240 The Broadway, SW19 (0181 543 4888). Wimbledon South tube/Wimbledon tube/rail. **Admission** £5-£10.
Credit MC, V.
A beautiful purpose-built complex for the under-13s, with a 300-seat theatre, an Adventure Room for under-5s, a delightful playground, a café and two shops. The thriving company has put on several award-winning shows. Closed in September.

Puppet Theatre Barge
Blomfield Road, W9 (0171 249 6876). Warwick Avenue tube. **Performances** *Term time* 3pm every weekend; *school holidays & half-term* 3pm daily. Private parties by prior arrangement. **Admission** £6; £5.50. **Credit** MC, V.
Map 1 C4
Moored in Little Venice in the winter and the Thames in summer, this unique floating marionette theatre stages regular family shows and performances for adults (phone for details).

Unicorn Theatre for Children
6 Great Newport Street, WC2 (0171 836 3334). Leicester Square tube. **Performances** *Term time* 10.15am, 1.30pm, Tue-Fri (phone to check); 11am, 2.30pm, Sat; 2.30pm Sun; *school holidays* phone to check. **Admission** £5-£10. **Credit** AmEx, MC, £TC, V. **Map 8 K7**
Founded in 1948, London's oldest professional children's theatre puts on an adventurous programme of commissioned plays and other entertainment for ages 4-12.

Annual events

There are surprisingly few events in London geared specifically towards children, although the spectacles of the **Lord Mayor's Show** (*see page 10*), **Trooping the Colour** (*see page 8*) and **Changing of the Guard** (*see page 5*) are usually hits. Another sure-fire winner is the annual **Punch and Judy Festival** in Covent Garden (*see page 9*). For details of puppet shows that take place in the summer in London's royal parks, phone 0171 298 2100. There are also several funfairs a year at **Alexandra Park**, **Battersea Park** and **Hampstead Heath** (*see page 5*).

Teddy Bears' Picnic
Battersea Park, SW11 (0181 871 8107). Battersea Park rail/49 bus. **Date** usually the first Friday afternoon in August. **Admission** free. **Map 4 F13**
An annual picnic, held for thousands of children and their furry friends. There are entertainers, and activities include face-painting and workshops.

Shopping for children

See pages 190 and 214.

Taking a break

Childminders
6 Nottingham Street, W1 (0171 935 3000/2049).
Open 8.45am-5.45pm Mon-Thur; 8.45am-5pm Fri; 9.30am-4.30pm Sun. **Map 5 G5**
A large agency with over 1,000 babysitters, mainly nurses and infant teachers (all with references), who live all over London and the suburbs.

Pippa Pop-ins
430 Fulham Road, SW6 (0171 385 2458/fax 0171 385 5706). **Open** by appointment. **Fees** from £30 per morning; £25 per afternoon; £45 all day. **Credit** AmEx, MC, £TC, V. **Map 3 C12**
A crèche, nursery school, children's overnight hotel and babysitting service run by NNEB- and Montessori-trained nursery teachers and nannies in a large, bright, specially adapted house and garden. For children aged 2-12.

Universal Aunts
(daytime childminding 0171 738 8937/evening babysitting 0171 386 5900). **Open** 9.30am-5pm Mon-Thur; 9.30am-4pm Fri. **Rates** £5.50 per hour (daytime).
This London agency, founded in 1921, can provide reliable people to babysit, meet children from trains, planes or boats, or take them sightseeing.

Information

For more information and helplines, see *Kids Out* magazine.

Circusline *(0891 343341).* **Open** 24 hours daily.
Recorded information on circuses around the country.
Kidsline *(0171 222 8070).* **Open** *Term time* 4-6pm Mon-Fri; *school holidays* 9am-4pm Mon-Fri.
Information on films, shows, attractions and activities.
LTB Children's Information
(0839 123404/436/437). **Open** 24 hours daily.
The London Tourist Board's recorded what's on service.

Clubs

The sheer number and diversity of London's clubs can bewilder even the most experienced hipster. Navigate the waters with our round-up of the best.

London has one of the best club scenes in the world and over the last decade clubbing has become an essential part of mainstream British culture. No other European capital offers such an amazing variety of nightlife experiences: a culture that is constantly changing in response to new ideas bubbling from 'underground' club and dance music scenes. The best way to keep up-to-date with the club scene is to check *Time Out*'s weekly listings. In recent years British Asian club culture, break-beats, new British house and the resurgence of hip hop culture have been nightlife highlights, while bars with later opening times and DJs (dubbed 'club bars' for want of a better name; *see page 222*) have begun to offer serious competition to night-clubs, especially as there is no or little admission if you arrive before 9pm.

Dance! Dance! Dance!

All this diversity is fine, but it's still house music that packs the dancefloors at weekends. The most famous dance club in London is the **Ministry of Sound**. Situated south of the river near the Elephant & Castle (a part of town which won't be on any regular tourist itinerary), it usually looks like a prison yard from the outside, yet draws all-night dancers like moths to a flame. Big-name guest DJs (from the USA and the UK) spinning garage and house are the principal attraction, but the sheer energy and enthusiasm of the place will take your breath away. On the downside the queues can be long, the security crew at the door are rarely friendly and admission is £10-£15, but then you are paying to party on until 9am. While

Asian beats

For addresses of the following venues see p227 **Club index**.

Even though British Asians have been firing up the dancefloors long before bands like Cornershop or Asian Dub Foundation hit the charts, the late '90s has seen a vibrant and exciting new scene develop.

It's built around club events hosted by Talvin Singh, Outcaste Records, Earthtribe, the Joi Sound System and the 2nd Generation magazine crew – but new club nights, DJs and cross-cultural fusions are popping up all the time. The music draws inspiration from all quarters – incorporating elements of drum 'n' bass and techno, breakbeats or hip hop, alongside classical music from the Indian subcontinent, Bollywood film soundtracks or qawwali devotional chants – a partial explanation of why the scene has been given so many different names, including sitardelia, tablatronica, Stoned Asia, tabla 'n' bass, and 'ethnocyberfunk'.

Tabla virtuoso Talvin Singh, whose brilliant album *OK* was released late in '98, DJ-ed and played at **The End** from '94 until recently.

The Outcaste record label (home to talented musicians like Nitin Sawhney and Badmarsh and Shri) has also hosted clubs since '94. Compilations, like *Outcaste Too Untouchable*, are probably the best introduction to the sounds. It now hosts a monthly Saturday outing at the **Notting Hill Arts Club** – well worth catching if you're in London at the right time.

DJ Pathaan was hired as a tour DJ by David Bowie in 1997 after he'd only been DJ-ing for a few months. He plays his freestyle selection of Brit Asian beats mixed with all kinds of house and rock sounds at 'Stoned Asia' (Tuesdays at **Loughborough Junction**) and at 'Air Swaraj' (at **Mass** on monthly Fridays) and 'Audio Sutra' (at **Bar Rumba**, monthly on Fridays), which both fuse Asian sounds with the best new breakbeats.

Just as the music is multicultural, so the DJs aren't limited to only playing at Asian-run events. Look out for the State of Bengal, the Joi Sound System, Bobby Friction (of Swaraj), DJs Badmarsh and Ges-E (Outcaste), DJ Ritu (Club Kali) and Imran Khan (2nd Generation).

the Ministry is unquestionably London's 'super-club' (with its own merchandise shop in Covent Garden and hugely successful record label) there are many more major dance venues worth checking out. Among these are **The End**, **Turnmills**, **Heaven**, **The Complex** (formerly the Blue Note; *see below* **North London nights**), the **Fridge** (*see below* **Southside steppin'**), and, no doubt, **Fabric** (*see below*).

The West End's **The End** is the most sophisticated dance venue in the heart of London; a cutting-edge homage to minimal styling and maximum sound quality. It's hosted by Mr C, of the techno-pop band, The Shamen, who is often seen on the decks, and it boasts proper air-conditioning and spectacularly smart toilets, not to mention a monthly series of the best funky techno, drum 'n' bass and deep house parties in London. Last year the club opened a sister bar and restaurant, **AKA** (*see box below*), right next door; a good pre-club joint or a place to go when you're too tired to dance.

Turnmills in Farringdon is famous for its 'underground' dance nights, but it has more nooks and crannies than your granny's cupboards and plenty of space to sit and chill out, as well as sweat it out on the dancefloor. The full-on housey party, 'The Gallery' on Fridays, and the drunken revelry at the 'Heavenly Jukebox' on Saturdays are both ram-jammed popular. 'Heavenly Jukebox' closes at 3.30am, to be followed by 'Trade', a marathon, predominantly gay event which continues for the next ten hours until Sunday afternoon (*see page 241*). Most nights aren't quite so demanding on the stamina, usually finishing at a respectable 6am at weekends. Like The End, Turnmills has expanded over the past year, adding two floors which dramatically improve the layout of the club.

Heaven, a maze of bars, dancefloors and corridors behind Charing Cross station, had a major refit during 1998. It's London's most famous gay venue (*see page 240*); 'straight' clubbers are only likely to test its charms at the monthly parties – like 'Bedrock' and 'Metalheadz' – on Thursdays, or at the popular mixed-gay 'Wildlife' on Fridays, where hard house meets new breakbeats on three dancefloors.

Club bars

The term 'club bar' has been coined to describe a growing number of bars that stay open later than 11pm, entertain with DJs, have admission charges (after a certain time), and by doing all of this combine the conversation culture of pubs with the style, fashion and music of clubs. So if you're looking for somewhere that's musically credible and fills the gap between pre-club hangout and full-on all-nighter, here are some of our favourites, from Brixton to Islington.

AKA
18 West Central Avenue, WC2 (0171 836 0110).
Holborn or Tottenham Court Road tube. **Open** noon-3am Mon-Fri; 6pm-3am Sat. **Map 6 L6**
New bar and (highly rated) restaurant venture by former Shamen frontman Mr C, who also owns **The End** club (*see p222*) next door.

Blue Bar
257-259 Pentonville Road, N1 (0171 837 3218).
King's Cross tube/rail. **Open** 5pm-1am Wed; 9pm-3am Thur-Sat; 7.30pm-1.30am Sun. **Map 6 M3**
A respite from the general sleaze of King's Cross, this funky hangout (formerly the Cross bar) offers decent grub and a chilled atmosphere before the music cranks up.

Bug Bar
The Crypt, St Matthew's Peace Garden, Brixton Hill,
SW2 (0171 738 3184). Brixton tube/rail. **Open** 5pm-2am Mon-Sat; 5-11pm Sun. **Admission** varies.
Laid-back yet resolutely alive, the Bug Bar lays on regular entertainment such as bands, stand-ups and DJs.

Dogstar
389 Coldharbour Lane, SW9 (0171 733 7515).
Brixton tube/rail. **Open** noon-1am Mon-Thur; noon-3am Fri, Sat; noon-11pm Sun. **Admission** £3 9-10pm, £4 10-11pm, £5 11pm-3am, Fri, Sat.
The burgeoning southside club crowd would be lost without this vibey and happening converted pub. Comedy is currently big here (*see p229*).

Dust
27 Clerkenwell Road, EC1 (0171 490 5120).
Farringdon tube/rail. **Open** 11am-11pm Mon-Wed; 11am- midnight Thur, Fri; 6pm-midnight Sat; noon-6pm Sun. **Map 9 N4**
This classy DJ bar, within staggering distance of **Turnmills** (*see p222*), is a clever, simple space clad in wood and coppery paintwork. And the drinks and food are pretty good too.

Embassy Bar
119 Essex Road, N1 (0171 226 9849). Angel tube/
38, 56, 73, 171A bus. **Open** 5-11pm Mon-Thur; 5pm-1am Fri; 2pm-1am Sat; 2-10.30pm Sun.
Map 9 O1
A suave, retro Hollywood-style glamour design and an up-to-the-minute music policy, with guest DJs on Fridays and Saturdays.

Fridge Bar
1 Town Hall Parade, SW2 (0171 326 5100). Brixton
tube/rail. **Open** 10am-2am Mon-Thur; 10am-4am Fri, Sat; 10am-12.30am Sun.
At weekends the Fridge Bar functions as an agreeable chill-down session for the club nights next door. A nice laid-back crowd.

Fabric is a brand-new venue due to open in April 1999. Spread over five floors and 16 railway arches (and a garden) in Clerkenwell it should be sensational, featuring DJs, live music and comedy while also boasting the best sound systems and air-conditioning anywhere. It's run by the people who also promote The Cross so there's plenty of nightlife experience going into it: see *Time Out* magazine for more details nearer the time.

Dressed to kill

Let's assume that what you're really looking for is not the trendiest bar or the loudest sound system, but a nightclub where you can dress up and party in style. The West End's **Browns**, **Café de Paris** and **Stringfellows** spring to mind, while the **Roof Gardens** in Kensington is probably the most beautiful club location in the city. These are popular with people of all ages and positively encourage smart attire.

Browns is a sleek and chic two-floor club in Holborn that is best known as a haunt of celebrities and location for after-show parties.

Ion
165 Ladbroke Grove, W10 (0181 960 1702).
Ladbroke Grove tube. **Open** noon-midnight daily.
A new opening in 1998, this DJ bar from the Mean Fiddler music venue people is wonderfully light and airy, with a great terrace and decent restaurant on the mezzanine level.

Jerusalem
33-34 Rathbone Street, W1 (0171 255 1120).
Tottenham Court Road tube. **Open** noon-2am Mon-Thur; noon-3am Fri, Sat. **Map 5 J5**
A capacious basement bar where massive chunks of wood serve as bench tables and trendy staff serve trendy food and drinks to a trendy crowd. Pretty good DJs midweek.

Medicine Bar
181 Upper Street, N1 (0171 704 9536). Highbury & Islington tube/rail. **Open** 5pm-midnight Mon-Thur; noon-1am Fri, Sat; noon-11pm Sun.
Admission *(membership may be required)* 7pm-1am Fri; 6pm-1am Sat.
A stylish and comfortable hangout that fills up with pre-clubbers as the after-work drinkers fade away.

Notting Hill Arts Club
21 Notting Hill Gate, W11 (0171 460 4459).
Notting Hill Gate tube. **Open** 5pm-1am Mon-Sat; 4-11pm Sun. **Admission** £3-£5 8pm-1am Mon-Sat; 7-11pm Sun. **Map 1 A7**
A whitewashed basement that packs in local trusta-farians and clubbed-out drinkers. Good DJs too.

WKD
18 Kentish Town Road, NW1 (0171 267 1869).
Camden Town tube/Camden Road rail.
Open noon-2am Mon-Thur; noon-3am Fri, Sat; noon-1am Sun.
Varied live music and DJs from 9.30pm daily. The snack food is decent too. *See also p182.*

Samba magic

For addresses of the following venues see p227 **Club index**.

London has a great selection of Latin clubs and one-nighters. Always welcoming to interested, enthusiastic strangers, they tend to attract a broader age range and more cosmopolitan crowd than 'trendy' dance clubs and they're noticeably smarter too. Most of the dancers aren't Latinos, though regular dance classes and practice have transformed them into brilliant movers – don't be put off, as dance classes are often held before Latin clubs begin, so you can brush up your steps or learn a few beginner's moves to get you going…

Cuba, on Kensington High Street, is a good place to start. It's a relaxed club (and there's a restaurant and bar upstairs) with six nights of diverse Latin beats (Mon-Sat) often featuring live bands. If you're in the heart of the West End, then **Salsa!** on Charing Cross Road is a bar-cum-club that's well worth a visit, with a similarly broad range of nights aimed at dancers and Caipirinha cocktail drinkers. If you're staying south of the river, the **Loughborough Hotel** in Brixton is a rambling corner pub that's been transformed into an excellent two-floor Latin venue (open Thur, Fri; *see picture below*). Close by in Vauxhall (just south of the river), **Club Soneros** is best known for putting on live Latin bands three nights a week (Thur-Sat); it has a 'no trainers or jeans' dress code.

Apart from the venues devoted to latin rhythms there are a couple of other long-running latin one-nighters that are well worth checking. 'Rumba Pa'ti', **Bar Rumba** (Tue), is ideal for beginners and has a young and dressed-down crowd. 'Sunday School' at **Villa Stefano** (Sun) is pure 'hardcore salsa' for the real aficionados.

The Cambridge School of English
7-11 Stukeley Street
Covent Garden,
London WC2B 5LT
Tel: ++44(0) 171 242 3787
Fax: ++44(0) 171 242 3626
E-mail: cambse@cerbernet.co.uk
Website: http//www.cerbernet.co.uk/cambse

GREAT VALUE FOR MONEY IN CENTRAL LONDON!

Start any Monday

- Cambridge English in Central London's Covent Garden
- General English, Business English and various Cambridge Examination courses available, starting from 10 lessons per week upwards
- Tailor-made Courses for individuals, groups and executives
- Tuition for IELTS and TOEFL tests
- English for Specific and Academic Purposes
- English for Marketing with Interviews and Negotiation skills
- Qualified, experienced and friendly teachers
- Friendly international school environment with small classes
- An organised social programme
- A variety of accommodation options
- We have a lively in-house café with affordable prices

5% DISCOUNT FOR TIME OUT READERS
WITH A COPY OF THIS ADVERT

The more weird, the more wonderful at **The Fridge**'s *Friday-night* Escape from Samsara.

Café de Paris, a classic 1920s ballroom, was lavishly restored ain 1996 and has a lovely balcony from where you can spy on the dancefloor below. There's a restaurant too, which is great if you want a hassle-free night out. The **Roof Gardens** is a members club (non-members are admitted on Thursday and Saturday; the £40 admission includes a three-course dinner) and has the atmosphere and appearance of a plush restaurant rather than a disco, it is six floors above ground and, as its name suggests, boasts three stunning garden areas in addition to the restaurant and dancefloor. However, *the* place to go if you're all dressed up is

The Emporium, in the centre of town – it's known to be a hang-out for celebs, and once had to refuse a request to hold a party for Prince (or should that be The Artist…?) as it was too busy.

More famous and much less discreet is **Stringfellows**, another nightclub which can claim an à la carte (French) restaurant. It's a West End institution for suit-and-tie hedonists, and is hosted by the irrepressible self-styled 'king of clubs', Peter Stringfellow, and like its owner, it's neither new in town or trendy. In fact, for most of the week (Monday to Thursday) it hosts table dancing; disco-house beats take over from the girls at weekends.

Getting in with the in crowd

Many of London's clubs are phenomenally popular. It can be a major feat of stamina to survive the queuing and of bravado to get past the security staff. Door policies are one of the most frustrating aspects of clubbing, and one area that club owners are rarely specific about. Very few clubs have strict membership rules although you may find that they claim to have a members-only policy when you get to the door. To avoid such an experience, phone the club in advance to check on the best time to arrive and whether there are any dress requirements. Note that most club do not allow you in if you're wearing jeans and trainers. Also, **be sure to phone first to check that a specific night is on**. Clubs come and go with astonishing speed. *Time Out* magazine is the best source to find out what's happening week to week. Good luck, and have a happy nightlife.

Mayfair play

Mayfair is quiet at night, so clubs here rely on reputation rather than passing trade, and are more stylish and comfortable than most other dance clubs. The **Hanover Grand** (just off Regent Street), with its balconied dancefloor upstairs, and groovy bar below, is home to the best midweek R 'n' B and hip-hop ('Fresh 'n' Funky' on Wednesday), and seriously trendy dance clubs on Thursday, Friday and Saturday when only the most gorgeous club-people are likely to get past the style police on the door. **Iceni**, situated just off Piccadilly, has plenty of diversity with its five rooms on three floors. Its décor ranges from avant-garde to opulent as you ascend the stairs. The sleek and modern **Legends** stands in stark contrast. Designed by Eva Jirickna, the restaurant and bar upstairs has a huge window onto the street (if the area was busier it would be a perfect poseurs' parade) and a dressed-up good-looking crowd bops to house dance beats on the shiny floors at weekends.

West is best

If you're staying in west or south-west London then **Subterania** is an excellent night-time destination. Live music gigs entertain during the week and DJs spin funky sounds at the weekend to a

Do the funky Carwash *at* **LA2**.

trendy West London crowd – both Friday's 'Rotation' and Saturday's 'Soulsonic' are hard to get into unless you arrive early (and dress up for the latter). The **Leopard Lounge** on Fulham Broadway provides another good excuse not to hike up to the West End. It's a spacious and lavish new club, predictably decked out with a zebra- and leopard-skin décor (and full of flares-wearing '70s party people on Thursday nights).

North London nights

The Complex (formerly the Blue Note) in Islington is the club that has most successfully caught the musical moods of the last couple of years; the diversity ranges from soulful funk to radical breakbeats, and often within the same night. It moved from Hoxton Square in 1998 to a new four-floor venue where the whole of the top level 'Love Lounge' is devoted to chilling out and socialising in a warm womb-red glow. Saturday night is a freestyle feast of funk, swing and garage beats called 'Camouflage'.

Despite its location, in the wastelands behind King's Cross, **The Cross** has a reputation for great monthly dance parties at the weekend, when the brick arches shake to the latest grooves. It's well worth a cab fare but like so many of these clubs, it's already a hit with the locals, so arriving early is always a good idea. The **Scala** in King's Cross is due to open in the spring of 1999. This former theatre has been radically remodelled into a two-floor venue for live music, club events and film screenings, with a large bar overlooking King's Cross station.

The huge old music hall venue of the **Camden Palace** was transformed into a multi-level inferno of sound and light back in the early '80s. It's showing its age now but is still worth visiting for Tuesday's indie-rock club 'Feet First' and for some of the special events on Saturdays, but otherwise leave it alone.

Soho & Covent Garden

Dozens of bars, cafés, clubs and restaurants are situated in Soho and Covent Garden; the best way to explore is to cruise around on foot, although a few venues stand out. **Bar Rumba**, one of the best dance clubs in town, plays host to a series of excellent one-nighters: Monday has jazz, funk and drum 'n' bass; Tuesday, Latin; it's deep house on Wednesday; drum 'n' bass on Thursday; New Skool beats on Friday and garage on Saturday. Each night is among the best of its type. Equally popular is **The Wag**, a stylish club on three floors which similarly plays host to a wide variety of music. Midweek sees indie-rock nights; Friday, an '80s retro session; and 'Blow Up' is one of the best parties around on Saturday, a night that takes its inspiration from '60s soul and pop, but which plays all kinds of 'lounge' tunes and big beat too.

The **Velvet Room** (on Charing Cross Road) is a luxuriously-appointed 'club bar' that also hosts an excellent drum 'n' bass Wednesday nighter ('Swerve') and a great techno and deep house night on Thursdays. Stylish 'club' clothes should normally guarantee admission. Nearby, right opposite the Centrepoint building, is **LA2**, home to 'Carwash' on Saturdays, the best disco night in town but one for which you absolutely must dress the part

Southside steppin'

There's a growing nightlife scene in and around Brixton. The biggest venue is **The Fridge**, a transformation of a former theatre that is hardly glamorous but can look spectacular with clever use of visuals and décor. Saturday is a major gay night but it goes 'straight' on Fridays for the trancey, techno all-nighter 'Escape From Samsara'. Right opposite the Fridge is **Mass**, a two-room nightclub high up a circular stairwell in a converted church. It opened at the end of 1998 and is home to (yet another) series of cutting-edge monthly dance parties. Smaller in scale but not in ambition are the 'club bars' (*see also page 222* **Club bars**). The **Dogstar** on Coldharbour Lane has set the trend; it's free to get in for most of the night and attracts some of London's most interesting DJs. **The Junction**, much further up Coldharbour

Lane, and the **Bug Bar** (next to Mass) have a similarly adventurous line-up, while the **Fridge Bar** (adjacent to the Fridge, not surprisingly) adopts a more global dance perspective.

Disco nights

Alternatively, if you're simply reading this in the hope of finding a disco in the heart of the city, then head for Leicester Square and try the **Equinox** or the **Hippodrome**. These are heavyweight monster discos with chunky sound systems and spectacular flashing lights and lasers, playing a more 'commercial' (ie mainstream) selection of dance tunes. The Hippodrome is a chrome-clad dinosaur as far as its interior goes. It usually attracts a smart crowd of tourists and out-of-towners, with trapeze artists swooping over the dancefloor to surprise you in mid-step. The Equinox can be a lot of fun when it's rammed full of around 1,500 cheery punters at the weekends.

Game on

And for something completely different, why not book a table at Wednesday night's 'Double Six Club' at **The Office**. This longstanding board-game club offers a wonderful menu of silly and serious games, served up to you against a sleazy listening soundtrack. Top fun.

Club index

Comedy

Titter, guffaw, chuckle and roar – London's a right larf.

London can offer more live comedy than any other city in the world. In any one week throughout the year dozens of clubs provide an exciting mixture of stand-up and other forms of comedy. Major clubs, such as the **Comedy Store** and **Jongleurs Battersea**, feature top performers, while smaller venues combine established comics with new acts or mount specific newcomer competitions.

This festival of humour continues unabated from January to December, though the torrent of laughs slackens to a steady stream in the summer months. In August, many London-based comics head north for the Edinburgh Fringe Festival. But just as many stay behind to keep the huge circuit of London clubs alive and kicking.

In 1999, London celebrates the 20th anniversary of the Comedy Store, and with it the birth of the new movement in live comedy. Through performers such as Lee Evans, Harry Hill, Jo Brand and Frank Skinner, it has now successfully spread to television and the movies. All *you* need to do is buy a copy of *Time Out* magazine and take your pick of whatever tickles your fancy.

Below are some of the best comedy venues in town. At the end of this section we list the cream of the less-frequent comedy nights, as well as a brief introduction to the small but dedicated spoken word circuit.

Comedy

BAC
Lavender Hill, SW11 (0171 223 2223). Clapham Junction rail. **Performances** phone for details. **Admission** varies; phone for details. **Credit** MC, V.
BAC (Battersea Arts Centre) is a great venue with four performance areas. Short runs by well-known comics and an annual two-week pre-Edinburgh comedy festival (July) mean it's well worth checking out for top-class laughs. *See also p268.*

Backyard Comedy Club
231-237 Cambridge Heath Road, E2 (0171 739 3122). Bethnal Green tube. **Performances** 8.30pm Fri, Sat. **Admission** £10; £7 concs. **Credit** MC, V.
Comedian Lee Hurst's purpose-built comedy club opened in a former dress factory in Bethnal Green in September 1998. His industry clout and avowed intention to treat comics with the respect they don't always command in other clubs means that consistently excellent bills are likely. There's a disco after shows and food to soak up the beer.

Banana Cabaret
The Bedford, 77 Bedford Hill, SW12 (0181 673 8904). Balham tube/rail. **Performances** 9pm Fri, Sat. **Admission** £7; £5 concs.
One of the most enterprising and enjoyable clubs in London, with two separate spaces running simultaneously in the same building on Saturday nights. Food served until 9pm.

Bearcat Club
Turk's Head, Winchester Road, Twickenham, Middx (0181 891 1852). St Margaret's rail. **Performances** 9.15pm Mon, Sat. **Admission** £8, £7 concs, members, Sat; £6, £5 concs, members Mon.
One of the longest established clubs around, with fine bills almost guaranteed.

Canal Café Theatre
The Bridge House, Delamere Terrace, W2 (0171 289 6054). Royal Oak or Warwick Avenue tube. **Performances** daily; phone for details. **Admission** varies; phone for details. **Annual membership** £1. **Credit** MC, V. **Map 1 C4**
Housed in an upstairs room in a pub next to the picturesque canal running through Little Venice, the Canal Café Theatre hosts a wide range of entertainment, from the long-running topical sketch show *Newsrevue* (Thur-Sun) to cabarets and serious drama.

Comedy Brewhouse
Camden Head, 2 Camden Walk, Camden Passage, N1 (0171 359 0851). Angel tube. **Performances** 9pm Fri, Sat. **Admission** £5; £4 concs. **Map 9 O2**
Improv from the Laughing Cavaliers plus a selection of newish stand-ups.

Comedy Café
66 Rivington Street, EC2 (0171 739 5706). Old Street tube/rail. **Performances** 9pm Wed-Sat. **Admission** free Wed; £2 Thur; £10 Fri; £12 Sat. **Credit** MC, £TC, V. **Map 10 R4**
One of the few clubs in London to have been customised for comedy. The free Wednesday shows are for new acts. There's an after-show club until 2am on Fridays and Saturdays.

Comedy Store
Haymarket House, 1A Oxendon Street, SW1 (info 01426 914 433/bookings 0171 344 4444). Leicester Square or Piccadilly Circus tube. **Performances** 8pm Tue-Sun; also midnight Fri, Sat. **Admission** £11, £7 concs Tue, Wed; £12, £7 concs Thur, Fri (midnight show only); £13 Sat; £12, £8 concs Sun. **Credit** AmEx, MC, V. **Map 8 K7**
The most famous club in the country and the place where the new movement in comedy was launched in the late 1970s. All the best stand-ups appear here. On Wednesdays and Sundays the Comedy Store Players serve up high-class improvisation. Tuesday's innovative Cutting Edge show features a group of comics exploring different ways to interact on the same stage. Note that concessionary prices are only available to those who book in person.

Cosmic Comedy Club
177 Fulham Palace Road, W6 (0171 381 2006). Hammersmith tube. **Performances** 9pm Tue-Thur; 8.30pm Fri, Sat. **Admission** free Tue, Wed; £3 Thur; £8 Fri, Sat. **Credit** MC, V.
A lovely, long-established, purpose-built club, run by knowledgeable promoters. Tuesday nights are devoted to untried acts, with better-known faces appearing on other nights.

Chuckles all round at the **Backyard Comedy Club**.

Food is available and there's a disco until 2am on a Friday and Saturday.

Downstairs at the King's Head
2 Crouch End Hill, corner of The Broadway, N8 (0181 340 1028/admin 01920 823 265). Finsbury Park tube/rail then W7 bus. **Performances** 8.30pm Wed-Sun. **Admission** free-£7; free-£6 concs.
One of the oldest clubs in the capital and deservedly popular as the emphasis is on providing the best possible conditions for performers and giving audiences a good time. Resident host is Huw Thomas, and there's a try-out night every other Thursday.

East Dulwich Cabaret
East Dulwich Tavern, 1 Lordship Lane, SE22 (0181 299 4138). East Dulwich rail. **Performances** 9pm Wed, Sat; 8.30pm Thur. **Admission** £3, £2 concs, Wed; £5 Thur; £6, £5 concs, Sat. **Credit** MC, V.
There's theatre, music and comedy at this well-run, long-running club. Reliable line-ups often feature some of the circuit's biggest names such as Harry Hill, Eddie Izzard and Jenny Eclair. Wednesdays are devoted to new material. All this and a relaxed, pleasant atmosphere – what more could you possibly want?

Jongleurs Battersea
The Cornet, 49 Lavender Gardens, SW11 (0171 564 2500). Clapham Junction rail. **Performances** 8.45pm Fri; 7.15pm, 11.15pm, Sat. **Admission** £12, £9 concs, Fri; £10, £7 concs, Sat. **Credit** MC, V.
One of the leading London comedy clubs. The thing that distinguishes Jongleurs is its varied line-ups that are not confined just to stand-up. Food available.

Jongleurs Bow Wharf
221 Grove Road, E3 (0171 564 2500). Mile End tube. **Performances** 8.15pm Fri, Sat. **Admission** £12; £9 concs. **Credit** MC, V.
The newest of the Jongleurs' venues, this purpose-built club features some of the bigger names on the comedy circuit. Late bar. Food served.

Jongleurs Camden Lock
Dingwalls, Middle Yard, Camden Lock, Camden High Street, NW1 (0171 564 2500). Camden Town or Chalk Farm tube. **Performances** 8.15pm Fri; 7.15pm, 11.15pm, Sat. **Admission** £12, £9 concs, Fri; £10, £7 concs, Sat. **Credit** MC, V.
A comfortable, purpose-built comedy venue based on the American model, with excellent bills, a late bar and food. Be sure to book a table in advance to guarantee a seat. But remember, those at the front should be prepared to join in. A disco follows the show on Friday nights.

Meccano Club
Finnegan's Wake, 2 Essex Road, N1 (0171 813 4478). Angel tube. **Performances** 9pm Fri, Sat. **Admission** £6; £5 concs. **Map 9 O2**
A splendid, unpretentious basement venue that the comics love to play, so you'll generally see them at their best here. An excellent – if at times chokingly smoky – evening is almost always guaranteed.

Top Dog Comedy & Cabaret
The Dogstar, 389 Coldharbour Lane, SW9 (0171 737 3177). Brixton tube/rail. **Performances** 9pm Mon-Thur, Sun. **Admission** £5, £3 concs Tue-Thur, Sun; £3, £2 concs Mon. **Credit** MC, V.
This newish club in Brixton's ultra-trendy Dogstar bar is forging a name for itself on the comedy circuit. There's improv from the Top Dog Players on Thursdays. Club nights follow the shows and are included in the price.

Up the Creek
302 Creek Road, SE10 (0181 858 4581). Greenwich rail. **Performances** 9pm Fri-Sun. **Admission** £10, £6 concs, £2 local students, Fri; £12, £8 concs Sat; £6, £4 concs, £2 local students Sun. **Credit** AmEx, MC, V.
A fine, noisy, bearpit of a club which tests even the longest-established comics. Not for the faint-hearted. There's also food and a disco until 2am on Fridays and Saturdays.

Less-frequent clubs

One-off nights in venues that aren't dedicated to comedy tend to come and go with astonishing rapidity. Therefore, always phone first to check that the clubs listed below are still operating before setting out.

Aztec Comedy Club *The Borderland, 47-49 Westow Street, SE19 (0181 771 0885). Fri, Sun, weekly.*
Bound & Gagged Palmers Green *The Fox, 413 Green Lanes, N13 (0171 483 3456). Fri, weekly.*
Buccaneers Comedy *The Hope, Tottenham Street, W1 (0181 761 5319). Tue, weekly.* **Map 5 J5**
Camden Lock Comedy Revue *The Lock Tavern, 35 Chalk Farm Road, NW1 (0171 387 9304). Wed, weekly.*
Chiswick Comedy Club *Rowans Café Bar, Stile Hall Parade, Chiswick High Road, W4 (0181 742 1649). Sat, weekly.*
Chuckle Club *The London School of Economics, Houghton Street, WC2 (0171 476 1672/chuckler@ demon.co.uk). Sat, weekly (during term time).* **Map 6 M6**

Are you gonna laugh or what? **Comedy Café** *capers. See page 228.*

Comedy at Soho Ho *Crown & Two Chairmen, Dean Street, W1 (0956 996690).* **Map 6 K6** *Sat, weekly.*

Comedy Spot *The Spot, Maiden Lane, WC2 (0171 379 5900).* *Mon, weekly.* **Map 8 L7**

Comics on a Saturday Night *Fulmar & Firkin, 51 Parker Street, WC2 (0171 405 0590). Sat, weekly.* **Map 6 L6**

Fortnight Club *Moriarty's, 57 Liverpool Road, N1 (0171 837 5370). Mon, fortnightly.* **Map 9 N1**

Hampstead Comedy Club *The Washington, England's Lane, NW3 (0171 207 7256). Sat, weekly.*

Hecklers Comedy Club *Goose & Granite, 264 Hoe Street, E17 (0181 923 2127). Sat, weekly.*

Islington Comedy Revue *The Tramshed, 2a Corsica Street, N5 (0171 226 1026). Sat, weekly.*

Kal's East Sheen Comedy Club *Railway Tavern, 11 Sheen Lane, SW14 (0181 871 3396). Wed, weekly.*

Laughing Toucan *The Toucan, 94 Wimpole Street, W1 (0171 499 2440). Fri, weekly.*

Old Spontaneity Shop *The Troubadour, 265 Old Brompton Road, SW5 (0171 370 1434). Tue, weekly.* **Map 3 C11**

Oranje Boom Boom *Upstairs at De Hems, Macclesfield Street, W1 (0171 275 0118). Wed, weekly.* **Map 8 K6**

Oval Comedy Club *The Grosvenor, Sidney Road, SW9 (0171 733 1799). Wed, weekly.*

Red Rose Comedy Club *129 Seven Sisters Road, N7 (0171 281 3051). Sat, weekly.*

Screaming Blue Murder *Dog & Fox, 24 High Street, SW19 (0181 398 0298). Fri, weekly.*

Tut & Shive Cabaret *The Tut & Shive, 235 Upper Street, N1 (0171 359 7719). Tue, Sun, weekly.* **Map 9 O1**

Spoken word

One of the best sources for information on poetry readings and events is the **Poetry Society**, which hosts regular poetry-related bashes (and serves excellent food and wine) at its **Poetry Café** (22 Betterton Street, WC2; 0171 420 9880). The long-running **Apples & Snakes** group puts on fortnightly performances at the **BAC** in Battersea (*see page 228*). Presentations by **Big Word** every Thursday (Finnegan's Wake, 2 Essex Road, N1; 0171 354 2016) and the **Armadillo Beat Club** at Brady's (back bar), Atlantic Road, Brixton, SW4 at 9.30pm on Wednesdays (0973 442892) are accessible, noisy and often drunken affairs. **New River Writers** (Moriarty's, 57 Liverpool Road, N1; 0181 993 0285) is a friendly workshop-based group that deals in poetry, short stories and much more besides. **Vox'n'Roll** at Filthy McNasty's, 68 Amwell Street, EC1 (0171 837 6067), intersperses celebrity readings with music and a packed pub atmosphere (Tue-Thur 8.30pm).

Dance

Welcome to one of the world's most movin' cities.

The capital's thriving dance scene – measured through the sheer range of work regularly on view, the wealth of choreographic and performing talent, and the plethora of classes, workshops and more intensive studies – makes London a movement mecca comparable to New York and Paris.

In performance terms, there is fairly widespread recognition that the public and performers alike require better, more modern theatres for dance. Lottery funding has enabled high-profile venues such as **Sadler's Wells** and the theatre in the **Barbican Centre** to be completely refurbished. Others will undergo extensive facelifts in the coming years. **The Place** is expected to shut down during much of the latter half of 1999, with performances relocated to other sites like the South Bank and the Lilian Baylis (a studio theatre in the new Sadler's Wells that is scheduled to reopen in the spring). Meanwhile, the **Royal Opera House** is closed for major renovation at least until December (*see also pages 245-6*). This means that the much-beleaguered **Royal Ballet** will remain without a permanent home for the duration of the year. (The company performs at the Wells in July 1999; for details call 0171 863 8000/420 1166 or check out the Ballet's website: www.royalballet.org)

On the plus side, staggered throughout the capital's annual dance calendar are a number of notable dance festivals showcasing both up-and-coming and proven artists (*see below* **Festivals**). In addition, year-round there is usually ample opportunity to catch work from abroad. The extent to which some long-running West End shows (for instance, *Chicago* and *Saturday Night Fever*) depend on their dance content further points up the art form's continued popularity.

As well as the performances and venues below, check the weekly listings in *Time Out*. The magazine's dance pages include detailed information on a gamut of fringe shows and more 'mainstream' productions, the latter often held at venues not used solely for dance events (such as *Lord of the Dance* at Wembley Arena, 2-4 March, and English National Ballet's in-the-round *Swan Lake* at the Royal Albert Hall, 16-26 June).

The **London Dance Network Website** (www.london-dance.net) is a new and valuable resource comprising some 50 artists, venues, producers and agencies whose brief is to promote up-to-the-minute awareness of the strength and diversity of dance in London.

And make sure you drop by **Dance Books** at 15 Cecil Court, WC2 (off Charing Cross Road, close to the National Portrait Gallery; 0171 836 2314), the world's sole specialist shop for new and used dance books. CDs and videos related to dance are also available.

Finally, should Terpsichore inspire you to take a turn on the dancefloor yourself, London's range of dance classes is unrivalled (for a round-up of the best, *see below* **Dance classes**).

Major venues

Barbican Centre

Silk Street, EC2 (0171 638 8891/info 0171 638 4141). Barbican tube/Moorgate tube/rail. **Open** *box office* 9am-8pm daily. **Tickets** £6-£30. **Credit** AmEx, MC, £TC, V. **Map 9 P5**

The Barbican Theatre, with a newly sprung floor for dance, is wholeheartedly attempting to transform itself into a more inviting venue for all the arts. Working with **Dance Umbrella** (*see below* **Festivals**), it successfully launched its first dance season in 1998. The 1999 roster is slim on dance, however, with only French physical theatre magician Philippe Decouflé's phantasmagoric *Shazam!* confirmed for July at press time.

ICA

The Mall, SW1 (0171 930 3647/membership enquiries 0171 873 0062/info@ica.org.uk). Piccadily Circus tube/ Charing Cross tube/rail. **Open** *box office* noon-9.30pm daily; noon-6pm advance bookings. **Tickets** prices vary; average £8. **Credit** AmEx, DC, MC, £TC, V. **Map 8 K8**

The intimate space of the Institute of Contemporary Arts (ICA) is the setting for experimental, movement-based theatre and performance with an avant-garde flavour. A fine balance is struck between platforms for emerging talent and seasons for established British and international artists, including such renowned groups as Station House Opera, Goat Island and Forced Entertainment. The **London International Mime Festival** is also a regular visitor each January (*see also p10*). The price of a ticket includes day membership.

Website: www.ica.org.uk or tickets@ica.org.uk

London Coliseum

St Martin's Lane, WC2 (box office 0171 632 8300/ minicom 0171 836 7666). Leicester Square tube/ Charing Cross tube/rail. **Open** *box office* 24 hours daily. **Tickets** £2.50-£55; day tickets on sale to personal callers after 10am Mon-Fri; over the telephone from 2.30pm Mon-Fri. **Credit** AmEx, DC, MC, £TC, V. **Map 8 L7**

The beautiful, spacious Coliseum is home to the **English National Opera** for most of the year, and is usually visited by major dance companies over the summer and at Christmas. Christmas 1998, for example, saw the **English National Ballet** performing two favourites: *The Nutcracker* and *Cinderella*.

The Place

17 Duke's Road, WC1 (0171 387 0031/placetheatre@
easynet.co.uk). Euston tube/rail. **Open** *box office*
10.30am-6pm Mon-Fri; noon-6pm Sat. **Tickets** £6-£10.
Credit MC, V. **Map 6 K3**
This cracking dance theatre may not be in the West End,
but there's no better dance venue in town. It presents a broad
international sweep of contemporary dance during a handful of annual themed seasons (*see below* **Festivals**) at very
reasonable prices. Facilities include a comprehensive dance
video library, an information centre, top-notch dance training and evening classes for all levels of ability. It is also
home to the contemporary **Richard Alston Dance
Company**. The café is excellent too. The building is due to
be closed for refurbishment during the second half of 1999.
Website: www.theplace.org.uk

Riverside Studios

Crisp Road, W6 (0181 237 1000/box office 0181 237
1111). Hammersmith tube. **Open** *box office* noon-7pm
daily. **Tickets** £7-£15. **Credit** MC, V.
This leading arts and media centre occasionally hosts British
contemporary dance and physical theatre, and visiting international companies, in three auditoria. It is also likely to be
one of the venues for the 1999 **Dance Umbrella** (*see below*
Festivals). There's a pleasant bar/café, restaurant, bookshop, and wheelchair access to all ground-floor areas.

Royal Festival Hall

South Bank, Belvedere Road, SE1 (box office 0171 960
4242/recorded info 0171 633 0932). Embankment tube/
Waterloo tube/rail. **Open** *box office* 10am-9pm daily.
Tickets £5-£60. **Credit** AmEx, DC, MC, V. **Map 8 M8**
Architecturally it's not to everybody's taste, but in terms of
facilities and programming this arts complex is exemplary.
British and international dance companies perform regularly at its three venues: the massive **RFH1**, the medium-
sized **RFH2 (Queen Elizabeth Hall)** and the smaller
RFH3 (Purcell Room). Highlights for 1999 include two
community-based events, **Dance for Youth** (3 July) and
the annual **Blitz** (*see below* **Festivals**). Starting in
September with the gutsy **DV8 Physical Theatre**'s new
show, the SBC hopes to take a more pro-active role in British
and world dance by presenting up to ten new commissioned
pieces per season. This includes work by **Javier De
Frutos**, **Ricochet** and, in December, the return of **Alain
Platel**'s *iets op Bach*, winner of a 1998 *Time Out* Live
Award. Some of the higher-profile **Dance Umbrella** events
can also be seen here (*see below* **Festivals**). *See also p245.*
Website: www.sbc.org.uk

Sadler's Wells

Rosebery Avenue, EC1 (box office 0171 863 8000).
Angel tube. **Open** *box office* 10am-6pm Mon-Sat.
Tickets £7.50-£45. **Credit** AmEx, MC, V. **Map 9 N3**
Peacock Theatre, Portugal Street, off Kingsway, WC2
(box office 0171 314 8222). Holborn or Temple tube.
Open *box office* noon-8pm performance days, 10am-6pm
when no performances, Mon-Sat. **Tickets** £7.50-£35.
Credit AmEx, MC, V. **Map 6 M6**
An institution in the London dance world, Sadler's Wells
now attracts world-class contemporary and classical dance
companies to its totally rebuilt, ultra-modern theatre. At
press time, scheduled performances include **Green Candle
Dance Company**'s in-the-round fantasy *On the Road to
Baghdad* (9-14 March) and **Northern Ballet Theatre**'s
balletic chiller *Dracula* (17-27 March). **Rambert Dance
Company**'s spring and autumn seasons (May and October)
render them the nearest the Wells has to a resident troupe.
The considerably smaller, on-site **Lilian Baylis Theatre**
will reopen in the spring. The organisation is also retaining
its second home, the more centrally located Peacock Theatre
in Holborn, for longer runs of more populist fare (tango, flamenco and urban street dance).

Other venues

The Bhavan Centre

Old Church Building, Castletown Road, W14 (0171 381
3086). West Kensington tube. **Open** 9.30am-5.30pm
daily. **Tickets** £5-£15. **Credit** MC, V.
This institute of Indian art and culture promotes, and sometimes hosts, traditional Indian dance performances, along
with educational courses and classes in traditional Indian
dance in the style of Bharata Natyam and Kathak.

The Bull Theatre

68 High Street, Barnet, Herts (0181 449 0048).
High Barnet tube. **Open** 10am-8pm Mon-Sat;
1-8pm Sun. **Tickets** £3-£10. **Credit** MC, V.
The Bull hosts a broad range of dance performances
(approximately two a month), mostly by contemporary and
world (especially Asian) dance companies. Past troupes to
have graced the floors include Sakoba, Nina Rajarani and
Common Ground.

Chisenhale Dance Space

64-84 Chisenhale Road, E3 (0181 981 6617/mail@
chisenhale.demon.co.uk). Bethnal Green or Mile End tube.
Open *box office* 10am-6pm daily. **Tickets** £7.50; £5 concs.
A seminal research centre for contemporary dance and
movement-based performance of a more experimental,
work-in-progress nature, Chisenhale also features a spectrum of activities including workshops, often hosted by
international artists, plus children's classes.
Website: www.chisenhale.demon.co.uk

Cochrane Theatre

Southampton Row, WC1 (0171 242 7040). Holborn tube.
Open *box office* 10am-6pm Mon-Fri; noon-6pm Sat.
Tickets £4-£15. **Credit** MC, V. **Map 6 L5**
This small West End theatre programmes dance perfor-
mances from classical to contemporary.

Jacksons Lane Dancebase

*269A Archway Road, N6 (0181 341 4421). Highgate
tube.* **Open** 10am-10pm daily. **Tickets** £7; £3-£5 concs.
Credit MC, V.
This community centre presents an admirable number of
dance performances and activities, with lots of contemporary and new dance from young British and international
companies. Artists featured recently include Matthew
Hawkins and Wendy Houston. Look out for **Mosaics** in
summer 1999 (*see below* **Festivals**).

Laban Centre

*Laurie Grove, SE14 (0181 692 4070). New Cross or
New Cross Gate tube.* **Open** 8.30am-5.30pm Mon-Fri.
Tickets £5-£10; £3 concs.
The Laban Centre is an independent conservatory for dance
training and research, which runs undergraduate and postgraduate courses, evening and weekend classes, specialist
short courses and an international summer school. Other
facilities include a dance library and a 'body-control studio'
offering Pilates-based body conditioning. The Laban Centre
is also home to the dynamic **Transitions** dance company.
Shows featuring work by emerging contemporary dance
choreographers are regularly presented in the **Bonnie Bird
Theatre**. The centre publishes the excellent *Dance Theatre
Journal* (available by mail order).

Studio Theatre

*North Westminster Community School, North Wharf
Road, W2 (0171 641 8424). Edgware Road tube.* **Open**
10am-6pm Mon-Fri. **Tickets** £6; £4 concs. **Map 2 D5**
This theatre hosts about 70 shows a year, 20 of which are
dance (traditional to contemporary). **Bullies Ballerinas**
dance company is resident at the studio, and the likes of
BiMa and Union Dance make regular appearances.

Dance classes

In addition to classes mentioned in the preceding section, the following places all offer dance classes to help you polish, and then strut, your stuff. And that's just the tip of the iceberg in terms of what's available. For a list of accredited dance classes, call the **Council for Dance Education and Training** (0181 746 0076). Also, if you're interested in the strange blend of martial art and dance that is Capoeira, *see page 258* **London School of Capoeira Dance**.

Dance Attic
368 North End Road, SW6 (0171 610 2055). Fulham Broadway tube. **Membership** £1.50 per day; £30 per half year; £50 per year. **Map 3 A12**
This centre in Fulham has a wide range of dance classes, including ballet, jazz, flamenco, lambada, salsa and hip hop, for all levels of expertise. There is also a gym. Membership is required.

Danceworks
16 Balderton Street, W1 (0171 629 6183). Bond Street tube. **Membership** £15-£22 per month; £30-£75 per year. **Map 5 G6**
Danceworks runs an incredible variety of dance classes (including Afro, contemporary, salsa, ballet and tango), as well as aerobics classes, yoga, Pilates, martial arts and various therapies. Some dance classes require membership.

Drill Hall
16 Chenies Street, WC1 (0171 637 8270). Goodge Street tube. **Membership** £15-£50 per year. **Credit** AmEx, JCB, MC, V. **Map 6 K5**
This central fringe venue, close to Tottenham Court Road, provides classes in Egyptian, Latin American, tango, t'ai-chi, butoh, contemporary dance and more.

Greenwich Dance Agency
Borough Hall, Royal Hill, SE10 (0181 293 9741). Greenwich rail. **Membership** £4, £3 concs per class.
Daily professional-level classes, workshops and occasional intensives run by established artists are offered here, as well as beginner/intermediate adult classes in Egyptian, flamenco, jazz, salsa and other disciplines.

Islington Arts Factory
2 Parkhurst Road, N7 (0171 607 0561). Caledonian Road tube. **Membership** £3 per term; £8 per year.
Classes in ballet, Egyptian, jazz, contemporary, salsa and mime are available at this lively arts centre. Membership is required, but can be obtained on the day.

Morley College
61 Westminster Bridge Road, SE1 (0171 450 9232). Lambeth North tube. **Membership** £35-£46; £7-£30 per 10 classes. **Map 8 M9**
A broad portfolio of dance classes and courses at all levels is held at this adult education centre. The setting is fairly spartan, but you can't complain about the prices, nor the efforts made to accommodate beginners.

Pineapple Dance Studio
7 Langley Street, WC2 (0171 836 4004). Covent Garden tube. **Membership** £1-£4 per day; £40-£85 per year. **Map 6 L6**
Centrally located, this popular, trendy dance centre boasts a wide choice of classes, with an emphasis on ballet, jazz and commercial genres. There is also a gym, a studio for Pilates, treatments and therapists, sunbeds, a café and even a clairvoyant. Classes are for all levels. Membership is required.

*Hanging out by the barre at **Danceworks**.*

Festivals

The highly esteemed **Dance Umbrella** (0181 741 5881), now in its 21st year, is one of the world's top contemporary dance festivals. Held for five weeks from early October, it features a stimulating mix of proven British and international companies (as well as a number of lesser-known discoveries) performed at venues across London. The popular group led by American choreographer **Mark Morris** is expected to return in 1999. And English dance-maker **Lea Anderson** will also be busy: besides creating a cabaret evening for her two companies, the all-female Cholmondeleys and the guys-only Featherstonehaughs, she'll stage **The Big Match**, a massive community dance event at the Crystal Palace National Sports Centre. There are also workshops, talks, video screenings and forays into digital technology and dance.

The Place (*see above*) organises a superb series of dance festivals every year. Keep an eye out for **Resolution!** (Jan/Feb), featuring an almost overwhelming amount of work from emerging British and European choreographers; **Spring Loaded** (16 Feb-2 May), in association with the South Bank Centre, presents the best of British contemporary dance; and **The Turning World** (7 May-12 June), a season of international companies and artists. Later in the year The Place presents **Re:orient** (late September), bringing to London the latest cross-cultural contemporary dance from Britain and the Asian Pacific.

Each August the **South Bank Centre** (*see above*) hosts the month-long **Blitz**. Britain's biggest and most diverse community dance festival, it is a cornucopia of free dance performances, lectures and workshops. Also in August, **Sadler's Wells** and **Jacksons Lane Dancebase** (for both, *see above*) co-present **Mosaics**. This ambitious season of small-scale events, with more than 30 young companies performing new dance and physical theatre, is a veritable dance-athon.

Film

Though the Hollywood blockbuster still rides high, cult festivals and new formats take the London film scene into the next millennium.

Almost every conceivable cinematic taste is catered for in London. Leicester Square and the West End is the place to come for blockbusters, big screens (*see opposite page* **Size matters**) and state-of-the-art sound; you'll need to go further afield to enjoy the more varied and imaginative programmes of the repertory cinemas.

All feature films are classified under the following categories: **U** (universal) – suitable for all ages; **PG** – open to all, but parental guidance is advised; **12** – no one under the age of 12; **15** – no one under 15; **18** – no one under 18. Expect to pay up to £8-£10 for a first-run film in the West End; less in repertory cinemas. Some cinemas have concessionary rates for children, students and the unemployed, and many cinemas offer reductions on Monday and for the first couple of shows of the day, usually from Tuesday to Friday. It's a good idea to book by credit card for first-nighters, though you're generally charged a fee (around 30p)

for this service (most mainstream and first-run cinemas take credit cards, but some repertory cinemas don't). Some of the smaller rep venues ask for a nominal 'membership fee' at the door. For cinema screening details, check the weekly listings in *Time Out* magazine.

Mainstream & first run

The central booking and information number for **Odeon** cinemas is **0870 505 0007**.

Bloomsbury & the City

ABC Tottenham Court Road *Tottenham Court Road, W1 (recorded info 0171 636 6148/credit card bookings 0870 902 0414). Tottenham Court Road tube.* **Map 6 K5**

Barbican Centre *Silk Street, EC2 (recorded info & bookings 0171 382 7000). Barbican or Moorgate tube.* **Map 9 P5**

Renoir *Brunswick Centre, Brunswick Square, WC1 (0171 837 8402). Russell Square tube.* **Map 8 L4**

Take it to the IMAX

Spring 1999 marks the opening of the long-awaited **BFI London IMAX Cinema**, following a £20-million, 14-year project and an 18-month building plan. Situated on the roundabout next to Waterloo Station and the Museum of the Moving Image, the dramatic, drum-like 500-seat cinema cuts an impressive sight. Though not the first IMAX (Image Maximum) cinema in London (the elaborately named **Pepsi IMAX 3-D Theatre Trocadero** wins that award), at more than ten storeys high, and ten times bigger than a conventional 35mm film frame, the screen is not just the biggest in the capital, but in the whole of Europe.

The technology employed by IMAX is astonishing: projectors advance the film horizontally in a wave-like motion, surrounding the audience with huge 2-D images for 2-D films, and 3-D images for 3-D films (special headsets are provided for the latter). Sound is critical: 80 million tiny holes in the screen allow high-fidelity sound to filter through into the auditorium, and the building itself is on springs to cut out the noise

from surrounding traffic. Impressively, the cinema will also be fully accessible for visitors with special needs, and will also contain a shop, café and other facilities. Although until now most films made for IMAX cinemas have been documentaries about wildlife, travel or space, the subject matter is continually expanding – currently, though, only ten films are produced a year – to meet the demands of an audience more used to watching car chases and bomb blasts *à la* Bond. Not that there's a shortage of viewers: an estimated 510 million people (65 million in 1997 alone) have already seen an IMAX film in the 150 specially built cinemas around the world. And, with an Oscar already under its belt (for the Scientific and Technical category in the 1997 Academy Awards), IMAX looks set to take the future by storm.

BFI London IMAX Cinema

Waterloo Bullring, next to Museum of the Moving Image, South Bank, SE1 (information 0171 928 3535). Embankment tube/Waterloo tube/rail. **Map 8 M8**

*The pride of Brixton: the glitzy **Ritzy**. See page 238.*

Marylebone

ABC Baker Street *Marylebone Road, next to Baker Street tube station, NW1 (recorded info 0171 935 9772/credit card bookings 0870 902 0418). Baker Street tube.* **Map 5 G4**

Odeon Marble Arch *10 Edgware Road, W2. Marble Arch tube.* **Map 2 F6**

Screen on Baker Street *96 Baker Street, NW1 (0171 935 2772/recorded info 0171 486 0036). Baker Street tube.* **Map 5 G5**

Mayfair & St James's

ABC Panton Street *Panton Street, SW1 (recorded info 0171 930 0631/credit card bookings 0870 902 0404). Piccadilly Circus tube.* **Map 8 K7**

ABC Piccadilly *Piccadilly, W1 (recorded info 0171 437 3561). Piccadilly Circus tube.* **Map 7 J7**

Curzon Mayfair *38 Curzon Street W1 (0171 369 1720). Green Park or Hyde Park Corner tube.* **Map 7 H8**

ICA Cinema *Nash House, The Mall, SW1 (recorded info 0171 930 6393/credit card bookings 0171 930 3647/info@ica.org.uk/www.ica.org.uk). Piccadilly Circus tube or Charing Cross tube/rail.* **Map 8 K8**

Odeon Haymarket *Haymarket, SW1. Piccadilly Circus tube.* **Map 8 K7**

Plaza *Lower Regent Street, W1 (0171 930 0144/recorded info 0171 437 1234/credit card bookings 0990 888990). Piccadilly Circus tube.* **Map 8 K7**

Virgin Haymarket *Haymarket, W1 (recorded info & credit card bookings 0870 907 0712). Piccadilly Circus tube.* **Map 8 K7**

Soho to Leicester Square

ABC Shaftesbury Avenue *Shaftesbury Avenue, W1 (recorded info 0171 836 6279/credit card bookings 0870 902 0402). Leicester Square or Tottenham Court Road tube.* **Map 6 K6**

ABC Swiss Centre *Swiss Centre, 10 Wardour Street, Leicester Square, W1 (recorded info 0171 439 4470/credit card bookings 0870 902 0403). Leicester Square or Piccadilly Circus tube.* **Map 8 K7**

Curzon Soho *93-107 Shaftesbury Avenue, W1 (0171 734 2255/recorded info 0171 439 4805). Leicester Square or Piccadilly Circus tube.* **Map 8 K6**

Empire *Leicester Square, WC2 (recorded info & credit card bookings 0990 888990). Leicester Square or Piccadilly Circus tube.* **Map 8 K7**

Metro *Rupert Street, W1 (enquiries & bookings 0171 734 1506/recorded info 0171 437 0757). Leicester Square or Piccadilly Circus tube.* **Map 8 K7**

Odeon Leicester Square *Leicester Square, WC2. Leicester Square tube.* **Map 8 K7**

Odeon Mezzanine *Adjacent to Odeon Leicester Square. Leicester Square tube.* **Map 8 K7**

Odeon West End *Leicester Square, WC2. Leicester Square tube.* **Map 8 K7**

Pepsi IMAX 3-D Theatre Trocadero *Pepsi Trocadero, Piccadilly Circus, W1 (info & bookings 0171 494 4153). Piccadilly Circus tube.* **Map 8 K7**

Prince Charles *Leicester Place, WC2 (recorded info 0171 437 8181). Leicester Square or Piccadilly Circus tube.* **Map 8 K7**

Size matters

Screen size is roughly proportional to the number of seats, so, if you want the full monty for *The Full Monty*, here's where you'll find the 15 biggest screens in town:

	Seats
Odeon Leicester Square	1,943
Empire 1	1,330
Odeon West End 2	838
Plaza 1	732
Chelsea Cinema	720
Odeon Swiss Cottage 1	705
ABC Shaftesbury Avenue 1	616
Odeon Haymarket	600
ABC Shaftesbury Avenue 2	580
Virgin Trocadero 1	548
Curzon Mayfair	542
Odeon Kensington 1	520
Odeon West End 1	503
Prince Charles	488
Virgin Haymarket	448

Top tours: Movies, murder & the macabre

A bloodstained trail of film murder sites through Soho

The noirist of the noir – dark doings afoot in Peeping Tom *(1960).*

British Museum

Great Russell Street, WC1. **Map 6 K/L5**
Here's the roof over which the villain is pursued in the finale of Hitchcock's first talkie, *Blackmail*, the reading room in which a ghostly force manifests itself in Jacques Tourneur's eerie *Night of the Demon*, and the Hall of Egyptian Antiquities where Charlton Heston revives an evil princess in Mike Newell's *The Awakening*.

Newman Passage

off Rathbone Street (by Newman Arms pub). **Map 5 J5**
This obscure byway is the site of the murder that opens Michael Powell's 1960 masterpiece of London psychonoir, *Peeping Tom*. Seen partially through the viewfinder of the murderer's cine-camera, the scene follows prostitute Dora – a rare, realistic middle-aged tart – into the passage and up a stairway to the right, which should logically take her to the upper rooms of the pub, where she is murdered by Mark, who impales her with a spiked camera tripod, all the while filming her terror. Powell described Newman Passage as 'a narrow, arched passageway that gives you goose-pimples just to look at it'.

Wardour Street

W1. **Map 5 J6/6 K6**
This has been the administrative heart of the British film industry since the 1920s, but it's a curiously underfilmed thoroughfare. There are no studios here, just the offices of distributors, production companies, publicists and post-production facilities. Britain has produced few films about its film industry along the lines of Hollywood's *Sunset Boulevard* or *Singin' in the Rain*, so you have to make do with the glimpses of preview theatres and distributors' offices caught in Martin Campbell's *Eskimo Nell* (1974), a surprisingly apt insider's view of 1970s British porn filmmaking.

At 113 Wardour Street is **Hammer House**, once owned by Hammer Films, now a photographic services outlet. There's an in-joke in producer Herman Cohen's 1958 American movie *I Was a Teenage Frankenstein*, as Dr F plans on dissecting his creation and posting him in bits to 113 Wardour Street.

Diadem Court

between Dean Street & Great Chapel Street, W1.
Map 6 K6
Diadem Court is the obscure address of yet another murdered prostitute, Champagne Ivy, mistress of Fredric March's brutal Mr Hyde in Rouben Mamoulian's 1932 *Dr Jekyll and Mr Hyde*. Unlike *Peeping Tom*, it was shot an ocean and a continent away in Hollywood; but it's unusual that an American film of the period would take so much care as to give a real address for a throwaway character.

Falconberg Court

off Sutton Row, W1. **Map 6 K6**
Soho Square, a patch of green frequented by cycle messengers waiting for the call, abusers of various substances and (in summer) lunching employees of the British Board of Film Classification, Bloomsbury Publishing and 20th Century Fox is surprisingly rarely filmed. If you cross the square and feint towards Charing Cross Road via Sutton Row, you find Falconberg Court, a foul-smelling right angle around the back of the Astoria that was the given address of the Alan Howard character in *The Cook, the Thief, His Wife and Her Lover*, the library where Howard and Helen Mirren conduct their adulterous affair and where Howard is stuffed full of pages torn out of his books.

Old Compton Street

W1. **Map 6 K6**
Walking towards Old Compton Street, the Soho you see gets more like the Soho you imagine: the name is well-enough known internationally to crop up as a fantastical locale recreated on soundstages in Berlin or Budapest for *The Gorilla of Soho*, *The Hunchback of Soho* and *The Phantom of Soho*. It is this imaginary Soho that is the haunt of the fused image of Jack the Ripper and Mr Hyde: an actor possessed by the role of the Ripper stalks through the German *The Monster of London Town*, set in some Teutonic version of these streets, while *Edge of Sanity*, made in Hungary, has Anthony Perkins as a Dr Jekyll who becomes 'Jack Hyde' under the influence of nineteenth-century crack and murders yet more of the doomed tarts who are so indelibly associated with the region in the popular imagination.

Old Compton Street is the site of the strip club run by thin-moustached Christopher Lee in the 1962 classic *Beat Girl*, outside which Adam Faith is beaten so badly that he throws his guitar into a waste bin with a significance roughly equal to that of Dirty Harry chucking away his badge; and it's also the address of the private club in *Mona Lisa* where Bob Hoskins asks a lady in leather if there's any chance of a cup of tea and is told to piss off.

Soho clubs feature in many movies, but those that were actual places – like the ones featured in *The Krays* – are now as elusive as the imaginary sinkpots of iniquity explored in the forgotten *Noose* and the original, masterly *Night and the City*. The closest to the fantasised vision of a smoky collection of picturesque characters drinking late at night is probably Gerry's Club in Dean Street.

On Old Compton Street, you can still find espresso cafés and Italian restaurants, though you'd be hard-put to find the actual joints where Tony Hancock demands coffee 'with no froth' in *The Rebel*, Cliff Richard and Tommy Steele are 'discovered' in *Expresso Bongo* and *The Tommy Steele Story*, or a magic realist family saga plays itself out in *Queen of Hearts*.

Great Windmill Street

W1. See picture p23. **Map 8 K7**
The Windmill Theatre, known for its nude tableaux, was the subject of a fakey Hollywood biopic *Tonight and Every Night*, with Rita Hayworth standing up to the Blitz. But true connoisseurs of British tat much prefer *Murder at the Windmill*, a backstage whodunnit featuring Jon Pertwee and Jimmy Edwards doing their demob ENSA acts, and the undeservedly forgotten *Secrets of a Windmill Girl*, in which a very young Pauline Collins (who leaves it off her CV these days) suffers mightily for coming to the big city.

Piccadilly Circus

W1. **Map 8 K7**
Filmmakers have long complained that the London authorities are far less amenable to the staging of large-scale action sequences than those of many American cities, and so there are few equivalents to the breathless San Francisco, Los Angeles or New York car chases of *Bullitt*, *Speed* and *The French Connection*. But John Landis did stage the climax of *An American Werewolf in London* in the Circus, crashing a satisfying collection of vehicles and gunning down his lycanthrope in a handy alley.

Taken from Kim Newman's walk in the **Time Out Book of London Walks** *(£9.99).*

His Royal Highness Lord Cliff of Richard, making his name in Expresso Bongo *(1959).*

Virgin Trocadero *Trocadero, WC2 (recorded info & bookings 0870 907 0716). Leicester Square or Piccadilly Circus tube.* Map 8 K7

Warner Village West End *Leicester Square, WC2 (recorded info 0171 437 4347/credit card bookings 0171 437 4343). Leicester Square tube.* Map 8 K7

Knightsbridge & Chelsea

Chelsea Cinema *206 King's Road, SW3 (0171 351 3742). Sloane Square tube.* Map 4 E12

Curzon Minema *45 Knightsbridge, SW1 (0171 369 1723/www.minema.com). Hyde Park Corner or Knightsbridge tube.* Map 7 G9

Virgin Chelsea *279 King's Road, SW3 (recorded info & credit card bookings 0870 907 0710). Sloane Square tube then 11, 19, 22 bus.* Map 4 E12

North London

Odeon Camden Town *Parkway, NW1. Camden Town tube.*

Odeon Swiss Cottage *Finchley Road, NW6. Swiss Cottage tube.*

Screen on the Green *83 Upper Street, N1 (0171 226 3520). Angel tube.* Map 9 O2

Screen on the Hill *203 Haverstock Hill, NW3 (0171 435 3366). Belsize Park tube.*

South London

Clapham Picture House *76 Venn Street, SW4 (recorded info 0171 498 2242/credit card bookings 0171 498 3323). Clapham Common tube.*

Greenwich Cinema *180 Greenwich High Road, SE10 (credit card bookings 0181 293 0101/recorded info 01426 919020). Greenwich rail.*

Ritzy *Brixton Oval, Coldharbour Lane, SW2 (recorded info 0171 737 2121/credit card bookings 0171 733 2229). Brixton tube/rail.*

Virgin Fulham Road *142 Fulham Road, SW10 (recorded info & credit card bookings 0870 907 0711). South Kensington tube.* Map 4 D11

West London

Gate Cinema *87 Notting Hill Gate, W11 (0171 727 4043). Notting Hill Gate tube.* Map 1 A7

Notting Hill Coronet *Notting Hill Gate, W11 (0171 727 6705). Notting Hill Gate tube.* Map 1 A7

Odeon Kensington *Kensington High Street, W8. High Street Kensington tube.* Map 3 A9

UCI Whiteleys *2nd floor, Whiteleys Shopping Centre, Queensway, W2 (recorded info 0171 792 3332/credit card bookings 0990 888990). Bayswater or Queensway tube.* Map 1 C6

Repertory

See also **ICA**, **Metro** and **Ritzy Cinema** above. The following are distinguished by well-chosen, off-the-wall material. The **Phoenix** and **Watermans Arts Centre** also show new releases.

Ciné Lumière *Institut Français, 7 Queensberry Place, SW7 (0171 838 2144/838 2146). South Kensington tube.*

Everyman Cinema *Hollybush Vale, NW3. Hampstead tube. Closed at time of going to press; due to reopen early 1999 – see Time Out magazine for details.*

Goethe Institut *50 Princes Gate, Exhibition Road, SW7 (0171 411 3400/www.goethe.de/london). South Kensington tube.* Map 4 D9

Lux Cinema *2-4 Hoxton Square, N1 (0171 684 0201/684 0200). Old Street tube/rail.* Map 10 R3

Pick of the flicks

Best for...

- latest late shows: **Odeon Marble Arch**
- first-night blockbusters: **Odeon Leicester Square**; **Empire**
- smoking: **Notting Hill Coronet**
- comfortable surroundings: **Curzon Minema**
- foreign flicks: **Goethe Institut** (subtitled German films); **Institut Français** (subtitled French films)
- cheap admission (mainstream/first-run): **Prince Charles**
- impressing your friends by pretending you're into arty films: **Renoir**; **Lux Cinema**
- taking the kids to: **Ritzy**; matinées at the **NFT** (irregular Sats & Suns)
- bar for a pre-/post-film drink: **Screen on the Hill**; **Ritzy**

National Film Theatre (NFT) *South Bank, SE1 (0171 928 3232/www.bfi.org.uk). Embankment tube/ Waterloo tube/rail.* Map 8 M7

Phoenix *52 High Road, N2 (0181 444 6789/recorded info 0181 883 2233). East Finchley tube.*

Rio Cinema *107 Kingsland High Street, E8 (0171 254 6677). Dalston Kingsland rail/67, 76, 149, 243 bus.*

Riverside Studios Cinema *Crisp Road, W6 (0181 237 1000/credit card bookings 0181 237 1111/ www.riversidestudios.co.uk). Hammersmith tube.*

Watermans Arts Centre *40 High Street, Brentford, Middx (0181 568 1176). Kew Bridge/Brentford rail.*

Festivals

The annual **London Film Festival** (4-18 Nov 1999), aimed at reflecting the full range of world cinema, is a must for any film-lover. Throughout the festival, hundreds of films are shown at the South Bank's **National Film Theatre** (*see above*) and selected West End cinemas. Other annual film festivals hosted by the NFT include the **London Lesbian and Gay Film Festival** (8-18 Apr 1999), the **London Jewish Film Festival** (date unconfirmed as this guide went to press; phone for details) and the **Fantasm Festival of Horror and SF** (usually the last weekend in July; phone to check). The NFT also hosts regular talks and previews, attracting the likes of Clint Eastwood and Quentin Tarantino. The **Metro** (*see above*), meanwhile, is home to the **Latin American Film Festival** (3-16 Sept 1999), the **German Film Festival** (one week in Dec; phone for exact dates) and the **Raindance Film Festival** (7-15 Oct 1999), Britain's only independent film festival, featuring works by first-time filmmakers.

Gay & Lesbian

London is coming out for the next millennium.

Cheer if you're glad to be queer. London's gay scene has advanced enormously in recent years. The idea of a specific, unified 'gay culture' is slowly being replaced by a celebration of healthy heterodoxy – there's greater strength in diversity than unity. Thus, 'queer' encompasses everything and everybody with leanings away from the straight and narrow. There is still, alas, plenty of attitude to be overcome: in clubs and bars, if your face and bearing don't fit, you'll often be made all too aware of it.

This neanderthal ethos is under attack, though. Not least from the sharp-tongued humour of iconoclast avant-garde performer The Divine David (who has broken into the mainstream with his *The Divine David Presents...* TV show on Channel 4). Further positive signs are the increasingly visible lesbian and non-white gay scenes, as demonstrated by London's hosting of the world's first lesbian beauty contest and Europe's first Black and Asian gay beauty contest. These days, anything goes – so if you long to be showered with flowers by an Indian drag queen, get picked up in a gay skater's club by a green-haired teenager, have tea with young gay professionals, swim naked in a gay pool or sing at a lesbian karaoke, you'll find something to suit your tastes.

One of London's biggest marches and festivals, **Pride**, has been in trouble recently. The festival was cancelled in 1998 (though the march went ahead), and at the time of going to press it was not certain whether the march would be taking place in 1999. However, there are definite plans for a **Pride Arts Festival** (18 June-11 July 1999), which will feature a wide range of events in a number of venues. Check the weekly *Time Out* magazine nearer the time for details. The gay-oriented **Summer Rites** (0171 278 0995) bash in Brockwell Park near Brixton has been hugely popular in recent years. In 1999, it takes place on 7 August, and you can expect bucketloads of events, market stalls, bars, a funfair and live performances.

London's lesbian and gay nightlife is well organised. Clubs advertise their events in the gay press, including *Time Out* magazine, and in freebie publications (the 'gaypers') such as *Boys* and *QX,* available in many of the bars and clubs listed below. Of the rest of the gay press, the *Pink Paper* is good for news and lifestyle features, while light relief can be had from (lipstick) lesbian mag *Diva* and fashion-led *Attitude*.

Royal Vauxhall Tavern's **Duckie**. *See p241.*

Admission prices vary from place to place and from night to night. The trendiest clubs often charge in excess of a tenner, depending on what time you get past the door. Keep an eye out for discount vouchers and flyers. At most pubs, though not all, admission is free.

Clubs

Soho is still the gay mecca, but recently clusters of gay nightlife have been appearing away from the West End, in places such as Brixton and Camden. Earl's Court, the centre of Gay London life in the 1970s, is also experiencing a renaissance. Clubs tend to come and go with bewildering speed, so be sure to phone ahead before you order your rubber gear. Note that venues that put on more than three nights a week are listed by venue; others are listed by name of club night. Central London is served by an extensive network of night buses (bus numbers are prefixed with an N); only those for venues outside of central London are listed below. 'Women only' means lesbians. Note that many bars also host excellent club nights; *see page 179*. Also worth looking out for is **Helmut Slang**, previously held at Gossips on a Wednesday; in early 1999 it will move to a new venue in Soho and will take place on a Saturday (see *Time Out* or phone 0171 733 4506 for details).

Ace of Clubs
52 Piccadilly, W1 (0171 408 4457). Piccadilly Circus tube. **Open** 9pm-4am Sat. **Map 7 J7**
Long-running, perennially packed women-only club with DJs Rachel and Charlotte. Perhaps not the trendiest place in town, but definitely fun.

Club Kali
The Dome, 1 Dartmouth Park Hill, N19 (no phone). Tufnell Park tube/N20. **Open** 10pm-3am third Fri of the month.
The gorgeous Rita welcomes a mixed crowd into what must be the world's biggest, friendliest and most attitude-free club for Indian and South Asian lesbians and gays. You're likely to be chatted up by several Bollywood diva lookalikes before you get to dance to captivating bhangra, Hindi and Arabic rhythms, infused with house, soul and swing. All are welcome, and drinks are cheap. Look out also for **Shakti Disco** on the first Friday of the month, which is a South Asian lesbian, gay, bisexual and transgender people's club night.

Club Travestie Extraordinaire
Stepney's, 373 Commercial Road (entrance in Aylward Street), E1 (0181 788 4154). Aldgate East tube. **Open** 8.30pm-2am every other Sat.
This TV/drag club has been running for 19 years and is as popular as ever, attracting not only TVs but gays,lesbians, straights, you name it. Fun, disco tunes are expertly mixed by DJ Keith DeMaggio, and nights are often themed: check current listings for the latest. There are plans to run the club every Saturday in 1999, but phone to check first.

Club V
The Garage, 20-22 Highbury Corner, N5 (0171 607 1818). Highbury & Islington tube/rail/N43. **Open** 9pm-3am every other Sat.
An excellent alternative alternative to **Popstarz** *(see below)*. DJs Mel, Neil, Phil and Sarit satisfy a mixed crowd with the Smashing Pumpkins and other choice indie artists.

Coco Latté
Chocolate Bar & Club, 59 Berkeley Square, W1 (0956 198267). Green Park tube. **Open** 10pm-late Fri. **Map 7 H7**
Pricey, classy mixed gay club night with funky house and chunky garage on the main floor and '70s classics and rare groove upstairs. Recommended.

DTPM
The End, 16A West Central Street, WC1 (0181 586 0344). Tottenham Court Road tube. **Open** 8pm-late Sun. **Map 6 L5**
A glossy, hi-tech design club with a stylish clientele to match, who finish their weekend to funky sounds pumped out by The End's superb sound system.

Factor 25
Saint, 8 Great Newport Street, WC2 (0171 240 1551). Leicester Square tube. **Open** 5pm-late Sun. **Map 8 K6**
Busy dance session for a post-Trade, pre-DTPM party crowd, hosted by Paul and Yan. Top-notch stuff.

G.A.Y
The Astoria (LA1) & LA2, 157 Charing Cross Road, WC2 (0171 734 6963). Tottenham Court Road tube. **Open** 10.30pm-4am Mon, Thur; 11pm-4am Sat. **Map 6 K6**
Jeremy Joseph hosts London's biggest gay trash bash, attracting mainly a young, unpretentious crowd. Monday's and Thursday's **G.A.Y Pink Pounder** at LA2 and Friday's **G.A.Y Camp Attack** ('70s/'80s music) at the Astoria have cheap drinks and entry (£1 with flyer) and are heavy on the cheese; for big commercial beats and bigger sound systems, head for **G.A.Y** at the Astoria on Saturdays.

Gay Tea Dance
The Limelight, Shaftesbury Avenue, W1 (0171 437 4303). Leicester Square tube. **Open** 6-11pm Sun. **Map 6 K6**
A Sunday institution, this feast of '70s, '80s and '90s pop is hosted by Dusty O, with slightly harder sound downstairs.

Heaven
The Arches, Villiers Street, WC2 (0171 930 2020). Embankment tube/Charing Cross tube/rail. **Open** 10pm-3am Mon, Wed; 10pm-6am Fri; 10.30pm-6am Sat. **Map 8 L7**
The best-known and longest-established gay venue in town has just undergone a massive refurbishment, which has given birth to a new sibling club, **The Soundshaft** (open on Fridays and Saturdays), accessible from Heaven, and left the club itself with an extra bar, coffee bar and VIP lounge. Three floors, each with different music, keep a diverse crowd happy. Fabulous drag hostess Miss Kimberly manages the upstairs attitude-free lounge to the sound of oldies, disco and singalong tunes (and also **Powder Room** on a Wednesday), while the mid-floor offers the widest array of top-notch British DJs to entertain the New York house and R&B loving clientele. Downstairs, you'll find mainly tourists and out of towners, hoping to spot a star while listening to the latest techno/rave tunes. Monday's **Popcorn** offers a mix of bubblegum pop, disco trash and dance, and Sheena Showgirl hosting the Dakota cabaret bar (while there's a friendly indie night, **Room Two**, in the Star Bar); **Fruit Machine** on Wednesdays finds soul in the Star Bar and some heavy funk downstairs. Friday night is **Wildlife**: hard house and techno beats. The ultimate night at Heaven, though, is Saturday's **Heaven** itself: NY house and speed garage. Be warned, though, Heaven's popularity has moved it towards the mainstream, bringing in lots of non-gays (in fact, Saturday night is the only strictly gay night) and giving the staff an arrogance verging on the offensive.

Kitty Lips
No longer at Mars, this popular club, playing hard house and friendly techno for young lesbians and their male guests, was looking for a new home at the time of going to press. Check the gay press for details.

Love Muscle
The Fridge, Town Hall Parade, Brixton Hill, SW2 (0171 326 5100). Brixton tube/rail/N2, N3, N35, N37, N109. **Open** 10pm-6am Sat; *Fridge Bar* 8pm-12.30am Sun.
The queues for this busy party night stretch into the distance. Once inside, expect dance and fluffy techno aimed at a mixed crowd of (mainly) muscle boys, disco dykes and club freaks. Superb light effects, steamy stage shows and a chill-out room are all part of the fun. Also watch out for **Space Race** at the Fridge Bar on Sundays, with its global beats, drum 'n' bass, dub and space funk.

Mis-shapes
Plastic People, 37/39 Oxford Street, W1 (0171 738 2336). Tottenham Court Road tube. **Open** 10pm-2am Sun. **Map 6 K6**

A mixed gay club for 'mis-shapen types bullied at school', and alienated by the attitude of the gay scene – indie pop, funky rock, beaty swing.

Popstarz
No longer at Holborn's Leisure Lounge, the grandaddy of gay indie clubs, Simon Hobart's Popstarz, was looking for a new home at the time of going to press. Check the gay press for details.

Royal Vauxhall Tavern
Vauxhall Tavern, Kennington Lane, SE11 (0171 582 0833). Vauxhall tube/rail/N2, N36, N44. **Open** 9pm-2am Wed, Thur, Fri, Sat; 2pm-midnight Sun.
High-school ball meets avant-garde testing ground for upcoming comedians and performance artists at **Duckie** (Sat). Incredibly and deservedly successful, Amy Lamé and Mr Strange's cheery, attitude-free club affirms the need for non-conformist queer spaces. Nostalgic tunes and whining Morrissey are the soundtrack for a fun night of cheap drinking. Thursday night is **Frolics**, a mixed gay drag show with Regina Fong, while Friday sees **Vixens at the Vauxhall Tavern**, rightly regarded as one of the few long-standing, safe, women-only havens, where weekly cabaret is enjoyed by a cool, convivial crowd. On Wednesdays there's **Wig'n'Casino**, a gay northern soul revue, while **Adrella's Sunday Skool**, logically enough on Sundays, combines drag show with uplifting house.

Stuff
The Artful Dodger, 139 Southgate Road, N1 (0171 281 7690). Angel or Highbury & Islington tube. **Open** 10pm-2am every other Sat.
Hip hop, bigbeat and alternative dance entertain a happy crowd at this newish alternative night for gays.

Substation Soho
1A Dean Street, W1 (0171 287 9608). Tottenham Court Road tube. **Open** 10.30pm-3.30am Tue-Thur; 10pm-5am Fri; 10pm-6am Sat. **Map 6 K6**
Substation Soho puts on a popular, friendly and fabulously diverse collection of nights. It all starts with **Twisted** (Tue), a garage fest 'for those who feel a bit twisted after the weekend', followed on Wednesday by the indie night **Love Bite**, and Thursday's **Get Over It** with DJs Rolf and Jamie B. The weekend lineup consists of long-running **Spunk** (Fri), with sexy gogos and a cruisey party atmosphere, and Saturday's **Renegades**, with house, hard house and 'tribal energy'. All of these nights are mixed gay nights.

Substation South
9 Brighton Terrace, SW9 (0171 737 2095). Brixton tube/rail/N2, N3, N37, N109. **Open** 10pm-3am Mon, Wed; 10pm-2am Tue; 10pm-3am Thur; 10.30pm-5am Fri; 10.30pm-6am Sat; 9pm-2am Sun.
People who know what they want come here (as it were). The reputation of Substation Soho's south London brother is strictly no-frills and down-to-business. **Y-front** (Mon) is a men-only grope'n'grind fest – underwear only; **ToolBox** (Tue) and **Blackout** (Thur) are men-only cruise nights; **Boot Camp** (Wed) is for male fetish fans (uniforms, leather, jocks, boots), with proceeds to the Eddie Surman Trust. Weekends start up with gay/lesbian **Dirty Dishes** (Fri), followed by Saturday's the NY style house/garage of **Queer Nation** (mixed gay). On Sundays the indie kids flock in for fun-packed **Marvellous**, also mixed gay.

Trade
Turnmills, 63B Clerkenwell Road, EC1 (0171 250 3409). Farringdon tube/rail. **Open** 4am-1pm Sat; 10pm-6am Sun, Mon. **Map 9 N4**
Classic late night, playing raunchy techno to an enthusiastic, mixed crowd dominated by muscle boys. Lawrence Malice hosts. Turnmills also hosts **Melt** (Sun), with tech-

no/trance on the main floor and speed garage/funky house upstairs, and the mixed/gay **Club Epsilon** (Mon).

Wig Out
The Tube, Falconberg Court, W1 (0171 287 3726). Tottenham Court Road tube. **Open** 10.30pm-5am Fri. **Map 6 K6**
This popular club at the bottom of the Tottenham Court Road is alive with '70s, '80s and '90s trash on a Friday night, bringing in a happy clubby crowd.

Bars & pubs

Most of the places below are open to gay men and lesbians unless specified; we've tried to make clear which have less to offer female customers.

The Bar
Chariots House, Fairchild Street, EC2 (0171 247 5222). Old Street or Shoreditch tube/Liverpool Street tube/rail. **Open** 11am-11pm Mon-Sat; noon-10.30pm Sun. **Map 10 R4**
Large, airy café-bar adjoining Chariots Roman Spa. DJs and regular cabaret. Friendly service and excellent food.

BarCode
179A Finborough Road, SW10 (0171 734 3342). Earl's Court or West Brompton tube. **Open** 1pm-midnight Mon-Thur; 1pm-1am Fri, Sat; 1-10.30pm Sun. **Map 8 K7**
Having moved from its Soho location, this men's cruise and dance bar is due to open at this address in March 1999.

The Box
32-34 Monmouth Street, WC2 (0171 240 5828). Leicester Square tube. **Open** *café* 11am-5.30pm Mon-Sat; noon-6.30pm Sun; *bar* 5.30-11pm Mon-Sat; 6.30-10.30pm Sun. **Map 6 L6**
Busy, modern bar just off the Seven Dials, Covent Garden, serving drinks, coffee and food. Mixed crowd.

BJ's White Swan
556 Commercial Road, E14 (0171 780 9870). Aldgate East tube. **Open** 9pm-1am Mon; 9pm-2am Tue-Thur; 9pm-3am Fri, Sat; 5.30pm-midnight Sun. **Map 12 S6**
Busy local bar/club featuring discos and drag/cabaret on a Tuesday and Thursday, and strip shows on a Monday and Wednesday.

Brief Encounter
42 St Martin's Lane, WC1 (no phone). Charing Cross tube/rail. **Open** 11am-11pm Mon-Sat; noon-10.30pm Sun. **Map 8 K7**
Busy men's bar.

Brompton's
corner of Old Brompton Road & Warwick Road, SW5 (0171 370 1344). Earl's Court tube. **Open** *bar* 6pm-2am Mon-Sat; 8.30pm-midnight Sun; *club* 10.30pm-2am Mon-Thur; 10pm-2am Fri, Sat; 5.30pm-midnight Sun. **Map 3 B11**
Popular men's venue with two bars, a video screen and a cabaret stage. The bar, with a separate club (cabaret Mon, Thur), caters to gays and lesbians every night except Tuesday when it's men only. Also check out **Fleas and Tease**, with male strippers, on a Sunday.

Candy Bar
4 Carlisle Street, W1 (0171 494 4041). Tottenham Court Road tube. **Open** *bar* 5pm-midnight Mon-Thur; 5pm-2am Fri, Sat; 5-10.30pm Sun; *club* 8pm-midnight Mon-Thur; 8pm-2am Fri, Sat; 7-11pm Sun. **Map 6 K6**
The UK's first and only seven-nights-a-week lesbian bar hosts an exceptional series of club nights, including the

sleaze, glam and bubblegum pop of **Suffragette City** on Mondays, **Disco Bunny** on Tuesdays, Wednesday's superbly named **Opportunity Knockers**, Thursday's house night **Kix**, Friday's **Booby Trap**, and **Dolly Mixtures**, Saturday's party night for girls. Sunday nights vary. Male guests are welcome every night.

Central Station
37 Wharfdale Road, N1 (0171 278 3294). King's Cross tube/rail. **Open** 5pm-2am Mon-Wed; 5pm-3am Thur; 5pm-4am Fri; noon-4am Sat; noon-midnight Sun. **Map 6 L2**
This award-winning 'community pub' combines meeting place, cabaret and late-night cruising. **Bulk** (Wed) is a serious men-only night; **Handsome Devil** is a queer indie session (second Tue of month); while male latex-lovers can check out **Gummi** (second Sun of month). Rubber gear only.

Duke of Clarence
140 Rotherfield Street, N1 (no phone). Angel tube then 38, 73, 56, 171A, 277 bus. **Open** 6pm-midnight Mon-Fri; 7pm-midnight Sat; 3-11.30pm Sun. **Map 9 P1**
Mixed gay pub with a separate women-only bar.

First Out
52 St Giles High Street, WC2 (0171 240 8042). Tottenham Court Road tube. **Open** 10am-11pm Mon-Sat; 11am-10.30pm Sun. **Map 6 K6**
The first lesbian and gay veggie eaterie in London. On Fridays, there's a pre-club night, **Girl Friday** (8-11pm; for women and male guests), described by the owners as 'house and garage with a funky twist'.

Freedom Café-Gallery-Bar
60-66 Wardour Street, W1 (0171 734 0071). Piccadilly Circus tube. **Open** 11am-3am Mon-Sat; 11am-midnight Sun. **Map 6 K6**

*Break all the rules at **Regulation**. See p191.*

A busy joint that serves booze and food to a hip mixed crowd. There are various themed nights; see *Time Out* magazine for details.

Glass Bar
West Lodge, Euston Square Gardens, 190 Euston Road, NW1 (0171 387 6184). Euston tube/rail. **Open** 5pm-late Tue-Fri; 6pm-late Sat; 2-7pm Sun. **Map 5 J4**
London's largest women-only members bar (with a staggering 10,000 members), on two floors and with pub prices. No admission after 11.30pm.

The Hoist
Railway Arch 47C, South Lambeth Road, SW8 (0171 735 9972). Vauxhall tube/rail. **Open** 10pm-3am Fri, Sat; 9pm-1am Sun.
Men's cruise bar. Dress: leather, rubber, uniform, etc.

Joiner's Arms
116-118 Hackney Road, E2 (0171 739 9854). Old Street or Liverpool Street tube/rail. **Open** noon-11pm Mon-Sat; noon-10.30pm Sun. **Map 10 R3**
Gay pub providing regular entertainment, including DJs and quizzes.

King Edward VI
25 Bromfield Street, N1 (0171 704 0745). Angel tube. **Open** noon-midnight daily. **Map 9 N2**
Busy, mixed gay pub with café-bar upstairs, plus beer garden. Friendly, welcoming crowd.

Ku Bar
75 Charing Cross Road, W1 (0171 437 4303). Leicester Square tube. **Open** 4-11pm Mon-Sat; 4-10.30pm Sun. **Map 8 K7**
Stylish bar, popular with a young, scene-friendly crowd.

Kudos
10 Adelaide Street, WC2 (0171 379 4573). Charing Cross tube/rail. **Open** 11am-11pm Mon-Sat; noon-10.30pm Sun. **Map 8 L7**
Smart, busy boys' bar. Large video screen downstairs, café upstairs.

Retro Bar
2 George Court, off Strand, WC2 (0171 321 2811). Charing Cross tube/rail. **Open** noon-11pm Mon-Sat; noon-10.30pm Sun. **Map 8 L7**
Mixed gay indie/retro bar playing '70s, '80s, New Romantic, goth and alternative sounds.

Rupert Street
50 Rupert Street, W1 (no phone). Piccadilly Circus tube. **Open** 11am-11pm Mon-Sat; noon-10.30pm Sun. **Map 8 K7**
Busy gay boys' bar.

West Central
29-30 Lisle Street, WC2 (0171 479 7981). Leicester Square tube. **Open** noon-11.30pm Mon-Sat; *basement bar* 10.30pm-3.30am Mon-Sat. **Map 8 K7**
A newish and very happening three-floor bar. On the first Friday of the month, the popular **Shake Your Tail Feather** pumps out a quality mix of funk, rare groove and northern soul until 3.30am. Look out also for another Friday monthly, **Shinky Shonky**.

Dining clubs

A relatively recent phenomenon, these increasingly popular organisations put together (for a price) civilised nights out in restaurants for those who are tired of the gay bar and club scene. The

Champagne Dining Club (0181 696 0829) organises men-only, lesbian-only and mixed gay evenings; the **Out and Out Dining Club** (0181 723 9245) is strictly for the boys.

Sport

Covent Garden Health Spa
29 Endell Street, WC2 (0171 836 2236). Covent Garden tube. **Open** 11am-11pm daily. **Admission** £13.50; *students* £7 before 4pm; £10 after 4pm. **Credit** MC, £TC, V. **Map 6 L6**
Come here for a beauty treat, Jacuzzi or massage. There's a woman-only night, **Flirt**, held on the first Saturday of the month after closing time (11pm-3.30am). Otherwise it's for men only.

Soho Athletic Club
10-14 Macklin Street, WC2 (0171 242 1290). Holborn tube. **Open** 7am-10pm Mon-Fri; 10am-10pm Sat; noon-6pm Sun. **Membership** £325-£440 per year; £18-£22 per week; £6-£8 per day. **Map 6 L6**
A huge, friendly gym open to men and women, with excellent cardiovascular and resistance machines and plenty of free weights. It's become one of the first London gyms to embrace the new New York craze of spinning, low impact aerobics on exercise bikes. There's also normal aerobics, a therapy room and a beauty therapist on site. The real beauty is the hidden extras, which include the Revival Café and cable TV.

Accommodation

The **London Holiday Accommodation Bureau** (*see page 151*) can organise holiday apartments for gays and lesbians, and also throws in a free airport/tube pick-up, theatre tickets and a tour of Soho.

Lesbian & Gay Accommodation Outlet
32 Old Compton Street, W1 (0171 287 4244/homes@ outlet.co.uk). Leicester Square tube. **Open** 10am-7pm Mon-Fri; noon-5pm Sat. **Map 6 K6**
A service for lesbian and gay flat-seekers, landlords and those looking for short term holiday accommodation. It also runs a hostel in Holborn with rooms from £25 a night and, as part of its holiday accommodation service, can find rooms in the West End from £45.

Number Seven
7 Josephine Avenue, SW2 (0181 674 1880/hotel@ no7.com). Brixton tube/rail. **Rates** *single* £59-£69; *double* £82-£105; *suite* £112; *triple* £116; *quad* £147. **Credit** AmEx, MC, V.
A Victorian townhouse in a quiet tree-lined street in buzzing Brixton. Run by friendly John and Paul (and their dog Dougal), this small (though not cheap) B&B is clean and comfortable. Clubbers take note: it's handy for the **Fridge** (*see p240*) and **Substation South** (*see p241*). **Hotel services** *Fax. Garden. Laundry. Parking. Safe.* **Room services** *Air-conditioning. Hairdryer. Radio. Refrigerator. Satellite TV. Telephone. Website: www.no7.com*

Philbeach Hotel
30-31 Philbeach Gardens, SW5 (0171 373 1244). Earl's Court tube. **Rooms** 40 (14 en suite). **Rates** (incl continental breakfast) *single* £35-£55; *double* £58-£75. **Credit** AmEx, DC, JCB, MC, £TC, V. **Map 3 A11**
A well-established gay hotel, particularly favoured by trans-vestites (there's a cross-dressing party every other Monday). The interiors of some of the rooms are not quite up to scratch, but there is at least a late-opening bar and restaurant, Wilde about Oscar, which has just been refurbished. **Hotel services** *Bar. Fax. Garden. Laundry. Multilingual staff. Restaurant. Safe. TV Lounge.* **Room services** *Room service (24 hour). Telephone. TV.*

Health & information

For further helplines, *see page 291*.

Audrey Lorde Clinic
Ambrose King Centre, Royal London Hospital, Turner Street, E1 (0171 377 7312). Whitechapel tube. **Open** 10am-5pm Fri.
Weekly lesbian health clinic, offering smears, HIV testing, information and counselling.

Axis
Mortimer Market Centre, Mortimer Market, off Capper Street, W1 (0171 530 5050). Warren Street tube. **Open** 7-9pm Thur. **Map 5 J4**
Sexual health clinic for gay and bisexual men and women under 26. No appointment necessary. Also drugs information for gay men.

Bernhard Clinic
GU Medicine Department, Charing Cross Hospital, Fulham Palace Road, W6 (appointments 0181 846 1576/7). Hammersmith or Baron's Court tube. **Open** 2-7pm Wed.
Sexual health clinic for women.

Big Up Helpline
(0171 501 9315). **Phone enquiries** 6-8pm Tue, Thur. An organisation run by and for gay African and Afro-Caribbean men, providing support and health information. Postal enquiries should be directed to: Unit 41, Eurolink Business Centre, 49 Effra Road, London SW2 1BZ.

Black Lesbian & Gay Helpline
(0171 620 3885). **Phone enquiries** 5.30-7.30pm Tue; 11am-4pm Sat. Also drop-in and advice.

London Friend
(0171 837 3337). **Phone enquiries** 7.30-10pm daily. Lesbian and gay helpline offering confidential information, counselling and support.

London Lesbian Line
(0171 251 6911/minicom 0171 253 0924). **Phone enquiries** 2-10pm Mon, Fri; 7-10pm Tue-Thur. Advice, info and support.

London Lesbian & Gay Switchboard
(0171 837 7324). **Phone enquiries** 24 hours daily. Everything you want to know about queer life in the capital, but be prepared for a long wait before you get through.

Metroline
(0181 741 3355). **Phone enquiries** 7-10pm Mon-Thur. Information and support for lesbians, gay men, bisexuals and those questioning their sexuality.

Naz Project
(0181 741 1879). **Phone enquiries** 9.30am-5.30pm Mon-Fri.
Serving the (gay and straight) Asian community, with counselling and information on HIV, AIDS and sexual health in South Asian, Middle Eastern, South American, Horn of African and North African languages.

Music: Classical & Opera

Despite the ongoing Royal Opera House saga, there are still reasons to be cheerful about London's classical and opera scene.

Over the past 18 months, London's classical music and opera world has been dominated by squabbles and shenanigans at the **Royal Opera House** (*see page 246* Who's in the House?). But it's not *all* bad news… The Royal Opera House aside, there's still a lot to enjoy at the moment, with classical music in London as healthy as it's ever been. Quite aside from the four big orchestras – and no other city can boast of such a surfeit of world-class large ensembles – there are plenty of smaller groups well worth the price of admission, and hundreds of young musicians plying their trade at small concerts. For example, there's the **London Symphony Orchestra**, resident at the **Barbican Centre** (*see below*). Under conductor Sir Colin Davis, it has consolidated its position as undoubtedly the best orchestra in the capital, and among the finest in Europe.

Then there's the **Philharmonia**, arguably second only to the LSO of the London orchestra quartet, and based at the **Royal Festival Hall** (*see below*), which is also home to the improved **London Philharmonic Orchestra**. The **Royal Philharmonic Orchestra**, meanwhile, is unique in two respects: it doesn't benefit from state funding and isn't tied to any one venue. It is also rather less reliable than the others.

Smaller groups worth a look include the painfully modernist **London Sinfonietta**, the manageably eclectic **Nash Ensemble** and the wholeheartedly traditional **Gabrieli Consort**. You can also expect to see some of the top musicians from around the world on London stages, both ensembles and solo performers, and often performing at one of the capital's many excellent music festivals, the largest of which is the **Proms**, held annually at the **Royal Albert Hall** (*see below*). At the other end of the spectrum, students at the three big music colleges in the capital – the **Royal College of Music** (*see below*), the **Guildhall School of Music and Drama** (next door to the Barbican Centre, with which it often links up) and the **Trinity College of Music** – are often to be found performing in small venues

for a nominal admission fee. Variety, then, and quality too. Now, if only we could do something about that bloody Opera House…

Major venues

Barbican Centre

Silk Street, EC2 (0171 638 8891/info 0171 638 4141). Barbican tube or Moorgate tube/rail. **Open** *box office* 9am-8pm daily. **Tickets** £6-£30. **Credit** AmEx, MC, £TC, V. **Map 9 P5**
First of all, don't expect to be able to negotiate the Barbican easily. Quite aside from having the ugliest exterior of any concert hall in London, it's implausibly difficult to find your way around if you're a first-time visitor. Still, once you're firmly ensconced in your seat, do expect an excellent programme of classical music in the Barbican Hall. The Centre finally seems to be ridding itself of the aura of irredeemable naffness that has long pervaded its music programme (tip for visitors: avoid any concert bannered with the phrase 'Raymond Gubbay presents'). A lot of this is due to its fantastic and inspired **Inventing America** festival that dominated 1998 – and won the *Time Out* award for best live music event that year – but even though the fest has now finished, there are further signs that things are on the up-and-up. The **London Symphony Orchestra**, which has been here since the bad old days, is still resident, while the Centre also hosts regular concerts by guest orchestras. A programme of free music in the foyer and one of the capital's best music libraries round things off nicely at this vastly improved concert venue.

London Coliseum

St Martin's Lane, WC2 (box office 0171 632 8300/ fax credit card bookings 0171 379 1264/minicom 0171 836 7666). Leicester Square tube or Charing Cross tube/rail. **Open** *box office* 24 hours daily. **Tickets** £2.50-£55; *day tickets* on sale to personal callers after 10am Mon-Fri and over the phone from 2.30pm Mon-Fri. **Credit** AmEx, DC, MC, £TC, V. **Map 8 L7**
The grandly named and grandly proportioned Coliseum is the home of the **English National Opera**, the matey cousin to the noticeably more stuffy Royal Opera. The ENO, which hands over the Coliseum to ballet companies during the Christmas and summer seasons, likes to think of itself as an approachable, slightly populist company. To a large extent it's entitled to: ticket prices are considerably lower than the ROH's, while the productions are, on the whole, more challenging than those at Covent Garden, and all the works are sung in English so's the common people can, like, understand it. Since the Royal Opera's ongoing problems began to spiral out of control, culminating in the fact that it is presently without a venue, ENO has grasped the mettle with some fine productions and a return to the form that made it so popular in the 1980s. Well worth a look.

Relive days of empire at **The Proms**.

Royal Albert Hall

Kensington Gore, SW7 (0171 589 3203/info 0891 500252/box office 0171 589 8212). Gloucester Road, Knightsbridge or South Kensington tube/9, 10, 52 bus. **Open** *box office* 9am-9pm daily. **Credit** AmEx, MC, V. **Map 4 D9**

This massive, labyrinthine all-purpose arena, built over 100 years ago, puts on any number of events from boxing to popera. It is best known, though, as home to the **Proms**, a wonderful summer-long festival of music that takes in any number of styles and a broad international mix of ensembles and performers. Remarkably, though the Proms (it's short for Henry Wood Promenade Concerts, after its founder) has been running for over a century, it has somehow managed to maintain its freshness, and is now as essential as ever. Best of all, tickets for the so-called 'promenade' area (the bit in front of the stage with all the seats removed) are a giveaway at only a few pounds. A word of warning though: the Albert Hall is a good 15-minute walk from the nearest tube station, and the traffic can be awful. Allow plenty of time to get there, and you'll have a lovely evening.

Royal Festival Hall

South Bank, Belvedere Road, SE1 (box office 0171 960 4242/recorded info 0171 633 0932). Embankment tube or Waterloo tube/rail. **Open** *box office* 10am-9pm daily. **Tickets** £5-£60. **Credit** AmEx, DC, MC, £TC, V. **Map 8 M8**

Now that the Barbican has pulled its socks up, London has two excellent arts complexes – this is the other. The **Royal Festival Hall** actually consists of three concert halls. The main venue, now officially known as **RFH1**, is the largest of the three auditoria and stages mainly symphony concerts and events at the more popular end of the spectrum, although the acoustics arguably don't suit amplified music. **RFH2** (formerly the **Queen Elizabeth Hall**) is about a

third of the size, and takes care of chamber groups, semi-staged operas and the occasional idiosyncratic theatrical event. Finally, small chamber groups and recitals can be found in the comparatively cosy **RFH3** (previously known as the **Purcell Room**). In addition, there's a good-sized bookshop, free foyer music, an overpriced record store, a poetry library and performance room, several bars, a few restaurants, including the classy **People's Palace**, and a number of cafés. Looking out across the river, glass of wine in hand, is as lovely a way to spend a concert interval as you'll find anywhere in the world.

Royal Opera House

Covent Garden, WC2 (0171 240 1200). Covent Garden tube. **Closed until December 1999**. **Tickets** £5-£150. **Credit** AmEx, DC, MC, £TC, V. **Map 6 L6**

Not so long ago, the Royal Opera House was the symbol of all things British and traditional: grandiose, snobby, impeccable, old-fashioned, expensive. Now, though, some more global attributes can be added to the ROH's list of characteristics: inept, disorganised, clueless and very, very skint (*see introduction*). As things stand, there will be no performances anywhere by the Royal Opera until December 1999 (presuming, that is, the building is ready in time, which is hardly guaranteed). When they do restart, it'll be with a substantially reduced programme. Sorry... the music? Excellent, of course. But at £150 a ticket, so it should be.

St James's Church, Piccadilly

197 Piccadilly, W1 (0171 734 4511). Piccadilly Circus tube. **Open** *enquiries* 10am-6pm Mon-Fri. **Admission** *lunchtime concerts* free (donations appreciated); *evening concerts* £4-£17; tickets available at the door an hour before start of performance. **Credit** £TC. **Map 7 J7**

An odd yet delightful little Wren church, not far from the hubbub of Piccadilly Circus but, inside, as far removed from the chaos outside as it's possible to be. The programme of events here is impressively varied, if hardly essential: aside from the fine lunchtime concerts (Mon, Wed, Fri) given by young musicians, there's also a series of talks and lectures each month. Look out too for the evening concerts: there's no set day/date plan, nor is there any real thread running through the programme, but the music is often delicious.

St John's Smith Square

Smith Square, SW1 (box office 0171 222 1061). Westminster tube. **Open** *box office* 10am-5pm Mon-Fri; until start of performance on concert nights; from 6pm and at weekends bookings for that evening's performance only. **Tickets** £5-£30. **Credit** MC, £TC, V. **Map 8 K10**

A converted church tucked away in an impossibly posh area just around the corner from the Houses of Parliament, and, as such, something of a hidden gem. It's far from the perfect venue, however: the seats are among the least comfortable in town, it can get a bit nippy, and the acoustics don't seem to suit large ensembles (not least for the musicians, who often can't hear what they're playing). Still, for recitals and chamber concerts (including lunchtime shows every other Thursday) it's a winningly atmospheric place, while the restaurant in the crypt is a terrific spot for a pre-concert snack or an after-show drink or three.

St Martin-in-the-Fields

Trafalgar Square, WC2 (church 0171 930 0089/concert info & box office 0171 839 8362). Charing Cross tube/rail. **Admission** *lunchtime concerts* donation requested (1.05pm Mon, Tue, Fri); evening concerts £6-£16. **Credit** MC, £TC, V. **Map 8 L7**

After the National Gallery just across the street, St Martin's is the second best place to escape from the chaos of Trafalgar Square. The series of lunchtime recitals largely feature student musicians performing a wide range of music. These are supplemented by weekly concerts on Thursdays, Fridays

Who's in the House?

Every year, we wonder how on earth it could possibly get any worse for the **Royal Opera House**. And every year, it somehow manages to do just that. As has become normal in the late 1990s, all the good news about the classical music scene in London – and there's been plenty of it, including a greater variety of performers, refurbished concert halls, good box office takings and, last but not least, some tremendous music – has been swallowed up by the atrocious state of affairs that has befallen the Royal Opera House. Public opinion of the Opera was already at a low in 1995 – thanks to years of huge public subsidy and ridiculous ticket prices – when a fly-on-the-wall BBC documentary portrayed those in charge of the organisation as inept almost beyond belief. Following a public outcry, the Opera's public relations plummeted still further when it was awarded £78.5 million to do up its building in Covent Garden, which closed for two years in 1997.

In 1998, just when it looked like things couldn't get any worse, they did. A government report damned the Opera House, with the net result that the entire board resigned. The Opera House then admitted it couldn't afford to keep going and asked for an extra £15 million a year. After a proposed residency at Sadler's Wells fell through, the Opera was left with nowhere to perform for the duration of 1999. And then, the *coup de grâce*: the board announced that in order to save money, there would be no opera performances until the end of 1999, with technical staff and musicians asked to take a pay cut or face mass redundancy. Unsurprisingly, this didn't go down too well.

So, by the start of the millennium, the problems should have been sorted out, right? Well, no. The longterm downside is that the Royal Opera House's problems have affected, and will continue to affect, other arts organisations in the UK, particularly the big ones. Thanks in no small part to the carry-on, public perception of the arts in the UK – which wasn't exactly great before all of this started – has fallen so low that the government is now far more cautious about giving hand-outs to arts organisations. As it is, the government's arts budget has been cut dramatically during the '90s, with more cuts rumoured to be on the way. The knock-on effects from the Royal Opera's troubles are yet to be fully felt, but if and when they do – and the smart money says that they will – the arts scene in the capital, and particularly the classical music scene, could be in very serious trouble. What we're saying, essentially, is enjoy it while it lasts.

and Saturdays at 7.30pm, invariably featuring baroque repertoire (including the weekly performance of *The Four Seasons*, which has been running for some six years). In addition, occasional Tuesday evening concerts feature young musicians, many of whom have 'graduated' from the lunchtime programme. The lovely **Café-in-the-Crypt**, beneath the church, is a top place for a contemplative pot of tea first thing in the morning or a light lunch.

Wigmore Hall

36 Wigmore Street, W1 (0171 935 2141). Bond Street tube. **Open** *box office, personal callers* 10am-8.30pm Mon-Sat; *Nov-Mar* 10.30am-5pm Sun; *Apr-Oct* 10.30am-8pm Sun; *telephone bookings* 10am-7pm Mon-Sat; *Nov-Mar* 1-4pm Sun; *Apr-Oct* 1-6.30pm Sun. **Performances** 7.30pm Mon-Sat; *Nov-Mar* 11.30am, 4pm, Sun; *Apr-Oct* 11.30am, 7pm, Sun. **Tickets** £5-£35. **Credit** AmEx, DC, JCB, MC, £TC, V. **Map 5 G6**

The connoisseur's concert hall. The Wigmore is resolutely traditional – while other venues have tried, with varying degrees of success, to attract younger, hipper audiences through a variety of marketing techniques and gimmickry, the Wigmore has remained staunchly old-fashioned. Long may it continue to be so too, if it means the concerts – including the bargain Monday lunchtime series, recently poached from St John's Smith Square, which are recorded for transmission on BBC Radio 3 – maintain such a superlative standard. The décor, though, is recent, the hall having been refurbished a couple of years ago. As a result, the Wigmore is a wonderfully comfortable place to listen to music, something no doubt helped by the friendly staff and reasonable ticket prices. A must-visit.

Festivals & open-air venues

London is blessed with a feast of music festivals good enough to gorge even the most voracious of music-lovers. From low-key lunchtime seasons at City churches to high-profile month-long bashes in the West End, there's normally some sort of festival running at any given time. Similarly, there are also a number of open-air venues in the capital (which, for obvious reasons, normally limit their events to the summer months). Just make sure that, with the notoriously unpredictable British weather, you remember to pack a brolly.

BOC Covent Garden Festival

Venues in and around Covent Garden, WC2 (info 0171 379 0870). **Tickets** prices vary; phone for details. **Credit** AmEx, MC, £TC, V. **Date** 17 May-5 June 1999. The Covent Garden Festival is a real treat. The programming tends to focus on new performers, while some of the events are wonderfully imaginative: opera in Bow Street Magistrates' Court anyone? Some events are held in St Paul's Church, Freemasons' Hall and the Peacock Theatre.

City of London Festival

Venues in and around the City (festival box office 0171 638 8891/info 0171 377 0540). **Date** 22 June-15 July 1999.

The great escape: a free lunchtime recital at **St Bride's**. *See page 249.*

Run on similar principles to the Covent Garden Festival (*see above*), albeit with a slightly more traditional programme, the CoL Festival is a month-long series of events in and around London's financial district. Venues include the Barbican, St Paul's Cathedral and the many gorgeous churches dotted across the Square Mile, and the crowd is a mix of City suits and dignitaries, plus a fair number of curious outsiders.

Hampton Court Palace Festival

Hampton Court, East Molesey, Surrey (festival box office 0171 344 4444). Hampton Court rail/riverboat from Westminster or Richmond to Hampton Court Pier (Apr-Oct). **Tickets** £25-£85. **Credit** AmEx, MC, V. **Date** 10-19 June 1999.
The olde worlde-ness of Hampton Court Palace can, depending on your mood, be either marvellously charming or incredibly grating. However, the relaxed music festival held during the summer is worth a visit, should you have the money: tickets start at a terrifying £25 each.

Holland Park Theatre

Holland Park, Kensington High Street, W8 (box office 0171 602 7856/info 0171 379 0870). High Street Kensington or Holland Park tube. **Performances** 7.30pm. **Tickets** £13-£24. **Credit** AmEx, MC, £TC, V. **Date** early June-mid-Aug 1999. **Map 1 A8**
A variety of music, dance and theatre events takes place every summer here in the grounds of one of London's most picturesque and civilised parks (check out the fab peacocks). Both stage and audience are covered by a canopy, which is a blessed relief in dodgy weather, but can be frustrating when it's fine and you fancy a bit of sun.

Kenwood Lakeside Concerts

Kenwood House, Hampstead Lane, NW3 (info 0171 973 3427). Archway, Golders Green or Highgate tube/ 210 bus/East Finchley tube then courtesy bus on concert nights. **Tickets** £7.50-£20; *day tickets box office* on site from 2pm on the day. **Credit** MC, £TC, V. **Date** early July-early Sept 1999.
A quite spectacularly populist series of summer concerts held in the lush green confines of Kenwood House. The programme is at a strictly *Best Classical Album in the World… Ever!* level (Mozart, the '1812' Overture, Handel's Water Music, etc) and the audience 2.4-children types up from Surrey for the evening, but don't let that put you off: bring a six-pack and a load of French bread, lie back and soak up some lovely scenery and some even lovelier music.

Marble Hill Concerts

Marble Hill Park, Richmond Road, Twickenham, Middx (info 0171 973 3427). St Margaret's rail or Richmond tube/rail then 33, 90, 290, H22, R70 bus. **Tickets** £10.50-£15; *day tickets* on site from 2pm on the day. **Credit** MC, £TC, V. **Date** late July-late Aug 1999.
The Marble Hill concerts, held every Sunday during the summer, are similar to Kenwood: undemanding music – normally including a selection of popular classics – watched by folks from most walks of life seated on the grass or on deckchairs. The summer concerts end with a fireworks display. Hurrah!

Spitalfields Festival

Christ Church, Commercial Street, E1 (box office 0171 377 1362). Aldgate or Aldgate East tube or Liverpool Street tube/rail. **Tickets** £3-£25. **Credit** MC, £TC, V. **Date** 9-30 June 1999, 13-23 Dec 1999. **Map 10 S5**
Thanks in part to the emergence of the area around Spitalfields as A Cool Place, the Spitalfields Festival has finally begun to get the recognition it deserves in recent years. Many, though by no means all, of the concerts take place in what is many people's favourite Hawksmoor building, **Christ Church Spitalfields** (*see p93*).

City lunchtime concerts

Couple gorgeous, historic church architecture with London's surfeit of starving musicians – many of them students – and what do you have? A wonderful and largely unadvertised programme of concerts in the City, that's what. The area in and around London's financial centre is also one of its most historic (despite the impression given by some of the unabashedly modern office blocks). There are scores of old churches in this neck of the woods, plenty of which host regular lunchtime concerts by the aforementioned starving musicians. The acoustics are often marvellous, the settings unique, and the musicians frequently excellent. What's more, concerts are normally either free or with an 'admission by donation' policy, though if you like the concert, pop across to

FOR £18 WE'LL INTRODUCE YOU TO THE MOST INTERESTING PERSON YOU'VE EVER MET

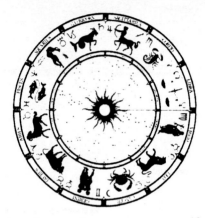

You! As you've never seen yourself. Because you'll get, in 5 minutes, a unique 20 page Equinox Astrological Character Portrait. For £32 we'll also include a 20 page forecast of the next year of your life. You know it'll be a worthwhile meeting.

THE ASTROLOGY SHOP

78 Neal Street, Covent Garden, London WC2

Open: 9am-7pm Mon-Sat. 11am-7pm Sun.

Tel: 0171-497 1001 Fax: 0171-497 0344

equinox@equinox.uk.com

www.equinox.uk.com.

the nearest pub afterwards and buy the performers a drink. The **City Information Centre** (0171 332 1456), just south of St Paul's Cathedral, can provide further details.

In addition to the venues below, regular lunchtime organ concerts are also held at several churches (officially) outside the City, including **Temple Church**, off Fleet Street, EC4 (0171 353 1736), **Grosvenor Chapel**, South Audley Street, W1 (01923 828592) and **St James's**, Clerkenwell Close, EC1 (0171 251 1190); phone for details.

St Anne & St Agnes
Gresham Street, EC2 (0171 606 4986). St Paul's tube. **Performances** 1.10pm Mon, Fri. **Map 11 P6**
Damaged in World War II and rebuilt during the 1960s, this (single) red-brick church features an erratic timetable of concerts.

St Bride's
Fleet Street, EC4 (0171 353 1301). Blackfriars tube/rail. **Performances** 1.15pm Tue, Wed, Fri (except in Aug, Advent, Lent). **Map 11 N6**
Performers at St Bride's are normally either professional musicians or senior students. The spire of this Wren church is said to have inspired the design of the traditional layered wedding cake. *See picture p247.*

St Lawrence Jewry
Guildhall, EC2 (0171 600 9478). Bank or St Paul's tube. **Performances** 1pm Mon, Tue. **Date** (festival) Aug. **Map 11 P6**
This Wren church, the local for the Corporation of London, has lunchtime piano recitals on Mondays and organ recitals on Tuesdays. Also look out for the August festival of lunchtime concerts.

St Margaret Lothbury
Lothbury, EC2 (0171 606 8330). Bank tube. **Performances** 1.10pm Thur (except Aug). **Map 12 Q6**
St Margaret's outstanding feature is its wonderful 1801 George England pipe organ. The church also holds the occasional evening concert (phone for details).

St Martin within Ludgate
Ludgate Hill, EC4 (0171 248 6054). St Paul's tube or Blackfriars tube/rail. **Performances** 1.15pm Tue, Wed (occasional). **Map 11 O6**
Lunchtime recitals in this 1684 Wren church are somewhat irregular; phone for details.

St Mary-le-Bow
Cheapside, EC2 (0171 248 5139). Bank or St Paul's tube. **Performances** 1.05pm Thur. **Map 11 P6**
Escape the bustle of Cheapside by listening to the recitals at this beautiful white Wren church.

St Michael
Cornhill, EC3 (0171 626 8841). Bank or Monument tube. **Performances** 1pm Mon. **Map 12 Q6**
It's believed that Handel once played the organ at St Michael and, although you're unlikely to find anyone so notable there nowadays, the weekly organ recitals are still well worth attending.

St Olave
Hart Street, EC3 (0171 488 4318). Tower Hill tube/ Fenchurch Street rail. **Performances** 1.05pm Wed, Thur. **Map 12 R7**
Lovely St Olave's is where Samuel Pepys and his wife worshipped and are buried.

St Stephen Walbrook
39 Walbrook, EC4 (0171 283 4444). Bank tube or Cannon Street tube/rail. **Performances** 12.30pm Fri (except Good Friday and Friday nearest Christmas). **Map 11 P7**
Wren's wonderful church is a suitable setting in which to hear the fabulous William Hill organ in action.

Around & about

Almeida Theatre
Almeida Street, off Upper Street, N1 (0171 359 4404). Angel tube or Highbury & Islington tube/rail. **Open** *personal callers* 9.30am-6.30pm Mon-Sat; *phone bookings* 24 hours daily. **Tickets** £6.50-£19.50. **Credit** AmEx, DC, MC, £TC, V. **Map 9 O1**
This scarily intimate theatre in Islington is usually home to drama of the literary rather than the musical kind, but does stage the occasional concert and (extremely small-scale) opera. *See also p268.*

Blackheath Concert Halls
23 Lee Road, Blackheath, SE3 (box office 0181 463 0100). Blackheath rail/53, 54, 75, 108, 202 bus. **Open** *box office* 10am-7pm Mon-Sat. **Tickets** £2.50-£50. **Credit** AmEx, MC, V.
It's a bit of a trek down here, sure, but the programme at Blackheath Concert Halls deserves investigation: expect anything from Mozart to Jools Holland. But, thankfully, not at the same time.

British Music Information Centre
10 Stratford Place, W1 (0171 499 8567/www.bmic.co.uk). Bond Street tube. **Open** noon-5pm Mon-Fri. **Recitals** 7.30pm Tue, Thur (excl Aug). **Tickets** £3-£5. **Map 5 H6**
British composers, unsurprisingly, dominate the BMIC. If you want to find out anything about any Brit composer – new or old – this is where to head. The library holds all manner of books, scores, recordings (both audio and video), and there are occasional lectures. The BMIC also holds twice-weekly recitals of modern British music, which ranges from the unmissable to the unlistenable.

Lauderdale House
Waterlow Park, Highgate Hill, N6 (0181 348 8716/341 2032). Archway tube/143, 210, 271 bus. **Open** 11am-4pm Tue-Fri. **Tickets** £4-£10.
Kind of a baby stately home, Lauderdale House is one of those places favoured by out-of-towners after a traditional, genteel English tea. Don't be put off: quite aside from being a gorgeous wee building, Lauderdale stages the occasional evening concert featuring London-based musicians. And if it's boring, take a wander in the lush confines of **Waterlow Park** (*see p83*).

National Sound Archive
British Library, 96 Euston Road, NW1 (0171 412 7440). Euston tube/rail. **Open** 10am-5pm Mon-Fri. **Map 6 K3**
The National Sound Archive does exactly what it says on the tin. If you've ever made a record – or, perhaps, done a vox-pop for radio – then you'll be in here, such is the diversity of the Archive's stock. Listening is free, though it's advisable to call ahead with your request.

Royal College of Music
Prince Consort Road, SW7 (0171 589 3643). South Kensington tube. **Map 4 D9**
London's leading music college stages at least one chamber concert every weekday during term time (normally at around 1pm), with the occasional larger event held back for the evening. Most concerts are free and open to the public, and here, as at the other two big London music colleges, you get the chance to catch tomorrow's stars today.

Music: Rock, Roots & Jazz

Rock, reggae, soul, salsa, blues, bhangra – it's all here.

Few cities in the world have a live music scene as thriving as London's, to the extent that choosing where to go and what to see can be quite bewildering. On a typical Friday night, well over a hundred venues will be staging gigs – with most of them having at least two bands. Check *Time Out* magazine's listings for day-by-day details.

Prices for gigs vary greatly and can go as high as £30 for the big names. However, the average price for a well-known band is between £10 and £15, while many lesser-known indie, jazz and folk groups can be seen for less than a fiver.

Buy tickets as far in advance as you can – many gigs sell out – and avoid booking fees by paying by cash or cheque directly from the concert venue. Beware touts selling tickets outside gigs; they may be forgeries, are sure to be overpriced and the practice itself is illegal.

Most of all, don't be afraid to experiment with different types of music. The beauty of London's rich cultural diversity is that you never know what you might discover.

Major venues

Astoria (LA1)

157 Charing Cross Road, WC2 (box office 0171 434 0403). Tottenham Court Road tube. **Open** *box office* 10.30am-5.30pm Mon-Sat. **Admission** £8-£15. **Credit** MC, V. **Map 6 K6**
This is a popular mid-size venue with a great central location. Bands come from across the board, with an emphasis on alternative rock acts. Good views can be had throughout, but if downstairs gets too sweaty, you can always relocate to one of the intimate tables for two upstairs. On the down side, drinks are pricey and the security and bar staff can be surly.

Brixton Academy

211 Stockwell Road, SW9 (0171 924 9999). Brixton tube/rail. **Open** *box office* 10am-6pm Mon-Fri; noon-6pm Sat. **Admission** £9-£22.50. **Credit** MC, V.
This large (4,300-capacity) and atmospheric venue slopes down towards the stage, which is great for views, but not so good on your calves! The upstairs balcony is seated, with an excellent view of the stage, but it can feel a bit removed from the action. Popular with the bigger indie, rap and rock bands who've not quite reached arena level.

Earl's Court Exhibition Centre

Warwick Road, SW5 (0171 385 1200/credit card bookings 0171 373 8141). Earl's Court tube. **Open** *box office* 9am-6pm Mon-Sat. **Admission** varies. **Credit** AmEx, MC, V. **Map 3 A11**
This arena (with a capacity around 20,000) is used as a London stopoff for big names on world tours, including U2, Oasis, Pink Floyd and, on the entertainment grounds that previously stood on the site, Buffalo Bill's Wild West Show (no kidding). It is the most easily accessible of London's arenas, but unfortunately suffers from the usual view problems associated with venues of this size.

Forum

9-17 Highgate Road, NW5 (Mean Fiddler info line 0181 963 0940/box office 0171 344 0044). Kentish Town tube/rail/N2. **Open** *box office* 10am-6pm Mon-Sat. **Admission** varies. **Credit** MC, V.
Previously the much-loved Town & Country Club, the Forum (now part of the Mean Fiddler group) is still one of London's top concert venues, attracting a range of well-known acts such as Natalie Imbruglia, Dr John and Ash. However, the venue is let down by a sound system that isn't what it was, moody bar staff and aggressive security. Saturday night from 10pm-2am is **House of Fun**, playing cheesey '70s and '80s music.

Hackney Empire

291 Mare Street, E8 (0181 985 2424). Hackney Central rail/30, 38, 242, 277 bus. **Open** *box office* noon-6pm Mon-Sat. **Admission** £8.50-£18.50. **Credit** MC, V.
Although this original music hall traditionally stages more comedy than music, acts including Dodgy, Tricky, Shalamar and Christy Moore have all played in recent years. The views and sound are excellent, as are the great local atmosphere and pub prices. Let's hope the future brings more music.

London Arena

Limeharbour, Isle of Dogs, E14 (0171 538 1212). Crossharbour & London Arena DLR. **Open** *box office* 10am-6pm Mon-Fri; 10am-3pm Sat. **Admission** varies. **Credit** MC, £TC, V.
A huge (12,500-capacity) venue that has recently reopened after a £10-million refurbishment, the arena hosts big-name acts like Massive Attack and Culture Club as well as events such as the Smash Hits Poll-Winners' Party. However, like the other arena-sized places, the sound and vision are only good for those at the front, and refreshments are pricey.

Shepherd's Bush Empire

Shepherd's Bush Green, W12 (0171 771 2000). Shepherd's Bush tube. **Open** *box office* 10am-6pm Mon-Fri; noon-6pm Sat. **Admission** varies. **Credit** MC, V.
Formerly the BBC Television Theatre, the Empire has become one of London's top venues. The three-tiered seating arrangement ensures good views of the top rock, country, soul and indie bands who play here. Tip: buy a ticket for one of the (jolly comfy) seats upstairs as, strangely, the ground floor slopes down towards the back.

Wembley Arena, Stadium & Conference Centre

Empire Way, Wembley (info 0181 902 8833/box office 0181 900 1234). Wembley Park tube/Wembley Central tube/rail. **Open** *box office* 8am-9pm Mon-Sat; 9am-8pm Sun. **Admission** varies. **Credit** AmEx, MC, V.

For a glimpse (and that's about the best you'll get) of the biggest stars, join the 80,000 people in the outdoor Stadium (where Band Aid was held), the 12,500 in the indoor Arena or the 7,500 in the Conference Centre. The fact that it's a nightmare to get to, however you travel, coupled with the general unfriendliness and impersonality of the venues, prove that size isn't everything.

Pubs & bars

Bull & Gate

389 Kentish Town Road, NW5 (0171 485 5358). Kentish Town tube/rail. **Open** 11am-11pm Mon-Sat; noon-10.30pm Sun. **Music** 8.30-11.15pm Mon-Sat; 8.45-10.45pm Sun. **Admission** £2-£5.

Long-standing indie favourite – see them here before they make it big. And with three or four bands playing every night there's enough choice to keep you interested. Pub rock it ain't, but if you go for minimalist décor and high volume, you'll love it.

Camden Falcon

234 Royal College Street (entrance on Wilmot Place), NW1 (0171 485 3834). Camden Town tube. **Open** 5-11pm Mon-Sat; 7-10.30pm Sun. **Music** 8-11pm Mon-Sat; 8-10.30pm Sun. **Admission** £3.50-£5.

Up to 150 punters can cram into the dingy black-painted music bar of this Camden pub, also known as the Barfly, which has one of the busiest rock and indie line-ups of any London venue. Stick to bottled drinks rather than draught.

Dublin Castle

94 Parkway, NW1 (0171 485 1773). Camden Town tube. **Open** noon-midnight Mon-Sat; noon-11pm Sun. **Music** 9pm-midnight Mon-Sat; 8.30-11pm Sun. **Admission** £3.50-£4.

Once the centre of Camden's vibrant pub music scene, the Castle's small music bar at the back is a black-painted hole, totally the wrong shape and has the stage in the worst possible position. And there's not even a dressing room! But, dammit, it's got a great atmosphere and with three bands playing virtually every night, it's always worth a visit.

Hope & Anchor

207 Upper Street, N1 (0171 354 1312). Highbury & Islington tube/rail. **Open** noon-midnight Mon-Thur, Sun; noon-1am Fri, Sat. **Music** 9pm-midnight Mon-Thur, Sun; 9pm-1am Fri, Sat. **Admission** £3-£4. **Map 9 O1**

Once a well-known punk venue, the stage here has seen many a famous face (Elvis Costello, The Stranglers). Up-and-coming indie bands (mainly first-giggers) feature now, and although the pocket-sized basement suffers from over-crowding and restricted sound and vision, it's still a great venue with a fab vibe.

Station Tavern

41 Bramley Road, W10 (0171 727 4053). Latimer Road tube/295 bus. **Open** 11am-11pm Mon-Sat; noon-10.30pm Sun. **Music** 9-11pm Mon-Sat; 2-5.30pm, 8.30-10.30pm, Sun. **Admission** free.

A dedicated blues venue with (free) live music (of variable quality) every night.

Torrington Arms

4 Lodge Lane, High Road, N12 (0181 445 4710). Woodside Park tube. **Open** *main bar* 11am-11pm Mon-Sat; noon-10.30pm Sun (function room till midnight when a band is playing). **Music** 8pm-midnight.
Admission £3-£6. **Credit** MC, V.

A great north London back-room pub venue, which features Brit blues on Sundays, indie on Thursdays, tribute bands on Saturdays and a regular folk club on Wednesdays.

Water Rats

328 Gray's Inn Road, WC1 (0171 837 7269). King's Cross tube/rail. **Open** 8pm-midnight Mon-Sat. **Music** 8.30-11pm Mon-Sat. **Admission** varies. **Map 6 M3**

It doesn't look much, and it's not situated in the most salubrious of areas, but this is the best of London's small indie venues; the two-level room has adequate views and a reliable PA. Things can get very packed and sweaty – but that's part of the fun.

World's End

21-23 Stroud Green Road, N4 (0171 281 8679). Finsbury Park tube/rail. **Open** 11am-midnight Mon-Thur; 11am-12.30am Fri, Sat; noon-10.30pm Sun. **Music** 9.30pm-close. **Admission** free.

A large, lively pub, next to Finsbury Park tube, rail and bus station, offering a variety of music – generally fun and undemanding blues and rock, washed down with a good range of reasonably priced beers.

Club venues

100 Club

100 Oxford Street, W1 (0171 636 0933). Tottenham Court Road tube. **Open** 7.45pm-midnight Mon-Thur; noon-3pm, 8.30pm-2am, Fri; 7.30pm-1am Sat; 7.30-11.30pm Sun. **Admission** £5-£8. **Map 6 K6**

Famed cellar club with a broad booking policy but specialising in quality traditional and mainstream jazz, blues, rhythm and blues, jive and swing. Mainstream indie and retro rock acts are brought in some Tuesdays and Thursdays, but the venue will always live in the shadow of its past glories, which include the Sex Pistols, the Clash, the Who, the Kinks and the Stones.

The Borderline

Orange Yard, Manette Street, off Charing Cross Road, W1 (0171 734 2095). Tottenham Court Road tube. **Open** *gigs* 8-11pm Mon-Fri; *club* 11.30pm-3am Mon-Sat. **Admission** *gigs* £5-£10; *club* £3-£8. **Credit** MC, V. **Map 6 K6**

Run by the group that owns the Shepherd's Bush Empire (*see above*), this consistently good, centrally located hole-in-the-wall is little more than a small basement (beneath a Tex-Mex restaurant) and can get very crowded, at which point the sound and views of the stage start to suffer. However, many top-name artists have played here, including REM, Blur, Jeff Buckley, Crowded House and Oasis (who filmed the video for *Cigarettes and Alcohol* here). Gigs often attract an older muso crowd and on a good night the atmosphere can be electric.

Dingwalls

Middle Yard, Camden Lock, Chalk Farm Road, NW1 (recorded info 0171 267 1577/box office 0171 267 3142). Camden Town or Chalk Farm tube. **Open** 7.30pm-midnight Mon-Thur; 7.30-11pm Sun. **Admission** £5-£12.

With its multi-level layout and cosy tables and chairs, Dingwalls offers a slightly more civilised night out than other north London indie venues. The sound tends to be good, but sightlines range from decent to dire.

The Garage

20-22 Highbury Corner, N5 (0171 607 1818/ info 0181 963 0940). Highbury & Islington tube/rail. **Open** (times vary, phone to check) 8pm-midnight Mon-Thur; 8pm-3am Fri, Sat. **Admission** £4-£10. **Credit** MC, V (advance bookings only).

The Garage's main room, which has consistently good sound, plays host to industrial, rock and punk in addition to the usual UK and international indie acts. In the separate, smaller upstairs room you'll find a line-up of less well-known acts that are often worth checking out. Stay late on Friday and Saturday for the indie disco after the show, but beware that when packed, as it often is, it can be hotter than hell.

Improv Theatre

161 Tottenham Court Road, W1 (0171 387 4173). Warren Street tube. **Open** varies. **Admission** varies. **Credit** MC, £TC, V. **Map 5 J4**
Previously an awful tourist-trap theme restaurant called The Cockney, this is one of London's best new gig venues/comedy clubs. Attracting small to mid-size indie bands, the theatre, with its dimmed chandeliers, plush wallpaper and split-level floor, feels like it's straight out of *Bugsy Malone*.

LA2

For listings, see **Astoria (LA1)** *above.*
An indie-oriented venue, with the occasional dancier outfit, for acts who can't quite drum up the 2,000 punters needed to fill its big sister next door, the Astoria (LA1). As with the Astoria, the LA2's central location is its strongest asset.

Mean Fiddler

22-28A High Street, NW10 (0181 961 5490/info line 0181 963 0940). Willesden Junction tube/rail. **Open** 8pm-2am Mon-Thur, Sun; 8pm-3am Fri, Sat. **Admission** varies. **Credit** MC, V.
A good ear for music and a knack for giving people good service in comfortable and stylish surroundings helped the owner of the Mean Fiddler launch an empire that now encompasses half of London's best venues, from the Forum to the Jazz Café. This is the place where it all began. Most famous for Irish and country music, the 600-capacity Mean Fiddler also hosts rock and pop acts.

Roadhouse

Jubilee Hall, 35 The Piazza, WC2 (0171 240 6001). Covent Garden tube. **Open** 5.30pm-3am Mon-Fri; 6.30pm-3am Sat; 5.30pm-1am Sun. **Music** 11pm. **Admission** £3-£10. **Credit** AmEx, MC, V. **Map 8 L6**
Specialising in party-style cover and tribute bands, as well as genuine '60-'80s pop favourites who are still doing the rounds (Imagination, the Real Thing and the Supremes have all played recently), this American-look basement also offers the best burgers of any London music venue.

Rock Garden

The Piazza, Covent Garden, WC2 (0171 240 3961). Covent Garden tube. **Open** 5pm-3am Mon-Thur; 5pm-5am Fri, Sat; 7pm-midnight Sun. **Admission** £5-£8. **Credit** AmEx, DC, MC, V. **Map 8 L6**
In the early 1980s, the Rock Garden was the unlikely site of many a cool indie booking (the likes of Microdisney and the Higsons); now the bands showcased are generally indie bill-fillers or covers/tribute bands. But it's a pleasant, central spot with late closing times, and attracts a truly international crowd.

The Sound Republic

Swiss Centre, Leicester Square (entrance at 10 Wardour Street), W1 (0171 287 1010). Leicester Square tube. **Open** varies. **Admission** £8-£15. **Map 8 K7**
This multimillion-pound, purpose-built, 700-capacity venue, which opened in October '98, looks set to become one of London's most popular mid-sizers. Attracting big names from across the range – Puff Daddy, Spice Girls, Five, Herbie Hancock and Transglobal Underground all played here within its first two months – the venue is the first in a planned global chain of Sound Republics. MTV and Channel Five film shows here, and the restaurant next door hosts regular free jazz, funk and soul gigs.

Spitz

Old Spitalfields Market, 109 Commercial Street, E1 (0171 392 9032). Liverpool Street tube/rail. **Open** 7pm-midnight Tue-Thur, occasional Sun; 7pm-1am Fri, Sat. **Admission** £4-£7. **Credit** MC, V. **Map 10 R5**
One of the more interesting new places to have opened since the arrival of the trendy set in EC1, Spitz offers groovy club nights mixing live music (often jazz) and DJ-ing of an experimental and avant-garde nature.

Subterania

12 Acklam Road, W10 (0181 960 4590/info 0181 963 0940). Ladbroke Grove tube. **Open** 8pm-2am Mon-Thur; 10pm-3am Fri, Sat; 7pm-midnight Sun. **Admission** £5-£12. **Credit** MC, V.
Sparse, double-tiered west London club venue that concentrates on a broad spectrum of black music, from hip hop and R&B, to acid jazz and reggae. Door policy can be a little heavy but, once you're inside, the venue is usually buzzing.

ULU (University of London Union)

Manning Hall, Malet Street, WC1 (0171 664 2030). Goodge Street tube. **Open** varies. **Admission** £5-£10. **Map 6 K4**
This 800-capacity, all-standing venue has adequate sound and vision, but is perhaps best loved for the fact that, being a student union, it has the cheapest bar prices in central London. It attracts upcoming indie acts like Moloko, Elliot Smith and Idlewild, and has helpful and discreet security.

The Underworld

174 Camden High Street, NW1 (0171 482 1932). Camden Town tube. **Open** *gig nights* 7.30-11pm daily (until 3am on club nights). **Admission** £3.50-£12.
The Underworld features a surprising number of well-known bands, and sits in a prime Camden location beneath the World's End pub, directly opposite the tube station. Sightlines are not brilliant as it's standing only.

West One Four

3 North End Crescent, North End Road, W14 (0171 381 0444). West Kensington tube. **Open** 8.30pm-midnight Mon-Sat; 7.30-10.30pm Sun. **Admission** £4-£5.
Reasonable views of the stage, and often good music (a lively mix of indie bands, funky stuff and songwriters' nights). The West One Four (previously known as The Orange) is a compact venue that can comfortably accommodate 350.

WKD

18 Kentish Town Road, NW1 (0171 267 1869). Camden Town tube/Camden Road rail. **Open** noon-2am Mon-Sat; noon-midnight Sun.
A surprisingly successful combination of café, bar, club and exhibition space. Music ranges from reggae, soul and world music to jamming sessions (there are DJs from 9.30pm daily).

Roots venues

Africa Centre

38 King Street, WC2 (0171 836 1973). Covent Garden tube. **Open** *club* 10pm-3am Fri, Sat; *music* varies. **Admission** £5-£7. **Credit** MC, V. **Map 8 L7**
The Africa Centre plays host to top African bands most Friday nights as well as staging occasional gigs on other nights. During the day the ground-floor shop offers a range of African goods. There's also a specialist bookshop on the first floor and a basement restaurant/café.

Bread & Roses

68 Clapham Manor Street, SW4 (0171 498 1779). Clapham Common tube/37, 88, 133, 137, 345 bus. **Open** 11am-11pm Mon-Sat; noon-10.30pm Sun. **Music** 1-5pm Sun. **Admission** free.

Top tours:
Anarchy in the West End

Punk's seminal central sights

Thames TV/Capital Radio
Euston Tower, 306 Euston Road (corner with Hampstead Road), NW1. **Map 5 J4**
It was here on 1 December 1976 that the Sex Pistols' infamous expletive-filled Thames TV interview with Bill Grundy took place, gaining them instant notoriety, sacking by their label EMI and the effective end of Grundy's career.

Another occupant of the Euston Tower was the subject of the Clash's *Capital Radio*, written to mock the station's bland output. The band sprayed 'White Riot' on the foyer windows in March 1977.

Speakeasy
(now Cameo nightclub) 48-50 Margaret Street, W1.
Map 5 J5
Originally a '60s club, Joe Strummer was once beaten up in the toilets, and the Pistols angrily confronted Bob Harris here for refusing to allow them on his *Old Grey Whistle Test* music show, leading A&M to drop the band.

100 Club
100 Oxford Street, W1. **Map 5 J6**
A jazz club for most of its long history, the 100 Club is nevertheless forever associated with punk. On 30 March 1976 the Pistols played to a small crowd and began a Tuesday night residency *(see picture above)*. In June, the future Sid Vicious (not yet a member of the band) attacked music journalist Nick Kent in the club. On 20-21 September, a punk festival featured the Pistols, the Clash, Siouxsie & the Banshees (with Vicious on drums), the Buzzcocks, the Damned and the Vibrators.

Vortex
(now Vogue nightclub) 201 Wardour Street, W1.
Map 5 J6
The Buzzcocks headlined this club's opening night on 4 July 1977 (supported by The Fall among others). Siouxsie & the Banshees and the Slits also played here.

Notre Dame Hall
5 Leicester Place, WC2. **Map 8 K7**

The Pistols played live here for the first time with Sid Vicious in March 1977. The church hall has also hosted the Clash and Wire. Check out the Cocteau murals in the church (that's Jean, not Twins).

Central St Martin's College of Art & Design
107 Charing Cross Road, WC2. **Map 6 K6**
Glen Matlock, while a student at St Martin's, got the Sex Pistols their first gig at the college on 6 November 1975. They were so bad that the plugs were pulled after a few songs.

La Gioconda Restaurant
(now Barino sandwich bar), 9 Denmark Street, WC2.
Map 6 K6
In their early days, the Pistols and Banshees used to hang out here, three doors down from their rehearsal room at no.6 behind Zeno Greek bookshop. Steve Jones and Paul Cook lived over the shop.

The Roxy
(now Scribbler's & Red or Dead), 41-43 Neal Street, WC2. **Map 6 L6**
The first specialised punk venue opened in January 1977 with a Clash gig, but only lasted four months. The Adverts, Wire, the Buzzcocks, X-Ray Spex and the Slits all played.

Rock Garden
The Piazza, Covent Garden, WC2. **Map 8 L6**
This former banana warehouse opened as a theme restaurant/venue in 1976. In the same year the Stranglers were pelted with spaghetti here by unimpressed diners.

Charing Cross Pier
Victoria Embankment, just east of Hungerford Bridge, SW1. **Map 8 L7**
The Queen Elizabeth, chartered by Malcolm MacLaren to promote *God Save the Queen*, docked here after a boisterous Thames cruise that included blasting out *Anarchy in the UK* opposite the Houses of Parliament. Eleven arrests were made during scuffles on disembarkation.

This pleasant mid-nineteenth-century pub is host to 'The Mwalimu Express', one of London's best world music events, which takes in the live music and food of a different city each Sunday, whether it be Oran, Algeria, or Accra, Ghana. The event also features family workshops on particular instruments relating to that week's music. Winner of *Time Out*'s 1998 Pub of the Year award.

Cecil Sharp House

2 Regent's Park Road, NW1 (0171 485 2206). Camden Town tube. **Open** varies. **Admission** £3-£6.
A folkie's dream, with all sorts of traditional English music and dancing. File Gumbo (first Friday of the month) is cajun dancing at its best and includes a beginner's session (7.30-10pm). At the monthly Monday Musicians anyone can join in, just bring your own instrument. And the Folk Club (8-11pm Tuesdays in the real ale cellar bar) hosts friendly trad folk sessions and singalongs. It also runs regular Balkan, jive, Irish, clog and barn dancing nights.

Hammersmith & Fulham Irish Centre

Blacks Road, W6 (0181 563 8232). Hammersmith tube. **Open** varies. **Admission** £3-£6.
This small and friendly venue plays hosts to all manner of Irish music events from free Ceilidhs to biggish-name Irish acts like Shane McGowan's the Popes. If you like Irish music, this is your place.

Swan

215 Clapham Road, SW9 (0171 978 9778). Stockwell tube. **Open** 5pm-midnight Mon-Wed; 5pm-2am Thur; 5pm-3am Fri; 7pm-3am Sat; 7pm-2am Sun. **Music** 9.30pm daily. **Admission** £1.50-£6 (normally free Mon-Wed and before 9pm Thur, Sun).
An Irish pub that specialises in semi-traditional music most evenings, with big names and rock acts in the upstairs dancehall at weekends. Views are good even when the place is busy, and the atmosphere, like the music, is raucous.

Twelve Bar Club

22-23 Denmark Place, off Denmark Street, WC2 (0171 916 6989/credit card booking 0171 209 2248). Tottenham Court Road tube. **Open** 8pm-1.30am daily. **Music** 9pm. **Admission** £5-£10. **Credit** MC, V. **Map 6 K6**
Mostly acoustic-oriented folk, country and blues regularly pack out the Twelve Bar, one of London's best acoustic venues (Noel Gallagher, Johnny Marr and Sinéad O'Connor have all been spotted in the crowd in the past). The sound is good, and, as the room is so tiny, the atmosphere is often electrifying, or should that be acoustifying.

Union Chapel

Compton Terrace, N1 (box office 0171 226 1686). Highbury & Islington tube/rail/73, 171A, 341. N92 bus. **Open** varies. **Tickets** £3.50-£12.50.
A 50-ft (31-m) high ceiling in the main chapel helps make the acoustics here among the best in London for certain types of music (electronic, jazz, folk) and one of the worst for others (indie and rock). The chapel, which is still a functioning church, has an eclectic, serious selection of music and excellent sightlines, although toilets and bar are a bit of a trek. A leaflet available at the entrance gives a full history of this most attractive of London gig venues.

Weavers

98 Newington Green Road, N1 (0171 226 6911). Highbury & Islington tube/rail/73, 171A, 341. **Open** 8.30pm-midnight Mon-Sat; 8-10.30pm Sun. **Music** 8pm. **Admission** £3-£7.
The owners' total dedication to music has made this one of the best roots venues in Europe. A constant stream of top-name acoustic, cajun and country acts from around the world make a point of playing at Weavers. Though off the beaten track, it is well worth seeking out.

Jazz venues

Pizza on the Park (11 Knightsbridge; 0171 235 5273) has nightly jazz sessions from 9.15-11.15pm (cover charge variable).

606 Club

90 Lots Road, SW10 (0171 352 5953). Fulham Broadway tube/11, 22 bus. **Open** 8.30pm-2am Mon-Sat; 8.30-11.30pm Sun. **Music** 9.30pm Mon-Thur, Sun; 10pm Fri, Sat. **Music charge** £4.75 Mon-Thur, Sun; £5.95 Fri, Sat. **Credit** MC, V. **Map 3 C13**
An unusual venue in that it (admirably) hosts mainly local and young jazz bands. There is no admission fee, just a music charge that funds the musicians and is added to your bill. On Fridays and Saturdays, visitors must have a meal; Monday to Thursday you can only consume alcohol if you eat (otherwise it's soft drinks). Food is good, if pricey.

Bull's Head

373 Lonsdale Road, SW13 (0181 876 5241). Barnes Bridge rail. **Open** 11am-11pm Mon-Sat; noon-10.30pm Sun. **Music** 8.30-11pm Mon-Sat; 2-4.30pm, 8-10.30pm, Sun. **Admission** £3-£7.
Some of the finest musicians in jazz history have played at this riverside pub. American artists are a favourite, along with old-school London stalwarts like Art Themen, Don Weller and Stan Tracey. Good views and sound, and drinks at pub prices.

Jazz Café

5 Parkway, NW1 (0171 916 6060/Mean Fiddler info line 0181 963 0940). Camden Town tube. **Open** 7pm-1am Mon-Thur; 7pm-2am Fri, Sat; 7pm-midnight Sun. **Admission** £6-£20. **Credit** AmEx, MC, V.
Voted *Time Out*'s 1998 Live Venue of the Year, this intimate, two-level venue has a great booking policy that means that everything from country and jazz to nu soul and indie gets an airing. The sound is better than it used to be and views are mostly very good. There's a wide range of reasonably priced drinks, classy food, the staff are generally friendly and, when it gets going, the atmosphere is electric.

Pizza Express Jazz Club

10 Dean Street, W1 (0171 439 8722/437 9595). Tottenham Court Road tube. **Music** from 9pm daily. **Admission** £8-£20. **Credit** AmEx, DC, MC, V. **Map 6 K6**
A revamp has rid Pizza Express of its old-fogeyish reputation and put it up there with the best as an excellent, intimate venue for mainstream and contemporary jazz. Look out for residencies by big names. The pizzas are great too.

Ronnie Scott's

47 Frith Street, W1 (0171 439 0747). Leicester Square or Tottenham Court Road tube. **Open** 8.30pm-3am Mon-Sat; 7.30-10.30pm Sun. **Music** 9.30pm daily. **Admission** £4-£20. **Credit** AmEx, DC, MC, £TC, V. **Map 6 K6**
A Soho legend, run by the eponymous saxophonist until his death in 1996. The club's hallowed reputation continues to attract some of the top names of modern jazz, including James Moody, Elvin Jones and Joe Lovano, as well as top British artists and Latin bands. It will never be quite the same without Ronnie there, but the atmosphere remains excellent.

Vortex

139-141 Stoke Newington Church Street, N16 (0171 254 6516). Stoke Newington rail/67, 73, 76, 106, 243 bus. **Open** 10am-11.30pm Mon-Thur; 10am-midnight Fri, Sat; 11am-11pm Sun. **Music** 9pm daily. **Admission** £3-£10. **Credit** MC, V.
One of London's more relaxed and friendly venues. Musicians from across the jazz spectrum play, and the (mainly vegetarian) food is reasonable and fairly priced.

Festivals

While large-scale, big-name events such as Glastonbury, Reading and the Notting Hill Carnival (*see page 108*) dominate Britain's summer festival season, London offers plenty of smaller events, often organised locally. Most of the capital's fields and open spaces will, at some time during the year, stage some sort of bash – keep an eye on *Time Out* for details of festival line-ups. Phone the numbers listed below nearer the time for confirmed dates ticket prices (generally on sale about two to three months before the event). Though most of these festivals are outside London, they are well worth the trip.

35th Charles Wells Cambridge Folk Festival

Cherry Hinton Hall Grounds, Cambridge (box office 01223 357851). **Date** 30 July-1 Aug 1999. **Tickets** £45 (approx). **Credit** AmEx, MC, V.
In clement weather, the Cambridge bash makes for a perfect, mellow weekend and, employing an admirably wide definition of what constitutes 'folk' (such as blues, country, gospel and cajun), there's always something for everyone. Recent acts have included Elvis Costello, the Levellers and Eddi Reader. The box office opens in May and the festival's 10,000 tickets are quickly snapped up. It's a relatively grown-up affair as music festivals go but is still often as much fun for kids as adults. Also check out the **Cambridge Shakespeare Festival** while you're in town (*see page 286*).

Essential

Stanmer Park, Brighton, Sussex (info 0891 230190/ credit card bookings 01273 709709). **Date** 17-18 July 1999. **Tickets** £30. **Credit** AmEx, MC, V.
This reasonable newcomer evolved, somewhat surprisingly, from an annual campus barn dance (it takes place next to Sussex University campus). Although it's no longer a student event, the audience is generally youngish and laid-back. The weekend usually consists of a dance day, an indie day and a roots day, and tickets are sold on a daily basis. No camping.

Fleadh

Finsbury Park, N4 (0181 961 5490/bookings 0171 344 0044). Finsbury Park tube. **Date** June/July (phone to check). **Tickets** £28 (approx). **Credit** AmEx, MC, V.
This one-day, open-air event is a boozy, good-humoured celebration of Irish music. Recently, the Fleadh (pronounced 'flar', the Gaelic word for a party or celebration) has featured an admirably eclectic range of acts, and pulled in big names such as Bob Dylan, James, Van Morrison and Christy Moore.

Glastonbury Festival

Worthy Farm, Pilton, Somerset (no phone at time this guide went to press). **Date** 25-27 June 1999. **Tickets** £80. **Credit** AmEx, MC, V.
The mother of them all. The brainchild of farmer Michael Eavis, Glastonbury was first held in the 1960s and just grew and grew. Today's festival plays host to some 90,000 chilled-out revellers who flood in to hear (in 1998) the likes of Blur, Robbie Williams, Bob Dylan and Pulp and otherwise commune with the area's mystic past. The quality of Eavis' line-ups are legendary, the chemical loos notorious. The box office opens in April (a phone number for bookings will be advertised in *Time Out* magazine from March) and soon sells out, although for the past two years, the event has been blighted by biblical amounts of rain, and the consequent mud.

Guildford Festival

Stoke Park, Guildford, Surrey (info 01483 536270). **Date** 23-25 July 1999. **Tickets** £24 per day (approx). **Credit** AmEx, MC, £TC, V.
In a summer where many UK festivals were hit by bad weather and/or poor ticket sales, Guildford '98 was something of a surprise success. The 10,000-capacity festival, which has three stages and is held over three days, has the feeling of a village fête crossed with a major festival. It doesn't have the big-name bills of other festivals (although headline bands last year were Space, Shed Seven and Lightning Seeds), but the friendly vibe and family feel more than make up for it. Tickets go on sale from March.

Meltdown

Royal Festival Hall, on the South Bank, SE1 (info/box office 0171 960 4242). **Date** 19 June-2 July 1999. **Tickets** £10-£15 (approx). **Credit** AmEx, DC, MC, V.
One of the most significant players in identifying and breaking music in Britain, Meltdown is a wide-ranging fortnight-long event championing music, performance and more. Always recommended, and, if last year's John Peel-led bash is a benchmark, it's likely to be a resounding success again in 1999.

Reading Festival

Richfield Avenue, Reading, Berkshire (info 0181 963 0940/box office 0171 344 0044). **Date** 27-29 Aug 1999. **Tickets** £30 per day; £75 weekend. **Credit** AmEx, MC, V.
Traditionally the festival season finale, Reading's August bank holiday weekend shindig used to be seen as something of a hard rock get-together. Last year's bill, which included New Order, Beastie Boys, Prodigy, Page & Plant and Garbage, highlighted the fact that these days Reading, like Glastonbury, is home to all kinds of music. What really makes Reading stand out is that, unlike other major festivals, the site is within walking distance of shops, banks, public transport and other forms of civilisation. Tickets are on sale from May or June.

V99

Hylands Park, Chelmsford, Essex (info/credit card hotline 0870 165 5555/0171 344 4444). **Date** 21-22 Aug 1999. **Tickets** £30 per day (approx); £64 weekend camping ticket (approx). **Credit** AmEx, MC, V.
Now in its fourth year, this Virgin-run bash in Chelmsford has quickly established itself as one of the biggest UK music festivals. Also operating in Leeds, with the whole bill playing one site on Saturday and the other on Sunday, the festival is known for its civilised nature – with surprisingly decent toilets and plenty of cashpoints. Standouts from 1998's lineup included the Verve, Robbie Williams, All Saints, James Brown and the Charlatans, although the most memorable moment came when oh-so-naughty US punksters Green Day set fire to the stage. The booking line opens in March or April.

Best of the rest

Jazz is pretty much sewn up by the year's two big productions: the **Soho Jazz Festival** (30 Sept-10 Oct; 0171 437 6437) and the **Oris London Jazz Festival** (phone 0171 405 5974 for dates). In addition, the **Coin Street Festival** (6 June-19 Sept; 0171 620 0544) offers a wide array of performances, and incorporates the **Latin American Gran Gran Fiesta** on 4 July (0171 620 0544). The festival usually ends with Thameside fireworks.

Sport & Fitness

Where to see it and where to do it.

See the sport section of *Time Out* for the pick of the weekly action, as well as details of contacts and classes in virtually every kind of physical activity. Alternatively, phone **Sportsline** (0171 222 8000) or contact your nearest leisure centre.

See the sport section of *Time Out* for the pick of

Participation sports

Baseball

British Baseball Federation
Wendy MacAdam, PO Box 45, Hessle, East Yorkshire HU13 0YQ (01482 643551).
The BBF runs the National Baseball League, which has a northern and southern premier division and four regional conferences (London is covered by the southern conference). Write for details of your local teams.

Bungee jumping

UK Bungee Club/Adrenalin Village
Chelsea Bridge Tower, Queenstown Road, SW8 (0171 720 9496). Sloane Square tube then 137 bus. **Open** *Apr-Sept* 5-9pm Wed; 4-8pm Fri; 11am-6pm Sat, Sun; *Oct-Mar* 4-8pm Fri; 11am-6pm Sat, Sun. **Admission** *cage ride to viewing tower* £5; *bungee jump* £35 plus £15 membership fee. **Credit** AmEx, MC, V.
A 300-ft (92-m) observation tower is the centrepoint of London's only static bungee jump. The UK Bungee Club also organises mobile bungees; phone for details.

Cycling

Lee Valley Cycle Circuit
Temple Mills Lane, E15 (0181 534 6085). Leyton tube. **Open** *summer* 8am-8pm daily, but check availability; *winter* 8am-3.30pm Mon-Fri. **Admission** *with bike hire* £4.05, £3 under-16s; *with own bike* £2.05, £1 under-16s.
BMX, road racing, time-trialing, cyclo-cross and mountain biking are catered for with various purpose-built tracks. King computerised cycle testing can pick up powerless pedalling (£20 first test; £14 subsequently). Events (with international riders) are held most weekends and on summer evenings.

Dance

For details of dance classes, *see page 233*.

Golf

Ring the **English Golf Union** (01526 354500) for more information about courses in the capital.

Courses
Airlinks *Southall Lane, Hounslow, Middx (0181 561 1418). Hayes & Harlington rail then 195 bus.* **Course** 18 holes. **Fees per round** £10 Mon-Fri; £16 Sat, Sun.

Brent Valley Church Road *Cuckoo Lane, W7 (0181 567 1287). Hanwell rail.* **Course** 18 holes. **Fees per round** £6 Mon; £9.50 Tue-Fri; £14 before noon Sat, Sun; £10 after noon Sat, Sun.

Chingford Golf Course *Bury Road, E4 (0181 529 5708). Chingford rail.* **Course** 18 holes. **Fees per round** £10.10 Mon-Fri; £13.80 Sat, Sun; £5.05 under-18s after 10am Mon-Fri.

Lee Valley Golf Course *Picketts Lock Lane, N9 (0181 803 3611). Ponders End rail.* **Course** 18 holes. **Fees per round** *members* £8 Mon-Fri, £11 Sat, Sun; *non-members* £11 Mon-Fri, £13.50 Sat, Sun.

Richmond Park *Roehampton Gate, Priory Lane, SW15 (0181 876 3205). Richmond rail.* **Course** two 18-hole courses. **Fees per round** £5-16.80.

Stockley Park Golf Course *off Stockley Road (A408) Uxbridge, Middx (0181 813 5700). Heathrow Terminals 1, 2 & 3 tube then U5 bus.* **Course** 18 holes. **Fees per round** *Hillingdon residents* £21 Mon-Fri, £27 Sat, Sun; *non-residents* £23 Mon-Fri, £33 Sat, Sun.

Regent's Park Golf School
Outer Circle, Regent's Park, NW1 (0171 724 0643). Baker Street tube. **Open** 8am-9pm daily.
Membership from £60, phone for details. **Map 5 G2**
Services include club adjustment, lessons with pros (£20 for 30 mins; £90 six lessons) and driving range sessions (*non-members* £5 for 50 balls; *members* £2). You could even go so far as to have your golf swing computer-analysed, for £35.

Horse riding

Belmont Riding Centre
Belmont Farm, The Ridgeway, NW7 (0181 906 1255). Mill Hill East tube. **Open** 9am-9pm Tue-Fri; 9am-6pm Sat, Sun. **Fees** *group lessons weekday* £18 per hour, £15 child; *weekend* £20 per hour, £18 child; *individual lessons* £25 per hour, £22 child; £16 per 30 mins, £14 child.
Apart from its 160 acres (65 hectares) and cross-country course, Belmont has an indoor school and three manèges. Facilities are suitable for novices through to the advanced rider, and there's also a British Horse Society-approved pre-novice course. All equestrian disciplines are catered for, including polo.

Hyde Park Stables
63 Bathurst Mews, W2 (0171 723 2813). Lancaster Gate tube. **Open** *summer* 7.15am-7pm, *winter* 7.15am-5pm, Tue-Sun. **Fees** *group lessons* £28 per hour, £25 children; *individual lessons* £60 per hour; *ride around Hyde Park* £25; £23 under-15s. Reservations essential. **Map 2 D6**
Smart stables offering pleasant treks through Hyde Park.

Wimbledon Village Stables
24 High Street, SW19 (0181 946 8579). Wimbledon tube/rail. **Open** 8am-5pm Tue-Sun. **Fees** from £20 per hour Tue-Fri; £25 Sat, Sun.
These British Horse Society-approved stables have small classes and horses to suit both beginners and experienced riders. Rides are on Wimbledon Common, Putney Heath and Richmond Park.

Ice skating

Ice rinks need regular resurfacing and sweeping. As a result, session times vary from day to day, and from season to season. Generally, sessions last about two hours, and rinks are open from approximately 10am to 10pm; ring for more specific details.

Broadgate Ice Rink
Broadgate Circus, Eldon Street, EC2 (0171 505 4068). Liverpool Street tube. **Admission** £5; £3 concs; **Skate hire** £2; £1 concs. **Map 10 Q5**
The UK's only outdoor ice rink is compact, friendly and caters for skaters of all ages and abilities. Teams play a game called broomball here (6-9pm Mon-Wed) in which players try to 'sweep' a football into goals – spectators are welcome. Phone for details of private hire. Open only late October-early April.

Lee Valley Ice Centre
Lea Bridge Road, E10 (0181 533 3154). Blackhorse Road tube. **Admission** £4.20 adults, £3.20 children. **Skate hire** 80p.
Though not exactly centrally located, this is a large, well-maintained rink running popular disco nights.

Leisurebox
17 Queensway, W2 (0171 229 0172). Bayswater or Queensway tube. **Admission** £3-£5; *disco* £6.50. **Skate hire** £1. **Map 1 C6**
Friday and Saturday nights are disco night at this fashionable Bayswater rink. Students are catered for on Wednesday nights and there are various after-school sessions and family hours. If you find you're spending more time on your backside than on your blades, the tenpin bowling lanes might prove a more steadying experience.

Streatham Ice Rink
386 Streatham High Road, SW16 (0181 769 7771). Streatham rail. **Admission** £4.50; £3.50 under-12s. **Skate hire** £1.50.
This spacious rink offers skating courses and sometimes stages junior league ice-hockey games.

Karting

Playing at Formula One on zippy karts (and they are exhilaratingly fast) is very popular in London, particularly for companies and groups of friends. All the tracks below have daily sessions; phone for details.

Daytona Raceway *54 Wood Lane, W12 (0181 749 2277). White City tube.* **Rates** £20 15-min practice session; from £40 standard private entry fee for race.

Playscape Pro Racing *Battersea Kart Raceway, Hester Road, SW11 (0171 801 0110). Sloane Square tube then 19 bus.* **Rates** £37.50 per driver for two hours. **Map 4 E13**

Playscape Pro Racing *Streatham Kart Raceway, 390 Streatham High Road, SW2 (0171 801 0110). Streatham rail.* **Rates** £37.50 per driver for two hours.

Raceway *Central Warehouse, North London Freight Terminal, York Way, N1 (0171 833 1000). King's Cross tube/rail.* **Rates** £20 per driver for 15 mins; £30 per driver for 30 mins.

Trak 1 Racing *Unit 2A, Wyvern Way, Barnsfield Place, Uxbridge, Middx (01895 258410/811303). Uxbridge tube.* **Rates** £40 per person per race meeting.

Park life

London's parks offer a wealth of sporty activities. Note that some facilities must be booked in advance; phone for details. Here's a summary of what's on offer at six of the main parks:

Battersea Park
See p104 (0181 871 7530).
Athletics track. Boating lake. Cycle/rollerblading tracks. Football pitch. Rugby pitch. Softball pitch. Tennis courts.

Hampstead Heath
See pp78-80 & p82 (0171 485 3873).
Athletics track. Bowls. Cricket pitch. Cycle paths. Football pitch. Hockey pitch. Horse riding. Kite flying. Model boat sailing pond. Putting. Swimming ponds (women's, men's and unisex). Tennis courts.

Hyde Park
See p73 (0171 298 2100).
Boating. Boules and bowls. Fishing and cycle tracks. Horse riding paths. Putting. Tennis courts.

Regent's Park
See p55 (0171 486 7905).
Athletics track. Boating lakes (one for children). Football, hockey, and rugby pitches (winter). Golf school. Softball, cricket and rounders pitches (summer). Tennis courts and school.

Richmond Park
See p106 (0181 948 3209).
Cycle and pedestrian path (shared). Fishing. Horse riding. Model aeroplane field. Model boat sailing pond. Swimming pool (outdoor).

Victoria Park
See p93 (0181 533 2057).
Athletics track. Bowling (Apr-Sept). Combined cycle and pedestrian paths. Cricket and softball pitches (summer). Fishing (July-Feb). Football, mini-football and rugby pitches (winter). Model boating lake. Tennis courts.

Martial arts

Jujitsu Club of London
Church Hall, Church of St Anne & All Saints, corner of South Lambeth Road & Mile Street, SW8 (0171 352 7716). Vauxhall tube/rail. **Classes** many and varied; phone for details. **Fees** £3 per lesson. **Map 7 J9**
Tuition in all levels of jujitsu, and also in karate, aikido and t'ai chi.

London School of Capoeira Dance
Studio 8, The Place, 17 Dukes Road, WC1 (0171 281 2020). Euston tube/rail. **Classes** 8-10pm Tue, Wed, Fri. **Fees** £75 (£65 concs) beginner's course (four lessons). **Map 6 K3**
Capoeira is an increasingly popular blend of dance and martial art from Brazil. Free demonstration sessions are held every Friday evening (9-10pm), and introductory workshops every month.

Softball

British Softball Federation/London Softball Federation

Bob Fromer, Birchwood Hall, Storridge, Malvern, Worcestershire WR13 5EZ (01886 884204).
There are 350 organised softball teams in London. Bob Fromer offers info both for beginners and seasoned players, ranging from contacts for local London teams, leagues and coaching sessions to advice on how to become an umpire.

Sport & leisure centres

Aerobics, step, badminton, squash, swimming and various other indoor sports and exercise classes are on offer at many sports centres. Always phone ahead if you're hoping to book a court or hall. For further centres, look in *Yellow Pages* under 'Leisure Centres', or call Sportsline (0171 222 8000).

Admission prices for the following centres vary depending on the activity. Ask about membership prices if you're planning on using the facilities of a gym over a long period of time.

Chelsea Sports Centre

Chelsea Manor Street, SW3 (0171 352 6985). Sloane Square tube. **Open** 7am-10pm Mon-Fri; 8am-6.30pm Sat; 8am-10pm Sun. **Map 4 E12**
A good selection of facilities including swimming pool, weights, sports hall and aerobics classes.

Jubilee Hall Leisure Centre

30 The Piazza, WC2 (0171 836 4835). Covent Garden tube. **Open** 7am-10pm Mon-Fri; 10am-5pm Sat, Sun. **Map 8 L7**
A huge, busy, well-equipped gym with London's biggest selection of free-weights is one of the main attractions here. It also offers martial arts, aerobics and step classes.

Michael Sobell Leisure Centre

Hornsey Road, N7 (0171 609 2166). Finsbury Park or Holloway Road tube. **Open** 9am-10.30pm Mon-Fri; 9am-6pm Sat; 9am-10pm Sun.
This huge north London centre has excellent facilities including a climbing wall, trampolines and gym; the sports hall is often used as a basketball venue.

Mornington Sports & Leisure Centre

142-150 Arlington Road, NW1 (0171 267 3600). Camden Town tube. **Open** 7am-9.30pm Mon-Fri; 10am-5.30pm Sat, Sun. **Map 5 J2**
The usual range of team sports (volleyball, basketball and football) are offered here, as well as a gym, sunbeds and various fitness and karate classes.

Porchester Centre

Queensway, W2 (0171 792 2919). Bayswater or Queensway tube. **Open** 7am-10pm Mon-Fri; 8am-8pm Sat, Sun.
A pool, gym, classes, squash courts, sauna, sunbed and excellent spa make this a popular venue. *See also p206.*

Queen Mother Sports Centre

223 Vauxhall Bridge Road, SW1 (enquiries 0171 630 5522/bookings 0171 630 5511). Victoria tube/rail. **Open** 6.30am-10pm Mon-Fri; 8am-8pm Sat, Sun. **Map 7 J10**
This sports centre boasts a gym, two dance studios, sauna and steam room, badminton, swimming and diving, martial arts and aerobics classes.

Seymour Leisure Centre

Seymour Place, W1 (0171 723 8019). Edgware Road or Marble Arch tube. **Open** 7am-10pm Mon-Fri; 7am-8pm Sat; 8am-8pm Sun. **Map 2 F5**
The centre has a 30-m pool, sports hall, cardiovascular fitness room, steam room, sauna, Jacuzzi and snooker room with a bar. It also runs body-conditioning, aerobics and step classes.

Swiss Cottage Sports Centre

Winchester Road, NW3 (0171 413 6490). Swiss Cottage tube. **Open** 7am-9.30pm Mon-Fri; 9am-8.30pm Sat, Sun.
As well as a gym and two indoor swimming pools, there are facilities for squash, badminton, table tennis, tennis and football.

Swimming (indoor)

To find your nearest swimming pool, try the *Yellow Pages* or **Sportsline** (0171 222 8000). A few of the better-known ones follow (*see also above* **Sport & leisure centres**). For pools that are particularly suitable for children, *see page 218.*

Highbury Pool *Highbury Crescent, N5 (0171 226 4186). Highbury & Islington tube/rail.* **Open** 7am-9pm Mon-Fri; 7.30am-5pm Sat; 7.30am-9pm Sun. *Women only* 6.30-9pm Tue. **Admission** £2.60; £1.10 under-16s; free under-4s.

Ironmonger Row Baths *Ironmonger Row, EC1 (0171 253 4011). Old Street tube/rail.* **Open** 7.30am-8pm Mon; 7.30am-8.30pm Tue, Thur; 7.30am-10pm Wed; 7.30am-7pm Fri; 9am-5pm Sat; noon-6pm Sun. **Admission** £2.60; £1.10 under-16s; free under-3s. **Map 9 P4**

Oasis Sports Centre *32 Endell Street, WC2 (0171 831 1804). Covent Garden or Holborn tube.* **Open** *indoor pool* 6.30am-9pm Mon-Fri; 9.30am-5pm Sat, Sun; *outdoor pool* 7.30am-8.30pm Mon, Wed, Fri; 7.30am-8pm Thur; 9.30am-5pm Sat, Sun. **Admission** £2.65; £1 under-16s; free under-5s. **Map 6 L6**

Swimming (outdoor)

See also above **Oasis Sports Centre** *and* **Finchley Lido** (*page 218*).

Brockwell Lido *Dulwich Road, SE24 (0171 274 3088). Herne Hill rail.* **Open** *May-Sept* 6.45-10am, noon-7pm, Mon-Fri; 11am-7pm Sat, Sun. **Admission** *morning* £1.50, £1 children; *afternoon* £3, £2 children.

Hampstead Heath Ponds *Hampstead Heath, NW3 (Parliament Hill 0171 485 4491). Hampstead tube/ Gospel Oak or Hampstead Heath rail/C2, C11, 214.* **Open** 7am-dusk daily.

Parliament Hill Lido *Hampstead Heath, Gordon House Road, NW5 (0171 485 3873). Gospel Oak rail/ C11 bus.* **Open** *Apr-Sept* 7am-9.30am, 10am-6pm, daily. **Admission** £1-£4 (no charge before 10am).

Richmond Pools on the Park *Old Deer Park, Twickenham Road, Richmond, Surrey (0181 940 0561). Richmond tube/rail.* **Open** *May, Sept* 6.30am-8pm Mon-Fri; 7am-7pm Sat, Sun; *June-Aug* 6.30am-10pm Mon, Wed, Fri; 6.30am-9pm Tue, Thur; 7am-7pm Sat, Sun. **Admission** £2.25-£2.90.

Serpentine Lido *Hyde Park (0171 298 2100). Hyde Park Corner, Knightsbridge, Lancaster Gate or Marble Arch tube.* **Open** usually for two months over summer; phone for details of times and admission prices.

Tooting Bec Lido *Tooting Bec Road, Tooting Bec Common, SW16 (0181 871 7198). Tooting Bec tube/Streatham rail.* **Open** *May-Oct* 10am-8pm daily. **Admission** £2.40, £1.90 children Mon-Fri; £2.95, £2.10 children Sat, Sun.

Going to the dogs? **Wimbledon Stadium** *is as good a place as any. See page 262.*

Tennis

Many London parks have courts, which usually cost little or nothing to play on (*see page 258* **Park life**). Private facilities and coaching will cost more, but **Sportsline** (0171 222 8000) may be able to help you shop around for the best bargain. Phone or write (enclosing a stamped self-addressed envelope) to the **Lawn Tennis Association Trust**, Queen's Club, West Kensington, W14 9EG (0171 381 7000) for its leaflet, *Where to Play Tennis in London.*

Islington Tennis Centre

Market Road, N7 (0171 700 1370). Caledonian Road tube. **Open** 7am-11pm daily. **Fees** *outdoor courts* £4.70-£5.70 per hour; *indoor courts* £13-£14 per hour.
The centre provides three floodlit outdoor courts, three indoor courts and three mini-courts for general use. Coaching courses are held at the centre itself, and during the summer at Highbury Fields, for beginners, improvers and advanced improvers, priced £19-£34.

Tenpin bowling

Tenpin bowling is becoming increasingly popular. Here are a few of London's best bowling alleys; for other choices check the *Yellow Pages.* All have food and drink facilities, although don't expect much in the way of quality. *See also* **Leisurebox**, *page 258.*

Airport Bowl *Bath Road, Harlington, Middx (0181 759 1396). Hatton Cross or Hounslow West tube/Hayes Town rail.* **Open** 10am-late Mon-Fri; 7am-late Sat, Sun. **Lanes** 36.

GX Superbowl *15-17 Alpine Way, E6 (0171 511 4440). East Ham tube then 101 bus/Beckton DLR.* **Open** noon-midnight Mon, Thur-Fri; 10am-midnight Sat, Sun. **Lanes** 22.

Rowans Leisure Centre *10 Stroud Green Road, N4 (0181 800 1950). Finsbury Park tube/rail.* **Open** 10.30am-12.30am Mon-Thur; 10.30am-2.30am Fri, Sat; 10.30am-1.30am Sun. **Lanes** 24.

Streatham Mega Bowl *142 Streatham Hill, SW2 (0181 671 5021). Streatham rail.* **Open** 10am-midnight daily. **Lanes** 36.

Watersports

All manner of watery pursuits can be enjoyed on London's river and reservoirs.

Capital Rowing Centre

Polytechnic Boathouse, Ibis Lane, off Hartington Road, W4 (0181 395 2190/0973 314199). Chiswick rail. **Open** phone for details.
If you're a glutton for punishment, enroll on one of the centre's courses on the river for virgin oarspeople. Prices start at £4 for 90 minutes of tuition.

Docklands Sailing & Watersports Centre

Millwall Dock, E14 (0171 537 2626). Crossharbour & London Arena DLR. **Open** 9.30am-11pm Mon-Fri; 9.30am-5pm Sat, Sun.
If you enjoy messing about on the water, this school offers both practical and theoretical training. Dragon-boat racing is also available. Phone for prices.

Docklands Watersports Club

Gate 14, King George V Dock, Woolwich Manor Way, E16 (0171 511 7000). Gallions Reach DLR/North Woolwich rail. **Open** 10am-dusk Mon, Tue, Thur-Sun.
The Docklands Watersports Club provides good training facilities for jet-ski riders at all levels. Prices start at around £30 for 30 minutes (including hire of craft, wetsuit and use of club facilities).

Lee Valley Watersports Centre

Banbury Reservoir, Harbet Road, E4 (0181 531 1129). Walthamstow Central tube. **Open** 10am-dusk daily.
Windsurfing, sailing, water-skiing and canoeing are the main pursuits on 90-acre (36-ha) Banbury Reservoir. The centre runs Royal Yachting Association-approved courses in all these activities.

Royal Docks Water-ski Club

Inside London City Airport, King George V Dock, E16 (0171 511 2000). Stratford tube/rail then 473 bus/ Canary Wharf DLR then London City Airport bus/ Silvertown rail. **Open** phone for details.
Beginners and experienced water-skiers are welcomed at London's most central water-ski club. There are courses for all skill levels, and more experienced skiers can select from mono, slalom, jump and tricks courses. You can also try speedboat driving or wakeboarding – like snowboarding on water.

Yoga

Yoga Therapy Centre

4th floor, Royal London Homeopathic Hospital, 60 Great Ormond Street, WC1 (0171 419 7195). Holborn or Russell Square tube. **Open** phone to check. **Map 6 L4**
Founded by the Yoga Biomedical Trust (a registered charity), the centre provides treatment for asthma, hypertension, arthritis, diabetes, ME, menstrual problems, pregnancy and childbirth, and general stress-related illnesses. Remedial classes are available for asthma and back pain and general classes run at weekday lunchtimes and evenings. Personal tuition and children's classes are also available.

Spectator sports

Basketball

This growing sport has spawned a number of London teams. The Leopards and the Towers play in the Budweiser Basketball League; for details on where to see these games phone the **Basketball League** (0121 749 1355). Barking & Dagenham and the Brixton Topcats play in the National Basketball League; for details of these games phone the **English Basketball Association** (0113 236 1020).

Boxing

Details of big fights tend to be fly-posted throughout the city. Seats can cost anything between £20 and £150. For boxing nostalgists, the famous **Henry Cooper** pub (0171 232 0887) on the Old Kent Road has a ringside gym upstairs. Most of London's up-and-coming talent can be seen fighting in the East End at **York Hall**, Old Ford Road, E2 (0181 980 2243). Championship fights are often held in hotels and theatres. For details on where to see boxing in London call the **British Boxing Board of Control** (0171 403 5879).

Cricket

Most league matches take four days to complete, so it's advisable to catch one of the limited-overs matches on Sunday afternoons. The season runs

from April to September. For a more informal but quintessential English experience, take a deckchair and relax at one of the regular weekend games on Kew Green (*see page 111*).

Lord's

St John's Wood Road, NW8 (MCC 0171 432 1066/ switchboard & bookings 0171 289 1611). St John's Wood tube.
The immaculate playing surface of Lord's is the spiritual and administrative home of the game. It's the base of Marylebone Cricket Club (MCC) – governing body of the sport – and Middlesex County Cricket Club, and hosts league and cup matches. Tickets for county matches are easy to obtain, and often cost less than £10. For the **MCC Museum**, *see p122.*

Foster's Oval

Kennington Oval, SE11 (0171 582 6660). Oval tube.
Immediately recognisable by the gasometer behind the main stand, the Oval has one of the finest batting pitches in the country and a reputation for producing thrilling cricket. Also home to Surrey County Cricket Club, the Oval traditionally stages the final – often the deciding – game in each summer's International Test Series.

Cycling

Herne Hill Velodrome

Burbage Road, SE24 (0171 525 1540). Herne Hill rail. **Open** phone for details. **Admission** from £4.50; from £1.50 under-16s.
Founded over 100 years ago, Herne Hill Velodrome is the oldest cycle stadium in the country (although the track itself is only about five years old), and the only velodrome in London. International events are staged here over holiday periods, the biggest of which is on Good Friday.

Football

As British football draws increasing numbers of world-class foreign players, and London clubs begin to make their mark on the European stage, ticket availability for the Premier League clubs is becoming increasingly restricted (unless you have a season ticket). London clubs feature in all divisions, from the FA Carling Premiership to the Nationwide League Division 3; tickets are cheaper and more readily available the lower the division. Most clubs offer concessions for kids and OAPs.

Clubs

Arsenal *Arsenal Stadium, Avenell Road, N5 (0171 704 4000). Arsenal tube.* **Tickets** £14-£34. FA Carling Premiership.

Barnet *Underhill Stadium, Westcombe Drive, Barnet, Herts (0181 441 6932). High Barnet tube.* **Tickets** *standing* £8; *seats* £10-£14. Nationwide League Div 3.

Brentford *Griffin Park, Braemar Road, Brentford, Middx (0181 847 2511). Brentford rail.* **Tickets** *standing* £8; *seats* £9-£15. Nationwide League Div 3.

Charlton Athletic *The Valley, Floyd Road, SE7 (0181 333 4000). Charlton rail.* **Tickets** £9-£22. FA Carling Premiership.

Chelsea *Stamford Bridge, Fulham Road, SW6 (0171 385 5545). Fulham Broadway tube.* **Tickets** £10-£28. FA Carling Premiership. **Map 3 B13**

Crystal Palace *Selhurst Park, Whitehorse Lane, SE25 (0181 771 8841). Norwood Junction, Selhurst or Thornton Heath rail.* **Tickets** £9-£25. Nationwide Div 1.

Fulham *Craven Cottage, Stevenage Road, SW6 (0171 736 6561). Putney Bridge tube.* **Tickets** *standing* £9-£10; *seats* £14. Nationwide League Div 2.

Leyton Orient *Matchroom Stadium, Brisbane Road, E10 (0181 926 1111). Leyton tube.* **Tickets** *standing* £10; *seats* £11-£13. Nationwide League Div 3.

Millwall *The Den, Zampa Road, SE16 (0171 232 1222). South Bermondsey rail.* **Tickets** £11-£15. Nationwide League Div 2.

Queens Park Rangers *Loftus Road Stadium, South Africa Road, W12 (0181 740 0503/743 0262). White City tube.* **Tickets** £10-£20. Nationwide League Div 1.

Tottenham Hotspur *White Hart Lane, High Road, N17 (0181 365 5000). White Hart Lane rail.* **Tickets** £21-£41. FA Carling Premiership.

Watford *Vicarage Road, Watford, Herts (01923 496010). Watford High Street rail.* **Tickets** £5-£16. Nationwide League Div 1.

West Ham United *Boleyn Ground, Green Street, E13 (0181 548 2748). Upton Park tube.* **Tickets** £18-£35. FA Carling Premiership.

Wimbledon *Selhurst Park, Park Road, SE25 (0181 771 2233). Norwood Junction, Selhurst or Thornton Heath rail.* **Tickets** £10-£22. FA Carling Premiership.

Golf

Two of the UK's most famous courses lie within easy reach of London. Wentworth has become the regular venue for the Toyota World Matchplay tournament every October. Phone for details.

Sunningdale *Ridgemount Road, Sunningdale, Ascot, Berks (01344 621681). Sunningdale rail.*

Wentworth *Wentworth Drive, Virginia Water, Surrey (01344 842201). Virginia Water rail.*

Greyhound racing

Greyhounds chase a dummy hare around the track, and punters place bets on likely-looking dogs between beers. It's great fun for an evening out with friends. All tracks have a bar and restaurant (the quality of food varies).

Catford Stadium *Adenmore Road, SE6 (0181 690 8000). Catford or Catford Bridge rail.* **Admission** £4. **Races** 7.30pm Thur, Sat.

Walthamstow Stadium *Chingford Road, E4 (0181 531 4255). Walthamstow Central tube.* **Admission** £2-£4.50. **Races** 7.30pm Tue, Thur, Sat.

Wembley Stadium *Stadium Way, Wembley, Middx (0181 902 8833). Wembley Park tube/Wembley Stadium rail.* **Admission** £3-£3.50. **Races** 7.30pm Tue, Fri.

Wimbledon Stadium *Plough Lane, SW17 (0181 946 8000). Wimbledon Park tube.* **Admission** £3-£4.50. **Races** 7.30pm Tue, Fri, Sat.

Horse racing

The horse-racing season is roughly divided between flat racing from April to September, and National Hunt racing (jumps) from October to April. Trackside bookies usually accept a minimum stake of £5 on a win-only bet. Bets can also be made with the Tote, which gives no odds until all the bets have been placed, and divides the pool between the winners.

Ascot

High Street, Ascot, Berks (01344 622211). Ascot rail. **Admission** *silver ring* £5; *grandstand* £10-£15; *members* £15-£25.

Big hats invade Ascot in mid-June for the highlight of the racing society calendar, the Royal Meeting, when the Queen drops in for a flutter. Ascot is Britain's premier flat-racing course; the racing is always highly competitive. In 1999 the race will be held from 15-18 June (Ladies' Day is on the 17th); *see also p8.*

Epsom

Epsom Downs, Epsom, Surrey (01372 470047). Tattenham Corner or Epsom Downs rail. **Admission** *enclosure* £5; *grandstand* £10; *club* £16.

The Oaks and the Derby are both run in June at Epsom (4 and 5 June 1999 respectively) – one of the world's oldest and most idiosyncratic flat-racing courses. Epsom is characterised by meandering slopes and a lopsided home straight, but it is still one of the fastest courses in the country. *See also p7.*

Kempton Park

Staines Road East, Sunbury-on-Thames, Surrey (01372 470047). Kempton Park rail. **Admission** *silver ring* £5; *grandstand* £10-£16; *club* £14-£27.

The course holds races throughout the year, and the annual highlight is the King George VI stakes, run on Boxing Day (26 Dec). Facilities include a 400-seater restaurant with views over the racecourse.

Sandown Park

The Racecourse, Portsmouth Road, Esher, Surrey (01372 470047). Esher rail. **Admission** *silver ring* £5; *grandstand* £10-£15; *club* £16-£26 (£10-£13 concs).

Generally deemed to be the best equipped of the London tracks, Sandown's major annual occasions include the Whitbread Gold Cup (24 Apr 1999) and the Coral Eclipse Stakes (3 July 1999).

Windsor

Maidenhead Road, Windsor, Berks (01753 865234). Windsor Central/Windsor & Eton Riverside rail. **Admission** *silver ring* £4; *tattersalls* £10; *club* £15.

Overlooked by Windsor Castle, this course takes advantage of its Thames-side setting with a shuttle boat service operating from the town before and after race meets. The figure-of-eight course, with a head-on view of the last five furlongs, can make it difficult to work out which horse is winning, though in the balmy ambience of the evening, you may not care.

Motor sport

Brands Hatch
Fawkham, Longfield, Kent (0990 125250). Swanley rail.
Car and bike races take place most Sundays throughout the year and, if you fancy a go at Formula First, rally driving or off-roading yourself, then Brands Hatch has racing schools to provide the wherewithal.

Silverstone Circuit
Silverstone, near Towcester, Northants (01327 857271). Northampton rail.
The UK's number one circuit is home to the British Formula 1 Grand Prix (9-11 July in 1999; book early). Ironically, transport to Silverstone is troublesome; you'll need a car and plenty of patience. There are races, including classic cars and Formula 3, from February to November.

Wimbledon Stadium
Plough Lane, SW17 (enquiries 01256 333277). Tooting Broadway or Wimbledon Park tube.
Admission £8; £4 concs.
Bangers, hot-rods and stock-car racing. Sunday evening is the regular night; the season takes a break in June and July.

Rugby league

London Broncos
Stoop Memorial Ground, Langhorn Drive, Twickenham, Middx (0181 410 5000/tickets 0181 410 5005). Twickenham rail.
Owned by Richard Branson's Virgin, the Broncos, London's only rugby league team, hope to break the traditional indifference of the South to the 13-man form of rugby. The Super League season runs from March to September, in order to fit in with the Australian season.

Rugby union

The rugby revolution has brought professional status, extra tournaments and big bucks to a game previously run on gentleman's agreements. Several leading internationals play their club rugby here, most notably the Harlequins, Saracens, Wasps and London Irish. The season runs from September to May; games are played on Saturday afternoons, and sometimes weekdays. Ticket prices can cost anything between £5 and £20.

Clubs
Blackheath *Rectory Field, Charlton Road, SE3 (0181 858 1578). Blackheath rail.*
Harlequins *Stoop Memorial Ground, Langhorn Drive, Twickenham, Middx (0181 410 6000/0839 664414). Twickenham rail.*
London Irish *The Avenue, Sunbury-on-Thames, Surrey (01932 783034). Sunbury rail.*
London Scottish *as Harlequins above. (0181 410 6002). Twickenham rail.*
London Welsh *Old Deer Park, Kew Road, Richmond, Surrey (0181 940 2368). Richmond tube/rail.*
Richmond *Athletic Ground, Kew Foot Road, Richmond, Surrey (0181 940 0397). Richmond tube/rail.*
Rosslyn Park *Upper Richmond Road, Priory Lane, Roehampton, SW15 (0181 876 1879). Barnes rail.*
Saracens *Vicarage Road Stadium, Vicarage Road, Watford, Herts (01923 496009). Watford High Street rail.*
Wasps *Rangers Stadium, South Africa Road, W12 (0181 902 4220). White City tube.*

Twickenham
Rugby House, Rugby Road, Twickenham, Middx (0181 892 8161/box office 0181 744 3111). Twickenham rail.
Twickenham is the home of English rugby, hosting internationals, league games and cup finals. The stadium has been magnificently rebuilt in recent years, raising capacity to 60,000 and making it the country's most impressive modern stadium. Tickets for matches in the Five Nations Championship (Jan-Mar) are distributed via clubs and almost impossible for casual spectators to obtain. Those for cup finals and other matches are easier to come by (phone the box office for details). For the **Museum of Rugby**, *see p123*.

Tennis

All England Lawn Tennis Club
PO Box 98, Church Road, SW19 (0181 944 1066/recorded info 0181 946 2244). Southfields tube or Wimbledon tube/rail.
Gaining admission to the one-they-all-want-to-win remains one of life's less attainable quests. Centre Court and Number One Court seats are allocated by ballot: write (enclosing an SAE) for an application form between 1 September and 31 December. For most people, the outer courts are a more realistic proposition. You'll need hours to spare for the inevitable queueing, but once you're in, the freedom to wander from court to court means you're never far from the action. Take an umbrella, suncream, a sunhat and plenty of cash for the pricey strawberries. Wimbledon is from 21 June-4 July 1999.

Queen's Club
Palliser Road, W14 (0171 385 3421). Barons Court tube.
In June, these west London grass courts host the Stella Artois tournament, featuring most of the stars from the men's circuit as they limber up for the Big One down the road at Wimbledon. Plan ahead, as it's getting increasingly popular with spectators. In 1999 it will be held from 7-13 June.

Major stadiums

Crystal Palace National Sports Centre
Ledrington Road, SE19 (0181 778 0131/9876). Crystal Palace rail.
London's premier athletics stadium hosts a Grand Prix meeting every summer, and the sports centre itself is a venue for a host of events and tournaments including basketball, martial arts, hockey and weightlifting. Following repeated threats of closure, Crystal Palace was reprieved in late 1997. It has since been made a Grade II listed building, and though doubt still persists over its long-term future, it is secure in its present form until at least March 2000.

London Arena
Limeharbour, E14 (box office 0171 538 1212). Crossharbour & London Arena DLR/D8, D9 bus.
In the shadow of Canary Wharf, London Arena provides a modern, comfortable and atmospheric setting for major indoor sports such as boxing and wrestling. Londoners know it best as the home of the hoop-dreaming Leopards.

Wembley Stadium/Wembley Arena
Empire Way, Wembley, Middx (0181 900 1234). Wembley Park tube/Wembley Stadium rail.
Open box office 9am-9pm Mon-Sat; 9am-7pm Sun.
Wembley Stadium (capacity 80,000) hosts many of Britain's greatest sporting occasions. Top football matches, such as the FA Cup Final (*see p7*), are played here (and are normally sold out months in advance). The Rugby League Cup Final (*see p7*), pop concerts and greyhound racing (*see p262*) are also staged here. The indoor Wembley Arena accommodates major snooker, gymnastics, equestrian, tennis, ice hockey, boxing and basketball events.

Theatre

There are big musicals, there are tiny pub productions – and there's a lot of good stuff in between.

The London theatre scene is a swirling vortex of eddies and currents between the Scylla and Charybdis of the West End and the Fringe. They will swallow up the imprudent punter as easily and indifferently as they swallow up productions and performers themselves. The following is a guide on how to navigate these treacherous waters.

'**West End**' refers to the part of central London lying to the west of the City, but it also refers to the cultural status of theatres (the **Royal National Theatre**, for example, is classified as West End even though it is located south of the river). However, West End theatres are concentrated in the geographical West End and are most famous for musicals and commercial theatre. Musicals can be divided into three categories: oldies, middle-agers and newies. Some of the oldies from the 1970s – *Cats*, for example – are beginning to look a little mangy, but others, like *Starlight Express*, have had bionic overhauls. Middle-aged musicals from the 1980s such as *Les Misérables* and *Miss Saigon* are in better shape, but aren't as fresh as the more recent 1990s arrivals like *Chicago*.

West End drama is usually pretty reliable whether new work or revivals. Plays like *Art, An Inspector Calls* and *The Woman in Black* are relatively sophisticated, as are those that enjoyed shorter tenures in 1998 such as Patrick Marber's *Closer*, Conor McPherson's *The Weir* and Mark Ravenhill's *Shopping & Fucking*. Many of these plays originated from the major repertory companies.

The most reliable of these rep companies are building-based and include the **Royal National Theatre**, with three stages in the South Bank Centre producing all manner of drama; the **Royal Shakespeare Company**, with two theatres in the **Barbican** (during the winter months), focusing largely, but not exclusively, on Shakespeare; and **Shakespeare's Globe**, which has settled down as more than just a heritage gimmick. **Royal Court**, meanwhile, is the country's most dynamic new writing theatre, and is due to return to its Sloane Square home in autumn 1999, while Peter Hall's adventurous repertory company is looking to return to the prestigious **Old Vic** after a successful interlude at the Piccadilly Theatre.

Taking its cue from the New York classification of 'Off Broadway', '**Off-West End**' refers to the next rung down in terms of financial means and it is this section that generally provides the best mix of both quality and originality. These theatres are usually heavily subsidised, paying minimum wages or, in some cases, no wages at all. Top writers, directors and actors are lured instead by the prospect of artistic liberty. But even these places have their own pecking order with wealthier theatres like the **Donmar Warehouse** and the **Almeida** drawing names as big as Nicole Kidman and Kevin Spacey. Theatres like **The Gate** and the **King's Head** are often dependent on fresh-out-of-drama-college hopefuls who are prepared to work for nothing.

'**The Fringe**', meanwhile, is scattered all over London – it is a theatrical underclass where the risk of getting artistically mugged is all too high. There is, of course, a lot of good work to be found, and many of the biggest names in British theatre cut (and in some cases broke) their teeth here. But finding such shows is, in truth, a complete lottery. Leading the way are theatres such as **The Finborough**, struggling in adverse financial circumstances to develop bold artistic policies – a fuller list follows at the end of this section.

Finally, it is the nature of theatre that it changes capriciously, much like the British weather, and from week to week reputations rise and fall like the front-of-stage curtains. To keep abreast of developments, *Time Out* magazine, with full, up-to-date listings and reviews, is indispensable.

INFORMATION & TICKETS

Tickets for West End musicals can be the most difficult to obtain and are easily the most expensive at £10-£35 a pop. In association with many theatre box offices, **Ticketmaster** (0171 344 4444) and **First Call** (0171 420 0000) provide advance tickets, but watch out for those big bad booking fees, which can bump up the price up by ten per cent or more. The cheapest option is to buy your tickets in person with cash direct from the theatre.

Note that in the listings below, the hours given in brackets after the phone number are the times that bookings are taken over the phone. If no hours are specified here, then the phone line is open the same hours as the box office.

Theatre tokens are available from branches of WH Smith, John Menzies, Books etc, Hammicks and James Thin Booksellers (in Scotland) or by phone on 0171 240 8800 or e-mail from theatretokens@solttma.co.uk. They are accepted at over 180 theatres nationwide.

Half-Price Ticket Booth

The Clocktower Building, Leicester Square Gardens,
Leicester Square, WC2 (no phone). Leicester Square or
Piccadilly Circus tube. **Open** noon-6.30pm Mon-Sat; noon-
3.30pm Sun. **Tickets** for some shows half-price plus £2
service charge (£1.25 on tickets under £12.50). **Map 8 K7**
Run by the Society of London Theatres, this has a limited
number of tickets for West End shows on the day of performance at half-price (cash only) on a first-come, first-
served basis (there are plans to make more tickets available,
including those for some of the most popular shows at 25%
discount). Tickets are restricted to four per person and you
cannot return tickets to the booth (though the theatre itself
may sometimes accept returns). Beware of touts trying to
flog tickets while you queue and make sure you are queueing at the right booth and not one of the other (more expensive) ticket outlets in Leicester Square. A list of theatres
using the standby scheme is available from SOLT, 32 Rose
Street, WC2 (0171 557 6700).

Building-based repertory companies

The Peter Hall Company

After a highly successful sojourn in the West End's
Piccadilly Theatre, this boldly traditional repertory company, run by one of the elder statesmen of British theatre, is
intending to return to its original camp in the **Old Vic** (on
The Cut, close to Waterloo Station) in autumn 1999, funding
permitting. Former home of the National Theatre, the Old
Vic has an illustrious history and it is to be hoped the company can return with its imaginative programme of new and
classical work featuring big names such as Dame Judi Dench.

Royal Court Theatre (English Stage Company)

(Reopening autumn 1999). Sloane Square, SW1 (0171
565 5000; 10am-6pm Mon-Sat). Sloane Square tube.
Box office 10am-performance time Mon-Sat. **Tickets**
10p-£25; £5 all tickets Mon. **Credit** AmEx, MC, £TC, V.
Map 7 G11
The Royal Court has long been the undisputed epicentre of
new writing in this country, having fostered such names
as John Osborne, Christopher Hampton, Howard Barker,
Caryl Churchill and Mark Ravenhill. Like the National
Theatre, the Court is in a period of transition, having been
moved from its long-time Sloane Square home while it
undergoes a £25-million refurbishment (due to be completed autumn 1999) and a change of artistic directors.
Its two spaces, 'Upstairs' (small studio theatre) and
'Downstairs' (proscenium arch main stage), which previously occupied the same building, are now divided between
two West End theatres: the **Ambassadors** ('Upstairs') and
the **Duke of York** ('Downstairs'). Not only this, Stephen
Daldry, the artistic director who oversaw this move and
transformed the theatre's image from worthily intelligent
and middle-aged to youthful and dynamic, is moving on to
pastures new. The indubitably competent Ian Rickson
takes his place.

Royal National Theatre

South Bank, SE1 (box office 0171 452 3000/info 0171
452 3400). Waterloo tube/rail. **Box office** 10am-8pm
Mon-Sat. **Tickets** *Olivier & Lyttelton* £8-£27; *Cottesloe*
£12, £18. **Credit** AmEx, MC, V. **Map 8 M7**
The captaincy of the UK's theatrical flagship recently
passed from the innovative and imaginative Richard Eyre
to the able, populist ex-RSC and West End musical maestro
Trevor Nunn. Nunn's production of the musical *Oklahoma!*
is set to run in the West End in 1999 and he has continued
to build on the diversity that characterised Eyre's tenure,
mixing in the expressionistic (Théâtre de Complicité), the

innovative (Robert Lepage) and the contemporary (Terry
Johnson) to accompany its diet of stalwart classics. The concrete mausoleum of the RNT contains three theatres: the
Olivier's large, open platform for big shows, the Lyttelton's
traditional and focused proscenium arch, and the Cottesloe's
flexible studio-like space accommodating smaller, more cutting-edge shows. In 1999, watch out for an Alan Ayckbourn
adaptation of Ostrovsky's *The Forest* starring Frances De
La Tour, Robert Lepage's *Geometry of Miracles* and a Hanif
Kureishi play *Sleep with Me*. There will also be 'platform'
events analysing 'the 100 most important English plays of
the twentieth century' in the run up to the millennium.

Royal Shakespeare Company

Barbican Centre, Silk Street, EC2 (info 0171 638
4141/box office 0171 638 8891). Barbican tube/
Moorgate tube/rail. **Box office** 9am-8pm daily.
Tickets £6-£24. **Credit** AmEx, MC, £TC, V. **Map 9 P5**
The RSC is the principal custodian of Shakespeare's rich
legacy and, between national tours, it divides its time
between its main home in Stratford-upon-Avon where it has
three theatres (**Royal Shakespeare Theatre**, the **Swan**
and **The Other Place**; *see p278*), the Barbican's two theatres (the huge **Barbican Theatre** and the more intimate
space of **The Pit**) and now also the **Young Vic** in Waterloo
(*see below*). There has of late been a trend for heritage-
industry and sponsorship-friendly productions, but there is
no question that the RSC has nurtured some fine acting and
directing talents like Ralph Fiennes and Deborah Warner.
The RSC also puts on works by new and classical writers
of relevance to the Bard, as well as running a sideline in
money-spinning musicals like *Les Misérables*. Highlights
for 1999 include a new production of *Measure for Measure*,
an adaptation of *The Lion, the Witch and the Wardrobe* and
a touring production of *Richard III* with Robert Lindsay,
which is due to finish in the West End.

Shakespeare's Globe

New Globe Walk, SE1 (0171 401 9919). Blackfriars tube or
London Bridge tube/rail. **Box office** 10am-6pm Mon-Sat.
Tickets £5-£20. **Credit** AmEx, MC, £TC, V. **Map 11 O7**
Under the guidance of actor Mark Rylance, this fascinating
venue has established itself as a thinking person's tourist
trap staging plays from May to September. The artistic standard of works by Shakespeare and his contemporaries is
reasonably strong, but the theatre is dominated by its status as an open-air replica of Shakespeare's original Globe.
With all the background noise of the modern day and tran-
sient interest of coach parties, the theatre is no great friend
of artistic nuance. However, the venue provides interesting
insights into how Shakespeare dealt with mob dynamics
and the productions are nothing if not fun. Plans for 1999
include four plays in rep, at least two of which will be by
Shakespeare. The Inigo Jones Theatre, a replica Jacobean
indoor playhouse that will stage plays in winter, is due to
open in 2000. *See also p33.*

Long-runners & musicals

Most theatres have evening shows Monday to
Saturday (starting 7.30-8pm) and matinées on one
weekday (usually Wednesday), Saturday and
sometimes Sunday. Phone the theatres for details.

An Inspector Calls

Garrick Theatre, 2 Charing Cross Road, WC2
(0171 494 5085; 24 hours daily). Leicester Square tube.
Box office 10am-8pm Mon-Sat. **Tickets** £10-£27.50.
Credit AmEx, JCB, MC, V. **Map 8 K7**
Stephen Daldry's much-lauded production of JB Priestley's
previously stale old repertory warhorse is rediscovered as
an expressionist psychological and social parable.

Annie

Victoria Palace Theatre, Victoria Street, SW1 (0171 834 1317). Victoria tube/rail. **Box office** 10am-6pm Mon; 10am-8.30pm Tue-Sat; noon-4.30pm Sun. **Tickets** £12.50-£32.50; from £7.50 children. **Credit** AmEx, JCB, MC, V. **Map 7 J10**
Weepie about a little orphan girl saved by a billionaire bachelor that, by all accounts, will melt the hardest of hearts.

Art

Wyndhams Theatre, Charing Cross Road, WC2 (0171 369 1736; 9am-9pm daily). Leicester Square tube. **Box office** 10am-6pm Mon-8pm Tue-Sat. **Tickets** £9.50-£25. **Credit** AmEx, DC, MC, V. **Map 8 K7**
Yasmina Reza's lightweight satire of three middle-class men's friendship blown apart when one of them buys an overpriced painting has top actors falling over themselves for a part and punters falling over themselves for tickets.

Beauty & The Beast

Dominion Theatre, Tottenham Court Road, W1 (0171 656 1888; 8.30am-10pm daily). Tottenham Court Road tube. **Box office** 10am-7.30pm Mon-Sat. **Tickets** £18.50-£35. **Credit** AmEx, DC, MC, V. **Map 6 K5**
London's most expensively produced musical, based on the famous fairytale, leaves nothing to the imagination and parades panto-like sets.

Blood Brothers

Phoenix Theatre, Charing Cross Road, WC2 (0171 369 1733; 9am-9pm Mon-Sat, 10am-6pm Sun). Leicester Square or Tottenham Court Road tube. **Box office** 10am-7.45pm Mon-Sat. **Tickets** £11.50-£32.50. **Credit** AmEx, DC, MC, V. **Map 6 K6**
Willy *'Educating Rita'* Russell's grand, ambitious melodrama, filled with sentiment and toe-tapping songs, is beginning to feel its age after ten-plus years in the West End.

Buddy

Strand Theatre, Aldwych, WC2 (0171 930 8800; 10am-8pm Mon-Sat, 12.30-4pm Sun). Charing Cross tube/rail. **Box office** 10am-6pm Mon; 10am-8pm Tue-Sat; 12.30-4pm Sun. **Tickets** £10-£30 (half-price Fri matinée). **Credit** MC, V. **Map 6 M6**
A jolly, nostalgic review of the songs that made Buddy Holly world-famous before his untimely death in an air crash.

Cats

New London Theatre, Drury Lane, WC2 (0171 405 0072). Covent Garden or Holborn tube. **Box office** 10am-7.45pm Mon-Sat. **Tickets** £10-£35. **Credit** AmEx, DC, MC, V. **Map 6 L6**
Based on TS Eliot's *Old Possum's Book of Practical Cats*, Andrew Lloyd Webber's patchwork show is London's longest-running musical ever and is showing the strain.

Chicago

Adelphi Theatre, Strand, WC2 (Ticketmaster 0171 344 0055; 24 hours daily). Charing Cross tube/rail. **Box office** 10am-8pm Mon-Sat. **Tickets** £16-£36. **Credit** AmEx, MC, V. **Map 8 L7**
Well-praised cabaret and dance satire of Al Capone's Chicago. A film version of the show is in the pipeline.

Complete Works of William Shakespeare/Complete History of America (both abridged)

Criterion Theatre, Jermyn Street, W1 (0171 369 1737; 9am-9pm Mon-Sat, 10am-6pm Sun). Piccadilly Circus tube. **Box office** 10am-8pm Tue-Sat; 10am-4pm Sun. **Tickets** £10-£25. **Credit** AmEx, DC, MC, V. **Map 7 J7**

American iconoclasts of Shakespeare's oeuvre and their own national history started as a fringe comedy act, but a few years down the line their jokes are wearing rather thin.

Doctor Dolittle

London Apollo, Queen Caroline Street, W6 (0870 606 3400; 8.30am-9.30pm daily). Hammersmith tube. **Box office** 10am-6pm Mon-Sat. **Tickets** £15-£32.50. **Credit** AmEx, MC, V.
Omni-smiling children's TV presenter Philip Schofield talks to the impressively electronically animated animals.

Grease

Cambridge Theatre, Earlham Street, WC2 (0171 494 5040; 24 hours daily). Covent Garden/Leicester Square tube. **Box office** 10am-7.30pm Mon-Sat. **Tickets** £12.50-£30. **Credit** AmEx, MC, V. **Map 6 L6**
This coach-party favourite, taken from the movie about courtship in 1950s America, has a gushy heart the size of a Cadillac engine.

Les Misérables

Palace Theatre, Shaftesbury Avenue, W1 (0171 434 0909; 24 hours daily). Leicester Square tube. **Box office** 10am-8pm Mon-Sat. **Tickets** £8.50-£35. **Credit** AmEx, DC, MC, V. **Map 6 K6**
Boublil and Schonberg's 13-year-old RSC money-spinner idealises the struggle between paupers and villains in Victor Hugo's revolutionary Paris.

Miss Saigon

Drury Lane Theatre, Catherine Street, WC2 (0171 494 5000; 24 hours daily). Covent Garden tube. **Box office** 10am-8pm Mon-Sat. **Tickets** £5.75-£35. **Credit** AmEx, MC, £TC, V. **Map 6 K6**
Boublil and Schonberg again in a spectacular plundering of the Madame Butterfly story set in Vietnam and featuring a real helicopter on stage.

The Mousetrap

St Martin's Theatre, West Street, WC2 (0171 836 1443). Leicester Square tube. **Box office** 10am-8.30pm Mon-Sat. **Tickets** £10-£24.50. **Credit** AmEx, MC, V. **Map 6 K6**
Agatha Christie's absurdly long-running murder mystery is camped up to the max to keep it alive.

Phantom of the Opera

Her Majesty's Theatre, Haymarket, SW1 (0171 494 5000/5400; 24 hours daily). Piccadilly Circus tube. **Box office** 10am-6pm Mon-Sat. **Tickets** £10-£35. **Credit** AmEx, MC, V. **Map 8 K7**
Lloyd Webber's world-famous non-autobiographical musical about the hideous theatre-goer who becomes obsessed with a beautiful opera singer.

Rent

Shaftesbury Theatre, 210 Shaftesbury Avenue, WC2 (07000 211221/0171 344 4444; 24 hours daily). Piccadilly Circus tube. **Box office** 10am-7.45pm Mon-Sat. **Tickets** £12.50-£35. **Credit** AmEx, DC, MC, V. **Map 8 K7**
Jonathan Larson's international musical celebrates a community of young East Villagers, as they struggle with the soaring hopes and tough realities of today's New York.

Saturday Night Fever

London Palladium, Argyll Street, W1 (0171 494 5020; 24 hours daily). Oxford Circus tube. **Box office** 10am-8pm Mon-Sat. **Tickets** £10-£35. **Credit** AmEx, MC, V. **Map 5 J6**
Heavy-handed revival of the Travolta classic jumping aboard the '70s revival gravy train.

Starlight Express

Apollo Victoria Theatre, Wilton Road, SW1 (0171 416 6070; 8am-10pm daily). Victoria tube/rail.
Box office 10am-8pm Mon-Sat. **Tickets** £12.50-£30.
Credit AmEx, MC, V. **Map 7 H10**
Revamped Lloyd Webber musical depending less on the music than the spectacle of the cast flying round on rollerblades impersonating trains.

West Side Story

Prince of Wales Theatre, Coventry Street, W1 (0171 839 5972; 24 hours daily). Leicester Square or Piccadilly Circus tube. **Box office** 10am-7pm Mon-Sat. **Tickets** £18.50-£35. **Credit** AmEx, DC, MC, V. **Map 8 K7**
Fortieth anniversary production of the renowned New York musical.

Whistle Down the Wind

Aldwych Theatre, The Aldwych, WC2 (0171 416 6003; 8.30am-10pm Mon-Fri, 8.30am-9pm Sat, 10am-8pm Sun). Covent Garden tube. **Box office** 10am-8pm Mon-Sat. **Tickets** £10-£35. **Credit** AmEx, DC, MC, V.
Map 8 M6
Lloyd Webber's '50s-set musical about an adolescent girl and a runaway killer has been critically deplored – but it's booking way ahead just the same.

The Woman in Black

Fortune Theatre, Russell Street, WC2 (0171 836 2238). Covent Garden tube. **Box office** 10am-8pm Mon-Sat. **Tickets** £8.50-£23.50. **Credit** AmEx, DC, JCB, MC, V.
Map 6 L6
Susan Hill's ghost story performed by just two actors has become a West End spine-chilling potboiler.

Off-West End

Almeida

Almeida Street, N1 (0171 359 4404; 24 hours daily). Angel tube/Highbury & Islington tube/rail.
Box office 9.30am-6pm Mon-Sat. **Tickets** £6.50-£19.50. **Credit** AmEx, DC, MC, V. **Map 9 O1**
For ten years now actor-directors Ian McDiarmid and Jonathan Kent have maintained a steady flow of lively, highbrow drama involving top actors and writers. Such is their success they have developed a semi-permanent West End ancilliary for stars as big as Juliette Binoche and Kevin Spacey. The 1999 programme includes Cate Blanchett appearing in the old David Hare play *Plenty*.

BAC

Lavender Hill, SW11 (0171 223 2223; 10.30am-7pm Mon-Sat, 4-7pm Sun). Clapham Junction rail/77, 77A, 345 bus. **Box office** 10.30am-6pm Mon; 10.30am-9pm Tue-Sat; 4-7pm Sun. **Tickets** £4-£12.50; 'pay what you can' Tue. **Credit** MC, V.
Situated in a crusty Victorian town hall, BAC (Battersea Arts Centre) has been turned around under the tenacious directorship of Tom Morris and has earned its self-appointed oxymoronic pseudonym 'National Theatre of the Fringe'. It contains three theatres (main house and two studios), carrying much of the capital's best fringe while promoting a lot of physical, experimental and visual theatre. Look out in particular for the 'I Wish I'd Seen That' season, giving a second chance to catch the best of the previous year's fringe shows, and also the Festival of Visual Theatre.

The Bush

Shepherd's Bush Green, W12 (0181 743 3388; 10am-7pm Mon-Sat). Goldhawk Road or Shepherd's Bush tube. **Box office** 6-8pm Mon-Fri; 7-8pm Sat. **Tickets** £7-£10. **Credit** MC, V.
This is the second most important venue for new writing in

Scary hair 'n' flares: **Saturday Night Fever**.

London and perhaps even England, after the Royal Court. Dedicated to new plays, often by first-time writers, The Bush is the springboard for many young writers into the bigger theatres (such as the gab-gifted Conor McPherson, writer of the Irish film *I Went Down*) or television soap opera. Seating is on a large squidgy bank so the best seats are at the back where you won't get anyone's knees rammed in your head.

Donmar Warehouse

Thomas Neal's, Earlham Street, WC2 (0171 369 1732; 9am-9pm Mon-Sat, 10am-6pm Sun). Covent Garden tube. **Box office** 10am-8pm Mon-Sat. **Credit** AmEx, DC, MC, V. **Map 6 L6**
Under the artistic direction of Sam Mendes, the Donmar Warehouse has continued to put out a combination of old and new plays, visiting and in-house shows produced to a very high standard and pitched to West End prices. One of the big successes of 1998 was Nicole 'theatrical Viagra' Kidman in *The Blue Room*, capping the vogue for Hollywood stars walking the West End boards.

Drill Hall

16 Chenies Street, WC1 (0171 637 8270; 11am-7pm Mon-Sat, 11am-6pm Sun). Goodge Street tube. **Box office** 10am-7.30pm Mon-Fri; 12.30-7.30pm Sat. **Tickets** £6-£10. **Credit** AmEx, MC, V. **Map 6 K5**
London's biggest, loudest and liveliest gay and lesbian theatre stages its own work and shows from all over the world while keeping the flag of resistance flying in an increasingly apathetic political climate. Monday evenings are women-only from 6pm and Thursday is no-smoking day, but this is not a hostile or separatist venue. There's a popular vegetarian café in the basement.

The Gate

The Prince Albert, 11 Pembridge Road, W11 (0171 229 0706). Notting Hill Gate tube. **Box office** 10am-6pm Mon-Fri. **Tickets** £6-£12. **Credit** MC, V. **Map 1 A7**

The days when the former Royal Court director Stephen Daldry forged this theatre's national reputation are long gone, but the Gate still has an estimable reputation for producing high-quality, low-budget world drama (past and present) on a shoestring, now under Mick Gordon's direction. One of its other hallmarks is radical set designs. Young actors and directors sell loved ones down the river to work here for nothing.

Hampstead Theatre

Avenue Road, NW3 (0171 722 9301). Swiss Cottage tube. **Box office** 10am-7.30pm Mon-Sat. **Tickets** £9-£16. **Credit** MC, V.

Not really in Hampstead, and housed in what looks like a reinforced caravan on the Swiss Cottage roundabout, but do not be deceived: the Hampstead Theatre under the artistic direction of Jenny Topper is revered for promoting contemporary drama. The programme for 1999 features *Perfect Days* by Liz Lochhead, *Snake* by Rona Monroe, *Celine* by Matt Parker and *Falling* by David Eldridge.

King's Head

115 Upper Street, N1 (0171 226 1916). Angel tube/ Highbury & Islington tube/rail. **Box office** 10am-8pm Mon-Sat; 10am-4pm Sun. **Tickets** £4-£12. **Credit** MC, V. **Map 9 O1**

As the proprietors never tire of telling you, this is London's oldest pub theatre, and they are forever launching appeals for its maintenance. However, far from showing signs of wear, this quintessential Islington venue will probably survive the apocalypse with its variable diet of small-scale musicals and revues in the evening (preceded by optional, cheap and cheerful school dinners) as well as its lunchtime plays (short shows taken with burger and chips). The unspoilt pub's late licence (midnight) and impromptu musical evenings make it a busy all-round winner.

Lyric

King Street, W6 (0181 741 2311; 10am-7pm Mon-Sat). Hammersmith tube. **Box office** 10am-8pm Mon-Sat. **Tickets** £5-£18. **Credit** AmEx, DC, MC, V.

The Lyric, although not strictly a producing house, has established a serious reputation for more alternative mainstream work, often with a gay slant, under the directorship of Neil Bartlett. Other productions on the large proscenium main stage tend to feature major touring companies, while the studio space is usually taken by smaller-scale touring productions, but always by companies with good track records. Bartlett will be collaborating with the RSC in 1999 on Marivaux's *La Dispute*.

Open Air Theatre

Regent's Park, NW1 (0171 486 2431/1933). Baker Street tube. **Repertory season** May-Sept, phone for details. **Tickets** £8-£22. **Credit** AmEx, DC, MC, V. **Map 5 G3**

A well-equipped theatre with a buffet bar and barbecue in a leafy Regent's Park bower, this is a delightful venue for watching plays in the summer months. Usually very popular (and not just with tourists), the company has a robust reputation – although its productions are at the mercy of the fickle English weather, it is remarkable how few of the mixed repertory shows are cancelled. You can always count on a couple of alfresco Shakespeares, one musical and a family show as well as Sunday concerts.

Theatre-going on the cheap

1. The **Half-Price Ticket Booth** in Leicester Square has discounted tickets for most West End shows. These are sold on a first-come, first-served basis (cash only). *See page 265.*

2. Matinée performances are much cheaper than evenings, although, in some instances, understudies replace stars. Seats for Monday to Thursday evening performances in the West End are cheaper than Friday or Saturday nights.

3. Pay for a restricted-view seat in the stalls (not all theatres have them), then quietly slip into a better seat when the lights go down. Of course, this won't work if the auditorium is full or the ticket-holder of the seat to which you've moved turns up late.

4. The cheapest seats are usually in the 'gods' at the top of the theatre, but visibility can become faint – especially if vertigo sets in.

5. Buy tickets direct (in person or by phone) from the theatre's box office to save on insidious 'booking fees' – a parasitic blight sweeping the world of entertainment.

6. Go to previews of West End and Off-West End shows. Tickets are considerably cheaper and, despite the melodramatic assertions of highly strung luvvies, there's usually no difference between a preview and the 'real' thing: a turkey's a turkey no matter how long it's cooked.

7. The **Royal National Theatre** sells a number of the cheapest tickets (£10, £12) for shows on the day from 10am at the box office: 40 tickets at the Olivier, 40 at the Lyttleton and 20 at the Cottesloe. Queues start as early as 8am for popular shows.

8. Some theatres have reduced-price nights. For example, the **BAC** has a 'pay what you can' night on Tuesdays, the **Royal Court** has some standing tickets for as little as 10p, while all tickets on a Monday are £5, and the **Theatre Royal Stratford East** has the lowest concessionary rates around for the unwaged, students and pensioners. Also, it's always worth scanning the Society of London Theatres' information website for details of periodic deals (www.officallondontheatre.co.uk).

9. Look out for occasional special offers in *Time Out*'s weekly magazine.

Orange Tree

1 Clarence Street, Richmond, Surrey (0181 940 3633).
Richmond tube/rail. **Box office** 10am-7pm Mon-Sat.
Tickets £5-£14.50. **Credit** MC, V.
This small, smart bearpit of a venue has been flourishing under the directorship of Sam Walters and his prescribed Richmond diet of closely directed costume drama in the round with little or no set. It's not exactly ground-breaking, but is high quality and attracts big names.

Riverside Studios

Crisp Road, W6 (0181 237 1111/1000; 24 hours daily).
Hammersmith tube. **Box office** noon-7pm Mon-Sat.
Tickets £6-£10. **Credit** MC, V.
With one hangar-like space and one studio, the Riverside boasts a repertory cinema and its own gallery while hosting a commendable range of international travelling theatre, dance and larger-scale domestic works, usually with an avant-garde tilt. Watch out for Declan Donellan's production of Corneille's *Le Cid* as part of the **French Theatre Season** as well as the hit-and-miss **New Play Festival** in the spring, the **Sitcom Festival** in the summer and **Dance Umbrella** *(see p233)* in the autumn.

Tricycle

269 Kilburn High Road, NW6 (0171 328 1000).
Kilburn tube. **Box office** 10am-8pm Mon-Sat.
Tickets £8-£13.50. **Credit** MC, V.
A smaller-scale West London rival to Stratford East's Theatre Royal, the Tricycle specialises in high-quality Black and Irish drama, musical and revue aimed at its local population, but also receives shows by major touring companies like Shared Experience. Under the directorship of Nicholas Kent, the theatre maintains a strong identity as well as one of Kilburn's more agreeable bars with its own art gallery. Highlights for 1999 include *Inner City*, a musical by the Black Theatre Co-op and a production by South African satirist Pieter-Dirk Uys.

Young Vic

66 The Cut, SE1 (0171 928 6363). Waterloo tube/rail.
Box office 10am-7pm Mon-Sat. **Tickets** £6-£20.
Credit MC, V. **Map 11 N8**
Artistic director Tim Supple has turned around the fortunes of this theatre standing in the shadow of the venerable Old Vic, making it an altogether more thrusting venue with a not inconsiderably proportioned studio space and a large main house playing host to touring companies as big as the Royal Shakespeare Company. Plays for 1999 include an RSC production of Stephen Poliakof's *Talk of the City* and *Bartholomew Fair* by Ben Jonson. There will also be a production of *Hamlet* by the Plymouth Theatre Royal.

The Fringe

Check out the venues below to sample the best of London's ever-active fringe.

The Bridewell *Bride Lane, off Fleet Street, EC4*
(0171 936 3456). Blackfriars tube/rail.
Box office 10.30am-6pm Mon; 10.30am-8pm Tue-Sat; noon-4pm Sun. **Map 11 N6**
A good-sized theatre with a decent mixture of musicals and new works, often produced by national theatre companies.

Chelsea Centre *King's Road, SW10 (0171 352 1967).*
Sloane Square tube then 11, 22, 211 bus/Earl's Court tube then 31 bus. **Box office** 7pm-11pm Mon-Sat.
Map 3 C13
This large, versatile but rather underexploited space is set for fuller artistic exploitation in the future thanks to Lottery funding.

Etcetera Theatre *Oxford Arms, 265 Camden High Street, NW1 (0171 482 4857). Camden Town tube.*
Box office 10am-8pm Tue-Sun.
Classic tiny pub theatre with a perenially lively programme of works by ambitious young theatre folk. Two different shows a night (phone for details).

The Finborough *Finborough Arms, Finborough Road, SW10 (0171 373 3842). West Brompton/Earl's Court tube.* **Box office** 11am-8pm Mon-Sat. **Map 3 B12**
Pub venue run by the ever-resourceful Steam Industry and nurturing new writing, some of which has gone on to theatres like the Royal Court.

Grace Theatre *Latchmere Pub, 503 Battersea Park Road, SW11 (0171 223 3549). Clapham Junction rail.*
Box office 9am-11pm daily.
Burgeoning, ambitious venue trying to raise its profile with a thrusting programme.

Man in the Moon *392 King's Road, SW3 (0171 351 2876/5701). Sloane Square tube then 11, 19, 22, 319 bus/South Kensington tube then 49, 345 bus.* **Box office** 1-11pm Mon-Fri; 6-11pm Sat, Sun. **Map 4 D12**
Oblong theatre receiving a variable but often spirited quality of work. Two different shows a night (7.30pm & 9.30pm).

New End Theatre *27 New End, NW3 (0171 794 0022). Hampstead tube.* **Box office** 2-7pm daily.
Small, very Hampstead theatre staging very Hampstead plays: faintly risqué but basically conventional and tailored for affluent locals.

Old Red Lion *St John Street, EC1 (0171 837 7816). Angel tube.* **Box office** 10am-11pm daily. **Map 9 N3**
One of the London fringe's oldest and most respected venues for new writing, located over an always-busy bar.

Oval House *52-54 Kennington Oval, SE11 (0171 582 7680). Oval tube.* **Box office** 3-9pm Thur-Sun.
London's second gay and lesbian venue after the Drill Hall has two theatres hosting work often by respected, subsidised companies.

Pentameters *Three Horseshoes Pub, 28 Heath Street, NW3 (0171 435 3648). Hampstead tube.*
Box office *telephone bookings* 24 hours daily.
Another very Hampstead venue, but a little more eccentric and adventurous than the New End Theatre *(see above)*. Famous alumni include Harold Pinter.

Pleasance *Carpenters Mews, off North Road, N7 (0171 609 1800). Caledonian Road tube.*
Box office 10am-6pm daily.
This offshoot of one of the Edinburgh Fringe Festival's most successful venues is a large, commercially ambitious fringe venue with generally sound productions.

The Room *above Orange Tree Pub, 1 Clarence Street, Richmond (0181 940 3633). Richmond tube/rail.*
Box office 10am-7pm Mon-Sat.
Small sibling to the Orange Tree next door, The Room is seeking to arrange a programme of lively, varied work.

Southwark Playhouse *63 Southwark Bridge Road, SE1 (0171 620 3494). Borough tube/35, 40, 133, 344, bus.* **Box office** 11am-7.30pm Mon-Sat. **Map 11 P8**
Small, isolated but thrusting venue with grand ambitions.

Warehouse Theatre *Dingwall Road, Croydon (0181 680 4060). East Croydon rail.* **Box office** 10am-6pm Mon; 10am-8.30pm Tue; 10am-10pm Wed-Sat; 3-7pm Sun.
Alternative, suburban theatre (with a little more emphasis on suburban than alternative) funded for its mix of conventional and unconventional new work.

White Bear *138 Kennington Park Road, SE11 (0171 793 9193). Kennington tube.* **Box office** 10am-6pm Mon-Sat; noon-6pm Sun.
Occupying the back room of a seedy bar, this can be fringe theatre at its most depressing, but it can also rise to adventurous and original heights.

Trips Out of Town

Trips Out of Town

Take a break – make the great escape.

Myriad though the thrills of the big city are, there comes a time when we all need to escape the traffic, the noise, the pollution and the crush. Many visitors (and most Londoners) are unaware of the attractions lurking outside the M25 – and how easily accessible they are.

Planning a trip

The best place to start is at the new **British Visitor Centre** (*see below*), which opened in 1998. Here you can get guidebooks, free leaflets and advice on any destination in the UK and Ireland, you can book rail, bus, air or car travel, reserve tours, theatre tickets and accommodation; there's even a bureau de change, a branch of Thomas Cook, a ticket agency and a bookshop.

British Travel Centre

1 Regent Street, SW1 (no phone). Piccadilly Circus tube. **Open** *June-Sept* 9am-6.30pm Mon-Fri; 9am-5pm Sat; 10am-4pm Sun; *Oct-May* 9am-6.30pm Mon-Fri; 10am-4pm Sat, Sun. **Credit** AmEx, MC, V. **Map 8 K7**
Personal callers only.

Getting there

Most of the places of interest we list in this chapter are within an hour and a half's rail journey of London (although some will then require a further bus or taxi ride). In the listings for each destination, we include the approximate train (and, where appropriate, coach) journey time.

By train

To find out train times and ticket prices, call National Rail Enquiries on **0345 484950**. (If you want to reserve your tickets in advance by credit card, ask the operators on the above line for the appropriate number.) Always make sure you ask about the cheapest ticket for the journey you are planning. The **rail travel centres** in all of London's mainline stations (as well as in Heathrow and Gatwick airports and the British Travel Centre) will also be able to help with timetable information and ticket booking. The train journey times we give in the listings below are the fastest available.

London mainline rail stations

Charing Cross *Strand, WC2.* **Map 8 L7**
For trains to and from south-east England (including Dover, Folkestone and Ramsgate).

Euston *Euston Road, NW1.* **Map 6 K3**

For trains to and from the north and north-west of England, and a suburban line to Watford (via Kilburn).

King's Cross *Euston Road & York Way, N1.* **Map 6 L2**
For trains to and from the north and north-east of England and Scotland, and suburban lines to north London and Hertfordshire.

Liverpool Street *Liverpool Street, EC2.* **Map 10 R5**
For trains to and from the east coast (including Harwich) and Stansted Airport; also trains to East Anglia and suburban services to east and north-east London.

Paddington *Praed Street, W2.* **Map 2 D5**
For trains to and from the south-west, west, south Wales and the Midlands.

Victoria *Terminus Place, SW1.* **Map 7 H10**
For fast trains to and from the Channel ports (Folkestone, Dover, Newhaven); also trains to and from Gatwick Airport, plus suburban services to south and south-east London.

Waterloo *York Road, SE1.* **Map 8 M8**
For fast trains to and from the south and south-west of England (Portsmouth, Southampton, Dorset, Devon), plus suburban services to south-west London.

By coach

Coach and bus travel is almost always cheaper than rail travel, and almost always slower. **National Express** (0990 808080) runs routes to most parts of the country; its coaches depart from Victoria Coach Station on Buckingham Palace Road, five minutes' walk from Victoria rail and tube stations. **Green Line** buses (0181 668 7261) operate within an approximate 40-mile (64-km) radius of London. Their main departure point is Eccleston Bridge, SW1 (Colonnades Coach Station, behind Victoria Station).

Victoria Coach Station

164 Buckingham Palace Road, SW1 (0171 730 3466). Victoria tube/rail. **Map 7 H11**
Britain's most comprehensive coach company **National Express** (0990 808080) – which runs services to destinations all over England, Scotland and Wales – and **Eurolines** (01582 404511) – which travels to the Continent – are based at Victoria Coach Station. There are many other companies operating to and from London (some departing from Marble Arch). *See also p301.*

By car

If you are in a group of three or four, it may be cheaper (and more flexible) to hire a car (*see page 304*). And if you plan to take in several sights within an area, then this is probably the only realistic way of getting around. The road directions given in the listings below should be used in conjunction with a map. (Note that, for example, 'J13 off M11' means 'come off the M11 motorway at junction 13'.)

How this chapter is arranged

This chapter has been split into nine broad categories: **Town & city breaks**, **Castles**, **Country houses**, **Family attractions**, **Gardens**, **Homes of the famous**, **Life on the ocean wave**, **Out in the country** and **Seaside**.

Opening times & admission prices

For main entries below we include full details of opening times, admission and transport details, but be aware that these can change without notice. If you are planning a trip around one particular sight **always phone first to check that it is open**. Many attractions close down during the winter (typically between November and March inclusive), although major sights are open year round. We supply phone numbers for sights listed within entries; again, phone first to find out opening times. In the 'Where to stay' sections, the accommodation prices listed are the range for a double room. Note that credit cards are only accepted where specified.

Town & city breaks

Bath

Bath is a stunner; a sleek, immaculately groomed supermodel of a city. With its slender Georgian streets, tanned stone, beautifully proportioned curves and voluptuously hilly situation it puts most of frumpy, flyblown Britain to shame. It's no surprise that this is the only city in Britain with the distinction of being a World Heritage Site.

The Romans, realising the curative powers of the local hot springs, called the city Aquae Sulis. For centuries, the Roman baths were buried under medieval buildings but were rediscovered in the eighteenth and nineteenth centuries. The **Roman Baths Museum** (01225 477785) offers an excellent acoustiguide tour of what are the most impressive non-military Roman remains in Britain – made all the more evocative by the fact that the waters still bubble up from the earth here (250,000 gallons a day at 46.5°C), just as they did 2,000 years ago. You can taste the waters in the adjoining **Pump Room** (immortalised by Jane Austen), but a pot of Earl Grey might go down better.

Overlooking the baths is **Bath Abbey**, a fifteenth-century rebuilding of an earlier Norman structure, itself built on the site of a Saxon church where Edgar, the first king of a united England, was crowned in 973. It's a beautifully light, harmonious building, boasting some fine fan vaulting and stained glass.

Bath has close on 20 museums, most of them excellent. These include **The Building of Bath Museum** on Lansdown Road (01225 333895), the highlight of which is a spectacular model of the city, and, in Bennett Street, the **Museum of East Asian Art** (01225 464640), which contains a fine collection of Chinese jade carvings. Opposite, in the grand **Assembly Rooms** (once the social focus of Georgian high society in Bath), there's the renowned **Museum of Costume** (01225 477789), illustrating high society togs since the late sixteenth century. The **American Museum** (01225 460503) at Claverton Manor, which offers a fascinating series of reconstructed seventeenth- to nineteenth-century American domestic interiors, is well worth the short trip out of town (bus 18).

But Bath's greatest attraction is simply its streets, the grandest of which is the much-photographed **Royal Crescent**, a breathtaking sweep of 30 houses designed by John Wood the Younger (1767-75). **No.1 Royal Crescent** (01225 428126) is furnished in authentic period style with a fully restored Georgian garden and is open to the public. Nearby is the magnificent **Circus**, which was designed by the elder John Wood and completed by his son, composed of three crescents forming a circle. In terms of its exquisite proportions (its diameter is exactly that of Stonehenge) and architectural detail, it's an even finer creation than Royal Crescent. Stand in the middle and try out the powerful echo.

Not all of Bath's streets are so imposing – there are also plenty of narrow alleyways, particularly in the area to the north of Abbey Churchyard, an open space popular with street entertainers. There is plenty of good shopping too, centred around Milsom, Union and Stall streets and Southgate.

The **River Avon** adds greatly to the appeal of the city and is spanned by **Pulteney Bridge**, an Italianate masterpiece by Robert Adam, which recalls the bridges of Florence and Venice. There are walks beside the river and the adjacent Kennet and Avon Canal. Boats may be hired in summer from the Boating Station on Forester Road.

Further information

Getting there *by train* from Paddington (1 hour 15 mins); *by coach* National Express (3 hours 20 mins); *by car* J18 off M4 then A46, use park 'n' rides to get into the centre.

Where to stay *Haydon House* (01225 444919/427351; £60-£80) offers superior B&B and splendid breakfasts, five minutes' drive from the centre. If you want to stay on Bath's most famous street, the grand but discreet *Royal Crescent* (01225 823333; £222-£727) will oblige – for a hefty price. More affordable is *Paradise House* (01225 317723; £65-£110), with its lovely walled gardens, and quiet, secluded *Cranleigh* (01225 310197; £68-£75).

Eating & drinking *Sally Lunn's Refreshment House & Museum* (01225 461634) in North Parade Passage is the oldest house in Bath and you can sample the famous buns made fashionable by Sally Lunn in the 1680s. The best of Bath's many restaurants are the long-serving *Hole in the Wall* at 16 George Street (01225 425242), the *Moon & Sixpence* wine bar/bistro at 6A Broad Street (01225 460962), the fine French fare of *Clos du Roy*, next to the Theatre Royal (01225 444450) and the classy, cosy *Moody Goose* (01225 466688) on Kingsmead Square.

Popular pubs include the *Coeur de Lion* in Northumberland Place, the *Boater* on Argyle Street (by the river) and the *Saracen's Head* on Broad Street.

Tourist Information Centre *Abbey Chambers, Abbey Churchyard (01225 477101).* **Open** Oct-Apr 9.30am-5pm Mon-Sat; 10am-4pm Sun; *May-Sept* 9.30am-6pm Mon-Sat; 10am-4pm Sun.

Brighton

The stunning sight of the **Royal Pavilion** alone is worth a ticket from London – especially at night when it is magically illuminated. Its bizarre blend of architectural styles – Indian, Chinese, Gothic – was conceived by John Nash in 1823 for the Prince Regent (later George IV), and it stands in gardens that have been restored to their original Georgian condition. The adjacent **Brighton Museum & Art Gallery** (01273 290900) is home to a good crop of twentieth-century and ethnic art and artefacts.

Brighton has much else to offer the visitor. The English Channel for a start: it may be freezing cold most of the year and the beach steep and pebbly rather than sandy, but it's still the sea. The gaudy **Palace Pier** is packed with archetypal seaside attractions – slot machines, funfair, fish and chips. On a clear day you can gaze west from the top of the helter skelter to the Isle of Wight, or along the shore to the derelict West Pier (currently undergoing restoration) and genteel Hove.

Between the piers, beachfront arches house cafés, bars and clubs – notably the **Zap** (01273 202407) and **Honey** (01273 202807) clubs. Contrast these with the neighbouring **Brighton Fishing Museum** and crafts shops or the **Sea Life Centre** (01273 604234).

When the sea loses its fascination, lose yourself in **The Lanes**, a warren of antique and specialist shops punctuated by pubs and cafés, between West Street and the Old Steine. If these prove too expensive, cross North Street and explore the vibrant **North Laine** area for vintage clothing, street fashion, records, kitsch and cafés of every kind, or visit the **Duke of York's** (01273 626261) at Preston Circus, quite possibly the cosiest independent cinema in the UK.

However, there's more to Brighton than sea, sights and shops. More and more people come (and return) here for the atmosphere – an eclectic cocktail of traditional seaside resort and liberal lifestyles. Brighton will embrace anyone – as the town's large gay community, anarchists, artists, eccentrics and celebs will testify.

Further information

Getting there *by train* from Victoria (from 50 mins), or from King's Cross (1 hour 10 mins); *by coach* National Express (1 hour 50 mins); *by car* M23 then A23.
Where to stay *The Adelaide* (01273 205286) is old, four-star and mid-priced (£65-82); the *Twenty One* (01273 686450) offers a friendly welcome and a tasty

breakfast for £54-£95; while *Marina House* (01273 605349) does B&B from around £40.
Where to eat & drink For food, try the enticing anglo-asian dishes at the unpromisingly sited *Black Chapati* (12 Circus Parade, New England Road; 01273 699011), north of the rail station, or the inspired vegetarian café *Terre à Terre* at 71 East Street (01273 729051). *The Dorset* on Gardener Street (01273 605423) is a relaxed café, bar and restaurant. Drink in *The Cricketers*, 15 Black Lion Street or the *Regency Tavern*, Russell Square, modelled loosely on the Royal Pavilion. The Lanes are lined with pubs.

Events Second only to Edinburgh, the Brighton Festival (01273 292951) fills the first three weeks of May with theatre, comedy, art, music and literature. On Sundays throughout the year Madeira Drive on the seafront hosts diverse events – notably the London to Brighton Bike Ride in June and the London to Brighton Veteran Car Run in November. Monthly listings guides *Impact* and *The List* are available from newsagents, or find out what's going down by tuning in to Surf 107FM (6.30-7pm Mon-Fri). For gay listings, see the monthly *G Scene* or visit Scene 22 (129 St James Street; 01273 626682).

Tourist Information Centres *10 Bartholomew Square (01273 292599).* **Open** 9am-5pm Mon-Fri; 10am-5pm Sat; 10am-4pm Sun. *Hove Town Hall, Church Road, Hove (01273 292589).* **Open** 9am-5pm Mon, Tue, Thur-Fri; 10am-5pm Wed.

Cambridge

The university has dominated life in Cambridge since the fourteenth century. The oldest college is **Peterhouse** on Trumpington Street, endowed in 1284. The original hall still survives, though most of the present buildings are nineteenth century. Just up the road is **Corpus Christi**, founded in 1352. Its Old Court dates from that time and is linked by a gallery to the eleventh-century **St Bene't's Church**, the oldest building in town. Just across the road is fifteenth-century **Queens'**. Most of the original buildings survive and the inner courts are wonderfully picturesque.

Next to Queens' is, logically enough, **King's**, founded by Henry VI in 1441, and renowned for its **chapel** (1446-1515). Considered one of the greatest Gothic buildings in Europe, the chapel's interior, containing its original stained glass, is breathtaking. Famous King's alumni include EM Forster, Rupert Brooke and John Maynard Keynes. To the north is **Trinity**, founded in 1336 by Edward III and refounded by Henry VIII in 1546. The apple tree outside the gate is a direct descendant of the one that dropped its fruit on Sir Isaac Newton's head to such inspirational effect. A fine collection of Tudor buildings surrounds the Great Court where, legend has it, Lord Byron used to bathe naked in the fountain with his pet bear (the university would not allow him to keep a dog). Wittgenstein studied and taught at Trinity; the library where he occasionally worked, designed by Wren, is open to visitors for two hours after lunch each day. Further on, at the corner of Bridge Street and St John's Street, you'll find the **Round Church** (the oldest of the four remaining round

*Two sides of the annual artsy **Brighton Festival**. See page 286.*

churches in England) and now also the home of the **Cambridge Brass Rubbing Centre**.

Behind the main group of colleges is **The Backs**, a series of beautiful meadows, some still grazed by cows, bordering the willow-shaded **River Cam**, which is spanned by several fine footbridges. It's a perfect spot for summer strolling or you can hire a punt and drift lazily along the river.

The city also has its non-collegiate attractions: visit the **Fitzwilliam Museum** on Trumpington Street (01223 332900) for its outstanding collections of antiquities and Old Masters; climb the tower of **Great St Mary's Church** on King's Parade for far-reaching views; take a short walk to the **Scott Polar Research Institute** (01223 336540) in Lensfield Road; admire the **Botanical Gardens** (01223 336265) in Bateman Street; or simply wander along the charming streets. Unsurprisingly, Cambridge is an excellent place to buy books – new, second-hand and antiquarian.

Further information

Getting there *by train* from King's Cross (50 mins); *by coach* National Express (1 hour 50 mins); *by car* J11 or J12 off M11.

Where to stay Cambridge is short on characterful accommodation. Two decent options are *Arundel House* (01223 367701; £62-£89) at 53 Chesterton Road, a fine early Victorian terrace overlooking the Cam, and *De Freville House* (01223 354993; £50-£55) at 166 Chesterton Road.

Where to eat & drink Sup a jar in the comfy, well-worn *Eagle* on St Bene't Street or the rowing-mad (no-smoking) *Free Press* on Prospect Row, which also offers decent lunchtime food. For posh nosh, try the quality

*Stereotypical, but still typical, images of sedate **Cambridge**.*

The Duke of Marlborough's prize for beating the Frenchies: **Blenheim Palace**. *See p281.*

French cooking at *Midsummer House* (01223 369299) on Midsummer Common or the global cuisine at *22 Chesterton Road* (01223 351880).

Tourist Information Centre *The Old Library, Wheeler Street (01223 322640).* **Open** *Nov-Mar* 10am-5.30pm Mon-Fri; 10am-5pm Sat; *Apr-Oct* 10am-6pm Mon-Fri; 10am-5pm Sat; *Easter-Sept* also 11am-4pm Sun.

Canterbury

When St Augustine converted King Ethelbert to Christianity in 597, Canterbury became the cradle of English Christianity: long stretches of its medieval walls still stand and the magnificent **cathedral**, with its superb stained glass, stone vaulting and vast Norman crypt, is now the Mother Church of Anglicans worldwide. A plaque near the altar marks the spot where Archbishop Thomas à Becket was murdered in 1170 by four overzealous knights who had overheard King Henry II moaning, 'Will no one rid me of this turbulent priest?' Becket's tomb has been a site of pilgrimage ever since. **Trinity Chapel** contains the site of the original shrine plus the tombs of Henry IV and the Black Prince.

The small city centre can become overcrowded in summer but still retains its charm. **Eastbridge (St Thomas's) Hospital**, on the High Street, dates from the twelfth century and contains a medieval mural, sundry antique treasures and a crypt; there are the remains of a Roman townhouse and mosaic floor at the **Roman Museum** on Butchery Lane (01227 785575); and the **Royal Museum** (01227 452747), The Beaney, High Street, covers the history of the area. **King's School** is where Elizabethan playwright Christopher Marlowe, author of *Dr Faustus*, was educated. **Canterbury Heritage** (01227 452747), at the medieval poor Priest's Hospital, offers a journey through the city's past, as does **Canterbury Tales** (01227 454888) in St Margaret's Street. The latter is an animated 'darkride' interpretation of Chaucer's *The Canterbury Tales*, complete with fourteenth-century sounds and smells.

Further information

Getting there *by train* from Victoria to Canterbury East (1 hour 20 mins), or from Charing Cross to Canterbury West (1 hour 30 mins); *by coach* National Express (1 hour 50 mins); *by car* A2 then M2 and A2.

Where to stay Try the 600-year-old *Falstaff* (01227 462138; £85-£95) on St Dunstan's Street or the flower-strewn B&B *Magnolia House* (01227 765121; £68-£95) at 36 St Dunstan's Terrace.

Where to eat & drink The *Falstaff* (*see above*) is one of the most characterful pubs in town. *Cate's Brasserie*

Broadway in the **Cotswolds**. *See page 285.*

Discover the villages of London and their famous country houses

KENWOOD HOUSE, HAMPSTEAD. *An Old Master painting collection, including Rembrandt, Vermeer and Gainsborough in a unique setting on Hampstead Heath.*

RANGER'S HOUSE BLACKHEATH. *Home to the magnificent Suffolk collection of Jacobean portraits.*

MARBLE HILL HOUSE, TWICKENHAM. *The pretty Thames-side home of Henrietta Howard, mistress of King George II*

CHISWICK HOUSE & GARDENS, CHISWICK. *A stunning villa set in splendid Italianate gardens.*

DOWN HOUSE: HOME OF CHARLES DARWIN DOWNE, NR ORPINGTON. *See Darwin's Study where he wrote his world-famous 'On the Origin of Species'.* Tickets must be prebooked on 0870 603 0145

For information on travel details, opening hours and admission prices, guided tours and special events call Customer Services on 0171 973 3434.

ENGLISH HERITAGE

(01227 456655) on Church Street is good for an informal meal, or, for something posher, try *Sully's* (01227 766266) in the County Hotel on the High Street or the accomplished French cooking at *La Bonne Cuisine* (01227 450551) in the Canterbury Hotel at 71 New Dover Road. Canterbury is stuffed with tea rooms and coffee shops.

Tourist Information Centre *34 St Margaret's Street (01227 766567).* **Open** *Apr-Dec* 9.30am-5.30pm daily; 10am-4pm Sun; *Jan-Mar* 9.30am-5pm Mon-Sat.

Oxford

Founded by the Saxons, Oxford began its development in the early eighth century around a priory established by St Frideswide on the site where Christ Church now stands. Its slow but steady growth in importance and influence received the royal seal of approval when Henry I built his Palace of Beaumont there in the early twelfth century, at much the same time as the first students were beginning to gather. Their numbers were boosted in 1167 when Paris University was closed to the English, and by the end of the century Oxford was firmly established as England's first university town. Today, the university comprises a federation of 41 independent colleges and halls, mostly occupying the sort of buildings that lend substance to Oxford's claim to be 'one of the great architectural centres of the world'.

Most are usually open to the public, and a shortlist of the finest includes **Christ Church**, with its famous Tom Tower, and a chapel so grand that it serves as Oxford's cathedral. Nearby **Merton**, founded in 1264, boasts a marvellous medieval library and garden, but **University College** was Oxford's first college, endowed in 1249. **Magdalen** (pronounced 'mórd-lin') is often said to be the loveliest college. Its extensive grounds include a deer park and a meadow where the rare snakeshead fritillary still blooms every April.

Other centres of academia in Oxford include the **Ashmolean Museum** (01865 278000) in Beaumont Street, and the **Bodleian Library** off Broad Street, begun in 1598. The elegant **Radcliffe Camera** is England's earliest example of a round reading room (1737). You can see, hear and smell the history of academe at **The Oxford Story** (01865 790055) on Broad Street, a popular animatronic 'dark-ride' giving a one-hour introduction to the university's history.

But Oxford is as much town as gown, and there's more to see than centres of learning. The **Museum of Modern Art** (01865 722733) in Pembroke Street has established an international reputation for its pioneering exhibitions of contemporary and twentieth-century work. At another extreme, the **Pitt Rivers Museum of Archaeology & Anthropology** (01865 270949) is a remarkable Victorian pile crammed with one of the strangest collections of ancient ethnic artefacts in the world.

Little Clarendon Street and the recent development at Gloucester Green offer some interesting specialist shops. Best of all is the classy **Covered Market**, linking High Street and Market Street. Opened in 1774, it's a foodie's delight. If shopping for antiques, you should investigate Park End Street between the bus and railway stations.

The countryside pushes green fingers into the heart of the town, with the **Oxford Canal**, the **River Thames** (sometimes called the Isis, from the Latin 'Thamesis') and the **Cherwell** (pronounced 'Chár-well') providing opportunities for strolling and punting. For the classic view of Matthew Arnold's 'dreaming spires' you must climb Boar's Hill three miles to the south-west.

Further information

Getting there *by train* from Paddington (1 hour), then use your rail ticket for a free ride into the centre on one of Oxford's pioneering electric buses (every ten mins); *by coach* frequent, cheap, fast services from several London departure points; details from National Express (1 hour 40 mins), Stage Coach (01865 727000) and Oxford Bus Company (01865 785400); *by car* J8 off M40 then A40; use the park 'n' rides.

Where to stay The *Norham Guesthouse* (01865 515352; £54) at 16 Norham Road offers reliable B&B within 15 minutes' walk of the centre. The ever-popular seventeenth-century *Old Parsonage* (01865 310210; £145-£160) at 1 Banbury Road is a more upmarket alternative, with a good bar and food.

Where to eat & drink Oxford is well supplied with taverns – the busy sixteenth-century *King's Arms* at 40 Holywell Street can be overwhelmed by students but has good beer and decent pub grub, or try the *Eagle & Child*, favoured watering hole of CS Lewis and JRR Tolkien. Of the restaurants, there's upmarket fare in somewhat basic surroundings at the riverside *Cherwell Boat House* (01865 552746) off Bardwell Road, classy French/fusion cooking at the fine *Bath Place* (01865 791812) off Holywell Street and Raymond Blanc's swish, metropolitan brasserie *Le Petit Blanc* (01865 510999) at 71-72 Walton Street.

Tourist Information Centre *The Old School, Gloucester Green (01865 726871).* **Open** 9.30am-5pm Mon-Sat; *May-Sept* 10am-3.30pm Sun, public hols.

Salisbury & Stonehenge

In its first incarnation Salisbury was an Iron Age hill fort, subsequently taken over by the Romans, the Saxons and finally the Normans. The latter called it Sarum and built a castle and cathedral, but the site at Old Sarum, still worth a visit for its impressive ruins, wasn't big enough for both to co-exist happily and in 1220 the bishop embarked on the building of a new cathedral two miles to the south. The settlement that grew up around it became New Sarum, now Salisbury.

The **cathedral** (01722 555120) took only 38 years to complete, so it's unusually consistent in style, except for the spire, the tallest in Britain, which was added in 1334. The cathedral library contains one of only four original copies of the Magna Carta (1215) and, in the north aisle, you can see the country's oldest working clock (1386). Cathedral Close is a haven of peace lined with beautiful houses and lawns to soothe the eye. Many of the houses are thirteenth century but with Georgian façades. Two of the finest are **Malmesbury House** (01722 327027) and **Mompesson House** (01722 335659), both of which are open to the public, while the **Salisbury & South Wiltshire Museum** (01722 332151), in the King's House, is one of the country's most enjoyable local museums.

The town centre is a jumble of jettied, gabled, timber-framed buildings overhanging narrow streets. Names such as Butcher Row, Fish Row and Poultry Cross hint at Salisbury's true character as a regional trading centre; it really comes alive on market days (Tuesdays and Saturdays), as it has for the past 400 years.

For all its considerable charms, it seems that most visitors to Salisbury are just stopping off on their way to **Stonehenge**, a World Heritage Site about ten miles (16km) to the north, near Amesbury. Why it was built we don't know, and never will. How it was built is staggering enough. Construction began around 3000 BC and continued intermittently over a period of 1,500 years. The stones were transported over land and water (from Pembrokeshire and the Marlborough Downs) using sledges and rafts. It has been estimated that each of the largest stones would have required 500 men to pull the sledge, and 100 more to lay rollers in front of it. What remains today is only a small part of the original complex. Stonehenge is only one of more than 500 known prehistoric sites in an area of just ten square miles (26sq km).

Officially sanctioned vandalism has surrounded the monument with roads, car parks, facilities and fencing. There is talk of re-routing the road system. In the meantime, visitors have to work hard to conjure up the appropriate atmosphere.

Further information

Getting there *by train* from Waterloo to Salisbury (1 hour 90 mins); *by coach* National Express (2 hours 45 mins); *by car* J8 off M3 then A303 and A338; *local buses* Wilts & Dorset (01722 336855) is the main operator and runs daily services to Stonehenge from Salisbury bus and rail stations.

Where to stay The *Old Mill at Harnham* (01722 327517; £70-£90) offers comfy rooms in a great location, while the cheaper *Old Bakery* (01722 320100; £34-£44) has more basic rooms in a sixteenth-century building.

Where to eat & drink The fourteenth-century *Haunch of Venison*, on Minster Street, is the oldest tavern in town, and serves decent food; the *King's Arms* on St John Street isn't much younger; while the *New Inn* is also anything but new and puts on a good spread.

Tourist Information Centre *Fish Row, Salisbury (01722 334956)*. **Open** Oct-Apr 9.30am-5pm Mon-Sat; *May* 9.30am-5pm Mon-Sat; 10.30am-4.30pm Sun; *June, Sept* 9.30am-6pm Mon-Sat; 10.30am-4.30pm Sun; *July, Aug* 9.30am-7pm Mon-Sat; 10.30am-5pm Sun.

Stratford-upon-Avon

Shakespeare was born in Stratford in 1564, and died there in 1616. His birthplace soon became a place of literary pilgrimage. Top of the list for vis-

itors are the Shakespeare properties, five picturesque Tudor houses that function as museums and are worth visiting in their own right. There are three in the town centre: **Shakespeare's Birthplace** (01789 204016), on Henley Street; **Hall's Croft** (01789 292107), home of his daughter Susanna, on Old Town; and **Nash's House** (01789 292325), on Chapel Street, which belonged to the first husband of his granddaughter. Its garden contains the foundations of **New Place**, Shakespeare's last home, demolished in 1759.

A mile and a half away at Shottery, and accessible from Stratford by public footpath, is **Anne Hathaway's Cottage** (01789 292100), where Shakespeare's wife lived before her marriage. The girlhood home of his mother, **Mary Arden's House** (01789 293455), is at Wilmcote, a pleasant 3½-mile (5½-km) stroll along the towpath of the Stratford Canal. Both may also be reached by bus, and there are trains to Wilmcote.

Shakespeare was educated at **Stratford Grammar School**, which you can see on Church Street, and he was buried in **Holy Trinity Church**, which has a fine riverside setting and supposedly the playwright's tomb (the whereabouts of his body are disputed). The dramatist's most meaningful memorials are his plays, and the **Royal Shakespeare Theatre** is the place to see them (tickets sell out fast though). The adjoining **Swan Theatre** stages a variety of classics, while **The Other Place** is for modern and experimental work. For bookings call 01789 295623. If you can't get a ticket, make do with a backstage tour or a visit to the **RSC Collection**, a museum of props and costumes.

Relief from all things Shakespearian is easily achieved. Stratford has been a market town since 1169 and, in a way, that's still what it does best. See it on a Friday, when the awnings go up over the stalls at the top of Wood Street, and locals flock in from the outlying villages. And wander round the town centre, which still maintains its medieval grid pattern. Many fine old buildings survive, among them **Harvard House** on the High Street, dating from 1596. It was the home of Katharine Rogers who married Robert Harvard of London. It was their son John who founded Harvard University.

The town's charms are enhanced by the presence of the **River Avon** and the **Stratford Canal**. The canal basin is usually crammed with narrowboats and there are walks beside both waterways.

Further information

Getting there *by train* from Paddington (2 hours 10 mins); *by coach* National Express (2 hours 45 mins) or Guide Friday (01789 294466) from Euston; *by car* J15 off M40 then A46.

Where to stay The pick of the many B&Bs is *Caterham House* (01789 267309; £68-£72) at 58 Rother Street, close to the Royal Shakespeare Theatre. Another good choice is *Victoria Spa Lodge* (01789 267985; £55-£60) on Bishopton Lane.

Where to eat & drink Drink with the thespians at the *Dirty Duck* (aka the *Black Swan*) on Waterside, or the heavily beamed *Garrick* on the High Street. Among the many eating options is the excellent bistro fare at *The Opposition* (01789 269980) on Sheep Street.

Tourist Information Centre *Bridgefoot (01789 293127).* **Open** *Apr-Oct* 9am-6pm Mon-Sat; 11am-5pm Sun; *Nov-Mar* 9am-5pm Mon-Sat.

Castles

Arundel

West Sussex. **Getting there** *by train* from Victoria (1 hour 30 mins); *by car* A24 then A280 and A27. **Open** *1 Apr-30 Oct* noon-5pm Mon-Fri, Sun (last admission 4pm). **Admission** £6.20; £4.20 5s-15s; £5.70 OAPs; £18 family.

Arundel's picturesque hilltop setting inevitably draws in summer crowds, but the medieval settlement remains one of the region's most charming and least spoiled towns. The major sight is the castle, home of the Dukes of Norfolk since the sixteenth century. The original castle was Norman, but it has been rebuilt many times, most recently in the nineteenth century. There's plenty to see inside, including the imposing Barons Hall and some good paintings by Van Dyck and Holbein. Don't miss the unusual Fitzalan Chapel in the grounds. It contains the tombs of past Dukes (the leading Catholic family in post-Reformation England) and is separated from the altar of the main (Anglican) church of St Nicholas by a glass screen and an iron grille – it paid to be discreet about your Catholicism in those days.

Arundel also has its own neo-Gothic nineteenth-century cathedral, more impressive outside than in, plus some agreeable shopping streets and a handful of decent alehouses – try the busy *Eagle* on Tarrant Street.

Five miles (8km) north-east of Arundel is **Parham**, a near-perfect Elizabethan house in a near-perfect English country setting, beneath the South Downs (01903 744888). A couple of miles west of Parham are the evocative remains of a Roman villa at **Bignor** (01798 869259), site of the longest surviving extent of mosaic pavement in the country.

Bodiam

near Robertsbridge, East Sussex (01580 830436).
Getting there *by train* Charing Cross to Robertsbridge (1 hour 15 mins), then 10-min taxi journey; *by car* J5 off M25 then A21. **Open** *13 Feb-1 Nov* 10am-6pm (last admission 5pm) Tue-Sun; *2 Nov-3 Jan* 10am-4pm Tue-Sun (last admission 3pm). **Admission** £3.50; £1.75 child; £8.75 family. **Credit** AmEx, MC, V.

All that remains of fourteenth-century Bodiam Castle is its shell, yet this is one of southern England's most evocative castles. It's great fun exploring the ruins with its turreted tower, thick walls, moat and drawbridge. At the beginning of the twentieth century the castle was a favourite excursion for society in search of the picturesque and it retains a romantic appeal. The surrounding countryside is also a treat.

Hever

Hever, Edenbridge, Kent (01732 865224).
Getting there *by train* Victoria to Edenbridge (1 hour), then 5-min taxi journey, or Victoria to Hever (1 hour), then 1-mile walk; *by car* J5 off M25 then B2042 and B269 or J6 off M25 then A22, A25 and B269. **Open** *1 Mar-30 Nov* noon-6pm (last admission 5pm) daily; *1 Dec-28 Feb* noon-4pm daily. **Admission** £7.30; £4 child; £6.20 OAPs; £18.60 family; *garden only* £5.80; £3.80 5s-16s; £4.90 OAPs; £15.40 family. **Credit** MC, V.

Eight miles (13km) north-west of Tunbridge Wells, in the magnificent gardens of this enchanting, double-moated, thirteenth-century castle, Henry VIII is said to have courted Anne Boleyn. The ill-fated queen certainly spent much of her childhood here. More recently, the American millionaire William Waldorf Astor bought the estate (in 1903) and

spent a huge amount of time, money and effort in restoring the place. The grounds now boast splendid Italianate gardens with loggia, classical sculpture and a colonnaded piazza, as well as a large lake and rose garden. Hever's newest attraction, a water maze, invites bravehearts to reach a folly in the middle of large pond, by means of stepping stone paths, while avoiding water obstacles made by jets of water.

Leeds

Maidstone, Kent (01622 765400). **Getting there** *by train* Victoria to Bearsted (1 hour), then 10-min bus transfer; *by car* J8 off M20. **Open** *Mar-Oct* 10am-5pm daily; *Nov-Feb* 10am-3pm daily. **Admission** £9.30; £6-£7.30 concs; £25 family; *park & gardens only* £7.30; £4.50-£5.80 concs; £20 family. **Credit** MC, V.

Leeds Castle, five miles (8km) east of Maidstone, is stunningly sited on two small islands in the midst of a lake. Built by the Normans nearly 900 years ago, it was converted into a royal palace by Henry VIII and now contains a mishmash of medieval furnishings, paintings, tapestries and, bizarrely, the world's finest collection of antique dog collars. The castle's greatest attractions, however, are external. Apart from the flower-filled gardens, there's the Culpeper Garden (an outsize cottage garden), an aviary containing over 100 rare bird species and, best of the lot, the maze, which centres on a spectacular underground grotto adorned with stone mythical beasts and shell mosaics. Facilities for disabled visitors are good (a leaflet is available in advance). Special events are held throughout the year (phone for details). The combined train journey, transfer and entrance ticket (book at Victoria Station) is the best deal going; £19.20 adult, £8.35 child.

Six miles (10km) from Leeds Castle (and a mile north of Maidstone) is the excellent **Museum of Kent Life, Cobtree** (01622 763936) at Sandling, an award-winning open-air re-creation of ye olde Kent complete with an oast house, hop gardens, an eighteenth-century farmhouse, hop-pickers' huts, working craftspeople and an adventure playground. The **North Downs Way** (*see p287*) is also within easy reach of Leeds Castle.

Lewes

East Sussex (01273 486290). **Getting there** *by train* Victoria to Lewes (1 hour); *by car* M23 then A23 and A27. **Open** 10am-5.30pm Mon-Sat; 11am-5.30pm Sun. **Admission** £3.50; £1.80-£3 concs; £10 family. **Credit** MC, V.

Nearby **Lewes**, worth a visit in its own right, is blessed with a handsome town centre and a fine setting amid the South Downs. There are splendid views of the countryside from the towers of the ruined eleventh-century **castle**. The admission price includes the **Barbican House Museum** (same hours), a distinctly superior town museum, opposite the castle entrance. Also worth a look is Tudor **Anne of Cleves House** (01273 474610). Henry VIII's queen was given the house as part of her divorce settlement, although she never lived there. The oak-beamed bedroom is stunning. Lewes' **Bonfire Night** celebrations (5 Nov) are famed, not only because of their scale and extravagance, but also because they commemorate the 17 Protestants burned here in 1556 as part of Mary I's crackdown on the new religion, rather than Guy Fawkes' 1605 plot to blow up James I and Parliament (*see p10*).

Rochester

The Lodge, Rochester, Kent (01634 402276). **Getting there** *by train* from Victoria (45 mins); *by road* A2. **Open** *1 Apr-1 Nov* 10am-6pm daily; *2 Nov-31 Mar* 10am-4pm daily. **Admission** £3.50; £2.50 concs. **Credit** MC, V.

Rochester, Chatham and Gillingham form an almost continuous urban sprawl known as the Medway Towns. The hilly setting is lovely; the towns themselves are, in the main, distressingly ugly. Yet this is an area rich in history.

*A defender's-eye view of **Lewes** from the castle. See page 279.*

Rochester's biggest draw is its castle. Commanding a wide bend on the River Medway, the vast keep of Rochester, built in the late eleventh century by the architect of the White Tower in London, is one of the finest Norman castles in the country. Its early history was particularly lively, including occupation by Wat Tyler and his ragged-trousered forces in the Peasants' Revolt of 1381.

The castle dominates the town, and overlooks the small but beautiful cathedral. Also Norman in origin, it has been much altered over the centuries, but retains some splendid early paintings. Charles Dickens spent his youth in Rochester and, although he was not overly impressed with the place, it appeared in a number of his works (variously disguised as 'Mudfog' and 'Dullborough'); his last, unfinished novel *The Mystery of Edwin Drood* was set here. The entertaining **Charles Dickens Centre** in Eastgate House on the High Street is well worth a look (01634 844176). The **Guildhall Museum**, making the most of the area's rich history, is also worth visiting (01634 848717). **Gad's Hill Place** at Higham (3 miles/5km from Rochester; 01474 822366) is where Dickens lived from 1857 until his death in 1870 and has been evocatively preserved.

Windsor

Windsor (01753 868286). **Getting there** *by train* Paddington to Slough, then change for Windsor Central (45 mins); Waterloo to Windsor Riverside (1 hour); *by car* J6 off M4. **Open** *Mar-Oct* 10am-5.30pm (last entry 4pm), *Nov-Feb* 10am-4pm, daily (last admission 3pm). **Admission** £10 adults; £5-£7.50 concs; £22.50 family. **Credit** AmEx, MC, £TC, V.

The largest castle in England squats bulkily above the Thames near Slough. There has been a royal home here since William the Conqueror built the first fortifications in 1070 to protect the western approaches to London, although the modern edifice is a hotchpotch thrown up by various monarchs' fancies down the ages. George V liked the place so much that he changed his family name in 1918 to Windsor (Saxe-Coburg-Gotha being none too popular during a war against Germany). Not to be missed is **Queen Mary's Dolls' House**, designed by Edward Lutyens and built over three years by 1,500 craftsmen. Even the toilets flush. The **State Apartments** have reopened following the 1992 fire. The Perpendicular Gothic **St George's Chapel** is where Henry VIII is buried. There are other royal tombs inside – as well as the most beautiful roof you may ever see.

Country houses

Althorp

Althorp, near Northampton (24-hour booking 01604 592020). **Getting there** *by train* Euston to Northampton (1 hour-1 hour 20 mins) then coach link (4 times per day) or 20-min taxi ride; *by car* J16 off M1 then A45 and A428. **Open** *1 July-30 Aug* 9am-5pm daily (4pm last admission). **Admission** (tickets only available in advance by phone) £9.50; £5-£7 concs. **Credit** MC, V.

Althorp (pronounced, don't ask why, 'orlthrup') has been the Spencer family home since 1508. The house is nothing special, although it does contain some decent paintings, but nobody will be coming to Althorp for the house. On an island in the middle of the Round Oval lake, designed by André Le Nôtre, the man behind the gardens at Versailles, lie the mortal remains of **Diana, Princess of Wales**. During July and August visitors can see (but not stand on) the island, the lakeside temple that has been dedicated to Diana, the house itself and an exhibition in the splendid 1730s Stable Block commemorating the Princess's life and work. There's also a restaurant and a shop selling 'a select range of goods inspired by Diana but not cheapening her memory in any way'. Note that entry is only by pre-booked ticket, and you should book as far in advance as possible – tickets in 1998 were snapped up almost as soon as they left the presses. Be warned: if you arrive without a ticket you'll be turned away.
Website: www.althorp.com

Audley End

Saffron Walden, Essex (01799 522399). **Getting there** *by train* Liverpool Street to Audley End (1 hour) then 1-mile walk or 2-min taxi ride; *by car* J8 off M11 then B1383. **Open** *1 Apr-30 Sept* 11am-6pm Wed-Sun (last admission 5pm); *1 Oct-1 Nov* 10am-3pm Wed-Sun. **Admission** £6; £3 child; £4.50 concs; £15 family; *grounds only* £4; £2 child; £3 concs; £10 family. **Credit** MC, V.

The magnificent Jacobean mansion of **Audley End** was the largest house in the country when it was built for Thomas Howard, 1st Earl of Suffolk, in 1614. It was later owned by Charles II, but given back to the Howards in the eighteenth century, who demolished two-thirds of it to make the place more manageable. More than 30 rooms are open to the public today, many of which have been restored to Robert Adam's 1760s designs. Capability Brown landscaped the grounds. Phone if you want to book a guided tour.

Saffron Walden (1 mile/1.5km from Audley End) is an appealing market town containing many timber-framed houses with decorative plastering (known as 'pargeting'). Eight miles (13km) south-west of here is the village of **Thaxted** where Gustav Holst wrote much of *The Planets* and site of a superb three-tiered, half-timbered **Guildhall**, dating from the fifteenth century (01371 831339). There are many other fine villages and much great walking in the area.

Blenheim Palace

Woodstock, Oxfordshire (01993 811091).
Getting there *by train* Paddington to Oxford (1 hour) then 30-40-min bus ride; *by car* J8 off M40 then A40 and A44. **Open** *palace & gardens 15 Mar-31 Oct* 10.30am-5.30pm (last admission 4.45pm); *park* 9am-5pm, daily. **Admission** *palace & gardens* £8.50; £4.50-£6.50 concs;

£22 family; *park* £6 per car (including occupants); £2 adult; £1 concs. **Credit** AmEx, DC, MC, V.

As a prize for beating the French at the Battle of Blenheim, John Churchill, Duke of Marlborough, was promised the money to build this immense, extravagant baroque fantasy. Its construction was acrimonious, as Parliament refused to stump up all the necessary cash and Churchill's wife quarrelled with the architect, Sir John Vanbrugh (she had wanted Wren for the job). Baroque masterpiece it may be, but the scale of the building means that it overwhelms rather than charms, and the speedy tours of the plush, antique-packed interior don't leave much time for reflection. The gardens, landscaped by the ubiquitous Capability Brown, are splendid (and contain a butterfly house, adventure play area, maze, putting greens and mini-train). Winston Churchill was born at Blenheim in 1874 (five rooms are dedicated to the wartime PM) and is buried with his wife and parents in the nearby church at **Bladon**.

The handsome, well-scrubbed town of **Woodstock** has a long history of royal connections but now chiefly services visitors to Blenheim and the Cotswolds. It's an agreeable refreshment stop. If you want to avoid the worst of the crowds, try the Black Prince pub on Oxford Street, just north of the centre.

Hatfield House

Hatfield, Hertfordshire (01707 262823).
Getting there *by train* from King's Cross to Hatfield (25 mins); *by car* J4 off A1(M). **Open** *25 Mar-26 Sept house* noon-4pm Tue-Thur; 1-4.30pm Sat, Sun; 11am-4.30pm public hols; *park* 10.30-8pm Mon-Thur, Sat, Sun. **Admission** *house, park & gardens* £6; £3 5s-15s; *park* £1.50; 80p 5s-15s.

Hatfield House is one of the largest and most impressive Jacobean mansions in the country. Built in 1607-11 for Sir Robert Cecil (and remaining in the hands of his family today), it stands on the site of Tudor Hatfield Palace, where Elizabeth I spent much of her childhood. Cecil demolished most of the sixteenth-century building, although one wing survives. The grand interior contains some fine furniture and wonderful Tudor and Jacobean portraits. Outside, the seventeenth-century formal gardens were laid out by John Tradescant (whose pioneering work is detailed in the Museum of Garden History in London; *see p127*). The entrance to the house is opposite the rail station.

Highclere Castle

Highclere, Hampshire (01635 253210). **Getting there** *by train* Paddington to Newbury (45 mins) then 10-min taxi ride; *by car* J13 off M4 then A34 or J8 off M3 then A303 and A34. **Open** *1 Jul-5 Sept* 11am-5pm daily (last admission 4pm, 2.30pm Sat). **Admission** £6; £4.75 student; £3 child; *gardens only* £3; £1.50 child. **Credit** MC, V.

Four miles (7km) south of Newbury is over-the-top Gothic Highclere Castle. Sir Charles Barry, the man largely responsible for the Houses of Parliament, let his imagination run wild, both inside and out, when augmenting the original Georgian mansion. Highclere is the ancestral home of the Earls of Carnarvon, and there are artefacts belonging to the 5th Earl who, together with Howard Carter, excavated the tomb of Tutankhamun in 1922.

Knebworth House

Knebworth, Hertfordshire (01438 812661).
Getting there *by train* from King's Cross to Stevenage (19 mins), then 5-min taxi ride; *by car* J6 or J7 off A1(M). **Open** phone for details. **Admission** *house, park, gardens & railway* £6; £5.50 5s-16s, OAPs; *park & gardens only* £5; £17.50 family. **Credit** MC, V.

Not as grand as its near-neighbour **Hatfield House** (*see above*), Knebworth is nevertheless well worth a visit. The gargoyled Gothic exterior was slapped on the original Tudor mansion in 1843 by romantic novelist Edward

Bulwer-Lytton (the house has been in the Lytton family for 500 years). Inside, Dickens once acted in private theatricals in the fine Jacobean banqueting hall. Beautiful parkland, ideal for picnics and deer-watching, surrounds the house. Garden connoisseurs can admire Gertrude Jekyll's unique quincunx-pattern herb garden; kids can frolic in the large adventure playground or on the miniature railway.

Knole

Sevenoaks, Kent (01732 462010). **Getting there** *by train* Charing Cross to Sevenoaks (31 mins); *by car* J5 off M25. **Open** *1 Apr-1 Nov* noon-4pm Wed-Sat (last admission 3.30pm); 11am-5pm Sat (last admission 4.30pm). **Admission** £5; £2.50 child; £12.50 family. **Credit** MC, V.

With fast connection to London, Sevenoaks is well placed to allow easy access to a number of sights in north-west Kent. As a town, it has little to entice visitors beyond the massive noble pile of Knole. The house was largely created by Archbishop of Canterbury Thomas Bourchier in 1456 and carefully planned to be in harmony with the calendar (seven courtyards, 52 staircases, 365 rooms – only 13 of which are open to the public). Knole was again remodelled by the Sackville family in 1605 and it has remained in the family ever since. Deer roam the vast grounds.

The most interesting historical sight within easy reach of Sevenoaks is seven miles (11km) to the north – **Lullingstone Roman Villa** (01322 863467). This excavated first-century residence is thought to have been home to a farmer – he must have been a very wealthy farmer, for some of the finest mosaic pavements in the region have been uncovered here.

Penshurst Place

Penshurst, near Tonbridge, Kent (01892 870307). **Getting there** *by train* Charing Cross to Tonbridge (45 mins) then 15-min taxi ride; *by car* J5 off M25 then A21, A26 and B2176. **Open** *Mar* noon-5.30pm Sat, Sun; *1 Apr-1 Nov* noon-5.30pm daily. **Admission** *house* £5.70; £5.30 concs; £3.20 child; £15 family; *garden only* £4.20; £3.70 concs; £2.80 child; £12 family. **Credit** AmEx, MC, V.

The Penshurst estate, four miles (6km) west of Tonbridge, was founded by merchant Sir John de Poultney in 1341, and has been in the hands of the Sidney family since 1552. The highlight of the interior is the fourteenth-century Baron's Hall; outside, the grounds include an intricately laid-out Italian garden, and an adventure playground, nature trail and toy museum for children.

Petworth House

Petworth, West Sussex (01798 342207).
Getting there *by car* A3 then A283. **Open** *house 27 Mar-31 Oct* 1-5.30pm Mon-Wed, Sat, Sun (last admission 4.30pm); *park* 8am-sunset daily. **Admission** *house* £5.50; £2.50 child; £13.50 family; *park* free. **Credit** MC, V.

Petworth House is one of the finest stately homes in the South-East. JMW Turner was a frequent guest at the late seventeenth-century house and immortalised it in a series of paintings, some of which form part of the superb art collection on display, which includes works by Titian, Bosch and Gainsborough. A highlight of the interior is the ornate Carved Room, decorated with Grinling Gibbons' intricate wood carvings of musical instruments, flowers and birds. The grounds were one of Capability Brown's earliest works of landscaping. A few miles north-east of Petworth, the vegetarian restaurant **Clements** (01403 871246) is a good place for a healthy lunch.

Polesden Lacey

Surrey (01372 458203). **Getting there** *by train* Waterloo to Westhumble or Dorking (40 mins) then 10-min taxi ride; *by car* A3 then A243 and A24. **Open** *house 27 Mar-1 Nov* 1.30-5.30pm Wed-Sun; *grounds* 11am-

6pm/dusk daily. **Admission** £6; £15 family; *grounds only* £3; £7.50 family.

Three miles (5km) west of **Box Hill** (*see p287*) is the Regency villa of Polesden Lacey. This was the honeymooning ground for the Queen Mother and the late George VI more than 70 years ago. Tucked into the folds of the North Downs, the house and gardens give way to splendid views over woodland and commons. Within the grounds, tree-lined walks, walled rose gardens and a charming thatched bridge over a typical Surrey sunken lane all make for a right royal day out.

Waddesdon Manor

Waddesdon, Buckinghamshire (01296 651226). **Getting there** *by train* Marylebone to Aylesbury (53 mins) then bus; *by car* J9 off M40 then A41. **Open** *Apr-mid-Oct* 10am-5pm Thur-Sun. **Admission** £9; £7.50 child; *grounds only* £3; £1.50 child. **Credit** MC, V.

Five miles (8km) north-west of Aylesbury, château-like Waddesdon Manor looks fantastically out of place in the English countryside. Built by the obscenely wealthy Rothschild family between 1874 and 1889, the house contains a magnificent collection of seventeenth- and eighteenth-century decorative arts. Panelling from nineteenth-century Parisian houses lines the walls, Savonnerie and Aubusson carpets cover the floors, and fine gold boxes, majolica and rare books are among the exhibits. The star attraction is one of the world's finest selections of Sèvres porcelain. The splendid rococo aviary in the grounds is also worth a look, as are the Rothschild wine-packed cellars (where tastings are on offer).

Woburn Abbey

Woburn, Bedfordshire (01525 290666). **Getting there** *by train* Euston to Bletchley (30 mins) then 25-min taxi ride; *by car* J13 off M1 then A4012. **Open** *21 Mar-26 Sept* 11am-4pm Mon-Sat; 11am-5pm Sun; *Oct* 11am-4pm Sat; 11am-5pm Sun; *1 Jan-20 Mar* 11am-4pm Sat, Sun. **Admission** £7.50; £3-£6.50 concs. **Credit** MC, V.

Home of the Dukes of Bedford for more than 350 years, eighteenth-century Woburn Abbey is hugely popular with daytrippers, due in large part to its **Safari Park** (half-price admission with a ticket for the Abbey; *see p283*). The Abbey itself – so called because it was built on the foundations of a twelfth-century Cistercian monastery – is a grand old house, containing some superb Tudor portraits.

Family attractions

Many of the other destinations in this chapter are great for families – particularly the castles and seaside towns.

Chessington World of Adventures

Leatherhead Road, Chessington, Surrey (01372 729560/ recorded info 01372 727227). **Getting there** *by train* Waterloo to Chessington South (30 mins); *by coach* Flightline 777 bus from Victoria Coach Station (1 hour); *by car* J9 off M25 or A3. **Open** *24 Mar-31 Oct* 10am-5.15pm daily (last admission 3pm).
Admission £19; £15 child; £7.50-£8.50 concs; free under-4s; £56 family ticket.
Credit AmEx, MC, V.

This frenetic 65-acre (26-ha) theme park and zoo is certainly fun (if a little tacky), but boy do you pay through the nose for the pleasure. If you take the train, hang on to your tickets as there's usually reduced-price admission for rail passengers. Attractions include Rameses Revenge, the Vampire (a suspended rollercoaster), the Safari Skyway Monorail, and the Rattlesnake, a rollercoaster ride 'that bites back'! Make sure you arrive early to pre-empt the worst of the queues.

Chislehurst Caves

Chislehurst, Kent (0181 467 3264). **Getting there** *by train* Charing Cross to Chislehurst (23 mins); *by car* A222. **Open** *45-min tour every hour* 10am-4pm Wed-Sun (daily during school hols); *90-min tour* 2.30pm Sun. **Admission** *45-min tour* £3; £1.50 concs; *90-min tour* £5; £2.50 concs.

On the outskirts of south-east London, and close to Chislehurst rail station, are the highly recommended Chislehurst Caves. Take a lamplight tour (45 or 90 mins) through this maze of ancient man-made chalk tunnels and caves. Previous occupants include Druids, Romans and wartime Londoners sheltering from air raids.

Drusillas Zoo Park

Alfriston, East Sussex (01323 870656). **Getting there** *by car* A22 then A27 or M23 then A23 and A27. **Open** *Apr-Oct* 10am-5pm daily; *Nov-Mar* 10am-4pm daily. **Admission** £6.95; £5.75 3s-12s. **Credit** MC, V.

This deceptively large wildlife park is imaginatively designed. Children and agile adults can scramble through tunnels to re-emerge in mini-domes amid meerkats or rats. Impressively clean and well organised – almost to the point of military precision; you have to wind your way along a pre-ordained path to earn that cuppa in the café at the end, where there is also a huge playground with (free) activities including gargantuan slides and train rides.

Legoland Windsor

Windsor Park, Berkshire (0990 040404). **Getting there** *by train* Paddington to Windsor Central, change at Slough (30 mins) or to Windsor & Eton Riverside (49 mins) then shuttle service (small charge); *by car* J6 off M4, J3 off M3 or J13 off M25, then follow signs; *by coach* Golden Tours runs a daily service with pick-up at 50 London hotels (0171 233 7030). Green Line runs a daily service from Victoria (0181 668 7261). **Open** *13 Mar-31 Oct* 10am-6pm daily; 10am-8pm in school summer holidays. **Admission** £16.50; £13.50 child; £10.50 OAPs; free under-3s. **Credit** AmEx, MC, V.

Modelled on the Danish original, Legoland is a slick affair and a sure-fire hit with most two- to 12-year-olds. The huge site is split into different activity zones. In Miniland, there are miniature versions of famous European buildings. Duplo Gardens has a water-play area and cascades of chunky plastic. Kids can get their Legoland licence in the Driving School, before heading on to Wild Woods to pan for gold and ride the Pirate Falls. New in 1998 was the CastleLand adventure area with its Dragon Knight's rollercoaster ride. Phone for details of special events and for an advisory sheet on facilities and access for guests with disabilities. New for 1999 are the Junior Dragon Ride, for smaller kids, and the Balloon Ride, where four people get to ride in a balloon.
Website: www.legoland.co.uk

Mountfitchet Castle & Norman Village

Stansted Mountfitchet, Essex (01279 813237). **Getting there** *by train* Liverpool Street to Stansted Mountfitchet (45 mins); *by car* J8 off M11 then A120 and B1383. **Open** *castle mid-Mar-mid-Nov* 10am-5pm, *toy museum mid-Jan-mid-Dec* 10am-4pm, daily. **Admission** *castle* £4; £3.20 concs; *toy museum* £3.50; £2.50 concs. **Credit** MC, V.

Stansted Mountfitchet, eight miles (13km) south of Saffron Walden, is the site of this superb reconstruction of an eleventh-century Norman castle, which vividly brings history to life. There is also a good toy museum in the village. A great place for kids.

Thorpe Park

Staines Road, Chertsey, Surrey (01932 569393). **Getting there** *by train* Victoria to Staines, change at Clapham Junction (45 mins), or Hatton Cross tube, then

*A fruit bat snacks at **Drusillas Zoo Park**.*

link bus; *by car* J11 or J13 off M25. **Open** *27 Mar-16 July* 10am-6pm daily; *17 July-1 Nov* generally 9.30am-7.30pm daily. **Admission** £16.50; £10-£13 concs; free children under 1m in height. **Credit** AmEx, DC, MC, V.
A Disneyesque theme park in Surrey, attracting around one million visitors a year. The pleasantly landscaped site covers 500 acres (1,235 ha) and rounds up the usual suspects: rides, stunt shows, a working farm, 'fungle jungle' adventures, ghost rides, oversized and overfriendly cartoon characters and, if you dare, No Way Out, a backwards ride in the dark.

Whipsnade Wild Animal Park

Dunstable, Bedfordshire (01582 872171).
Getting there *by train* King's Cross to Luton (33 mins) or Euston to Hemel Hempstead (25 mins), then bus or 20-min taxi ride; *by car* J9 off M1 then A5 and B4540.
Open *Easter-Aug* 10am-6pm Mon-Sat; 10am-7pm Sun; *Feb-Easter, Sept, Oct* 10am-dusk daily; phone for winter opening times. **Admission** £9.50; £7 concs. **Credit** AmEx, MC, V.
Set in 600 acres (243 ha) of beautiful parkland, Whipsnade is one of Europe's largest conservation centres. It is home to over 2,500 animals (many of them endangered species), including wallabies, Chinese water deer, elephants, lemurs and a hippo pool. Kids especially love the Runwild Play Area, Children's Farm and Great Whipsnade Railway, but there are many attractions that adults can enjoy too, including the Birds of the World demonstration, Squirrel Monkey Island and Tiger Falls.

Woburn Safari Park

Woburn Park, Bedfordshire (01525 290407). **Getting there** *by car* J13 off M1. **Open** *6 Mar-31 Oct* 10am-5pm daily; *Nov-Feb* 11am-3pm Sat, Sun. **Admission** *summer* £11.50 adults; £8-£8.50 concs; free under-3s; *winter* £6.50 adults; £5-£5.50 concs; free under-3s. **Credit** MC, V.
The Duke of Bedford's vast grounds have been turned over to a grand safari park, home to lions, tigers, bears, monkeys and rhinos. There are five adventure playgrounds to explore (and two designed for under-5s). Children should enjoy the full programme of animal demonstrations and feeding times, including training sessions with the park's three Asian ele-

phants. Other attractions include Rainbow Landing (where visitors can be swooped at by rainbow lorikeets) and the new walk-through squirrel monkey exhibit. While you're here, you might also want to look at **Woburn Abbey** (half-price admission with a ticket for the Safari Park; *see opposite*).

Gardens

Groombridge Place Gardens

Groombridge, Kent (01892 863999). **Getting there** *by rail* Charing Cross to Tunbridge Wells (53 mins) then 10-min taxi ride; *by car* J5 off M25 then A21, A264 and B2110. **Open** *31 Mar-31 Oct* 9am-6pm daily. **Admission** £6.50; £5.50 concs. **Credit** AmEx, MC, V.
It comes as little surprise that this medieval site (the current house – closed to the public – dates from the seventeenth century), surrounded by parkland, has inspired artists and writers over the centuries (including filmmaker Peter Greenaway and Sir Arthur Conan Doyle for *The Valley of Fear*).With a listed walled garden set against a seventeenth-century moated mansion, walks through the award-winning 'Enchanted Forest', spring-fed pools and waterfalls giving way to dramatic views over the Weald, the possibilities for waxing lyrical are endless. Great for kids.

Leonardslee

Lower Beeding, West Sussex (01403 891212). **Getting there** *by train* Victoria to Horsham (1 hour 8 mins) then 15-min taxi ride; *by car* M23 then A23 and B2110. **Open** *Apr, Jun-Oct* 9.30am-6pm, *May* 9.30am-8pm, daily. **Admission** *Apr, Jun-Oct* £3.50; £2 child; *May* £4.50; £2 child.
Perhaps the most charming of Sussex gardens, Leonardslee, set in a wooded valley three miles (5km) south-west of Nymans (*see below*), is particularly impressive for its floral displays. Six lakes, originally built in the sixteenth century to provide water power for iron foundries, are linked by paths; deer and wallabies roam free.

Nymans

Handcross, West Sussex (01444 400321). **Getting there** *by train* Victoria to Three Bridges (35 mins) then 10-min taxi ride; *by car* M23 then A23 and B2114. **Open** *1 Mar-1 Nov* 11am-6pm/sunset Wed-Sun; *house* noon-4pm Wed-Sun. **Admission** £5; £2.50 child; £12.50 family. **Credit** MC, V.
Four miles (6km) south of Crawley is one of the finest of all English gardens. Set high on the edge of the Sussex Weald, Nymans is a showpiece of rare shrubs and trees. Highlights include the walled garden, the hidden sunken garden and some wonderful woodland walks. Parts of the house are now open to the public.

Sheffield Park

near Uckfield, East Sussex (01825 790231). **Getting there** *by train* Victoria to Hayward's Heath (45 mins) then 15-min taxi ride; *by car* J10 off M23 then A264, A22 and A275. **Open** *Jan, Feb* 10.30am-4pm Sat, Sun; *Mar* 10.30am-4pm Tue-Sun; *1 Apr-31 Oct* 10.30am-6pm Tue-Sun, bank hol Mon; *2 Nov-23 Dec* 10.30am-4pm Tue-Sun. **Admission** £4.20; £2.10 child; free under-5s, members of National Trust; £10.50 family.
The major draw of the sleepy heart of Sussex is its array of splendid gardens. The most majestic of these is Sheffield Park, ten miles (16km) north of Lewes. Yet another eighteenth-century Capability Brown creation, the gardens were modified in the early twentieth century but retain a grand landscape feel. There are five lakes connected with cascades and waterfalls in the early spring, fine specimens of azalea and rhododendron in early summer, and autumn hues from rare trees. Close by is the southern terminus of the nine-mile (14-km) **Bluebell Railway** (01825 722370) and the lovely village of **Fletching**. The **Griffin Inn** here is a great spot for lunch.

Sissinghurst

Sissinghurst, Cranbrook, Kent (01580 715330). **Getting there** *by train* Charing Cross to Staplehurst (53 mins) then 10-min taxi ride; *by car* J5 off M25 then A21 and A262. **Open** *1 Apr-15 Oct* 1-6.30pm Tue-Fri; 10am-5.30pm Sat, Sun. **Admission** £6; £3 child. **Credit** AmEx, MC, V.

Sissinghurst is the greatest of the Kent gardens. Here Vita Sackville-West and her husband Harold Nicolson transformed a ruined sixteenth-century mansion (closed to the public) and grounds into a paradise of colour and fragrance. Alas, the edenic lure of Sissinghurst is so powerful that coachloads of trippers frequently swamp the place and timed tickets are the norm.

Stowe

Buckinghamshire (01280 822850). **Getting there** *by train* Euston to Milton Keynes (40 mins) then bus to Buckingham (30 mins) then 5-min taxi ride; *by car* J10 off M40 then A43 and A422 or J14 off M1 then A5 and A422. **Open** *gardens 20 Mar-12 Apr, 5 July-4 Sept* 10am-5pm daily; *14 Apr-4 July, 5 Sept-31 Oct* 10am-5pm Mon, Wed, Fri, Sun; *27 Dec-4 Jan* 10am-5pm/dusk daily (last admission one hour before closing); *house 20 Mar-12 Apr, 5 July-4 Sept* 2-5pm Mon-Sat; noon-5pm Sun. **Admission** *gardens* £4.50; £2.50 concs; £11.50 family; *house* £2; £1 child.

Three miles (5km) north-west of Buckingham, Stowe is possibly the most important and spectacular eighteenth-century landscaped garden in the country. Its 325 acres (132ha) were first laid out in 1680 but transformed over the following 100 years by tree-plantings, (six) lake-makings and (32) temple-buildings. To Capability Brown's naturalistic landscape-shaping were added monuments by almost every big-name architect of the time, including James Gibbs, John Vanbrugh and William Kent. Little of the interior of the house can be seen as it is occupied by Stowe School. Buckingham itself is a relatively lively town, with some jumping, studenty pubs.

Woolfs' lair: **Monk's House** *in Rodmell.*

Homes of the famous

For **Gad's Hill Place** (Dickens), *see page 280;* for **Flatford Mill** (Constable), *see page 287.*

Bateman's

Burwash, Etchingham, East Sussex (01435 882302). **Getting there** *by car* J5 off M25 then A21 and A265. **Open** *27 Mar-31 Oct* 11am-5.30pm Mon-Wed, Sat, Sun (last admission 4.30pm). **Admission** £5; £2.50 child; £12.50 family. **Credit** MC, V.

Rudyard Kipling lived at Bateman's from 1902 until his death in 1936. The seventeenth-century house has been preserved as the author left it, and the attractive grounds contain a watermill that Kipling converted to generate electricity.

Charleston Farmhouse & around

near Firle, East Sussex (01323 811265). **Getting there** *by train* Victoria to Lewes (1 hour 5 mins) then 10-min taxi ride; *by car* M23 then A23 and A27. **Open** *1 Apr-31 Oct* 2-5pm Wed-Sun; *July, Aug* 11.30am-5pm Wed-Sat, 2-5pm Sun; *Nov, Dec* open *only* 2-5pm Sat, Sun. **Admission** £5.50; £3.50 child, concs. **Credit** MC, V.

Six miles (10km) east of Lewes stands this shrine to Bloomsbury Groupies. Virginia Woolf's sister Vanessa Bell moved here with her husband Clive and lover Duncan Grant during World War I so that the two men, as conscientious objectors, could become farm labourers and, thus, exempt from military service. Admission includes a guided tour of the house, which is hung with superb paintings by the likes of Picasso and Renoir, as well as more minor daubings.

Four miles (6km) west of here is another Bloomsbury site – **Monk's House** in Rodmell, home of Leonard and Virginia Woolf from 1919 (01892 890651; *27 Mar-30 Oct*

2-5.30pm Wed, Sat; £2.50, £1.25 child). Close by is the spot on the River Ouse where Virginia drowned herself in 1941, walking into the water, her pockets full of stones. She and Leonard (who lived here until his death in 1969) are both interred in the garden.

Chartwell

Westerham, Kent (01732 866368). **Getting there** *by train* Charing Cross to Sevenoaks (33 mins) then Chartwell Explorer bus; *by car* J5 off M25 then A25 and B2026 or J6 off M25 then A22, A25 and B2026. **Open** *27 Mar-31 Oct* 11am-5pm Wed-Sun, bank hol Mon; *July, Aug* 11am-5pm Tue-Sun (last admission 4.15pm). **Admission** £5.50; £2.75 children; £13.75 family; free members of National Trust; *combined ticket* £12 adults; £6 children. **Credit** V.

Six miles (9km) west of Sevenoaks lies one of the South-East's most-visited sights: Chartwell, home of **Winston Churchill**. The wartime PM lived in the much-restored Tudor building from 1924 until his death in 1965 and it contains a large hoard of Churchillabilia. Guided tours are available on Wednesday mornings; phone for details. The combined ticket, covering the train and bus journey and admission to Chartwell, is available by calling 0345 484950.

Down House

Luxted Road, Downe, Kent (info 01689 859119/ bookings 0870 603 0145). **Getting there** *by train* Charing Cross to Orpington (23 mins) then 20-min taxi ride; *by car* A223 or A21. **Open** *10 Apr-31 Sept* 10am-6pm Wed-Sun; *1 Nov-31 Jan* 10am-4pm Wed-Sun; *Mar* 10am-4pm Wed-Sun. **Admission** £5; £3.80 concs; £2.50 child. **Credit** MC, V.

A couple of miles outside Orpington is the recently restored home of probably the most significant figure of the nineteenth century: **Charles Darwin**. The naturalist's world-shaking theory of evolution was partly written in this large house, where he lived for 40 years. On the ground floor are the original drawing room and study; the first floor houses temporary topical exhibitions.

Jane Austen's House

Chawton, Hampshire (01420 832262). **Getting there** *by train* Waterloo to Alton (1 hour); *by car* J5 off M3 then B3349. **Open** *1 Mar-1 Jan* 11am-4.30pm daily; *Jan, Feb* 11am-4.30pm Sat, Sun. **Admission** £2.50; £2 concs; 50p 8s-18s. **Credit** MC, V.

A mile south-west of Alton is the village of Chawton, where **Jane Austen** lived between 1809 and 1817. She wrote or revised all of her six books in this modest red-brick house, which now contains a collection of Austen first editions and other memorabilia.

Alton is one terminus of the **Mid Hants Watercress Line**, which runs steam trains between here and Alresford (01962 733810). Four miles (6km) south of Chawton is little Selborne where eighteenth-century naturalist **Gilbert White**'s house **The Wakes** (01420 511275) has been preserved as a memorial to his pioneering work.

Shaw's Corner

Ayot St Lawrence, Hertfordshire (01438 820307). **Getting there** *by train* from King's Cross to Welwyn North (55 mins) then 10-min taxi ride; *by car* J6 off A1(M). **Open** *1 Apr-31 Oct* 1-5pm Wed-Sun, public hols. **Admission** £3.30; under-16s £1.65; free members of National Trust; £8.25 family.

George Bernard Shaw lived for more than 40 years (until his death in 1950) in the village of Ayot St Lawrence amid some of Hertfordshire's prettiest scenery. The playwright's house has been preserved much as he left it, and his famous revolving writing shed, which turned to follow the path of the sun, was restored to full working order in 1998.

Life on the ocean wave

Chatham Historic Dockyard

Kent (01634 823800). **Getting there** *by train* Victoria to Chatham then 1-mile walk, 2-min taxi ride or bus; *by car* J2 off M25 then A2. **Open** *29 Mar-Oct* 10am-5pm daily; *Nov-28 Mar* 10am-4pm Wed, Sat, Sun. **Admission** phone for details. **Credit** MC, V.

Close neighbour to **Rochester** (*see p280*), **Chatham**, founded by Henry VIII, had become England's biggest naval base within 100 years. Not surprisingly, the town's major attraction is the excellent **Chatham Historic Dockyard**, a restored Georgian river dockyard with a 'Sail and Colour Loft', where you can learn how flags and sails are made. Vessels to explore include restored sloops, gunships and paddlesteamers. Other attractions are the Dockyard's shire-horses and a collection of naval guns. Nearby **Fort Amherst** was built to defend the dockyard in the mid-eighteenth century and extended during the Napoleonic Wars (01634 847747). There are tunnels, nature trails, barracks and batteries to be explored and occasional military re-enactments to enjoy on Sundays (phone for details). Chatham town itself is decidedly lacking in the charm department.

Historic Ships, Portsmouth

Hampshire (01705 861512/861533). **Getting there** *by train* Waterloo to Portsmouth Harbour (1 hour 30 mins); *by car* A3 or M3 then M27. **Open** *Mar-Oct* 10am-6pm, *Nov-Feb* 10am-5pm, daily (last admission one hour before closing). **Admission** *passport ticket to see all attractions* £14; £10 child; £33 family (phone for details of charges to individual attractions).

Portsmouth is rich in naval associations but poor in looks (the two are connected: its importance as a port meant it was bombed to bits during World War II). The city's greatest draw is undoubtedly the **Historic Ships**. This encompasses a number of museums and three ships: Britain's first armoured battleship, HMS *Warrior*, dating from 1860; Nelson's flagship at Trafalgar, HMS *Victory*; and Henry VIII's *Mary Rose*, which sunk in front of the King while engaging the French just off the coast in 1545.

It is also worth making the short ferry journey to Gosport to look around the claustrophobic vessels in **Submarine World** (01705 529217). Military enthusiasts can press on to the **D-Day Museum** on Clarence Esplanade (01705 827261), centred around the 272-ft (83-m) embroidery commemorating Operation Overlord, in which Portsmouth played a major role. Next to the museum is **Southsea Castle** (01705 827261), from which Henry VIII may have watched his beloved *Mary Rose* sink beneath the waves. A mile further along the front is the **Royal Marines Museum** (01705 819385), complete with junior assault course.

Portsmouth's one non-military attraction is **Dickens' Birthplace** at 393 Commercial Road, north of the town centre (01705 827261). There's not a lot to see, though, beyond a couple of recreated rooms.

Out in the country

Despite appearances, London's sprawl does not go on forever. There's wonderful walking country within easy reach of the city, particularly in the North Downs, south of London, the Chilterns to the north-west, and the Cotswolds to the west. For further details, see below.

Shameless self-promotion it may be, but we recommend the pocket-sized *Time Out Book of Country Walks* (Penguin, £9.99) for walking enthusiasts. The book details 52 walks in the countryside around London.

Country Lanes *9 Shaftesbury Street, Fordingbridge, Hampshire SP6 1JF (01425 655022).* Take the train from London and be met at your destination by representatives from Country Lanes who will then lead you on cycling or walking tours of the New Forest, the Cotswolds, Dorset and other areas. There are day trips, short breaks and six-day tours. Write or phone for a brochure.

The Chilterns

Getting there *by train* from Paddington to Henley (55 mins); Paddington to Maidenhead then change for Marlow (55 mins); *by car Henley/Marlow* J8 off M4 then A404(M) and A4130 or J4 off M40 then A404 and A4155. *Wendover* J20 off M25 then A41 and A4011 or A40 and A413.

Stretching in a broad arc around the north-west of London, the Chilterns rarely receive more than a glance out of the window from tourists powering through to Oxford and Stratford. Yet this gently hilly region has some great walking and excellent pubs (if also some charmless towns) and is easily and quickly accessible from the capital.

At the place where Oxfordshire, Berkshire and Buckinghamshire meet is cocky little **Henley** (tourist office: 01491 578034). This wealthy commuter burg becomes the centre of braying-toff life for five days at the end of June when the Henley **Royal Regatta** hits town (*see p8*), but is otherwise most useful as a base from which to explore the wonderful villages and countryside to the north. Some of the best walking in the Chilterns can be found around **Frieth** and **Nettlebed**, and the **Prince Albert** pub in the former and **Carpenters Arms** in **Crocker End** near the latter are good spots to hole up with a pint after a hike. There's also fine walking further north around **Wendover**.

Another good (if very popular) town from which to explore the southern Chilterns and the Thames Valley, **Marlow** is a relaxed little town with some good Georgian architecture and a fine pub – the **Two Brewers** on St Peter's Street – where Jerome K Jerome wrote part of *Three*

Calendar of out of town events

For out of town music festivals and sporting events, *see page 256 and pages 7-10.*

Brighton Festival   1-23 May
Brighton, East Sussex (enquiries 01273 292951/ box office 01273 709709/info@brighton-festival. org.uk). Brighton rail. **Open** *box office 10am-5.30pm Mon-Sat.* **Admission** *varies depending on event.* **Credit** AmEx, DC, MC, V.
England's largest arts festival. Attractions in 1999 include the Nederlands Dans Theatre, the Bruckner Symphony Orchestra and productions by the Royal Shakespeare Company. Tickets go on sale from March.
Website: www.brighton-festival.org.uk

Newbury Spring Festival   8-22 May
Newbury, Berkshire (01635 32421/box office 01635 522733). Newbury rail. **Open** *box office (from 26 Feb 1999) 10am-6pm Mon-Sat.* **Admission** *varies depending on event.* **Credit** MC, V.
Held at a number of venues in Newbury and the surrounding villages. The wide range of events on offer include various classical concerts, jazz, world music, opera, film, family events and a visual arts programme.

Aldeburgh Festival   11-27 June
in and around Aldeburgh and at the Snape Maltings Concert Hall, Snape Bridge, Saxmundham, Suffolk (01728 453543). Saxmundham or Ipswich rail. **Open** *enquiries/box office 9.30am-5pm Mon-Sat.* **Admission** £9-£28. **Credit** MC, V.
Established by Benjamin Britten in 1948, this classical and contemporary music festival is one of the largest in England, attracting 20,000 people. Events for 1999 will include Thomas Adès' opera *Powder Her Face* and a piano recital by Alfred Brendel. Tickets are available from April.
Website: www.aldeburgh.co.uk

Cambridge Shakespeare 5 July-28 Aug Festival
various Cambridge colleges, Cambridge (enquiries 01223 511139/box office 01223 504444). Open enquiries 9am-9pm daily; box office 10am-6pm Mon-Sat. **Admission** £9, £6 concs. **Credit** AmEx, MC, V.
Each year several of Shakespeare's plays are produced using professional actors and directors in a number of colleges. There is an emphasis on authenticity, and performances remain true to the text, with the help of period costume. Most of the plays take place outdoors, and people are welcome to bring along picnics. Tickets go on sale from June, or you can buy them on the door.

RAC British Grand Prix   8-11 July
Silverstone, Northamptonshire (enquiries 01327 857271/box office 01327 857273). Milton Keynes or Northampton rail. **Open** *box office 8am-7pm Mon-Fri; 10am-2pm Sat, Sun.* **Admission** *phone box office for details.* **Credit** AmEx, DC, MC, V.
This four-day event is part of the FIA Formula 1 World Championships. Practice events take place on Thursday and Friday, Saturday is the qualifying race and Sunday the final race day. Other races include the Formula 3000 championship, and there are also track parades and air displays. Tickets go on sale the previous autumn, and sell out quickly, especially for the Sunday race.
Website: www.silverstone-circuit.co.uk

War & Peace Military Show 23-25 July
Hop Farm Country Park, Beltring, near Paddock Wood, Kent (01622 872068). Paddock Wood rail then 6 bus. **Open** *enquiries 9am-6pm daily.* **Admission** *Fri £6, £4 concs; Sat, Sun £8, £6 concs.* **Credit** DC, MC, £TC, V.
The world's largest collection of military vehicles and memorabilia are on display here. There are re-enactments aplenty, and the more enthusiastic visitors dress up as famous military figures. Various events take place throughout the weekend, including 'tank crashing'. There are also trade stalls selling military related items. If you're planning on camping out, you need to buy tickets in advance; otherwise you can buy them at the event.

History in Action IV   14-15 Aug
Kirby Hall, Northamptonshire (enquiries 01536 203230). Kettering rail. **Open** *enquiries 10am-4pm Sat, Sun; from 1 Apr 10am-6pm daily.* **Admission** *varies; phone for details.* **Credit** EC, MC, V.
Europe's largest festival of multi-period living history is now in its fourth year (1999). Visitors can watch re-enactments of almost every era from the first to the twentieth centuries, including the Saxons and Vikings, and a World War II battle. Other attractions are a living history encampment, historical crafts market and opportunities to take part in a grand period dance. Tickets are only available on the gate.

Airbourne 1999   19-22 Aug
The Western Lawns, King Edward's Parade, Eastbourne, East Sussex (enquiries 01323 415442). Eastbourne rail. **Open** *enquiries 9am-5pm Mon-Fri.* **Admission** *free.*
A seafront airshow of Britain's historic jets and planes, including the famous Red Arrows. There are parachute displays and aerobatic wing walking. The event also includes simulator rides, trade stands and exhibits.

Cheltenham Festival   8-24 Oct of Literature
Cheltenham, Gloucestershire (box office 01242 227979). Cheltenham rail. **Open** *box office 9.30am-5.30pm Mon-Sat.* **Admission** *free-£8 (concs available), varies depending on event.* **Credit** MC, V.
The Cheltenham Festival of Literature celebrates its 50th anniversary in 1999. Events, which are held in various venues such as theatres, include author appearances, signings, readings, lectures and discussions. A children's sub-festival, **Book It!**, runs along side the main festival, and both children and adults can enjoy the multimedia education centre. There is also a celebration of other art forms; with music, theatre, performance poetry, cabaret and art work. Each year the festival has a theme (phone for details of this year's). Tickets go on sale from mid-August.

Aldeburgh Poetry Festival   5-7 Nov
Aldeburgh Jubilee Hall, Crabbe Street, Suffolk (enquiries/box office 01728 453543). Saxmundham or Ipswich rail. **Open** *enquiries/box office 9.30am-5pm Mon-Sat.* **Admission** *varies depending on event.* **Credit** MC, V.
England's most successful poetry festival includes readings, poet appearances, lectures, book stalls, cabaret, and children's events. You can buy tickets from September.

Men in a Boat. Other notable literary residents have included Percy and Mary Shelley, and TS Eliot.

The cutesy village of **Cookham**, four miles (7km) east of Marlow, is famed as the home of one of Britain's greatest and most idiosyncratic twentieth-century painters, **Stanley Spencer**. Several of his deceptively naïve, sex-and-God-obsessed works are displayed in the **Wesleyan Chapel** on the High Street.

The Cotswolds

Getting there *by train* Paddington to Moreton-in-Marsh (1 hour 20 mins); *by car* M40 then A40 and A44.

Nowhere in England is there such a harmonious relationship between buildings and landscape as in the Cotswolds. The enchanting stone villages and incomparable 'wool churches' that characterise the area were built by the medieval merchants who grew rich from the profits of the local wool trade. Routinely described as 'honey-coloured', the stone is actually extremely variable, yet its ubiquitous use helps to unify a region that sprawls generously over six counties.

Parts of the Cotswolds suffer horrible congestion on summer weekends, but it's always localised. While crowds buzz around **Bourton** and **Bibury**, equally charming villages such as **Stanton** and **Stanway** slumber gently on, almost undisturbed. The small Cotswold towns are often even more memorable than the villages. Places such as **Stow-on-the-Wold**, whose elegant seventeenth-century houses look down on The Square (the tourist information centre is found here; 01451 831082); **Winchcombe**, with its gargoyle-encrusted church and its wonderful setting; **Broadway**, where cottage gardens of wisteria, clematis and old roses spill out on to the High Street; and, best of all, **Chipping Campden**, with its 600-year-old houses and glorious wool church.

Chipping Campden is also the starting point of the long-distance footpath, the **Cotswold Way**. Fortunately, Cotswold footpaths are as suitable for Sunday strollers as hardened hikers. Well-maintained and waymarked, they converge on every town and village. The ancient **Eight Bells Inn** in Chipping Campden (01386 840371), the **Old White Lion** in Winchcombe (01242 603300) and the pricier **Grapevine Hotel** in Stow-on-the-Wold (01451 830344) are all recommended bases. For **Stratford-upon-Avon**, *see p278*.

Epping Forest

Information Centre, High Beech, Loughton, Essex (0181 508 0028). **Getting there** *by train* Loughton tube then 2-mile walk or 5-min taxi ride; *by car* J26 off M25. **Open** *summer* 10am-5pm Mon-Sat; 11am-5pm Sun; *winter* 11am-3pm Mon-Fri; 10am-dusk Sat; 11am-dusk Sun.

The 6,000 acres (2,430ha) left of this once massive ancient forest are still mighty impressive, and perfect for walking, cycling, horse riding, picnicking, blackberrying and mushrooming. Wander down wheelchair- (and buggy-) friendly paths, among ancient oaks adjacent to the visitors' centre and around Connaught Water. The friendly staff can offer suggestions for walks around the acres, or supply leaflets and a detailed map to help with explorations. Be warned that the visitors' centre is a two-mile uphill walk from Loughton tube station. You're best off buying a map of the Forest beforehand (try **Edward Stanford**; *see p188*), having a coffee in Loughton town when you get off the tube, and then walking to the information centre through the forest rather than along the main roads. Alternatively, continue on the tube for a couple of stops to Theydon Bois, a pretty, largely unspoiled village with a green and duck pond, and wander into the forest from there.

The North Downs

Getting there *by train* Waterloo to Westhumble or Dorking (40 mins) then 10-min taxi ride; *by car* A3 then A243 and A24.

The bones of the landscape of England south of London are the Downs – North and South – long chalk ridges facing each other across the Weald. The South Downs are more spectacular, but the North Downs are much closer to the capital; so close that you can enjoy some of the South-east's best views little more than 20 miles (32km) from the heart of London.

A long-distance footpath, the **North Downs Way**, runs for 140 miles (224km) from Farnham in Surrey to the White Cliffs of Dover. Opportunities for shorter walks are plentiful, and the ancient market town of **Dorking** is a good centre. There's easy access from here to **Box Hill**, which has been a popular picnic spot since the days of Charles II – avoid weekends if you can. The **William IV** pub in nearby Mickleham is a popular place for liquid and solid refreshment. Not far away is **Polesden Lacey** (*see p282*) and **Ranmore Common**, which offers good walks on the south slopes of the Downs. Another good spot for walking, six miles (9km) south-west of Dorking, is **Leith Hill**, the highest point in south-east England.

The Stour Valley

Essex & Suffolk. **Getting there** *by train* Liverpool Street to Sudbury (1 hour 7 mins); *by car* J28 off M25, then A12 and A134.

Despite its dour reputation, parts of Essex are very pretty, particularly where the county meets Suffolk at the Stour Valley. This tranquil, gently undulating region is known for its good walking, handsome towns and villages (impressively built on the wealth of the area's medieval wool and weaving trade) and, most of all, as **John Constable** country. The birthplace of Britain's best-loved painter at **East Bergholt** is long gone, so the Constable heritage industry is now based around **Flatford Mill**, the house his father owned, and the setting for *The Hay Wain*.

Good-looking **Sudbury**, the biggest town in the Stour Valley, makes a decent base for touring a region where the chief pleasures are the soothing landscape and the fine architecture. Among the area's most beguiling villages are **Castle Hedingham**, **Long Melford**, **Kersey** and medieval picture-postcard-perfect **Lavenham** (the **Great House** French restaurant with rooms is a good place to eat and sleep; 01787 247431; from £138 including dinner, bed and breakfast). If you're in the area treat yourself to a meal at the wonderful **White Hart** in Great Yeldham near Halstead (01787 237250) or the Californian-influenced fare at the **Stour Bay Café** in Manningtree (01206 396687).

Thames Path

The Thames Path follows a 180-mile (288-km) stretch of river from its source near Kemble in Gloucestershire via the Cotswolds, Oxford, the Chilterns, Windsor and through London to the Thames Barrier at Woolwich. Set up by the Countryside Commission, the Path is claimed to be the only long-distance route that follows a river for most of its length. You can join it at any point and enjoy the riverside scenery for a short walk or a longer hike.

Leaflets are available from tourist information centres, although it's worthwhile buying a copy of the *National Trail Guide: The Thames Path* by David Sharp (Aurum Press, £12.99), which includes Ordnance Survey maps and details of public transport and refreshment stops.

Vale of the White Horse

Getting there *by train* Paddington to Didcot (40 mins-1 hour); *by car* J13 off M4 then A34 and A417 or J14 off M4 then A338 or J8 off M40 then A40, A4142 and A34.

The **Lambourn Downs**, south-west of Oxford, between Didcot and Swindon, are fine for walking and ancient sites. The 5,000-year-old **Ridgeway** path qualifies as both. The 374-ft (127-m) long figure of a prancing horse, after which the area is named, was carved into the chalk sometime in the second millennium BC, making it the oldest chalk figure in Britain. Its origins are shrouded in legend – no one knows who created it or why.

The horse is located near the village of **Uffington**, six miles (9km) west of Wantage. The prehistoric fort of **Uffington Castle** is just above the mysterious horse. There's not much to see beyond the earthworks, but its size, and the location, are impressive. Two miles (3km) west of here is **Wayland's Smithy**, a well-preserved 5,000-year-old neolithic burial mound.

Six miles (9km) east of Wantage, **Didcot Railway Centre** (01235 817200) celebrates the glory days of the Great Western Railway from the 1850s to the 1950s with its collection of locomotives and regular 'Steam Days'; phone for details. **The Harrow** (01635 281260) in West Ilsley, five miles (8km) south-west of Didcot, is worth a detour for its superb, and distinctly upmarket, pub grub.

Seaside

See also page 274 **Brighton**.

Aldeburgh

Suffolk. **Getting there** *by car* J28 off M25 then A12 and A1094.

There can be something otherworldly about the Suffolk coast, and the little town of Aldeburgh is a perfect spot to experience its uniqueness and escape the capital's crowds – that is unless you come in June or November when the place is overwhelmed by visitors to the world-famous **Aldeburgh Festival** of classical music and **Aldeburgh Poetry Festival** respectively (*see p286*). Local boy **Benjamin Britten** founded the music festival in 1948 and is buried in the churchyard by the side of his long-term partner, the tenor Peter Pears; the two of them lived in Crag House on Crabbe Street from 1947 to 1957. The tourist office on the High Street (01728 453637) can help with places to stay, or try B&B at **Ocean House** (01728 452094; £50-£60). There are a number of good restaurants in town, including the **Lighthouse** (01728 453377), which isn't and never was a lighthouse. Other beguiling spots on the Suffolk coast include Orford and Southwold.

Hastings & Battle

Getting there *by train* from Charing Cross or Victoria (1 hour 30 mins-2 hours); *by car* M25 then A21.

Apart from having the most famous battle on British soil named after it, there is little of distinction about **Hastings**. Its fading-resort air sits oddly with an arty quarter popular with painters and the still-active fishing port. Of the sprinkling of museums, the commandingly situated ruins of the **Norman castle** hold **The 1066 Story**, an explanation of William the Conqueror's invasion (01424 781112). More exciting is the **Smugglers' Adventure** in St Clement's Caves (01424 422964). Until the early nineteenth century, smuggling was one of Hastings' major industries, and the caves, once used for stashing contraband, now contain some excellent dioramas detailing the nefarious activities of the locals. The tourist office is in the town hall (01424 718888).

The literally named town of **Battle**, five miles (8km) inland, gives a big clue as to the actual spot where William and King Harold slugged it out for the English crown more than 900 years ago. To thank God for his victory William built **Battle Abbey** (01424 773792) on the spot where Harold was killed. The abbey is in ruins now, but wonderfully evocative ruins they are, and an audio-visual display gives a low-down of the battle and the demise of the English King (who was clubbed to death, not shot in the eye with an arrow as a misinterpretation of the Bayeux Tapestry popularly led us to believe). The town itself is rather touristy, but the fourteenth-century **Almonry** (01424 772772) on the High Street is worth a look for the Battle of Hastings model and the 300-year-old Guy Fawkes effigy, which is paraded through the streets on the Saturday nearest to 5 November.

Rye

East Sussex. **Getting there** *by train* Charing Cross to Ashford then change for Rye (1 hour 40 mins); *by car* J10 off M20 then A2070 and A259 or J5 off M25 then A21 and A268.

When is a seaside town not a seaside town? When the river it sits on silts up, the sea retreats and it finds itself two miles inland. Such is the case with the wonderful town of Rye, one of the original Cinque Ports. The skewiff little houses tumbling down steep streets are tremendously snappable – a fact that draws the summer hordes to Rye and has resulted in rather too much commercialisation. Still, this is a great place to visit, and is rich with literary connections. Radclyffe Hall and EF Benson lived here, as did **Henry James**, whose former residence **Lamb House** (call the National Trust for information on 01892 890651) is open to the public. Also worth a peek are **Rye Castle** (01797 226728) and **Rye Art Gallery** (01797 222433). Two of the best B&Bs in town are **Jeake's House** on Mermaid Street (01797 222828; £49-£89) and **Little Orchard House** on West Street (01797 223831; £64-£84). Eating options include the **Landgate Bistro** (01797 222829) and the **Mermaid** inn (01797 223065).

If you want to avoid the Rye crowds, you need only travel a couple of miles south-west to **Winchelsea**, another little town abandoned by the sea. It was planned on a grid pattern by Edward I in the thirteenth century and contains a wonderfully evocative ruined church. There's a shingly beach a mile or so south of here.

Walmer, Deal & Dover

Getting there *by train* from Charing Cross to Walmer, Deal or Dover Priory (1 hour 40 mins-2 hours); *by car* to Walmer and Deal, J13 off M20 then A258; to Dover, J13 off M20.

Part of the chain of coastal forts built by Henry VIII to protect Britain from the fury aroused in the remaining Catholic countries of Europe by the Reformation, Walmer and Deal, only a mile apart, make a satisfying comparison. **Walmer Castle** (01304 364288), next to the beach where Julius Caesar landed in 55 BC, has been converted into a stately home for the Warden of the Cinque Ports (HM the Queen Mother) with splendid gardens. **Deal Castle** (01304 372762) remains almost unchanged: a sturdy, menacing structure (shaped like a Tudor rose) with long gloomy passages.

Eight miles (13km) to the south, **Dover Castle** (01304 201628) was once the most strategically important castle in Britain, dominating the narrowest point of the English Channel and has been in constant use for the last 800 years. Within the cliffs on which it perches are a warren of tunnels to explore. Walking along the castle's walls you are closer to that distressingly Eurosceptic island spirit of complacent security than almost anywhere else in the land. Other attractions in not-very-attractive Dover include the **White Cliffs Experience** (01304 214566), which recreates the town in Roman times and during World War II, and the informative **Dover Museum** (01304 201066).

Whitstable

Kent. **Getting there** *by train* from Victoria (1 hour 15 mins); *by car* J7 off M2 then A99.

Much of the north Kent coast is not particularly appealing, but the civilised little town of Whitstable is an exception. The seafront, looking out on to a neat shingle beach, is unobstrusive and well mannered, but most people come to Whitstable to eat. The town has long been famous for its oysters (previously considered a poor man's food) and fine seafood now fills the menus of a number of excellent restaurants, the pick of which is probably the **Royal Native Oyster Stores** (01227 276856), which also offers quirky, characterful rooms for the night at the **Hotel Continental** (01227 280280) just a few hundred yards away (£40-£60). You can brush up on your bivalve knowledge in the **Oyster & Fishery Exhibition** (01227 262003) or of the town itself in the **Whitstable Museum & Gallery** (01227 276998).

Directory

Resources A-Z

Customs

When entering the UK, non-EU citizens and anyone buying duty-free goods should be aware of the following import limits:

- 200 cigarettes **or** 100 cigarillos **or** 50 cigars **or** 250 grams (8.82 ounces) tobacco;
- 2 litres still table wine **plus either** 1 litre spirits or strong liqueurs (over 22 per cent alcohol by volume) **or** 2 litres fortified wine (under 22 per cent abv), sparkling wine or other liqueurs;
- 60cc/ml perfume;
- 250cc/ml toilet water;
- other goods to the value of £32 for non-commercial use;
- the import of meat, meat products, fruit, plants, flowers and protected animals is restricted or forbidden;
- no restrictions on import and export of currency.

Since the Single European Market agreement came into force at the beginning of 1993, people over the age of 17 arriving from an EU country have been able to import limitless goods for their own personal use, if bought tax-paid (not duty-free). But Customs officials may need convincing that you do not intend to sell any of the goods.

Embassies

For other embassies, consulates and high commissions check the telephone directory and *Yellow Pages* under 'Embassies'.

American Embassy *24 Grosvenor Square, W1 (0171 499 9000). Bond Street or Marble Arch tube.* **Open** 8.30am-5.30pm Mon-Fri. **Map 7 G7**

Australian High Commission *Australia House, Strand, WC2 (0171 379 4334). Holborn or Temple tube.* **Open** 9.30am-3.30pm Mon-Fri. **Map 8 M6**

Canadian High Commission *38 Grosvenor Street, W1 (0171 258 6600). Bond Street tube.* **Open** 8-11am Mon-Fri. **Map 7 H7**

French Embassy *58 Knightsbridge, SW1 (0171 201 1000). Knightsbridge tube.* **Open** *phone enquiries* 9.30am-1pm, 2.30-6pm, Mon-Fri. **Map 2 F9**. **Consulate General** *21 Cromwell Road, SW7 (0171 838 2000). South Kensington tube.* **Open** 8.45am-3pm Mon-Thur; 8.45am-noon Fri. **Map 4 D10**. **Visa section** *6A Cromwell Place, SW7 (0171 838 2050/24-hour visa helpline 0891 887733). South Kensington tube.* **Open** 9-10am, 1.30-2.30pm, Mon-Fri. **Map 4 D10**

German Embassy *23 Belgrave Square, SW1 (0171 824 1300). Hyde Park Corner or Knightsbridge tube/rail.* **Open** 9am-noon Mon-Fri. **Map 7 G9**

New Zealand High Commission *80 Haymarket, SW1 (0171 930 8422). Piccadilly Circus tube.* **Open** 9am-5pm Mon-Fri. **Map 8 K7**

South African Embassy *South Africa House, Trafalgar Square, WC2 (0171 451 7299). Charing Cross tube/rail.* **Open** 9am-1pm, 2-5pm, Mon-Fri. **Map 8 K7**

Health

Free emergency medical treatment under the National Health Service (NHS) is available to:

Emergencies

In the event of a serious accident, fire or incident, call **999** and specify whether you require ambulance, fire service or police. *See also below* **Health**.

- European Union nationals, plus those of Iceland, Norway and Liechtenstein. People from these countries are also entitled to specific treatment for a non-emergency condition on production of form E112.
- Nationals (on production of a passport) of Bulgaria, Czech and Slovak Republics, Gibraltar, Hungary, Malta, New Zealand, Russia, former Soviet Union states (except Latvia, Lithuania and Estonia) and former Yugoslavia.
- Residents, irrespective of nationality, of Anguilla, Australia, Barbados, British Virgin Islands, Channel Islands, Falkland Islands, Iceland, Isle of Man, Montserrat, Poland, Romania, St Helena, Sweden, Turks & Caicos Islands.
- Anyone who at the time of receiving treatment has been in the UK for the previous 12 months.
- Anyone who has come to the UK to take up permanent residence.
- Students and trainees whose course requires them to spend more than 12 weeks in employment during their first year. Students and others living in the UK for a settled purpose for more than six months may be accepted as ordinarily resident and not liable to charges.
- Refugees and others who have sought refuge in the UK.
- Anyone formally detained by the Immigration Authorities.
- People with HIV/AIDS at a special clinic for the treatment of sexually transmitted diseases. The

treatment covered is limited to a diagnostic test and counselling associated with that test.

There are no NHS charges for the following:

- Treatment in Accident & Emergency departments.
- Certain district nursing, midwifery or health visiting.
- Emergency ambulance transport.
- Diagnosis and treatment of certain communicable diseases including STDs.
- Family planning services.
- Compulsory psychiatric treatment.

Any further advice should be obtained from the Patient Services Manager at the hospital where treatment is to be sought.

Accident & emergency

Below are listed most of the hospitals with 24-hour casualty departments. Those within central London are marked on the maps at the back of this guide by a white cross on a red square.

Charing Cross Hospital
Fulham Palace Road, W6 (0181 746 5555). Barons Court or Hammersmith tube.

Chelsea & Westminster Hospital
369 Fulham Road, SW10 (0181 746 8000). Bus 14, 73, 211. **Map 3 C12**

Guy's Hospital
St Thomas Street (entrance Snowsfields, off Weston Street), SE1 (0171 955 5000). London Bridge tube/rail. **Map 12 Q8**

Hackney & Homerton Hospital
Homerton Row, E9 (0181 510 5555). Homerton rail/22B bus.

Royal Free Hospital
Pond Street, NW3 (0171 794 0500). Belsize Park tube/Hampstead Heath rail.

Royal London Hospital
Whitechapel Road, E1 (0171 377 7000). Whitechapel tube.

St George's Hospital
Blackshaw Road, SW17 (0181 672 1255). Tooting Broadway tube.

St Mary's Hospital
Praed Street, W2 (0171 886 6666). Paddington tube/rail. **Map 2 D5**

St Thomas's Hospital
Lambeth Palace Road, SE1 (0171 928 9292). Waterloo tube/rail or Westminster tube. **Map 8 L9**

University College Hospital
Grafton Way, WC1 (0171 387 9300). Euston Square or Warren Street tube. **Map 5 J4**

Whittington Hospital
St Mary's Wing, Highgate Hill, N19 (0171 272 3070). Archway tube.

Chemists

For late-opening chemists, *see page 211.*

Contraception/abortion

Family planning advice, contraceptive supplies and abortions are free to British citizens on the National Health Service. This also applies to EU residents and foreign nationals living, working and studying in Britain. Two doctors must agree that an abortion is justified within the terms of the Abortion Act 1967, as amended, whether it's on the NHS or not. If you decide to go private, contact one of the organisations listed below.

British Pregnancy Advisory Service

7 Belgrave Road, SW1 (0171 828 2484). Victoria tube/rail.
Open phone first for an appointment; *phone lines* 8am-8pm Mon-Fri; 8.30am-6pm Sat; 9.30am-1pm Sun. **Map 7 H10**
Contraception advice, contraceptives and the morning-after pill are available. The service carries out pregnancy tests and makes referrals to BPAS nursing homes for private abortions.

Brook Advisory Centre

233 Tottenham Court Road, W1 (enquiries 0171 323 1522/ appointments 0171 580 2991/ 24-hour helpline 0171 617 8000). Tottenham Court Road tube.
Open *enquiries/appointments* 9.30am-7.30pm Mon-Thur; 9.30am-3pm Fri; noon-2pm Sat.
Map 6 K5
There are 14 Brook Advisory family planning clinics in central London. Call the above number to find your nearest. Advice is given on contraception, sexual problems and abortion with referral to an NHS hospital or private clinic.

Family Planning Association

2-12 Pentonville Road, N1 (0171 837 5432/Contraceptive Education Service helpline 0171 837 4044). Angel tube. **Open** 9am-5pm Mon-Thur; 9am-4.30pm Fri; *helpline* 9am-7pm Mon-Fri. **Map 9 N2**
There are more than 1,800 NHS-run Family Planning Clinics in Britain.

Phone the first number to find your nearest.

Marie Stopes House

Family Planning Clinic/ Well Woman Centre *108 Whitfield Street, W1 (0171 388 0662/family planning 0171 388 2585/sterilisation 0171 388 5554). Warren Street tube.* **Open** 9am-5pm Mon, Thur-Sat; 9am-8pm Tue, Wed. **Map 5 J5**
Contraceptives, treatment and advice for gynaecological complaints, counselling for sexual problems and referral for abortion. Fees vary.

Dental services

Dental care is free under the NHS to the following British residents:

- Under-18s.
- Under-19s in full-time education.
- Pregnant women and those with a baby under the age of one when treatment begins.
- People receiving Income Support, Jobseeker's Allowance, Family Credit or Disability Working Allowance.

All other patients, NHS or private, must pay. NHS charges start from around £4 for a check-up or a filling. To find an NHS dentist, get in touch with the local Health Authority or a Citizens' Advice Bureau (*see page 292*). Private dentists can charge whatever they like. We list emergency services below.

Dental Emergency Care Service

(0171 955 2186). **Open** 8.45am-3.30pm Mon-Fri.
The Dental Emergency Care Service refers callers to a surgery open for treatment (private or NHS).

Guy's Hospital Dental School

Guy's Tower, St Thomas Street, SE1 (0171 955 4317). London Bridge tube/rail. **Open** 9am-3pm Mon-Fri.
Map 12 Q8
Walk-in dental emergency service. Free, except weekends.

Doctors & medication

If you are a British citizen or working in the UK, you can go to any general practitioner (GP). If you are not visiting your usual GP, you will be asked for details of the doctor with whom you are registered. People who are ordinarily resident in the UK, such as overseas students, can also register with an NHS doctor.

Many drugs cannot be bought over the counter. A pharmacist will dispense medicines on receipt of a prescription from a GP. An NHS prescription costs £5.80 at present (some people, such as children under the age of 16 and people over 60, are exempt from paying). If you are not eligible to see an NHS doctor, you will be charged cost price for medicines prescribed by a private doctor.

Great Chapel Street Medical Centre

13 Great Chapel Street, W1 (0171 437 9360). Tottenham Court Road tube. **Open** 11am-12.30pm Mon, Tue, Thur; 2-4pm Mon-Fri (phone for available times). **Map 6 K6**
Walk-in NHS surgery for anyone without a doctor.

Medicine: complementary

British Acupuncture Council

Park House, 206 Latimer Road, W10 6RE (0181 964 0222). **Open** *phone enquiries* 9.30am-5.30pm Mon-Fri.
Phone or write for your local registered specialist. The Council will provide lists of acupuncture practitioners.

British Holistic Medical Association

59 Landsdowne Place, Hove, East Sussex, BN3 1FL (01273 725951).
Networking organisation run by a group of doctors for practitioners, clients and anyone interested in holistic healing.

British Homeopathic Association

27A Devonshire Street, W1N 1RJ (0171 935 2163). **Open** *phone enquiries* 1.30-5pm Mon-Fri.
The BHA will give you the address of your nearest homeopathic chemist and doctor (send a stamped self-addressed envelope for a list).

Opticians

See page 209.

Physiotherapy

Chartered Society of Physiotherapy

14 Bedford Row, WC1R 4ED (0171 242 1941). **Open** *phone enquiries* 9am-5pm Mon-Fri.
This is the professional body of phys-iotherapists. The CSP can check whether any practitioner is a qualified member.

STDs/HIV/AIDS

NHS Genito-Urinary Clinics (such as the **Centre for Sexual Health**; *see below*) are affiliated to major hospitals. They provide free, confidential treatment of sexually transmitted diseases (STDs) and non-sex-related problems, such as thrush and cystitis. They offer information and counselling about HIV and other STDs, and can conduct a confidential blood test to determine HIV status. Government and Health Education Authority pamphlets – *AIDS: The Facts, Safer Sex and the Condom* and *AIDS: The Test* – are available from clinics and (with a stamped self-addressed envelope) by post from: Health Education Authority, Hamilton House, Mabledon Place, WC1H 9TX. *See also below* **Helplines & information**.

AIDS Helpline

(0800 567123/minicom 0800 521361). **Open** 24 hours daily; *minicom* 10am-10pm daily.
A free and confidential information service. The helpline caters for ten languages at certain times and days, including Bengali (0800 371132; 6-10pm Tue), Gujarati and Urdu (both 0800 371134; 6-10pm Wed).

Body Positive

14 Greek Street, W1 (0171 287 8010/helpline 0800 616212). Tottenham Court Road or Leicester Square tube. **Open** 11am-7pm Mon-Fri; noon-5pm Sat; *helpline* 7-10pm Mon-Fri; 4-10pm Sat, Sun. **Map 6 K6**
Run by and for people who are HIV-positive, Body Positive offers comple-mentary therapies and counselling by appointment. A course is available for those who have been recently diagnosed and a newsletter is published monthly.

Centre for Sexual Health

Genito-Urinary Clinic, Jefferiss Wing, St Mary's Hospital, Praed Street, W2 (0171 886 1697). Paddington tube/rail. **Open** 8.45am-7pm Mon; 8.45am-6pm Tue, Fri; 10.45am-6pm Wed; 8am-1pm Thur; 10am-noon Sat (new patients must arrive at least 30 mins before closing). **Map 2 D5**
Walk-in clinic; free and confidential.

Terrence Higgins Trust

52-54 Gray's Inn Road, WC1 (admin 0171 831 0330/helpline 0171 242 1010/legal line 0171 405 2381). **Open** *helpline* noon-10pm daily; *legal line* 7-9pm Mon, Wed.
The Trust advises and counsels those with HIV/AIDS, their relatives, lovers and friends. Free leaflets about AIDS are available. The Trust also gives advice about safer sex.

Helplines & information

See also **STDs/HIV/AIDS**.

Alcoholics Anonymous

(0171 352 3001). **Open** *helpline* 10am-10pm daily.
A helpline for the London area. Operators put you in touch with a member in your area who can act as an escort to your first meeting.

Capital Radio Helpline

(0171 484 4000). **Open** *helpline* 10am-10pm Mon-Fri; 10am-4pm Sat, Sun.
Run in conjunction with Capital Radio, this helpline tackles queries about anything. If the staff can't answer your query themselves, they'll put you in touch with someone who can help. The line is always busy, so keep trying.

Childline

Freepost 1111, London N1 OBR (0800 1111/0171 239 1000). **Open** *phone lines* 24 hours daily.
Free and confidential national helpline for children and young people in trouble or danger.

Gamblers Anonymous

(0171 384 3040). **Open** 8am-11pm daily.
Advice is offered by members of the fellowship and referrals to meetings.

Healthline

(0345 678444). **Open** 10am-5pm Mon-Fri.
A free (except for the call) telephone information service. Ask to listen to any of the 400 health-related tapes. These give details of symptoms and contact names of groups involved with treatment or support for sufferers. Health advice can also be gleaned from staff.

Directory

Just Ask

46 Bishopsgate, EC2 (0171 628 3380). Liverpool Street tube/rail. **Open** *counselling* 10am-9pm Mon-Thur; 10am-5pm Fri; *helpline* 10am-6pm Mon-Thur; 10am-5pm Fri (after-hours answerphone). **Map 12 R6**

Counselling is targeted at people aged 35 and under who are homeless, unemployed or on a low income, but advice will be given to anyone with a personal problem. Closed for counselling in August.

London Rape Crisis Centre

(0171 837 1600).

Free, confidential rape counselling. Due to cuts in funding, there are no set opening times for this line.

London Women's Aid

(0171 392 2092). **Open** 10am-1pm, 2-4.45pm, Mon-Fri.

Refuge referral for women suffering domestic violence. An after-hours answerphone gives alternative numbers for immediate help.

Medical Advisory Service

(0181 994 9874). **Open** 5-10pm Mon-Fri.

Helpline for most medical problems.

MIND

Granta House, 15-19 Broadway, E15 (0181 519 2122/info line 0181 522 1728/0345 660163). **Open** *info line* 9.15am-4.45pm Mon-Fri.

Callers to the mental health charity MIND will be referred to one of 34 London groups. MIND's legal service advises on maltreatment, wrongful detention and sectioning.

Narcotics Anonymous

(0171 730 0009). **Open** 10am-10pm daily.

Run by members of the fellowship, this helpline offers advice, and informs callers of their nearest meeting.

National Association of Citizens' Advice Bureaux

Greater London Office, 136-144 City Road, EC1 (0171 251 2000). **Open** *phone enquiries* 9am-5pm Mon-Fri.

CABs are run by local councils, offering free advice on legal, financial and personal matters. The above office does not give advice itself but will direct callers to their nearest CAB. Alternatively, check the phone book.

National Childbirth Trust

(0181 992 8637). **Open** 9.30am-4.30pm Mon-Fri.

Independent charity offering information and support to women in pregnancy, childbirth and early parenthood.

Rape and Sexual Abuse Centre

(0181 239 1122). **Open** noon-2.30pm, 7-9.30pm, Mon-Fri; 2.30-5pm Sat, Sun.

Offers support and information to those who have experienced rape or sexual abuse.

Refuge Crisis Line

(0181 995 4430). **Open** 24 hours daily.

Refuge referral for women experiencing domestic violence.

Rights of Women

(0171 251 6577). **Open** noon-2pm, 7-9pm, Tue, Thur; 3-5pm, 7-9pm, Wed; noon-2pm Fri.

Provides legal advice for women.

Samaritans

(0171 734 2800). **Open** 24 hours daily.

The Samaritans will listen to anyone with emotional problems. It's a popular service and you may have to phone several times before getting through.

Victim Support

National Office, Cranmer House, 39 Brixton Road, SW9 (0171 735 9166 with after-hours answerphone/fax 0171 582 5712). Oval tube. **Open** 9am-5.30pm Mon-Fri.

Victims of crime are put in touch with a volunteer who provides emotional and practical support, including information on legal procedures and advice on compensation. Interpreters can be arranged.

Insurance

Insuring personal belongings is highly advisable, and difficult to arrange once you have arrived in London, so organise it before you leave home.

Medical insurance is often included in travel insurance packages, and it's important to have it unless your country has a reciprocal medical treatment arrangement with Britain (*see page 289*). EU citizens (and those from Iceland, Norway and Liechtenstein) are entitled to free emergency healthcare in hospitals under the NHS. Those wanting specific treatment under the NHS will need form E112, while citizens of these countries studying in the UK for less than six months are entitled to full NHS treatment if they have form E128.

Left luggage

Airports

Gatwick Airport
(South Terminal 01293 502014/ North Terminal 01293 502013).

Heathrow Airport
(Terminal 1 0181 745 5301/ Terminal 2 0181 759 3344/ Terminal 3 0181 745 4599/ Terminal 4 0181 745 7460).

London City Airport
(0171 646 0000).

Luton Airport
(01582 405100).

Stansted Airport
(01279 663213).

Railway stations

To find out which stations will store luggage call 0171 928 5151.

Lost property

Always inform the police if you lose anything (to validate insurance claims). Go to the nearest police station. Only dial the emergency number (999) if violence has occurred. A lost passport should be reported to the police and to your embassy (*see page 289*).

Airports

The following lost property offices deal only with items lost in the airports concerned. For property lost on the plane contact the airline or handling agents dealing with the flight.

Gatwick Airport
(01293 503162).

Heathrow Airport
(0181 745 7727).

London City Airport
(0171 646 0000).

Luton Airport
(01582 395219).

Stansted Airport
(01279 680500).

Bus & tube

London Transport *Lost Property Office, 200 Baker Street, NW1 (recorded info 0171 486 2496). Baker Street tube.* **Map 5 G4.** Allow three days from the time of loss. If you lose something on a bus, call 0171 222 1234 and ask for the phone numbers of the depots at either end of the route. Pick up a lost property form from any tube station.

Railway stations

If you have lost property in an overground station or on a train call 0171 928 5151; an operator will connect you to the appropriate station.

Taxis

Taxi Lost Property *15 Penton Street, N1 (0171 833 0996). Angel tube.* **Map 9 N2**
This office off Pentonville Road deals only with property that has been found in registered black cabs. For items lost in a minicab you will have to contact the office from which you hired the cab.

Money

Until the UK catches up with the rest of the Europe and adopts the euro, the nation's currency remains the pound sterling (£). One pound equals 100 pence (p). 1p and 2p coins are copper; 5p, 10p, 20p and the seven-sided 50p coins are silver; £1 is a yellowy-gold coin; the new £2 coin is silver in the centre with a circle of yellowy-gold around the edge. Paper notes are as follows: blue £5, orange £10, purple £20 and red £50. Note, though, that you will probably find an increasing number of places pre-empting the government and accepting euros – but don't rely on this.

You can exchange foreign currency at banks and bureaux de change (*see below*). If you're here for a long stay, you may need to open a bank or building society account. To do this, you'll probably need to present a reference from your bank at home, and certainly a passport as identification.

Banks

Minimum opening hours are 9.30am-3.30pm Monday to Friday, but most branches close at 4.30pm. Cash can be obtained at any time from machines outside most banks.

Banks generally offer the best exchange rates, although rates can vary considerably from place to place and it pays to shop around. Commission is sometimes charged for cashing travellers' cheques in foreign currencies, but not for sterling travellers' cheques, provided you cash the cheques at a bank affiliated to the issuing bank (get a list when you buy your cheques). Commission is charged if you change cash into another currency. You always need identification, such as a passport, when exchanging travellers' cheques.

Bureaux de change

You will be charged for cashing travellers' cheques or buying and selling foreign currency at a bureau de change. Commission rates, which should be clearly displayed, vary. **Chequepoint** (16 London branches), **Lenlyn** (24 London branches) and **Thomas Cook** (73 London branches; many within branches of Midland Bank) are reputable bureaux. Major rail and tube stations in central London have bureaux de change, and there are many in tourist areas. Most are open 8am-9pm, but those listed below are open 24 hours daily.

Chequepoint

548 Oxford Street, W1 (0171 723 1005). Marble Arch tube. **Map 5 G6**
222 Earl's Court Road, SW5 (0171 370 3238). Earl's Court tube. **Map 3 B11**
2 Queensway, W2 (0171 229 0093). Queensway tube. **Map 1 C6**
37 Coventry Street, SW1 (0171 839 3772). Leicester Square tube. **Map 8 K7**

Lost/stolen credit cards

Report lost or stolen credit cards immediately to both the police and the 24-hour services listed below. Inform your bank by phone and in writing.

American Express *(Personal Card 01273 696933/Corporate Card 01273 689955).*
Diners Club/Diners Club International *(General enquiries &*
emergencies 01252 513500/ 0800 460800).
Eurocard *(00 49 697 933 1910). This German number will accept reversed charges in an emergency.*
JCB *(0171 499 3000).*
MasterCard *(0800 964767).*
Visa *(0800 895082).*

Money transfers

Western Union

(0800 833833).
The old standby for bailing cash-challenged travellers out of trouble – but it's pricey. Expect to pay a whopping 10%-plus commission.

Police & security

The police are a good source of information about the locality and are used to helping visitors find their way. If you have been robbed, assaulted or involved in an infringement of the law, look under 'Police' in the phone directory for the nearest police station, or call directory enquiries (free from public payphones) on 192.

If you have a complaint to make about the police, there are several things you can do. Make sure that you take the offending police officer's identifying number, which should be prominently displayed on his or her epaulette. You can then register a complaint with the **Police Complaints Authority**, 10 Great George Street, SW1P 3AE (0171 273 6450). Alternatively, contact any police station or visit a solicitor or a Law Centre. Dial 999 only in an emergency.

Violent crime is relatively rare in London, but, as in any major city, it is unwise to take any risks. Thieves and pickpockets specifically target unwary tourists. Use common sense and follow these basic rules:

● **Keep** your wallet and purse out of sight. Don't wear a wrist wallet (they are easily snatched). Keep your handbag securely closed.

● **Don't** leave a handbag, briefcase, bag or coat unattended, especially in pubs, cinemas, department stores or fast-food shops, on public transport, at railway stations and airports, or in crowds.

- **Don't** leave your bag or coat beside, under or on the back of your chair.
- **Don't** put your bag on the floor near the door of a public toilet.
- **Don't** wear expensive jewellery or watches that can be easily snatched.
- **Don't** put your purse down on the table in a restaurant or on a shop counter while you scrutinise the bill.
- **Don't** carry a wallet in your back pocket.
- **Don't** flash your money or credit cards around.
- **Avoid** parks after dark. Late at night, travel in groups of three or more.

Postal services

Post office opening hours are usually 9am-5.30pm Monday to Friday; 9am-noon Saturday, with the exception of **Trafalgar Square Post Office** (24-28 William IV Street, WC2; 0171 930 9580; Charing Cross tube/rail), which is open 8am-8pm Monday to Friday; 9am-8pm Saturday. The busiest time of day is usually 1-2pm. Listed below are the other main central London post offices.

43-44 Albemarle Street, W1 (0171 493 5620). Green Park tube. **Map 7 J7**

111 Baker Street, W1 (0171 935 3701). Baker Street tube. **Map 5 G5**

202 Great Portland Street, W1 (0171 636 9935). Great Portland Street tube. **Map 5 H4**

3-9 Heddon Street, W1 (0171 734 5556). Piccadilly Circus tube. **Map 7 J7**

43 Seymour Street, W1 (0171 723 0867). Marble Arch tube. **Map 2 F6**

24 Thayer Street, W1 (0171 935 0239). Bond Street tube. **Map 5 G5**

32A Grosvenor Street, W1 (0171 629 2480). Bond Street tube. **Map 7 H7**

19 Newman Street, W1 (0171 636 9995). Tottenham Court Road tube. **Map 5 J5**

Cracking the codes

London led the way in the development of postcodes. Post office pioneer Sir Rowland Hill split the capital into 10 postal districts corresponding to the points of a compass in 1857-8 – northern, north-eastern, eastern, south-eastern, southern, south-western, western, north-western, plus western central and eastern central. A decade later the southern and north-eastern districts were merged into south-western/south-eastern and eastern districts respectively, meaning that today there are no 'S' or 'NE' codes.

World War I played a role in subsequent changes to the system. With most of the Post Office's experienced post sorters away being blown to bits in the trenches, a numbering system was introduced to aid the neophyte sorters. This was based not on proximity to the centre, but on the position of the initial letter of each sub-district in the alphabet. Thus, SE2 is Abbey Wood on the far eastern boundary of London, more than ten miles (16km) from the

centre, while Walworth SE17 is not much more than a mile from the Houses of Parliament. Hardly very intuitive.

At a later date various districts were merged and new ones created, making it necessary to start again from the beginning of the alphabet for the SE and SW districts (so although Woolwich is SE18, Dulwich is SW21). A further refinement of the system was implemented between 1968 and 1971 resulting in some codes gaining an extra letter (eg SW1 to SW1A) and ways continue to be sought to update and improve the system today.

Below are the postcodes that crop up most frequently in this guide:

WC1	Bloomsbury, Holborn, St Pancras
WC2	Covent Garden, Strand
EC1	Holborn, Clerkenwell, St Luke's
EC2	Barbican, Liverpool Street
EC3	Tower Hill, Aldgate
EC4	Temple, St Paul's, Cannon Street

W1	West End (Mayfair, Soho, Marylebone)
W2	Bayswater
W4	Chiswick
W6	Hammersmith
W8	Kensington
W11	Notting Hill
SW1	Westminster, Victoria, St James's, Belgravia
SW2	Brixton
SW3	Chelsea
SW4	Clapham
SW5	Earl's Court
SW6	Fulham
SW7	Kensington (South)
SW10	West Brompton
SW11	Battersea
SW15	Putney
SW19	Wimbledon
SE1	Southwark, Lambeth, Borough
SE3	Blackheath
SE10	Greenwich
SE16	Rotherhithe
SE21	Dulwich
E1	Aldgate, Stepney, Whitechapel
E2	Bethnal Green
E3	Bow
E8	Hackney
E11	Leytonstone
E14	Poplar, Isle of Dogs
E15	Stratford
E17	Walthamstow
N1	Barnsbury, Islington, Canonbury
N16	Stoke Newington
NW1	Camden, Regent's Park
NW3	Hampstead

Directory

Poste restante

If you intend to travel around Britain, friends from home can write to you care of a post office, where mail will be kept at the enquiry desk for up to one month. Your name and 'Poste Restante' must be clearly marked on the letter above the following address: Post Office, 24-28 William IV Street, London WC2N 4DL. Bring ID when you come to collect mail.

Stamp prices

You can buy stamps at all post offices and also at many news-agents. Current prices are 20p for second-class and 30p for first-class letters and letters to EU countries. Postcards cost 30p to send within the EU and 37p to countries outside Europe. Rates for other letters and parcels vary according to weight and destination.

Express delivery services

DHL
181 Strand, WC2 (0345 100300). **Open** *phoneline* 24 hours daily; *office* 8am-9pm Mon-Fri. **Credit** AmEx, DC, MC, V. **Map 8 L7**
Worldwide express delivery service. Next-day deliveries can be made within the EU (though not guaranteed), and the USA if booked before 2pm.

Federal Express
9 Elms Lane, SW8 (0800 123800). **Open** *phoneline* 7.30am-7.30pm Mon-Fri; *office* 9am-7pm Mon-Fri. **Credit** AmEx, MC, V.
Fed Ex can deliver day by day by 8am to certain destinations across the USA (mainly NY and other major cities). More than 210 countries are served.

UPS
UPS House, Forest Road, Middlesex (0345 877877). **Open** 8am-8pm Mon-Fri; 8am-1pm Sat. **Credit** AmEx, MC, V.
UPS offers express delivery to more than 200 countries; cheaper, slower services are also available. Deliveries to some destinations can be guaranteed to arrive by 8.30am or 10.30am the next day.

Public holidays

On public holidays (known as bank holidays) many shops

remain open, but public transport services are less frequent. The exception is Christmas Day, when almost everything closes down.

New Year's Eve Fri 31 Dec 1999.
New Year's Day Sat 1 Jan 2000; Mon 1 Jan 2001.
Good Friday Fri 2 Apr 1999; Fri 21 Apr 2000.
Easter Monday Mon 5 Apr 1999; Mon 24 Apr 2000.
May Day Holiday Mon 3 May 1999; Mon 1 May 2000.
Spring Bank Holiday Mon 31 May 1999; Mon 29 May 2000.
Summer Bank Holiday Mon 30 Aug 1999; Mon 28 Aug 2000.
Christmas Day Sat 25 Dec 1999; Mon 25 Dec 2000.
Boxing Day Sun 26 Dec 1999; Tue 26 Dec 2000.

Religion

Anglican
St Paul's Cathedral
For listings details see p43.
Services 7.30am, 8am, 12.30pm, 5pm, Mon-Fri; 8am, 8.30am, 12.30pm, 5pm, Sat; 8am, 10.15am, 11.30am, 3.15pm, 6pm, Sun. **Map 11 O6**
Times vary due to special events, phone to check.

Westminster Abbey
For listings details see p70.
Services 7.30am, 8am (Holy Communion), 12.30pm, 5pm (choral evensong, except Wed), Mon-Fri; 8am, 9.20am, 3pm (evensong), Sat; 8am, 10am (sung matins), 11.15am (abbey eucharist), 3pm (evensong), 5.45pm organ recital, 6.30pm (evening service), Sun. **Map 8 K9**

Baptist
Bloomsbury Central Baptist Church
235 Shaftesbury Avenue, WC2 (0171 836 6843/240 0544). Tottenham Court Road tube. **Open** *office* 10am-5pm daily; *Friendship Centre* (closed Aug, Sept) 11.30am-2.30pm Tue; 10.30am-8.30pm Sun. **Services** 11am, 6.30pm, Sun. **Map 6 L6**

Buddhist
Buddhapadipa Temple
14 Calonne Road, SW19 (0181 946 1357). Wimbledon Park tube. **Open** *temple* 1-6pm Sat; 8.30-10.30am, 12.30-6pm, Sun; *meditation retreat* 7-9pm Tue, Thur.

Catholic
Brompton Oratory
For listings details see p73.
Services 7am, 7.30am, 8am (Latin

mass), 10am, 12.30am, 6pm, Mon-Fri; 7am, 7.30am, 8am, 10am, 6pm, Sat; 7am, 8am, 9am, 10am (tridentine), 11am (sung Latin), 12.30pm, 3.30pm (vespers and benediction), 4.30pm, 7pm, Sun. **Map 4 E10**

Westminster Cathedral
For listings details see p70.
Services eight daily masses Mon-Fri; seven daily masses Sat; 7am, 8am, 9am, 10.30am, noon, 5.30pm, 7pm, Sun. **Map 7 J10**

Hindu
Swaminarayan Hindu Mission
105-119 Brentfield Road, NW10 (enquiries to Amrish Patel on 0181 961 5031). Neasden tube or Harlesden tube/rail. **Open** 9am-6.30pm daily. **Services** 11.45am, 7pm, daily.
In addition to a large prayer hall, this huge complex provides north-west London's Hindu community with a social and cultural centre, comprising a conference hall, a 2,000-capacity marriage suite, sports facilities, a library and a health clinic. *See also p112.*

Islamic
London Central Mosque
146 Park Road, NW8 (0171 724 3363). Baker Street tube/74 bus. **Open** dawn-dusk daily.
Services phone to check.

East London Mosque
84-98 Whitechapel Road, E1 (0171 247 1357). Aldgate East or Whitechapel tube. **Open** phone to check. **Services** *Friday prayer* 1.25pm (1.10pm in winter).
Map 12 S6

Jewish
Liberal Jewish Synagogue
28 St John's Wood Road, NW8 (0171 286 5181). St John's Wood tube. **Open** *enquiries* 9am-5pm Mon-Thur; 9am-3pm Fri.
Services 6.45pm Fri; 11am Sat.

West Central Liberal Synagogue
109 Whitfield Street, SW1 (0171 636 7627). Warren Street tube.
Services 3pm Sat. **Map 5 J4**

Methodist
Methodist Church
Westminster Central Hall, Storey's Gate, SW1 (0171 222 8010). St James's Park tube. **Open** *Chapel* 9am-5pm Mon-Fri. **Services** 12.45pm Wed; 10am, 11am, 6.30pm, Sun. **Map 8 K9**

Quaker
Religious Society of Friends (Quakers)
Friends House, 173-177 Euston Road, NW1 (0171 387 3601). Euston tube/rail. **Open** 8am-9pm Mon-Fri. **Meetings** 11am Sun.
Map 6 K3

Telephones

To phone London from outside the UK, dial 00 (the international dialling code), followed by 44 (the code for Britain), then the ten-digit number starting with 171 or 181 (ie omitting the first 0).

International dialling codes

Australia (*00 61*); **Austria** (*00 43*); **Belgium** (*00 32*); **Brazil** (*00 55*); **Canada** (*00 1*); **Czech Republic** (*00 42*); **Denmark** (*00 45*); **France** (*00 33*); **Germany** (*00 49*); **Greece** (*00 30*); **Hong Kong** (*00 852*); **India** (*00 91*); **Iceland** (*00 354*); **Ireland** (*00 353*); **Israel** (*00 972*); **Italy** (*00 39*); **Japan** (*00 81*); **Netherlands** (*00 31*); **New Zealand** (*00 64*); **Norway** (*00 47*); **Portugal** (*00 351*); **Russia** (*00 7*); **South Africa** (*00 27*); **Spain** (*00 34*); **Sweden** (*00 46*); **Switzerland** (*00 41*); **USA** (*00 1*).

Operator services

Operator

Call **100** for the operator in the following circumstances: when you have difficulty in dialling; for an early-morning alarm call; to make a credit card call; for information about the cost of a call; and for international person-to-person calls.

Dial **155** if you need to reverse the charges (call collect) or if you can't dial direct, but be warned that this service is very expensive.

Directory enquiries

Dial **192** for any number in Britain, or **153** for international numbers. Phoning directory enquiries from a private phone is expensive, and only two enquiries are allowed per call. However, if you phone from a public call box, directory enquiries calls are free.

Talking Pages

This service lists the numbers of thousands of businesses in the UK. Dial **0800 600900** and tell them what type of business you require, and in what area of London. Calls are free and the line is open 24 hours a day.

International telemessages/telegrams

Call **0800 190190** to phone in your message and it will be delivered by post the next day (£8.99 for up to 50 words, an additional £1 for a greeting card). There is no longer a domestic telegram service, but you can still send telegrams abroad. Call the same number if you urgently need to contact someone abroad.

Public phones

Public payphones take coins, credit cards or prepaid phonecards (sometimes all three). The minimum cost is 10p, but some payphones (such as counter-top ones found in many pubs) require a minimum of 20p.

British Telecom phonecards

Available from post offices and many newsagents. **Cost** 10p per unit; cards in denominations of £2, £5, £10 and £20. Call boxes with the green Phonecard symbol take prepaid cards. A notice in the call box tells you where to find the nearest stockist. A digital display shows how many units you have remaining on your card. Though British Telecom no longer has a monopoly on public phones, its phones swallow your money at a slower rate than most others.

Telephone directories

There are three phone directories for London: two for private numbers and one for companies. These are available at post offices and libraries. Hotels have them too and they are issued free to all residents with telephones, as is the *Yellow Pages* directory, which lists businesses and services.

Time & the seasons

Every year in spring (28 Mar 1999; 26 Mar 2000) the UK puts its clocks forward by one hour to give British Summer Time (BST). In autumn (31 Oct 1999; 29 Oct 2000) the clocks go back by one hour to rejoin Greenwich Mean Time (GMT).

Prepare yourself for the unpredictability of the British climate. For some guidance try **Weathercall** on 0891 500401 (50p per minute at all times). The figures in the chart opposite have been provided by the Met Office and give a rough indication of what to expect.

Spring extends approximately from March to May, though winter often seems to stretch well beyond February. March winds and April showers may turn up either a month early or a month late. May is generally very pleasant.

Summer – June, July and August – can still be unpredictable. Searing heat one day followed by sultry greyness and thunderstorms the next. The combination of high temperatures, humidity and the city's pollution can create problems for anyone with hayfever or breathing difficulties – so head for the open spaces.

Autumn starts in September, although the weather can still have a summery feel as the skies tend to remain clear and the weather mild. Real autumn comes with October when the leaves start to fall. Then the cold sets in and November hits with a reminder that London is situated on a fairly northerly latitude.

Winter may contain the odd mild day, but don't bank on it. December, January and February are generally pretty chilly in London, although snow is rare.

Tipping

In Britain it's accepted that you tip in taxis, minicabs, restaurants (some waiting staff are forced to rely heavily on gratuities), hairdressers, hotels and some bars (not pubs) – ten per cent is normal, with some restaurants adding up to 15 per cent. Be careful to check whether service has been added automatically to your bill. Too many restaurants include service in the bill and then leave the space for a gratuity on your credit card slip blank. Beware.

Tourist information

The **London Tourist Board** (LTB; 0171 932 2000) runs the information centres listed below; these centres can supply a free map of central London. You can also ring **Visitorcall** (0839 123456), a recorded information service with several different lines providing information on events and entertainment. The LTB also runs a fax-back service (phone 0171 971 0026 to order a leaflet), recorded information lines for children (0839 123404/123436/123437) and a website (www.Londontown.com). Calls on 0839 numbers cost 50p per minute.

Weather report

Average daytime temperatures, rainfall and daily hours of sunshine in London

	Jan	Feb	Mar	Apr	May	June
Temperature °C/°F	6/43	6/43	8/46	10/50	13/55	16/61
Rainfall mm/in	45/1.8	30/1.2	43/1.7	37/1.5	47/1.9	44/1.8
Hours of sunshine	1.9	2.5	3.3	5.3	6.3	6.2
	July	**Aug**	**Sept**	**Oct**	**Nov**	**Dec**
Temperature °C/°F	19/66	19/66	16/61	13/55	9/48	7/45
Rainfall mm/in	46/1.8	42/1.7	39/1.6	56/2.2	46/1.8	49/2.0
Hours of sunshine	6.7	6.6	5.0	3.5	2.3	1.5

Heathrow Terminals 1, 2, 3
Tube station concourse, Heathrow Airport. **Open** 8.30am-6pm daily.
Liverpool Street Station *Tube station, EC2.* **Open** 8am-6pm Mon-Fri; 8.45am-5.30pm Sat, Sun. **Map 10 R5**
Victoria Station *Victoria Station forecourt, SW1.* **Open** 8am-7pm daily (reduced hours in winter). **Map 7 H10**
Waterloo International Terminal *Arrivals Hall, SE1.* **Open** 8am-10.30pm daily. **Map 8 M8**

For information on travel in the rest of Britain, *see page 272.*

Visas

Citizens of EU countries do not require a visa to visit the UK; citizens of other countries, including the USA, Canada and New Zealand, require a valid passport for a visit of up to six months.

To apply for a visa, and to check your visa status **before you travel**, contact the British Embassy, High Commission or Consulate in your own country. The visa allows you entry for a maximum of six months. For information about work permits, which must be arranged before entering the UK, *see page 298.*

To obtain visas to other countries, contact the embassies concerned (*see page 289*), or have the paperwork handled for you – for a fee – by **Rapid Visa** or **Ferguson Snell**. However, certain countries, including Italy, Canada, Guyana and Japan, require personal applications.

Ferguson Snell & Associates
10/11 Heathfield Terrace, W4 4JE (0181 747 3004). Chiswick Park tube. **Open** 9am-5.30pm Mon-Fri. Ferguson Snell will sort out work permits and extensions to your UK visa for up to six months. It charges from £350 for the service and also arranges visas for other countries.

Home Office
Immigration & Nationality Department, Lunar House, 40 Wellesley Road, Croydon CR9 2BY (0181 686 0688). **Open** *phone enquiries* 9am-4.45pm Mon-Wed; 10am-4.45pm Thur; 9am-4.30pm Fri. The immigration department of the Home Office deals with queries about immigration matters, visas and work permits for citizens from Commonwealth and a few other countries.

Rapid Visa
Adventure Travel Centre, 135 Earl's Court Road, SW5 (0171 373 3026). Earl's Court tube. **Open** 9am-5.30pm Mon-Fri; 9.30am-12.30pm Sat.

Credit £TC. **Map 3 B11**
Rapid Visa can arrange visas to most countries for £11; £12.75 for US requirements.

Working in London

Finding temporary employment in London can be a full-time job in itself. But providing you can speak English well, are an EU citizen or have a work permit, you should be able to find something in catering, labouring, bar/pub or shop work. Graduates with an English or foreign-language degree could try teaching. If your English isn't great, there's always the mind-numbing distributing of free magazines. Try for seasonal work in tourist spots; local councils sometimes take on summer staff such as playgroup leaders or swimming pool attendants. Ideas can be found in *Summer Jobs in Britain*, published by Vacation Work, 9 Park End Street, Oxford, OX1 OHJ (£8.99 plus £1.50 p&p). The **Central Bureau for Educational Visits & Exchanges** (*see below*) has other publications.

To find work, look in the *Evening Standard*, local and national papers and news-agents' windows. Employers advertise vacancies on Jobcentre noticeboards; there is often temporary and unskilled work available. Most districts of London have a Jobcentre; look in *Yellow Pages* under 'Employment Agencies'.

For office work, sign on with temp agencies. If you have good shorthand, typing (40 words per minute upwards) or wordprocessing (WP) skills, and dress the part, such agencies might find you well-paid assignments. If you're desperate, try a fast-food chain.

Work for foreign visitors

With few exceptions, citizens of non-European Economic Area (EEA) countries (*see below*) need a work permit before they are legally able to work in the UK. One of the advantages of working here is the opportunity to meet people, but for any em-ployment it's essential that you speak reasonable English. For office work you need a high standard of English and relevant skills.

Work permits

EEA citizens, residents of Gibraltar and certain categories of other overseas nationals do not require a work permit. How-ever, others who wish to come to the UK to work must obtain a permit before setting out.

The prospective employer who has a vacancy that they are unable to fill with a resident or EEA national must apply for a permit to the Department for Education & Employment (*see below*). Permits are issued only for jobs that carry a high level of skill and experience. The employer must be able to demonstrate to the DfEE that there is no resident/EEA labour available.

There is a Training & Work Experience Scheme that enables non-EEA nationals to come to the UK for training towards a professional or specialist qualification, or to undertake a short period of managerial-level work experience. Again, this should be applied for before coming to the UK. Listed below are other possibilities.

Au pairs

The option of au pairing is only open to citizens of certain countries (*see below*) who are aged between 17 and 27. Try contacting an agency in your own country or look in *Yellow Pages* under 'Employment Agencies'. Such work usually provides free accommodation, but wages tend to be low. The following countries are included in the **Au Pair Scheme**: Andorra, Bosnia-Herzegovina, Croatia, Cyprus, Czech Republic, Faroe Islands, Greenland, Hungary, Macedonia, Malta, Monaco, San Marino, Slovak Republic, Slovenia, Switzerland and Turkey.

Sandwich students

Students at a recognised UK university or college can undertake work placements that are essential to obtain their qualifications. Approval for such placements must be obtained by the college from the DfEE's **Overseas Labour Service** (*see below*).

Students

Visiting students from the US, Canada, Australia or Jamaica can get a blue BUNAC card enabling them to work in the UK for up to six months. BUNAC cards are not difficult to obtain, but you must get it before entering the country. Contact the Work in Britain Department of the **Council on International Educa-tional Exchange** or call **BUNAC** (*see below*), a non-profit-making org-anisation that arranges work exchange programmes for students from these countries. BUNAC students should obtain an application form OSS1 (BUNAC) from BUNAC before starting work in the UK. This should be submitted to the nearest Jobcentre to obtain permission to work.

Non-EEA nationals in the UK as students who wish to take casual part-time or vacation employment unconnected to their course of study must obtain the permission of their local Employment Service Jobcentre. The Jobcentre will provide an application form (OSS1) for completion by the student, their college and the prospective employer.

Voluntary workers

Voluntary work in youth hostels (*see p150*) can provide board, lodging and some pocket money. For advice on voluntary work with charities contact the **Home Office** (*see below*).

Working holidaymakers

Citizens of Commonwealth countries, aged 17-27, may apply to come to the UK as a working holidaymaker. This allows them to take part-time work without a DfEE permit. They must contact their nearest British Diplomatic Post to obtain the necessary entry clearance before travelling to the UK.

Useful addresses

Aliens Registration Office

10 Lamb's Conduit Street, WC1 (0171 230 1208). Holborn tube. **Open** 8.45am-4.30pm Mon-Fri. **Map 6 M5**
It costs £34 to be registered, if you have a work permit.

BUNAC

16 Bowling Green Lane, EC1 (0171 251 3472). Farringdon tube/rail. **Map 9 N4**

Central Bureau for Educational Visits & Exchanges

British Council, 10 Spring Gardens, SW1 (0171 930 8466). Charing Cross tube/rail. **Open** 9.15am-5.30pm Mon-Fri. **Map 8 K8**
This office deals with the organisa-tion of visits outside the UK, but you can obtain copies of its useful publications.

Council on International Educational Exchange

Work in Britain Department, 205 East 42nd Street, New York, NY 10017 (00 1 212 822 2600).

Department for Education & Employment

Overseas Labour Service, Level 5, Moorfoot, Sheffield S1 4PQ (0114 259 4074). **Open** *phone enquiries* 9am-5pm Mon-Fri.
Not open to personal visits, but you can call the above enquiry line. Employers seeking work permit application forms should phone 0990 210224.
Website: www.open.gov.uk/dfee/ols

Home Office

Immigration & Nationality Directorate, Lunar House, 40 Wellesley Road, Croydon CR9 9BY (0181 686 0688). East Croydon rail. **Open** 8.30am-4pm Mon-Fri.
Will give advice on whether a work permit is required.

Getting to London

By air

Gatwick Airport

(01293 535353). About 30 miles (50km) south of central London, off the M23.
Three rail services link Gatwick to London. The **Gatwick Express** to Victoria Station takes about 30-35 minutes and runs 24 hours daily, every 15 minutes, then every hour between 1.35am and 4.35am. Tickets cost £9.50 single, £19 return (valid for one month), £11 day return (after 9.30am); half-price for under-15s.

Connex South Central also runs a service from Gatwick to Victoria, with trains running approximately every 15 minutes during the day and every hour between 1.05am and 5.05am. It takes between three and eight minutes longer than the Gatwick Express but tickets are cheaper, costing £8.20 single, £16.40 return (valid for one month), £8.30 day return (after 9.30am); half-price for under-15s; free for under-5s.

There is also a **Thameslink** service that might be more convenient if you are staying in the Bloomsbury area or want to connect with trains at King's Cross or Euston. It runs via Blackfriars, Farringdon and King's Cross, and frequency and journey times are equivalent to the Connex South Central service. Tickets (to Blackfriars) cost £9.50 single, £19 return.

The **Flightline 777** bus (0181 668 7261/01737 242411) to Victoria Coach Station (*see below*) is the cheapest option, but the journey time is about 90 minutes. Buses run 5am-8pm daily, every one or two hours (phone to check). Tickets cost £7.50 single, £11 return (valid for three months); half-price under-15s; free for under-5s. There is also an **Airbus Hotel Shuttle** (book by fax on 0181 759 5452 or e-mail on book@airbus.co.uk). For £18 you will be met at the airport, taken to the Gatwick Express train, met at Victoria Station and taken on to your hotel by minibus. Forget **taxis** unless you are seriously wealthy – you'll do well to get away with paying less than £50. The journey to central London will take at least an hour.

Heathrow Airport

(0181 759 4321). About 15 miles (24km) west of central London, off the M4.
The **Heathrow Express** service (15-20 minutes to Paddington station), which began operating in 1998, is the quickest and most efficient way of travelling between Heathrow and central London. The train can be boarded at one of the airport's two underground stations (Terminals 1, 2 & 3 or Terminal 4). Tickets cost £10 each way; half-price for under-15s; free for under-5s. Note that if you're planning to continue your journey into town from Paddington by taxi, queues can be extremely long, though a taxi-share scheme means you can jump the queue and pay a fixed fare.

A longer but cheaper journey is by tube on the **Piccadilly Line** (50-60 minutes to Piccadilly Circus). Tickets to central London cost £3.30 one way (£1.60 under-16s). Trains run from about 5.30am to 11.30pm. There's a station at Terminal 4 and one for Terminals 1, 2 & 3.

The **Airbus Heathrow Shuttle** (0171 222 1234/0181 400 6655) runs four buses an hour (5am-10.30pm) from all four terminals at Heathrow to 23 points within central London (journey time is about 60 minutes to Victoria; 80 minutes to Russell Square). These special double-deckers have ample room for luggage and are all accessible to wheelchair users. Tickets cost £6 single, £10 return (£3 single, £5 return concs). There's also an excellent **Airbus Hotel Shuttle** service. Passengers are greeted at the airport and taken to a minibus which will drop them at their hotel's door. The service costs £12 per person and can be booked by fax on 0181 759 5452 or e-mail on book@airbus.co.uk. **Taxi** fares to central London are high (£30 or more) and the journey time is about 45-60 minutes (often far longer during the rush hour).

London City Airport

(0171 646 0000). About 9 miles (14km) east of central London, in Docklands.
Silvertown & City Airport rail station, on the Silverlink line (*see p303*), is a couple of minutes' walk from the terminal. Its services are approximately every 20 minutes and run via Stratford (interchange with the Central Line tube). Most people travel to London on the blue-and-white **Airbus** service (0171 222 1234), which goes to Liverpool Street Station (30 minutes journey time) via Canary Wharf. The shuttle bus leaves every 10 minutes 6.50am-9.10pm Mon-Fri, 7.30am-1.10pm Sat, 11am-9.10pm Sun; tickets cost £4 to Liverpool Street Station (£2 to Canary Wharf). The journey by **taxi** to the City takes about 30-40 minutes and costs upwards of £15.

Luton Airport

(01582 405 100). About 30 miles (50km) north of central London, off the M1 at junction 10.
The building of Luton Airport Parkway rail station will enable people to travel direct from the airport to central London. The service is due to open some time in 1999 and will be run by **Thameslink** (0345 484950). Until the new station is open there is a shuttle bus that runs every 15 minutes from Luton airport to Luton rail station. The journey takes about 10 minutes and costs £1.60. From the station there is a rail service running to a number of central London stations including King's Cross. Trains leave every 15 minutes and take 35-45 minutes. Tickets cost £10.20 single, £18.90 day return, and £20.20 for an open return. There are also cheap day returns available after 9am costing £11.10.

For a cheaper but longer journey, the **Green Line** coach service (0181 668 7261) runs from Luton to Victoria Station at 40 minutes past each hour. The journey takes 90 minutes, and costs £7 single, £11.50 return; half-price for under-5s. A **taxi** from the airport into central London takes at least an hour and will set you back at least £70.

Stansted Airport

(01279 680500). About 35 miles (60km) north-east of central London, off the M11.
The quickest way to get to London is on the **Stansted Express** train (0345 484950) to Liverpool Street Station; the journey time is 45 minutes. Trains leave every 30 minutes 8am-8pm, and every hour from 6am to 8am and 8pm to midnight, Mon to Sat; every 30 minutes 8am-11pm (plus a last train at midnight) Sun. Tickets cost £10.40 single, £10.50 day return (after 9.30am Mon-Fri), £15 return within five days (after 9.30am), £20.80 open return; half-price under-15s. **Flightline 777** buses run to Victoria Coach Station; the journey takes about 1 hour 40 minutes, with stopoffs at Hendon Central and Finchley Road tube stations and Marble Arch. Prices are £9 single, £13 return (valid for three months), half-price under-16s. By car, the journey to central London takes about an hour. A **taxi** to central London will cost upwards of £50.

By train

Eurostar

Waterloo International Terminal, SE1 (0990 186186). Waterloo tube/rail. **Map 8 M8**
Probably the most fun way to reach (and escape from) London is via the

Directory

Channel Tunnel and Eurostar. The company now operates five routes – Paris, Disneyland Paris, Brussels, Lille and the ski train which goes to Bourg St Moritz and Moutiers (Sat only). Compared with first-class air fares, Leisure First at £199 return to Paris or Brussels (minimum stay three nights) is very reasonable, but the standard fares work out more expensive than standard-class flights: a return to Paris is £229 Mon-Thur and £169 Fri; £75 for a weekend day trip; and £89 Saturday night away fare (book one week in advance). Look out, though, for special offers. Journey time to Paris is three hours, Brussels two hours 40 mins, the tunnel section taking 22 mins. There are currently between 16 and 19 trains a day to Paris from Monday to Saturday, and either ten or 11 to Brussels. On Sundays between ten and 12 run to Paris and seven or eight to Brussels.

Getting around London

LT Travel Information Centres

London Transport (LT) centres provide maps and information about the tube, buses and Docklands Light Railway (DLR). You can find them in the following stations:

Euston 7.15am-6pm Mon-Sat; 8.30am-5pm Sun. **Map 6 K3**

Hammersmith Bus Station 7.15am-6pm Mon-Fri; 8.15am-6pm Sat.

Heathrow Airport *Terminals 1, 2 & 3 tube station* 6.30am-7pm Mon-Sat; 7.15am-7pm Sun. *Terminal 1* 7.15am-10pm daily. *Terminal 2* 7.15am-5pm Mon-Sat; 8.15am-5pm Sun. *Terminal 4* 6am-3pm Mon-Sat; 7.15am-3pm Sun.

King's Cross 8am-6pm Mon-Sat; 8.30am-5pm Sun. **Map 6 L2**

Liverpool Street 8am-6pm Mon-Sat; 8.45am-5.30pm Sun. **Map 10 R5**

Oxford Circus 9am-6pm Mon-Sat. **Map 5 J6**

Piccadilly Circus 9am-6pm daily. **Map 8 K7**

St James's Park 8am-5.30pm Mon-Fri. **Map 8 K9**

Victoria 8am-7pm Mon-Sat; 8.45am-7pm Sun. **Map 7 H10**

Fares & Travelcards

Bus and tube fares are based on a zone system. There are six zones stretching 12 miles (20km) out from the centre of London. Beware of on-the-spot £10 fines for anyone caught travelling without a valid ticket.

Adult fares

The single underground fare for adults in Zone 1 is £1.40; for Zones 1 and 2, £1.70; rising to £3.40 for an all-zone single fare. Single bus fares start at 60p for a short hop and rising to £1.20 for all zones. Buying individual tickets is the most expensive way to travel. If you are likely to make three or more journeys in one day, or if you are staying in London for more than a day, it's always better value to buy a Travelcard (*see below*).

Child fares

On all buses, tubes and local trains, children are classified as under 16. Under-5s travel free. Under-16s pay a child's fare until 10pm; after 10pm (buses only) they pay an adult fare. Fourteen- and 15-year-olds must carry Child Rate Photocards, available from any post office: take a passport-size photo and proof of age (passport or birth certificate) with you. The single tube fare for children in Zone 1 is 60p; for Zones 1 and 2, 80p; rising to £1.40 for an all-zone ticket. Single child bus fares are 40p anywhere in London.

One-Day LT Cards

One-Day LT Cards are valid on buses (but not N-prefixed night buses), underground services (although not those running to and from Bakerloo Line stations north of Queen's Park; this section of track is not run by London Transport) and Docklands Light Railway (DLR) services. The tickets cost £4.80 for Zones 1 & 2; £6 for Zones 1, 2, 3 & 4 and £7.50 for all the zones (child £2.40 Zones 1 & 2; £2.90 Zones 1, 2, 3 & 4; £3.20 all zones).

Travelcards

The most economical way to get around London is with a **Travelcard**. These can be used on the tube sytem, buses (except N-prefixed night buses), rail services, DLR and some Green Line bus services. Travelcards can be bought at all tube and rail stations and also at appointed newsagents. The most convenient cards for short-term visitors are the One-Day or One-Week Travelcards; monthly tickets are also available.

One-Day Travelcards can be used after 9.30am Mon-Fri and all day at weekends. You can make unlimited journeys within the zones you select. They cost £3.80 for Zones 1 & 2; £4 for Zones 1-4; £4.50 for all zones (£1.90 for a child all-zone ticket). Note that these tickets are not valid on night buses.

One-Week Travelcards offer unlimited journeys throughout the selected zones for seven days, including use of night buses. Weekly Travelcards cost £14.30 for Zone 1; £17.60 for Zones 1 & 2; £21.50 for Zones 1-3; £26.70 for Zones 1-4; £32 for Zones 1-5; £36.90 for all zones (child £5.20 Zone 1; £6.50 Zones 1 & 2; £9 Zones 1-3; £11.50 Zones 1-4; £12.50 Zones 1-5; £13.50 all zones).

Weekend Travelcards allow travel on consecutive weekend days or bank holidays (not valid on N-prefixed night buses). The cost is £5.70 for Zones 1 & 2 rising to £6.70 for all six zones (child £2.80 for an all-zone ticket).

Family Travelcards are available for families and groups of one or two

Tube, bus & train enquiries

The tube and buses in Greater London are run by London Transport (LT), which has a 24-hour telephone enquiry service: call London Travel Information on **0171 222 1234** (often engaged, so keep trying, or settle for the 24-hour recorded information line on 0171 222 1200).

For information on overland rail services, both in London and the UK, call National Rail Enquiries on **0345 484950**.

adults travelling with between one and four children. They are valid after 9.30am Mon-Fri, and all day weekends and public holidays (but not on N-prefixed night buses) and cost £3 for Zones 1 & 2, rising to £3.60 for all zones (child 60p for all zones).

Carnet

If you're planning on making a lot of short-hop journeys within Zone 1 over a period of several days, it makes sense to buy a carnet of ten tickets for £10 (£5 for children). This saves you £4 on the standard Zone 1 fares. Note that if you exit a station outside of Zone 1 and are caught with only a carnet ticket, you are liable to a £10 penalty fine.

Photocards

Photocards are required for all bus passes and Travelcards except one-day versions. Child-rate photocards are required for five-15-year-olds using child-rate Travelcards and bus passes. Fourteen and 15-year-olds need a child-rate photocard if buying any ticket at child-rate.

Buses

Certain routes still use the venerable 30-year-old red Routemaster buses (the ones you can hop on and off), but modern buses are taking over: they are cheaper to run as they are operated by a single driver/conductor, although this can make them slower. Travelling by bus is one of the most pleasurable ways of getting about (and getting to know) London, although progress can be very slow during rush hours.

Night buses

Night buses are the only form of public transport that runs through the night. They operate from around midnight to 6am, about once an hour, on most routes. All pass through central London, and the majority stop at Trafalgar Square, so head there if you're unsure which bus to get. Night buses have the letter 'N' before their number (note that One-Day Travelcards – *see above* – are not valid on night buses). Pick up a free map and timetable from one of the LT Travel Information Centres (*see page 300*).

Green Line buses

Green Line buses (0181 668 7261) serve the suburbs and towns within a 40-mile (64-km) radius of London. Their main departure point is Eccleston Bridge, SW1 (Colonnades Coach Station, behind Victoria).

Two wheels good; four wheels bad?

An increasing number of Londoners think so. The issue has received high-profile attention in recent years through street-party-cum-road-blocks – or 'organised coincidences' – arranged by direct-action groups and coalitions such as **Critical Mass** (fax 0171 326 0353/bill@bill.co.uk/www.critmass.org.uk) and **Reclaim the Streets** (0171 281 4621; rts@gn.apc.org/www.gn.apc.org/rts) in protest at soaring pollution levels and apalling road congestion.

However, despite the efforts of some local councils, London remains, on the whole, an unfriendly place for bike-riding commuters who, mostly without cycle lanes, have to contend with pitted roads and pit-bull motorists. A safety helmet, filter-mask and determined attitude are advisable. However, cyclists shouldn't forget that they have as much responsibility as motorists for driving safely. So no jumping those red lights.

London Cycling Campaign

228 Great Guildford Business Square, 30 Great Guildford Street, SE1 0HS (0171 928 7220). **Open** *phone enquiries* 1-6pm Mon-Fri.
Get the definitive guide to pedalling around London, *On Your Bike*, and the *Cyclists' Route Map* (£4.95 for both), from the London Cycling Campaign. It includes tips on maintenance, security and the law. Members of the LCC enjoy a host of other benefits (membership from £5.50).

Cycle hire & storage

Bikepark

14½ Stukeley Street, WC2 (0171 430 0083/bikepark@easynet.co.uk). Covent Garden or Holborn tube. **Open** 7.30am-7.30pm Mon-Fri; 10am-6pm Sat. **Hire** £10 first day; £5 second day; £3 per day thereafter. **Deposit** £200. **Credit** MC, £TC, V.
Map 6 L6
Leave your bike in secure parking (50p for 4 hours, £1 for 8 hours; £1.50 for 12 hours; £2 for 24 hours; £15 a month), and make use of the changing facilities at this branch (there are shower facilities at the new Chelsea branch; *see below*). There's also a repair service and you can hire a hybrid or mountain bike and accessories for commuting or touring. Season tickets also available.
Branch: Bikepark Chelsea The Courtyard, 250 King's Road, SW3 6NT (0171 565 0777).
Website: www.bikepark.co.uk

London Bicycle Tour Company

1A Gabriel's Wharf, 56 Upper Ground, SE1 (0171 928 6838/london.bicycle@btinternet.com). Blackfriars tube/rail. **Open** *Easter-Oct* 10am-6pm daily; *Nov-Easter* by appointment. **Hire** £2 per hour; £4 half a day; £9.95 first day; £5 per day thereafter.
Deposit £100. **Credit** AmEx, DC, MC, £TC, V.
Map 9 N7
In addition to bike hire, this company, as the name implies, conducts bicycle tours (approx three hours) of the East End on Saturdays and the West End on Sundays, costing £11.95. It also offers weekend breaks in the countryside around London, which are accompanied by a guide.
Website: www.londonbicycle.com

Stationlink bus

The red-and-yellow Stationlink buses (0171 222 1234) are convenient for the disabled, the elderly, people laden with luggage or those with small children. The service connects all the main London rail termini on a round trip. Buses run every hour from about 9am to 7pm (phone for details). The fare is £1 for adults, 50p for 5s-15s.

The underground

Travelling on the tube is the quickest way to get around London (although short distances may be faster on foot). However, lines frequently suffer from delays, escalators are sometimes out of action and, occasionally, there are station and line closures (typically at the weekend because of engineering work). Smoking is illegal anywhere on the Underground system. Crime is not a major problem on the tube, although you would be wise to avoid getting into an empty carriage on your own, and beware of pickpockets.

Using the system

Tickets can be purchased from a station ticket office or self-service machines. (Unfortunately, staff in ticket offices rarely speak foreign languages and can be remarkably gruff and unhelpful.) You can buy most tickets, including carnets and One-Day Travelcards (see above), from self-service machines, but for anything covering a longer period you need to show a valid photocard to a ticket officer. Note that, because of staff shortages, ticket offices in some of the less busy stations often close early (around 7.30pm).

Put your ticket through the automatic checking gates (and pull it out of the top to open the gates). If you have a single journey ticket, it will be retained by the gate at the exit station. There are 11 underground lines, colour-coded on the tube map. The much delayed £1.9-billion Jubilee Line extension (which was originally scheduled to open during 1999, but may well not even be completed by the start of 2000) will link Green Park to Stratford via Waterloo, Bermondsey, North Greenwich and Canary Wharf.

Underground timetable

Trains run daily, starting at around 5.30am Mon-Sat, 7.30am Sun. The only exception is Christmas Day, when there is no service. Generally you won't have to wait more than ten minutes for a train; during peak times the service should run every couple of minutes. Times of last trains vary; usually 11.30pm-1am Mon-Sat, and 11.30pm Sun. The only all-night public transport is by night bus (see above).

Access all areas?

Compared to some European cities, such as Madrid and Rome, London is relatively friendly to the mobility-impaired. But this is only relative. While many of the capital's sights make provision for wheelchair users, the great headache for those who have problems getting around is transport.

London Transport publishes a booklet called *Access to the Underground*, which gives information on lifts and ramps at individual underground stations. It's available free from LT ticket offices or from LT's Unit for Disabled Passengers (172 Buckingham Palace Road, SW1 9TN; 0171 918 3312/minicom 0171 918 3015/fax 0171 918 3876) and at LT Travel Information Centres (see page 300). The unit also provides details on buses and Braille maps. All DLR stations have wheelchair access.

In 1998 the London Tourist Board launched a newsletter, *London for All*, giving an update of tourist facilities for people with special needs in London, including access to sights, hotels, shops and entertainment venues. It is available in London Tourist Information Centres (see page 296) or by post from the LTB at Glen House, Stag Place, London SW1E 5LT.

We thoroughly recommend *Access in London* by Gordon Couch, William Forrester and Justin Irwin (Quiller Press, 1996). Admirably comprehensive, it is written and researched by a team of able-bodied and disabled people and includes detailed maps of step-free routes and accessible tube stations. There are tips on travelling around, who to contact for help, a guide to adapted loos, sections on accommodation, shopping and entertainments from pubs to racecourses. The guide is available at some (but not all) bookshops, priced at £7.95, or free of charge (although a donation is appreciated) from Access Project, 39 Bradley Gardens, W13 8HE.

The organisations below offer help to disabled visitors to London.

Artsline

54 Chalton Street, NW1 (tel/minicom 0171 388 2227/fax 0171 383 2653). Euston tube/rail. **Open** 9.30am-5.30pm Mon-Fri. **Map 6 K3**
Gives information on disabled access to arts and entertainment events in London and on adapted facilities at venues such as cinemas, art galleries and theatres.

Can Be Done

7-11 Kensington High Street, W8 5NP (0181 907 2400). **Open** 9am-5.30pm Mon-Fri; noon-1pm Sat. **Map 3 A9**
This small tour operator can tailor holidays and tours in London to the needs of disabled people.

Docklands Light Railway (DLR)

(0171 363 9700).
The DLR is administered as part of the tube system. Its driverless trains run on a raised track from Bank (Central Line/Waterloo & City Line) or Tower Gateway, close to Tower Hill tube (Circle and District Lines). Trains run from 5.30am to around 12.30am Mon-Fri; 6-12.30am Sat; 7.30am-11.30pm Sun.

The DLR is keen to promote itself as much as a tourist attraction as a transport system. To this end it offers 'Sail and Rail' tickets that combine unlimited travel on the DLR with a riverboat trip between Greenwich and Westminster Piers (boats departing from 10.30am to 6.30pm) plus discounts on selected museums and sights. Starting at Tower Gateway, special trains leave on the hour (from 10am) with a DLR tour guide giving passengers the lowdown on the area as the train glides along. Tickets cost £7.50 for adults, £3.80 for children.

Rail services

Independently owned commuter services run out of all of London's mainline rail stations (*see page 272*). Travelcards are valid on these services within the relevant zones. The **Silverlink Line** is a useful and relatively underused overground service that carves a huge arc through the north of the city, running from Richmond (in the south-west) to North Woolwich (in the east). The line connects with the tube network at several stations. Trains run about every 20 minutes Mon-Sat, every 30 minutes Sun. It offers a refreshing alternative to the tube with great views of London's back gardens.

Rail & coach discounts

Various annual discount cards are available for the elderly, children, students and families. Enquire at mainline railway stations (*see page 272*), rail-appointed travel agents or Victoria Coach Station.

Driving

If you've heard that driving in central London is tough, just wait till you try to find somewhere to park. If you park illegally, you'll probably get a £30 parking ticket or find your car has been immobilised by a yellow triangular wheel clamp, or it may be towed away and impounded. The retrieval procedure is no easy ride (*see below*).

DAIL (Disability Arts in London)

Diorama Arts Centre, 34 Osnaburgh Street, NW1 (0171 961 6351/minicom 0171 691 4201/fax 0171 916 5396/enquiries@dail.dircon.co.uk).
Open 10.30am-6.30pm Mon-Fri.
Produces a monthly magazine that contains up-to-date listings, reviews and articles on the arts and the disabled (free for disabled people).

DIAL (National Association of Disablement Information & Advice Lines)

(01302 310123). **Open** 9am-5pm Mon-Thur; 9am-4pm Fri.
Call DIAL for details of local groups in the UK who can offer free information and advice on all aspects of disability.

William Forrester

1 Belvedere Close, Guildford, Surrey GU2 6NP (01483 575401).
William Forrester is a London Registered Guide and, as a wheelchair user himself, has extensive experience in leading tours in the capital for disabled individuals and groups. Book early.

Greater London Association of Disabled People (GLAD)

336 Brixton Road, SW9 (0171 346 5800/infoline 0171 346 5819). Brixton tube/rail. **Open** *general phone enquiries* 9am-5pm Mon-Fri; *infoline* 1.30-4.30pm Mon-Fri.
GLAD is a voluntary organisation providing, via local associations, valuable information for disabled visitors and residents. Its publications include *Update*, produced every two weeks and containing extracts from anything that has appeared in the national newspapers and

magazines that relates to the disabled, and the monthly *London Disability News.*

Holiday Care Service

For listings details, see p138.
An advisory service specialising in holiday accommodation for disabled visitors.

Royal Association for Disability & Rehabilitation (RADAR)

12 City Forum, 250 City Road, EC1 (0171 250 3222). Old Street tube/rail. **Open** 8am-5pm Mon-Fri.
Map 9 P3
The central organisation for disabled voluntary groups. Through RADAR you can get advice on almost any aspect of life. The Association publishes *Bulletin*, a monthly newsletter, which has articles on news-oriented subjects such as housing and education.

Tripscope

The Courtyard, Evelyn Road, W4 5JL (0181 994 9294). **Open** *phone enquiries* 9am-4.45pm Mon-Fri.
Jim Bennett and Adrian Drew's information/advice service for the elderly and disabled can help with all aspects of getting around London, the UK and overseas. It's chiefly an enquiry line, but you can write in or visit by appointment if you have difficulty with the phone.

Wheelchair Travel & Access Mini Buses

1 Johnston Green, Guildford, Surrey GU2 6XS (01483 233 640).
An excellent source of converted vehicles for hire, including adapted minibuses (with or without driver), plus cars with hand controls and 'Chairman' cars.

Trips & tours

Balloon tours

Adventure Balloons *3 Queen's Terrace, W7 (0181 840 0108)*. **Flights** *Apr-Oct* morning & evenings daily, weather permitting. **Fares** £115 per person. **Duration** 1 hour. **Credit** MC, V. Drift over the capital from the launch site a couple of miles from Tower Bridge.

Bicycle Tours

London Bicycle Tour Company *(0171 928 6838)*. Guided bike tours and independent bike hire. *See p301.*

Bus tours

Big Bus Company *(0181 944 7810)*. **Open-top bus tours** four different routes, 40 mins-1 hour; all with live commentary. **Departures** every 15 mins from Green Park, Victoria and Marble Arch *summer* 8.30am-7pm daily; *winter* 8.30am-4.30pm daily. **Pick-up** Green Park (near The Ritz Hotel); Marble Arch (Speaker's Corner); Victoria (outside Royal Westminster Hotel, Buckingham Palace Road, SW1). **Fares** £15; £7 children; tickets are valid for 24 hours, and are interchangeable between routes, allowing you to hop on and off the bus at over 50 different locations.
London Pride *(01708 631122)*. **Departures** *Jan-Jun/Sep-Dec* 8.30am-7pm daily; *Jul, Aug* 24 hours daily; *grand tour* 1 hour 30 mins. **Fares** *from* 50p; £12 for grand tour, £6 5s-15s, valid 24 hours. Also routes from London Zoo to Buckingham Palace, Russell Square to the South Kensington Museums, Bayswater to Euston Station and Bloomsbury to Tate Gallery.
Original London Sightseeing Tour *(0181 877 1722)*. **Departures** *summer* 9am-7pm daily; *winter* 9.30am-5pm daily. **Pick-up** Victoria Street; Grosvenor Gardens; Marble Arch (Speaker's Corner); Baker Street tube (forecourt); Haymarket (at bus stop L); Charing Cross Station (Strand); Charing Cross Pier. **Fares** £12; £6 concs.

Helicopter tours

Cabair Helicopters *Elstree Aerodrome, Hertfordshire (0181 953 4411)*. *Elstree rail.*

Flights *from* 11.30am Sun. **Fares** £125 per person for 30 mins. **Credit** MC, £TC, V.

Personal tours

Tour Guides *(0171 495 5504)*. Tailor-made tours with Blue Badge guides for individuals, small or large groups, on foot, by car, coach or boat.

River tours

To find out about events, sights and excursions on the river get a copy of the London Tourist Board booklet, *Discover the Thames*, from one of the LTB information centres (*see p296*). Further information on return services and evening cruises is available from Westminster Passenger Services Association (0171 930 2062). Upstream trips run only during the summer. The trips listed below all depart from Westminster Pier, Victoria Embankment, SW1 (Westminster tube. **Map 8 L9**).

Downriver
Services run daily.
To Greenwich *(0171 930 4097)*.
6 Apr-May, Sept, Oct 10.30am-4pm every 30 mins; *June-Aug* 10am-5pm every 30 mins; *Nov-24 Mar* 10.40am-3.20pm every 40 mins. **Duration** 45 mins. **Fares** *single* £5.80; £3.10-£4.60 concs; £15.70 family; *return* £7; £3.60-£5.80 concs; £18.60 family.
To Tower of London *(0171 930 9033)*. *Apr-Oct* 10.30am, 11.30am; noon-3pm every 20 mins; 3-6pm every 30 mins; 6-9pm every hour; *Nov-Mar* 10.30am-3.45pm every 45 mins. **Duration** 30 mins. **Fares** *single* £4.60; £2.30 under-16s; free under-4s; *return* £5.80; £2.90 under-16s; group discount available.
To Thames Barrier via Canary Wharf *(0171 930 3373)*. *14 Mar-4 Apr, 24 Oct-7 Nov* 11.15am, 1.45pm; *5 Apr-2 May, 5 Sept-24 Oct* 10.15am, 12.45pm, 3.15pm; *3 May-4 Sept* 11.15am, 12.15pm, 1.45pm, 2.45pm. **Duration** 75 mins. **Fares** *single* £5.75; £3.20-£4.55 concs; *return* £6.95; £3.70-£5.75 concs.

Car hire

To hire a car you must have at least one year's driving experience with a full current driving licence. If you are an overseas visitor, your current driving licence is valid in Britain for a year. Prices for car hire vary considerably; always ring several competitors for a quote (see *Yellow Pages*). Below are two reputable companies.

Avis *(Central reservations 0990 900500)*. **Credit** AmEx, DC, MC, £TC, V. You must be over 23. Chauffeur-driven cars are also available. Rental prices vary within different areas of London.
Europcar BCR *30 Woburn Place, WC1 (0171 255 2339)*. *Russell*

Square tube. **Open** 8am-6pm Mon-Fri; 8am-1pm Sat. **Credit** AmEx, DC, MC, £TC, V. **Map 6 L4**
You must be over 23 to hire a car at BCR. Cheapest rental is £36 per day inclusive. There is a £150 deposit on all rentals.

Motorbike hire

Scootabout *1-3 Leeke Street, WC1 (0171 833 4607)*. *King's Cross tube/rail*. **Open** 9am-6pm Mon-Fri. **Credit** AmEx, DC, MC, £TC, V. **Map 6 M3**
Any driving licence or foreign motorbike licence qualifies you to drive a 50cc moped. The hire charge for a Honda 100 starts at £23.50 per day; £135 per week. Hiring an ST1100 Pan European costs £75.50 per day; £375 per week. All rental prices include unlimited mileage, AA

cover, insurance, VAT and helmet. Note that a (sometimes substantial) deposit will be required unless you are paying by credit card.

Clamping

The immobilising of vehicles by attaching a clamp to one wheel is becoming an increasingly common way of combating illegal parking in London. If you've been clamped call the Clamping and Vehicle Section 24-hour hotline (0171 747 4747). There will be a label attached to the car telling you which payment centre to phone or visit. Some boroughs let you pay over the phone with a

Upriver

To Hampton Court
(0171 930 4721). 30 Mar-Oct tides vary, phone to
check; 10.30am, 11.15am, noon, daily. **Duration**
approx 3-4 hours. **Fares** *single* £8; £4-£7 concs;
return £12; £7-£10 concs.

To Kew *(0171 930 4721)*. *Mar-Oct* 10.15am, 10.30am,
11.15am, noon, 2pm, daily. **Duration** approx 90 mins.
Fares *single* £6; £3-£5 concs; *return* £10; £5-£8 concs.

To Putney *(0171 930 4721)*.
Mar-Oct 10.15am, 10.30am, 11.15am, noon, 2pm, daily.
Duration approx 45 mins. **Fares** *single* £5; £2.50-£4
concs; *return* £8; £4-£6 concs.

To Richmond *(0171 930 4721)*.
Mar-Oct tides vary, phone to check 10.30am; 11.15am,
noon, daily. **Duration** approx 2 hours. **Fares** *single* £7;
£3.50-£6 concs; *return* £11; £6-£9 concs.

Specialist tours

Architectural Dialogue
(0181 341 1371).
Departures 10.15am. **Meeting point** outside Royal
Academy, Piccadilly, W1 (Piccadilly Circus tube).
Tickets £17.50; £11 concs. *Advance booking
advisable.*

Beatles Walks
(0171 624 3978).
Beatles Magical Mystery Tour **Departures** 2pm Wed;
11am Thur, Sun. **Pick-up** Dominion Theatre,
Tottenham Court Road, W1 (Tottenham Court Road
tube). *Beatles In My Life Tour* **Departures** 11am Tue,
Sat. **Meeting point** Baker Street tube (Baker Street exit).
Duration (both) 2 hours 30 mins. **Tickets** (both)
£4.50; £3.50 concs.

Bus Trip to Murder
(0181 857 1545).
Departure 7pm Tue, Thur-Sun. **Meeting point**
Grosvenor Hotel, Victoria, SW1. **Duration** 3 hours 30
mins. **Tickets** £16.50 including fish and chip supper.
Trip with Tragical History Tours.

Garden Day Tours
(0171 720 4891/from USA 1 800 873 7145).
Departures May-Sept 8.45am Wed, Thur, Sun,
alternate Tues (return 6pm). **Meeting point** Victoria
Coach Station. **Tickets** £54 per day (lunch not incl).

Jack the Ripper Mystery Walk
(0181 558 9446/mobile 07957 388280). **Departures**
8pm Wed, Sun. **Meeting point** Aldgate tube. **Tickets**
£4; £3 concs.

London Show Boat
Departures *May-Oct* 7pm Thur-Sun; *Nov-Apr* 7pm
Fri, Sat (return 10.30pm). **Meeting point** Westminster
Pier. **Tickets** £42 per head including one drink, four-
course meal, half-bottle of wine, live show and dancing.

Royal & Celebrity Tour
(01932 854721). **Departures** Wed, Fri, Sat (phone for
times). **Pick-up** Victoria Station (Tourist Information
Centre). **Tickets** £13.

Taxi tours

Black Taxi Tours of London *(0171 289 4371)*.
Cost £65.
A tailored two-hour tour for up to five people.

Walking tours

Ever-increasing numbers of companies and individuals
are running (often themed) walks around London. One
of the best and longest established is **The Original
London Walks** (0171 624 3978/www.walks.com),
which encompasses walks on everything from Sherlock
Holmes to riverside pubs to ghosts. Other walk
companies include: **Citisights** (0181 806 4325); **Historical Tours** (0181 668 4019), **Capital Walks** (0181 650
7640), **Cityguide Walks** (01895 675389) and
Stepping Out (0181 881 2933). There are even art
guided tours in Hebrew (0171 586 1455).
   If you want to do it yourself, the excellent **Green
Chain** walks connect many of the green spaces of
south-east London (0181 312 5884).
   The *Time Out Book of London Walks* (£9.99) details
30 walks by writers around the capital.

Directory

---

credit card, others insist you go
in person. Either way, you'll
have to stump up a £38 clamp
fee and you have 28 days in
which to pay a parking fine,
which is £40-£60 (50 per cent
discount if you pay within
14 days).
   Staff at the payment centre
promise to de-clamp your car
within the next four hours but
can't tell you exactly when. You
are also warned that if you
don't remove your car within
one hour of its being de-
clamped, they will clamp it
again. This means you may
have to spend quite some time
waiting by your car.

Vehicle removal

If your car has mysteriously
disappeared, chances are that,
if it was legally parked, it's
been nicked; if not, it's probably
been hoisted on to the back of a
truck and taken to a car pound,
and you're facing a stiff
penalty: a fee of £105 is levied
for removal, plus £12 per day if
you don't collect it within 24
hours. To add insult to injury,
you'll probably get a parking
ticket of £20-£30 when you
collect the car. To find out
where your car has been taken
and how to retrieve it call the
Clamping and Vehicle Section
24-hour hotline (0171 747 4747).

24-hour car parks

NCP (0171 404 3777) has a
number of (phenomenally
expensive) 24-hour car parks in
and around central London,
including the following.

**Arlington House, Arlington
Street, SW1** *(0171 499 3312)*.
Rates £11.50 for 3 hours; £22.50 for
6 hours; £32 for 9 hours; £37 for 12
hours; £45 for 24 hours. **Map 7 J8**
21 Bryanston Street, W1 *(0171
499 7050)*. **Rates** £5.80 for 2 hours;
£10.80 for 4 hours; £15.70 for 6
hours; £21 for 9 hours; £31.50 for 24
hours. **Map 2 F6**
2 Lexington Street, W1 *(0171
734 0371)*. **Rates** £7.50 for 2 hours;
£14.80 for 4 hours; £20.50 for 6 hours;
£30 for 9 hours; £37 for 24 hours.
Map 7 J7

Car breakdown

If you are a member of a motoring organisation in another country, check to see if it has a reciprocal agreement with a British organisation.

AA (Automobile Association)

119-121 Cannon Street, EC4 (info 0990 500600/breakdown 0800 887766/new members 0800 444999). **Open** 24 hours daily. **Credit** MC, V.

You can call the AA if you break down. Become a member on the spot, and it will cost you £75 to join. The first year's roadside service membership starts at £40.

Environmental Transport Association

Freepost KT4021, Weybridge, Surrey KT13 8RS (01932 828882). **Open** *office* 8am-6pm Mon-Fri; 9am-4pm Sat; *breakdown service* 24 hours daily. **Credit** MC, V.

The green alternative, if you don't want part of your membership fees used for lobbying the government into building more roads, as happens with the AA and RAC. Basic membership is £20 a year for individuals and £25 for families.

RAC

RAC House, 1 Forest Road, Feltham TW13 7RR (emergency breakdown 0800 828282/office & membership enquiries 0990 722722). **Open** *office* 9am-5pm Mon-Fri; *breakdown service* 24 hours daily. **Credit** AmEx, DC, MC, V.

Ring the general enquiries number and ask for the Rescue Service. Membership costs from £39 for basic cover to £135 for the most comprehensive, plus £75 for European cover.

Taxis

Black cabs

Licensed London taxis are called black cabs (even though many of them are not black). They all have a yellow 'For Hire' sign and a white licence plate on the back of the vehicle. Drivers of black cabs must pass 'The Knowledge' to prove they know the name of every street in central London, where it is and the shortest route to it. Any complaints or enquiries should be made to the Public Carriage Office (0171 230 1631/lost property 0171 833 0996; 9am-4pm Mon-Fri). Remember to note the number of the offending cab. When a taxi's 'For Hire' sign is switched on, it can be hailed in the street.

Radio Taxis (0171 272 0272) and **Dial a Cab** (0171 253 5000) both run 24-hour services for black cabs.

Minicabs

Minicabs (saloon cars) are generally cheaper than black cabs, especially at night and weekends. However, the drivers are unlicensed, untrained, frequently uninsured, not always reliable and very occasionally dangerous. There are, though, plenty of trustworthy firms – always ask for a recommendation. Ask the price when you book and confirm it with the driver when the car arrives. Minicabs can't legally be hailed in the street: avoid drivers touting for business (common at night) as it's illegal and can be very risky. **Addison Lee** (0171 387 8888) is one of the bigger, more reliable companies, and it also claims to do pick-ups from all areas. Women travelling alone may prefer to use **Lady Cabs** (0171 254 3501/254 3314), which employs only women drivers.

Business services

The proudly pink *Financial Times* (daily) is the most authoritative newspaper for facts and figures in the City and all over the world. If you are after in depth analysis, and some considered domestic and international news, try *The Economist* magazine (weekly).

Communications

British Monomarks

Monomarks House, 27 Old Gloucester Street, WC1 (0171 419 5000/404 5011/fax 0171 831 9489/ bm@monomark.co.uk). Holborn tube. **Open** 9.30am-5.30pm Mon-Fri; *telex bureau* 8am-6.30pm Mon-Fri. **Credit** AmEx, MC, £$TC, V. **Map 6 L5**

You can use any number of British Monomarks services including arranging to have your mail forwarded, use of the telex or fax machine, or arranging to use the 24-hour telephone answering service. If you leave a deposit, you can phone in your telex messages, during the times listed above.

Conferences

London Tourist Board

Glen House, Stag Place, SW1 (0171 932 2010/fax 0171 932 2013). Victoria tube/rail. **Open** 9am-5.30pm Mon-Fri. **Map 4 J9**

LTB will assist with the organisation of conventions or exhibitions. Request (by letter or fax) its free guide, *Convention, Exhibition and Incentive London*, which lists hotels and centres that host events, together with their facilities.
Website: www.LondonTown.com

Queen Elizabeth II Conference Centre

Broad Sanctuary, SW1 (0171 222 5000/enquiries 0171 798 4000/fax 0171 798 4200). St James's Park tube. **Open** 8am-6pm Mon-Fri; 24-hour conference facilities. **Map 8 K9**

This unattractive, purpose-built centre close to the Houses of Parliament has some of the best conference facilities in the capital. There are rooms with capacities from 30 to 1,100, and communications equipment is available including a TV studio equipped to broadcast-specifications.

Dinners

Funevents

2nd floor, Berkeley Square House, Berkeley Square, W1 (0171 887 6110).

A unique idea. For a fee of £150, Funevents will link up individual business travellers to 'exchange ideas and business cards over a good meal'. The cost of dinner and taxis to and from your hotel is included in the price.
Website: www.funevents.com

Equipment hire

ABC Business Machines

59 Chiltern Street, W1 (0171 486 5634). Baker Street tube. **Open** 9am-5.30pm Mon-Fri; 9.30am-12.30pm Sat. **Credit** JCB, MC, £TC, V. **Map 5 G5**
Answerphones, calculators and audio equipment are among the items on hire at ABC. Electronic typewriters cost £35.25 a month, fax machines £52.88 a month; copiers and computers start at £90 a month.

Reference libraries

City Business Library

1 Brewer's Hall Garden, off London Wall, EC2 (0171 638 8215/recorded info 0171 480 7638). Moorgate tube/rail. **Open** 9.30am-5pm Mon-Fri. **Map 12 Q6**
The City Business Library keeps an excellent range of business reference works, including newspaper cuttings, Extel cards and world trade and professional directories. It also has a free enquiry service and fee-based research service.

Guildhall Library

Aldermanbury, EC2 (0171 332 1868/bookshop 0171 332 1858). Bank, Moorgate or St Paul's tube. **Open** 9.30am-5pm Mon-Fri (restricted service on Sat). **Admission** free. **Map 11 P6**
Most of the material deals with the history of London. On the ground floor are books, while the first floor has maps, prints and manuscripts.

There is also a bookshop selling material relevant to the library and the Guildhall Art Gallery.

London Business School Library

Taunton Place, Regent's Park, NW1 (0171 262 5050). Baker Street tube or Marylebone tube/rail. **Open** 8.30am-10pm Mon-Fri; 9am-5pm Sat; 11am-7pm Sun. **Admission** £20 per day; free for postgraduate students & members of the UN.
The library has a comprehensive stock of standard business reference works and by-country and by-industry information files. The LBS Research Service (0171 723 3404) will do the work for you at a rate of £70 per hour.

Westminster Reference Library

35 St Martin's Street, WC2 (0171 641 4634). Leicester Square tube or Charing Cross tube/rail. **Open** 10am-8pm Mon-Fri; 10am-5pm Sat. **Admission** free. **Map 8 K7**
A public reference library with government publications, international phone directories and business on the ground floor; an arts collection, including performance arts, and maps on the first floor; a large art and design collection on the second floor.

Secretarial

Reed Employment, Staff Agency

143 Victoria Street, SW1 (0171 834 1801/fax 0171 821 5593). Victoria

tube/rail. **Open** 8am-6pm Mon-Fri. **Map 7 J10**
Reed supplies secretarial, computing, accountancy and technical services to registered companies. This branch specialises in secretarial and administration services.

Typing Overload

67 Chancery Lane, WC2 (0171 404 5464/fax 0171 831 0878). Chancery Lane tube. **Open** 9.30am-5.30pm Mon-Fri. **Credit** AmEx, DC, MC, £STC, V. **Map 6 M5**
Come here for a speedy and professional typing service for any job that can be done on a wordprocessor. **Branch**: 35 Brompton Road, SW3 (0171 823 9955).

Translation

Central Translations

2-3 Woodstock Street, W1 (0171 493 5511). Bond Street tube. **Open** 9am-5pm Mon-Fri. **Map 5 H6**
Be it typesetting, proofreading, translation or the use of an interpreter, Central can work with almost every language under the sun. Rates for translation into English range from about £9 to £25 per 100 words.

1st Translation Company

24 Holborn Viaduct, EC1 (0171 329 0032/fax 0171 329 0035). Chancery Lane tube. **Open** 10am-6pm Mon-Fri. **Map 11 N5**
More than 50 languages can be translated (£8-£21 per 100 words, depending on the complexity of the language). Interpreters cost £220-£500 per day.

Media

Newspapers

National newspapers fall broadly in to three categories. At the lofty, serious news end of the scale are the broadsheets – the rightish-wing *Daily Telegraph* and *The Times* are balanced by the (increasingly unindependent) *The Independent* and the *Guardian*. All have bulging Sunday equivalents (except the *Guardian*, but it does have a sister Sunday paper: the *Observer*). The right-wing middle-market leader has long been the *Daily Mail* (and *Mail on Sunday*), although its rival, the *Daily Express*, is currently making huge efforts

to claw back its market share. At the bottom of the pile are the most popular papers of them all: the tabloids. Still undisputed leader of the rat pack is the *Sun* (and the Sunday *News of the World*), selling around seven million copies daily (more than half the daily total of all newspapers sold). The *Daily Star* and the *Mirror* are the other main lowbrow contenders. The *People* and the *Sunday Mirror* provide sleaze on Sunday. London's only daily paper, which comes out in several editions through the day, is the right-wing *Evening Standard*, a sort of *Mail* for London.

Magazines

There are more than 6,500 titles available. Two thirds of this total are professional magazines, the others are consumer publications. The women's market is the most profitable (and saturated), with *Marie Claire*, selling close to half a million copies a month, leading the way. The men's market continues to expand, with *FHM* doing particularly well at the moment. Style magazines, such as *i-D*, *Dazed & Confused* and *Mixmag*, have established themselves in a profitable niche. Sport magazines have proliferated wildly in recent

Directory

years; football fans are particularly well served. If you're looking for something more serious and hard-hitting, there's not much to choose from. *The Spectator*, the *New Statesman* and *Prospect* are the closest you will get. *Private Eye* offers a fortnightly satirical look at politics and news. *The Big Issue*, sold on the street by homeless people, is also worth a look. *The Economist* covers international political and business issues, and you'll find the international editions of *Time* and *Newsweek* at most newsagents.

Radio

BBC Radio 1 *98.8 FM.*
Youth-oriented music station – pop, rock, dance and more unusual genres.
BBC Radio 2 *89.1 FM.*
Fairly bland, middle-of-the-road – both the music and the DJs.
BBC Radio 3 *91.3 FM.*
The BBC's classical music station.
BBC Radio 4 *93.5 FM, 720 MW, 198 LW.*
Speech-only station, particularly loved for its six-mornings-a-week *Today* news programme.
BBC Radio 5 Live *693, 909 MW.*
News and sport, 24 hours a day. Live coverage of major sporting events.
BBC GLR (Greater London Radio) *94.9 FM.*
The BBC's excellent station for London. Good music, good chat and unusually intelligent DJs.
BBC World Service *648 MW, 6.195, 9.410 SW.*
Transmitted worldwide but available in the UK for a distillation of the best of all the other BBC stations.
Capital FM *95.8 FM.*
London's liveliest commercial station offers music, quizzes and ads.
Capital Gold *1548 MW.*
Plays '60s to '80s pop.
Choice FM *96.9 FM.*
South London soul station.
Classic FM *100.9 FM.*
Classical easy listening.
Country *1035 MW.*
The name says it all.
Heart *106.2 FM.*
More MOR music, less talk.
Jazz FM *102.2 FM.*
There's still *some* jazz left on this station, which had to go mainstream in order to survive.
Kiss *100.0 FM.*
Wide selection of dance music for the seriously funked up.

Liberty *963 MW.*
Liberty took over from the women's station, Viva!
London Greek *103.3 FM.*
Only available in the Haringey area of north London.
London Newstalk (LBC) *1152 MW.*
Phone-ins and chat.
LTR *1584 MW.*
Turkish radio.
Melody *105.4 FM.*
Cabbies' favourite. Music as bland as you can get.
News Direct *97.3 FM.*
24-hour news, weather, motoring and business information.
Premier Radio *1335, 1332 MW.*
Christian radio station.
Spectrum *558 MW.*
Researched, produced and presented by various ethnic communities.
Sunrise *1458 MW.*
Asian-oriented programming.
Talk Radio *1053, 1089 MW.*
As the name implies…
Virgin *105.8 FM, 1215 MW.*
Adult rock.
XFM *104.9FM.*
Indie music station.

Television

With the launch of digital TV in 1998 things are about to change for British television. People with the facility will be able to access extra channels. Below are the main channels that can be accessed by analogue terrestrial, cable and satellite television.

BBC1

BBC1 represents all that is 'Auntie BBC' – the Corporation's mass-market station. No commercials. There's a smattering of soaps and game shows, also the odd quality programme. Daytime programming, however, stinks.

BBC2

Another commercial-free station but, in general, BBC2 is also free of crass programmes. That doesn't mean the output is riveting, just not insulting. It offers a cultural cross-section and plenty of documentaries; recently it has also been competing with Channel 4 in the Friday-night comedy stakes.

ITV – Carlton

Mass-appeal programmes punctuated by frequent commercial breaks. It's not quite the lowest common denominator, more the highest possible audience. Any successful formula is repeated *ad infinitum*. The odd sparkler of a drama.

ITV – London Weekend Television

LWT takes over from Carlton at the weekend to offer much of the same, if not more downmarket.

Channel 4

C4's output includes some pretty mainstream fare, especially its extremely successful US imports, but it still comes up with some gems of programmes, particularly its films.

Channel 5

Britian's newest terrestrial channel arrived amid much fanfare in 1997. So far, output has failed to match the hype, except for viewers for whom made-for-TV films and re-runs pass as entertainment.

Satellite & cable

Bravo
Retro channel offering TV classics from the 1960s and 1970s.
CNN
News and current affairs reporting, the American way.
Eurosport
One of three sport-only channels; marginal-interest events.
FilmFour
Launched in late 1998, this admirable Channel 4 venture shows 12 hours of films every day, including independent flicks and director's cuts.
Family
Safe programming policy. Dullsville.
Granada Talk TV
News, views, current affairs – like Radio 5 Live but on TV.
Movie Channel
More films.
MTV
Rock/pop channel that borrows from its US counterpart.
QVC
Home shopping channel.
Sky Movies
Blockbusters and interview snippets.
Sky Movies Gold
Classic movie channel.
Sky News
24-hour news and features.
Sky One
Channel with general appeal.
Sky Sports
Major sporting events. There are also Sky Sports 2 and Sky Sports 3.
TNT
Cartoons all day then classic repeats.
UK Gold
Buys wholesale from BBC and ITV, repeating yesterday's successes.
UK Living
For those who spend all day at home.
VH-1
Rock station featuring extensive album coverage.

Students

Being a student in London can be an exciting, if initially daunting, not to mention, disconcertingly expensive, affair. Whether you are here to study or just visiting, *Time Out*'s annual *Student Guide* magazine, available in many bookshops and newsagents, provides a comprehensive low-down on what London has to offer students and how to survive in the big city. This section lists some practical information for students plus tips on saving money, and the pick of the student bars in which to drink away your savings. We also list some of the many English-language classes available to foreigners wanting to brush up their local lingo.

In addition to the money-savers listed (*see page 311*), see also the section within the Restaurants chapter on budget eateries (*see page 160*) and cheap accommodation (though be warned that no accommodation in London is *that* cheap; *see page 149-52*). Throughout this guide, entry prices for students at museums, art galleries, sights, sports venues and other places are usually designated 'concs' ('concessions'). Students (whether EU citizens or not) wanting to find work in the UK as a way of boosting their funds, *see page 297* **Working in London**.

National Bureau for Students with Disabilities
Chapter House, 18-20 Crucifix Lane, SE1 (0800 328 5050). **Open** *phone enquiries 1.30-4.30pm Mon-Fri.* Information and advice.

Universities

Brunel University
Clevedon Road, Uxbridge, Middx, UB8 (01895 274000/Students Union 01895 462200). Uxbridge tube.

City University
Northampton Square, EC1 (0171 477 8000/Students Union 0171 505 5600). Angel or Barbican tube. **Map 9 O3**

Guildhall University
2 Goulston Street, E1 (0171 320 1000/Students Union 0171 247 1441). Aldgate East tube. **Map 12 S6**

South Bank University
Borough Rd, SE1 (0171 928 8989/Students Union 0171 815 6060). Elephant & Castle tube. **Map 11 O9**

University of East London (Stratford Campus)
Romford Road, E15 (0181 590 7722/Students Union ext 4210). Stratford tube/rail.

University of Greenwich
Wellington Street, SE18 (0181 331 8000/Students Union 0181 331 8268). Woolwich Arsenal rail.

University of Kingston
Penrhyn Road, Kingston, Surrey (0181 547 2000/Students Union 0181 255 2222). Kingston rail.

University of London
(see below)

University of Middlesex
Trent Park, Bramley Road, N14 (0181 362 5000/Students Union 0181 362 6450). Cockfosters or Oakwood tube.

University of North London
166-220 Holloway Road, N7 (0171 607 2789/Students Union 0171 753 3361). Holloway Road tube.

University of Westminster
309 Regent Street, W1 (0171 911 5000). Oxford Circus tube. **Map 5 H4**

University of London
A large proportion of all students studying in London attend one of the 34 colleges, spread out all over the city, that make up the gargantuan University of London; only the six largest are listed below. All London universities (except Imperial College) are affiliated to the **National Union of Students (NUS)**.

NUS London Regional Office
(0171 272 8900/www.nus.org.uk). **Open** 9.30am-5pm Mon-Fri.

Goldsmiths' College
Lewisham Way, SE14 (0171 919 7171/Students Union 0181 692 1406). New Cross/New Cross Gate tube/rail.

Imperial College
Prince Consort Road, SW7 (0171 589 5111/Students Union 0171 594 8060). South Kensington tube. **Map 4 D9**

King's College
Strand, WC2 (0171 836 5454/Students Union 0171 836 7132). Temple tube. **Map 8 M7**

London School of Economics (LSE)
Page Building, Houghton Street, WC2 (0171 405 7686/Students Union 0171 955 7158). Holborn tube. **Map 6 M6**

Queen Mary & Westfield College (QMW)
Mile End Road, E1 (0171 975 5555/Students Union 0171 975 5390). Mile End or Stepney Green tube.

University College London (UCL)
Gower Street, WC1 (0171 387 7050/Students Union 0171 387 3611). Goodge Street or Warren Street tube/Euston tube/rail. **Map 6 K4**

Student bars

All the student unions in London have some sort of programme of events. The quality varies immensely – some are dreary and amateurish but many are imaginative and excellent. Many student unions, however, will only let in students with the relevant ID, so be sure to carry your NUS or ISIC card with you at all times to ensure entry. Below are the six best student venues in the capital, where you can normally expect an entertaining night out at friendly prices. For other bars and pubs in town, *see page 179*.

Directory

Fly in and out of Gatwick.

Whether you've just landed or you're preparing for take off,
the fastest and most convenient way to travel between Gatwick Airport
and Victoria Station is on the Gatwick Express.
With trains leaving every 15 minutes during the day and hourly through the night,
it really is the only way to travel to and from the airport.
For more information, call us on 0990 30 15 30 or visit our website at
http://www.gatwickexpress.co.uk

Student money-savers

London can be an expensive place, especially if you're counting every penny. But do not despair – student status can turn out to be a real money-saver. First, you need to equip yourself with a student card: either a **National Union of Students (NUS) Card**, or, if you're visiting London and don't have an NUS card (but have some other form of student ID), then get an **International Student Identity Card (ISIC)**, available from most students' unions or student travel agencies.

Both cards work as a passport to savings on all sorts of goods and services in town. These range from clothing to cheap hairdos and driving lessons. Check the NUS website (*www.nus.org.uk*) for details of the latest savings available. Be aware that while some organisations advertise their student discounts heavily, others are rather more coy: a flash of your student card won't do you any harm and might just net you a considerable discount.

Entertainment

Many cultural events in London – from indie gigs to art exhibitions – offer some form of student reduction. For details of current discounted events, see *Time Out*'s weekly student section, or the free fortnightly newspaper *London Student*.

London cinemas are queueing up to give students concessions, and not just during the day. Most **ABC** and **Virgin** cinemas in central London offer cheap tickets for students all day every day (though there are some exceptions). Many other West End movie houses offer discounts to everyone, not just students, while most rep houses, including the estimable **National Film Theatre** (0171 928 3232), have reduced-price tickets for students.

The majority of the big classical music venues operate a student standby scheme. Most concerts at the **Royal Festival Hall** (0171 633 0932) have discounted student tickets – some in advance and some as standbys; expect to pay under £10 for most events. Major cultural centres, including the **English National Opera** (0171 632 8300) and the **Barbican Centre** (0171 382 7272), plus lesser-known venues such as **Wigmore Hall** (0171 935 2141), run their own student standby schemes for some, if not all, performances.

Student theatre buffs need not despair: a fair few of the big houses run some sort of discount scheme (*see page 269*). Another useful innovation is the **Stage Pass**, available to anyone aged 16-29 for £15 a year. This gives members discounts on a wide variety of shows in London and, unlike the standby schemes so popular in Theatreland, enables you to buy discounted seats in advance.

Stage Pass *28 Charing Cross Road, London WC2H 0DB (0171 379 6722/stagepass@dial.pipex.com). Leicester Square tube.* **Open** *phone enquiries 10am-6pm Mon-Fri.* **Map 8 K7**
Discounts on plays, musicals, concerts, opera, comedy and the like.

Travel

Increased competition within the travel trade is resulting in cheaper than ever travel to many destinations around the globe (less so, alas, within Britain), and for students (and under-26s in general) savings can be outstanding. Surprisingly, perhaps, the most economical way of travelling is often by air. In addition to the places listed below (which specialise in cheap air, rail and coach fares for students and young people), there is a heavily subsidised travel programme run by the **International Students House Travel Club** (0171 631 8300).

Campus Travel
52 Grosvenor Gardens, SW1 (Europe 0171 730 3402/North America 0171 730 2101/worldwide 0171 730 8111/www.campustravel.co.uk). Victoria tube/rail. **Open** 9am-6pm Mon-Fri; 10am-5pm Sat; 10am-4pm Sun. **Map 7 H10**
Branches: UCL Union, 25 Gordon Square, WC1 (0171 383 5337); South Bank University, Keyworth Street, SE1 (0171 401 8666); 14 Southampton Street, WC2 (0171 836 3343); 174 Kensington High Street, W8 (0171 938 2188).

STA Travel
6 Wright's Lane, W8 (Europe 0171 361 6161/worldwide 0171 361 6262/guide & brochures 0171 361 6166). High Street Kensington tube. **Open** 9am-6pm Mon-Fri; 10am-4pm Sat. **Map 3 B9**
Branches: 86 Old Brompton Road, SW7 (0171 581 4132); 117 Euston Road, NW1 (0171 465 0484); 38 Store Street, WC1 (0171 580 7733); 11 Goodge Street, W1 (0171 436 7779).

Trailfinders
194 & 215 Kensington High Street, W8 (Europe & transatlantic 0171 937 5400/long haul 0171 938 3939/3366). High Street Kensington tube. **Open** 9am-6pm Mon-Wed, Fri, Sat; 9am-7pm Thur; 10am-6pm Sun. **Map 3 A9**
Branch: 42-50 Earl's Court Road, W8 (0171 938 3366).

Directory

Imperial College

*Beit Quad, Prince Consort Road,
SW7 (0171 589 5111). South
Kensington tube.* **Open** noon-2pm,
5-11pm, Mon, Tue, Thur; noon-2pm,
5pm-midnight, Wed; noon-2pm, 5pm-
1am, Fri; 12.30-11pm Sat; 12.30-
10.30pm Sun. **Map 4 D9**
No-frills union hospitality at its most
basic and best. Imperial has a large
union, a fact reflected in its excellent
entertainments programme. The
main bar, Da Vinci's, is a lively and
friendly place, with cheap beer and
constant MTV. Imperial, though, is
the only college in the UK not to be
affiliated to the NUS, so check if
you'll be able to get in or not before
you go.

International
Students House

*229 Great Portland Street, W1
(0171 631 8300 ext 744).
Great Portland Street tube.*
Open noon-2pm, 5-11pm, Mon-Thur;
noon-2pm, 4.30pm-2am, Fri; 5.30-
11pm Sat; 5.30-10.30pm Sun.
Map 5 H4
Part refuge, part social mecca,
International Students House
attempts to be all things to all
students – and it largely succeeds.
Aside from keeping rooms to rent for
visiting students on a long- or short-
term basis (*see p152*), there are also
sports facilities, a number of eateries
and a bar, which holds events
throughout the year, including a
decent club night on Fridays.
Look out, too, for the excellent and
heavily subsidised Travel Club.
Some colleges automatically enroll
their students here: check to see if
this is the case before forking out
for membership.

King's College

*Macadam Building, Surrey Street,
WC2 (0171 836 7132). Temple
tube.* **Open** *Waterfront* noon-11pm
Mon-Fri; 8-11pm Sat. *Tutu's* 9pm-
2am Fri; 10pm-2am Sat.
Map 8 M7
King's is the best student venue in
London: no question. This is all the
more surprising when you consider
that a couple of years ago, this place
was an utter dump. Now, though,
there's the newly refurbished and
always lively and entertaining
Waterfront Bar, which also serves
pretty decent food, and Tutu's, a 600-
capacity live venue that puts on
some great bands every couple of
weeks at the geekily named Colin's
Kitchen night.

School of Oriental &
African Studies

*Thornhaugh Street, WC1 (0171
637 2388). Goodge Street or
Russell Square tube.* **Open** noon-

2pm, 5pm-9pm, Mon-Fri.
Map 6 K4
A capacious, scruffy bar that
generates a great atmosphere most
nights of the week. The beer's cheap
– which goes some way towards com-
pensating for the decidedly dodgy
décor – there are three pool tables,
and they even serve pies. What more
could you want?

University of London
Union (ULU)

*Malet Street, WC1 (0171 664 2000).
Goodge Street or Russell Square tube.*
Open noon-11pm Mon-Fri; noon-
1am Fri, Sat; noon-10.30pm Sun.
Map 6 K4
The big London student venue,
recently done up at no small expense.
There are two decent bars – Room
101, a cod-wine bar, and the Duck &
Dive, a more pubby bar where you
can also get food – and where there's
often a band or two playing on
Friday or Saturday nights.

University of North
London

*166-220 Holloway Road, N7 (0171
607 2789 ext 2532). Holloway Road
tube.* **Open** 11am-11pm Mon, Tue,
Thur; 11am-1am Wed; 11am-
midnight Fri; 11am-2am Sat.
In keeping with the university's reputation for design, the bar has been
refurbished in a postmodern style
and renamed the Rocket Bar. The
huge function hall upstairs is the
venue for the Big Fish club night
every Wednesday.

University of Westminster

*35 Marylebone Road, W1 (0171
911 5000). Baker Street tube.*
Open 11.30am-11pm Mon-Fri.
Map 5 G4
The location doesn't seem very
promising, and the building itself is
hardly inspiring, but the University
of Westminster is blessed with one of
the most upmarket union bars in the
UK. Banish all thoughts of the beer-
soaked, fag-burned carpet, peeling
paint and peeling posters. This is a
practically postmodern union bar; the
décor is far too extravagant and
splendid for a humble student
drinking hole. There's also a decent
entertainment programme.

English language
classes

It can sometimes seem that half
the foreign students in London
are earning pocket money
handing out leaflets for English
language schools, particularly
around Tottenham Court Road
tube station. All the following

are reputable schools,
recommended by the British
Council and ARELS
(Association of Recognised
English Language Schools),
offering English language
classes to foreigners of all
levels of ability.

Anglo-World Education

*3-4 Southampton Place, WC1 (0171
404 3080/fax 0171 404 3443/
Learn@angloworld.com). Holborn
tube.* **Map 6 L5**
As well as offering a range of English
language courses, this educational
centre puts students in touch with
host families.
Branch: 8 Queen's Road, NW4 (0181
202 4351).

Central School of English

*1 Tottenham Court Road, W1 (0171
580 2863/fax 0171 255 1806/
efl@cselond.demon.co.uk).
Tottenham Court Road tube.*
Map 6 K5
Students can benefit from one-to-one
tuition in this excellently located
and long-established school of
English.
Website: www.edunet.com/cselond

Frances King School
of English

*195 Knightsbridge, SW7 (0171 838
0200/fax 0171 838 0303/info@
fkse.ac.uk). Knightsbridge tube.*
Map 2 F9
A study year in London and teacher
training courses are just two of the
special programmes available here.
Website: www.fkse.ac.uk

London Study Centre

*Munster House, 676 Fulham Road,
SW6 (0171 731 3549/fax 0171 731
6060/english-language@compuserve.
com). Parsons Green tube.*
Set up over 20 years ago, this centre
offers such useful courses as English
for tourism.

Sels College

*64-65 Long Acre, WC2 (0171 240
2581/fax 0171 379 5793/
english@sels.co.uk). Covent Garden
tube.* **Map 6 L6**
Founded in 1975, Sels runs a range of
English courses, with an emphasis on
tuition in small groups.
Website: www.sels.co.uk

Shane English School

*59 South Molton Street, W1 (0171
499 8533/fax 0171 499 9374/
info@saxoncourt.com). Bond Street
tube.* **Map 5 H6**
Intensive daytime and evening
courses are offered by this school
just off Oxford Street.
Website: www.saxoncourt.com

Directory

Further Reading

Fiction

Peter Ackroyd *Hawksmoor/The House of Doctor Dee/ Dan Leno & the Limehouse Golem/Great Fire of London*
Intricate studies of arcane London.

Jonathan Coe *The Dwarves of Death*
Mystery, music, mirth, malevolence.

Norman Collins *London Belongs to Me*
Witty saga of goings-on in Kennington in the 1930s.

Wilkie Collins *The Woman in White*
A midnight encounter has dire consequences.

Joseph Conrad *The Secret Agent*
Anarchism in seedy Soho.

Charles Dickens *Oliver Twist/David Copperfield/ Bleak House/Our Mutual Friend*
Four of the master's most London-centric novels.

Sir Arthur Conan Doyle *Complete Sherlock Holmes*
Reassuring sleuthing shenanigans.

Aidan Andrew Dun *Vale Royal*
Epic poet engages with myths of King's Cross and St Pancras.

Christopher Fowler *Disturbia/Soho Black*
Conspiracy theories and class war/Walking dead in Soho.

George Gissing *New Grub Street*
Trials and tribulations of hack writers.

Graham Greene *The End of the Affair*
Adultery, Catholicism and Clapham Common.

Patrick Hamilton *20,000 Streets Under the Sky/ Hangover Square*
Yearning romantic trilogy set among Soho sleaze/Love and death in darkest Earl's Court.

M John Harrison *The Ice Monkey*
The dark spiritual heart of Camden.

Alan Hollinghurst *The Swimming Pool Library*
Shimmering evocation of gay life around Russell Square.

Stewart Home *Come Before Christ and Murder Love*
Blend of paranoia, food sex and tour-guide psycho-rap.

Hanif Kureishi *The Buddha of Suburbia*
Funny take on suburban boredom, ethnicity and hippies.

Maria Lexton (ed) *Time Out Book of London Short Stories*
London-based writers pay homage to their city.

Colin MacInnes *City of Spades/Absolute Beginners*
Coffee and jazz, Soho and Notting Hill.

Wolf Mankowitz *A Kid for Two Farthings*
Boy meets goat in East End market.

Herman Melville *The Paradise of Bachelors*
Bizarre story set in the all-male enclave of the Inner Temple.

Michael Moorcock *Mother London*
Love-letter to London.

Oscar Moore *A Matter of Life and Sex*
Moving tale of love, sex and cottaging in AIDS-hit London.

Iris Murdoch *Under the Net*
Picaresque adventures of a talented but wastrel writer.

Courttia Newland *The Scholar*
Life is full of choices for a kid on a West London estate.

Kim Newman *The Quorum*
Web of intrigue surrounds Docklands-based media magnate.

George Orwell *Keep the Aspidistra Flying*
Saga of struggling writer and reluctant bookshop assistant.

John Preston *Ghosting*
Existential, dourly funny novel with broadcasting theme.

Derek Raymond *I Was Dora Suarez*
Blackest London noir.

Alan Ross (ed) *London Magazine*
Essential bi-monthly mix of fiction, reviews, poetry, articles.

Nicholas Royle *The Matter of the Heart*
Sex and death in disused hospital at Hyde Park Corner.

Geoff Ryman *253*
Glimpse into lives of passengers on a Bakerloo Line train.

William Sansom *Selected Short Stories*
Lyrical tales of Londoners at large.

Will Self *Grey Area*
'There are only eight people in London…'. Short stories.

Iain Sinclair *Downriver/Radon Daughters/ White Chappell, Scarlet Tracings*
The Thames's own Heart of Darkness by London's laureate/William Hope Hodgson via the London Hospital/ Ripper murders and bookdealers.

Tobias Smollett *The Expedition of Humphry Clinker*
Assault on eighteenth-century sensibilities and strawberries.

Muriel Spark *The Ballad of Peckham Rye*
The devil incarnate spreads mayhem in Peckham.

Evelyn Waugh *Vile Bodies*
Satire on the too-shamemaking antics in 1920s Mayfair.

Angus Wilson *The Old Men at the Zoo*
London faces down oblivion.

Virginia Woolf *Mrs Dalloway*
Joyce's *Ulysses* transplanted to London, with female lead.

Non-fiction

Felix Barker & Ralph Hyde *London as it Might Have Been*
Schemes that never made it past the drawing board.

Quentin Crisp *The Naked Civil Servant*
'Blind with mascara… I paraded the dim streets of Pimlico…'

Daniel Farson *Soho in the Fifties*
Affectionate portrait of the pubs and characters of Soho.

Derek Hammond *London, England – A Day-tripper's Travelogue from the Coolest City in the World*
Witty, endlessly enthusiastic celebration of the capital.

Samantha Hardingham *London: A Guide to Recent Architecture*
Excellent pocket-sized guide.

Stephen Inwood *A History of London*
Recent, readable, encyclopaedic London biog.

Jack London *The People of the Abyss*
Extreme poverty in the East End.

Nick Merriman (ed) *The Peopling of London*
Fascinating account of 2,000 years of settlement.

George Orwell *Down and Out in Paris and London*
Grim autobiographical account of waitering and starving.

Samuel Pepys *Diaries*
Fires, plagues, bordellos and more.

Roy Porter *London – A Social History*
All-encompassing history of London.

Iain Sinclair *Lights Out For the Territory*
Time-warp visionary walks across London.

Richard Trench *London Under London*
Investigation of the subterranean city.

Ben Weinreb/Christopher Hibbert (eds)
Encyclopaedia of London

Index

Street Index

Advertisers' Index

Please refer to the relevant sections for addresses/telephone numbers

Places of interest or entertainment	▮
Railway stations	▮
Underground stations	⊖
Parks	▮
Hospitals	▮
Casualty units	✚
Churches	✚
Districts	MAYFAIR

0   500 m

Maps

London Overview

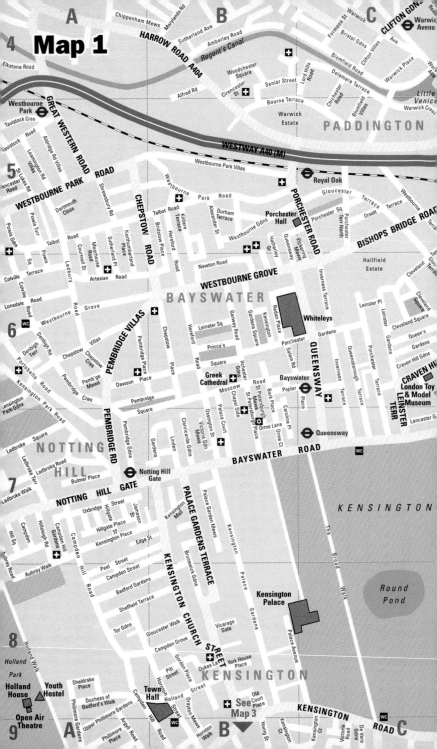

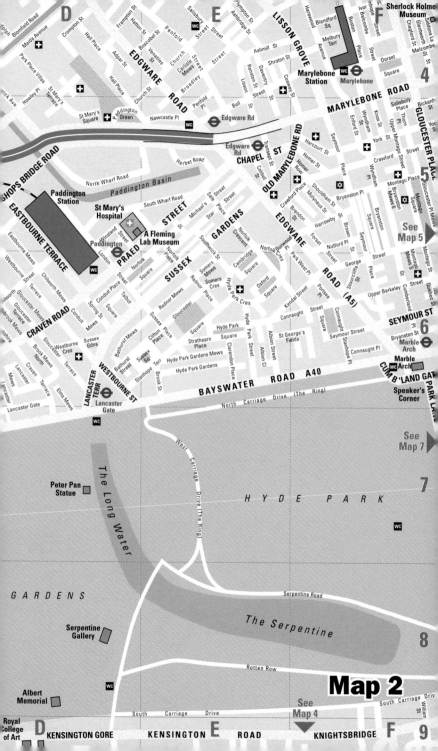

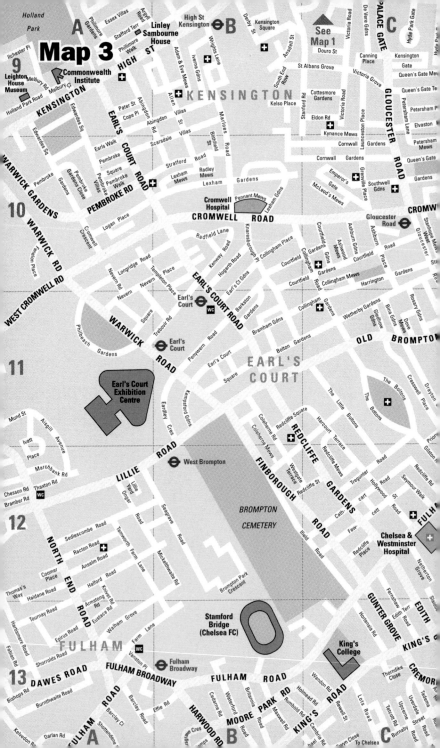

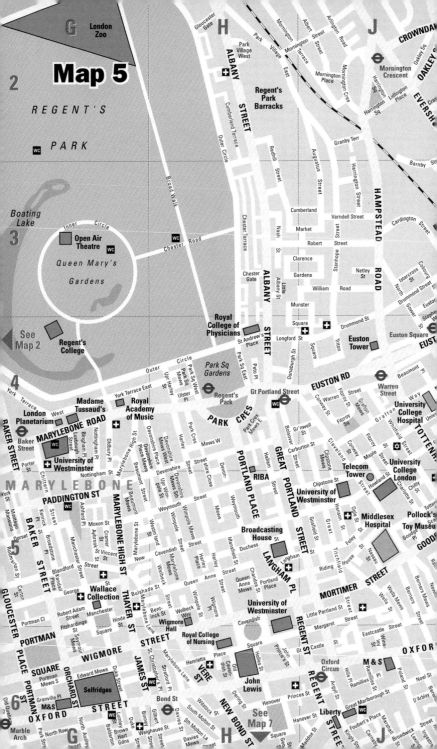

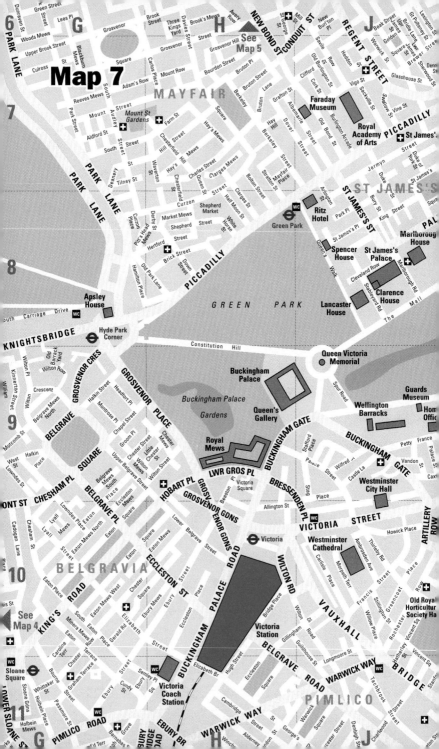

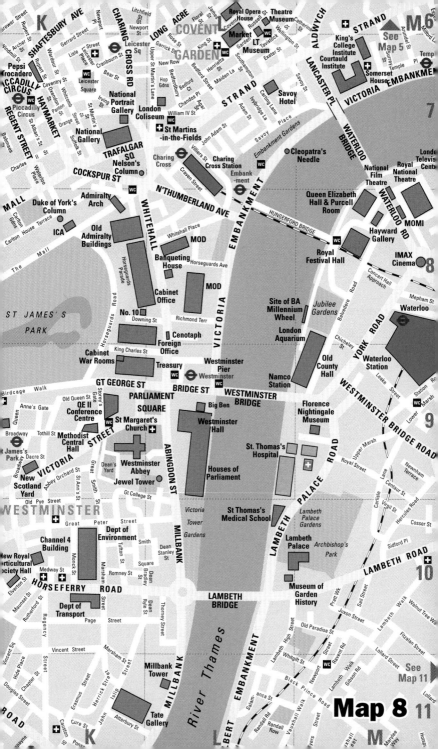

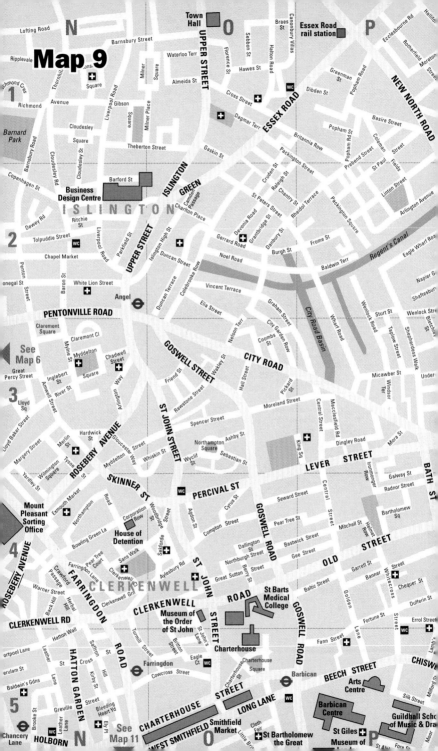

Map 10

Q   **R**   WC   **S**

De Beauvoir   **DALSTON**   Mapledene Rd

Morston Rd   Northchurch Road   De Beauvoir   Holly St   Road   Lavender Gr

Halliford Street   Almorah Rd   Cleveland Road   Lawford Road   Square   Albion   **1**

Southgate Gr   Ufton Road   Mortimer Rd   Square   Albion   Queensbridge   Drive

Downham   Road   Hertford   Lee Street   Livermore Rd   Shrubland Road

Sherbourne St   Southgate   Road   Acton Mews   Scriven St   Brownlow Rd

Balmes Road   De Beauvoir   Clarissa St   Pownall Row

Wilton   Crescent   Dunston Rd   Dunston Rd

Square   Baring Street   Whitmore Road   Orsman Road   Mill Row   *Regent's Canal*

Bridport Place   Penn St   Hyde Rd   Halcomb St   Phillipp Street   Laburnum Road   Whiston Road

NEW NORTH ROAD   Poole St   Whiston Road   **HAGGERSTON**   Kent St   *Haggerston Park*   **2**

Wimbourne St   *Shoreditch Park*   Hemsworth St   Nuttall St   Hows Street   Thurtle Rd   Queensbridge Road

Copley Street   Mintern Street   Pitfield Street   Ivy St   Geffrye   Ormsby   Appleby Street   Weymouth Ter

Murlock Street   Buckland St   Purcell St   WC   Pearson   Street   Horchio St

Murray Grove   Cherbury   Regan Way   Stanway Street   **Geffrye Museum**   Dunloe   ROAD   Cadell Cl   Shipton Street   Ropley St

New Norm Rd   Crondall Street   Shenfield St   Cremer Street   **HACKNEY**   Ravenscroft St   **3**

Provost Street   **HOXTON**   Falkirk Street   Nazral St   Columbia   Road

Nile Street   Bevenden St   Fanshaw   St   Union Wk   Long St   Quilter St

Vestry St   Haberdasher St   Waterson   **COLUMBIA ROAD**   Wellington Row

EAST ROAD   Buttesland St   St   GOSSET ST

Chart St   Hoxton   Austin St   Virginia Rd   Chambord St   Turin Street

Moorfields Eye Hospital   Corsham St   Chart St   Square   Drysdale St   Calvert Ave   Arnold   Satchwell St

Peerless Street   Brunswick Place   Baches St   Charles   Pitfield   Boot St   **KINGSLAND ROAD**   Circus   Padbury Ct   Granby St

Old Street   Crawood St   Square   **OLD STREET**   Old Nichol   Chilton St   **4**

OLD   WC   **STREET**   Rivington   Street   Bateman's Row   Redchurch   Street   WC   Bacon Street   St Matthews Row

Featherstone St   Cowper St   Willow St   Charlotte   New Inn Yard   **GREEN**   **ROAD**

Mallow St   Leonard   Street   **GREAT EASTERN STREET**   Boundary Street   **BETHNAL**   **CHESHIRE ST**

Bunhill Fields Burial Grounds   **John Wesley's House**   Tabernacle   Paul   Luke   Street   Philip St   Holywell   Lane   **SCLATER ST**   Shoreditch   **5**

CITY   Epworth St   Scrutton   St   Curtain   **SHOREDITCH**   Pedley St

ROAD   Bonhill St   Holywell Row   Hearn St   Plough Yard   **SHOREDITCH HIGH STREET**   Fleur de Lis St   Quaker   Street   Buxton Street

Bunhill Fields   Worship   Street   Worship   Street   Blossom   St   Elder St   Calvin St   Grey Eagle St   **BRICK LANE**   Spital St   Hunton St   Deal St

Finsbury   Dysart St   Snowden   St   Folgate   Street   Woodseer St

MOORGATE   Finsbury Pavement   Christopher St   Clifton St   Pindar St   Primrose St   Spital Sq   Hanbury   Street

Shoemaker   Earl   Sun Street   Appold St   Sun Street   Lamb St   Wilkes St   Princelet   Street

Lackington St   **Broadgate Centre**   Steward Street   **Spitalfields Market**   **COMMERCIAL ST**   Fournier   Street

South Place   Eldon St   **Liverpool Street Station**   Brushfield   Street   Heneage   St

Moorgate   **Q**   **R**   Christ Church   **S**

See Map 12

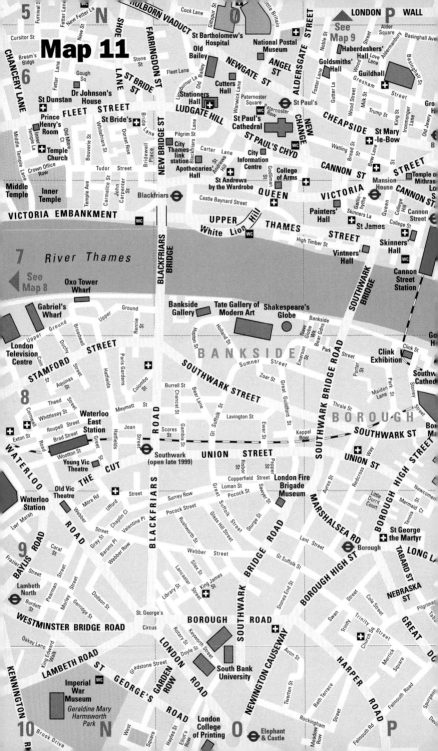

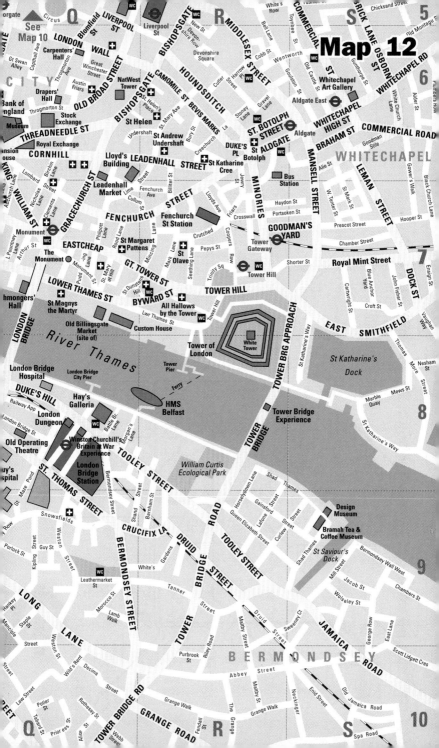

Map 12

See
Map 10

Q

Circus

Blomfield Street

LIVERPOOL

Liverpool St

BISHOPSGATE

R

MIDDLESEX STREET

White's Row

New St

Devon-
shire Row

Devonshire
Square

Toynbee St

Cobb St

Bell Lane

COMMERCIAL

S

BRICK LANE

Chicksand Street

Old Montagu St

OSBORN ST

Plumber's Row

5

LONDON
WALL

Carpenters'
Hall

Gt Swan
Alley

Coothall Ave

Blomfield Street

Throgmorton
Ave

Great
Winchester
Street

CITY

Austin
Friars

Throgmorton St

NatWest
Tower

OLD BROAD STREET

St Helen's
Place

HOUNDSDITCH

CAMOMILE ST BEVIS MARKS

Cutler
Street

Harrow
Pl

Wentworth

Stoney
Lane

Gravel
Lane

Goulston St

Old Castle St

Whitechapel
Art Gallery

Aldgate East

Gunthorpe St

WHITECHAPEL RD

White Church
Lane

Alder St

6

Bank of
England

Museum

Drapers'
Hall

Stock
Exchange

BISHOPSGATE

St Helen

St Mary Axe

Bury St

Creechurch
Lane

ST BOTOLPH

Aldgate

WHITECHAPEL
HIGH ST

BRAHAM ST

COMMERCIAL ROAD

Goodman
Stile

WHITECHAPEL

Black Church Lane

THREADNEEDLE ST

Royal Exchange

Undershaft

St Andrew
Undershaft

DUKE'S
PL

St
Botolph

ALDGATE

Mansell St

Alie St

W. Tenter St

St Mark St

Gower's Walk

LEMAN

STREET

CORNHILL

Lombard
Street

Birchin
Lane

Lloyd's
Building

LEADENHALL STREET

St Katharine
Cree

Jewry
St

Bus
Station

Haydon St

Portsoken St

Prescot Street

Goodman St

Hooper St

ansion
ouse

KING
WILLIAM ST

Clements Lane

Nicholas Lane

Abchurch Lane

Leadenhall
Market

GRACECHURCH ST

Lime Street

Fenchurch
Ave

FENCHURCH STREET

Billiter St

Lloyds Ave

Friars

Crosswall

GOODMAN'S
YARD

Chamber Street

Royal Mint Street

Blue Anchor
Yard

Cartwright St

Croft St

Cartwright St

John Fisher St

DOCK ST

Ensign St

7

Monument

EASTCHEAP

Philpot Lane

Rood Lane

St Margaret
Patterns

Mincing Lane

Mark Lane

Seething Lane

Pepys St

Coopers
Row

Crutched
Friars

Tower
Gateway

Shorter St

EAST

Vaughan
Way

The
Monument

L Pountney
Lane

Arthur St

Monument St

Pudding
Lane

GT. TOWER ST

St Mary
at Hill

St
Olave

Trinity Sq

Tower Hill

WC

SMITHFIELD

Thomas More St

Nesham
St

hmongers'
Hall

LOWER THAMES ST

St Dunstan's
Hill

BYWARD ST

TOWER HILL

Tower Hill

St Magnus
the Martyr

All Hallows
by the Tower

Lwr Thames St

Marble
Quay

Mews St

London
Bridge

Old Billingsgate
Market
(site of)

Custom House

Tower of
London

White
Tower

TOWER BRG APPROACH

St Katharine's Way

St Katharine's
Dock

River Thames

Tower
Pier

8

London Bridge
Hospital

London Bridge
City Pier

Ferry

TOWER

St Katharine's Way

DUKE'S
HILL

Railway App

London
Bridge App

Hay's
Galleria

Battle Br.
Lane

Morgan's Lane

HMS
Belfast

BRIDGE

Tower Bridge
Experience

Old Operating
Theatre

Guy's
spital

London
Dungeon

Winston Churchill's
Britain at War
Experience

London
Bridge
Station

TOOLEY STREET

Bermondsey Street

Shand Street

William Curtis
Ecological Park

Shad
Thames

Horselydown Lane

Gainsford Street

Lafone Street

Cullen Street

Queen Elizabeth Street

Shad Thames

Design
Museum

9

Snowsfields

ST. THOMAS STREET

Gt Maze Pond

CRUCIFIX LA

Shand

Barnham St

DRUID

ROAD

TOOLEY STREET

Shad Thames

Bramah Tea &
Coffee Museum

St Saviour's
Dock

Bermondsey Wall West

Mill Street

Jacob St

Wolseley St

Chambers St

Porlock St

Kipling
Street

Guy St

Weston St

White's
Gardens

BERMONDSEY STREET

BRIDGE

Tanner
Street

Leathermarket St

WC

Morocco St

Lamb
Walk

TOWER

STREET

Maltby Street

Druid
Street

Sweeney Ct

Riley Road

George Row

East Lane

JAMAICA

ROAD

LONG

Hankey
Pl

Staple
St

Manciple
Street

LANE

Weston Street

Decima
Street

Street

Purbrook
St

Riley Road

Maltby
Street

Neckinger

Enid Street

Old Jamaica Road

Scott Lidgett Cres

10

Q

Law Street

Tabard St

Prior ess's

R

Alice St

Rothsay St

TOWER BRIDGE RD

GRANGE ROAD

Webb
St

Fendall
Street

BERMONDSEY

Abbey

Street

Maltby St

Grange Walk

Grange Walk

The
Grange

ROAD

S

Spa Road

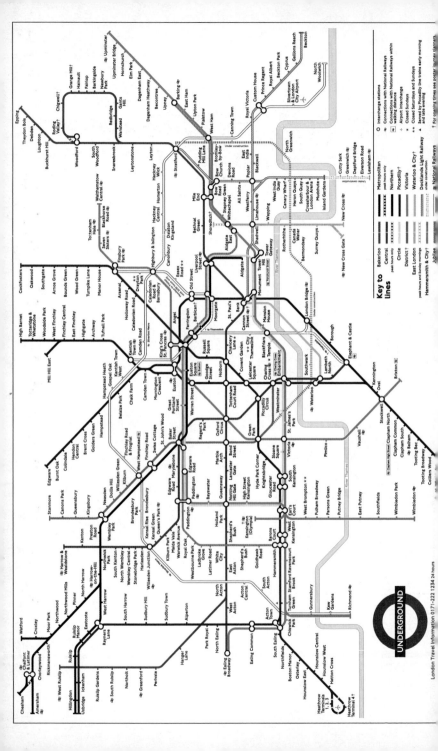

Time Out London Guide Please let us know what you think

About this guide...

1. How useful did you find the following sections?

	Very	Fairly	Not very	
London In Context	☐	☐	☐	(5)
Sightseeing	☐	☐	☐	(6)
Accommodation	☐	☐	☐	(7)
Eating & Drinking	☐	☐	☐	(8)
Shopping	☐	☐	☐	(9)
Arts & Entertainment	☐	☐	☐	(10)
Trips	☐	☐	☐	(11)
Directory	☐	☐	☐	(12)
Maps	☐	☐	☐	(13)

2. Did you travel to London: (17)

Alone? ☐ With partner? ☐
As part of group? ☐ With children? ☐
On business? ☐ I Live here. ☐

3. How long was your trip to London? (18)

Less than three days ☐
Three days to one week ☐
One to two weeks ☐
Over two weeks ☐

4. Did you visit any other destinations in the UK? If so, which ones?

_____
_____
_____

5. Where did you get additional travel information from? (19)

Tourist Board ☐
Internet ☐
Travel agents ☐
Another guide book (please specify) (20/22)
_____
Other
_____

6. Is there anything you'd like us to cover in greater depth?

_____
_____

7. Are there any places that should/should not be included in the guide?

_____
_____

8. How many other people have used this guide? (23)

none ☐ 1 ☐ 2 ☐ 3 ☐ 4 ☐ 5+ ☐

About other Time Out publications...

9. Have you ever bought/used Time Out magazine? (24)

Yes ☐ No ☐

10. Have you bought any other Time Out City Guides? (25)

Yes ☐ No ☐

If yes, which ones? (26,28)
_____

11. Have you ever bought/used other Time Out publications? (29)

Yes ☐ No ☐

If yes, which ones? (30)

Film Guide
Kids Out magazine
London Eating & Drinking Guide
London Pubs & Bars Guide
London Visitors' Guide
ici Londres
Paris Eating & Drinking Guide
Paris Free Guide
London Shopping Guide
Student Guide
Book of Country Walks
Book of London Walks

☐☐☐☐☐☐☐☐☐☐☐☐ (31)

Book of New York Short Stories
Time Out New York magazine
Time Out Roma
Time Out Diary
www.timeout.com

☐☐☐☐☐

About you...

12.
First name: _____
Surname: _____
Address: _____

Postcode: _____

13. Year of birth (32)
_____

14. Sex: male ☐ female ☐ (43)

15. Are you: (44)

employed full-time ☐
employed part-time ☐
self-employed ☐
unemployed ☐
student ☐
homemaker ☐

16. At the moment do you earn: (45)

under £10,000 ☐
over £10,000 and up to £14,999 ☐
over £15,000 and up to £19,999 ☐
over £20,000 and up to £24,999 ☐
over £25,000 and up to £39,999 ☐
over £40,000 and up to £49,999 ☐
over £50,000 ☐

☐ Please tick here if you don't want to receive further information on related promotions or products.

Time Out Guides

FREEPOST 20 (WC3187)
LONDON
W1E 0DQ

Time Out City Guides are available from all good bookshops or through Penguin Direct.
Simply call 0181 899 4036 (9am-5pm) or fill out the form below, affix a stamp and return.

ISBN	title	retail price	quantity	total
0140273115	Time Out Guide to **Amsterdam**	£9.99		
0140273123	Time Out Guide to **Barcelona**	£9.99		
0140257187	Time Out Guide to **Berlin**	£9.99		
0140284052	Time Out Guide to **Boston** (published 4/99)	£9.99		
0140273166	Time Out Guide to **Brussels**	£9.99		
014026745X	Time Out Guide to **Budapest**	£9.99		
0140266879	Time Out Guide to **Dublin**	£9.99		
0140266844	Time Out Guide to **Edinburgh**	£9.99		
0140266860	Time Out Guide to **Florence & Tuscany**	£9.99		
0140270620	Time Out Guide to **Las Vegas**	£9.99		
0140273158	Time Out Guide to **Lisbon**	£9.99		
0140259767	Time Out Guide to **London**	£9.99		
0140274456	Time Out Guide to **Los Angeles**	£9.99		
014027443X	Time Out Guide to **Madrid**	£9.99		
0140266852	Time Out Guide to **Miami**	£9.99		
014027314X	Time Out Guide to **Moscow**	£9.99		
0140274480	Time Out Guide to **New Orleans**	£9.99		
0140273107	Time Out Guide to **New York**	£9.99		
0140270647	Time Out Guide to **Paris**	£9.99		
0140257160	Time Out Guide to **Prague**	£9.99		
0140266887	Time Out Guide to **Rome**	£9.99		
0140267468	Time Out Guide to **San Francisco**	£9.99		
0140259732	Time Out Guide to **Sydney**	£9.99		
0140284060	Time Out Guide to **Venice** (published 4/99)	£9.99		
		+ postage & packing		£1.50
		Total Payment		

(Please Use Block Capitals)

Cardholder's Name

Address

Town _____ Postcode

Daytime Telephone Number

Method of Payment (UK Credit cards only)

Barclaycard/Visa

Access Card/Mastercard

Signature (if paying by credit card)

Expiry date

Cheque
I enclose a cheque £ _____ made payable to Penguin Direct

Delivery will normally be within 14 working days. The availability and published prices quoted are correct at time of going to press but are subject to alteration without prior notice. Order form valid until May 2000. **Please note that this service is only available in the UK.** Please note your order may be delayed if payment details are incorrect.

Penguin Direct
Penguin Books Ltd
Bath Road
Harmondsworth
West Drayton
Middlesex
UB7 0DA